"Few Protestant, let alone Catholic, interpreters of Karl Barth read him with as much skill and conviction as does Paul Molnar. Here again we find him making important and timely interventions not only in Barth studies, but also in theology in general, challenging the present dominance of a 'historicized Christology.' Molnar shows the deep difficulties such a Christology generates, and how Barth is not their ally. He then situates the Barth-Torrance position within the contemporary theological landscape defending its viability admirably. The result is compelling and deserves the attention of evangelical, Protestant and Catholic theologians."

D. Stephen Long, Marquette University

FAITH, FREEDOM
and the SPIRIT

THE ECONOMIC TRINITY IN BARTH, TORRANCE AND CONTEMPORARY THEOLOGY

PAUL D. MOLNAR

IVP Academic
An imprint of InterVarsity Press
Downers Grove, Illinois

InterVarsity Press
P.O. Box 1400, Downers Grove, IL 60515-1426
ivpress.com
email@ivpress.com

InterVarsity Press® is the book-publishing division of InterVarsity Christian Fellowship/USA®, a movement of students and faculty active on campus at hundreds of universities, colleges and schools of nursing in the United States of America, and a member movement of the International Fellowship of Evangelical Students. For information about local and regional activities, visit intervarsity.org.

Previously published material by Paul D. Molnar used with permission:

"The Role of the Holy Spirit in Knowing the Triune God." In Trinitarian Theology After Barth, *edited by Myk Habets and Phillip Tolliday, foreword by John B. Webster, pp. 3-47. Eugene, OR: Pickwick Publications, 2011. Used by permission of Wipf and Stock Publishers (www.wipfandstock.com).*

"The Perils of Embracing a 'Historicized Christology.'" Modern Theology *30, no. 4 (2014): 454-80. Used by permission of John Wiley & Sons Ltd., Blackwell.*

"The obedience of the Son in the theology of Karl Barth and of Thomas F. Torrance." Scottish Journal of Theology 67, no. 1 (2014): 50-69. Used by permission of Cambridge University Press.

"Can Jesus' Divinity be Recognized as 'Definitive, Authentic and Essential' if it is Grounded in Election? Just how far did the Later Barth Historicize Christology?" Neue Zeitschrift Für Systematische Theologie Und Religionsphilosophie Band 41 Heft 1 (2010): 40–81. Used by permission of Walter de Gruyter.

Cover design: Cindy Kiple
Interior design: Beth McGill

ISBN 978-0-8308-3905-6 (print)
ISBN 978-0-8308-8018-8 (digital)

Printed in the United States of America ∞

 As a member of the Green Press Initiative, InterVarsity Press is committed to protecting the environment and to the responsible use of natural resources. To learn more, visit greenpressinitiative.org.

Molnar, Paul D., 1946-
  Faith, freedom, and the Spirit : the economic Trinity in Barth,
Torrance and contemporary theology / Paul D. Molnar.
     pages cm
  Includes bibliographical references and index.
  ISBN 978-0-8308-3905-6 (pbk. : alk. paper)
  1. Trinity--History of doctrines—20th century. 2. Trinity—History
of doctrines—21st century. 3. Barth, Karl, 1886-1968. 4. Torrance,
Thomas F. (Thomas Forsyth), 1913-2007. I. Title.
  BT109.M65 2015
  231'.044--dc23

                                                          2014044445

P 23 22 21 20 19 18 17 16 15 14 13 12 11 10 9 8 7 6 5 4 3 2 1

Y 34 33 32 31 30 29 28 27 26 25 24 23 22 21 20 19 18 17 16 15

Contents

Preface

My first book on the Trinity[1] was rightly perceived as a ground-clearing exercise that was meant to illustrate why a doctrine of the immanent Trinity was important and needed to function in theological reflection by directing theologians to the need to recognize and to maintain the freedom of God's grace. This book is intended as a discussion of just how a properly conceived pneumatology would assist theologians speaking of the economic Trinity to think more accurately about divine and human interaction in the sphere of faith and knowledge within history. Toward that end I begin with an extensive discussion of the role of faith in knowing God and in relating with God in and through his incarnate Word and thus through the Holy Spirit. I then move to a discussion of how and why a properly functioning pneumatology will lead to an appropriately theological understanding of God's actions within the economy, and of why natural theology can never be seen as the ground for a theology of revelation. Rather, natural theology is seen as an approach to God that bypasses God's revelation and thus diverts attention away from the action of the Holy Spirit enabling knowledge of God acting for us within history.

In this context, one of the key themes of this book will be to explore and explain exactly why it is imperative always to begin and end theology from within faith. That means of course that any attempted apologetic approach to Christology, to knowledge of God and thus to the doctrine of the Trinity that

---

[1]Paul D. Molnar, *Divine Freedom and the Doctrine of the Immanent Trinity: In Dialogue with Karl Barth and Contemporary Theology* (New York: T & T Clark, 2005).

begins by focusing on our experience of faith instead of focusing on the God experienced in faith will always tend to confuse or separate not only nature and grace but reason and revelation. Any such confusion, I will contend, will weaken a strictly theological understanding of divine and human freedom and thus undermine the need for the Holy Spirit in order to see and to understand how exactly Christology relates with the doctrine of the Trinity and with pneumatology to point us to the constant need to rely on God himself both to know God and to love God within the sphere of history.

In this book I will rely on the thinking of Karl Barth and of Thomas F. Torrance to explicate such thinking in contrast to those theologians (Catholic and Protestant) who do not begin and end their reflections in faith. I will also argue against attempts to historicize Christology in inappropriate ways by discussing the kinds of resources that are available in the theology of Barth and Torrance from which one could develop a properly historical view of Christology, and thus of God acting within history in his Word and Spirit without falling into the Hegelian trap of making God in some sense dependent on history. Any assumption therefore that suggests that Jesus' human history is constitutive of his divine being, I will argue, is an assumption that effectively is based on a kind of theology that operates, perhaps unwittingly, with a type of false apologetic approach that attempts to ground theology in history, experience and reason instead of in God's actions for us within history that enable our knowledge of the truth.

After discussing what I would consider to be an appropriate understanding of faith and how theological knowledge operates within pneumatology, I will proceed to consider in detail divine freedom once again as the basis for true human freedom. This time, however, I will consider criticisms and misunderstandings that arose in connection with various misreadings of my first book on the Trinity. Since the publication of that first volume on the Trinity, the doctrine of election has become something of a flashpoint for contemporary discussions of divine and human freedom. After considering various proposals with regard to how election and the Trinity relate to our understanding of the immanent and economic Trinity, I will argue that those who emphasize Barth's actualism in such a way as to undercut his view that God's being and act are one tend to confuse time and eternity because they unwittingly embrace a type of thinking that was rejected when Origenism was rejected. Relying on the thought of Thomas F. Torrance, I will propose an alternative way of understanding the connection between time and eternity that is christologically focused and pneumatologically informed.

Since there is a critical connection between Christology and the doctrine of the Trinity, I will spend some time considering some of the perils of embracing a historicized Christology, that is, a Christology that is supposed to offer a view of Jesus' divinity without having to acknowledge the continued relevance of the *Logos asarkos* for reflection on the God who acts as our reconciler within the economy. What does it mean to recognize that Jesus' divinity must, as Barth once put it, be understood to be "definitive, authentic and essential"? Can Jesus' divinity be recognized as the decisive factor that gives meaning to revelation and reconciliation within the economy if for a moment his divine Person is thought to be a reality that results in any sense from Jesus' human relation to his Father in history? I will explain why that question must be answered negatively in order to perceive the true meaning of God's actions as the basis of and enabling condition of our human actions within history.

Closely related to this issue, a consideration of Karl Barth's early and later Christology will follow, with a view toward explaining why I think the evidence suggests that he never did and never would have abandoned his early position that the Word would still be the eternal Word without the incarnation, just as God would be none the less the eternal Father, Son and Holy Spirit if he had never decided to create, reconcile and redeem the world. This discussion will focus on debates among Barth scholars as to whether Barth so historicized his Christology that he could no longer espouse his earlier view, but that he changed his thinking in light of his doctrine of election and that this new view was expressed in what he had to say in the fourth volume of the *Church Dogmatics*, titled *The Doctrine of Reconciliation*. I will argue that Barth always held that revelation and reconciliation do not create the deity of Jesus Christ. Instead, Christ's deity creates revelation and reconciliation. Thus he never would have accepted the idea that Jesus' antecedent existence as the eternal Word was in any sense constituted by his human history. I explain how and why I think that those who claim that Barth's later Christology changed and required that he therefore should reject his earlier views or be considered inconsistent in his thinking are mistakenly engaging in "untheological metaphysical speculation" just because their historicist presuppositions lead them to discredit Christ's antecedent existence as "authentic, definitive and essential." After considering this crucial issue, we will focus more particularly on Christology once again to see where some of the problems bequeathed to contemporary theology come from.

To do this I will engage in a close comparison of the views of Thomas F. Torrance and Karl Barth, comparing their understanding of the obedience of the Son as that act on the basis of which reconciliation and redemption become events within the sphere of history. The main issue to be discussed in this regard will be whether and to what extent obedience and subordination can be read back into the immanent Trinity. When such a reading occurs, it will be my contention that the order of the trinitarian persons actually is confused with their being because an extraneous concept of causality is, perhaps inadvertently, imported into the relations of the Father, Son and Holy Spirit, thus weakening the positive point that the Son of God did not hold himself aloof from us but in his incarnation, death and resurrection he really was God acting *as* man for us both from the divine and the human side, reconciling the world to the Father. And as the ascended and advent Lord, he remains the one Mediator between us and the Father in the time between his first and second appearance within history. It is the Holy Spirit who enables us to experience and to live that reconciliation that is our justification and sanctification by grace and by faith; this is what empowers Christian hope here and now as well. In connection with this issue I will explain why I think that Torrance had a more consistently theological view of this matter than Barth because he made important distinctions between the missions and the processions in order to assert God's freedom *in se* and *ad extra* in ways that closed the door to reading back elements of the economy into the immanent Trinity. It is that problematic aspect of Barth's theology that opens the door to those who think the processions within the Trinity should be resolved into the missions. But I will argue that any such thinking historicizes the person of the Mediator in just the wrong way.

Finally, in order to develop a positive view of how human beings may live within the economy by grace and thus through the Holy Spirit uniting us to Christ and therefore through faith, I discuss at length how the doctrine of justification by faith relates to the living of the Christian life in the power of the Holy Spirit. In order to accomplish this I rely once again on the thinking of Barth and Torrance, as I do throughout this book, which itself is once again also a dialogue with other contemporary theologians about divine and human freedom. This time the emphasis is on our experience of God within the economy without forgetting what was learned from a properly functioning doctrine of the immanent Trinity. It is hoped that when the full picture that is presented here is considered in detail, thoughtful readers will see just why God's freedom as the one who loves must be upheld at all costs, even and especially when speaking about our Christian life as the life of those who are justified and sanctified in and through the one Mediator precisely as the Holy Spirit actualizes that reconciliation in our lives here and now. Whenever the Holy Spirit is confused with the human spirit, as it certainly is when it is thought that trinitiarian life is our life or that simply by loving others we love God, there and then the all-important union and distinction between us and God is lost, and theology becomes once again little more than our conversation with ourselves using theological categories.

Acknowledgments

A book such as this takes years to develop. Thus, there are many colleagues and friends who must be thanked for their support, friendship and assistance along the way. First, I would like to thank Myk Habets who invited me to participate in an International Symposium, "Trinitarian Theology After Barth," held at Carey Baptist College, Auckland, New Zealand in May, 2009. What is now chapter two was first presented as a lecture at that Symposium. What is now chapter six was first presented as a lecture to the faculty and graduate students at Laidlaw Carey Graduate School in Auckland in May, 2009. During my visit to Auckland, I taught a graduate course in the doctrine of the Trinity at the invitation of Myk Habets. I am extremely grateful to Myk and his wife, Odele, who went to great lengths to make my visit a wonderful and memorable experience. Thanks are also due to Nicola Hoggard Creegan for her boundless hospitality and friendship during my stay in Auckland. Next, I would like to thank Ivor Davidson, who invited me to the University of Otago in Dunedin to lecture in early June of 2009, where I presented what is now chapter six once again as a lecture and had a chance to interact with students and faculty. This was an exciting and happy visit, and Ivor went to inestimable lengths to make me feel most welcome. The students and the faculty both in Auckland and Dunedin helped me think through the many issues related to Karl Barth's early and later Christology.

Thanks are due to David A. S. Fergusson for his invitation to give a lecture at the University of Edinburgh in March of 2011. Through his good offices, that lecture developed into an article that was published in the *Scottish*

Journal of Theology, and later into what is now chapter seven. As always,
David helped me to think through important and difficult theological issues.
Both he and his wife, Margot, went out of their way to extend hospitality and
friendship to me and to see that my visit to Edinburgh was a great success.
When he introduced me to the students and faculty at the University, David
noted, with his usual sense of humor, that this was the first stop on my "east
coast Scottish tour"! From Edinburgh I travelled to St. Andrews and at the
invitation of Alan Torrance and Ivor Davidson I presented what is now
chapter seven as a lecture to a group of graduate students and faculty at
Alan's seminar. My deepest gratitude must be expressed to Alan and to Ivor
for making me most welcome as a colleague and friend at the University
during my visit there. Additionally, I must thank John Webster for inviting
me to present that same lecture to a group of graduate students and faculty
at the University of Aberdeen during the final leg of my visit to Scotland in
March of 2011. John also went to immeasurable lengths to extend hospitality
and friendship to me during my visit to Aberdeen. From the questions and
interaction with the many students and faculty at the University, I learned
a great deal that helped me to further refine the contents of chapter seven.

I am grateful to St. John's University for providing me with a research
leave during spring 2012 semester and for subsequent research reductions
in support of my work. I especially wish to thank the Dean of St. John's
College of Liberal Arts and Sciences, Jeff Fagen, for his constant support. In
addition I must thank the present Chair of the Department of Theology and
Religious Studies, Chris Vogt; my esteemed colleagues on the Personnel
and Budget Committee; as well as the former Chair of the Department,
Mike Whalen, CM, for their constant support, friendship and collegiality.
St. John's is a wonderful place to work because of those with whom I work.
I would especially like to thank my friends and colleagues Nick Healy, David
Haddorff and Mike Dempsey for many hours of conversation and collabo-
ration in the work of serious theology.

In addition I must thank my valued friend Iain R. Torrance for his constant support, encouragement and friendship. I would also like to thank another dear friend and colleague, George Hunsinger with whom I have spent
much time exchanging important ideas and insights. George generously took
the time to read and comment on sections of this book as it developed. His

insights were and are always of great value to me. It was for good reason that he won the Karl Barth prize in 2010! Thanks are also due to my colleagues and friends in the Karl Barth Society of North America and in the Thomas F. Torrance Theological Fellowship, especially Elmer Colyer, Gary Deddo, Todd Speidell, Chris Kettler and Myk Habets. Finally, I would like to offer my sincere gratitude to another good friend, John J. McCormick, who once again, generously gave his time and expertise in reading and re-reading my manuscript in its various stages and offering valuable advice, support and editorial suggestions along the way. His assistance was an invaluable factor enabling me to complete this book. Thanks are also due to Christoph Schwöbel for his willingness to accommodate an extra-long article discussing Barth's early and later Christology, and for his support. I also need to acknowledge the help and support that I received from my editors at InterVarsity Press, starting with Gary Deddo and Brannon Ellis and continuing with Andy Le Peau. Their knowledge and professionalism made it a much easier task to complete this work. Andy in particular has been especially helpful in moving the manuscript seamlessly into its final form. Naturally, it goes without saying that the sole responsibility for any errors resides with me.

Abbreviations

Karl Barth's *Church Dogmatics*

I/1   Vol. I, *The Doctrine of the Word of God*, pt. 1, ed. G. W. Bromiley and T. F. Torrance, trans. by G. W. Bromiley (Edinburgh: T & T Clark, 1975)

I/2   Vol. I, *The Doctrine of the Word of God*, pt. 2, ed. G. W. Bromiley and T. F. Torrance, trans. G. T. Thomson and Harold Knight (Edinburgh: T & T Clark, 1970)

II/1   Vol. II, *The Doctrine of God*, pt. 1, ed. G. W. Bromiley and T. F. Torrance, trans. T. H. L. Parker, W. B. Johnston, H. Knight and J. L. M. Harie (Edinburgh: T & T Clark, 1964)

II/2   Vol. II, *The Doctrine of God*, pt. 2, ed. G. W. Bromiley and T. F. Torrance, trans. G. W. Bromiley, J. C. Campbell, Iain Wilson, J. Strathearn McNab, Harold Knight and R. A. Stewart (Edinbugh: T & T Clark, 1967)

III/1   Vol. III, *The Doctrine of Creation*, pt. 1, ed. G. W. Bromiley and T. F. Torrance, trans. J. W. Edwards, O. Bussey and Harold Knight (Edinburgh: T & T Clark, 1970)

III/2   Vol. III, *The Doctrine of Creation*, pt. 2, ed. G. W. Bromiley and T. F. Torrance, trans. Harold Knight, G. W. Bromiley, J. K. S. Reid and R. H. Fuller (Edinburgh: T & T Clark, 1968)

III/3   Vol. III, *The Doctrine of Creation*, pt. 3, ed. G. W. Bromiley and T. F. Torrance, trans. G. W. Bromiley and R. J. Ehrlich (Edinburgh: T & T Clark, 1976)

III/4   Vol. III, *The Doctrine of Creation*, pt. 4, ed. G. W. Bromiley and T. F. Torrance, trans. A. T. MacKay, T. H. L. Parker, Harold Knight, Henry A. Kennedy and John Marks (Edinburgh: T & T Clark, 1969)

IV/1	Vol. IV, *The Doctrine of Reconciliation*, pt. 1, ed. G. W. Bromiley and T. F. Torrance, trans. G. W. Bromiley (Edinburgh: T & T Clark, 1974)
IV/2	Vol. IV, *The Doctrine of Reconciliation*, pt. 2, ed. G. W. Bromiley and T. F. Torrance, trans. G. W. Bromiley (Edinburgh: T & T Clark, 1967)
IV/3.1	Vol. IV, *The Doctrine of Reconciliation*, pt. 3, first half, ed. G. W. Bromiley and T. F. Torrance, trans. G. W. Bromiley (Edinburgh: T & T Clark, 1976)
IV/3.2	Vol. IV, *The Doctrine of Reconciliation*, pt. 3, second half, ed. G. W. Bromiley and T. F. Torrance, trans. G. W. Bromiley (Edinburgh: T & T Clark, 1969)
IV/4	Vol. IV, *The Doctrine of Reconciliation*, pt. 4, Fragment, *Baptism as the Foundation of the Christian Life*, ed. G. W. Bromiley and T. F. Torrance, trans. G. W. Bromiley (Edinburgh: T & T Clark, 1969)
IV/4	Vol. IV, *The Christian Life*, pt. 4, Lecture Fragments, trans. Geoffrey W. Bromiley (Grand Rapids: Eerdmans, 1981)

GREEK AND LATIN TEXTS

C. Ar.	Athanasius, *Orations Against the Arians*
De. Trin.	Hilary, *On the Trinity*
Or. Bas.	Gregory of Nazianzen, *Oratio in laudem Basilii*

JOURNALS

IJST	*International Journal of Systematic Theology*
NZSTh	*Neue Zeitschrift für Systematische Theologie und Religionsphilosophie*
SJT	*Scottish Journal of Theology*

OTHER ABBREVIATIONS

Atonement	Thomas F. Torrance, *Atonement: The Person and Work of Christ*, ed. Robert T. Walker (Downers Grove, IL: InterVarsity Press, 2009)
Christian Doctrine of God	Thomas F. Torrance, *The Christian Doctrine of God: One Being Three Persons* (Edinburgh: T & T Clark, 1996)
FCF	Karl Rahner, *Foundations of Christian Faith: An Introduction to the Idea of Christianity*, trans. William V. Dych (New York: Seabury, 1978)
Incarnation	Thomas F. Torrance, *Incarnation: The Person and Life of Christ*, ed. Robert T. Walker (Downers Grove, IL: IVP Academic, 2008)
PTNC	Karl Barth, *Protestant Theology in the Nineteenth Century: Its Background & History*, trans. Brian Cozens and John Bowden (Valley Forge, PA: Judson Press, 1973)
STI	Robert W. Jenson, *Systematic Theology*, vol. 1, *The Triune God* (New York: Oxford University Press, 1997)
Systematic Theology I	Wolfhart Pannenberg, *Systematic Theology*, vol. 1, trans. Geoffrey W. Bromiley (Grand Rapids: Eerdmans, 1991)
TI	Karl Rahner, *Theological Investigations* (London, Baltimore and New York: 1961–1992)
Trinitarian Faith	Thomas F. Torrance, *The Trinitarian Faith: The Evangelical Theology of the Ancient Catholic Church* (Edinburgh: T & T Clark, 1988)
Trinitarian Perspectives	Thomas F. Torrance, *Trinitarian Perspectives: Toward Doctrinal Agreement* (Edinburgh: T & T Clark, 1994)

1

Thinking About God Within Faith

The Role of the Holy Spirit

In his review of my book *Divine Freedom and the Doctrine of the Immanent Trinity*, John Webster noted that it was "a piece of polemic in the best sense of the term: critical analysis and clarification with an eye kept firmly on a rich and fruitful set of dogmatic commitments."[1] As such he suggested that it should be read as "a ground-clearing exercise: part protest, part alarm signal, part dismantling of the shaky edifice of modern economic trinitarianism." That such a "ground-clearing" exercise was needed at the time I think will be acknowledged by anyone who realizes the importance of recognizing that a properly conceived doctrine of the Trinity cannot simply be the embodiment of our human experience of relationality or of our religious ideas writ large. Any serious understanding of the doctrine of the Trinity must be shaped by who God eternally was and is as Father, Son and Holy Spirit. Many reviewers saw clearly that what I had to say about the immanent Trinity as the indispensable premise of what takes place in the economy was based on God's personal economic self-communication in his Word and Spirit. Thus it was not arbitrary. Yet, for some strange reason there were some who claimed that I held that a proper understanding of the doctrine could not begin with the economic Trinity because I was critical of those who claimed that one could not begin thinking about the

---

[1]John Webster, "Review of *Divine Freedom and the Doctrine of the Immanent Trinity: In Dialogue with Karl Barth and Contemporary Theology*," *Journal of Theological Studies* 56, no. 1 (April 2005): 288-90.

immanent Trinity from experience.[2] Of course that is not what I said at any point in the book. Any such idea would have circumvented revelation at the outset in an attempt to know God directly instead of mediately through his incarnate Word and through faith that is enabled by the Holy Spirit. Knowing God the Father through his Son and in and by the Spirit means acknowledging that it is always God, who alone exists self-sufficiently as the one who loves, who enables our knowledge of him and our actions as those who live as his witnesses here and now. What I argued was that a proper theology that begins in faith does indeed involve our experience of God, but in that experience we know that it is God and not our experience of God who is the object of faith and of knowledge. This chapter will involve a careful analysis and comparison of the view of mediated knowledge offered by Karl Barth with the view offered by Karl Rahner. Barth's view, it will be argued, does justice both to knowledge and experience of God just because it takes the action of the Spirit seriously and operates explicitly within faith all along the line. Rahner's view, which intends to speak of our knowledge and experience of God, as does Barth's, differs from Barth's approach by its apologetic attempt to validate knowledge of faith from the experience of self-transcendence. By contrasting these views I hope to clarify why fideism is unacceptable while thinking within faith is required in order to properly understand human and divine interaction, especially when it comes to knowing that our experience of God really is an experience of God and not just an experience of ourselves extended to the nth degree.

FAITH AND THE KNOWLEDGE OF GOD

Very early in II/1 Barth objected to Augustine's description of a type of knowledge of God in his *Confessions* that he considered to be problematic because it was an attempt to know God by way of "a timeless and non-objective seeing and hearing" (II/1, p. 11).[3] While Barth also noted that else-

---

[2]See, e.g., the review of *Divine Freedom and the Doctrine of the Immanent Trinity* by Brian M. Doyle in *Horizons* 36, no. 2 (Fall 2009): 356-57.

[3]Barth was not alone in this. Thomas F. Torrance also opposed any sort of what he called "non-conceptual" or non-objective knowledge of God, and opposed the thinking of those who did not allow their concepts to be shaped by God himself acting for us in his Word and Spirit. See, e.g., Paul D. Molnar, *Thomas F. Torrance: Theologian of the Trinity* (Aldershot, UK: Ashgate, 2009), pp. 33-34, 172, etc. Both Barth and Torrance followed Hilary and argued that it is reality that determines meaning and not our words in and of themselves. We will discuss non-conceptual knowledge of God in more detail toward the end of this chapter.

where in his *City of God* Augustine himself advanced the kind of "mediate, objective knowledge" that Barth himself believed was the only way we could have knowledge of God through his Word and Spirit, Barth persistently rejected any sort of "non-objective" knowledge of God because any such knowledge necessarily and always bypasses the place and manner in which God reveals himself to us, namely, his incarnate Word. Any attempt to know God that seeks some form of direct knowledge of God (a knowledge without the mediation of his incarnate Word), in Barth's view, always would mean the inability to distinguish God from us; and that would then mean our inability to speak objectively and truly about God at all. Barth therefore understood faith to mean "the knowledge of God" (II/1, p. 14). But this meant the knowledge of God as an object; knowledge of the truth. Yet, because God is not an object within a series of other objects, it is impossible to come to an objective knowledge of God via "a general understanding of man's consideration and conception, but only in particular from God as its particular object" (II/1, p. 15). For Barth, "God is not God if He is considered and conceived as one in a series of like objects. . . . Faith will have to be denied if we want to take our stand on this presupposition. God, as the object of knowledge, will not let Himself be placed as one in a series" (II/1, p. 15). For this reason Barth insisted that he did not teach "this distinction between the knowledge of God and its object on the ground of a preconceived idea about the transcendence and supramundanity of God," and neither did he teach it "in the form of an affirmation of our experience of faith"; instead he insisted that he taught it because of what he found "proclaimed and described as faith in Holy Scripture" (II/1, p. 15). And that faith, according to Barth, "excludes any faith of man in himself—that is any desire for religious self-help, any religious self-satisfaction, any religious self-sufficiency" (II/1, p. 13) precisely because faith in the biblical sense "lives upon the objectivity of God. . . . Take away the objectivity of this *He* [namely, the Father, Son and Holy Spirit] and faith collapses, even as love, trust and obedience" (II/1, p. 13).

I mention this understanding of faith here because, while my first book on the Trinity was an attempt to explain that unless our God-talk is grounded in God's own existence, that is, an existence that God retains even in his closest union with us, which does indeed take place in revelation (which includes God's actions as reconciler and redeemer) and in faith (which involves our

acknowledgment of God *as* God and our fellowship [communion] with God),
all our talk about God and our relations with God become simply descriptions
of our own religious experiences and agendas instead of descriptions of who
God is, what God does for us in history and how God enables us to live the
life of faith. The fact that so many theologians thought they could begin their
theologies not only with some sort of self-confidence in the strength of their
religious experiences, but that they could even claim that "trinitarian life is
also our life"[4] suggested to me that those approaches to God had missed God's
objectivity precisely because they did not in fact begin and end their thinking
in faith by acknowledging God's objectivity as just described.

Because I followed Barth to insist that unless God's actions for us in
history are seen against the background of God in himself who was and
remains eternally triune and could have remained the triune God without
us, even though in fact he chose not to, some readers erroneously concluded
that I had adopted a view of God as independent of us in the sense that God
remained locked up within his own trinitarian relations and thus remained
apart from us. Any careful reader of my first book on the Trinity certainly
never could have reached that conclusion. Those who did reach that conclusion did so, I suspect, because they had already collapsed the immanent
into the economic Trinity by implicitly and explicitly arguing for a "dependent" deity, that is, a God whose eternal being was and is in some sense
constituted either by his decision to be in relation with us or by his actually
relating with us in history. My first book was an attempt to show that when
a properly formulated doctrine of the immanent Trinity is allowed to
function throughout one's theology, then one of the things that is necessarily
excluded as a possibility is the idea that God's relations with us in history
were or are in *any sense necessary* to him. In this regard I made a distinction
between factual necessities and logical necessities, the former referring to
the fact that when God acts toward us in his Word and Spirit, we can then
say that it was necessary for God to be incarnate, for instance, but only in

---

[4]See, e.g., Catherine Mowry LaCugna, *God for Us: The Trinity and Christian Life* (San Francisco:
HarperSanFrancisco, 1991), p. 228. Thus, "The life of God is not something that belongs to God
alone. *Trinitarian life is also our life.*" She continues with the logic implied in this remark and
concludes that "The doctrine of the Trinity is not ultimately a teaching about 'God' but a teaching about *God's life with us and our life with each other.*" Nothing could be further from the truth,
as I showed in my previous work.

the sense that, in light of the fact that that is how God has chosen to reconcile the world to himself, we cannot think of God in himself at all without thinking of God through his incarnate Son as the reconciler and redeemer. But that does not mean and can never mean that God realizes his Sonship or any aspect of his eternal triunity by means of suffering for us or by means of his becoming incarnate and acting for us as the reconciler and redeemer. We will consider some of these ideas once again as the book develops.

THINKING ABOUT GOD FROM WITHIN THE ECONOMY

All of this is by way of saying that in this sequel to my first book on the Trinity, I will still be in dialogue with Karl Barth and contemporary theology. But this time, instead of doing a ground-clearing exercise by showing how and why a doctrine of the immanent Trinity is crucial to every aspect of theology, I will attempt to show (without forgetting what was established in that book) exactly how one might begin a theology with "man in the presence of God, his action over against God's action."[5] In other words, instead of beginning with the doctrine of God, I will begin from the human side with our human experience of God. But I will attempt to do so in such a way that what is said derives from an understanding of God's actions in relation to us as the basis on which all human action flourishes and has meaning. Karl Barth once said that "Trinitarian thinking compels theology . . . to be completely in earnest about the thought of God in at least two places: first, at the point where it is a question of God's action in regard to man, and secondly, at the point where it is a question of man's action in

---

[5]*PTNC*, p. 459. When asked whether he really believed that he could begin his *Church Dogmatics* with any doctrine other than the Trinity, Barth responded that because Christian truth is a "living whole" where every point aims toward the center, it must be possible to begin dogmatics with any doctrine, including the doctrine of the Holy Spirit. Indeed, Barth said, "we might even begin with the Christian man!" (*Karl Barth's Table Talk*, recorded and ed. John Godsey [Richmond, VA: John Knox, 1962], p. 13). Noting that he had opposed Friedrich Schleiermacher and subjectivism because it was necessary at the time, he suggested that at another time theologians might even "begin with Christian subjectivism" (p. 13). Barth insisted that theology must be free enough to proceed as Schleiermacher did by "*ending* with the Trinity" and still be correct. Of course, for Barth freedom meant finding the truth in Christ alone through the power of the Spirit, and to that extent even his understanding of faith and experience is shaped by his trinitarian understanding throughout. Here, though I now will begin with our experience of God in the economy, I still argue, with Thomas F. Torrance, that any doctrine that is held apart from the doctrine of the Trinity becomes seriously distorted whenever that happens. See, e.g., *Christian Doctrine of God*, p. 31.

regard to God" (*PTNC*, p. 458). This means that whether theology begins
with God or with the human, it must be aware of the fact that God the
Father encounters us in his Word that is spoken to us; and through the
Spirit of the Father and the Son, God himself enables us to hear his Word.
Because God encounters us in this way, Barth said, a theology guided by
the Trinity "cannot seek to have merely one centre, one subject. . . . To the
extent that it sought to resolve itself into a mere teaching of God's action in
regard to man, into a pure teaching of the Word, it would become metaphysics" (*PTNC*, p. 459). Yet, any theology that "sought to resolve itself into
a teaching of man's action in regard to God, into a pure teaching of the
Spirit . . . would become mysticism" (*PTNC*, p. 459). Either way, we would
end with a God who is not the Father, Son and Holy Spirit because this God
cannot be known via metaphysics, that is, by exploring being, because theology is focused not on being in general as is metaphysics but on the specific being and action of the Father, Son and Holy Spirit in himself as the
one who loves in freedom and as the one who loves us in his actions for us
and with us in history. Or we might conjure a God who can be known directly and not mediately. Such a God would end up being identical with
ourselves, such that one might then say "trinitarian life is also our life"! In
this book I will follow Karl Barth once again and argue that "A pure teaching
of the Word will take into account the Holy Spirit as the divine reality in
which the Word is heard, just as a pure teaching of the Spirit of the Son will
take into account the Word of God as the divine reality in which the Word
is given to us" (*PTNC*, p. 459). Beginning in this way does not mean I am
abandoning what I said previously about the immanent Trinity. What it
does mean is that a serious theology properly focused on the Holy Spirit as
the enabling condition of our knowledge of and love of God will always
allow for the fact that knowledge of and relationship with God means
union with Christ and thus union with the Father.[6] Trinitarian thinking

---

[6]Again Barth claimed that "There is no reason why the attempt of Christian anthropocentrism
should not be made. . . . There is certainly a place for legitimate Christian thinking starting from
below and moving up, from man who is taken hold of by God to God who takes hold of man.
Let us interpret this attempt by the 19th-century theologians in its best light! Provided that it in
no way claims to be exclusive and absolute, one might well understand it as an attempt to formulate a theology of the third article of the Apostles' Creed, the Holy Spirit. . . . Theology is in
reality not only the doctrine of God, but the doctrine of God and man. Interpreted in this light,
19th-century theology would not have forgotten or even suppressed, but rather stressed, the fact

thus will always allow God himself to be the determining factor in all that we think, say and do.

THE IMPORTANCE OF THE HOLY SPIRIT

As is well known, Barth was critical of Schleiermacher for focusing too much on our human relations with God, although he did not condemn him out of hand because he believed that "A genuine, proper theology could be built up from such a starting-point" (*PTNC*, p. 459). That anthropocentric starting point might work, according to Barth, but only with "an honest doctrine of the Holy Spirit and of faith" (*PTNC*, p. 459). In spite of the dangers, which were all too obvious to Barth, and which I tried to point out in my first book on the Trinity, namely, the danger of reducing God to a description of our own experiences of ourselves and the danger of confusing God with ideas developed on such a basis, I agree with Barth that theology could begin with the human as long as it is "the pure theology of the Holy Spirit; the teaching of man brought face to face with God by God, of man granted grace by grace" (*PTNC*, p. 460). But it is crucial to note that for Barth one cannot have a proper theology of the Holy Spirit without recognizing "the divinity of the *Logos*"; a theology of the Holy Spirit must be a theology of faith that proves itself such by the fact that "it is the divine Word that forms its true centre" (*PTNC*, p. 460). In contrasting Martin Luther's view of faith with Schleiermacher's, Barth discloses what would become a persistent theme throughout the *Church Dogmatics*, namely, that true faith arises as a *necessity* because it is a miraculous creation of the Holy Spirit. That does not mean that the Spirit replaces our human decision of faith; rather it means that our free human decision is an act of obedience that is constrained by the hearing of God's Word spoken to us through the scriptural witness. That is why, in contrast to Schleiermacher, Barth could say

> He [Luther] neither needed to model the concept of faith to comply with a certain world view, nor did he need first to work out the indispensable nature of this concept. The concept of faith, rather, is already posited, both in its content and in its range, in and with his conception of the Word. (*PTNC*, p. 462)

---

that man's relation to God is based on God's dealings with man, and not conversely" (Karl Barth, *The Humanity of God*, trans. Thomas Wieser and John Newton Thomas [Richmond, VA: John Knox, 1968], pp. 24-25).

The difference, in Barth's view, lay in the fact that "the divinity of the *Logos* is pre-supposed as unequivocally as . . . the divinity of the Holy Spirit" (*PTNC*, p. 462). Without this decisive connection, in Barth's view, one must wonder whether it is the Holy Spirit that is in view at all!

Among contemporary theologians, Barth's student Thomas F. Torrance saw and maintained this connection with unparalleled determination by taking his cue from Athanasius, who insisted that our understanding of the Spirit must be governed by our understanding of the Son who is *homoousion* with the Father so that the Spirit, who is one in being with both the Father and Son and who is sent by the Father and by the Son, must never be confused with the human spirit. That, for Torrance, was the crucial error embedded, for instance, in the theologies of Rudolf Bultmann and Paul Tillich. I will not develop Torrance's important and helpful thinking here because there will be occasions for that development as the book proceeds. Here I simply note the importance of connecting the Spirit and the Word in such a way that one could not in truth be referring to the Holy Spirit if and to the extent that one's thought is not necessarily and from the outset governed by the Word and by faith.

This insight led to another. While faith is indeed a human action, as just noted, most attempts at apologetic theology inevitably try to establish the divinity of Christ in a way that bypasses the Holy Spirit as the one who alone enables true faith. As Torrance emphasized, and Barth would agree, no one can say Jesus is Lord except by the Spirit. Hence, in his Christology, Torrance insisted that we must begin with the "fact of Christ," by which he meant that we had to begin our thinking by acknowledging his true divinity and his true humanity as witnessed in the Scriptures. There was no way we could build up to this recognition and knowledge, in his mind, because the only way to grasp it was through the actions of the Word and Spirit, on which we utterly depend.[7] In other words it had to be revealed to us, and revelation included the idea that the Holy Spirit was active here and now enabling our hearing of the Word spoken by and through that Spirit. It is extremely interesting to note that for Barth, Schleiermacher's mistake at this point was that "As an apologist he was bound to be interested in understanding revelation not strictly as revelation, but in such a way that it might also be comprehensible

---

[7]*Incarnation*, p. 2.

as a mode of human cognition" (*PTNC*, pp. 462-63). This led him to offer a
view of mediation that did not see faith as revelation and thus as "a correlate
to the concept of the Holy Spirit . . . but as a correlate to this human experience [religious consciousness as such]" (*PTNC*, p. 463). And this led him
to conceptualize faith and Christ by equating them with experience and
history so that he turned "the Christian relationship of man with God into
an apparent human possibility" (*PTNC*, p. 463). At this point Barth maintains
that the Reformation theologians never took this approach because there was
only one mediation of God to humanity, and that is the mediation of "the
Father in the Son through the Spirit in the strict irreducible opposition of
these 'persons' in the Godhead" (*PTNC*, p. 464). Because this mediation
simply cannot be conceptualized "as a mode of human cognition," Barth
insists that it "is unusable in apologetics" (*PTNC*, p. 464). This is an enormously important point because if theology is faith in the Word of God
seeking understanding, then any attempt to formulate a theology of faith that
tries to build up to it will automatically subvert the truth, which is that the
possibility of theology is and remains grounded only in God and not in us.

In the remainder of this chapter, then, I will spell out just how Barth
understood faith as a mode of revelation in a way that did not undermine
but rather enabled free human decisions—decisions that became free because they took place in obedience to the only one who could truly enable
human beings to act in freedom, namely, Christ himself. There are very
interesting descriptions of faith by Barth in *CD* I/1, II/1 and especially in IV/1.
I think it would helpful to see how Barth's thinking is shaped by his view of
the Trinity with a view toward developing the thesis of this book, namely,
that a proper understanding of theology starting from the anthropological
side can do justice both to divine and human freedom in a positive way as
long as it develops strictly within faith as enabled by the Holy Spirit. The
chapter will conclude with a brief comparison of some of the key points
stressed by Barth with another very different view of faith offered by Karl
Rahner. The comparison will set into relief the point of this book: when the
Holy Spirit is allowed to function as the one who both enables faith and
unites us to Christ, then we not only come to know God with a definite
certitude, but we come to know ourselves in Christ in positive ways that
would be closed to us apart from faith and revelation.

THE HOLY SPIRIT AND CHRISTIAN FAITH

In a sustained reflection on faith in §63 of *CD* IV/1 Barth begins by noting
that "The Holy Spirit is the awakening power in which Jesus Christ
summons a sinful man to His community and therefore as a Christian to
believe in Him" (IV/1, p. 740). The first, most important point to note in
this context is that Christian faith is not "a fact and phenomenon which is
generally known and which can, as such, be explained to everybody" (IV/1,
p. 740). Its possibility and reality simply cannot be explained "in the light
of a general anthropology" precisely because faith as a human action is
what it is by virtue of a divine action, namely, the action of the Holy Spirit.
It is, in other words, enabled by a miracle—a special, new act of God that
is not demonstrable by considering a general anthropology but can only be
acknowledged and lived.[8] As we shall see, this position is diametrically opposed to Karl Rahner's view that "theology itself implies a philosophical
anthropology which enables this message of grace [the Christian message]
to be accepted in a really philosophical and reasonable way."[9] Barth insisted that while the Christian religion is a "fact and phenomenon" that can
be considered and understood "historically, psychologically, sociologically
and perhaps even philosophically," the Christian faith cannot, because
"Christian faith is something concealed in the Christian religion (like the
true Church in its visibility)" (IV/1, p. 741). This is a crucial insight because
what is meant here is that faith is not grounded at all in itself and therefore
cannot in any sense begin with itself as a human experience *per se*. Faith
means allowing Jesus Christ, "the Judge who was Himself judged for us," to
shape our knowledge of God and of ourselves. When that happens we recognize that we are sinners who are opposed to Jesus Christ and in need of
reconciliation even in order to know him. The doctrine of justification

---

[8]The truth that we, as sinners who are justified by faith, actually experience the Word of God
occurs "in absolute independence of all the criteria of truth that secular or even the religious
man has first to provide and apply critically before he very kindly resolves to let what is true be
true. . . . The possibility of knowledge of God's Word lies in God's Word and nowhere else. In the
absolute sense its reality can only take place, and it can do so only as a miracle before the eyes of
every man, secular and religious, Greek and Jew" (I/1, pp. 222-23). Miracle means that we really
can know and experience God in faith. But the truth of what occurs in this experience "is not
dependent on man," cannot be reproduced in our experience and cannot be thought of as inher-
ing within our experience because it "rests in God's Word itself" (I/1, p. 223).
[9]*FCF*, p. 25.

therefore shapes one's understanding of what it means to be human as a Christian within the community of faith. What is it that distinguishes Christians from non-Christians?

This is an important question, given the fact that Barth adamantly insists that "faith stands or falls with its object" (IV/1, p. 742). That object of course is Jesus Christ himself risen from the dead and present even now because he is "like a circle enclosing all men and every individual man." Yet, "in the case of the Christian this circle closes with the fact that he believes" (IV/1, p. 742). In other words, Jesus Christ is the reconciler, the one in whom we have been converted back to God, the one who lives eternal life for everyone even now; he did what he did not just for believers but for unbelievers. Those who believe have the advantage of actually being there for the one who is there for all; one who believes enters into relationship with Christ himself. Faith, in Barth's view, therefore is a free, spontaneous action on the part of those who are compelled to find their true center outside themselves and in Jesus Christ himself. One can thus see the power of Barth's statement that

> To believe means to believe in Jesus Christ. But this means to keep wholly and utterly to the fact that our temporal existence receives and has and again receives its truth, not from itself, but exclusively from its relationship to what Jesus Christ is and does as our Advocate and Mediator in God Himself. . . . In faith we abandon . . . our standing upon ourselves . . . for the real standing in which we no longer stand on ourselves . . . but . . . on the ground of the truth of God. . . . We have to believe; not to believe in ourselves, but in Jesus Christ. (II/1, p. 159)

This free act of faith, however, is "a necessary work" that is "completely bound to its object" so that we are not in any sense in control. We simply find ourselves, Barth says, "in that orientation" and "accept it" (IV/1, p. 744). This is a work that can only be described as "renunciation in favour of the living Lord Jesus Christ." Nonetheless, it is a genuinely free human work as an act of responsibility to Jesus Christ himself. "It is really ours, the possibility of the entire creaturely and sinful man; yet not in such a way that contemplating this man one can discover it or read it off somewhere in him or on him. . . . The possibility given to us in faith is that it arises and consists absolutely in the object of real knowledge" (I/1, p. 237).

FAITH AS A FREE HUMAN ACT

While Barth thinks of faith as obedience in order to guard against any idea of a self-grounded faith or any idea that we might control the subject matter here, he unequivocally insists that this is a "free human act—more genuinely free than any other" precisely because "It is also the work of Jesus Christ who is its object" (IV/1, p. 744). Both of these factors must be held together because, following John 8:36, it is the case that "The Son makes a man free to believe in Him. Therefore faith in Him is the act of a right freedom, not although but just because it is the work of the Son" (IV/1, p. 745). Importantly, no one can be said to have this freedom "unless the Son makes him free" because Christians are sinful just like everyone else. There is a gulf between ourselves and faith, even though things did not have to turn out that way. Barth says, "Believing might have been more natural to [us] than breathing," since we were created to be "the covenant-partner[s] of God and therefore for God" (IV/1, p. 745). In this sense the great gulf between us and faith is something that is "contrary to nature" and is created only by our "being in the act of pride." No one has ever overcome this, not even the Christian— even the slightest slip toward supposing that we can believe *of ourselves* would simply continue that prideful activity. Any sort of "self-fabricated faith" on whatever basis is in fact "the climax of unbelief." Why does Barth take such a hard line here? The answer is simple: it is because it is not a matter of our doing something here for ourselves; rather it is a matter simply of "following Him, of repeating His decision" (IV/1, p. 745). The freedom experienced by Christians who have faith, then, is true freedom not because it implies an ability to choose between belief and unbelief, like Hercules at the crossroads. That idea itself is a great illusion. Any such prospect means that one has always already chosen unbelief. There is instead, Barth says, a "necessity of faith." In what does that consist? To answer this question it is important to see that faith does not stand "somewhere in face of the possibility of unbelief (which is not a mere possibility but the solid actuality of sinful man)" (IV/1, p. 746). Faith in this sense is no mere possibility vying for respectability alongside unbelief. No. "Faith makes the solid actuality of unbelief an impossibility. It sweeps it away" (IV/1, p. 746). Beyond this, faith actually replaces unbelief. That is what takes place "in the necessity of faith." It is necessary because it is the only possible act that remains for us, that is, "the genuinely free act of faith" (IV/1, p. 746).

The foundation of faith, then, that is grounded in this necessity consists in the fact that it is a joyful and unquestioning act that simply "cannot be compared even remotely with the certainty of any other human action" (IV/1, p. 747). But the whole point of this discussion is this: the necessity of faith just described cannot be found within us at all. It cannot be found in our good nature as God created it or in our sinful nature that as such has no possibility of faith. Indeed, "it does not even lie in faith in itself and as such. It is to be found rather in the object of faith" (IV/1, p. 747).

> One is not to seek this capability [of conformity to God in faith] among the stock of his own possibilities. The statement about the indwelling of Christ that takes place in faith must not be turned into an anthropological statement. There must be no subtraction from the lostness of natural and sinful man, as whom the believer will for the first time really see himself. (I/1, p. 240)

This, because this sinful person that I see myself to be in faith "is dead in faith, in Christ, according to Romans 6:3f., and I am alive in faith, a miracle to myself, another man, and as such capable of things of which I can only know myself to be absolutely incapable as a natural sinful man" (I/1, p. 240). This object, namely, Jesus Christ himself, "forces itself necessarily on man and is in that way the basis of his faith" (IV/1, p. 747).

This seems a strange way of putting the matter since it appears to suggest that what takes place in faith is not the supreme act of freedom, but an act of being dominated by another—an act that would, by any human standard, be considered abhorrent. This would be a monstrous misunderstanding of the matter, however. Barth speaks of necessity here because what happened in the life of Jesus Christ himself was "an absolutely superior actuality" in that our sin and ourselves as sinners have been destroyed in his life of obedience for us, so that our "unbelief, is rejected, destroyed and set aside," and we are "born again" as those who are obedient and now have the freedom for faith. It is in that "destroying and renewing of man as it took place in Jesus Christ" that "there consists the necessity of faith" (IV/1, p. 747). What Barth is saying is that, objectively, Jesus Christ died and rose from the dead for everyone so that "ontologically there is a necessity of faith for them all" (IV/1, p. 747). This means that since Jesus Christ did what he did for all people, he is "not simply one alternative or chance which is offered to man, one proposition which is made to him. He is not put there for man's choice, à prendre ou à laisser [to take or leave]" (IV/1, p. 747). Rather, "The other alternative is, in fact, swept away in Him" (IV/1, p. 747). That is what Barth means here when he speaks of necessity. There is only the possibility of obedience to a fact that has been established—a fact that is alone the enabling condition of what it means to be truly human. That fact is that we are now free in Christ to live as God intended us to live, that is, as those who find their truth again and again in Jesus Christ himself, who is God acting for us as well as the human mediator living faithfully in our place. This is what makes unbelief "an objective, real and ontological impossibility and faith an objective, real and ontological necessity for all men and for every man" (IV/1, p. 747).

Barth goes on to indicate that it is the Holy Spirit who is the "awakening power" of both this impossibility and this necessity. Confronted by these, we discover in faith that our only possibility is to choose that for which we have been already chosen. While the divine decision is not made in us, it can be repeated in us. It is not made in us because we cannot destroy our old sinful selves and establish ourselves as new creatures. In this sense believing is "an absolute necessity" because it is our "most proper and inward necessity"; something that is not strange but "self-evident." In fact Barth says that faith is the only human action that is self-evident because it is the only free choice there is beside which there is no other choice! Once again, "The Holy Spirit is the power in which Jesus Christ the Son of God makes a man free, makes him genuinely free for this choice and therefore for faith" (IV/1, p. 748). And what is discovered is the fact that in Jesus Christ, we come to know that we are at one with God and that by the power of his resurrection we have faith to accept the fact that things are objectively the way they are because of him. Even though a person becomes and is a Christian inasmuch as faith "is orientated and based on Him [Jesus Christ] as its object, there takes place in it the constitution of the Christian subject. . . . In this action there begins and takes place a new and particular being of man" (IV/1, p. 749).

Just as sinners are what they do, so those who as sinners who now live a new birth in Christ by faith are what they do when they are "awakened to faith and can live by it" (IV/1, p. 750). People awakened to faith by the Holy

Spirit pray the Lord's Prayer, call on God the Father, recall the apostolic message. They are drawn from "both Jews and Gentiles" and become the body of Christ, their head, and partake of salvation because they are brought into peace with God as they have been "reconciled by Him to Himself in Jesus Christ" (IV/1, p. 750). This has occurred for every person. But Christians are those who "are the first-fruits and representatives of the humanity and the world to which God has addressed Himself in Jesus Christ" (IV/1, p. 750). They must give glory to the God who has done this, "the glory which the others do not give Him, and in so doing to attest to them that which they do not know although it avails for them" (IV/1, p. 750). All of this means that each individual who has faith lives in community with others in a

> royal freedom [which] is the freedom to stand in [the community] as a brother or a sister, to stand with other brothers and sisters in the possession granted to it and the service laid upon it. If faith is outside the Church it is outside the world, and therefore a-Christian. It does not have as its object "the Saviour of all men, and specially of them that believe." (IV/1, p. 751)

Does faith merely have a cognitive character for Barth? He has been understood this way. But this would be a mistake. Barth really thinks that, while faith has no creative character, because "It is not their faithfulness which makes them this [Christian subjects]" (IV/1, p. 752), nonetheless

> the event of their faith . . . is more than cognitive in character. . . . It is clearly the positing of a new being, the occurrence of a new creation, a new birth of these men. In their act these sinful men confirm that they are the witnesses of the alteration of the human situation which has taken place in Jesus Christ: not the men who are altered in it—for as such they cannot so far be seen—but certainly, and this is the astonishing thing—as those for whom it has happened and not not happened, as the witnesses of it. (IV/1, p. 752)

People have the characteristic of being witnesses to this alteration of the human situation in Jesus Christ. And while their faith does not cause them to be who they are in Christ, still their faith has a "certain creative character" in that they actually do become Christians in the midst of others and thus have the characteristic of believers. Here is where the emphasis on the Holy Spirit is important. Christ himself, risen from the dead, has proven himself to be "stronger by the irresistible awakening power of His Holy Spirit" (IV/1, pp. 752-53). And it is because the Holy Spirit awakens people to faith through Christ's active power that itself is "effected by Him, the event of his faith is not merely cognitive as a human act but it is also creative in character" (IV/1, p. 753). This new being that is effective and revealed—this "new creation"— all "are the mystery of the One in whom he believes and whom he can acknowledge and recognise and confess in faith" (IV/1, p. 753). When Christ encircles such a person, then that person necessarily does what must be done in faith. Faith means that I discover myself as one of those for whom "from all eternity God has thought of . . . acted for . . . and called . . . to Himself in Him as His Word" (IV/1, p. 753). My resulting activities are those of one who lives life in accordance with this new situation. The work of the Holy Spirit then consists in the fact that in Him we are called to responsibility and claimed as those for whom Christ died and rose from the dead— those whose pride was overcome and who in him live a new life. The mystery and creative fact that occurs here is that each person recognizes that grace, salvation and justification all took place just for each of us; that Jesus Christ is there just for us. "That this shines out in a sinful man is the mystery, the creative fact, in the event of faith" (IV/1, p. 754). What, then, is the new creation? Simply that each of us is compelled to acknowledge that "Jesus Christ is, in fact, just for me, that I myself am just the subject for whom He is. . . . That is the newness of being, the new creation, the new birth of the Christian" (IV/1, p. 755). This does not occur in isolation, because Christ died for all of us. Yet this death for all includes us as individuals as well. In spite of the danger of existentializing the gospel at this point, one cannot abstract from the fact that all that God in Christ has done for humanity, he has done just for me. Yet again, this cannot be understood in terms of a general anthropology but only as a reality in and from Jesus Christ himself. Let me conclude this discussion of faith by illustrating how Barth develops his view of the specific act of faith with the concepts of acknowledgment, recognition and confession. This is important because I will argue throughout this book that a proper view of our experience of God can never find its true meaning *in* our experience but only in Christ himself and thus only in faith, and in that way theologians can do justice both to their experiences of God in faith and to the fact that it is the triune God and not their experience that is truly known in the process.

Faith as Acknowledgment

We begin by noting that one might think that recognition should come before acknowledgment. And Barth says that in other cases this may be true; but it is not true in the case of Christian faith. In that case recognition is included in the acknowledgment but "it can only follow" because it is an act of "obedience and compliance" (IV/1, p. 758). This is an extremely interesting point. What is meant here is that the knowledge of faith "is not preceded by any other kind of knowledge, either recognition or confession" (IV/1, p. 758). Obedience closes the door in a real sense to apologetics because what is known in faith makes itself known precisely in such a way that no one and nothing else can claim our attention in the same way. That is why recognition and confession "are included in and follow from the fact that they are originally and properly an acknowledgment, the free act of obedience" (IV/1, p. 758).[10]

Barth traces his view of obedience not only to John Calvin but to Romans 1:5, where Paul describes the task of the apostolate as obedience. Specifically, this faith as acknowledgment "will start with the fact that the calling of sinful man to faith in Jesus Christ is identical with his calling to the community of Jesus Christ built on the foundation of the apostles and prophets, the community which is his body, the earthly-historical form of His existence" (IV/1, p. 759). Faith, then, will always involve some encounter with the relative authority and freedom of the Christian community in its preaching or teaching such that the person who experiences this will be compelled to accept and "submit to its law and desire to associate himself with it and join it" (IV/1, p. 759). Such a person will not base his or her decision on what the community is and does as a "worldly phenomenon." Wisely, Barth notes that it always was and is the "more than doubtful Christians who are impressed by the phenomenon of the Church as such and won by it to submit to it and join it" (IV/1, p. 759). A church that tries to impress others in this sense is also quite problematic, because anyone who comes to true Christian faith will necessarily encounter Jesus Christ himself *through*

---

[10]As we will note in chap. 2, Barth allows for the fact that there is a good apologetics and a bad apologetics. Good apologetics will be incidental and implicit because it will be based on the reality and possibility of the knowledge of God grounded in the Word of God, and it will not be based on our free choices but on God's choice of us. An apologetics based on our free choices is a bad apologetics because it is self-grounded instead of being grounded in the enabling power of the Holy Spirit (pp. 102-5, 113).

the community, that is, in an encounter with the community. That means that such a person does not submit to the church "but to its law and therefore to the Lord Jesus Christ Himself, and that in so doing he will necessarily desire to associate with it and join it" (IV/1, p. 759). The key here is to realize that the church does not win people "for itself," but through its ministry Jesus Christ wins people for himself; hence acknowledgment means that faith that gives rise to recognition and confession means acceptance of Jesus Christ himself, the living Lord.

Negatively, this means that faith as acknowledgment cannot mean acceptance of some doctrine or proposition or report, because it is obedient acceptance of Jesus himself who "is sovereign" and simply cannot be replaced by the apostolic witness to him. This does not mean that Barth is here reverting to some sort of non-objective knowledge of God. What it means is that, even though he thinks we cannot come to faith without "the articles of faith" or the statements of the creed, the power and truth of faith come from the God who meets us in that encounter and empowers that faith. That is why Barth insisted early on that

> what gives faith its seriousness and power is not that man makes a decision, nor even the way in which he makes it. . . . Faith lives by its *object*. . . . The seriousness and power of faith are the seriousness and power of the *truth*, which is identical with God Himself, and which the believer has heard and received in the form of definite truths, in the form of articles of faith.[11]

This acknowledgment does not take place in a vacuum but in accordance with the witness of the Bible and the creed; but it is acknowledgment of Jesus Christ himself and nothing and no one else. Substitution of the church's witness or of certain statements for Christ at this point would lead either to the worst kind of false orthodoxy or perhaps even to a Modernist dogmatics that, as Barth once suggested, "hears man answer when no one has called him. It hears him speak with himself" (I/1, pp. 61-62). Instead, Barth insists that even as a fully human act, faith has its reality only in the direct encounter with its object and thus "only as the gift of the Holy Spirit of Jesus Christ Himself, only as the work of obedience which is pledged to Him and the freedom which is given by Him" (IV/1, p. 761). In rejecting "false or-

---

[11]Karl Barth, *Credo* (New York: Charles Scribner's Sons, 1962), p. 2.

thodoxy" Barth himself noted that his thinking might appear to be in agreement with both Wilhelm Herrmann and Rudolf Bultmann. Yet, he doubted that for these theologians Jesus Christ alone was the "basis of the act of faith" such that the negation had to be made only on that ground and not on the ground of some sort of "ethico-anthropological propositions" (IV/1, p. 761).[12]

FAITH AS RECOGNITION

Having defined faith as a basic act of obedience that consists in "compliant taking cognisance" (IV/1, p. 761), Barth moves on to explain what he means by recognition. And it is more than a little interesting. Here is where those who mistakenly accuse Barth of fideism miss something truly indispensable. Following Calvin and Paul, Barth wishes to stress that "All true knowledge of God (*omnis recta Dei congitio*) is born of obedience" in order to show that as a basic act of faith "this obedience is not an obedience without knowledge, a blind obedience without insight or understanding, an obedience which is rendered only as an emotion or an act of will" (IV/1, p. 761). This, because recognition is, in Barth's view, contained already in the acknowledgment as a second thing enclosed within the first. That is why Barth notes that Calvin sharply rejected the scholastic idea of *implicit faith*, which he equated with "a readiness to subject reason to the teaching of the Church" (IV/1, p. 761). This, for Calvin, was a falsehood "which would not merely bury the true faith but completely destroy it," because faith is not based on or located in ignorance but in knowledge, and in this case it is based in knowledge of God's revealed will and thus in the graciousness of the Father and in the atonement made by Christ himself.

Here is where Barth's rejection of non-objective knowledge and Torrance's rejection of non-conceptual knowledge (which amount to the same thing) pay dividends. There is recognition in the basic act of acknowl-

---

[12]For a full and quite interesting discussion of acknowledgment see I/1, pp. 205-8, where Barth presents nine points aimed at stressing the ideas just discussed by noting that human *ratio* includes all of our experience (feeling, will and conscience) as well as action, such that our free human self-determination is not at all limited or put aside but rather, in obedience to the Word, it is governed by God's own self-determination to be our God. Obedience suggests that we are in a personal relationship to God and thus we must yield to God who has supremacy. God's Word bends us but does not break us by bringing us "into conformity with itself" (I/1, p. 206).

edgment because the living Lord Jesus Christ makes himself known through
the biblical witness and the proclamation of the church not as some formless
reality or in

> some featureless way which is at the mercy of every possible conception and
> interpretation, but He does so as a genuine object with a very definite form
> which cannot be exchanged or mistaken for any other form, which is deter-
> mined by His own being and His own revelation of His being, which is His
> authentic form. (IV/1, p. 762)

And this occurs only within the sphere of the biblical revelation and the
church's proclamation as they present the true knowledge of faith in and
through their own obedient witness. But what form does Barth have in mind
here? In a more general or basic sense he is thinking of Calvin's statement
that God the Father is favorable to us because of the reconciliation accomplished in Christ. But in a more developed sense he is thinking of Luther's
statement that he believed that Jesus Christ is his Lord and then followed
that with further statements of the creed, namely, that he was begotten of
the Father, that he was truly human, was born of the virgin Mary, that he
redeemed him and freed him from sin, death and the devil's power through
his blood and not with silver or gold, and that he is free to live righteously
in his kingdom since Jesus has been raised from the dead and "lives and
reigns to all eternity" (IV/1, p. 763).

Nonetheless, Barth contends that Christian faith should be varied because, as the true Son of God who presents himself to believers, Jesus Christ
is "eternally rich." Even though Jesus himself is "single, unitary, consistent
and free from contradiction" as the one witnessed by Scripture and proclaimed by the community, his form is "inexhaustibly rich"; that is why
believers must see him "in new lights and new aspects" (IV/1, p. 763). But it
is also important to stress here that the limit of true knowledge of Jesus
Christ is also found in the scriptural witness and in the proclamation of the
church. Respecting this limit is the only way to know whether we have true
knowledge of Jesus Christ. Why is this so? The answer is simple. It is because
outside the scriptural witness and the church's proclamation "Jesus Christ
has no form for us; He is not an object of our knowledge and He cannot be
known by us" (IV/1, p. 763). To this extent, believers whom he has encoun-

tered in this sphere "will not even try to seek Him outside this sphere" (IV/1, p. 763). This is a critically important point, especially today when so many think that they not only can but that they must seek Jesus by identifying him with whatever actions of reconciliation one may find anywhere in the world.[13] Barth is absolutely adamant about this: to seek Jesus outside this sphere would have to mean that "both Jesus Christ and [that person's] faith would dissolve into nothingness" (IV/1, p. 763).

This is where the authority of Scripture and, in subordination to Scripture, the propositions, confessions and dogmas of the church have their place. Knowledge of faith in this sense means that those who believe in Jesus Christ attested in Scripture and proclaimed by the church are associated with a community that is in that same school and learns together with that community. What, then, is the ultimate judge or criterion of whether one knows the truth or has true faith? It is certainly not the church or any individual within it. Rather, it is Jesus Christ himself who "is the ultimate Judge who they are that truly recognise Him when they acknowledge Him" (IV/1, p. 764). Going further, Barth asserts that we must not be taken in by any sort of "anti-intellectualism" to suppose that "there is not a definite element of knowing" within this sphere of Scripture and the church because "If we believe, then . . . we know in whom we believe" (IV/1, p. 764). While there may be much that we need to learn, Barth says "we are never complete ig-noramuses, who cannot distinguish and think and speak" (IV/1, p. 764). In this sense everyone who has faith will have some knowledge and in fact "without an initial knowing there can be no initial faith, for faith takes place only in that sphere of Scripture and the community in which Jesus Christ has form and is an object of knowledge and can be known" (IV/1, pp. 764-65). To that extent every Christian is a theologian, even if only in a very basic

---

[13]See, e.g., my discussion of the thinking of Gordon Kaufman in Paul D. Molnar, *Incarnation and Resurrection: Toward a Contemporary Understanding* (Grand Rapids: Eerdmans, 2007), pp. 202-13. Instead of salvation referring to a unique action of God in Christ and through his Spirit, Kaufman redefines salvation in a purely social way to mean "all the activities and processes within human affairs which are helping to overcome the violence and disruptions and alien-ations . . . promoting personal and social deterioration and disintegration" (Gordon D. Kaufman, *Theology for a Nuclear Age* [Philadelphia: Westminster Press, 1985], p. 57). Because for Kaufman, Jesus is only a "paradigmatic exemplification" of various dispositions such as peace, joy and love, all activities of reconciliation and healing at work anywhere in the world should be equated with "the salvific divine spirit—the spirit of Christ—at work in the world" (p. 58).

way since they have true thoughts of Jesus Christ. Still, anyone who wants a
Jesus "without form" is not only no theologian, but such a person is not even
a Christian, according to Barth. "For Jesus Christ is not without form, but
in the sphere in which he [the Christian] encounters Him He is both form
and object" (IV/1, p. 765).

Moreover, the knowledge of faith, together with the recognition that
follows, is not in any sense "abstract" because while it is theoretical, it is also
practical, and it involves us in a definite relationship and leads directly to
knowledge about ourselves in that we know that we are the ones whom Jesus
Christ has freed from sin and the devil through his death and resurrection
(IV/1, p. 766). Here Barth breaks with the traditional order of moving from
a more general knowledge of God, faith, dogmatics, the Bible, then proceeding to assent, in the sense that people decided to accept these abstract
truths for themselves, and finally they attained trust (*fiducia*) in them and
grasped their true meaning. For Barth this procedure is impossible because
when faith is tied to Jesus Christ, then there can be no neutrality. There can
only be a "decision of obedience" (IV/1, p. 765). Abstract knowledge in this
context would have to be a knowledge that actually takes place outside faith
in Jesus Christ, and in Barth's eyes this would essentially describe "a theologian abstracted from the fact that he is a Christian." Barth rightly believes
that such an idea "is one which has no substance" (IV/1, p. 765). For Barth
our knowledge and our recognition can never be neutral but always an "existential knowledge" that involves "knowledge in the active recognition of
[one's] faith" (IV/1, p. 766). Going further, Barth insists that active recognition must lead from knowledge to awareness and thus to "the self-
understanding and self-apprehension, of the whole man, thus becoming an
action and decision of the whole man" (IV/1, p. 766). When we discover that
Jesus died for us and rose for us, this leads to a total disruption of our lives
that takes the form of a free action "which is characterised as a basic act by
the fact that it is . . . the act of [one's] heart" (IV/1, p. 767).

Here Barth notes that we are at a dangerous point because we are talking
about "penultimate things" and not "ultimate things," since what has been
described is a total disruption or disturbance of our lives but not an absolute
one. Here one speaks of a "radical" but not an "eschatological decision" and
indeed of a "free act of man, of the human heart, grounded in the act of God,

but not the act of God itself and as such" (IV/1, p. 767). The danger at this point, evident in the younger Luther's theology and in the theology of Rudolf Bultmann, is the tendency to confuse what happened decisively in the life of Christ for us with some sort of reenactment of that history in us. There simply cannot be an identification of what happened in the history of Jesus Christ and what he accomplishes in his Holy Spirit when "he makes Himself the object and origin of faith" (IV/1, p. 767) with our free action of faith. "What takes place in the recognition of the *pro me* of Christian faith is not the redemptive act of God itself, not the death and resurrection of Jesus Christ, not the presentation and repetition of His obedience and sacrifice and victory" (IV/1, p. 767). In this regard Barth claimed that Bultmann's conception was little more than an

> existentialist translation of the sacramentalist teaching of the Roman Church, according to which, at the climax of the mass, with the transubstantiation of the elements—in metaphysical identity with what took place then and there—there is a "bloodless repetition" of the sacrifice of Christ on Golgotha. (IV/1, p. 767)

With the later Luther, Barth wants to stress that faith means recognizing and apprehending Jesus Christ as the one who died and rose from the dead in our place without confusing faith with Jesus' dying and rising again, and without confusing Christ's own history with what takes place in faith. That is why one cannot speak of what takes place in faith as "an absolute disturbance or an eschatological decision or the redemptive act of God" (IV/1, p. 768). Barth repeatedly insists that Jesus Christ is and must always remain the "object and origin of Christian faith" (IV/1, p. 768). But that means that any focus on the saints or on ourselves with the idea that Jesus' life history is repeated or reenacted in such histories is a terrible mistake because it always means that Jesus Christ has ceased to be that object and origin in practice but not in theory. This was the counterquestion that Barth had for Hans Urs von Balthasar, whom Barth praised for his christocentrism and for his assessment of the *CD* while noting that Balthasar complained mildly about Barth's "christological constriction." It is this complaint that suggested to Barth that Balthasar had confused Christ and Christians in practice if not in theory, because such a complaint illustrates a tendency to allow the doctrine of justification to absorb that of sanctification, which is then understood as "the pious work of self-sanctification which man can undertake and accomplish in his own strength" (IV/1, p. 768). Hence Barth opposed not only the younger Luther and Rudolf Bultmann but also Balthasar and other Catholic theologians who claimed Christ as their center but then tended to confuse Christ with the lives of the saints and with their own sanctification. For Barth "The being and activity of Jesus Christ needs no repetition. It is present and active in its own truth and power" (IV/1, p. 769).

ANALOGY

At this point Barth introduces the concept of analogy to explain faith as a free human act that really does change our entire human situation. What happens to people when they come to faith is that they have to shape their existence in a manner "parallel to the One who as [their] Lord took [their] place" (IV/1, p. 769). One must conform oneself to the object of faith, namely, to Jesus Christ himself, whose death and resurrection occurred for that person. This is not the final thing because at this point the final thing can only be said of Jesus Christ himself; it is, Barth says, "the greatest penultimate thing" (IV/1, p. 769). And that means that such a person of faith is "with God" and "on the way to this end" (IV/1, p. 769). In faith we are free to live as Christians "in the likeness of Jesus Christ and His death and resurrection" (IV/1, p. 769). What we discover about ourselves is that we most certainly are not in any sense "a kind of second Christ" (IV/1, p. 769). That would lead us out of faith and knowledge of Christ because he would cease to be another, that is, an object of faith. We are not the reconciler who became a servant and obeyed the Father and was the Judge judged in our place. "The glory of God has not been revealed in me as in His resurrection. Far from being a Saviour, I am only a proud man like all other men, and as such I have fallen a prey to eternal death and perdition" (IV/1, p. 770). All that I can do is believe in Jesus himself, who alone is my savior. And even this is possible only "as He encounters me in the witness of Scripture and the proclamation of His community, only as He awakens me to it by the power of His Holy Spirit" (IV/1, p. 770). But Barth says that in this awakening and encounter with Jesus himself, we can see ourselves, without of course becoming like him, as determined by him and "stamped by Him" (IV/1, p. 770).

CHRIST AND CHRISTIANS

To see myself as stamped and determined by Jesus, and therefore in his light, means that there will be a likeness of Jesus' own justifying activity in mine. What Jesus did in his death for me was to vanquish my pride, that is, he removed, destroyed and put it to death in his "substitutionary being and activity," and this is what is shown in his resurrection (IV/1, p. 770). Barth freely admits that when I recognize myself as the one for whom Jesus did this, then something very definite happens for my own self-understanding and my entire attitude. In attempting to explain what it is that happens, Barth seeks to avoid confusing Christ and Christians, and so he insists that we say too much if we claim that the overcoming of our pride that has taken place for us in Jesus Christ and comes to us in him has actually "taken place in me" (IV/1, p. 771). Why? Because although it comes to me in Christ, "it has not taken place in me" (IV/1, p. 771). Even though we believe in Jesus Christ and see what has come to us in him, we still find in ourselves our pride and fall. Thus it would be a mistake to think that sin and death no longer have any power over us. Hence, "In relation to my being in Jesus Christ, I can and must maintain this, but better not in relation to myself. I have overcome in Him, but not in myself, not even remotely" (IV/1, p. 771). Only a bad theology, Barth thinks, will grasp at some sort of equality with Christ; there must instead be a clear distinction between Christ and us, a distinction that I believe is lost when one says that "the vocation and mission of *every* member of the church [is] to become Christ."[14]

Yet, Barth insists that we say too little if, in view of this distinction between Christ and us, we rest content to think that since it has not taken place in us, therefore we may use this as an excuse to continue in our condition as fallen in Adam and embracing sin, that is, embracing "impossible possibilities" (IV/1, p. 771). Only a poor theology, Barth says, "persists in the inequality between me and Jesus Christ—a pious cushion which is content to maintain the distinction from Him" (IV/1, p. 771). What, then, should we say with regard to the fact that our pride and fall have been vanquished in Christ's death and resurrection? We should, Barth thinks, be alarmed at ourselves and sorry for our condition, unwilling to boast of ourselves, and

---

[14]LaCugna, *God for Us*, p. 402.

think of our acts with remorse and penitence because we will recognize that together with the world we have been vanquished—put to death in Jesus Christ. That is the "total disturbance" that each of us must accept when we come to know Jesus and come to know ourselves in him (IV/1, p. 772). Barth identifies this as *mortificatio*. Heartfelt penitence will take place in those who know Jesus Christ as their Savior and are "determined and stamped and enlightened by Him" (IV/1, p. 772).

Penitence does not mean putting off the world. Rather it means that within the world we will experience the Word of God as cutting through the old Adam. This happens to the extent that we believe, so that, as "a new subject in the knowledge of faith (different from when [we] did not believe)," we will experience the pain of this in a way that we can never escape. From the center of our existence this pain "will continually accompany and penetrate all [our] thoughts and words and works" (IV/1, p. 772). This Word will thwart and disturb our pride. This disturbance will continually come to the person of faith as a call to resist evil in whatever form by resisting one's pride. Such a person, perhaps in only a small way, will dismiss potential evil acts because of what has come to him or her in Jesus Christ—not in himself or herself, Barth stresses, but in Jesus Christ. To the extent that this happens such a person "will exist in analogy with Him" (IV/1, p. 772). However dissimilar they may be, there will be a "correspondence" or a "parallelism" and a "similarity" between believers and Jesus Christ. In this regard Barth notes that the publican (Lk 18:9-14) and the prodigal son (Lk 15:1-32) "are a likeness of the One who as the Lamb of God took away the sin of the world: no more but no less," and all those who believe in Jesus and know themselves in him are, alongside the publican and the prodigal, minimally in the likeness of what Jesus "has been and done, and is and does for [us]" (IV/1, p. 772). What this looks like in detail is spelled out by Barth in *CD* IV/3.2, §71, The Vocation of Man.

This is the negative side of the life of faith. The positive side refers to the fact that I recognize that my life has been restored in Jesus Christ—not the life of all people in general—but my own "right and life" (IV/1, p. 772). Jesus Christ "stands in my place as my righteousness and life" (IV/1, p. 773). I therefore see myself and know myself in him as the one "to whom that right and life are given, as the one to whom He has given Himself as righteous and alive for me" (IV/1, p. 773). Once again, however, care is required when thinking about the implications of this. It would be too much to suggest that "my restoration as it is taken place in Jesus Christ . . . has taken place in me" (IV/1, p. 773) with the result that I might boast of something that is now my possession and can count as my very own. This, because my history is not in reality identical with Jesus' history. This triumphant restoration of my righteousness has not taken place in me, and therefore the glory of that right and life cannot be seen in me. There is nothing in ourselves at all that we can cling to. The failure of a theology that presumes to be able to find the assurance of salvation by assuming that everything in our lives is or can be different once again mistakenly supposes an exact similarity with Jesus Christ. In relation to Jesus himself I have my assurance. But it is only in him that I have it. Still, Barth thinks we say too little if we conclude from this that we don't have to do anything because what Jesus has done and is doing is so different from what we can and must do. If I still think I must continue to accuse myself of the things that I do wrong and continue to do wrong and that I must still fear death as though "nothing had happened" (IV/1, p. 773), then although my right and life have indeed been restored in Jesus Christ as my full consolation, they are in a sense bracketed or as Barth says, they are "in cold storage" (IV/1, p. 773) because in that situation they have no practical value. To the extent that I am thrown back on myself to provide my own consolation and answer for my own right and perhaps make myself worthy of it and "earn and attain my own life" (IV/1, p. 773), I lack the assurance of salvation. Any such conclusion once again results from a bad theology because it looks away from its true and solid assurance, namely, the fact that in Jesus Christ we have our right and life so that we move into an impossible situation when we fall back into some subtle or not-so-subtle form of works righteousness. This thinking is discordant with the knowledge of faith.

What, then, follows in our lives when we recognize that our right and life have been restored in the death of Jesus and disclosed in his resurrection? Even though we know we are still threatened by death and accused of the wrong things we do and have done, we still can have complete assurance that includes comfort and joyful confidence, because we can genuinely rely on what actually has taken place for us. I can have security and think and act in peace by doing "my few works" and look forward not "to the void of a better future" but to "the fulfilment of the promise given to me in Jesus

Christ" (IV/1, p. 774). I really can trust the verdict that was revealed in him that assigns right and life to me. Trusting in the promise cannot be equated with *fiducia*, because it is not something arbitrary but a very definite response to the Word of God that is spoken to me. It is a trust grounded in the knowledge of faith "as the knowledge of Jesus Christ" (IV/1, p. 774). We do not stand in isolation here but recognize that what Jesus Christ did, he did for the community and for entire world; it was disclosed for the world and therefore also for me. It is thus incumbent on me to recognize that what applies to me also applies to the community and to the world. As such I must conduct myself as a reflection of the world's reconciliation in Jesus Christ. A confidence that had given up the church and the world as lost would in reality be a very strange kind of confidence. To know that my right and life are sure in Jesus Christ means that, as I abide in that fact and live accordingly, I also realize that "my right and life are promised to them" (IV/1, p. 774).

Barth, however, makes an interesting observation here that separates his view from those who argue for a view of salvation that ascribes one's hope to an optimistic view of people's nature and ways. This would be but another form of self-justification and miss the surety of faith. One has this view of others only because of what has happened in the death and resurrection of Jesus Christ for the entire world. Barth notes that the older theologians called this *vivificatio*, which means that our right and life do not just come to us once but do so continually, so that these determine our lives everywhere and always and not just occasionally. Hence, when someone knows Jesus Christ as the savior of the world and is thus determined and enlightened by Christ himself, "his heartfelt act cannot be omitted" (IV/1, p. 775). Once again, though, no one is called to suppose that what he or she experiences in this heartfelt action is in reality the new heaven and the new earth promised for them and for the church and the world. It is crucial that we have confidence in the new creation "on the old earth and under the old heaven but resolutely grasped" (IV/1, p. 775). That means that there will be "little renovations and provisional sanctifications and reassurances" that will penetrate us inasmuch as we have become new people in the knowledge of faith. When a person believes, Barth says, that person becomes a free person in spite of all his or her limitations because of the knowledge of his or her right and life as they have taken place in Christ. As a free person one is called away from pride and to humility and thus to obedience, and is thus willing and able to live obediently. Accepting the pain of penitence, the person of faith will trust in God's grace and in that way such a person will be cheerful. Without illusion one will realize that there will be setbacks and assaults on faith, and that he or she will be knocked down and have to rise up again and again. Yet in all of this, both in relation to God and others, such a person of faith ultimately will be a peaceful person because he or she will know that each of us is "held by the One in whom [we are] already restored" because we are already righteous covenant partners of God (IV/1, p. 775). Once again it is important to emphasize that faith here means that even as we are exposed to questions and have no claim to this peace and surety because it is not to be found in us at all but only in Christ who acted and acts for us, we can and do live in likeness to what Christ has done for us. In and with our imperfections we still reflect Christ's perfection in thankfulness for God's "almighty grace" (IV/1, p. 775).

Faith as Confession

To acknowledge and to recognize Jesus Christ without confessing would mean that one is not a Christian. In Barth's thinking, "The goal of the freedom in which He makes a man genuinely free—free to believe in Him—is the freedom to be His witness" (IV/1, p. 776). That is why the goal of faith is confession (witness). With the glory of God manifested in Jesus Christ the radiance evident "breaks through and lights up the man himself" (IV/1, p. 776). Anyone who genuinely believes in Jesus Christ enacts a history—what Barth calls "a history of the heart," in which that person expresses outwardly the obedience of faith by communicating what it is that is known and recognized. Even if people do not wish to do this or are opposed to doing so, the fire and sword (Mt 10:24; Lk 12:49) are effective in the act of faith as confession. One cannot be a Christian without this. But what does it mean to confess?

Briefly, it means that to have faith involves taking one's stand on Jesus Christ himself, the object of faith, so that in acknowledging him and recognizing him, one outwardly confesses him before others (Mt 10:32). People of faith belong to Jesus Christ totally, that is, both inwardly and outwardly. One who is penitent and confident is only relatively and not absolutely different from others; one is only absolutely different "in the mystery of his existence as grounded in Jesus Christ, not in what he himself is and does on this basis" (IV/1, p. 777). One who confesses Jesus Christ may express that confession in surprising ways, especially in the eyes of those who do not have the categories to understand his or her actions. Indeed what one does thereby is simply to stand to what one now is in Christ. As such, one's actions acquire "the character of a venture" (IV/1, p. 777). Actions such as this, then, could possibly be annoying to others and even dangerous to the one who acts as a confessor. If one must suffer as a result, then it is not because that person intended to do so but because this proceeds from his or her action. No one can give this ability to provoke others to their actions. This occurs only from the mystery of their existence in Christ, who alone can do this. In other words, we are the little lights "reflecting the great light" (IV/1, p. 778) and as such, our actions stand out from the actions of others. We are thus witnesses "without especially willing to do so, and without in any way helping to do so" (IV/1, p. 778). Whoever does not hide his or her light under a bushel basket engages in the required act of confession.

Because by creation and by nature, to be human means to be in fellowship, the free human act of faith cannot simply be a private act that one might wish to conceal from others. Whatever their attitude to the person of faith may be, persons of faith cannot perform that act without their neighbors and therefore without communication with them. Here Barth makes the all-important point that the act of faith that involves acknowledgment, recognition and confession is not some arbitrary discovery of our own. Hence, "It is not on the basis of [our] own discovery and private revelation, but by the mediatorial ministry of the community which is itself in the school of the prophets and apostles, that a man comes under the awakening power of the Holy Spirit and therefore to faith" (IV/1, 778). That indeed is the "starting-point of the act of faith" (IV/1, p. 778). In this regard we all need the community, just as we need the awakening power of the Holy Spirit and just as we need the school of the prophets and apostles if we are to continue to stand in faith and to live by faith. Indeed the community also needs us, because its ministry is not done but must continue in and through our witness. Our witness is necessary for the ongoing ministry of the community. Every believer is called to this witness, and in certain situations a great deal may actually be at stake. One can "never escape the communion of the saints;

[one] can never leave it in the lurch" (IV/1, p. 778). To do this would be to deny one's faith. Because one must confess Jesus Christ publicly, such a person of faith will desire to be baptized. When this happens such a person will make it clear to all that he or she is the one for whom Christ died and in whom life has been restored. This will take place in thanksgiving.

None of this, however, implies escape from the world. Rather, even though we are surrounded by those who do not acknowledge, recognize or confess Jesus Christ, we make known the fact that God was in Christ reconciling the world to himself. In the midst of a world that does not know this, we are sure of that one decisive fact, namely, that Christ died and rose again not just for those who believe but for them as well. They therefore make that known in what they say, but also in what they do. They do so in small ways and not necessarily in great deeds. They do so just by being who they are as those who speak and act and make use of the freedom that has been given to them.

We have seen how Barth's understanding of faith is shaped by his belief that our experience of faith is fashioned by the action of the Holy Spirit and our union with Christ, and through Christ our union with the Father. In this last part of the chapter I would like to demonstrate with clarity the very different views of faith that follow when one does not exclusively allow the object of faith to determine the meaning and content of faith. I will do this by contrasting Barth's view with the views of Karl Rahner, focusing on two critical issues with wide-ranging implications, namely, Barth's belief that faith is not generally explicable, and why Barth and Torrance believe that non-conceptual knowledge undermines the very meaning of faith. I do this for two reasons. First, some theologians assume that Barth's thinking is quite close to Rahner's, and second, others think that Barth is simply a fideist. I hope to show that while both theologians have similar aims and perspectives and neither is a fideist, their methodologies and therefore their conclusions differ enormously.

FAITH IS NOT GENERALLY EXPLICABLE

Let us begin first by contrasting Barth's statement noted above that faith is not a phenomenon that is generally known and can be explained to everyone. Why does he say this? The answer is simple. What is known in faith is that Jesus Christ who is the divine-human Mediator between us and the Father has reconciled us to God and now meets us as the risen Lord enabling our belief in him and in his actions of justification and sanctification for us; he is the one in whom our conversion to God has taken place and the one in whom we can live freely as those who are now God's friends and not God's enemies. Since Jesus' divinity and humanity are not to be confused and since Barth consistently held that Jesus is not the revealer in his humanity as such, Barth concluded that no study of anthropology, of Jesus' humanity or of the church's visible structure could possibly disclose the true nature of Jesus as the revealer, the church as his earthly-historical form or the true meaning of faith. The truth of these historical realities can be known in their depth of meaning only by means of a miraculous action of the Holy Spirit enabling us to hear the Word of God active *as* the man Jesus reconciling us to God from both the divine and the human side. Simply put, no phenomenological analysis of human action, human belief or of any historical actions of church members—no analysis of general anthropology—can yield the truth recognized and acknowledged in faith, namely, that Jesus Christ is God's Word acting for our benefit as the incarnate, crucified, risen, ascended and coming Lord. Faith is bound to this particular object who gives us a knowledge that simply cannot be gleaned from elsewhere or outside faith itself, because what we come to know in faith is something that transcends the world of experience that can be analyzed sociologically, psychologically, historically and therefore phenomenologically. That is why Barth rejected any notion that knowledge of revelation could be had via any a priori sort of reasoning. That is also why, as we shall shortly see, he opposed apologetic attempts to prepare for the gospel through any such analysis; such preparation is rendered unnecessary and indeed impossible by the fact that Jesus himself is the truth of God and cannot be bypassed in an attempt to know what God is doing now within history.

Knowledge of revelation thus could only take place a posteriori because knowledge of faith follows and does not precede its object. The hard question here is this: can the truth of the Christian faith be seen, acknowledged and lived (as it is self-involving) by those who remain neutral in relation to the message of the gospel? Can the truth of the Christian faith be understood, in other words, by those who do not acknowledge Jesus' lordship, which acknowledgment, we have seen, is itself a human act begun, upheld and completed through the Holy Spirit enabling it by uniting us to the risen Lord himself? In one sense the answer is yes, because people might hypothetically understand the claims of Christian faith, namely, that Christ died for our sins and rose from the dead, on a theoretical level as one set of claims over against others. But, in Barth's understanding, any mere theoretical under-standing of the gospel (that Christ died and rose for all) is not true under-standing, since true understanding is indeed self-involving and thus ex-cludes embracing any sort of neutrality with regard to who Jesus was, is and will be for and in relation to the human race. To put the matter bluntly: any attempt to understand Jesus Christ as one religious figure among others means that one may grasp Christian preaching in a superficial and theo-retical manner, but that by the very attempt to compare Christ to others, one demonstrates that one is not and has not thought about who Christ was and is in faith, which by nature acknowledges his utter uniqueness as the one and only Word of God active in history and thus as the one Son of the Father who is the sole savior of the world.

Comparing Barth's thinking to Rahner's on this point is very instructive indeed. When Rahner's thinking is specifically focused on a theological theme such as our encounter with the risen Lord, his thinking appears to be in harmony with Barth's. Thus, for example, in analyzing Jesus' saying that he is the good shepherd as recorded in John's Gospel, Rahner makes the important point that the "I am" sayings mean that "Jesus is uttering the words 'I am' in an absolute sense that is self-subsistent and all-comprehending. . . . Thus one can only realise what is meant by the reference to the good shepherd when one has first understood what 'I am' means."[15] Rahner continues by stressing that "In this case the subject determines the predicate, and not the other way round" (*TI* 7:174). Hence, when for instance Jesus says he is the way, the truth and the life (Jn 14:6), he is the one who determines the meaning of each of those terms. Rahner thus can say that "the 'I am' of Jesus is in itself, and without further addition, the object of faith which pronounces judgment upon the sins of unbelief" (*TI* 7:174-75). Clearly, Barth and Rahner would be one in this affirmation based on the teaching of John's Gospel. Their agreement would go further. When Rahner says that since God himself "cannot be included in any system of reference pertaining

---

[15]"Encounters with the Risen Christ," in *TI* 7:169-80, on p. 174.

to our own existence" and "cannot be conceived of from any point outside his own being" so that God cannot be placed into any system that we could understand and apply, Barth would agree fully. And when Rahner says additionally that just as God is absolute since God is a subject

> in the absolute, and not one which is susceptible of predicates, just as he reveals himself in this guise to Moses as "I am who am," . . . so too Jesus is the "I am" in an absolute sense: God whose existence is absolutely sovereign, absolutely independent, and prior to the existence of any other being, and it is as such that he proclaims himself in the words "I am" (*TI* 7:175)

Barth would agree completely.

But things take a rather drastic turn when in another context Rahner claims that "It is possible to enquire about Jesus' resurrection today (if we are to do justice to the facts and talk in a way that inspires confidence) only if we take into account the whole of what philosophy and theology have to say about man" (*TI*: 17:16). On this basis Rahner claims that we must begin by assuming that "the hope that a person's history of freedom will be conclusive in nature (a hope which is given in the act of responsible freedom and which is transcendentally necessary) already includes what we mean by the hope of 'resurrection'" (*TI* 17:16). Rahner goes further and maintains that "anthropology and Christology mutually determine each other within Christian dogmatics if they are both correctly understood" (*TI* 9:28). He says this because he believes that "it is correct to say that in every philosophy men already engage inevitably and unthematically in theology" since they are "anonymous Christians . . . whether they know it or not" (*TI* 6:79). There is thus a "latent 'Christianness' in the history of human existence" (*TI* 6:79). And Rahner says this because he believes that Christian anthropology "understands man as the *potentia oboedientialis* for the 'Hypostatic Union'" (*TI* 9:28) so that Christology must develop an a priori demonstration of how human beings are always in search of a savior in order to make sense of Christology.[16]

---

[16]See Rahner, *FCF*, pp. 295-305. Rahner espouses an "existentiell Christology" that he says must be heard "with a certain amount of discretion and with some qualifications." He claims that "There is an implicit and anonymous Christianity" and believes that there must be an "anonymous" but real relationship between individuals who have not yet "had the whole, concrete, historical, explicit and reflexive experience in word and sacrament of this reality [the history of salvation, including Jesus Christ]." Such a person has this relationship "implicitly in obedience to his orientation in grace toward the God of absolute, historical presence and self-communication. He exercises this

Rahner says this because his theological anthropology presupposes that we can only explain the hypostatic union in a credible way today that avoids mythology if "the idea of the God-man" receives "proof of a transcendental orientation in man's being and history under grace. A purely a posteriori Christology, unable to integrate Christology correctly into an evolutionary total view of the world, would not find it easy to dismiss the suspicion of propounding mythology" (*TI* 9:28-29). From this Rahner concludes that it is not only important "for a true Christology to understand man as the being who is orientated towards an 'absolute Saviour' both a priori and in actuality . . . but it is equally important for his salvation that he is confronted with Jesus of Nazareth as this Saviour—which cannot, of course, be transcendentally 'deduced'" (*TI* 9:29-30). Here Barth and Rahner could not be farther apart, since Barth contends that, in light of the cross, human beings are disclosed as those who are not in fact oriented toward Jesus Christ but actually opposed to him such that they need the reconciling enlightenment of the Holy Spirit opening them to the truth of what Christ did on the cross for the human race and revealed in his resurrection. Consequently, it is reasonable to conclude that Rahner's remark that it is equally important to be confronted by Jesus and that this Jesus cannot be transcendentally deduced, while materially a true statement, has become void of force precisely because in his reflections the driving force is not exclusively Jesus Christ himself, but our supposed orientation toward an absolute Savior understood a priori and only then Jesus Christ. In other words, Rahner's a priori Christology undercuts the need for Jesus of Nazareth at root by assuming that one can indeed deduce the meaning of the resurrection in some sense from our transcendental, grace-filled experiences of hope. And these experiences themselves, in Rahner's thinking, can be described without any specific faith in Jesus himself as the risen Lord.

How then do these assumptions and statements shape Rahner's thinking about the resurrection? The answer is disturbing because Rahner concludes that he can "formulate the proposition that knowledge of man's resurrection given with his transcendentally necessary hope is a statement of philo-

---

obedience by accepting his own existence without reservation" (*FCF*, p. 306). Alongside this there is the "fullness of Christianity" that has "become conscious of itself explicitly in faith and in hearing the word of the gospel" and thus knows of its relation to Jesus of Nazareth (ibid.).

sophical anthropology even before any real revelation in the Word" (*TI* 17:18). This conclusion, from within Barth's understanding of faith, would represent an intolerable confusion of philosophy and theology, a denial of faith and a destruction of any possibility of Christian hope, which is inextricably tied not only to the risen Lord in whom we believe but also is in no sense whatsoever anthropologically grounded, as we have already seen. Here Rahner's thinking even is in conflict with his own reflections on the truth offered in John's Gospel. For if Jesus is the sovereign God and thus the subject determined by no predicate, then it is impossible to conclude that any Christian could know the meaning of the resurrection apart from an explicit encounter with the risen Lord himself conceptually and by means of the Holy Spirit enabling such knowledge.[17] In fairness to Rahner, he does go on to say that he would have to counter his initial proposition by saying that, "at least initially, the elucidation of man's basic hope as being the hope of resurrection was in actual fact made historically through the revelation of the Old and New Testaments" (*TI* 17:18). But this statement is rendered inconsequential by the fact that any elucidation of our basic hope of resurrection as shaped by the scriptural witness would never for an instant direct us to ourselves with the idea that we could philosophically demonstrate the meaning of the resurrection by analysis of general anthropology. One could respond to this analysis from Rahner's perspective by noting that he is thinking on the basis of "graced existence." Nevertheless, any appeal to the idea that human experience is "grace-filled," from Barth's perspective, would have already confused grace with nature by failing to notice that one simply cannot find God's grace by exploring human nature but only by acknowledging, recognizing and confessing Jesus Christ as the grace of God active for us in the sphere of anthropology.

It is for this reason that I think Barth's position here is more meaningfully and consistently Christian than is Rahner's. It is Rahner's theological anthropology, which he believes conditions and is conditioned by Christology, that is the problem here. There is neither space nor need to go into Rahner's view of the relation between philosophy and theology, nature and grace, and anthropology and Christology here. It is enough to note that in his anthro-

---

[17]We will discuss the problem of non-conceptual knowledge of God and of Christ in the next section, along with the notion of implicit faith.

pology, on the basis of which he believes it is possible to hear and under-stand the Christian message, "we do not have to be concerned about separating philosophy and theology methodologically in the sharpest pos-sible way" since "transcendental philosophy of human existence is always achieved only within historical experience" (*FCF*, p. 25). Thus "we can never philosophize as though man has not had that experience which is the expe-rience of Christianity." And that specifically refers to the experience "of what we call grace." Hence, "A philosophy that is absolutely free of theology is not even possible in our historical situation" (*FCF*, p. 25). This is why Rahner concludes that "theology itself implies a philosophical anthropology which enables this message of grace to be accepted in a really philosophical and reasonable way, and which gives an account of it in a humanly responsible way" (*FCF*, p. 25). Given these presuppositions, Rahner embraces the idea that Christianity as grace and historical message refers "to something which is accessible to every theoretical reflection upon and self-interpretation of human existence, and this we call philosophy" (*FCF*, p. 25).

This brief discussion at least explains why Rahner can say that one could demonstrate the meaning of the resurrection through philosophical anthro-pology and apart from revelation. And my point here is simply this: any assumption that Christianity can be explained to everyone is an assumption that is not governed by faith in Jesus Christ engendered by the Holy Spirit. Here Barth and Rahner differ. And this is an enormous difference because even though they may be at one when interpreting Scripture, it is clear that Rahner's thinking does not remain consistently theological precisely be-cause he does not consistently allow the object of faith to determine the truth of his reflections; one might even say he cannot do this consistently precisely because of his philosophical presuppositions. And this is con-firmed by Rahner's belief that "To lead to faith (or rather, to its further, ex-plicit stage) is always to assist understanding of what has already been ex-perienced in the depth of human reality as grace (i.e., as in absolutely direct relation to God)."[18] Thus, while Barth claims that one always comes from unbelief to faith, Rahner presumes that grace as God's self-communication is implanted within everyone such that everyone really believes, even if they

---

[18]Karl Rahner, ed., *Encyclopedia of Theology: The Concise Sacramentum Mundi* (New York: Seabury, 1975), p. 497.

are atheists, as long as they accept the dictates of conscience and their transcendental dynamisms, which are presumed to be oriented toward God
himself.[19] This leads to our next consideration, namely, the idea that for
Barth faith can only be obedience to Christ, whereas for Rahner faith can
be so described but is not necessarily so described. The result is that Rahner
thinks of faith as something universally discernible within all human beings,
while Barth insists that, as a free human act, faith cannot be read off from
somewhere within us. This is an extremely important point that divides the
thinking of Barth and Rahner not only with respect to their understanding
of faith but also with respect to their views of God, Christ and salvation.

WHERE DOES FAITH COME FROM?

Things get even more interesting when one asks where faith comes from.
Naturally both Rahner and Barth would insist that faith ultimately comes
from God. But, given Rahner's transcendental anthropology as briefly discussed above, he thinks that "The primary approach to faith is a man's direct
confrontation with himself in his whole nature as free and responsible and
thereby with the incomprehensible ground of this human reality, called
God."[20] Once again, when Rahner thinks strictly as a theologian he has some
very interesting and compelling things to say about faith, such as when he
says that "The man who has experienced God in Christ . . . wants to and
must confess him. . . . The man who has found Christ must bear witness to
him before his brethren" (*TI* 9:124). This is a statement with which, as we

---

[19]This is why it can be said from within Rahner's perspective that "Grace, therefore, is experienced,
though not as grace, for it is psychologically indistinguishable from the stirrings of human
transcendentality" (Stephen Duffy, "Experience of Grace," in *The Cambridge Companion to Karl
Rahner*, ed. Declan Marmion and Mary E. Hines [Cambridge: Cambridge University Press,
2005], p. 48). And quite naturally this leads to the idea that "nature is in continuity with and
positively open to grace" (p. 51). The difference here between Rahner's thinking and Barth's is
enormous, and this has decisive implications for one's understanding of faith. Since grace is and
remains identical with God's action in Christ, for Barth, and since the gift, namely, God's self-
communication, cannot be separated in any sense from the Giver (Christ himself and his Spirit),
Barth would never accept the idea that grace is indistinguishable in any sense from human
transcendentality. Moreover, Barth would consider the idea that nature is in continuity with
grace Pelagian in origin and outcome because what we learn from faith in the crucified and risen
Lord is that nature is fallen (opposed to God's grace and in need of reconciliation). Thus human
beings are not positively open to grace but only become open when the Holy Spirit actualizes
reconciliation in them by enabling belief in Christ himself and not in their horizon, which is
assumed by Rahner to be indistinguishable from the mystery of God himself.
[20]Rahner, *Encyclopedia of Theology*, p. 497, emphasis mine.

have seen, Barth would agree, even though when Rahner spells out the meaning of belief in Jesus he tends to detach faith from the historical Jesus as its object and goal in the very way that Barth insists we must not. This explains why Rahner thinks he can understand faith by analyzing our confrontation with ourselves, and Barth continually insists that faith directs us away from ourselves and toward Christ alone. Still, Barth would also agree with Rahner when he says that "one cannot demand (and it would be heretical Modernism to do so) that the attempt must be made simply to deduce strictly all theological statements *from* man's experience of himself as if they were the latter's objectifying conceptualisation and articulation" (*TI* 9:41).[21]

But things become a bit muddled when Rahner goes on to note that matters are more complex "than the traditional opponents of Modernism mostly think" (*TI* 9:41) and then concludes that "there *is* also an *experience* of grace, and this is the real, fundamental reality of Christianity itself" (*TI* 9:41). Whereas Barth identifies grace with Jesus Christ himself and thus consistently upholds our total dependence on Jesus Christ (as does Torrance), Rahner thinks of grace as part of our existential experience and thus speaks of a "supernatural existential," that is, of God's self-communication as the innermost experience of depth within everyone.[22] Because Rahner

---

[21]Modernism in both its Catholic and Protestant forms can be taken to refer to a kind of thinking that reduces the objective actions of God within history to the human experience of grace, faith and revelation. It thus tends to base revelation, grace and faith on experience rather than on who God is and what God is doing within history. Rahner certainly wanted to avoid any sort of rationalist explanation of dogmatics, as did Barth. As noted above, Barth amusingly stated that modernist dogmatics "hears man answer when no one has called him. It hears him speak with himself" (I/1, pp. 61-62). Barth consistently rejected what he labeled "Modernist Protestantism." See, e.g., below, p. 269.

[22]While Rahner believes his idea of a supernatural existential avoids "intrinsicism" (the confusion of nature and grace), it seems virtually impossible to distinguish nature and grace once one accepts this concept. Thus, for example, William V. Dych, S.J., *Karl Rahner* (Collegeville, MN: Liturgical Press, 1992), writes: "if God created human beings precisely for the life of grace, then the offer and the possibility of grace is given with human nature itself as this nature has been historically constituted" (p. 36). Consequently, in his view, "nature has a certain affinity for grace" (p. 37) so that Rahner maintains that "grace is utterly free and gratuitous and at the same time that it is utterly intrinsic to human nature and human existence" (p. 37). Bluntly put: in Barth's thinking, since one cannot detach the gift (grace) from the Giver (Christ), one could never claim that nature has an affinity for grace (because of sin and the need for reconciliation before living by grace is possible), and grace is no longer gratuitous once it is conceptualized as "utterly intrinsic to human nature," because then one could contemplate human nature in order to know of God's grace, whereas in reality one can only know oneself in the light of Christ, who always remains distinct from us in all our experiences, as discussed above.

thinks this way, he believes we can explore humanity's transcendental experiences (which he assumes are inherently graced in light of God's universal will to save) in order to make sense of Christian faith. It also allows him to conclude about someone that

> Without reflection he accepts God when he freely accepts himself in his own
> unlimited transcendence. He does this when he genuinely follows his con-
> science with free consent, because by such an action he affirms as well the
> condition of possibility of such a radical option which is implicitly bound up
> with this decision, i.e. he affirms God. (*TI* 16:55-56)

Consequently, "If a man freely accepts himself as he is, even with regard to his own inner being whose basic constitution he inevitably has not fully grasped, then it is God he is accepting" (*TI* 16:67).

Here once more there is a decisive difference between the two theologians' interpretation of faith. For Barth faith means obedience to the call of Jesus Christ himself, which meets us after the resurrection in the witness of the church's proclamation of the gospel and its witness to Christ. It meets us as the risen Lord himself frees us as only the Son can, to follow him and to live our new life in and from him alone in the power of his Holy Spirit. Obedience, to Barth, means that our faith does not contribute to the freedom we now have as God's justified and sanctified creatures. It is a free human decision. But its truth cannot be found in us, as we have seen, because we are and remain the sinners that Christ has reconciled, and the change or transformation of human nature has taken place in him and not directly in us; it can only be reflected in our lives of obedience analogously, as we have seen. Justification thus shapes Barth's view of faith, and so he claims it is not a free choice between possible alternatives but the only possible choice, given the fact that Christ has freed us to live as his children in faith looking forward to the final consummation when redemption will be complete. By contrast Rahner thinks of freedom in the first instance as our choice of the moral law in obedience to conscience. That is why Rahner can claim that such obedience to conscience means that even if one is a professed atheist, such a person can be a believer and thus justified and saved even anonymously, that is, without explicitly confessing Jesus Christ.[23] Here we come

---

[23]Rahner frequently mentions this as the teaching of Vatican II. Thus, "The *fides quae* [the content

to another very thorny issue, the question of non-conceptual knowledge or implicit faith. It should be obvious from what has been said that Rahner affirms such knowledge and faith while Barth opposes it.

NON-CONCEPTUAL KNOWLEDGE AND IMPLICIT FAITH

Because Barth has been accused of being a fideist, it is important to explain why it would be a mistake to do so before discussing why he rejects non-conceptual knowledge. To my knowledge no one has ever accused Rahner of being a fideist. Thus, while neither Barth nor Rahner can be considered fideists, nonetheless, certain distinctions are required to avoid confusing the object of faith with the experience of faith. Some theologians understand fideism to mean "that faith is its own ground, and that it cannot and should not appeal to reason."[24] A lot depends, however, on what one means by such a statement. If faith is its own ground, then such a faith is contrary to Barth's quite proper emphasis on the fact that it is only the object of faith that determines the truth of our faith. In other words Christian faith is never self-grounded; such a view would always amount to some form of self-justification, and that would be the very antithesis of a faith that is obedient and that lives by grace. Such thinking would undercut the all-important connection between the Holy Spirit and faith by suggesting that it is our believing rather than the Spirit who guarantees the truth of what is believed.[25] What is implied when it is said that faith cannot and should

---

of faith] may be quite minimal in content; in certain circumstances (as mediation and the free acceptance of grace) it can consist of that fidelity to one's own conscience in which, according to Vatican II, even persons who in a reflexive way consider themselves to be atheists can still be in union with the salvific mystery of Christ" (*TI* 21:158). This is the basis for Rahner's assertion that self-acceptance is the same as accepting the Christian God in faith: "If a man freely accepts himself as he is . . . then it is God he is accepting" (*TI* 16:67). Rahner continues: "The justification for such an assertion lies ultimately in the teaching of the Second Vatican Council, that genuine faith, whose object is revelation and whose consequence is salvation, is possible for *all* men. It can be found in people who consciously believe they are and must be atheists, as long as they are completely obedient to the absolute demands of conscience. . . . They accept themselves unconditionally . . . fulfilling that primordial capacity of freedom" (*TI* 16:67). Unfortunately, this thinking implies that salvation is conditional on our obedience to conscience, whereas salvation refers to God's unconditional act of reconciliation given once for all in Jesus Christ.

[24]Avery Dulles, S.J., *The Assurance of Things Hoped For: A Theology of Christian Faith* (New York: Oxford University Press, 1994), p. 208.

[25]In answer to a question about Rom 3:23-24 to the effect that Barth might have forgotten the previous verse where Paul wrote that while justification is a free gift for all, nonetheless, justification is "for all *who believe*," Barth responded that the "for" must be understood as a looking

not appeal to reason? Does that mean that in some sense reason is necessary as a factor that validates faith? It certainly seems so when, for example, one reads that "religious faith depends to some extent upon reason."[26]
Given Barth's view of faith as acknowledgment and recognition, he could
never be considered a *fideist* in this sense, since for him all true knowledge
of God that is born of obedience is not blind and thus not without
knowledge; it is not rendered only as an emotion or as an act of will.
Moreover, since faith lives by its object, one would have to say that for Barth
the ground of faith could never be faith itself, since any self-grounded faith
would be in conflict with true faith, which always finds its basis and goal
in Christ through the Holy Spirit. In this context it would be better to describe fideism as "The view that faith rather than reason . . . is the means
by which Christian truth is known."[27] In Barth's thinking it is not a matter
of *either* faith *or* reason but of the priority of the object of faith, which determines the validity of both faith and reason such that any proper use of
reason will never abstract from Jesus Christ because we never live our lives
as Christians outside Christ or apart from him. Faith enables reason to
understand the truth that comes to us as an act of God himself. So we can
at least all agree that neither Rahner nor Barth are *fideists*. The main difference between Rahner and Barth, however, concerns the fact that Rahner
thinks of faith as a possibility imparted to human beings in their experiences of self-transcendence, while Barth insists that there can be no syn-

---

forward to the good news that must be accepted by faith; thus Paul was announcing the gospel
"all over the Mediterranean world, for people did not yet know about the good news." In that
sense he noted that faith "can only look back upon what has become true. The Apostle can only
cry out: 'Believe!'—not in his faith, but in Christ. I have a suspicion that there is a hidden Pelagianism in the Anglo-Saxon mind!" and that that can be seen in the question that was asked.
Finally, Barth says, "the truth is that the relation between the objective reality of reconciliation
and subjective affirmation is a gift of the Holy Spirit" (Godsey, *Karl Barth's Table Talk*, pp. 94-95).
[26]Avery Dulles, S.J., *The Craft of Theology: From Symbol to System* (New York: Crossroad, 1992),
p. 144. Here Dulles explains further that "Theology, as a methodical inquiry into the significance
and coherence of the revealed message, is eminently a work of reason." Yes, of course, theology
is a work of reason. But it is a work of reason enabled by and controlled by the object of faith,
namely, God the Father revealing himself through his Son and in his Spirit. Consequently, while
I would agree with this further statement, I would reject the first statement that faith depends
to some extent on reason. True faith means precisely our recognition of total dependence on
God and not on what we consider reasonable or verifiable apart from Christ.
[27]Donald K. McKim, *Westminster Dictionary of Theological Terms* (Louisville, KY: Westminster
John Knox, 1996), p. 104.

thesis of the Word of God with our experience of it in faith.[28]

BARTH AND NON-CONCEPTUAL KNOWLEDGE

Still, as seen above, Barth rejected Augustine's idea that we could acquire a type of knowledge of God that is timeless and unmediated by the incarnate Word. In Barth's thinking non-objective or non-conceptual knowledge of God refers to any claim to know God that is not in fact grounded in the revelation of God in his Word and Spirit. In other words, we have objectively true knowledge of God because in a very real sense the God who meets us in Christ and in the power of his Holy Spirit enables us to know God with what Barth calls apodictic certainty by allowing us to participate in God's own self-knowledge, which meets us in Jesus Christ. But to experience this and to know this means that we must have a conceptual grasp of the particular reality of God who reveals himself to us in and through the human history of Jesus Christ himself, and in and through the scriptural and ecclesial witness to that particular history. Any attempt to portray that specific reality without a concept of it, perhaps by claiming an unthematic or unconceptualized knowledge of it, could be considered a form of non-conceptual knowledge. For Barth we have no capacity in ourselves for God. But since we have been reconciled to God in Jesus Christ and no longer stand apart from God in ourselves (selves who in their attempted independence of God brought Jesus to the cross and now have been removed from the picture), we are now ready for God because of God's readiness for us expressed in his Word and Spirit. In Barth's words:

> About man as such, about autonomous man, existing otherwise than in Jesus
> Christ, the only thing we need to know is that he has brought Jesus Christ to
> the cross and that in this same cross his sins are forgiven; that in his indepen-
> dence he is judged and removed, really removed, i.e., moved and taken up

---

[28]This is why Rahner speaks quite deliberately about the "infused" virtues of faith, hope and love (*TI* 6:241), and Barth maintains that when human beings are determined by God's Word in their own self-determination this must not be conceptualized in such a way that one supposes that the determination by the Word "passes out of God's hand into the hands of man . . . in the sense that it is really put in his hands" (I/1, p. 212). Were this to happen, then "A conjunction or synthesis has taken place. Man's consciousness now has a divine content of spirit in the light of which it can be contemplated and investigated. . . . There arises in the reality of this experience as something that is present and can be demonstrated and presupposed a new man, new not only in the sense that he is man addressed by the Word of God, new, then, not only in Christ—who could or would oppose that? —but new in himself, changed in the immanent constitution of his humanity" (I/1, p. 212). This difference between the two theologians is at the heart of the problem now to be discussed.

into fellowship [communion] with the life of the Son of God. Absolutely everything that is to be said about his relationship to God, and therefore about
his whole truth, his sin therefore, and the Law against which he has sinned,
and his creaturely existence as such, has now to be said and can only be said
from this point, from his being in Jesus Christ. (II/1, p. 162)

For Barth, then, we may have apodictically certain knowledge of God. But
that is possible only as our knowledge of God is the knowledge that comes
from Jesus Christ himself and is thus never grounded in our experience of
God, not even in our experience of Jesus Christ.[29] Barth was at pains to indicate even in *CD* II/1 that knowledge of God that takes place in faith means
acknowledgment, joyful thanksgiving and living exclusively by grace (II/1,
pp. 218-23). Hence Barth could also say that

> If the revelation reaches us, if it becomes for us the necessary basis of our
> knowledge, this does, of course, mean that it approaches us from without, but
> it also means—how else can it reach us?—that it does actually come to us and
> therefore into us. It does not cease to transcend us, but we become immanent
> to it, so that obedience to it is our free will. (II/1, p. 219)[30]

Because God remains transcendent to us even in revelation, we are, Barth
says, elevated "above ourselves," and this makes our knowledge of God "a
joyful action. A gratitude that consists in an involuntary, mutinous and
therefore forced and unjoyful action is not thanksgiving. A tribute paid to
tyranny, however paid, is not thanks" (II/1, p. 219). This does not mean that
we must or even could leave the sphere of human experience and of space
and time to know God—it means rather that we reach out above ourselves
while remaining the people we are in space and time by witnessing to what
transcends us based on God's encounter with us in his Word and Spirit. Our
thinking and language, Barth believed, have no ability to enable our

---

[29]Thus, "If this rule [that everything said in dogmatics can only be said from our being in Jesus
Christ] . . . is followed, the statement that God is knowable to man can and must be made with
the strictest possible certainty, with an apodictic certainty, with a certainty freed from any dialectic and ambiguity" (II/1, p. 162).

[30]True faith, for Barth, always at once includes obedience because it is not an idle faith. But true
faith always means our response to the summons of the living Christ; thus "faith in Jesus, as an
act of obedience to Him, is distinguished from every other step that he may take by the fact that
in relation to the whole of his previous life and thinking and judgment it involves a right-about
turn and therefore a complete break and new beginning" (IV/2, p. 538).

knowledge of God. But when God himself enables it, as he does in Jesus Christ, that which we cannot do actually occurs because "the kingdom of heaven has come to us" (II/1, p. 220). None of this can be explained from the human side but can only be acknowledged as a miracle. We receive God's grace but "We never let reception become a taking" (II/1, p. 223). That is why our knowledge of God "is always compelled to be a prayer of thanksgiving, penitence and intercession. It is only in this way that there is knowledge of God in participation in the veracity of the revelation of God" (II/1, p. 223). We really do know God with our views and concepts as an object mediated to us through the words of Scripture and witness of the church, but "We do not create the success. Nor do our means create it. But the grace of God's revelation creates it. To know this is the awe in which our knowledge of God becomes true" (II/1, p. 223).

Ultimately, Barth's understanding of our knowledge of God as the obedience of faith is shaped by his understanding of the doctrine of justification. Hence, while it is impossible for us as sinners to know God of ourselves, God is able to empower us to know him through our views and concepts. God even can be said to be in them (our views and concepts) in all his glory. Still, "It is not a question of a power to receive this guest being secretly inherent in these works of ours. . . . But there is a power of the divine indwelling in both the broad and the narrow which our works cannot withstand for all their impotence" (II/1, p. 212). However, this cannot refer to some "magical transformation of man, or a supernatural enlargement of his capacity, so that now he can do what before he could not do" (II/1, p. 212). People are still unable to accomplish knowledge of God even after their encounter with God in revelation; but a person is "taken up by the grace of God and determined to participation in the veracity of the revelation of God. . . . As a sinner he is justified" (II/1, p. 213). As forgiven sinners we are sanctified by this act of God so that even as sinners we are empowered truly to know God:

> The veracity of the revelation of God, which justifies the sinner in His Word by His Spirit, makes this knowledge of God true without him, against him— and yet as his own knowledge, and to that extent through him. By the grace of God we may view and conceive God and speak of God in our incapacity. (II/1, p. 213)

Finally, we can say that "The obedience to the grace of God in which a man acknowledges that he is entirely wrong, thus acknowledging that God alone is entirely right, is the obedience" that has the promise that whatever our capacity or incapacity, we have God's promise that he will confer his own truth on our views and concepts (II/1, p. 213).

Having said all of this, one can easily see why Barth would reject non-conceptual faith or implicit faith that could lead one to assert that people know God without reflecting on God as God truly is in his revelation to us in his Word and Spirit. That is why Barth rejected any sort of knowledge of Christ, as noted above, that is formless, that is, a knowledge that is not shaped by Jesus himself as attested in Scripture and by the witness of the church. There is no Christ to be found outside of that witness because Jesus, the incarnate Word, is not an idea and certainly not the content of an experience, but the man from Nazareth who died for our sins, rose from the dead, ascended into heaven and is coming again. This man, who is God himself calling us to faith and obedience here and now because he lives, cannot be had if it is some formless idea we have in mind when referring to him.

THOMAS F. TORRANCE AND NON-CONCEPTUAL KNOWLEDGE

Barth's student Thomas F. Torrance offers a very clear picture of why he rejects any sort of non-objective or non-conceptual knowledge of God, as well as any sort of implicit faith that claims knowledge of God without the mediation of his Word and Spirit. First, for Torrance it is imperative that faith be objectively and not subjectively grounded. That means we must find the basis of faith in the reality of God who exists self-sufficiently as Father, Son and Holy Spirit and is not in the least dependent on creation for his existence, even though out of his eternal love, God created us and will never be without us. That love of course was manifested in the fact that, in the face of our enmity against him, the Father nonetheless sacrificed his own Son for our sakes so as to overcome that enmity and enable not only true knowledge of God but the ability to live wholly in harmony with God in and through Christ and his Spirit. Hence, Torrance insisted that the basis of faith is not found in us but only in its object, namely, Jesus Christ who is God himself present and active among us. Citing Hilary of Poitiers, Torrance writes, "'In faith a person takes his stand on the ground of God's own being (*in sub-*

stantia dei)."[31] And for Torrance scientific theology always allows the unique object of knowledge to determine the truth of what is said. Torrance thus objected rather firmly to what he called, following Martin Buber, the tendency in modern theology toward a "conceptual letting go of God" as happened for instance in the thinking of Schleiermacher.[32] Torrance held that "Schleiermacher's refusal to think of God as the object of our conceiving and knowing on the ground that He cannot be exposed to our 'counter-influence', i.e. the objectifying force of our active reason" led him to claim that we could understand God only in so far as God was "'the co-determinant' of our feeling of absolute dependence."[33] But this thinking led Schleiermacher, in Torrance's estimation, to reduce theological statements to "accounts of 'religious affections set forth in speech.'"[34] And such a view amounted to nothing more than a discussion of human experience in place of the God who meets us in our experience of faith in his Word and Spirit.

That is why Torrance frequently objected to the thinking of Rudolf Bultmann and Paul Tillich. In his mind both of those theologians transformed scientific theology into an unscientific exercise by allowing theological language to be dictated not by who God is in himself as the eternal Father, Son and Spirit as experienced and known in faith, but by allowing their thinking to be dictated by their existential concerns and conclusions detached from the Holy Spirit. In Torrance's view Tillich tended to be rationalistic because for him

> the "direct object" of theology was "not God" but what he called "religious symbols" which mediated not objective content but power. Correspondingly, Tillich held that faith is essentially "non-conceptual," so that it can yield theology only if it borrows rational structures from something else and is conceptualized through them.[35]

Bultmann essentially cut himself off from scientific theology by existentializing theology, that is, by reducing theological categories to descriptions of people's existential reactions to the gospel instead of to objective descrip-

---

[31] *Trinitarian Faith*, p. 19.
[32] Thomas F. Torrance, *God and Rationality* (London: Oxford University Press, 1971; reissued Edinburgh: T & T Clark, 1997), p. 106.
[33] Ibid.
[34] Ibid.
[35] Ibid., p. 107.

tions of what God is doing in Christ, who meets us clothed with his gospel. The epitome of such existentializing is seen in Bultmann's equation of the resurrection with the rise of faith in the disciples; such thinking clearly confuses the objective act of God in the history of Jesus with the experience of faith on the part of the disciples and subsequently with our experience of faith. This thinking leaves us only with a theology that objectifies our experience of faith and never escapes the problem of projection in theology, precisely because it detaches knowledge of God from the Holy Spirit, who unites us to the historical Jesus through the scriptural witness and the proclamation of the church.

Since, for Torrance, faith is produced by the truth itself, and theology is thus faith seeking understanding and not understanding seeking faith, he held that faith could not be seen as some sort of "non-cognitive or non-conceptual relation to God." Because faith involves "acts of recognition, apprehension and conception, of a very basic intuitive kind" when human reason is confronted with God's self-revelation in Jesus Christ, one could never espouse non-conceptual faith or knowledge of the Christian God without obviating true scientific, theological understanding.[36] Following Anselm, Torrance insisted that "we cannot have experience of [God] or believe in Him without conceptual forms of understanding—as Anselm used to say: *fides esse nequit sine conceptione*."[37] Consequently, for Torrance, faith involved obedience grounded in God himself so that, with Barth, he embraced Hilary's dictum that realities are not subject to words but words are subject to realities.[38]

Torrance helpfully makes a distinction between apprehension and comprehension of God. The former means that we do not just grasp part of God since God is indivisible. But when we do grasp God, that action "does not exhaust His transcendent reality and mystery; but it is not less conceptual for that reason, since it is the form of conception rationally appropriate to His divine nature and majesty." The latter indicates that we cannot "bring the totality of God within the compass of our comprehension."[39] It does not follow from the fact that we only apprehend God, however, that our

---

[36]*Trinitarian Faith*, p. 20.
[37]Torrance, *God and Rationality*, p. 34.
[38]See ibid., p. 37. Barth insisted that anyone who does not accept Hilary's dictum methodologically is no theologian and never will be (*CD* I/1, p. 354).
[39]Torrance, *God and Rationality*, p. 22.

knowledge of God is not conceptual, since it is a form of conceptual knowledge appropriate to its object. Thus, one cannot argue from the fact that our concepts can never exhaust the divine being and that we therefore cannot conceptually define the reality of God with precision "that it cannot be conceptually grasped but may only be envisaged in some indefinite, non-conceptual way."[40] In a manner similar to Barth, Torrance insists that we may know God because we are known by God and are thus "seized by His reality" so that in response to God's "grasping of us" our "human grasping of Him takes place, in functional dependence upon Him."[41] Torrance thus argues quite rightly that when our thought leads us beyond what is for us imaginable, that does not mean that it leads us beyond what is conceivable, because in the case of God what is conceivable is precisely what does not correspond to what is to us "picturable." The fact that this is the case does not mean what we know is non-conceptual at that point. Thus Torrance claims that

> While there is no correspondence between the pictures latent in the language expressing our theological concepts and the realities to which we refer, this does not invalidate the concepts, for the conceptual relation they involve lies beyond the range of the imaginable. Indeed this is the only kind of conceptual relation that would be appropriate to God.[42]

Any denial of this, Torrance maintains, would mean that we would identify what is conceptual with what is imaginable to us, and this would have to imply that we have equated what is truly objective with what for us is "objectifiable." But, since the content of our creaturely conceptions does not correspond to anything in the reality of God, we might mistakenly conclude that "we have to reckon in the last analysis with a non-conceptual relation to Him." But that, says Torrance, "would be a serious lapse from rationality."[43] It is for these reasons that Torrance objected to Tillich's symbolic attempt to understand God and to Bultmann's existential redefinition of theological truth. In other words, Torrance rejects both projectionism and symbolic description of what is for us imaginable. And he does this because our concepts must be controlled from beyond us by the reality of God revealed in

---

[40]Ibid.
[41]Ibid.
[42]Ibid., p. 23.
[43]Ibid.

and by the Word and Spirit. Moreover, this can only be known in and through our concepts and not symbolically as an imaginative or aesthetic description of our experiences of ourselves. Consequently, true knowledge of God always involves concepts appropriate to God's own self-knowledge, into which we are drawn in faith by the Holy Spirit.

KARL RAHNER'S APPROACH TO GOD

Here, as we come to the end of this chapter, it will be especially helpful to contrast the positions of Torrance and Barth on non-conceptual knowledge of God with the thinking of Karl Rahner in order to make just one simple point. It is of course a point with profound and far-reaching implications. And that point is that whenever it is supposed that we can know God, faith, grace or revelation non-conceptually, our thinking no longer describes the reality of God and God's actions for us within history. To that extent, it becomes either projection of our understanding of ourselves and our world onto the reality of God revealed, or only a symbolic description of what is imaginable to us. Either way, such thinking represents a very serious lapse from scientific theology and rationality so that even though one may still speak of the trinitarian self-revelation and our inclusion in that revelation by grace and by faith, the meaning of those terms becomes seriously distorted.

Let me make my point first on a very basic level by comparing what Paul Tillich thinks about knowledge of God to what we have learned by thinking of God within faith along with Torrance and Barth. In a very famous quote referred to by those who wish to construct a theology of God non-conceptually in exactly the wrong way,[44] one can see the implications of a theology shaped by faith in Jesus Christ and one that clearly is not. In a sermon Tillich once said:

> Today . . . the so-called "psychology of depth" . . . leads us from the surface of our self-knowledge into levels where things are recorded which we knew nothing about on the surface of our consciousness. . . . It can help us to find

---

[44]See, e.g., John A. T. Robinson, *Honest to God* (Philadelphia: Westminster Press, 1963), p. 22; John Haught, *What Is God? How to Think About the Divine* (New York: Paulist, 1986), pp. 14-15; and Elizabeth A. Johnson, *She Who Is: The Mystery of God in Feminist Theological Discourse* (New York: Crossroad, 1992), who without directly citing this statement relies heavily on the thinking espoused here. For a discussion of how the thinking of John Haught, John Robinson and Paul Tillich relates to the knowledge of God in faith, see Paul D. Molnar, "'Thy Word Is Truth': The Role of Faith in Reading Scripture Theologically with Karl Barth," *SJT* 63, no. 1 (2010): 70-92.

the way into our depth, although it cannot help us in an ultimate way, because it cannot guide us to the deepest ground of our being and of all being, the depth of life itself. The name of this infinite and inexhaustible depth and ground of all being is *God*. That depth is what the word *God* means. And if that word has not much meaning for you, translate it, and speak of the depths of your life, of the source of your being, of your ultimate concern, of what you take seriously without any reservation. Perhaps, in order to do so, you must forget everything traditional that you have learned about God, perhaps even that word itself. For if you know that God means depth, you know much about Him. You cannot then call yourself an atheist or unbeliever. For you cannot think or say: Life has no depth! Life itself is shallow. Being itself is surface only. If you could say this in complete seriousness, you would be an atheist; but otherwise you are not. He who knows about depth knows about God.[45]

This statement is a perfect illustration of why Tillich's understanding of God represents a supreme misunderstanding of who God is as understood by faith. And it does so because it is a type of non-conceptual symbolic knowledge of God. It is non-conceptual inasmuch as it asserts rather bluntly that one could forget all that one has learned about God, perhaps from the Nicene Creed, in order to know God. It even says that one could forget the word God itself. And this suggestion follows the assumption by Tillich that if the word God does not have much meaning for you, it is perfectly acceptable, even advisable to translate it and to "speak of the depths of your life, of the source of your being, of your ultimate concern, of what you take seriously without any reservation." Here is the exact point that Torrance identified as the chief indication of a departure from scientific theology. In breaking free from a conceptual understanding of the reality of God revealed by God himself as he meets us and knows us in his Word and Spirit, Tillich ignores the knowledge of faith and directs our attention toward ourselves.

Now for Barth and for Torrance this will never do, since faith must be controlled by its object, namely, Jesus Christ himself. The object controlling Tillich's thinking very clearly is our own experience of ourselves and of what is for us supposed to be our ultimate concern. From this Tillich equates experiences of depth with experiences of God. And such experiences can be had by everyone without conceptual knowledge of God's reconciling grace, which is

[45]Paul Tillich, *The Shaking of the Foundations* (New York: Charles Scribner's Sons, 1948), pp. 56-57.

active, revealed and effective in Jesus Christ and which reaches us in the power
of his Holy Spirit. It is easy to see that everything that could go wrong in an
effort to understand God within faith has in reality gone wrong in this definition. Equating depth with God utterly subverts the Christian understanding
of God and supposes that knowledge of God, which only can take place in faith,
is in fact explicable to everyone, even those who do not believe in Jesus Christ.
That is the position Barth rightly rejected because he saw that such a procedure
transmutes the particular revelation of God in Jesus Christ into a universal
human experience, leads toward Pelagianism and, most importantly, changes
God's objectivity into the product of our human experiences of depth.

NON-CONCEPTUAL KNOWLEDGE: COMPARING RAHNER, BARTH AND TORRANCE

In an interesting explanation, Avery Dulles traces contemporary Catholic
thinking on the subject of non-conceptual knowledge to Jacques Maritain
and some mid-twentieth-century Thomists who based their thinking on
what he labels an obscure text in the *Summa Theologica* (I-2.89.6). Thomas
argued that when a child is first able to reason, that child chooses to be ordered toward the right end or not and is justified in the former instance but
commits a mortal sin in the latter instance. Dulles further maintains that
Maritain, "reflecting on this text, held that the moral option for the right end
involves a vital, non-conceptual knowledge of God."[46] Maritain linked this
text with another (*Summa Theologica* I-2.109.3) and claimed further that
fallen creatures could not order themselves toward the final end without the
assistance of grace. He concluded that

> when a child is faced by its first moral option, grace will in fact be given and
> that a virtuous response will be therefore elevated to the supernatural level. In
> this elevated act God will be sought as Savior. If it accepts the inner impulse of
> grace, the mind will be adhering to God's testimony, and thus making an act
> of faith that is formal and actual even though devoid of conceptual content.[47]

This so-called lived faith Maritain claimed was "a practical or existential
knowledge of God," and he also maintained that it could "coexist with

---

[46]Dulles, *Assurance of Things Hoped For*, p. 265.
[47]Ibid.

theoretical ignorance of God" so that even a person who thinks of himself or herself as an atheist could be "adhering to the reality of God known in a vital, preconscious manner."[48] Such a fundamental moral option, it seems, need not be restricted to a person's early life but could be made later on as well; and this could be understood to be an act of implicit faith. According to Dulles, this theory "insofar as it can appeal to the authority of Thomas Aquinas makes an important contribution. It brings out the value of non-conceptual knowledge through what Aristotle and Aquinas called 'connaturality.'"[49] In spite of this, Dulles goes on to note that this theory is difficult to reconcile with the insistence of Thomas and many others "that saving faith is a response to actual revelation, and not merely to an interior illumination."[50]

Unfortunately, however, Dulles does not seem to see that the real problem in this entire line of reasoning is the very idea of non-conceptual knowledge of God. Not only does such knowledge not make an important contribution to our understanding of Christian faith, but it completely distorts its meaning by claiming a knowledge of God that is overtly in conflict with knowledge of the Father that comes to us through the Son and by means of the Holy Spirit and thus through faith and by grace. It subverts Christian knowledge of God. Here a choice is required: either we freely obey the Word heard and believed *conceptually* through the hearing of the gospel or we equate knowledge of God with some sort of preconscious non-conceptual relation to our final end by choosing for or against the moral law. And it is thoroughly unhelpful to claim that such non-conceptual knowledge is upheld and enabled by grace because any such claim subverts the connection between the gift (knowledge of God) and the Giver (Jesus Christ and his Holy Spirit). Thus while Dulles certainly sees and wishes to maintain the connection between the Holy Spirit and faith, his openness to apologetics and to the idea that faith can and should be certified by reason and by the authority of the church, as well as his willingness to accept non-conceptual knowledge of God, all inevitably cut that connection.

With this background we can perhaps better understand why Rahner's

---

[48]Ibid.
[49]Ibid.
[50]Ibid.

embrace of non-conceptual knowledge of God in order to explicate his own understanding of the Trinity as well as other doctrines, including his view of faith, grace and revelation, is more than a little problematic. Rahner sees grace as an offer given to all human beings at every moment of their lives. This offer Rahner conceptualizes as a "supernatural existential." According to Dulles, that means that prior to its acceptance,

> grace gives a new horizon to human consciousness, so that our relationship to God is perceived in a different way than it would be in a purely natural order. To accept ourselves as we really are, that is to say, as ordered toward the vision of God, is to accept grace, and this acceptance, in its cognitive dimensions, is an act of faith.[51]

Here, as I have pointed out above and in detail elsewhere,[52] the very claim to a knowledge of God supposedly attainable by reflection on our transcendental dynamisms ends up detaching knowledge of God from God's specific actions in his Word and Spirit and locates grace and revelation within our self-experience. To put the matter directly, grace is identical with God's giving of himself in his Word and Spirit so that grace can never be detached from the giver of grace. But that also means that any assumption that our transcendental dynamisms or human consciousness have been altered by grace in the way imagined here necessarily means the confusion of nature and grace. And this happens precisely because the focus of Rahner's thought at this point is not the historical Jesus attested in the Scriptures, who is the very Word of God spoken to us and enabling faith through his Holy Spirit, but rather on our supposedly transformed horizon of reflection, which he mistakenly believes is ordered toward the God of Christian revelation. Of course that does not mean that Rahner has no interest in the historical Jesus and his significance for faith. He does indeed want to connect his transcendental deliberations with the his-

---

[51]Ibid., pp. 266-67. Dulles notes that Rahner's idea of a "supernatural existential" is widely embraced among contemporary Catholics. But he also notes that it has been criticized for making explicit faith "unimportant for salvation" and that "it is hard to reconcile with the biblical and traditional understanding of the salvific importance of Christian proclamation" (p. 267). Dulles theorizes that "These objections do not necessarily invalidate the theory, but until they are satisfactorily answered the theory must be regarded as vulnerable" (p. 267).

[52]See Paul D. Molnar, *Divine Freedom and the Doctrine of the Immanent Trinity: In Dialogue with Karl Barth and Contemporary Theology* (New York: T & T Clark, 2005), chaps. 3, 4 and 5, and *Incarnation and Resurrection*.

torical Jesus. But for him the historical Jesus is the one in whom self-acceptance has simply reached its irreversible final form. And the problem with this notion is that if Jesus is simply the irrevocable completion of human self-transcendence into God, as Rahner frequently asserts,[53] then, in spite of the fact that Rahner thinks his Christology from below properly ends with what he calls a descending Christology, he has in reality undermined the true meaning of the incarnation. It is true that what God has done and does in Jesus Christ is irrevocable and unsurpassable. But it is so not because he humanly gave himself over to God in a final way. It is so because he is God acting both from the divine and human side. The fact that Rahner never allows Jesus to be both the *first* and the *final* word in his thinking is a major indication that even his neo-Chalcedonian Christology is more than a little problematic.

This is a crucial point since, as we saw above, what Barth and Torrance learn from the cross and resurrection is that we discover, in light of God's saving grace actualized in these events, that we are sinners who are at enmity with the true God (since it is fallen humanity that brought Jesus to the cross). Furthermore, we need to rely on Christ himself, the risen Lord, to know God truly. Because Rahner thinks of grace as an offer made to

---

[53]This is why Rahner refers to Jesus understood from below as "a person who finds himself only by abandoning himself to the incomprehensibility of God. At the beginning of Christology the question is, 'What does he mean for us?' Then comes the question, 'Who must he be if he has this significance for us?'" (*TI* 21:224). There are three problems evident here. First, while it is true to say that Jesus lived a life of perfect obedience to God as his incarnate Son, it is problematic to express this by saying that Jesus is a person who finds himself by abandoning himself to the incomprehensibility of God. This latter understanding leaves out the fact that who Jesus was humanly from the first moment of his life on earth he was because and as he was the very Word of God acting for us. The difference here is simple: understood in Rahner's sense one could conclude that the incarnation is somehow the result of Jesus' human life of self-abandonment and that because that life was accepted by the Father, it then becomes unsurpassable and irrevocable. All of this has the appearance of suggesting that Jesus' uniqueness rests in his human self-abandonment, which is then regarded only as a higher degree of human self-transcendence than the rest of us can achieve. Second, the way Rahner asks the questions, What is Jesus' significance for us? And then who must he be? suggests that the two questions actually can be considered sequentially when in reality someone thinking in faith about Jesus could only begin by acknowledging his Lordship (that is who he is) in light of his resurrection, which is then seen as the fulfillment of his incarnate history as a history of salvation. But, third, that would mean that his history is not to be seen as the culmination of something taking place in all of history, that is, within everyone's experiences of self-transcendence. Rather it would have to mean that what took place in his history was something entirely new that came into history from outside. Hence it could not be conceptualized rightly at all as the culmination of a human history, since it was the history of God's fulfilling his act of incarnation by acting for us as the mediator and savior.

persons in their conscious acceptance or rejection of the moral law, he can speak of our graced nature and then conclude that since we tend toward a direct relation (the beatific vision) with God as human beings who are historically graced because of the incarnation, we therefore have unthematic (non-conceptual) knowledge of and experience of God in experiencing ourselves as those who transcend ourselves toward God himself. As we have been seeing, however, faith in the Christian sense never means self-acceptance; it always must mean turning from self and toward Christ as the only one who can justify our faith. Faith means acknowledging, recognizing and confessing that we have no genuine existence outside or apart from Jesus Christ. The very idea of non-conceptual faith leads Rahner to detach revelation (grace) from the Giver (Jesus Christ himself) and to locate God's self-revelation within our own experience as an a priori modality of human consciousness. Thus, in his attempt to explain God's universal offer of salvation to all, Rahner argues that

> It is not the case that we have nothing to do with God until we make God conceptual and thematic to some extent. Rather there is an original and unthematic experience of God, although it is nameless, whenever and to the extent that subjectivity and transcendentality are actualized. And correspondingly, man's supernatural transcendentality is already mediated to itself, although in an unobjectified and unthematic way, whenever a person appropriates himself as a free subject in the transcendentality of his knowledge and freedom. (*FCF*, p. 151)

Hence, for Rahner, God's self-revelation is not exclusively identical with the Word of God active in Jesus himself, as it is for Barth and for Torrance, but can and must be conceived as something present in our own transcendental experience of ourselves, that is, as

> an unreflexive but really present, and transcendental experience of man's movement and orientation towards immediacy and closeness of God, that is, the experience as such prior to being made thematic reflexively and historically, must be characterized as a real revelation throughout the whole history of religion and of the human spirit.

This transcendental knowledge, which is present unthematically wherever human beings act in knowledge and freedom and must be distinguished from "verbal and propositional revelation as such," nevertheless can be called "God's self-revelation." Indeed,

> This transcendental moment in revelation is a modification of our transcendental consciousness produced permanently by God in grace. But such a modification is really an original and permanent element in our consciousness as the basic and original luminosity of our existence. And as an element in our transcendentality . . . it is already revelation in the proper sense. (*FCF*, p. 149)

By wishing to distinguish this experience of revelation from verbal and propositional revelation as such (what Rahner calls transcendental revelation and categorical revelation), it is clear that Rahner wants to hold on to the traditional idea that revelation cannot be detached from Jesus himself. But once he ascribes revelation to us in our transcendental experiences of ourselves as a form of implicit faith and non-conceptual knowledge of God, that move eviscerates the meaning of faith as acknowledgment, recognition and confession of its object, namely, of Jesus Christ himself. It is just this thinking that leads him to espouse the idea that everyone who accepts himself/herself in the sense just described is an "anonymous Christian" and even has an "anonymous faith" (*TI* 16:58); that there is such a thing as an "anonymous" experience of the risen Lord;[54] that knowledge of God begins with an unthematic experience of and knowledge of the "nameless" (*TI* 4:50); and that Christology and anthropology mutually condition each other when rightly understood. And beyond that, this move ends up ascribing grace, revelation and faith to everyone who makes a positive moral decision and accepts himself/herself as he or she is.[55] It is this momentous move, which is thoroughly in harmony with the step made by Maritain, that is ultimately destructive of Christian faith and practice precisely because it

---

[54]See Karl Rahner and Karl-Heinz Weger, *Our Christian Faith: Answers for the Future*, trans. Francis McDonagh (New York: Crossroad, 1981), p. 113.

[55]That is why Rahner claims that "grace not only possesses an inner point of connection with human existence but also a seed in every man out of which the whole history of human salvation and revelation may grow, both in Christianity and in all the great religions" (*TI* 16:10). And it is also why he thinks that when we accept ourselves as those who have hope for the future we are simultaneously accepting God. Thus, "A Christian must grant every man who is faithful to his conscience this interior movement towards God, even when the other does not think of it in these terms and has not yet grasped its historical appearance in Jesus Christ in explicit faith" (*TI* 16:15). This makes sense to Rahner because he really believes that "The basic human hope and the experience of Jesus sustain and justify each other" (*TI* 16:15).

changes the content of our knowledge of God and the meaning of faith itself. Instead of allowing faith to be defined by the action of the Holy Spirit uniting us to Christ *conceptually* and *really*, this thinking confuses faith with our obedience to ourselves. Thus,

> Faith . . . is simply the obedient acceptance of man's supernaturally elevated self-transcendence, the obedient acceptance of his transcendental orientation to the God of eternal life. As an a priori modality of consciousness, this orientation has the character of a divine communication. (*FCF*, p. 152)

This thinking stands in stark contrast to the position espoused by Barth in a way that I believe requires a choice: either faith is conceptually and therefore genuinely tied to Christ through faith enabled by the Holy Spirit and thus as a miracle, or faith can be had simply by accepting our own transcendental dynamisms, which are uncritically assumed to be directed toward the God of Christian faith. Barth believes that we always come from unbelief to faith and that this can only occur in the power of the Holy Spirit enabling our acknowledgment of our new being in Christ. Rahner believes that a preacher very likely encounters a person who is already justified "because he was obedient to the dictates of his conscience . . . and therefore already believes, in the theological sense, even if what he explicitly believes is very little."[56] "Bringing someone to the faith" in this view "will mean the endeavor to develop this already existing faith into its full Christological and ecclesiastical, explicit, social, consciously professed form. . . . Christian faith is the historically and socially complete form of what the person to be converted already 'believes.'"[57] It is important to realize that Rahner holds this position because he ascribes grace universally to everyone in their transcendental experience as when he asserts that "the grace of faith . . . is nothing else than the self-communication of God to the human spirit in the depths of its being" (*TI* 16:57). Hence, one can have implicit faith and even what he calls a "Searching Christology" without ever having heard the gospel.

Moreover, instead of looking exclusively to the object of faith in order to understand faith itself, Rahner claims that "The primary approach to faith is a man's direct confrontation with himself . . . and thereby with the incom-

---

[56]Rahner, *Encyclopedia of Theology*, p. 496. See also *TI* 16:57-58.
[57]Rahner, *Encyclopedia of Theology*, p. 496.

prehensible ground of this human reality, called God."[58] That is why Rahner insists that "If a person by a free act in which he accepts himself unconditionally in his radical reference to God raised up by grace, also accepts the basic finality of this movement of his spirit, even if without reflection, then he is making a genuine act of faith, for this finality already means revelation" (*TI* 16:57-58). That, however, is exactly the problem with non-conceptual knowledge and implicit faith. Both ascribe grace and revelation to what is presumed to be a transformed human nature so that reflection on that transformed nature is then assumed to contain not only a reference to God but a reference to revelation itself. In both cases grace and revelation are detached from the action of God in the history of Jesus himself and from the action of the Holy Spirit in his essential union with the Father and the Son. And the indication of this is the fact that for Rahner one can speak of Jesus Christ, justifying faith, grace and of revelation without specifically adverting to the historical Jesus as the grace of God active in history through specific witness of Scripture and the church. For Rahner one can know these by reflecting on one's own transcendental dynamisms, which are already presumed to be in some sense revelatory and to that extent identical with God's self-communication. And that is why Rahner can speak both of an obediential potency for faith[59] as well as an anonymous faith (*TI* 16:57-58) and anon-

---

[58]Ibid., p. 497.

[59]It must be recalled that for Rahner "obediential potency" refers to our openness to being (as spirit in the world) and as such it refers to our openness to God's self-communication, at least as a possibility. According to John Galvin, "This potency is . . . our human nature as such. If the divine self-communication did not occur, our openness toward being would still be meaningful. . . . We are by nature possible recipients of God's self-communication, listeners for a possible divine word" ("The Invitation of Grace," in *A World of Grace: An Introduction to the Themes and Foundations of Karl Rahner's Theology*, ed. Leo J. O'Donovan, S.J. [New York: Crossroad, 1981], p. 72). The problem with this idea is that it stands in conflict with the fact that the possibility of receiving God's self-communication, according to what I have argued above, is to be found *only* in its actuality. And that actuality is the action of the Holy Spirit uniting us to Christ (conceptually and existentially) and thus through faith (as discussed above) to the Father, and therefore not to a holy mystery conceptualized in any one of a number of ways. Here I follow Barth and Torrance, who argue correctly that what is revealed in Christ himself is that we are not open to God's revelation but that, since the fall, by nature we are closed to this and must be made open through the Spirit actualizing the atonement accomplished in Christ's life, death and resurrection in us through the act of faith. See also Harvey D. Egan, who writes that the obediential potency refers to "the human person's natural ability to receive God's self-offer" (*Cambridge Companion to Karl Rahner*, p. 16). In my view any such ability was lost in the fall and restored in Christ and therefore cannot be located in our natural ability without moving in a Pelagian direction. To say or to suggest that "nature is in continuity with and positively open to grace"

ymous hope (*TI* 16:18-19) and then conclude, as seen above, that our basic experience of hope and our experience of Jesus sustain and justify each other. It must be remembered at this point that from within the perspective on faith elaborated by Barth and Torrance and discussed above, the idea that we have an obediential potency for grace undermines the sovereignty of grace and ignores the problem of sin and the need for reconciliation *before* we can live by grace. Such an idea inevitably allows theologians to look toward their own capacities rather than exclusively toward Christ, who through his Spirit alone gives people the capacity to know and love God. Indeed in the view of Barth and Torrance, as we have seen, any sort of anonymous hope in the resurrection or any sort of anonymous faith is clearly not shaped by a specific knowledge of the gospel, which teaches that Jesus died for our sins and rose from the dead and that as such he is the hope of the entire world because of who he is and what he has done and is now doing in and through his Holy Spirit. Consequently, he alone justifies our faith, and thus our experience of Jesus does not justify who he is. It is entirely the other way around: who he is justifies our faith, which is and always remains grounded in him alone and never in ourselves.[60] These difficulties highlight very clearly the problems inherent in any version of non-conceptual knowledge of God, revelation and faith. Rahner insists, of course, that none of these views undermine the need for explicit faith in Jesus. But in reality Jesus has been marginalized because he cannot have the *first* and the *final* word in this understanding, since both grace and revelation have been conceptualized as attributes of human transcendental experience; and knowledge of God and of Jesus becomes possible without any specific reference to God the Father through God the Son and by means of his Holy Spirit.

The ultimate difficulty here is not that Rahner does not speak about the Holy Spirit as grace but that he does not allow the Holy Spirit in his essential union with the incarnate Son to shape what he means by faith. Hence, it is my

---

(Steven J. Duffy, *Cambridge Companion to Karl Rahner*, p. 51) is to miss the fact that only the Holy Spirit can make us open to grace precisely by uniting us with Christ. Had we been in continuity with grace after the fall, Jesus never would have been crucified.

[60]For a full discussion of why I think there are serious problems in Rahner's view of an obediential potency and supernatural existential, see my *Divine Freedom and the Doctrine of the Immanent Trinity*, chaps. 2, 4, 5 and 6.

argument that whenever faith is detached from the Spirit in the sense described at the beginning of this chapter, it always becomes self-grounded even when it is referred to as grace and revelation. And that negative assertion is made in this book in order to present the positive view that it is crucial to speak more explicitly and thus more clearly about the role of the Holy Spirit, especially since it is the Spirit in union with the Word who alone brings true knowledge of God the Father. It is the Holy Spirit who imparts faith and enables hope and love through union with Christ and through him with the Father. This is a miraculous action, so that no one can control it and all must pray for the coming of the Spirit to enlighten our minds and hearts and to enable our participation in God's own self-knowledge and love. In order to make matters even clearer in this regard, we will next explore what theological knowledge looks like when one is consistently clear about the fact that the knowledge of faith is attainable only through faith as union with Christ that comes about exclusively through the miraculous act of the Holy Spirit.

2

The Role of the Holy Spirit
in Knowing the Triune God

I f contemporary theologians were to make explicit the role of the Holy Spirit in enabling our knowledge of the triune God, then there could be wide agreement that natural theology of whatever stripe is not only unhelpful but is directly excluded from any serious understanding of theological episte-mology. To develop this thesis I will rely on the theologies of Karl Barth and Thomas F. Torrance once again. My aim is to stress why it is crucial to rec-ognize the epistemological relevance of the Holy Spirit in our knowledge of God. In this remark I deliberately follow Torrance who, in agreement with Barth,[1] believes that there can be no epistemology *of* the Spirit because, while the Spirit is active in enabling our knowledge of God, that divine action cannot be explained from the human side.[2] My point here is that Torrance maintains that we may only speak of an "epistemological relevance of the Spirit" and not an "epistemology of the Spirit as such" since we cannot attribute actual knowledge of God to ourselves but only to the fact that such knowledge is genuinely a "freely given participation in [God's own] self-knowledge."[3] Three positive ideas therefore are to be stressed here: (1) since God is Spirit, we can only know God in truth in and through the Spirit, and therefore we cannot have true knowledge of God without the Spirit; (2) there

---

[1]See Barth, I/2, pp. 244-79 and 201.
[2]Thomas F. Torrance, *God and Rationality* (London: Oxford University Press, 1971; reissued Ed-inburgh: T & T Clark, 1997), p. 166.
[3]Ibid.

can be no "independent epistemology of the Spirit" because that would imply that the Spirit might have his own epistemological basis "apart from the Father and the Son;"[4] hence (3) in our knowledge of God our "epistemological forms break off" because "we are up against acts of God that are not only inexplicable from the side of man but quite ineffable."[5] For that reason the relevance of the Holy Spirit in our knowing God refers to the fact that we truly know God only as that knowledge is enabled by God himself in his act of uniting us to himself through faith by an act of the Spirit uniting us to Christ and thus to the Father. Before developing these ideas, let me first explain why I have chosen Barth and Torrance to explicate this theme.

My reason is simple. They are excellent examples of contemporary theologians who not only explicitly direct our attention to the role of the Holy Spirit in knowing God but also allow their own dogmatic thinking to be governed by what they assert to be true of the Holy Spirit as the enabling condition of such knowledge. While there are some differences between them regarding our natural knowledge of God, those differences, as far as I can tell, never surface in their strict dogmatic considerations. For instance, in his quest for a "new natural theology" Torrance refuses to embrace a traditional natural theology that claims that God can be known outside faith and apart from revelation. But at the same time he accepts remnants of that old natural theology with the claims that natural knowledge of God can be bracketed from revelation for purposes of clarification and that we find ourselves under an imperious constraint from beyond when we consider the intelligibility of the universe, and this suggests some reliable knowledge of God in that experience.[6] Barth certainly would not accept either of these claims, since for him there is no true knowledge of God apart from revelation, and any claim to knowledge of God based on the intelligibility of the universe could just as easily be knowledge of the devil as knowledge of the triune God. Nonetheless, these claims are seen in Torrance's thought only when he is trying to show the commonality of approaches to reality between

---

[4]Ibid., p. 165.

[5]Ibid., p. 166.

[6]See Paul D. Molnar, "Natural Theology Revisited: A Comparison of T. F. Torrance and Karl Barth," *Zeitshcrift Für Dialektische Theologie* 20, no. 1 (December 2005): 53-83. For more on this subject see Paul D. Molnar, "The Importance of the Doctrine of Justification in the Theology of Thomas F. Torrance and of Karl Barth," *SJT* (forthcoming).

theological and natural science. They never appear in his dogmatic work. Since Torrance's dogmatic theology is shaped by his understanding of the Trinity, there is substantial agreement between him and Barth on the role of the Holy Spirit in our knowledge of God that will help us see why a proper understanding of this matter marginalizes natural theology in the traditional sense and also shows why we can have true knowledge of God only as the Holy Spirit unites us to Christ and through him to the Father.

AN EXAMPLE OF A TRADITIONAL NATURAL THEOLOGY

Let us begin with a very brief example of the kind of thinking I believe is excluded and avoided when one's theological epistemology takes the Holy Spirit's activity seriously. I cite a book that was very popular in Roman Catholic circles some forty years ago, namely, John Courtney Murray's *The Problem of God Yesterday and Today*. I am aware that contemporary Thomists likely would not accept his basic premises because they tend to believe that even Thomas's so-called natural theology presented in his five ways was shaped by his faith commitments. That is pretty common fare today.[7] Whether that interpretation of Thomas is ultimately correct, I will leave to Thomists. I am interested in thinking that still pervades Catholic theology and perhaps not a few Protestant theologians today, with or without explicit reference to Thomas Aquinas. Let me explain that now. More than midway through his book, Murray explains that "we can know that God is but we cannot know what he is."[8] He explicitly follows Thomas's belief that "our

---

[7]See, e.g., Nicholas Healy, *Thomas Aquinas: Theologian of the Christian Life* (Aldershot, UK: Ashgate, 2007), pp. 5-7, 57. While Healy contends that the *Summa Contra Gentiles* "amounts in effect to a demonstration of our need for revelation" (p. 5), this does not explain Thomas's division of knowledge, assigning knowledge "that God exists" to natural reason and knowledge that God is triune to our knowledge of God through revelation. Thus, "Some truths about God exceed all the ability of the human reason. Such is the truth that God is triune. But there are some truths which the natural reason also is able to reach. Such are that God exists, that He is one, and the like. In fact, such truths about God have been proved demonstratively by the philosophers, guided by the light of the natural reason" (*Summa Contra Gentiles,* bk. 1, chap. 3, 2). Here the question concerns whether or not we know God's *actual* oneness apart from the Holy Spirit empowering us to know the Father through union with his Son. Eugene F. Rogers, *Thomas Aquinas and Karl Barth: Sacred Doctrine and the Natural Knowledge of God* (Notre Dame, IN: University of Notre Dame Press, 1995), attempts to show that Thomas's theology was grounded in Scripture rather than in an independent natural theology and then attempts to show that Thomas was really closer to Barth than is usually thought when considering the issue of natural theology. See my review of this book in *SJT* 55, no. 4 (2002): 496-98.
[8]John Courtney Murray, S.J., *The Problem of God Yesterday and Today* (New Haven, CT: Yale University Press, 1965), p. 71.

presence to him [God], which is real, is a presence to the unknown: 'to him we are united as to one unknown.'"[9] Therefore we must negate everything in this world as we know it, and then what remains in our minds is only the affirmation "that he is, and nothing more. Hence the mind is in a certain confusion."[10] The confusion is this: how can we affirm "that God is" while simultaneously claiming that God is not like anything else we know? Thomas's answer, according to Murray, is that it is by this very "ignorance" that we are united to God. Murray continues:

> Ignorance of God becomes a true knowledge of him only if it is reached, as Aquinas reached it, at the end of a laborious inquiry that is firmly and flexibly disciplined at every step by the dialectical method of the three ways. This method not only governs the search for the supreme truth but also *guarantees* that the search will end in a discovery.[11]

Our question is: What exactly is it that can be discovered by a method of negative theology that very clearly has not begun by acknowledging that the only guarantee of true knowledge of God is in reality the Holy Spirit? If this had been Thomas's working assumption, then both he and Murray would have had to admit that no method, not even a dialectical method, could be that guarantee. Here the problem of natural theology still rears its ugly head. Let us listen for a few more moments to Murray's reflections. He states that "Unlike the biblical problematic, which came down from heaven in a theophany, the Thomist statement rises up out of the earthly soil of experience."[12] And behind this, Murray says, is Thomas's assurance

> that it is within the native powers of the human intelligence, if it be trained in the discipline of philosophy, to make and to demonstrate the highest of metaphysical affirmations—to posit and to prove the judgment that God is; that it is further possible for reason to go on to articulate a complex conception of what God is not—a conception that, despite its negative form, is of positive cognitive value.[13]

---

[9]Ibid.
[10]Ibid., p. 72.
[11]Ibid., p. 73, emphasis mine. Murray describes this "first aspect of Thomist thought" as "definitional agnosticism" (p. 73).
[12]Ibid., pp. 73-74.
[13]Ibid., p. 74.

Murray goes on to say that "The fixed philosophical attitude today is to say that a natural theology is impossible," and that Protestants in particular think this type of natural theology is impossible because a philosophy of religion may be a possibility but "not a philosophy of God."[14] There is, he says, a gulf between what the philosopher recognizes by reason and the notion of God recognized in faith. But if this gulf exists, he says, then philosophers, who "must stand by reason, should also stand for atheism."[15] From this he concludes that "If the universe of reason and the universe of faith do not at any point intersect, it is unreasonable to accept any of the affirmations of faith, even the first, that God is."[16] For Murray that would mean that "The atheist denial is the reasonable position."[17] It is in this context, Murray believes, that Thomas Aquinas set out to demonstrate that "atheism is not the reasonable conclusion from the data of common human experience." And this is the case because while faith and philosophy are distinct, they nonetheless intersect "in the crucial instant when reason affirms, what faith likewise affirms, that God is."[18]

CONNECTING REASON AND FAITH WITHOUT ACCORDING PRIMACY TO REASON

With the help of Barth and Torrance we can see our way through this maze quite easily and quickly. *First*, for them, as seen in chapter one, it is impossible to assert "that God is" without first knowing "who God is" in faith. That means that while there is indeed an intersection of faith and reason in the affirmation "that God is," that point of intersection is not to be found either in human reason or in human experience but rather objectively in Christ and subjectively through his Holy Spirit. *Second*, to separate the question "that God is" from "what God is" or "who God is" is the first mistake that follows from failing to realize that our knowledge of who or what God is comes positively to meet us in Christ and thus through his Spirit as an act of God. *Third*, for that very reason, one can never discern either "that God is" or "who God is" by negating our experience of ourselves. Both Torrance

---

[14]Ibid.
[15]Ibid., pp. 74-75.
[16]Ibid., p. 75.
[17]Ibid.
[18]Ibid.

and Barth are consistently clear about this in their writings. And it is my contention that they are very clear about this because they both explicitly acknowledge, along with Irenaeus, Hilary and Athanasius, that it is by God that God is known.[19] They both explicitly claim our knowledge of God comes to us through a miraculous action of the Holy Spirit uniting us to Christ and through him to the Father. They also realize that as sinners we need to be reconciled to God by God actually to know God accurately.

What if John Courtney Murray had begun his reflections by acknowledging the role that the Holy Spirit plays in our knowledge of God? Then perhaps he could have seen that a proper doctrine of the Trinity would lead us to insist on the integrity of human reason, but not at the expense of faith's affirmation that God is both immanent and transcendent in his Word and Spirit in such a way that none of this can be explicated apart from faith. In other words, human reason cannot simply reach the true God by analyzing or by negating human experience. Torrance captures this situation perfectly when he says that we cannot have precise theological knowledge of God as the almighty creator "in terms of abstract possibilities and vague generalities—from what we imagine God is not, or from examining what God has brought into being in complete difference from himself."[20] It was the Gnostic Basileides from Alexandria who, relying on Plato's notion that "God is beyond all being," taught that "we cannot say anything about what God is, but can only say something about what he is not."[21] But Torrance insists that Gregory of Nazianzen (*Or. Bas.* 28.9) held in opposition to this thinking that "if we cannot say anything positive about what God is, we really cannot say anything accurate about what he is not."[22] As Torrance rightly explains, Nicene theologians refused to speak of God in empty, negative conceptions because if we do not think of the Father in his relation to the Son but only as creator in relation to creatures, then we will think of the Son himself as one of the works of the Father. And this will mean that we are then speaking of God "in a way that is not personally grounded in God himself, but in an

---

[19]Hilary, *De. Trin.* 5.20-21., cited in *Trinitarian Faith*, p. 21. This is also a theme that appears in Irenaeus. See Irenaeus, *Adversus haereses* 4.11, as cited in *Christian Doctrine of God*, p. 13. Athanasius will be cited below.

[20]*Trinitarian Faith*, p. 78.

[21]Ibid., p. 50.

[22]Ibid.

impersonal way far removed from what he is in himself."[23] Further, if we try
to reach knowledge of God from some point outside God, then there is no
point within God "by reference to which we can test or control our conceptions of him" and so we "are inevitably flung back upon ourselves."[24] In this
case our God-talk will be arbitrary and grounded in human experience
rather than God himself. And this is just what Athanasius accused the
Arians of doing. Hilary was also unhappy with such a procedure, arguing
that "the action of God must not be canvassed by human faculties; the
Creator must not be judged by those who are the work of his hands."[25]

The important point to be made here is that for Torrance we cannot attribute knowledge of God to ourselves since such knowledge is a "freely
given participation in [God's] self-knowledge."[26] Consequently, knowledge
of God takes place only in obedience to Christ as our minds conform to him.
And this can happen, Torrance says, "only as in the Spirit the being and
nature of God is brought to bear upon us so that we think under the compulsion of His Reality. That is the activity of the Holy Spirit whom Jesus
spoke of in this connection as the Spirit of Truth."[27] We will explore Torrance's thinking further later.

For now it is important to note that, left to itself, reason will always affirm
"that God is" based on a set of experiences that also could be interpreted as
pointing to any one of a number of gods or idols or perhaps even the devil, as
Barth once said.[28] Therefore it will never be compelling as true knowledge of
the Christian God. At the end of such a reasoning process, one may not be an
atheist, formally speaking. But materially one might just as well be an atheist

---

[23]Ibid.

[24]Ibid., p. 51.

[25]Hilary, *De. Trin.*, Book III, 26, at p. 70.

[26]Torrance, *God and Rationality*, p. 166.

[27]Ibid., p. 167.

[28]Speaking of the relation of science and philosophy to theology in answer to a question about the
   thinking of Karl Heim, Barth responded, "Is the presupposition true, that at the end of our
   thoughts we will always meet God? I do not think so. After all, it may be the devil!" (*Karl Barth's
   Table Talk,* recorded and ed. John Godsey [Richmond, VA: John Knox, 1962], p. 20). Interestingly, the questioner pressed Barth further, asking Barth how he might respond to the criticism
   that his theology was a "new mysticism." The questioner continued by saying that Barth claimed
   that the Holy Spirit makes the Bible God's Word for us and then asked, "Can we *trust* the Holy
   Spirit to continue to do this?" Barth's answer is instructive: "What an idea of the Holy Spirit, if
   He cannot be trusted! But the Holy Spirit is *God*, and God *can* be trusted. There is true continuity, but a continuity of the *actions of God*" (ibid.).

with regard to that very knowledge as far as Barth was concerned. Barth saw the matter very clearly when he insisted that his starting point for learning

> the lofty but simple lesson that it is by God that God is known . . . was neither an axiom of reason nor a datum of experience. In the measure that a doctrine of God draws on these sources, it betrays the fact that its subject is not really God. (II/2, 3)[29]

For Barth, as we shall see, it is the deity of the Holy Spirit that creates faith. That, unfortunately, is precisely what was systematically excluded from John Courtney Murray's reflections.

And in case there are those who might say that contemporary Roman Catholic theology has changed radically in the last forty years such that this example does not speak to us today, I would simply respond that they should read Elizabeth Johnson's recent *Quest for the Living God*.[30] The only difference between her and Murray is that she negates personal experiences of depth in order to attain knowledge of God. Thus she follows Rahner's basic turn to the subject to explain the meaning of Christianity. While claiming that the God she knows is the God of salvation history,[31] her theological method explicitly negates human experience on the assumption that we are basically good and that we therefore participate in the goodness of God so that we actually can know God's goodness by negating the goodness we experience humanly. In her words,

> Based on a belief that the created world is fundamentally good, analogy holds that all creatures participate in some way in the overflowing goodness, truth and beauty of the One who made them. Therefore, something of the creature's excellence can direct us back to God.[32]

Moreover, she explicitly argues both that "no expression for God can be taken literally"[33] and that

> From our experience of our own self and our interactions with other human beings, we develop an idea of what it means to be a person. Then we attribute

---

[29]See also Paul D. Molnar, *Divine Freedom and the Doctrine of the Immanent Trinity: In Dialogue with Karl Barth and Contemporary Theology* (New York: T & T Clark, 2005), p. 129.

[30]See Elizabeth A. Johnson, *Quest for the Living God: Mapping Frontiers in the Theology of God* (New York: Continuum, 2008).

[31]Ibid., p. 210.

[32]Ibid., p. 18.

[33]Ibid.

this excellence to God. . . . We affirm: yes, God is a person. We negate: no, God
is not a person in the finite way we know ourselves to be persons. We coun-
ternegate in order to affirm: still, God is a person in a supereminent way as
Source of all who are persons. In other words, God is not less than personal
but is super-personal, personal in a way that wonderfully transcends the
human way of being a person. At this point we've lost the literal concept. We
don't really understand what it means to attribute personhood to God. But in
the very saying, our spirits are guided into a relationship of personal communion with the Holy.[34]

But that is precisely the problem—we may envision ourselves in personal
communion with the holy, but that hardly means we have thereby described
our relationship with the triune God who alone can unite us to himself
precisely through the action of the Holy Spirit uniting us to his Son and thus
to the Father.

While Johnson claims she is thinking from the economy, she actually assumes that we can know God from our experience of ourselves and that
indeed, "If the Trinity is not grounded in the experience of salvation, the
triune symbol will remain in the dust, defeated."[35] How can anyone claim that
the Trinity is grounded in our experience of salvation without reducing the
content of the doctrine to a description of experience? No wonder she thinks
that God is *like* a Trinity,[36] and no wonder she espouses an agnosticism that
leaves it to us to construct the symbol God according to our social and religious agenda. No wonder also that she thinks we can never literally know
who God is. There must be many names for God, she claims, because "there

---

[34]Ibid., p. 19. Johnson thinks of God, with Rahner, as "holy mystery" and in that way breaks free
from a knowledge of God constrained by the triune God of Christian faith. For an analysis of
this, see chap. 1 of Molnar, *Divine Freedom,* and Cherith Fee Nordling, *Knowing God by Name:
A Conversation Between Elizabeth A. Johnson and Karl Barth* (New York: Peter Lang, 2010).
[35]Ibid., p. 211.
[36]See Elizabeth A. Johnson, *She Who Is: The Mystery of God in Feminist Theological Discourse* (New
York: Crossroad, 1992). She writes: "The symbol of the Trinity is not a blueprint of the inner workings of the godhead, not an offering of esoteric information about God. In no sense is it a literal
description of God's being *in se*. As the outcome of theological reflection on the Christian experience
of relationship to God, it is a symbol that indirectly points to God's relationality. . . . The Trinity is
itself an analogy referring to divine livingness. Our speech about God as three and persons is a
human construction that means to say that God is *like* a Trinity, *like* a threefoldness of relation" (pp.
204-5). But isn't the whole point of the doctrine to say that God *is* the Trinity? Stanley J. Grenz,
Rediscovering the Triune God: The Trinity in Contemporary Theology (Minneapolis: Fortress, 2004),
recognizes this problem in her thought, p. 181.

is no one such name," since "If human beings were capable of expressing the fullness of God in one straight-as-an-arrow name, the proliferation of names, images, and concepts observable throughout the history of religions would make no sense at all."[37] That is why human beings name God with many names, she says. By contrast, Barth and Torrance insist that because God *is* the Trinity, God can and does freely relate with us in the economy in his Word and Spirit and thus can be known only in faith through the Holy Spirit. This God cannot be known by negating any human experience, but only by knowing God as he has named himself to us in Jesus Christ and through his Holy Spirit. In other words, true and accurate knowledge of God can be attained analogically only through faith as that faith is based on God's self-revelation. It is worth noting here the connection between Johnson's symbolic approach to knowledge of God and Tillich's thinking, as well as the thinking of Bultmann, which, as we saw in chapter one, both Barth and Torrance categorized as an inappropriate form of non-conceptual knowledge that leaves us far from any scientific approach to the knowledge of God, which must be governed by who God actually is as the eternal Father, Son and Holy Spirit and as God acting for us in the economy in his Word and Spirit. Johnson explicitly appeals to the thinking of Paul Tillich, claiming that "Symbols . . . open up depths of our own being that would remain otherwise untouched. We cannot create symbols at will: they emerge from a deep level of consciousness. . . . Tillich considered 'God' the symbol of our ultimate concern."[38] But, as we saw in chapter one, this assumption that one could speak about God by speaking about the depths of their consciousness or of their ultimate concerns ends up equating God with our own depth experiences instead of recognizing who God is from God's own revelation of himself and thus through faith as the Spirit enables knowledge of the Father through his Son.[39]

Let me summarize the issue. If reason affirms "that God is" without faith in "who God is" as the eternal Father, Son and Holy Spirit, then the Holy Spirit, who unites reason and revelation, faith and knowledge, has been left out of the epistemology that is subsequently presented. And the crucial question

---

[37]Johnson, *Quest*, p. 21.
[38]Ibid., p. 20.
[39]See above, chap. 1, pp. 70-72.

then becomes whether the God affirmed by reason is the true God. In this approach to understanding God we will have no genuinely certain knowledge of God because it will always be thought in some way that reason can establish "that God is" without actually knowing "who God is" in faith as this is positively given to us in Christ objectively and through the Spirit subjectively.

MAPPING THE TERRAIN

Thomas F. Torrance frequently cited Athanasius's statement that it is more godly and accurate to know the Father through the Son than to name God the unoriginate from the works he has made.[40] There is a great deal in this statement, to be sure. And it is full of ecumenical significance, because the truth of that statement rests on the church's confession of the triune God as the source, meaning and goal of all its knowledge and action. When taken seriously, as both Barth and Torrance did in their theologies, this statement is full of meaning. *First*, this statement rules out any natural theology as a way to know God with accuracy. And natural theology is ruled out not on negative grounds but on very positive grounds: it is because God has made himself decisively known and knowable in his Son and by his Spirit and thus by grace and revelation that any other avenue into knowledge of God is recognized in faith to be at variance with the truth. That is, it is at variance with the truth of God's own self-knowledge into which we are drawn by grace through the Holy Spirit. *Second*, it implies, though it is not always stated in so many words, that one can really have true knowledge of God only through a special and miraculous action of the Holy Spirit. *Third*, it further implies that all knowledge of God is a kind of obedience; it is thus not simply theoretical, and so Barth could never be charged, as he sometimes is, with equating justification and sanctification merely with our knowledge and nothing more.[41] This has far-ranging implications for our understanding of how experience relates with doctrine in contemporary theology.

The fact that knowledge of God can take place only in obedience illustrates that we are dependent on the Holy Spirit at every moment really to relate with

---

[40]See, e.g., *Trinitarian Faith*, p. 49.
[41]See Alister E. McGrath, "Karl Barth's Doctrine of Justification from an Evangelical Perspective," in *Karl Barth and Evangelical Theology: Convergences and Divergences*, ed. Sung Wook Chung (Grand Rapids: Baker Academic, 2006), pp. 172-90, at pp. 182 and 187-88.

God and to know God. We cannot and indeed we must not attempt to do away with this neediness for the coming of the Spirit in any area of theology, but this is especially important in a Christian theological epistemology. *Fourth*, any claim to have the Holy Spirit and thus to know the triune God would be exposed as problematic if and to the extent that one is not immediately and self-evidently speaking of one's fellowship or communion with Christ himself. This implies that while we, with the full range of our experience, are fully involved in the present prophetic activity of Christ, the light of the world, the validity of our activity can never be traced to anything within that activity as such. Hence, there is no knowledge without experience of God. But, when God is known through God, we immediately know that the *guarantee* of that knowledge is and remains God and not our experience of God. This is why Barth insists that "To have the Holy Spirit is to let God rather than our having God be our confidence" (I/1, pp. 462-65, and I/2, p. 249). Any attempt to appeal to experience as the guarantee in this matter will always result in some false form of knowledge, whether it be pantheistic, panentheistic, dualistic or idealistic, because it will formulate its understanding without actually relying on the Holy Spirit, who alone unites us to Christ and thus to the Father. *Finally*, if the Holy Spirit is seen as the enabling factor in our knowledge of God, it will be extremely important to see that what Barth considered one of the hardest problems of Christology, namely, the issue of whether or not Jesus is the revealer in his humanity as such (I/1, p. 323), must be addressed in such a way that revelation has to be seen always as an act of God in the humanity of Jesus, which empowers our human being and actions without becoming confused with our self-experience (II/1, p. 56). Barth's insistence that there are no concepts or analogies that are true in themselves follows directly from this christological insight.

Here I would like to demonstrate that each of these points can be seen working together in the reflections of both Barth and Torrance; in fact, each of these points necessarily operates in unison because and to the extent that a theological epistemology recognizes and maintains its theological possibilities and limits on the basis of faith, grace and revelation. If one were to isolate any one of these insights, one might then castigate Barth and Torrance, perhaps for undercutting reason in their opposition to natural theology. Or one might chastise them for placing too much stress on faith to the exclusion of reason. But if one takes the factors just noted together and sees that opposing natural theology does not mean opposing human nature or human reason, and that stressing faith does not undermine human nature or human reason, then perhaps Christian theologians can find that they will agree about the truth of our knowledge of God when and to the degree that they specifically understand that such knowledge is a miracle, in the sense that it cannot be explained from the human side but can only be acknowledged and then genuinely understood.[42] In this context I hope to show that the attention Barth and Torrance pay to the Holy Spirit as the decisive factor in our knowledge of the Trinity will be extremely useful for a contemporary theological epistemology.

KNOWLEDGE OF GOD AND THE HOLY SPIRIT FOR BARTH

For Barth, "The knowledge of God occurs in the fulfilment of the revelation of His Word by the Holy Spirit, and therefore in the reality and with the necessity of faith and its obedience" (II/1, p. 3). Barth argues that since the triune God alone is the source and goal of true and certain knowledge of God, therefore "Knowledge of God is . . . an event enclosed in the mystery of the divine Trinity" (II/1, p. 181). In speaking of God's hiddenness Barth concludes that "The beginning of all knowledge of God has now to be understood as its end and goal—God the Father and God the Son by the Holy Spirit as the object of the knowledge of God." He continues by explaining that we humans are included secondarily, subsequently and improperly in this event

> in the height, in the being and essence of God, so that God is now the object
> not only of His own cognition, but also of that of man. . . . For if this is not
> the case he does not know God. Knowledge of God is then an event enclosed
> in the bosom of the divine Trinity. (II/1, p. 205)[43]

---

[42]It must be remembered here that for Barth as for Torrance miracle is an attribute of revelation, and it must not be understood in some extrinsicist, mechanical sense as an act of God on human nature. Rather it is "the special new direct act of God in time and in history. In the form in which it acquires temporal historical actuality, biblically attested revelation is always a miracle, and therefore the witness to it, whether direct or indirect in its course, is a narrative of miracles that happened. Miracle is thus an attribute of revelation" (I/2, pp. 63-64). The primary miracle that Barth had in mind was the resurrection; but faith itself is a miracle in the sense that it is a human act begun, upheld and completed by the action of the Holy Spirit here and now. That can only be acknowledged. It cannot be explained from the human side.

[43]In this context Barth is stressing that we are in the height with God because Jesus Christ is our reconciler and mediator. In other words, because of Christ our thinking is empowered to reach

This thinking reiterates an earlier position presented when Barth stated that "According to Scripture, everything which can be, everything which is either objectively or subjectively possible in relation to revelation, is enclosed in the being and will of the triune God" (I/2, p. 247).[44] If knowledge of God is an event enclosed within the bosom of the divine Trinity, then Barth must mean that we can have what he calls apodictically certain knowledge of God only in faith, by grace and therefore through the action of the Holy Spirit uniting us to the incarnate Son and thus to the Father (II/1, p. 162). Genuine knowledge of God then is a happening that is begun, upheld and completed by God himself.

That does not mean that it is an event that does not include us humanly with all we have and are, so that one might mistakenly criticize Barth for displaying an Apollinarian tendency in his theology of revelation.[45] One has only to pay attention to the fact that Barth insists that revelation claims us in our entirety without in any way changing our human being into something more or less than human (I/2, p. 266; II/1, p. 212).[46] What it does mean

---

God in spite of our sinful tendency to create God in our own image.

[44]This is why Barth speaks of the fact that the Spirit is not only the Spirit of the Father and Son here and now for us "but also for all eternity, in the hidden triune being of God which is revealed to us in revelation. It is because the Holy Spirit is from all eternity the communion between the Father and the Son and therefore not only the Spirit of the Father but also the Spirit of the Son, that in God's revelation He can be the communion between the Father and those whom His Son has called to be His brethren" (I/2, p. 250).

[45]See Alan Torrance, *Persons in Communion: Trinitarian Description and Human Participation* (Edinburgh: T & T Clark, 1996), p. 193, and Molnar, *Divine Freedom*, pp. 254-55.

[46]See especially I/1, "The Word of God and Experience," pp. 198-226. Barth insists that experience of God's Word takes place in a human act of self-determination but that in no way is it an experience of God's Word "as this act" (I/1, p. 199) because we do not give ourselves this determination—we cannot accomplish this in whole or in part; but neither does this mean that human self-determination is eliminated (I/1, p. 200). And for Barth no anthropological sphere is excluded from being determined by the power of the Word: will, conscience, subconscious, intuition and feeling included. Yet there is no hidden anthropological center where the Word may be found, either, because it is the act of God whereby we are upheld by God in our self-determination. In this regard Barth emphatically maintained that our new life as those who experience the Word and know God is not to be found in our "immanent constitution" (I/1, p. 212) but only in Christ. In Barth's view, "The possibility of knowledge of God's Word lies in the God's Word and nowhere else" (I/1, p. 222). Therefore it can take place "only as a miracle before the eyes of every man" (I/1, p. 223), and thus it takes place in faith. Hence one is "not sure of himself but of the Word of God, and he is not sure of the Word of God in and of himself but in and of the Word. His assurance is his own assurance, but it has its seat outside him in the Word" (I/1, pp. 224-25). Faith, Barth says, is "not one of the various capacities of man," but in faith we actually receive the Word, which is grounded only in itself (I/1, p. 238). In this section Barth speaks of faith as completely grounded in the objectivity of the Word. It is not until later in the volume that he specifically notes that "We may, of course, be strong and sure in faith—that we are so is the act of God we are confessing, the work of the Holy Spirit—but we cannot try specifically to make ourselves strong and sure again

is that since our inclusion in this event takes place by an act of God, that is, by God's grace, it is not something that can be traced directly to us in our experiences of God in Christ. It requires faith and the present activity of the Holy Spirit in order to be properly appreciated. Consequently, it rests on a miracle and thus is not in any sense under our control. Why does Barth insist that our knowledge of God rests on a miracle? We might say that it is because our knowledge of God' or readiness for God is enclosed in God's readiness for us. Barth says that God is "ready within Himself to be known by man" and that with and in that fact we are actually ready to know him. The error of natural theology, Barth stresses, is not that it treats the problem of our human readiness to know God but that it treats it by elevating human readiness for God "into an independent factor," so that God's actual readiness for us in his Word and Spirit is not the only possible basis for our knowledge; consequently it does not see human readiness as exclusively enclosed within this divine readiness (II/1, p. 129).

KNOWLEDGE OF GOD, MIRACLE AND GRACE

Barth says that God's readiness for us is "God's grace." Therefore our readiness must be readiness for grace. It must refer to our "openness for grace . . . openness for the majestic, the free, the undeserved, the unexpected, the new openness of God for man established entirely in God's own authority" (II/1, p. 129). Here Barth uses the word *miracle* to describe the fact that God is "not only open to Himself as the Father, the Son and the Holy Spirit, but that He is all this for men also" as "the Lord, the Creator, the Reconciler and Redeemer" (II/1, p. 129). This is a miracle because it is a free act of God for us that is neither demanded by God's essence nor conditioned by anything outside God and apart from God. It is something that is underserved and is to be seen as God's movement toward us in the incarnation, death and resurrection of Jesus himself (I/2, pp. 240-80). It is striking how many times Barth refers to our human inclusion in the event of revelation as a miracle in *CD* I/2. I think what he says there can be directly related to his understanding of our readiness for God in *CD* II/1 and illustrates why his theological epistemology is very precisely centered on his view that it is the Holy Spirit in

---

by contemplating ourselves as the strong and the sure. To have the Holy Spirit is to let God rather than our having God be our confidence" (I/1, p. 462).

union with the Father and Son who creates in us the possibility and actuality of our knowledge of God. For Barth this movement of God toward us in Christ is and remains offensive to us because it meets us in Jesus Christ and only in him. And it meets us as those who are sinners, those who actually resist God and are at enmity with God. This fact is not something that can be known in advance, Barth insists, because it is something that is revealed to us by Christ himself. It is and remains an act of God, who veils himself and who alone unveils himself to us. "The Holy Spirit," Barth writes,

> is holy because He is God's Spirit, and therefore the Spirit, the moving and unity of the Father and of the Son from eternity and in eternity. The fact that by the Holy Spirit we are ready for God in Jesus Christ is in the first instance and in itself only a confirmation of what we have just said. . . . In the Holy Spirit as the Spirit of the Father and of the Son there is, in the height of God, no "Against us" but only the "For us." (II/1, p. 157)

Here is where revelation and reconciliation must be seen together, since we are sinners who need to be reconciled with God in order to know God. That, for Barth, one might say, is the epistemological relevance of our justification by faith.[47] It is just this important fact disclosed to us in revelation that is always missing from theologies that claim reason knows "that God is" but not "what God is."

Barth is not only clear that knowledge of God takes place through a miraculous action of the Holy Spirit; his work is shaped by the fact that, at every point in his consideration of our knowledge of God, his thinking actually bears the mark of this particular truth because it operates under what he calls the constraint of the Word of God (II/1, pp. 7-9). Barth is simply being faithful to his insight that

> the work of the Spirit is nothing other than the work of Jesus Christ. . . . By the Holy Spirit whom He has given us, we know that the Word, that is Christ, abides with us, and so becomes ours and we His. . . . He Himself must give us

---

[47]Later, in his *The Doctrine of Reconciliation*, Barth identifies the sin known in light of the incarnation as pride and sloth—pride in the form of active displacement of God in his revelation and sloth in the form of evil inaction. God's response was to justify and sanctify us in the humiliation and exaltation of his Son. That is God's reconciling grace. See IV/2, p. 403. Importantly, Barth says that "The error of man concerning God is that the God he wants to be like is obviously only a self-sufficient, self-affirming, self-desiring supreme being, self-centered and rotating about himself. Such a being is not God. *God is for Himself, but He is not only for Himself*" (IV/1, p. 422, emphasis mine).

light to believe the Gospel, which is to make us new creatures, the temples of
God. (I/2, pp. 241-42)

Because he is the objective revelation of God for us, Barth maintains that
we are subjectively included in the fact that God was in Christ reconciling
the world to himself and that therefore our lives really are hidden with
Christ in God. For this reason, in him we are already "hearers and doers of
the Word of God" (I/2, p. 240). "When the Holy Spirit draws and takes us
right into the reality of revelation by doing what we cannot do, by opening
our eyes and ears and hearts, He does not tell us anything except that we
are in Christ by Christ" (I/2, p. 240). Barth is adamant that the subjective
reality of revelation, i.e., our human inclusion in the truth of our existence
in Christ, is not something that has to be added to who Christ is as our
savior and what he does for us; it is distinct from but not separable from
"objective revelation." Indeed, "Revelation is objective only in its irruption
into the subjective, in its redemptive objective assault upon man. We have
to follow objective revelation through its whole unified movement from
God to man" (I/2, p. 239). In this sense objective revelation comes to us and
is in fact "recognised and acknowledged by [us]. And that is the work of
the Holy Spirit" (I/2, p. 239). The work of the Holy Spirit opens our blind
eyes and empowers us thankfully to surrender and "acknowledge that it is
so" (I/2, p. 239). The truth of revelation as it is in God's actions in Christ
can never be added to, since "It is the truth, even if man is not in the truth,"
and "It is true from all eternity, for Jesus Christ who assumed our nature is
the eternal Son of God. . . . It is always true in time, even before we perceive
it to be true" (I/2, p. 238). Moreover, our perception that it is true is inexplicable from our side, since this is the work of the Holy Spirit (I/2, p. 239).
When we thankfully acknowledge the truth of our freedom for God as it is
in Christ, then we are living by faith, which itself is the work of the Holy
Spirit within us (I/2, pp. 242-43).

In speaking of the way objective revelation reaches us in the Holy Spirit,
Barth insists that the subjective reality of revelation "is simply the process
by which that objective reality becomes subjective. The Holy Spirit is the
Spirit of the Father and of the Son, of the Father who reveals Himself in His
Son and only in His Son. But that means that He is the Spirit of Jesus Christ"
(I/2, pp. 246-47). This is why Barth points firmly to the church as the place

"which corresponds to the particularity of the incarnation" (I/2, p. 247).[48] "The Church is the historical form of the work of the Holy Spirit and therefore the historical form of faith" because the Holy Spirit gathers people on the ground of what "in Jesus Christ is their common eternal truth" (II/1, p. 160). The church is the body of Christ as it is united to its heavenly head. But Barth does not fall into the trap of saying that Christ needs no other body than the church to be visible to us, since for Barth, the church is Christ's earthly, sacramental body precisely by being united to him as the risen and ascended Lord in his heavenly body.[49] Hence, "everything which can be, everything which is either objectively or subjectively possible in relation to revelation, is enclosed in the being and will and action of the triune God" (I/2, p. 247). Moreover, "The work of the Holy Spirit means that there is an adequate basis for our hearing of the Word, since it brings us nothing but the Word for our hearing" (I/2, p. 248). Furthermore, it means that "there is an adequate basis for our faith in Christ and our communion with Him, because He is no other Spirit than the Spirit of Jesus Christ" (I/2, p. 248). That precisely is the "life of the body of Christ, the operation of the prophetic and apostolic testimony, the hearing of preaching, the seeing of that to which the sacraments point" (I/2, p. 248). For Barth "The Holy Spirit is the Spirit of God, because He is the Spirit of the Word. And that is the very reason and the only reason why we acquire eyes and ears for God in the Holy Spirit" (I/2, p. 248).

Importantly, however, here Barth insists that we will never truly understand the Holy Spirit and his work on us if we "try to understand them abstractly and in themselves." What we will discover is "something extremely human, in which Christ is unrecognizable," and thus we will misunderstand the work of the Spirit or we will "confuse and equate the occurrence which we know, and therefore our human something, with Christ Himself, which means that we will seek Christ anywhere and everywhere and expose ourselves to every possible heresy" (I/2, p. 248). This will lead only toward skepticism or "mild or even a violent fanaticism" (I/2, p. 249). Here Barth reso-

---

[48]Barth works out the details of how he understands the church as the earthly-historical form of Christ's heavenly existence in IV/1, pp. 150-54 and 650-725.

[49]See II/1, p. 161. "As the earthly body of Jesus Christ it [the church] may—as is believed and proclaimed in the Lord's Supper—be nourished by its own eternal truth in its form as the heavenly body of Jesus Christ. It cannot be nourished in any other way. If it nourishes itself in any other way it can only die as the Church."

lutely insists that to avoid this problem "we must look at Christ Himself" and not our experiences of him, because the love of God is shed abroad in our hearts by the Holy Spirit (I/2, pp. 248-49, and Rom 5:5). We must, Barth says, point away from our or other people's "seizure" toward the "divine seizing, and therefore once again to Christ Himself" (I/2, p. 249). Barth never wavered on this point.

THE NECESSITY OF FAITH

That is why, in his doctrine of God, Barth insisted that "Faith does not consist in an inward and immanent transformation of man, although there can be no faith without such a transformation" (II/1, p. 158). For Barth, however, as described in detail in chapter one, "faith is more than all the transformation which follows it" precisely because it is "the work of the Holy Spirit" as our new birth from God "on the basis of which [we] can already live here by what [we] are there in Jesus Christ and therefore in truth" (II/1, p. 158). Faith is indeed the temporal form of our "eternal being in Jesus Christ"—a being "which is grounded on the fact that Jesus Christ intercedes for us before the Father. . . . Faith extinguishes our enmity against God by seeing that this enmity is made a lie, a lie confessed by ourselves as such, expiated and overcome by Jesus Christ" (II/1, p. 158). That is why Barth insists that the truth cannot be found within us. What we find in ourselves, he insists, "will only be our enmity against God." That very being, he says, "is a lie. It is the lie that is seen in faith. Our truth is our being in the Son of God, in whom we are not enemies but friends of God, in whom we do not hate grace but cling to grace alone, in whom therefore God is knowable to us" (II/1, pp. 158-59). This, Barth writes,

> is man's truth believed by faith. And it is the work of the Holy Spirit that the eternal presence of the reconciliation in Jesus Christ has in us this temporal form, the form of faith, which believes this truth. The man in whom Jesus Christ has this temporal form does not then in any sense believe in himself. (II/1, p. 159)

Faith, as seen in the previous chapter, means not standing at all on ourselves but only on Christ. And the point here is that the power to do this comes only from the Holy Spirit and not at all from ourselves. Thus, "We have to believe: not to believe in ourselves, but in Jesus Christ" (II/1, p. 159). Importantly, Barth maintains a strict unity here between the Word and Spirit.

As we saw in chapter one, Barth takes a similar line in his doctrine of reconciliation, insisting that the necessity of faith does not lie within us at all:

> It is to be found rather in the object of faith. It is this object which forces itself necessarily on man and is in that way the basis of his faith. This object is the living Lord Jesus Christ, in whom it took place, in whom it has taken place for every man, in whom it confronts man as an absolutely superior actuality, that his sin, and he himself as the actual sinner he is, and with his sin the possibility of unbelief, is rejected, destroyed and set aside, that he is born again as a new man of obedience, who now has the freedom for faith, and only in that faith his future. (IV/1, p. 747)

Because Christ has died and risen for all, he is not just one alternative put before us to choose, Barth says—rather the choice of unbelief—which is the choice not to acknowledge him, is rendered ontologically impossible. The only real possibility is faith and thus obedience. That is our only justification. Yet the power to do this does not lie within us, but "is the awakening power of the Holy Spirit. . . . The Holy Spirit is the power in which Jesus Christ the Son of God makes a man free, makes him genuinely free for this choice and therefore for faith" (IV/1, p. 748). As seen in chapter one, Barth concludes his discussion of faith at the end of *CD* IV/1 with his understanding of confession, saying that "confessing is the moment in the act of faith in which the believer stands to his faith, or, rather, to the One in whom he believes, the One whom he acknowledges and recognises, the living Jesus Christ; and does so outwardly, again in general terms, in face of men" (IV/1, p. 777). To Barth this means that someone who only acknowledges and recognizes but does not confess Jesus Christ by living as his witness in the genuine freedom that comes from Christ through his Spirit is not really a Christian at all. And it does not matter how a person feels about this, since we are not asked about our own wishes or aversions. Faith itself is the free act of confession. Consequently, Barth concludes that "It is not on the basis of his own discovery and private revelation, but by the mediatorial ministry of the community which is itself in the school of the prophets and apostles, that a man comes under the awakening power of the Holy Spirit and therefore to faith" (IV/1, p. 778).

KNOWLEDGE OF GOD AND APOLOGETICS

Thus, for Barth, there are good apologetics and bad apologetics. The former has "the character of a supplementary, incidental and implicit apologetics, comparable to the subsequent substantiation of a judgment of the supreme court which has already been given and come into force and hence whose validity cannot be questioned" (II/1, p. 8). The latter will not be bound by what has happened, namely, God's actually speaking his Word by his Holy Spirit, and so will think that knowledge of God is based on a person's free choice. Barth says that this approach to the knowledge of God will not only ask the false question of whether God is known (when it should be asking how it is that God has made himself known), just as a false understanding of revelation will lead one to ask whether he or she has understood instead of beginning in and by the Holy Spirit and asking about the fact that the Holy Spirit who does this has the power to do it (I/2, p. 243). But, additionally, this approach will create anxiety and doubt, since it will be unsure of its object, and it will thus be open to questioning from without. That, Barth claims, is the sure sign of all false knowledge of God as idolatry. Wisely, Barth depicts false apologetics by noting that its approach to understanding God will operate with "sublime, sovereign freedom, open on every side, interested in anything and everything, taking every possible and impossible knowledge of 'God' with a tragic seriousness" (II/1, p. 8) until it finally reaches the point of a "*sacrificium intellectus*" as its own final possibility. This final possibility may even take the form of a "leap into faith" (II/1, p. 9). At that point, "probably assuming a parsonic voice, it will praise this very *sacrificum* as the last and best choice" and will then speak of a "necessary constraint of the Word of God" and start talking about Jesus and the Bible or even church dogma. But, Barth says, then it is too late, since such thinking was not *originally* constrained by the Word, "even though it now declares and designates itself to be such" (II/1, p. 8). His point is simple, but with profound consequences: "We can only come from the real and original constraint by the Word; *we cannot come to it*" (II/1, p. 9, emphasis mine).

This is an enormously important point because it is false apologetics that separates the thinking of those who, like Karl Rahner, believe that they can and must begin their thinking about God with our self-transcending experiences. It is exactly for this reason that Rahner believes "we cannot begin with

Jesus Christ as the absolute and final datum, but we must begin further back than that."[50] He thus chooses to begin with "a knowledge of God which is not mediated completely by an encounter with Jesus Christ."[51] He begins with our transcendental experience, which he claims mediates an "unthematic and anonymous . . . knowledge of God,"[52] which, as seen in chapter one, both Barth and Torrance rightly rejected because such knowledge amounts only to a symbolic description of ourselves in place of the triune God. He thus claims that knowledge of God is always present unthematically to anyone reflecting on themselves, so that all talk about God "always only points to this transcendental experience as such, an experience in which he whom we call 'God' encounters man in silence . . . as the absolute and the incomprehensible, as the term of his transcendence."[53] This term of transcendence Rahner eventually calls a holy mystery because he believes that whenever this experience of transcendence is an experience of love, its term is the God of Christian revelation.[54] It is just this thinking that leads to Rahner's idea of "Searching Christology," which, as seen above in chapter one, essentially refers to the fact that anyone who truly loves another, for instance, is already an "anonymous Christian" in that search. In that sense Rahner believes their activity and thinking is in line with what traditional Christology teaches. This approach to Christology presumes that we must find a basis for belief in Christ in a transcendental anthropology. This led Rahner to embrace the idea that we have an *obediential potency* for revelation and that our lives are marked by a "supernatural existential," as seen in chapter one. Finally, it led him to the idea that self-acceptance is the same as accepting Christ and God himself. In this context I think one can see rather clearly that the crucial difference between Barth and Rahner is that Barth's thinking begins and ends with the Holy Spirit as the awakening power of faith—not faith in ourselves (our transcendental dynamisms)—but in the Word of truth, namely, Jesus Christ. And that of course rules out the idea of anonymous Christianity as the projection of

---

[50]*FCF*, p. 13.

[51]Ibid.

[52]Ibid., p. 21.

[53]Ibid.

[54]For more on this see Paul D. Molnar, "Is God Essentially Different from His Creatures? Rahner's Explanation from Revelation," in *The Thomist* 51, no. 4 (October 1987): 575-631; and chap. 4 of *Divine Freedom*. We have already noted how Elizabeth Johnson exploits Rahner's approach to the "holy" above.

an idea that is at variance with what is actually revealed by Jesus himself as the Word incarnate and through his Holy Spirit as the risen and ascended Lord here and now. It also rules out any notion that we have any "potency" or capacity for the revelation of God; that we have an existential on the basis of which we can rely on ourselves in our experience of grace to speak accurately about God; and that we can look to anyone or anything other than Jesus Christ himself to know who God is and what he has done and does for us as the reconciler and redeemer.

That is why Barth not only insists that our knowledge of God is based on his knowing us and enabling such knowledge but that the same is true regarding our knowledge of Christ's deity. We do not know this "on the basis of [our] knowledge and choice, but on the basis of [our] being known and chosen (not as the result but as the beginning of [our] thinking about Him" (I/1, p. 461). This, of course, sets Barth apart from those who like Rahner certainly would admit that our knowledge of the Trinity comes from and through the Holy Spirit, but then proceed to develop their knowledge of God from elsewhere than from the revelation of God in Jesus Christ.[55] For Barth this is impossible, because the Holy Spirit, who includes us in revelation as its "subjective reality," is the Spirit of the Father *and* the Son and simply cannot be separated under any circumstances from the Word, who is the Son.[56] This happens quite frequently, however. I will highlight just one more example.

PANNENBERG, APOLOGETICS AND THE KNOWLEDGE OF FAITH

Consider Wolfhart Pannenberg's approach elaborated in volume one of his *Systematic Theology*. He claims that "Dogmatics, although it treats all other themes from the standpoint of God and thus discusses them in exposition of the concept of God, cannot begin directly with the reality of God" (*Systematic Theology* I, p. 61). It must instead recognize that God is present initially only as "a human notion, word, or concept" and that to escape from confusing God with our ideas we must "engage in controversy" by clarifying "how we come to count on God as a reality" by publicly discussing the reality

[55]For a discussion of exactly how and why the methods of Barth and Rahner differ and cannot be reconciled as they stand, see Paul D. Molnar, "What Does It Mean to Say That Jesus Christ Is Indispensable to a Properly Conceived Doctrine of the Immanent Trinity?" *SJT* 61, no. 1 (2008): 96-106.
[56]Cf., e.g., I/2, p. 244.

of God witnessed in Scripture. This sounds acceptable, I realize, to many modern ears and is in many respects quite similar to Rahner's approach. But it is exactly the point that Barth emphatically contests because it represents a kind of apologetics that refuses to begin in faith with the reality of God made known in his Word and by his Spirit.[57] Thus Pannenberg can sound as though he is saying the same thing as Barth when he writes: "Materially only God, or his self-revelation in Jesus Christ, is fundamental" for a "fundamental theology" that seeks to lay the groundwork for dogmatics (*Systematic Theology* I, p. 61).

But Pannenberg is not even remotely close to Barth's position, because he believes that "The designation of Yahweh as God and the Christian attributing of deity to Jesus Christ make sense only on the condition of an established pre-Christian and extra-Christian use of the word 'God'" (*Systematic Theology* I, p. 68). No wonder Pannenberg reaches this conclusion:

> The natural theology of the philosophers had formulated a criterion for judging whether any God could be seriously considered the author of the whole cosmos, and Christian theology had to meet this criterion if its claim could be taken seriously that the God who redeems us in Jesus Christ is the Creator of heaven and earth and thus the one true God of all peoples.[58] (*Systematic Theology* I, p. 79)

This is exactly the thinking that Barth rejected as false apologetics precisely because of its refusal to begin thinking about God under the constraint of the Word of God. It refuses to acknowledge that it is the Holy Spirit *alone* who actually enables us to know this God. And it is no accident that Barth's entire theology is marked by the fact that he steadfastly refuses to begin thinking about God apart from Jesus himself as the incarnate Word,

---

[57]Pannenberg mistakenly accused Barth of "faith subjectivism" for beginning his theology in faith with the reality of God (*Systematic Theology* I, pp. 44-45). What Pannenberg did not realize is that unless one begins theology in faith with the reality of God revealed in his Word and by his Spirit and therefore as a witness (I/2, pp. 817-19), one will always be supposing that one can freely choose which concept of God one wishes based on a series of rational arguments (cf. also IV/3.1, p. 1). But in Barth's thinking that very approach displaces the Holy Spirit from the scene as the sole miraculous (because it cannot be explained or proven but only accepted as an act of God in faith) action that enables true and certain knowledge of God. See Paul D. Molnar, "Some Problems with Pannenberg's Solution to Barth's 'Faith Subjectivism,'" *SJT* 48, no. 3 (1995): 315-39.

[58]Barth was always very clear about the fact that "God can never be for dogmatic thinking and speaking an object which can be affirmed apart from God" (I/2, p. 819).

insisting that all thinking about God must begin with him because he is God's Son (I/1, p. 415). Indeed this is not something we can establish, as Pannenberg seems to believe, because Jesus simply is who he is, and that fact is grounded within the eternal relation of the Father to the Son and in the Spirit and can only be acknowledged in faith.[59]

This is why there is an air of adoptionism that pervades Pannenberg's Christology, as when he expresses his belief that the resurrection constitutes Jesus' Sonship.[60] There is no such ambiguity in Barth's thought, because Barth insists that the deity of the Holy Spirit can be contested (and is contested whenever one does not begin thinking about God from and through Jesus himself) "only if one has first explained away the fact that with its Ἰησοῦς Κύριος the New Testament community confessed its faith in Jesus Christ as faith in God Himself. If the Christ of the New Testament is a demigod from above or below, then naturally faith in Him becomes a human possibility" (I/1, p. 460). In Barth's words:

> The Spirit guarantees man what he cannot guarantee himself, his personal participation in revelation. The act of the Holy Ghost in revelation is the Yes to God's Word which is spoken by God Himself for us, yet not just to us, but also in us. This Yes spoken by God is the basis of the confidence with which man may regard the revelation as applying to him. This Yes is the mystery of faith, the mystery of the knowledge of the Word of God, but also the mystery of the willing obedience that is well-pleasing to God. All these things, faith, knowledge and obedience, exist for man "in the Holy Spirit."[61] (I/1, p. 453)

That is why, in his concept of analogy, Barth took a position diametrically opposed to Pannenberg's. "Can the ideas of lords and lordships even help us to know God?" Barth asks, before answering: "Of themselves they can only hinder. For in the last resort they do not point us to God, but to ourselves"

---

[59]This is a point also stressed by Torrance. See, e.g., *Christian Doctrine of God*, pp. 194-202.

[60]See Molnar, *Incarnation and Resurrection*, pp. 283-84. See also Iain Taylor, *Pannenberg on the Triune God* (New York: T & T Clark, 2007), pp. 111-13.

[61]See Karl Barth, *Credo* (New York: Charles Scribner's Sons, 1962), where he says that when we confess the Holy Spirit we recognize that human beings now come on the scene but that this is no warrant for pursuing an anthropology or theological anthropology *in order* to understand God and our relations with God (pp. 127-29). Is it any surprise that Barth reacted negatively to Pannenberg's Christology by stating that it appeared to him to be an outstanding example of a presupposed anthropology and cosmology? See *Karl Barth Letters 1961–1968*, ed. Jürgen Fangmeier and Hinrich Stoevesandt, trans. and ed. Geoffrey W. Bromiley (Grand Rapids: Eerdmans, 1981), p. 178.

(II/1, p. 76). Here Barth applies his doctrine of justification by faith once again to our knowledge of God, and he thus refuses to allow any self-grounding or any apologetic concern that would attempt to secure us from our neediness. In other words, we need God's grace and revelation. We need the Holy Spirit to have apodictic certainty here. We need to know the true God and our actual freedom as it exists in Christ for us. But for all this we must pray. And when we pray, we actually rely on God's promise to be our God, and so we believe and obey God's command, and we are thus in the truth—not, however, a truth that needs to be debated before freely deciding to commit ourselves—but a truth that constrains us to belief and thus to obedience to God's Word and Spirit, and therefore to the Father as the sole Lord of the covenant. Barth works these insights out with amazing consistency in his *The Doctrine of Reconciliation*.[62]

BARTH AND THE KNOWLEDGE OF GOD

In Barth's understanding, God knows himself immediately, and we never know God as God knows himself. Nonetheless, on the basis of revelation we do know God "mediately" as an "object" because God presents himself to us "in a medium" so that God is present to us in a "double sense. In His Word He comes as an object before man the subject. And by the Holy Spirit He makes the human subject accessible to Himself, capable of considering and conceiving Himself as object" (II/1, p. 10).

> As He is in the essence of God Himself the Spirit of the Father and of the Son, the Holy Spirit does not come independently, or for Himself, as immediate truth to man, but through the Son, and as the Spirit of the Son, as the power in which the truth of God lays hold of man in this very mediacy, in the incarnate Son of God. (II/1, p. 101)

Barth insists on two crucial points here. First, real knowledge of God thus described involves both God's relationship to us and his distinction from us.

---

[62]See, e.g., IV/1 §61, The Justification of Man, esp. pp. 608-642, and §62, The Holy Spirit and Christian Faith, pp. 725-79; IV/2 §68, The Holy Spirit and Christian Love, pp. 727-840; IV/3, §71, The Vocation of Man, §72, The Holy Spirit and the Sending of the Christian Community, and §73, The Holy Spirit and Christian Hope. See also the important chapter on the Holy Spirit by George Hunsinger, "The Mediator of Communion: Karl Barth's Doctrine of the Holy Spirit," in the *Cambridge Companion to Karl Barth*, ed. John Webster (Cambridge: Cambridge University Press, 2000), pp. 177-94.

This rules out all claims to knowledge of God that understand this as "the union of man with God" but "which do not regard it as an objective knowledge," since they "leave out the distinction between the knower and the known" (II/1, p. 10). Importantly, Barth is claiming that all attempts to know God that bypass Jesus Christ, the incarnate Word, will necessarily lead in this direction, namely, toward a non-objective knowledge and toward some form of confusion of divine and human being. As seen above in chapter one, this is why Barth insists that knowledge of God is knowledge of faith. "Faith is the total positive relationship of man to the God who gives Himself to be known in His Word. It is man's act of turning to God, of opening up his life to Him and of surrendering to Him" (II/1, p. 12). Indeed, "Knowledge of faith means fundamentally the union of man with the God who is distinct from him as well as from all his other objects" (II/1, p. 15). But this faith itself comes from God. In reality

> it is utterly and entirely grounded in the fact that God encounters man in the Word which demands of him this turning, this Yes, this obligation; becoming an object to him in such a way that in His objectivity He bestows upon him by the Holy Spirit the light of the clarity that He is God and that He is his God. (II/1, p. 12)

Barth proceeds to speak of God as an utterly unique object by positing what he calls God's primary objectivity, in distinction from his secondary objectivity. "In his triune life as such, objectivity, and with it knowledge, is divine reality before creaturely objectivity and knowledge exist," Barth writes (II/1, p. 16). That is God's "primary objectivity." Yet God "gives Himself to be known by us as He knows Himself." That is God's secondary objectivity. Barth maintains that God is "first to Himself, and then in His revelation to us . . . nothing but what He is in Himself. Here the door is shut against any 'non-objective' knowledge of God" (II/1, p. 16), as seen especially above in chapter one. It will be recalled that Barth's opposition to non-objective knowledge of God was based on the positive assertion that since God revealed himself to us in his Word and Spirit, we must know God objectively and conceptually as the eternal Father, Son and Holy Spirit who is active precisely in the history of Jesus Christ and in the community's witness to him through the power of his Spirit. With Barth's distinction between primary and secondary objectivity in place, then, he asserts that all our knowledge of God is knowledge of faith that rests on God's objectivity. But since it is mediated through the veil of secondary objectivity, it is indirect and not direct knowledge of God's "naked objectivity." That is why he says that

> the Word does not appear in His eternal objectivity as the Son who alone dwells in the bosom of the Father. No: the Word became flesh. God gives Himself to be known, and is known, in the substance of secondary objectivity . . . in the manhood which He takes to Himself, to which He humbles Himself and which He raises through Himself. (II/1, pp. 19-20)

Knowledge of God, however, takes place, Barth notes, as primary and secondary objectivity are distinguished without being separated and as long as God is understood as the living God, i.e., as the creator from whom we come even before we know him; he is our "Reconciler, who through Jesus Christ in the Holy Ghost makes knowledge of Himself real and possible," and he is our "Redeemer, who is Himself the future truth of all present knowledge of Himself. He and none other is the object of the knowledge of faith" (II/1, p. 21).

This knowledge of God is true and certain only as and because God in free grace "posits Himself as the object" of our knowledge (II/1, p. 22). Without any constraint and in the freedom of his love, God gives himself to be known and can be known as God only in this giving "which is always a bestowal, always a free action." This action of his can never be separated from his being, and we are completely unable to contemplate God *in abstracto* as if we might know God's being according to some prearranged "being of the contemplating man himself" (II/1, p. 22). Because our knowledge of God always depends on this preceding act of God to be true, we "must of necessity pray for its fulfilment as real knowledge of God. . . . The position of grace cannot be taken up and held in any other way than by asking and praying for it" (II/1, p. 22; I/1, p. 108; III/3, p. 266).

This is one of the reasons that Barth is so insistent on the fact that such knowledge must always be seen as a miracle (I/2, pp. 65-66, 68-69, 258). "Necessarily, it is all up with the truth of God's work and sign if we cease to adore its grace. For just as certainly as grace is truth, so certainly can truth only be had as grace" (II/1, p. 23). In the Bible, Barth insists, knowledge of God differs from all other human knowledge by the fact that "it coincides with some action of God. God is known, not simply because He is God in Himself, but because He reveals Himself as such; not simply because his work is there, but because He is active in His work" (II/1, p. 23). This is why Barth asserts further that knowledge of God is "obedience to God." And for Barth this is no coerced obedience but the free obedience that springs from one who has been set free for the service of God by the grace of God. Hence, for Barth, justification does not simply apply to human knowledge but to human being as it is in Christ. Human knowledge without corresponding acts of faith and obedience would not be true knowledge of the living God. Consequently, Barth insists that

> Knowledge of God according to the teaching of the Reformation does not therefore permit the man who knows to withdraw himself from God, so to speak, and to maintain an independent and secure position over against God so that from this he may form thoughts about God, which are in varying degrees true, beautiful and good. This latter procedure is that of all natural theology. . . . Knowledge of God according to the teaching of the Reformation is *obedience* to God and therefore itself already service of God.[63]

When God as object reaches out and grasps us, then knowledge of God takes place. But in that very occurrence we become new human beings, according to Barth. All of this is tied to faith, of course. And that means that we are set face-to-face with Jesus Christ as prophet, priest and king who not only tells us what we need to know but makes amends for us and will do so for everything, and has the power of God actually to accomplish all this. "That is why knowledge of God is nothing else than service of God."[64] Unless knowledge of God means service of God in Christ, our freedom in the Holy Spirit would only become a pretext for "new unfreedom" (I/1, p. 457). Moreover, unless we see knowledge of God as service of God, we would miss the fact that when the Holy Spirit actually is at work in our lives and thus when we "have our master unavoidably in Jesus Christ," we exist "in an ultimate and most profound irresponsibility" (I/2, p. 274). What could Barth mean by this?

He means that all other teachers or masters actually burden us with ob-

---

[63]Karl Barth, *The Knowledge of God and the Service of God According to the Teaching of the Reformation*, trans. J. L. M. Haire and Ian Henderson (London: Hodder and Stoughton, 1949), pp. 103-4. See also I/2, p. 846.

[64]Barth, *Knowledge of God and the Service of God*, p. 104.

ligations and responsibilities that we must fulfill by means of our own activities and achievements. But Jesus Christ, when he comes to us in his Holy
Spirit, actually "claims our response . . . claims the achievement which is, of
course required of us" (I/2, p. 274). Notice that Barth is no Apollinarian or
Docetist in his thinking. He really thinks that works follow from faith. But
they follow from faith not as autonomous activities that we must guarantee
but rather as acts of service "in the fulfillment of which we are borne and
covered by the work it does itself" (I/2, pp. 274-75). In this sense he states
that the outpouring of the Holy Spirit relativizes "the question who and what
we are in ourselves" because by this action we are placed under the
"command of the Word" (I/2, p. 275). We really "participate in that work of
the Word." But we do so "Not as those who have to finish the work, to reach
the goal, to bring in the results."

Our participation does not rest on our fitness for revelation, since we know
we are unfit for it. Our participation rests on our forgiveness. It is, Barth says,
"grace." What preserves us from the anxiety and worry about whether we are
truly able to do what God requires here is that we are permitted and enabled
to do exactly what we are unable to do of ourselves. "As those who cannot do
it of ourselves, and never could, we have to participate when the Word does
it" (I/2, p. 275). When we are placed under the command of the Word we are
genuinely free, that is, we do not have to worry about ourselves or others or
the development of the church or world, because we can pray, "Thy will be
done." In that prayer we admit that we need not worry about these things

> because that is not [our] business. I am not responsible. This burden, the
> burden of my own and others' sins, does not lie upon me. It lies solely and
> entirely upon Jesus Christ, upon the Word of God. . . . Jesus Christ alone bears
> it and can bear it. (I/2, p. 275)

This freedom is our "ultimate absence of responsibility," says Barth, because
we know in faith that Christ cares for us. And this is what the Holy Spirit of
Christ discloses to us. Of course Barth is not saying that we are not to be
responsible to the Word of God. But that responsibility is our obedience of
faith, and thus it cannot be traced back to us in some self-justifying fashion.

The key question in this context is, from where does faith come? Barth's
answer is direct and simple. It comes from the Holy Spirit so that the person

who lives by faith sees himself "convicted of his own unfaithfulness" and also sees that "he is in no position to have faith in himself, or to ascribe to himself a capacity or power by means of which he himself could somehow bring about his salvation, or co-operate in bringing it about."[65] Very bluntly, Barth states that "Faith, New Testament πίστις is . . . to be understood as a possibility which derives from a mode of being of God, from a mode of being which is in essential unity with Him who in the New Testament is described as Father and as Son" (I/1, p. 461). We have already seen that unlike those who think that some theological or philosophical method might guarantee our knowledge of God, Barth insists that only the Spirit is that guarantee and that our yes to God is the mystery of faith in which we are miraculously enabled by God to know him in spite of our sin and our tendencies to be self-reliant.

> It is God Himself who opens our eyes and ears for Himself. And in so doing He tells us that we could not do it of ourselves, that of our selves we are blind and deaf. To receive the Holy Spirit means an exposure of our spiritual helplessness, a recognition that we do not possess the Holy Spirit. (I/2, p. 244)

This is why Barth says it is a miracle. "It is a reality to be grounded only in itself" (I/2, p. 244). Thus, apart from this action of the Spirit including us in the life of Christ, "there is no other possibility of being free for God" (I/2, p. 244). Importantly, Barth insists here that he is not making a generally self-evident statement "after the manner of philosophical agnosticism" (I/2, p. 244). What the philosophical agnostic recognizes, Barth asserts, is not God, because we can have no actual view of God by speaking of our incapacity for God. The certainty of this agnosticism that speaks of "the above which is barred to us" is of our own disposing exactly because it is made so absolutely. Barth says that if the philosopher "did mean God, he would have to allow the renunciation he makes so absolutely to be bracketed and relativised by the reality of the Holy Spirit" (I/2, p. 244). An actual encounter with the Holy Spirit, Barth insists, would cause the agnostic to speak quite differently. Instead of making

> an absolute claim to renunciation, he would have to forego [sic] all claims and speak about the humility enjoined upon us. Instead of eyes which blink (and blink continually), he would have to speak about our blindness and the

---

[65]Ibid., 105.

healing of the blind. In fact, he would have to surrender his agnosticism all along the line. (I/2, p. 244)

Barth adds that he is not engaging in apologetics here because he simply wanted to make it clear that his statement that we cannot be free for God without the Holy Spirit has nothing to do with philosophical agnosticism. Hence, while it may seem that the philosophical agnostic and the theologian agree that we are not free for God, Barth maintains that the agnostic knows nothing about this because this can only be known by revelation and thus "by the Holy Spirit" (I/2, p. 245). Moreover and decisively, the fact that anyone really knows this is due to a miracle. The Holy Spirit is the "Teacher of the Word who reconciles us to God," and "He informs us both about God and also about ourselves" (I/2, p. 245). But he does not reveal to us that we are "petty finite creatures of little account in His presence (for this contrast would still not signify that we are not free for Him; the infinite needs the finite just as the finite needs the infinite)" (I/2, p. 245). What is revealed is that we are "rebels against this Lord" as those who are "unthankful for his kindness" and "as resisters of His call" (I/2, p. 245).

> In the Holy Spirit we are confronted by what we cannot deny even if we willed to do so. We know, therefore, that we cannot ascribe to man any freedom of his own for God, any possibility of his own to become the recipient of revelation. And we know it in a way which does not admit of any question. For the Holy Spirit is not a dialectician. And the negation is not our own discovery. Unlike our own positive or negative discoveries, it is not open to revision. (I/2, p. 246)[66]

But there is more to be said about the action of the Holy Spirit here. Barth also insists that "The Spirit gives man instruction and guidance he cannot give himself" (I/1, p. 454). However, this presupposes that "the Spirit is not identical, and does not become identical with ourselves. . . . As our Teacher and Leader He is in us, but not as a power of which we might become lords. He remains Himself the Lord" (I/1, p. 454). In this sense the Spirit is the power in which God "establishes and executes His claim to lordship over us by His immediate presence" (I/1, p. 454). In addition, "the Spirit is the great

---

[66]It is exactly here that one of the key differences between Barth on the one side and Rahner and Pannenberg on the other is to be seen.

and only possibility in virtue of which men can speak of Christ in such a way that what they say is witness and that God's revelation in Christ thus achieves new actuality through it" (I/1, p. 454). The Holy Spirit authorizes us to speak about Christ and summons us to be ministers of the Word. Therefore the very existence of the church consists in the fact that as individuals who are part of this community of faith, we are constrained by the Holy Spirit to speak about the "wonderful works of God" (I/1, p. 456). By the Holy Spirit we really become recipients of revelation, Barth says. How can a sinner become capable of receiving the Word of God? Barth answers by saying that we do not first become this in order to be it but that we are already capable of this because, in Christ, God has made us his children. As such, Barth says, we are free and can therefore believe. We are God's children as we receive the Holy Spirit. But in receiving the Holy Spirit a person "is what in himself and of himself he cannot be, one who belongs to God as a child to its father, one who knows God as a child knows its father" (I/1, p. 457). Interestingly, Barth identifies this freedom of ours as "the power of the resurrection" because it consists in a "transition from death to life" because the Holy Spirit sets us in Christ who died for us and also rose for us. This freedom cannot be seen as an "immanent freedom of [our] own, but as that which is conferred upon [us] by God" (I/1, p. 458). Hence, for Barth

> to stand under this Master is not only the normal thing, it is the only possible thing. The outpouring of the Holy Spirit exalts the Word of God to be the master over men, puts man unavoidably under His mastery. The miracle of the divine revealedness, the power of Christ's resurrection in a man, consists in this event. In it the "God became man" is actualised in us as "man has God."
> (I/2, p. 270)

In this event we participate "in this divine possibility" in spite of the fact that we exist as those who, as unredeemed, are unworthy of this.

THOMAS F. TORRANCE'S VIEWS

Now let us explore some of what Thomas F. Torrance has to say about the role of the Spirit in our knowledge of God in order to underscore the importance of allowing the Holy Spirit to dictate the truth of our knowledge of God and of our service of God. Torrance begins his chapter on the Holy

Spirit and knowledge of God in his important book *God and Rationality* by insisting, as he frequently does, that only God reveals God, and he proceeds to explain why he thinks we must speak of an "epistemological relevance of the Spirit."[67] We cannot attribute knowledge of God to ourselves, since such knowledge is a "freely given participation in [God's] self-knowledge."[68] Consequently, knowledge of God takes place only in obedience to Christ as our minds conform to him. And this can happen, Torrance says, "only as in the Spirit the being and nature of God is brought to bear upon us so that we think under the compulsion of His Reality. That is the activity of the Holy Spirit whom Jesus spoke of in this connection as the Spirit of Truth."[69] In this context Torrance mentions what we may say about the Spirit: "The Holy Spirit is not cognisable in Himself."[70] As the Spirit of Jesus Christ, the Holy Spirit bears witness to Christ and not to himself. According to Torrance, "By His very mode of being as Spirit He hides Himself from us so that we do not know Him directly in His own hypostasis, and in His mode of activity as transparent Light He effaces Himself that the one Triune God may shine through Him to us."[71] That Torrance speaks of the Holy Spirit hiding himself here is not meant to imply that the Spirit does not refer us decisively to the Word, that is, to the Son of the Father who is revealer and reconciler. Rather it is meant to say, as we shall see in a moment, that the Spirit is not directly knowable as the incarnate Son is and that the Spirit empowers our union with and knowledge of the Son and thus our union with and knowledge of the Father in faith. It is through the Holy Spirit that the Word became flesh and that the Word continues to be heard. It is by the operation of the Spirit that we know the unknowable God. We are confronted by the Holy Spirit in his own person, since the Spirit is of one substance with God. Yet unlike the Son, the Spirit did not become incarnate, and therefore he is not of one substance with us. This is an extremely important point when one considers how many contemporary theologians opt for indwelling Christologies claiming that Jesus differs from the rest of us only by the extent to which he was indwelt by the Spirit. Such thinking clearly rests on a confusion of the

---

[67]Torrance, *God and Rationality*, p. 166.
[68]Ibid.
[69]Ibid., p. 167.
[70]Ibid.
[71]Ibid.

work of the Holy Spirit with the work of the incarnate Word. For Torrance, the Spirit "incarnated the Son" and "utters the Word" and directs us to Christ.[72] Both he and Barth are consistent in stating this, since both theologians hold that there is an essential perichoretic relation both in eternity and in time of the Father, Son and Holy Spirit.

With regard to our knowledge of God, Torrance, like Barth, insists that such knowledge is a miracle.[73] The Holy Spirit functions here as the one who points us outside our human knowledge to reality beyond. It is the Spirit who enables us to distinguish what we know, namely, God himself, from our knowledge of him and from what we say about God. Through cognition and speech we are directed to objective realities, and thus we "speak of them under the compulsion of their being upon us."[74] In Torrance's view two things must be avoided: any attempt to "close the gap" between thought and being, and any attempt to "make the gap complete." In both cases, Torrance contends, knowledge is not just disrupted, but it is destroyed. In both cases we become "imprisoned in ourselves" either by reducing everything to the forms of our own thought and speech, or if we try to escape those forms to some world of "non-formal" reality beyond, "we grasp nothing and only engage in empty movements of thought."[75] In all genuine knowledge, Torrance insists, we need our "frames of thought," but we recognize that we must always be critical so as not to confuse those frames with reality, which must be allowed to break through our interpretations. In this context Torrance maintains that reality must show through our knowledge without being identified with it or separated from it.[76] But he insists no one can say *how* knowledge is related to reality. This is where the Holy Spirit functions.

Torrance insists that it is the Holy Spirit who makes God's being knowable to us so that "Apart from the Spirit we would not break through to the divine Being, or rather the divine Being would not break through to us."[77] While it is true that not everything we know can be objectified, Torrance insists that we cannot equate that limitation with the work of the Holy Spirit be-

---

[72]Ibid.
[73]Ibid., p. 168.
[74]Ibid., p. 169.
[75]Ibid.
[76]Ibid., p. 175.
[77]Ibid.

cause in the Holy Spirit we are up against God's very own transcendent truth and majesty so that it is *only* from the Spirit "that we learn what objectivity in knowledge really is."[78] The Holy Spirit therefore both creates the relation between us and God that is necessary if there is to be knowledge of God, and simultaneously reinforces the fact that we cannot explain "how our thought and speech are related to God."[79] In this sense all our thoughts and speech must point beyond themselves to God. We have what Torrance calls intuitive knowledge of God—but that does not mean we can control God by equating the Spirit with our intuitions. Rather it means that we come under God's control in our experience and knowledge. Had Torrance confused knowledge of God with our intuitions, he would not have claimed that our thoughts and speech must always point beyond themselves to God, and he would not have insisted that the Holy Spirit and not our experience dictates the truth of what is known.

As seen in chapter one, Torrance rejects what he calls "non-conceptual experience of God" as a leap into irrationality.[80] We cannot experience God or know God, Torrance claims, following Anselm, without concepts. And that is where the Spirit functions. For it is by the power and enlightenment of the Spirit that we think and speak "directly of God in and through the forms of our rational experience and articulation and we do that under the direction and control of the inner rationality of the divine Being, the eternal *Logos* and *Eidos* of Godhead."[81] Only through the Spirit, then, can we know the rational truth of God and distinguish this from our knowledge of it. In this way our knowledge is transformed by being rooted in the eternal Word and thus in the being of God.[82] Here Torrance makes four crucial points regarding the Holy Spirit that will enable him to explain the epistemological relevance of the Holy Spirit.

First, the Holy Spirit is not only the free and sovereign creator acting toward us, but is God enabling us to relate with God. Following Athanasius, Torrance notes that

---

[78]Ibid., p. 176.
[79]Ibid.
[80]Ibid., p. 170. This is fully in accord with Barth's rejection of non-objective knowledge of God discussed above and in chap. 1.
[81]Ibid.
[82]Ibid., pp. 170-71.

> For the grace and gift that is given is given in the Trinity, from the Father,
> through the Son, in the Holy Spirit. As the grace given is from the Father
> through the Son, so we can have no communion in the gift except in the Holy
> Spirit. For it is when we partake of him that we have the love of the Father and
> the grace of the Son and the communion of the Spirit himself.[83]

There is no *continuity* with God "that belongs to the creature in itself"; this
must be "continuously given and sustained by the presence of the Spirit
within the creation bringing creaturely relations to their *telos* in God."[84] For
this reason Torrance insists that there can be no concept of "a mutual correlation between the creature and the Creator." This is why Torrance insists
that there is "no necessary relation between God and the world he has
created, for he had no need of the creation to be who he is, while the world
he creatively brought into existence out of nothing contains no reason in
itself why it should be what it is and should continue to exist as it does."[85]
Here Torrance's thinking is fully in accord with Barth's. He even appeals to
Barth's own understanding of the matter to say:

> Coming from the inner Life and Communion of the Trinity, the Holy Spirit
> is the Creator God who in virtue to his presence to the creature, not just ex-
> ternally nor just from above, but from within and from below, effectuates the
> relation of the creature to himself by way of a relation of himself to himself.[86]

Second, the Holy Spirit is God himself freely opening creatures to know and
love God, creating in them a "capacity for God" and thus enabling knowledge
of God. The basis of this, says Torrance, is "the inner personal relations of
the Holy Trinity" in creation and revelation. And because the Father has
created and revealed himself in creation in his Word, all of this occurs only
"in the inseparable relation of the Spirit to the Word." Therefore the Spirit
does not come in his own name but "in the name of the Son."[87] This is an
exceptionally important point. As the Spirit is the Spirit of the Father and
Son in eternity, so the Spirit in creation and revelation cannot be conceptualized independently from the work of the Son "or apart from the incar-

---

[83]*Christian Doctrine of God*, p. 197.
[84]*God and Rationality*, p. 171.
[85]*Christian Doctrine of God*, p. 216.
[86]Ibid., p. 218.
[87]*God and Rationality*, p. 171.

nation of the Word."[88] As seen above, this thinking is wholly in line with Barth's insistence that the Spirit in no way and at no time can be separated theoretically or practically from the Son or from the Father.

What does this imply? For Torrance it means that we cannot think of the Spirit as a rational principle that informs all things with rationality and imparts form to humanity "which can be brought to expression within the cosmos as its inherent entelechy."[89] This statement of course eliminates at root the attempt of natural theology to approach knowledge of God with the claim that reason may know "that God is" but not "what God is." Because the Spirit actualizes within creation "its bond of union with the *Logos*," our minds learn of the truth of God only through God's Word and thus through union with Christ through the Spirit who recreates us in his image. Even though we are unable to relate our thoughts and speech to God, God himself acts on us and within us to enable us to know him.[90] That indeed is the epistemological function of the Spirit. Here, in the activity of the Holy Spirit, God himself is the object of our knowing in his activity of "creating from our side a corresponding action in which our own being is committed."[91] Torrance calls this "kinetic" thinking because it involves a movement of thought and experience that "corresponds to the movement of the Spirit and indeed participates in it."[92] In this sense theology is a spiritual activity. We know God by participating in what we seek to know. In this view Torrance says we may only know Jesus Christ as the eternal Word who became flesh according to the Spirit and in faith. Torrance says that what we have here is a leap of faith that is neither blind nor irrational. Importantly, Torrance understands that none of this depends on us but only on God, who acts on us. Were true knowledge of God here to depend on us, we would, as Heidegger claims, "leap into nothing or into death."[93] Here again Barth and Torrance can be seen to be one in rejecting any notion that we can rely on ourselves to understand God in truth.

Torrance maintains that when we think of God on the basis of revelation,

---

[88]Ibid., p. 172. See also *Trinitarian Faith*, pp. 200-203.
[89]Ibid.
[90]Ibid., p. 176. This is a persistent theme in all of Torrance's writings.
[91]Ibid., p. 177.
[92]Ibid.
[93]Ibid., p. 178.

we are confronted with something so totally *new* that we must engage in a "repentant rethinking" of all our presuppositions. We must, Torrance says, be carried beyond ourselves "to what is utterly beyond us."[94] Admittedly Torrance is not always this careful as when he says, "we bring our thinking under the compulsion of the inherent rationality of the divine Being."[95] But there can be no doubt that he intends to allow the doctrine of justification to shape his epistemology here just as Barth had done. Hence he insists that the Spirit comes to us from beyond our being to give us God's own Being as an object of knowledge and to realize our knowledge of God from our side. Here Torrance notes that we are at enmity with God without this knowledge, which is based on our reconciliation with God in Christ.[96] As seen above, this thinking reiterates Barth's important point that we may only know our enmity with God from the reconciliation of God that has taken place in Christ himself. And this is the place from which we may know God with certitude.

Third, because the Spirit "hides Himself from us" in the sense discussed above, we are not informed with "his own Form" but with the "Form of the Word." In this way we "participate in the communion of the Father and the Son." The Spirit never ceases being God himself even when he enables us who are incapable of relation with God to become free "from imprisonment in themselves" and "partake of His creative and eternal Life."[97] In the Holy Spirit we "come up against God in the most absolute and ultimate sense."[98] Thus God "resists all our attempts to be independent of him or to get alongside of Him or to manipulate Him."[99] The Holy Spirit distinguishes his own activity from all our "creative spirituality." God is thus revealed within the structures of our own experience but in such a way that he always encounters us as the Lord in his own way through his own Word of self-revelation. This thinking is fully in accord with Barth's view that although we experience and know God in faith, we can never control God or our knowledge of God and so must pray for the Spirit to come on us again and again.

---

[94]Ibid.
[95]Ibid., p. 170.
[96]Ibid., p. 179.
[97]Ibid., p. 172.
[98]Ibid., p. 173.
[99]Ibid.

Fourth, The Holy Spirit actually operates within us to realize our human response to God. He turns us away from our "in-turned" and "in-grown existence" toward God. Because the Holy Spirit "is the eternal communion of the Father and the Son,"[100] when he is sent into our hearts "by the Father in the name of the Son we are made partakers with the Son in His Communion with the Father and thus of God's own self-knowledge."[101] In this way we are "converted from ourselves to thinking from a centre in God and not in ourselves, and to knowledge of God out of God and not out of ourselves."[102] In the Spirit we actually know God in truth "together with Christ" and thus "always out of a centre in Him."[103] This thinking surely corresponds with Barth's view that the truth cannot be found directly within our self-experience and knowledge, but must always be sought and found in Christ himself and thus through the Spirit and in faith.[104]

Earlier I noted the importance of holding together God's Word and Spirit for Torrance. This means that God's being is not dark or mute but eloquent, because God speaks himself and utters himself both within the eternal Trinity in one way and in our hearts in another.[105] While "the Word of God remains eternally Word and does not disappear into Spirit," God nevertheless speaks in a way appropriate to his nature as Spirit. In us, however, the Spirit remains distinct from our spirits. Several crucial implications follow. *First,* because the Word is within God's eternal being, God himself is the Word he utters. Hence "The Word is not just the form that the shining of God's light or the going forth of His Spirit takes in the *opera Trinitatis ad extra* but is eternally in the depth of the divine Being what it is as Word towards us."[106] Through his Spirit and Word, Torrance insists, following Anselm and Calvin, God speaks to us—God "articulates Himself within our

---

[100]Ibid.

[101]Ibid., p. 174.

[102]Ibid.

[103]Ibid.

[104]Torrance offers a penetrating and illuminating discussion of how and why it is important to take seriously the fact that in the incarnation the Word assumed our sinful humanity in order to convert it back to God. This involved our minds, which, he believed, desperately needed to be redeemed and healed. This is why Torrance strongly opposed any Apollinarian view of the incarnation. See *Atonement*, pp. 437-47.

[105]*God and Rationality*, p. 180.

[106]Ibid. This is a frequently repeated insight, found in all of Torrance's major works. See, e.g., *Christian Doctrine of God*, p. 130; *Trinitarian Perspectives*, p. 38, and *Trinitarian Faith*, p. 233.

minds and makes Himself understood by us in accordance with His self-revelation."[107] This factor prevents genuine knowledge of God from becoming a human construct projected into God.

Second, "The co-ordinating principle of theological knowledge does not lie in theological activity itself but in the speaking of the Word by the Spirit and our participation in the Word through the Spirit."[108] In other words, we cannot think our way into God. That would be a form of self-justification, which Torrance abhors. Torrance asserts, "Theological knowledge must take the road from God to man before it takes the road from man to God."[109] For Torrance theology takes place in *acknowledgment* that we do not know God by the power of our own thought or spirituality but only by allowing the Spirit to lead us to recognize and respond to the truth of God's Word. The basis of theology therefore is "not in itself but in God."[110] All genuine theology must be open to "the questioning and speaking of the Spirit," and thus it can only be "*obedient* service to God's own testimony to himself."[111]

Third, theological knowledge can only take place in the form of "*recognition-statements*."[112] This is an enormously important point, because what Torrance means here is that genuine theological knowledge is neither creative nor inventive. If that were to happen, then theology would be self-grounded and would attempt to establish itself "as the basis of reality by building a world of reality on its own inventions and achievements."[113] For Torrance theology must allow its knowledge to be shaped by the given reality, namely, by God's own Word and Spirit. Theological knowledge in the form of recognition statements takes place only in acknowledgment[114] as our thinking points beyond itself to the Word "as their sole justification and truth."[115]

Fourth, the Holy Spirit works in our knowledge of God by personally being present to us and acting to open our minds to understand his revelation and to respond to God in faith and love. God uses the media of

---

[107]Ibid., p. 181.
[108]Ibid.
[109]Ibid.
[110]Ibid., p. 182.
[111]Ibid., emphasis mine.
[112]Ibid.
[113]Ibid.
[114]Ibid.
[115]Ibid., p. 183.

creation to do this in such a way that our minds do not "terminate on the media but on the Being of God Himself."[116] According to Torrance, God is personally present to us in space and time and uses "the sign-world of inter-human communication" to speak to us. God directs us, Torrance believes, "to immediate intuitive knowledge of Himself in His own ultimate Objectivity and Reality."[117] The sign-world God uses is the history of the covenant fulfilled in the incarnation and as witnessed in the Bible as inspired by the Spirit. Even now, Torrance says, God comes to us "clothed in the historical and biblical forms of His revelation which (whether B.C. or A.D.) direct us to Jesus Christ in the centre."[118] And it is the Holy Spirit who enables us to know God "directly and immediately in Jesus Christ." This is how God meets us in history objectively, and so this knowledge excludes "any possibility of non-objective knowledge." But God also meets us in His Spirit "as Supreme Subject, and thus in all His ultimate objectivity as Lord God."[119] Again, from what was said above, this thinking is fully in accord with Barth's understanding of our knowledge of God as mediated through history and thus through the prophetic and apostolic testimony, and ultimately through the incarnate Word.

All historical signs, however, in themselves cannot refer us to God because they refer only to intraworldly reality. To function properly they must (and this includes biblical statements) be made to point beyond themselves to God. That, according to Torrance, is where the Holy Spirit enters along with his "propriety to the Word of God."[120] He speaks the Word "in all His divine ineffability and transparence" so that through the created media he discloses himself to us by making us capable of "knowing Him beyond ourselves. Apart from the work of the Holy Spirit all the forms of revelation remain dark and opaque but in and through His presence they become translucent and transparent."[121]

How then can we think about that which utterly transcends our own thoughts by means of those same thoughts? How can we use human lan-

[116]Ibid., p. 184.
[117]Ibid.
[118]Ibid.
[119]Ibid.
[120]Ibid., p. 185.
[121]Ibid.

guage with merely intraworldly reference to speak of God, who transcends
them altogether? These are our most difficult questions, Torrance says, and
the answers can be found only in the "operation of the Holy Spirit"; what we
cannot do "by our thinking and stating is done by his *action* as Spirit of
God."[122] This means that a proper interpretation of Scripture cannot simply
look at linguistic and logical facts and the intentions of the authors but must
look to God himself and his truth. We must learn, Torrance says, that "the
truth of realities is independent of the statements we make in signifying
them." True statements about God thus have a "dimension of depth,"[123] since
they point beyond themselves to the truth of God.

Our concepts, Torrance believes, must be kept open. On our side they
are closed since we need to formulate them exactly and carefully. But they
are open on God's side. What does this mean? For Torrance it means that
"our acts of cognition are formed from beyond them by the reality disclosed so that the content of what is revealed constantly bursts through
the forms we bring to it in order to grasp it."[124] And the only way this can
happen is "under the power of the Spirit."[125] It is the Spirit who actually
keeps our concepts open, thus enabling us to know what is beyond them.
Without this action of the Spirit our concepts either obscure or obstruct
revelation. Open concepts, importantly, are not irrational because they are
open but because openness to God "is the true mode of their rationality."
But it does indicate that our concepts cannot control God's rationality and
thus are limited. Open concepts "do not describe, delimit or define the
Reality we seek to understand," rather, through them "we allow our minds
to come under the compulsion of the Reality so that we may think of it
only as we are forced to."[126] And when this happens, these concepts will
necessarily point beyond themselves. This can happen only through the
Spirit. Knowledge of God is rational and conceptual, but it is also "apposite
to the nature of God as *Spirit*," and so "we are carried right over to what
transcends us."[127]

---

[122]Ibid., p. 186.
[123]Ibid.
[124]Ibid., p. 187.
[125]Ibid.
[126]Ibid.
[127]Ibid., p. 188.

Fifth, knowledge of God takes place within the rational, personal and social structures of human life. This happens through the "personalizing Spirit." This means that as

> the living presence of God confronts us with His personal Being, addresses us in His Word, opens us out toward Himself, and calls forth from us the response of faith and love, He rehabilitates the *human subject*, sustaining him in his personal relations with God and with his fellow creatures.[128]

As human subjects, Torrance thinks, we can easily become concerned only with things and think mechanically and impersonally. Or we might react against such false objectivism and try to "subdue everything to [our] own subjectivity and so get locked up in [ourselves]."[129] Then we might actually objectify our own subjective states, cutting ourselves off from objective reality. It is the Spirit who frees us both from our "in-turned subjectivity"[130] for "genuinely objective experience" and from the "threat of impersonalizing objectivism and determinism"[131] so that we become free to stand before God and capable of spontaneous personal relations with others.

The personalizing work of the Spirit comes from "the inter-personal Communion of the Holy Trinity" and "establishes divine communion among us by reconciling us with God"[132] and creating social structures that are sustained through God's presence. While "theological statements take their rise from a centre in God and not in ourselves, the very nature of the divine Object makes it impossible for us to abstract them from the personal and community setting in which they take place."[133] A distinction between judgment and proposition is necessary. Judgments involve decisions within each individual's mind. But propositions occur within objective relations "between two or more subjects" so that together they "come under the compulsive reality of what is given in common to them."[134] Theology necessarily involves propositions that develop out of the church's obedient acknowledgment of God's self-revelation and are clarified and deepened through worship, dialogue and "repentant rethinking

---

[128]Ibid.
[129]Ibid., p. 189.
[130]Ibid., p. 188.
[131]Ibid., p. 189.
[132]Ibid.
[133]Ibid.
[134]Ibid, pp. 188-89.

within the whole communion of saints."[135] This requires them to be ecumenical
or open to the entire community to avoid distortion through a "false in-turned
subjectivity," but ultimately "it is not the Church but God Himself who is the
Object of their reference."[136] There is a danger here. The church could end up
reinterpreting God's Word "to suit contemporary thought and culture."[137] The
temptation is for the church to "transfer the locus of authority from the Word
and Truth of God to its own collective subjectivity, and to identify the Spirit of
God with its own spirit."[138] Torrance maintains that the church must also be on
guard against this danger by being critical of its own thinking in a disciplined
manner by testing its thought and speech to make sure that it is really speaking
about God and not itself. This, however, cannot simply be achieved "by method,
no matter how rigorous and scientific, for it is only by divine *action* that man's
thought may be related to God's Truth and his speech may actually refer to
God's Being."[139] That is precisely why the church must continually pray for the
Holy Spirit. It is the Holy Spirit alone who can free the church "from imprisonment in itself or deliver its mind from being engrossed in its own subjectivity
by confronting it with the implacable Objectivity of the divine Subject, and call
forth from it a faithful response to the divine self-revelation."[140] It is in this
regard that the role of the Holy Spirit in our knowledge of God is eschatological.
It is eschatological in the sense that only God himself can judge our theological
statements in such a way that they may actually signify God, who transcends
this world of time and space. The result of true knowledge of God will be the
recognition that when we really know God's being and act, we know that this
being and action cannot pass over into the church. If that were to happen we
would be thrown back on ourselves. But the Spirit constantly judges us and
points us to Christ as the objective source of our knowledge of God, and thus
the Spirit enables us to distinguish God's truth from our knowledge of it, "and
so to live ever out of Christ and not out of ourselves."[141]

---

[135]Ibid., p. 190.
[136]Ibid.
[137]Ibid.
[138]Ibid., p. 191.
[139]Ibid.
[140]Ibid.
[141]Ibid., p. 192. For more on Torrance's notion of the Spirit as it relates to our knowledge of and
   relationship with the triune God, see *Christian Doctrine of God*, pp. 147-55, and Torrance,
   Theology in Reconstruction (London: SCM Press, 1965), pp. 39-41.

One further point needs to be made here. Like Barth, Torrance links true knowledge of God to the power of the resurrection.

> It is in and through Jesus Christ . . . that we creatures of space and time may know God the Father, in such a way as to think and speak truly and validly of him, even in such a way that the forms of our thought and speech really terminate objectively on God himself. . . . Apart from the resurrection we could not say this.[142]

Torrance believes that because Jesus is the incarnate Word of God who is "full of grace and truth" he is "not simply the Word of God addressed to" humanity, but he is "the answering word of man addressed to God in the unity of his Person."[143] In him, therefore, there is what Torrance calls a hypostatic union of the truth of God and "the answering truth of man," so that the truth actualized in him creates in us a "counterpart."[144] In this way "Jesus Christ constitutes the bridge between the reality of God and the realities of our world, the connection between the transcendent Rationality of God and the created rationalities of this world."[145] Since he rose from the dead and now lives as the risen, ascended and coming Lord, in the power of his Holy Spirit he enables us in the very power of his resurrection to participate in God's own self-knowledge and thus to know God in truth. Hence we neither can nor should assume that we must get beyond the sphere of history in order to know God. For in the incarnation, death and resurrection of Jesus Christ himself God has come to us to enable us to know him from a center in himself through his incarnate Word and his Holy Spirit. In fact, Torrance maintains, had the resurrection not taken place there would have been a "final disjunction between God's Word and God's Act, e.g. in the forgiveness of our sins, but inevitably a final disjunction between our acts of knowing and the reality of God himself, or between our statements about God and their objective referent in God."[146]

Concluding Remarks

What I hope can be seen from this presentation of the function of the Spirit in knowledge of the triune God in the thought of Barth and Torrance is that

---

[142]Thomas F. Torrance, *Space, Time and Resurrection* (Edinburgh: T & T Clark, 1998), p. 71.
[143]Ibid.
[144]Ibid.
[145]Ibid.
[146]Ibid.

all genuine knowledge of the Christian God always begins in acknowledgment in the sense that it can only begin in faith in Christ and not at all in itself. And this beginning is not under anyone's power because it is itself a miracle enabled by the present action of the Holy Spirit uniting us to Christ and thus to the Father. It involves the very power of the resurrection. When knowledge of God is understood in this way, natural theology is simply marginalized as a way to understand God in truth. And as long as theologians recognize and maintain the importance of the Holy Spirit in knowing God, they will to that extent never attempt to know God outside faith in his Word and Spirit, and so their knowledge will never be grounded in reason or experience but only in grace as it meets us and heals our reason and enables our experience. What I have tried to illustrate here is that any apologetic attempt, outside of faith, to explain who God is, who Christ is or even who the Holy Spirit is must inevitably mean that such an attempt is untheological. Such an approach is self-grounded and does not think from a center in the risen and ascended Lord, as it must if it intends to speak about the truth of the triune God acting and enabling the church to be what it is in its union with Christ through his Spirit. Our focus thus must always be on the God experienced and known in faith and not on our experience and knowledge *per se*.

In light of what has been said in these two chapters, I think it might be helpful if I now consider God's freedom once again as I originally attempted to understand this in my first book on the Trinity. In light of theological developments in the years since that book first appeared, it has become even more important to clarify exactly why it is so important to stress, with Barth and the tradition, that God's freedom simply cannot be recognized in any properly consistent way unless we continue to admit that the God who meets us and enables our human freedom in the form of faith, action and knowledge is the God who could have been God without us but freely chose not to.

3

Considering God's Freedom Once Again

There is little doubt that, whatever difficulties may yet attend Barth's trinitarian doctrine,[1] he offered a very powerful understanding of God's relations with us and ours with God just because he based those actions *ad extra* on a positive consideration of who God eternally was and is. While many

---

[1]See, e.g., George Hunsinger, "Karl Barth's Doctrine of the Trinity, and Some Protestant Doctrines After Barth," in *The Oxford Handbook of The Trinity*, ed. Gilles Emery, O.P., and Matthew Levering (New York: Oxford University Press, 2011), who suggests that while Barth's presentation of the doctrine "was characteristically subtle, deep, and idiosyncratic" (p. 294), there was nonetheless a weakness, which was that he paid insufficient "attention (arguably) to the question of derivation" (p. 296). Hunsinger believes that if Barth had done this then he would have stressed both reconciliation and worship, since the doctrine arises because the church "confesses the full deity of Jesus Christ" and this mystery "is indispensable to the doctrine of revelation, reconciliation, and worship" (p. 296). Perhaps most importantly, however, in this context, it should be noted that for Hunsinger, Barth's "later use and development of the doctrine did not depart from these basic outlines" (p. 294), that is, the outlines he offered in I/1, pp. 295-489. This assertion, which I regard as quite accurate, is ignored or obviated by those who believe that Barth either had two doctrines of the Trinity, one expressed in I/1 and another in IV/1, or that his trinitarian presentation needed to be revised in light of his later thinking, especially after his presentation of the doctrine of election. See, e.g., Bruce L. McCormack, "The Doctrine of the Trinity After Barth: An Attempt to Reconstruct Barth's Doctrine in the Light of His Later Christology," in *Trinitarian Theology After Barth*, ed. Myk Habets and Phillip Tolliday (Eugene, OR: Pickwick, 2011), pp. 87-117. Ignoring or obviating this important point, unfortunately, leads to very different interpretations of theologians such as Rahner, Moltmann, Pannenberg and Eberhard Jüngel. Hunsinger is properly critical of these thinkers because he thinks Rahner's rule unwittingly threatened the relation of correspondence that Barth saw between the immanent and economic Trinity, while the others just mentioned never managed to uphold Barth's view of correspondence either (p. 310). It is no accident, then, that McCormack mistakenly believes that Rahner's axiom of identity does not collapse the immanent into the economic Trinity and that the views of Moltmann, Pannenberg and Jüngel do not compromise Barth's thinking either (Bruce McCormack, "The Lord and Giver of Life: A 'Barthian' Defense of the *Filioque*," in *Rethinking Trinitarian Theology: Disputed Questions and Contemporary Issues in Trinitarian Theology*, ed. Robert J. Woźniak and Giulio Maspero [New York: T & T Clark, 2012], p. 238). Hence, with respect to the question of whether or not

today still are unclear about this, there are others who are and remain clear in their thinking on this theme. For instance, in a recent article, John Webster writes: "We do not understand the economy unless we take time to consider God who is, though creatures might not have been."[2] Hence, "the starting point for a Christian doctrine of creation, as for any Christian doctrine, is God in himself. . . . Only out of the sheer antecedent perfection of God's life *in se* can we feel the force of the concept of creation."[3] This means that

> God is not one item in a totality, even the most eminently powerful item in the set of all things. . . . The creator can be conceived neither by thinking of him as in some fashion continuous with the world nor by conceiving of a purely dialectical relation between uncreated and created being; both . . . make creation intrinsic to God's fullness. Yet the triune God could be without the world.[4]

In his recent book on the eternal generation of the Son, Kevin Giles agrees.[5] And Adam Johnson focuses the question precisely when critically assessing the following remarks: "For Barth, the beginning of all the ways and works of God, *and therefore of the identity of God*, is the self-giving of God in Jesus Christ."[6] For Johnson the critical question con-

---

Rahner, Moltmann, Pannenberg and Jüngel had finally collapsed the immanent into the economic Trinity in some measure, McCormack says "such a collapse is not true of Rahner himself or any of the three Protestant theologians under consideration here" (p. 238). McCormack, of course, believes wholeheartedly in Rahner's axiom as long as it is modified by Jüngel's idea that the immanent Trinity must be identified with the economic at the point of Jesus' suffering and death. Among other things, McCormack exhibits no knowledge of Rahner's wider thinking and of how his theology of the symbol led him to problems in his Christology and in his view of God's relations with the world in terms of mutual conditioning (see Paul D. Molnar, *Divine Freedom and the Doctrine of the Immanent Trinity: In Dialogue with Karl Barth and Contemporary Theology* [New York: T & T Clark, 2005], chaps. 2, 4, 5 and 6). And he either never noticed or chose to ignore Moltmann's explicitly stated aim to move beyond Rahner's axiom of identity toward a view that asserts that the economic Trinity has a retroactive effect on the immanent Trinity, thus leading him toward patripassianism (see Molnar, *Divine Freedom*, chap. 7). Interestingly, the position for which McCormack now argues, as he has reconstructed it in light of his reading of Barth's later Christology, is amazingly similar to the views of Moltmann. See Han-Luen Kantzer Komline, "Friendship and Being: Election and Trinitarian Freedom in Moltmann and Barth," *Modern Theology* 29, no. 1 (January 2013): 1-17.
[2]John Webster, "Trinity and Creation," *IJST* 12, no. 1 (January 2010): 4-19, at p. 7.
[3]Ibid., p. 9.
[4]Ibid., p. 12.
[5]See, e.g., Kevin Giles, *The Eternal Generation of the Son: Maintaining Orthodoxy in Trinitarian Theology* (Downers Grove, IL: InterVarsity Press, 2012), pp. 203-4.
[6]Adam J. Johnson, *God's Being in Reconciliation: The Theological Basis of the Unity and Diversity of the Atonement in the Theology of Karl Barth* (New York: T & T Clark, 2012), p. 54, cites Paul Nimmo's book *Being in Action: The Theological Shape of Barth's Ethical Vision* (New York: T & T Clark, 2007).

cerns whether or not God's self-giving in Jesus Christ "is in fact an accurate interpretation of Barth's thought: does the self-giving of God in
Jesus Christ constitute the identity of God (with regards to the modes of
God's being or his perfections), or does it simply specify his being and
life in a new direction?"[7] Johnson notes further that Barth made repeated claims, even in his later theology, that "God would be triune
without us" and that this should be taken to mean that election is not
constitutive of God's triunity since

> The election of Jesus Christ is not the beginning of God's being and therefore
> his being as Father, Son and Holy Spirit, but the beginning of the triune God's
> interaction with all that is not God. . . . The act of election is the act of God at
> the beginning of all things (*ad extra*) by a God who Himself has no be-
> ginning—and the nature of this act is first and foremost with regards to
> himself by willing to become Jesus Christ.[8]

We may also note that George Hunsinger, in his definitive article "Election
and the Trinity," offers a thoroughly convincing and detailed case in favor
of understanding why it is important to hold, with Barth, that "God would
be no less God if He had created no world and no human being."[9] Yves
Congar clearly agrees when he writes: "As the Fathers who combated Arianism said, even if God's creatures did not exist, God would still be a Trinity
of Father, Son and Spirit, since creation is an act of free will, whereas the
procession of the Persons takes place in accordance with nature, *kata
phusin*."[10] Bruce Marshall concurs when he maintains that while our
human identities may "plausibly be regarded as contingent. . . . It seems
impossible that the identities of the divine persons could be contingent"
because our existence is completely dependent on God's gracious acts of
creation, incarnation, reconciliation and redemption, and God is dependent on no one and nothing. Further, these are free acts of the triune

---

[7]Ibid.

[8]Ibid., p. 55.

[9]See George Hunsinger, "Election and the Trinity: Twenty-Five Theses on the Theology of Karl
Barth," in *Modern Theology* 24 (2008): 179-98, and chap. 4 of *Trinity and Election in Contemporary Theology*, ed. Michael T. Dempsey (Grand Rapids: Eerdmans, 2011). We will discuss some
of Bruce McCormack's responses to Hunsinger later in this chapter.

[10]Yves Congar, *I Believe in the Holy Spirit*, vol. III, *The River of the Water of Life (Rev 22:1) Flows in
the East and in the West*, trans. David Smith (New York: Crossroad, 1997), p. 13.

God, who might not have made this or any world. Hence each person of the Trinity "would be the person he is, the person with whom we are allowed to become acquainted in time, even if there were no creatures—nothing besides these three divine persons."[11]

Finally, it is worth mentioning Torrance's helpful reminder that "we do not say that God is Father, Son and Holy Spirit, because he becomes Father, Son, and Holy Spirit to us. . . . He only becomes Father, Son, and Holy Spirit to us precisely because he *is* first and eternally Father, Son, and Holy Spirit in himself alone."[12] Hence, "The world needs God to be what it is, but God does not need the world to be what he is. . . . The Creator was free not to create."[13] And since God really does not need the world, we must say that "the Fatherhood of God is in no way dependent on or constituted by relation to what he has created outwith himself."[14]

Karl Barth's own thinking sums up the point rather nicely when he says:

> Why should God not also be able, as eternal Love, to be sufficient unto Himself? In His life as Father, Son, and Holy Spirit He would in truth be no lonesome, no egotistical God even without man, yes, even without the whole created universe. . . . He wants in His freedom actually not to be without man but *with* him and in the same freedom not against him but *for* him.[15]

Earlier in his *Church Dogmatics* Barth writes:

> We can certainly say that we see the love of God to man originally grounded upon the eternal relation of God, Father and Son. But as this love is already *free* and *unconstrained* in God Himself, so, too, and only then rightly, is it free in its realisation towards man. That is, in His Word becoming flesh, God acts with inward freedom and not in fulfilment of a law to which He is supposedly subject. *His Word will still be His Word apart from this becoming, just as Father,*

---

[11]Bruce D. Marshall, *Trinity and Truth* (Cambridge: Cambridge University Press, 2000), pp. 262-63. Marshall goes on to assert that since Nicaea, theologians have "uniformly insisted" that "the identities of the three divine persons who freely give themselves to us in creation, redemption, and consummation are the same as they would be even if the three had not decided to create and give themselves to us" (p. 264). See also Bruce D. Marshall, "The Absolute and the Trinity," *Pro Ecclesia* 23, no. 2 (Spring 2014): 147-64, and my response, "A Response: Beyond Hegel with Karl Barth and T. F. Torrance," *Pro Ecclesia* 23, no. 2 (Spring 2014): 165-73.

[12]Thomas F. Torrance, *The Doctrine of Jesus Christ* (Eugene, OR: Wipf and Stock, 2002), p. 107.

[13]Thomas F. Torrance, *Divine and Contingent Order* (Edinburgh: T & T Clark, 1998), p. 34.

[14]*Christian Doctrine of God*, p. 207.

[15]Karl Barth, *The Humanity of God*, trans. Thomas Wieser and John Newton Thomas (Richmond, VA: John Knox Press, 1968), p. 50.

Son and Holy Spirit would be none the less eternal God, if no world had been
created. (I/2, p. 135, emphases mine)[16]

In a later chapter we will consider whether and to what extent Barth's Christology changed. A key question will be whether Barth retracted this statement or so qualified it that one could or should no longer embrace it. My position is and will be that it is exactly this statement that underwrites the strength of what Barth has to say in his later Christology. It is akin to this statement which appears later in his *Church Dogmatics*:

> In the inner life of God, as the eternal essence of Father, Son and Holy Ghost, the divine essence does not, of course, need any actualisation. On the contrary, it is the creative ground of all other, i.e., all creaturely actualisations. Even as the divine essence of the Son it did not need His incarnation, His existence as man ... to become actual. As the divine essence of the Son it is the predicate of the one God. And as the predicate of this Subject it is not in any sense merely potential but in every sense actual. (IV/2, p. 113)

Closely connected with these remarks by Barth is another important statement, namely, that:

> The triune life of God which is free life in the fact that it is Spirit, is the basis of His whole will and action even *ad extra*, as the living act which He directs to us. It is the basis ... of the election of man to covenant with Himself; of the determination of the Son to become man, and therefore to fulfil this covenant ... of the atonement with its final goal of redemption to eternal life with Himself. (IV/2, p. 345)

Furthermore, speaking about how human love is grounded in God's love, Barth writes:

---

[16]It is worth noting that in his doctrine of creation Barth also states that God "could have remained satisfied with the fullness of His own being. If He had willed and decided in this way, He would not have suffered any lack. He would still be eternal love and freedom. But according to His Word and work which we have been summoned to attest He has willed and decided otherwise" (III/1, p. 69). And importantly, Barth insisted that "the Word of God is properly understood only as a word which has truth and glory in itself and not just spoken to us. *It would be no less God's eternal Word if it were not spoken to us*, and what constitutes the mercy of its revelation, of its being spoken to us, is that it is spoken to us in virtue of the freedom in which God *could be 'God in Himself'* and yet He does not will to be so and in fact is not so, but wills to be and actually is 'God for us'" (I/1, pp. 171-72, emphasis mine). This thinking is repeated many times by Barth, e.g., "While He [God] could be everything only for Himself (and His life would not on that account be pointless, motionless and unmotivated, nor would it be any less majestic or any less the life of love), He wills—and this is for us the ever-wonderful twofold dynamic of his love—to have it not only for Himself, but also for us" (II/1, pp. 280-81).

He reveals Himself as the One who, even though He did not love us and were not revealed to us, even though we did not exist at all, still loves in and for Himself as surely as He is and is God; who loves us by reason and in consequence of the fact that He is the One who loves in His freedom in and for Himself, and is God as such. It is only of God that it can be said that He is in the fact that He loves and loves in the fact that He is. . . . God loves, and to do so He does not need any being distinct from His own as the object of His love. If He loves the world and us, this is a free overflowing of the love in which He is and is God and with which he is not content, although He might be, since neither the world nor ourselves are indispensable to His love and therefore to His being. (IV/2, p. 755)

QUESTIONING BARTH'S VIEW OF GOD'S FREEDOM

The above-cited very traditional statements about the freedom of God's love in himself and in the incarnation have been questioned recently.[17] For example, relying on Rowan Williams and Bruce McCormack, Benjamin Myers claims that Barth's doctrine of the Trinity offers not just one doctrine of the Trinity but two.[18] And from this he concludes that "God's being as God is constituted by God's self-determined relation to the human Jesus"[19] and ultimately that "Jesus is not merely epistemologically significant, as the one who makes God known; *he is ontologically significant, as the one who (so to speak) makes God God.*"[20] All of this follows, he claims, from the fact that Barth's doctrine of God was radically changed with his doctrine of election in II/2, and that the doctrine of the Trinity that he presented in I/1 was formally based on revelation while the new doctrine presented in IV/1 was based on Jesus Christ as, in his mind, making God to be God! Now, from

---

[17]See Bruce L. McCormack, "Grace and Being: The Role of God's Gracious Election in Karl Barth's Theological Ontology," in McCormack, *Orthodox and Modern: Studies in the Theology of Karl Barth* (Grand Rapids: Baker Academic, 2008), pp. 183-200, at 193-94. This is a slightly altered version of his "Grace and Being: The Role of God's Gracious Election in Karl Barth's Theological Ontology," which first appeared in *The Cambridge Companion to Karl Barth,* ed. John Webster (Cambridge: Cambridge University Press, 2000), pp. 92-110.

[18]Benjamin Myers, "Election, Trinity, and the History of Jesus: Reading Barth with Rowan Williams," in *Trinitarian Theology After Barth,* ed. Myk Habets and Phillip Tolliday, (Eugene, OR: Pickwick Publications, 2011), pp. 121-37, at 121. Similar problematic assertions are made in Peter Goodwin Heltzel and Christian T. Collins Winn, "Karl Barth, Reconciliation, and the Triune God," in *Cambridge Companion to the Trinity,* ed. Peter C. Phan (Cambridge: Cambridge University Press, 2011), pp. 171-91.

[19]Myers, "Election, Trinity, and the History of Jesus," p. 130.

[20]Ibid., emphasis mine.

within any reasonable reading of Barth's *Church Dogmatics*, it should be quite obvious that these claims not only obviate God's freedom for us, but they destroy God's freedom as eternal Father, Son and Spirit precisely by making God's essence dependent on the historical existence of the man Jesus.

As can be seen from the several statements from Barth cited above, it is very clear that for him it is not Jesus who makes God God, since God eternally exists as Father, Son and Holy Spirit and would have so existed even if God had never even created the world.[21] Of course God did create the world, and God did determine to become incarnate and to reconcile and redeem the world. But the God who did these things and remains eternally united to us in his Word and Spirit did not *become* who he eternally was and is by virtue of those determinations to be God for us. As each of the theologians cited above properly recognize, any such viewpoint not only destroys God's freedom in himself, but it abolishes any possibility of distinguishing God's actions from history as the sphere in which he acts for us. This is the danger embedded in the assumption that Barth "historicized" God's being in light of the humiliation, death and resurrection of Jesus Christ because of an alleged radical change in his understanding of God that was supposed to have taken place in connection with his doctrine of election.

We will explore this thinking in more detail in a moment. For now it is important to ask: could the triune God, who freely and from eternity chose to be our creator, reconciler and redeemer, have been this God without us? As noted in my consideration of faith, experience and the Holy Spirit in chapter one, we are told today by a number of theologians that any such statement would embody a false idea of the divine freedom. My contention is that it is important to realize that this statement is tied to an acknowledgment of the importance of the *Logos asarkos* for a proper trinitarian theology and for a proper Christology. No doubt there are dangers involved in affirming the *Logos asarkos* in the context of the doctrine of reconciliation, because some theologians have done so precisely in order to advance a kind of natural theology that would speak of Christ's presence in history without attending to the fact that this presence can neither be seen nor understood

---

[21]George Hunsinger has compiled a full set of such statements and helpfully concludes that "the documentary record shows that his [Barth's] position did not change" on this matter. See Hunsinger, "Election and the Trinity," pp. 181-82.

apart from the historical Jesus who is and remains to all eternity the Word of God to us and for us. Nonetheless, it is crucial to recognize that the Word incarnate never ceased being who and what he was from all eternity as the Word: "The Word is what He is even before and apart from His being flesh. Even as incarnate He derives His being to all eternity from the Father and from Himself, and not from the flesh" (I/2, p. 136). It must be stressed here that these words are not only completely opposed to the thinking advanced by Benjamin Myers and those who think as he does, but they convey an insight that is lost in all historicized portrayals of the Trinity. They present us with a God who literally came into existence only for the sake of creating, reconciling and redeeming the world. In other words, while professing to have overcome Hegel's pantheistic view of the God/world relation, anyone who would claim that Jesus makes God God has in fact embraced a mutually conditioning view of God's relations with us and thus has spoiled the true meaning of John 1:14.[22] Put another way, Barth wished to maintain that the *Logos asarkos* was "the *terminus a quo*" while the *Logos ensarkos* was the "*terminus ad quem*" of the incarnation, without of course obviating the fact that there was a real union of natures in the incarnate Word.[23]

In spite of the fact that we have been told by some that he abandoned this view in *CD* II/2 and beyond, in light of the evidence we can say that Karl Barth certainly maintained these insights with respect to the freedom of God's love throughout his career. This chapter will build on Barth's understanding of faith as a human action that is grounded in God's freedom for us exercised in the incarnation and in the outpouring of his Holy Spirit. As such it embodies a proper view of human freedom as grounded in and shaped by God's freedom for us. In this chapter I begin by explaining exactly why it is still important to acknowledge that the God who is for us in Christ and his Spirit could have been God without us but freely chose not to. Here I will directly address once more the question of the proper relation between election and the Trinity. Much has been written on this subject since I de-

---

[22]For a proper understanding of how Jesus Christ should be understood as the subject of election, see Hunsinger, "Election and the Trinity," pp. 182-83. For Hunsinger, the eternal Son "is necessarily the eternal Son; he is only contingently *incarnandus*" (p. 183). One cannot say that Jesus Christ is the subject of election, Hunsinger rightly maintains, without qualification. Myers's statement certainly represents one that is made without qualification!

[23]I/2, pp. 169-71.

voted just a few pages to this issue in my first book on the Trinity.[24] I do not intend to repeat all of the discussion. But I will develop the thesis that unless this statement continues to be made in a serious way and not just as a type of throwaway statement, then and to that extent God's actual freedom for us, which is the very basis of human freedom (the freedom of faith and thus the freedom of the life of faith), is lost because it comes to be described as in some sense dependent on what happens within history.[25] In other words, just as Barth wished to avoid any notion of a mutually conditioning relationship between the Word and the flesh assumed by that Word in the incarnation, so too must we in our Christology avoid any idea that the Word was not fully the Word prior to and apart from the incarnation.[26]

This assertion is not one meant to underwrite a view that sees God as aloof from us in his divinity; rather it is meant to underscore the fact that the God who acts for us as creator, reconciler and redeemer is a God whose love of us on the cross and in the resurrection and outpouring of his Spirit in no way depends on us or on history in order to function effectively for us within history. Without this insight the specter of conditional salvation looms large in any consideration of the doctrine of reconciliation. In chapter one I referred briefly to those who advanced some idea of a dependent deity. In light of what I have just written, I think it should be clear why I do not believe that Barth ever would have countenanced the idea of such a deity. In this chapter I hope to explain why those whose thinking compromises the reality of the *Logos*

---

[24]See Molnar, *Divine Freedom*, pp. 61-64, 81.

[25]In a later chapter I will demonstrate that theologians who claim to accept the "value" of the *Logos asarkos* but reject these insights of Barth's end up embracing the mutual conditioning that Barth consistently rejected between humanity and divinity as they are united in the Person of the incarnate Word.

[26]What Barth wanted to avoid, of course, was Luther's idea that just as Christ's human nature has its reality only in and through the Word, "so too the Word only has reality through and in the humanity" (I/2, p. 166). In relation to this view Barth wondered whether such a position took sufficient account of "the freedom, majesty and glory of the Word of God" in such a way that "they are in no way merged and submerged in His becoming flesh" (I/2, pp. 166-67). Hence, "if the concept 'Word' and the concept 'flesh' are both taken seriously but are considered as *mutually conditioning* one another, is the statement of Jn. 1:14 an understandable statement at all? On the assumption of a *mutual conditioning* does it not mean that either the *vere Deus* or the *vere homo* is taken less than seriously, is in fact weakened down and altered in meaning?" (I/2, p. 167, emphasis mine). My answer to this question of course is yes, while the answer of those who claim that Barth's view of God's freedom changed after II/2 is to claim that Jesus' human history constitutes his being as the second person of the Trinity in some sense. For a full discussion of this point see below, chap. 5.

asarkos in relation to the *Logos ensarkos* do so precisely because they have reduced God to who and what God is for us. In other words, they have, in spite of their denials, collapsed the immanent into the economic Trinity. In chapter five I will develop this idea further by comparing the ideas of those who fail to respect God's preexistent divine being with the thought of one theologian, Thomas F. Torrance, whose thinking is shaped by election in just the right way. As this chapter develops I will respond to various characterizations of my first book on the Trinity while developing the ideas just introduced.

MISINTERPRETING GOD'S FREEDOM

Let us begin by considering Ben Myers's misguided interpretation of the view of divine freedom I presented in my first book on the Trinity. His thinking is hopelessly controlled by his confusion of the immanent and economic Trinity and of time and eternity from the start. Hence with respect to the *Logos asarkos* he writes that his "reading of Barth . . . is antagonistic to the notion of a *logos asarkos*, any moment at which God's identity was not already bound up with the human history of Jesus."[27] Myers's analysis is unacceptable in part because he ignores facets of Barth's thought that are present in the material he cites, and this leads him to misunderstand Barth's thinking as well as the importance of the *Logos asarkos* for trinitarian doctrine. First, there is a hermeneutical issue over how to interpret Barth that arises, because in the very same section Myers refers to, Barth himself insisted that the *Logos asarkos* "is the content of a necessary and important concept in trinitarian doctrine when we have to understand the revelation and dealings of God in the light of their free basis in the inner being and essence of God" (IV/1, p. 52). Indeed, Barth insists that the second person of the Trinity "in Himself and as such is not God the Reconciler. In Himself and as such He is not revealed to us. . . . He is not *Deus pro nobis*, either ontologically or epistemologically" (IV/1, p. 52). Second, Barth goes on to note that since he is now considering the Mediator in connection with the doctrine of reconciliation, it is impermissible to return "to the second person of the Trinity as such, *in such a way* that we ascribe to this person another form than that which God Himself has given in willing to reveal

---

[27]Benjamin Myers, "Election, Trinity, and the History of Jesus: Reading Barth with Rowan Williams," in *Trinitarian Theology After Barth*, p. 132.

Himself and to act outwards" (IV/1, p. 52). Myers either fails to notice or willfully chooses to ignore the fact that even here Barth not only does not deny the reality of the *Logos asarkos* but rather insists that we cannot retreat to this notion in this context (of the doctrine of reconciliation) in a way that separates the form of revelation from the shape it has taken in the one Mediator. In other words, he is opposing any use of a concept of the *Logos asarkos* to construct a natural theology, that is, an understanding of God that is not tied to the person and work of the Mediator.[28] The problem with Myers's assertion that there is no moment at which God's identity is not bound up with Jesus is that it amounts to a denial of the preexistent Son who has his eternal being from the Father in the Spirit and necessarily exists as the one who freely decides to become incarnate and live out a life of perfect obedience for us. We cannot pry into the eternal life of the Godhead to know how it is that God exists prior to creation and incarnation other than by acknowledging, on the basis of revelation, that God always existed as Father, Son and Holy Spirit who loves in freedom. To speak of moments with respect to God's eternal life without clearly distinguishing God's unique eternal time from created time runs the risk of projecting the limitations of our time into God's eternal time. I will discuss this important issue at length later in an attempt to move beyond the misguided thinking of those who logically reverse the doctrines of election and the Trinity.

Here it is important to note that the risk becomes a disaster because Myers does not make the careful distinctions made by Barth himself. He claims not to deny the Son's preexistence while actually denying it because he has already confused time and eternity. Hence, he says, "eternity here is not some anterior divine state that precedes the election of the human Jesus. The Son of God pre-exists precisely as a human being; the human history of

---

[28]John Webster thinks that Barth's assumption that the second person of the Trinity is an abstraction in III/1, p. 54 is unsatisfactory (Webster, "Trinity and Creation," p. 18). And that would be true if it weren't for the fact that both there and here in volume IV and elsewhere Barth clearly has in mind the reality of the Son's eternal existence as begotten of the Father before all worlds. And his stress, when focusing on the economy, is on what God the Son actually has become and is for all eternity, namely, the incarnate Word through whom God created the world and for whom the world was created. Hence, by abstraction Barth simply may mean that, given the reality of the incarnation, we must abstract from that in order to posit a *Logos asarkos* from the perspective of history in which God has acted for us. He is not denying the reality of the second person of the Trinity as such. Rather he is saying that any attempt to conceptualize this second person as such must not be formed in abstraction from what is revealed in Jesus Christ.

Jesus of Nazareth is already the form of God's eternal being."[29] What could this possibly mean? If Jesus' human history is "already the form of God's eternal being," then God has no eternal being prior to this human history. Such a conclusion implies either that God never existed prior to the incarnation or that God always was incarnate. Both of these choices mishandle Barth's thinking and leave Myers unable to acknowledge the basic truth of the incarnation as an act of free grace. It would of course be incorrect to think that God existed for a time and then decided to create, reconcile and redeem us. Such a view would falter because it attempts to understand God's eternity *by* created time instead of from itself as it has entered time and taken time into itself without any compromise of divine and human being and action. God's decision to elect us is indeed an eternal decision. But whenever that is taken to mean that God never existed without us, even in his pretemporal being and act, then and there the mystery of the Trinity is no longer respected, and a rationalistic attempt to explain something that can only be acknowledged takes over. This was the point I tried to make when I asked in my first book on the Trinity: "If God's election has always taken place, how then can it be construed as a decision; does it not then become a necessity?"[30] The question here concerned whether God could have been God without electing us. And the answer is no if and to the extent election is understood to be the ground of God's triunity. The point I was making was that God's triunity was and is eternally necessary, while his electing us is eternally contingent, as I explained later;[31] God could not not be Father, Son and Holy Spirit without ceasing to be God. But God could be the Father, Son and Holy Spirit without electing us. Nonetheless, out of sheer love, God eternally (but contingently) chose not be God without us.[32] Hence,

---

[29]Myers, "Election, Trinity, and the History of Jesus," p. 132.

[30]See Molnar, *Divine Freedom*, p. 62. That I was correct in this reading of McCormack is supported by the fact that he later claimed that since God's being in his second mode of existence is a determination of God's electing to be God for us, it "is a decision which has never *not* already taken place. So there is no 'eternal Son' if by that is meant a mode of being in God which is not identical with Jesus Christ" (*Orthodox and Modern*, pp. 213-19). If, however, the eternal Son cannot exist without being Jesus Christ, then that very assertion makes incarnation necessary to the divine being. And that undermines the divine freedom. This is discussed further in chap. 6 below.

[31]See note 58 below.

[32]Here I was following Barth's thinking that "We must guard against disputing the eternal will of God which precedes even predestination. We must not allow God to be subsumed in His relationship to the universe or think of Him as tied in Himself to the universe. . . . We confess the

God's election has always taken place, but the objects of his will *ad extra* are not ontologically necessary to God, and God could have refrained from deciding thus and would have been no less the eternal God he was and is.[33] Still, election of us, even as an eternal act of God, is new in a distinctive way, as we shall see in the next chapter.

In this context Myers is unable to acknowledge the incarnation as an act of free grace. In explaining his understanding of the Son's preexistence, Myers cites Barth's thinking about the *incarnate Word* in connection with the doctrine of *reconciliation* and writes: "For Jesus Christ—not an empty *Logos*, but Jesus Christ the incarnate Word . . . is the unity [of God and humanity]. . . . That he is both . . . is something which belongs to himself as the eternal Son of God for himself and prior to us. In this he is the pre-existent *Deus pro nobis.*"[34] It must, however, be recalled that Barth also says that in himself and as such the eternal Son is not *Deus pro nobis*, so that a distinction must be made between God's eternal existence as Son of the Father and his future (in God's eternal counsel) and actual existence as *Deus pro nobis*. Because Myers makes no such distinction, he reaches a number of bizarre conclusions. He says: (1) "The second person of the Trinity is a human being—or rather, the divine-human history enacted in Jesus";[35] (2) The "*logos asarkos* . . . represents . . . 'some image of God which we have made for ourselves'"; (3) "from all eternity, there is really no 'second person

---

eternal will of the God who is free in Himself, even in the sense that originally and properly He wills and affirms and confirms Himself" (II/2, p. 155).

[33]Scott R. Swain helpfully clarifies this point in *The God of the Gospel: Robert Jenson's Trinitarian Theology* (Downers Grove, IL: InterVarsity Press, 2013), p. 161. Swain thinks Torrance's emphasis on the priority of the Father/Son relation over the creator/creature relation is correct but imprecise and that it would be better to speak of a distinction between "objects of God's love that are 'eternally natural/necessary'" and those that are "'eternally free/contingent' objects." Torrance's thinking is indebted to Athanasius and makes more sense to me because it clearly suggests that God is necessarily Father, Son and Holy Spirit and would be even if he never had decided to create, reconcile and redeem the world. And it also implies that God's actions *ad extra* are new actions that cannot be understood to be coeternal with God, but must be understood as contingent on God's eternal decision to do something he had not previously done. So, as we shall see in the next chapter, there is a sense in which there is a "before" and "after" even in God's pretemporal eternity. Beyond that, we both agree that "God eternally but contingently wills the *ad extra* objects of his will." But it is not clear to me what objects of God's love are natural and necessary in Swain's understanding. God's act of willing is eternal and necessary. But the objects of God's love are his creatures and so they are, as we both agree, "not ontologically necessary."

[34]Myers, "Election, Trinity, and the History of Jesus," p. 132, citing IV/1, p. 53.

[35]Myers, "Election, Trinity, and the History of Jesus," p. 133.

of the Trinity," but only the divine-human history of Jesus of Nazareth";[36] and finally, (4) "God's deity is *constituted*—through God's own eternal decision— by the way God relates to this particular human being."[37]

Each of these conclusions stands in conflict with the trinitarian doctrine that Barth espoused and that is central to the faith of the church. First, to simply say that the second person of the Trinity is the human Jesus is to confuse the doctrines of reconciliation and the Trinity. This statement is a blatant collapse of the immanent into the economic Trinity—one that Barth never countenanced, although he is to some extent responsible for readings that go astray because in volume IV of the *CD* he did indeed inappropriately read back elements of the economy into the immanent Trinity, as I will note in a moment. Second, to suggest that for Barth the *Logos asarkos* is an image of an idol plain and simple, as an image of God we have made for ourselves, is to ignore the fact that it is so only when it is used to avoid knowing and relating with God through the reconciler, that is, the one Mediator. That would turn Jesus Christ, the incarnate Word, into a Christ-principle used to validate some naturally known God. Third, once again this remark that from all eternity there is no second person of the Trinity must be taken to be a denial of the *homoousion* of the Father and Son. This opens the door directly to some form of Arianism, as Kevin Giles never tires of reminding us. And the statement, however qualified, that God's decision to relate to the human being of Jesus *constitutes* his deity actually is a contemporary embodiment of the Arian view that without the human Jesus, God would not be the triune God. All four of these ideas must be rejected.

This, however, is not the end of it. Based on these ill-considered notions, Myers offers his critique of the view of divine freedom that I advanced in my book *Divine Freedom*. His thinking is therefore thoroughly confused and confusing. First, demonstrating a complete failure to understand that for Barth the basis of all that God does *ad extra* is his eternal act of being Father, Son and Holy Spirit, Myers says that Barth hints at a "kind of self-limitation in God," not in Moltmann's sense but "in the sense of God's freedom to restrict God's own possibilities to one particular course of action." Hence, Jesus' history "functions as a kind of inner 'necessity' for God, in as much as God is

[36]Ibid.
[37]Ibid., emphasis mine.

freely yet wholly self-determined towards this history."[38] This statement is more than a little problematic because Barth explicitly and repeatedly asserts that God's being is subject to no inner or outer necessities. When he speaks of the incarnation as necessary, it is only in light of the fact that that is what God decided to do in his gracious love and wisdom for us. In the sense that it is a *factual necessity* that can never be undone and that remains forever decisive for all history, it may be referred to as a necessity.[39] But to suggest that Jesus' history functions as a kind of inner necessity *for* God is precisely to imply that God needs Jesus' history in order to exist. That is exactly the opposite of what Barth intended. Based on this confused notion of God's freedom Myers claims that the Barth of IV/1 "knows nothing of Paul Molnar's picture of a sublime divine freedom that stands behind history, with differing possibilities balanced evenly on the scales."[40] This sort of statement is typical of Myers's caricatures and completely misses the point for which I argued in my first book.

In my prior book on the Trinity, I argued that God is free both positively and negatively. That is, God is free as the only self-moved being within himself and because God remains God in his relations with us, he acts for us and in relation to us without becoming dependent on us but rather by effectively creating and maintaining fellowship with us in spite of and against our sin. Moreover, while I did insist, with Barth and Torrance, that God remains who he is as Lord of the universe even in his incarnate Word and as the risen, ascended and advent Lord, I never argued that God's freedom is to be equated with something that stands behind history with evenly balanced possibilities between a freedom for us and one that might be against us. Quite the contrary. The whole point of my book was based on the fact that, although God *could have* chosen to be God without us, he chose not to so exist and did in fact create, reconcile and redeem us in his Word and Spirit. Without God's incarnation in Jesus Christ and without Jesus' resurrection from the dead we would have no genuine relations with God and no objective knowledge of

---

[38]Ibid.

[39]For a superb explanation of the difference between a factual necessity and a logical necessity (which leads to determinism and to arbitrary ideas of God's relations with creation), see Torrance, *Divine and Contingent Order*, pp. 22-23.

[40]Myers, "Election, Trinity, and the History of Jesus," p. 133. Interestingly, a check of the footnote for a reference to where I supposedly said this shows only a reference to my book with no page reference. That is because I never actually said this!

God.[41] So I argued that while the eternal God really exercised his freedom to be for us in Jesus Christ, that could never be taken to mean that God is wholly subsumed by the history of Jesus Christ as he must be if it is thought, with Myers, that "there is no second person of the Trinity."

The following statements from Barth found in my original work are decisive here:

> [God] does not need His own being in order to be who He is: because He already has His own being and is Himself. . . . If, therefore, we say that God is *a se*, we do not say that God creates, produces or originates Himself. . . . He cannot "need" His own being because He affirms it in being who He is. . . . What can need existence, is not God Himself, or His reality, but the reality which is distinct from Himself.[42]

It should be stressed here that all views that suggest that God becomes triune in order to relate with us falter when weighed against this important statement by Barth because they always assert that God needed to give himself his triunity for his relations with us. Moreover, in IV/2, where Barth speaks about the inner relations of the Father, Son and Holy Spirit as a history in partnership, he also insists that

> This history in partnership is the life of God before and above all creaturely life. . . . His inner union is marked off from the circular course of a natural process as His own free act, an act of majesty. . . . It is not subject to any necessity. The Father and the Son are not two prisoners. They are not two mutually conditioning factors in reciprocal operation. As the common source of the Spirit, who Himself is also God, they are the Lord of this occurrence. God is the free Lord of His inner union.[43]

Of course the force of this statement is meant to allow us to recognize that God is free, as God who loves, to enter into covenant relations with us

---

[41]Of course this is a true statement in light of the incarnation and resurrection of Jesus Christ. But it in no way is meant to imply that there was not true knowledge of God and of God's purposes in the history of Israel recounted in the Old Testament because it is that very God who became incarnate in Jesus Christ. In light of the resurrection we know God's internal relations in a way that could not be explicated prior to the events of incarnation and resurrection. But it is not a different God who is known in that way.

[42]II/1, p. 306. See also I/1, p. 354, where Barth insists that God does not need "a Second and then a Third in order to be One."

[43]IV/2, pp. 344-45.

without ceasing to be God. As a humble God who experiences our alienation and judgment as the man Jesus, God can and does act in history in
order to relieve our distress caused by sin. That is indeed what is revealed in
his resurrection and ascension. But that cannot be taken to mean that God
is *constituted* by this or that God needed to do this in order to be God or that
God "triuned" himself in order to relate with us.[44] Contrary to this, Myers
claims that God's freedom for Barth "is indeed a kind of necessity—but it is
simply the necessity of God's own loving self-consistency. God is necessarily
faithful to God's own decision about what the divine identity will be like."[45]
Hence, in Myers's view, Jesus "is *the* possibility, the free necessity of God's
deity."[46] This statement once again is confused and confusing.

In the section Myers cites from IV/1, when Barth writes of the "inner
necessity of the freedom of God and not the play of a sovereign *liberium
arbitrium*," he is not suggesting that God is subject to history in the sense
that there is no longer any Son of God or second person of the Trinity as
such. Rather he is saying that the condescension of the Son in his obedience to the Father acting as human for us is not the result of some arbitrary choice on God's part. What takes place in Jesus' humiliation and
exaltation on our behalf is the "divine fulfilment of a divine decree and
thus an act of obedience" (IV/1, p. 195). In light of the *fact* that God has
chosen to be God in this way *ad extra* from all eternity and has thus acted
for us as the savior in this history, Barth is explaining why it is important
to see that we do not have to do here "with one of the throws in a game
of chance which takes place in the divine being" (IV/1, p. 195). It is, in
other words, an act of divine "self-humiliation . . . as the presupposition
of reconciliation" (IV/1, p. 195). Here the all-important distinction
between a factual necessity and a logical necessity is once again ignored
by Myers. At this point, however, an issue arises in the thinking of
Barth that we will not consider in detail here. That issue concerns
whether and to what extent Barth illegitimately read back elements of the
economy into the immanent Trinity and thus, against his own intentions,

---

[44]For this way of stating the matter, see Kevin Hector, "Immutability, Necessity and Triunity:
Towards a Resolution of the Trinity and Election Controversy," *SJT* 65, no. 1 (2012): 64-81,
p. 67; and below, pp. 149-75.
[45]Myers, "Election, Trinity, and the History of Jesus," p. 134.
[46]Ibid.

uncharacteristically introduced an element of subordination into the immanent Trinity. We will treat this in a later chapter by comparing the thinking of Barth to that of Torrance, who, after a conversation with Barth late in his life, was asked by Barth to rewrite those sections of *CD* IV that did not take due consideration of Jesus' ongoing high-priestly mediation and thus led him to introduce some problematic notions into his thinking.[47]

Myers puzzlingly writes that

> God's freedom is not, as Molnar imagines, a mysterious abyss standing behind this event; rather it is fully realized in the event itself. This history is the form which God's freedom takes. And God's freedom *always already* takes this form, since Jesus is the content of God's eternal decision about who God will be.[48]

All of the confusion resident in Myers's original statement that Jesus makes God God is on display here. Instead of noting that God loves in freedom as the electing God who condescended to be the Judge judged in our place, as Barth did, Myers argues that God's triune being is constituted by Jesus' history and thus that it is "fully realized in the event itself" with the result that "Jesus is the content of God's eternal decision about who God will be." That would be a true statement except for one important thing, namely, Myers forgot to add that Barth here was referring once again to the incarnate Word or Son acting as our reconciler. And so he should have written that Jesus is the content of God's eternal decision about who God would be *for us* and *for our salvation*. But he did not write that, because from the very outset he had collapsed God's eternal Sonship into his actions *ad extra*. It is at this point that Myers thinks my notion of the divine freedom must be resisted because, while he says it is a faithful interpretation of the Barth of I/1 as perhaps "interpreted by T. F. Torrance, who shapes all Molnar's thinking about divine freedom and the immanent Trinity," still it embodies a type of thinking that is "structured by a tight sequence of paired opposites: the priority of eternity over history, the objective over the subjective, of reality over experience, of God *in se* over

---

[47]See Thomas F. Torrance, *Karl Barth, Biblical and Evangelical Theologian* (Edinburgh: T & T Clark, 1990), pp. 134-35, and then pp. 206-7, for Torrance's thinking about the obedience of the Son as a priestly obedience effected for us in order to "convert" us "back to true and faithful sonship through his own obedient self-offering to the Father."

[48]Myers, "Election, Trinity, and the History of Jesus," p. 134.

God-for-us."[49] And he claims the problem resident in interpreting God's freedom "through the lens of these metaphysical categories becomes clear" when one sees "how slight a place the human history of Jesus assumes in Molnar's thought" because "the human Jesus stands in the shadow of an antecedent *logos asarkos*."[50]

The real culprit then, according to Myers, is that in my thinking "God's decision is overshadowed by the ominous possibility that God might have chosen otherwise."[51] Hence, "the real history of Jesus is eclipsed by the sublime divine essence, which stands ineffably behind time and history. Behind the divine decision stands some nameless essence."[52] And we are told that this idea is captured by my statement that "if God's election has always taken place, how then can it be construed as a decision."[53] Here Myers finally exhibits his inability to comprehend the real point of affirming a *Logos asarkos*. It is not to assert that there is a God behind Jesus Christ, since anyone reading my previous book could see quite easily that, with Barth and Torrance, I consistently opposed both Ebionite and Docetic forms of Christology and specifically

---

[49]Ibid. The weakness of this analysis can be seen when one wonders exactly what Myers could possibly be affirming by rejecting the ideas that (1) eternity has priority over history; (2) the objective has priority over the subjective; (3) reality has priority over experience; and (4) God *in se* has priority over God for us. Both Barth and Torrance unfailingly maintained that God's relations with us were *irreversible* precisely in order to advance a realist view of theology, that is, one that allowed the unique object of the Christian faith to determine our subjective experiences of God in the economy. The content of these conceptions is not taken from metaphysics but from revelation in an attempt to think about God in faith and thus obediently without making God in his revelation dependent on or controlled by human experience or reflection. That is why Barth and Torrance insisted that God could be known only through God and that one could never be a real theologian unless one adopted Hilary's maxim that words are subject to realities and not realities to words. For a discussion of this, see Paul D. Molnar, *Thomas F. Torrance: Theologian of the Trinity* (Aldershot, UK: Ashgate, 2009), pp. 35-36. Just consider the fact that theology would become mythology if experience assumes priority over reality; that the creature indeed would become the creator (the original sin) if history assumed priority over eternity; that subjectivism (mythology) would rule the day if the subjective had priority over the objective, with the result that there never would be any true knowledge of God and of ourselves; and that if God for us assumed priority over God in himself, then we would inevitably have the God we want rather than, in the words of Colin Gunton, recognizing that in reality it is not the God we want who is the real God, but the God we are "damn well going to get"! In this argument Myers has let the cat out of the bag. What he is really after is a theology of irrationality and of mythology rather than one that is obedient to the Word of God incarnate and active in Jesus himself. That certainly would explain his bizarre idea that Jesus makes God to be God!

[50]Ibid.

[51]Ibid.

[52]Ibid., p. 135.

[53]Ibid. See above p. 140-41 for my discussion of this statement.

argued against the idea of a "nameless divine essence"; with Torrance and Barth, I emphatically and consistently opposed any God behind the back of Jesus Christ while simultaneously insisting that the God who is for us in Jesus Christ became incarnate *without ceasing to be God* so that God could act for us in Christ effectively both from the divine and from the human side.

What is really at stake in this statement "that God might have chosen otherwise" is the distinction between the God who eternally wills to be God for us with a freedom that expresses his eternal love as Father, Son and Spirit and the view that it is this decision for us that *determines* or *constitutes* God's triune being. With Hunsinger, Barth, Torrance and the others mentioned above, I have plainly argued for the fact that God could have been God without us but *freely* chose not to, not because I think that Jesus' history can be "reduced to one possibility among others, to be arbitrated by the indeterminate freedom of an unknowable divine essence,"[54] but because the history that was actualized in Jesus as the obedient Son acting as our savior from the divine and human side was indeed the history of the one God acting for us in that particular way. In other words, the statement that God could have been God without us but freely chose not to enables one to recognize that God acting for us *as* the man Jesus cannot be reduced to what he does for us, as clearly happens in Myers's thinking when he claims that Jesus makes God God. That is the issue at stake here and it is lost when Myers's convoluted thinking is embraced. While Myers does say that he agrees with me that "God does not contradict God's being when God enters into our history" and that he shares my "unease with the way a thinker like Moltmann introduces rupture and discontinuity within the being of God," the real point of contrast concerns his view that "the trinitarianism of IV/1 does not require any *logos asarkos* or any formalistic notion of divine choice in order to safeguard God's self-consistency."[55]

In light of this discussion, then, the problem that I tried to highlight in my first book and consistently thereafter is this: whenever the *Logos asarkos*, even in the restricted sense that Barth embraces it in IV/1, is jettisoned as in the thought of Robert Jenson or others, so also is the actual divinity of the man Jesus. And when that happens, an adoptionist or Ebionite Christology

---

[54]Ibid.
[55]Ibid., pp. 135-36.

looms large, and God the Son is then seen as dependent on history and merged with history in order to be God. But that is an idea of divinity that is useless because it can no longer allow God the freedom that is and remains his alone before, above and within history as a God who really is free for us and thus whose actions can be conceptually distinguished from the processes of history. I will take this question up once more in chapter five by comparing the thought of Torrance, Robert Jenson and Bruce Mc-Cormack on this issue to see what happens to the thinking of those who think a *Logos asarkos* is no longer required.

RECONSIDERING THE DIVINE FREEDOM

Now let me discuss a recent attempt to adjudicate the conflicts that have developed in connection with Bruce McCormack's thesis that Barth should have logically reversed the doctrines of election and the Trinity. A number of crucial issues should come clearly into view in this discussion. Kevin W. Hector argues, and I agree, that "It seems overwhelmingly likely . . . that Barth would reject McCormack's claim about the logical priority of election to triunity."[56] Nevertheless, he chooses to defend McCormack against charges of subordinationism and modalism while embracing the general aims of his thesis. It might be helpful to the reader here if I summarize Mc-Cormack's thesis through the prism of Hector's presentation. First, he claims that for McCormack "God determines to be triune as a result, as it were, of God's determination to be God-with-us."[57] This misguided refrain follows from the logical reversal of the doctrines of election and the Trinity, which is fundamental to McCormack's interpretation of Barth and his attempt to reconstruct Barth's doctrine of the Trinity. But it is, as I have pointed out on a number of occasions,[58] extremely problematic because, while God determines himself for us in electing us, that does not mean that he *thereby* gives himself his eternal being.[59] Why? Because a God who has to give himself his

---

[56]Hector, "Immutability, Necessity and Triunity," p. 70.

[57]Ibid., pp. 64-65.

[58]See Molnar, "The Trinity, Election and God's Ontological Freedom: A Response to Kevin W. Hector," *IJST* 8, no. 3 (2006): 294-306; and "Can the Electing God Be God Without Us? Some Implications of Bruce McCormack's Understanding of the Doctrine of Election for the Doctrine of the Trinity," *NZSTh* 49, no. 2 (2007): 199-222. These articles have been reissued in *Trinity and Election in Contemporary Theology*, ed. Michael Dempsey.

[59]George Hunsinger has demonstrated this with clarity. See, e.g., "Election and the Trinity:

being is in reality limited by the fact that he *needs* to do that. God eternally is the one he is and simply affirms this in his eternal act of being Father, Son and Spirit. In Barth's words:

> The freedom in which God exists means that He does not need His own being in order to be who He is: because He already has His own being and is Himself . . . this being does not need any origination and *constitution*. He cannot "need" His own being because He affirms it in being who He is. (II/1, p. 306, emphasis mine)

There is a great deal at stake here, because while McCormack claims he is only logically reversing election and the Trinity and not doing so in a chrono-logical or ontological way, the fact remains that any such logical reversal changes the meaning of both doctrines. It does so most decidedly by always implying that God could not be God without electing us and that he therefore needs to give himself the being he would have for eternity in order to do so. This misses the all-important point stressed by both Barth and Torrance that God's eternal election of us and his subsequent acts of creation, reconciliation and redemption are acts of grace that express God's eternal love and plan for us. But they do not in any way constitute his eternal being. That is why Barth specifically rejected the idea that God's aseity could be referred to as an act of "self-realisation," since "The God who takes His origin from Himself or is *con-stituted* by Himself is in a certain sense limited by the possibility of His non-being and therefore He is not the free God" (II/1, p. 305, emphasis mine).[60]

There is a critical distinction here that is lost by McCormack and his fol-lowers, and it is this: following Thomas Aquinas, Barth insists that God's triunity is both a work of his will and his nature because in God nature and will are one. Hence, the begetting of the Son

> is not an act of the divine will to the degree that freedom to will this or that is expressed in the concept of will. God has this freedom in respect of cre-

---

Twenty-Five Theses on the Theology of Karl Barth." McCormack's response to Hunsinger, "Elec-tion and the Trinity: Theses in Response to George Hunsinger," *SJT* 63, no. 2 (2010): 203-24, never actually addresses the real question, which concerns whether the position he espouses is Barth's. But, as Hector notes, McCormack admits that he has moved beyond Barth. The question I am raising concerns the fact that McCormack's main conclusions result precisely from this reversal. Therefore, for Hector to embrace his conclusions while rejecting this reversal leaves him in a position where he is still unable to recognize and maintain the freedom of God's love.
[60]It is no accident, as we shall see, that McCormack simply rejects this thinking, because in his view Barth here was only on the way toward his new antimetaphysical position that would no longer permit him to hold that God could have been triune without us.

ation—He is free to will it or not to will it. . . . But He does not have this freedom in respect to His being God. God cannot not be God. . . . He cannot not be Father and cannot be without the Son. (I/1, p. 434)

It is extremely important to realize that this is not simply an insight of Thomas Aquinas. It was a pivotal insight also espoused by Athanasius as when he wrote: "If He [the Word] be other than all things . . . and through Him the works rather came to be, let not 'by will' be applied to Him."[61] For Athanasius, because the Word is begotten from the Father's being, the Father "did not counsel beforehand" about the Word, because it was in him that the Father makes all else that he counsels. Since the will of God is in his Word, and his Word exists as begotten of the Father without beginning, any suggestion that the Word came into being by an act of will on the part of the Father would have to mean that "the will concerning Him consists in some other Word, through whom He in turn comes to be; for it has been shewn that God's will is not in the things which He brings into being, but in Him through whom and in whom all things made are brought to be" (*C. Ar.* III, 61). Therefore Athanasius argues that to say that the Son exists "by will" must mean that whoever says such a thing "places times before the Son; for counseling goes before things which once were not, as in the case of all creatures" (ibid.). In other words any suggestion that the Son exists because of an act of will on the part of the Father has to imply that the Word could not have coexisted with the Father as the one through whom the world was created.

Athanasius goes on to reject both the idea that the Son exists because of an act of will or because of some necessity within or outside God (*C. Ar.* III, 62). Athanasius thought the very idea that the Son or Word could have come into existence by an act of will on the part of the Father to be both an "unseemly" and a "self-destructive" and even "shocking" idea because God simply is who he is, and this applies both to the Father and to the Word. Hence,

He who is God not by will, has not by will but by nature His own Word. And does it not surpass all conceivable madness, to entertain the thought only, that God Himself counsels and considers and chooses and proceeds to have a good pleasure, that He be not without Word and without Wisdom, but have

[61] Athanasius, *C. Ar.* III, 61, in *A Select Library of Nicene and Post-Nicene Fathers of the Christian Church*, trans. and ed. Philip Schaff and Henry Wace, *Volume IV, St. Athanasius: Select Works and Letters* (Edinburgh: T & T Clark, 1987), p. 427.

both? For He seems to be considering about Himself, who counsels about what is proper to His Essence. (*C. Ar.* III, 63)

Athanasius answers that things "originate" have come into existence by an act of will and favor, but not the Son, because the Son is "not a work of will, nor has come after, as the creation, but is by nature the own Offspring of God's Essence" (*C. Ar.* III, 63). He is himself, Athanasius says, "the Father's Living Counsel, and Power, and Framer of the things which seemed good to the Father" (*C. Ar.* III, 63).

Athanasius concludes that it is blasphemous to say

that will was in the Father before the Word. . . . For if will precedes in the Father, the Son's words are not true, "I in the Father;" or even if He is in the Father, yet He will hold but a second place, and it became Him not to say "I in the Father," since will was before Him in which all things were brought into being and He Himself subsisted. (*C. Ar.* III, 64)

Finally, Athanasius asserts that it is madness to introduce "will and consideration between" the Father and the Son. While Athanasius is very clear that God's nature is not at all opposed to his will because who and what God is is not opposed to his will, nonetheless it is one thing to say "'Of will he came to be,'" because that implies that "once He was not" and also that "one might suppose that the Father could even not will the Son" (*C. Ar.* III, 66). But Athanasius says that to claim that the Son "might not have been" is

an irreligious presumption reaching even to the Essence of the Father, as if what is His own might not have been. For it is the same as saying "The Father might not have been good." And as the Father is always good by nature, so He is always generative by nature; and to say, "The Father's good pleasure is the Son," and "The Word's good pleasure is the Father," implies not a precedent will, but genuineness of nature. (*C. Ar.* III, 66)

For Barth, then, the begetting of the Son is a work of nature that "could not not happen just as God could not not be God," but creation is an act of God's will "in the sense that it could also not happen and yet God would not on that account be any the less God" (I/1, p. 434). In other words, there is an important distinction that Barth makes in II/1 that is fully in accord with the thinking of Thomas Aquinas and of Athanasius that must be stressed here: "There is, for example, the distinction between His willing of Himself and His willing of the possibility and reality of His creation as distinct from Himself" (II/1, p. 590). Strangely, McCormack claims that he is "as convinced as [I am] that God need not have created this world; God might have chosen to create a different world or to have created no world at all."[62] But nothing could be further from the truth. The logic of his thinking is such that, as Hector himself indicates, God *gave* himself the being he would have for all eternity as triune "for the sake of creation, reconciliation and redemption."[63] It is this very thinking that is at odds with the idea that God need not have created the world or might have chosen to create a different world or no world. And the problem resides in McCormack's refusal to acknowledge that the God who might never have created at all is indeed the very same triune God who meets us in the incarnate Word and in his Spirit. He claims that the issue here is not one of divine freedom. But that is exactly the problem. He says he questions whether anyone can "know what God would have been without us, to know, in fact, how the divine being would have been structured had God not deter-mined to be God for us in Jesus Christ."[64] But this assertion rests on the premise that God structured his triunity in order to elect us. That premise, however, is incorrect because, as Hunsinger rightly states,

> The Father does not eternally generate the Son for the purpose of pre-
> temporal election. If election were the purpose of the Son's eternal generation
> by the Father . . . the Trinity would *necessarily* be dependent on the world . . .
> the Son would be subordinated to an external end; and . . . the Son would be
> object but not the subject of election.[65]

This thinking seems fully in accord with the views of Athanasius discussed above and would certainly be in accord with Barth's important statement that "Of course, the fact that Jesus Christ is the Son of God does not rest on election" (II/2, p. 107).[66]

McCormack is unable to accept this or to acknowledge the problem here because he claims that Barth's idea that God would exist as eternal Father, Son and Holy Spirit even without creation, reconciliation and redemption was

---

[62]McCormack, *Orthodox and Modern*, p. 297.
[63]Hector, "Immutability, Necessity and Triunity," p. 65.
[64]McCormack, *Orthodox and Modern*, p. 297.
[65]Hunsinger, "Election and the Trinity," p. 192, emphasis mine.
[66]I emphasized this point in "Can the Electing God Be God Without Us?" p. 206.

something Barth affirmed from I/1 through II/1 "but that such a formulation
is not finally compatible with the statement that 'Jesus Christ is the electing
God.'"[67] But this thinking leads to the strange conclusion that it is important
to say that "God could be God without us" in order to safeguard the divine
freedom, but that any statement that God "would have been this way or that
way" is the result of "unwarranted speculation" that necessarily opens "a gap
in material content between the immanent and economic Trinity—as Molnar
does."[68] I say this is strange because in my book *Divine Freedom* I never
opened a gap between who God is for us and who God is in himself. Instead,
I consistently insisted, with Barth and Torrance, that what God is toward us,
he is eternally in himself. And I made it clear that for me that means that God
is eternally the Father, Son and Holy Spirit—the one who loves in freedom
and is free in his love. Therefore, I never had to make the incoherent assertion
that God could be God without us but that we could not identify that God as
the eternal Father, Son and Holy Spirit. To know the immanent Trinity from
God's actions within the economy means precisely to know that the triune
God who could have remained who he is in himself to all eternity without us
freely chose not to do so. And it is only on the basis of God's free grace and
love, which meet us in Christ, and in his Spirit uniting us to Christ that we
know this. Thus, from within a properly functioning doctrine of the Trinity
it is impossible to speak of God at all unless one is speaking of the triune God
precisely by thinking of the Father through the Son and by the Holy Spirit
enabling that speech. So, to claim that one could say that God could be God
without us without specifying who God is in his triunity truly represents an
exercise in unwarranted speculation. It is not thinking that is prompted by
the Holy Spirit. It is not thinking within faith as discussed in chapter one. If
it were, one could never speak of God without referring to the Father, Son
and Holy Spirit who is the one who loves in freedom *in se* and *ad extra*. And
it is exactly such reasoning that opens a gap in material content between the
immanent and economic Trinity, a gap that is then closed by improperly
reading back elements of the economy into the immanent Trinity and thus
allowing history itself to condition and to define God's triunity. What we have
here is simply another example of someone offering us a "dependent deity."

---

[67]McCormack, *Orthodox and Modern*, p. 297.
[68]Ibid.

Hence, when McCormack thinks of closing that imaginary gap, what he means is that God's actions *ad extra* actually must be understood to determine who God is *ad intra*. And that is precisely the difficulty that I have identified and rejected by insisting, with Barth, that the God who meets us in history is the triune God who had and has no need of us but who nevertheless in his grace and love does not will to exist without us and therefore does not in fact exist without us. Greater emphasis on the deity of the Holy Spirit here and on the *homoousion* of the Spirit with the Son would prevent any attempt to introduce the notion of a dependent deity at this point.

But McCormack is so intent on pressing his claims here that he simply dismisses Barth's clear statements about God's freedom to have existed as the triune God without us in I/1, I/2 and also in II/1, many of which have been meticulously documented by George Hunsinger.[69] Since I will be discussing some of this in other chapters in relation to Barth's Christology and in relation to the thought of Torrance and Jenson, there is no need to go into all the details of that argument here. But it is at least worth mentioning at this point that McCormack claims that there are "tensions" in Barth's thinking in II/1 such that Barth "is able to speak of the work of reconciliation and redemption as a 'fundamentally new work'"[70] and that this idea is something Barth later rejected, especially in IV/1.[71]

McCormack thus claims that in IV/1 Barth does not believe the incarnation "is a new event in God when it happens in time."[72] It is new to human beings because it is the revelation of what up to that point had been a mystery.

---

[69]See, e.g., "Election and the Trinity." An especially good example, among many others, is found in Barth's distinction between God's primary and secondary objectivity in II/1 (above, chap. 2, p. 108-9). Hunsinger rightly notes that "The one act in which the tri-personal God has his being therefore subsists in two modes at the same time. These modes represent God's primary and secondary objectivity. The one mode is immanent, the other is economic. The one is primordial; the other derivative. The one is self-existent; the other dependent on it. The one is necessary; the other contingent. *The one would exist whether the world had been created or not*; the other presupposes the creation and fall of the world" (p. 193, emphasis mine). Also: "For Barth, however, throughout the *Church Dogmatics* from beginning to end, God is seen as free not to have created the world, but he is not seen as free not to be himself, and therefore he is not seen as free not to be the Holy Trinity (to all eternity)" (p. 197).
[70]Bruce L. McCormack, "The Actuality of God: Karl Barth in Conversation with Open Theism," in *Engaging the Doctrine of God: Contemporary Protestant Perspectives*, ed. Bruce L. McCormack (Grand Rapids: Baker Academic, 2008), pp. 185-242, on p. 234.
[71]*Trinitarian Theology After Barth*, ed. Habets and Tolliday, p. 109.
[72]Ibid., p. 108.

But it is not new to God because it is the outworking in time of the eternal event in which God gave to himself the being he would have for all eternity. We have before us here another piece of significant evidence demonstrating that an important change has taken place within the bounds of the *Church Dogmatics*. In I/1 . . . Barth insisted that the incarnation was a new event in God's life. In IV/1, he denies it.[73]

It is crucial, however, to understand that the text McCormack cites (IV/1, p. 193) does not support this reading of Barth at all. Barth never says that the incarnation is in any sense an event in which "God gave to himself the being he would have for all eternity." He continues to insist that the incarnation is a free act of God the Son assuming human nature into union with his divine being in time and history, as he did in IV/2 as well: "Even as the divine essence of the Son it did not need His incarnation, His existence as man . . . to become actual. As the divine essence of the Son it is the predicate of the one God. And as the predicate of this Subject it is not in any sense merely potential but in every sense actual" (IV/2, p. 113). And, "The triune life of God which is free life in the fact that it is Spirit, is the basis of His whole will and action even *ad extra*, as the living act which He directs to us. It is the basis . . . of the determination of the Son to become man . . . of the atonement with its final goal of redemption to eternal life with Himself" (IV/2, p. 345). In IV/1, Barth says that Jesus "as the Son of God the Father and with God the Father the source of the Holy Spirit, united in one essence with the Father by the Holy Spirit . . . is God. He is God as He takes part in the event which constitutes the divine being" (IV/1, p. 129). Then he says,

We must add at once that as this One who takes part in the divine being and event He became and is man. This means that we have to understand the very Godhead, that divine being and event and therefore Himself as the One who takes part in it, in the light of the fact that it pleased God—this is what corresponds outwardly to and reveals the inward divine being and event— Himself to become man. In this way, in this condescension, He is the eternal Son of the eternal Father. (IV/1, p. 129)

While Barth is clear that we must understand God in light of what he has done in the incarnation, there is no hint that he argues here that God "gave

---

[73]Ibid.

himself" his being in an eternal event of determining to become incarnate so that the incarnation is only the outworking of the being God had given to himself in eternity for the purpose of becoming incarnate. If that were the case, then, once again, one would be advancing the idea that the Father eternally generated the Son based on his act of pre-temporal election. And that would make the Trinity dependent on the world as noted above because it would imply that God structured his triunity in order to elect us. This might then imply that incarnation is itself an eternal event in God even prior to the actual historical event of incarnation.

What he did was give himself to the human race without ceasing to be God so he could effectively reconcile us to the Father. He humbled himself "all without giving up His own form, the *forma Dei*, and His own glory, but adopting the form and cause of man into the most perfect communion with His own, accepting solidarity with the world" (IV/1, p. 187). Furthermore, when Barth speaks of the mystery of the Word humbling himself for us, he does not say that in the incarnation God makes suffering and death to be essential to God.[74] Rather, he argues that God takes our suffering and death into his divine being in order to overcome these for us. If suffering and death were to be thought of as essential to God, then God himself would stand in need of redemption.[75] Beyond this, when Barth says that the humility in which God "dwells and acts in Jesus Christ is not alien to Him, but proper to Him" and is thus not a *novum mysterium* to God but only a *novum mysterium* to us, he is clearly referring to the act of kenosis in which the Son did not grasp at equality with God but freely humbled himself for our benefit. This is not a new mystery to God because, Barth says, God does not become another God in condescending to give himself to us in this way. Rather he acts as the one he is from all eternity, that is, the eternal Father, Son and Holy Spirit, namely, "the one God Himself in His true Godhead" (IV/1, p. 193).

---

[74]Barth argues in fact that God's omnipotence is such that he "can assume the form of weakness and impotence and do so as omnipotence, triumphing in this form" (IV/1, p. 187). See also IV/2, p. 357, where Barth notes that the element of truth in the otherwise false position of patripassianism is that it is "God the Father who suffers in the offering and sending of His Son, in His abasement. The suffering is not His own, but the alien suffering of the creature, of man, which He takes to Himself in Him." God does not here make suffering part of his nature. For more on this see below, chap. 4, pp. 189-91; chap 7, pp. 246-48 and 301-5.

[75]For more on this see Molnar, *Divine Freedom*, pp. 220-27, and "A Response: Beyond Hegel with Karl Barth and T. F. Torrance," *Pro Ecclesia* 23, no. 2 (Spring 2014): 165-73.

There is no indication here that Barth intended to say that God gave to himself his eternal being in and by this event. It was rather the outworking of his eternal decision of love for us. Still, for Barth, this is a new act in that God was not always incarnate and God could well have existed without the incarnation if he had chosen to do so. Indeed God did not need to become incarnate in order to be the triune God.[76]

Additionally, Barth's explication of God's omnipotence is said to be extremely problematic because Barth "describes God's power as a power 'over everything that He actually wills *or could will.*'"[77] This, we are told, allows Barth to distinguish between God's omnipotence and God's omnicausality and to insist that

> we must reject the idea that God's omnipotence and therefore His essence resolves itself in a sense into what God actually does, into His activity, and that it is to be identified with it. It is not the case that God is God and His omnipotence omnipotence only as He actually does what He does. Creation, reconciliation and redemption are the work, really the work of His omnipotence. He is omnipotent in this work. . . . He has not lost His omnipotence in this work. It has not changed into His omnicausality in this work, like a piece of capital invested in this undertaking, and therefore no longer at the disposal of its owner. The love with which He turns to us in this work, and in which He has made Himself our God, has not made Him in the least degree poorer or smaller. It has its power and its reality as love for us too in the fact that it continues to be free love, that God has bound and still binds Himself to us as the One who is able thus to bind Himself and whose self-binding is the grace and mercy and patience which helps us, because primarily He is not bound, because He is the Lord, because stooping down to us He does not cease to be the Lord, but actually stoops to us from on high where He is always Lord. He is wholly our God, but He is so in the fact that He is not our God only. (II/1, p. 527)

McCormack claims that this thinking is dangerous and that it trespasses "against the very core of [Barth's] methodological commitments" since it

---

[76]In addition to the important statements to this effect adduced above, it would be very instructive here to add Barth's remark that "We must distinguish between God as such and God in His purpose (decree). From eternity the Son (as God *and man*) exists in God. But until the incarnation this has not happened. Nevertheless, this must be made clear; otherwise you have a fourth member of the Trinity" (*Karl Barth's Table Talk*, recorded and ed. John Godsey [Richmond, VA: John Knox, 1962], p. 52).

[77]McCormack, "Actuality of God," p. 235, citing II/1, p. 522.

opens the door "to speculation with regard to what God could have done—thereby looking away from the limits set for us by God's self-revelation in Jesus Christ."[78] Moreover, we are told that "none of this was necessary. Barth could have upheld the divine freedom simply by insisting that the eternal act of Self-determination in which God chose to be God in the covenant of grace and to be God in no other way is itself a free act."[79] Notice the way McCormack imposes his own thinking on Barth here. Barth was at pains to indicate that God is who he is both in himself and in his works. But God could never be reduced to what he does in his works *ad extra*. Because McCormack cannot agree with the distinction that led to that assertion, a distinction that is central to Barth's trinitarian theology, he reduces the divine freedom to what God actually chose to do in the economy by confusing God's choice to be God in the covenant of grace with God's eternal being as Father, Son and Spirit, with the result that he claims that God can be God in *no other way*. Put differently, McCormack clearly has moved beyond Barth by claiming that God's freedom exercised in his relations with us in the covenant must mean that God no longer has any existence in himself and thus apart from us. It is therefore no surprise that in quoting this text McCormack leaves out that last sentence that was crucial for Barth, namely, that God "is wholly our God, but He is so in the fact that He is not our God only."

That statement makes all the difference in the world. And it does not lead Barth into abstract speculation about what God could have done, that is, into natural theology. It only leads him to acknowledge and to assert the truth that the God who in fact meets us in his Word and Spirit could have remained perfectly God in himself without us but chose not to. That very distinction is lost by McCormack as when he writes, commenting on what he takes to be Barth's revised doctrine of the Trinity in IV/1, that "*There is no longer any room left here for an abstract doctrine of the Trinity. There is a triune being of God—only in the covenant of grace.*"[80] When compared to what Barth says in II/1 it is obvious that Barth never would have made this statement, because it overtly reduces God to his actions in the covenant of

---

[78]Ibid., p. 236.
[79]Ibid.
[80]McCormack, "Election and the Trinity," in Dempsey, *Trinity and Election in Contemporary Theology*, p. 128, emphasis mine.

grace.[81] That is exactly what Barth was trying to avoid, while simultaneously asserting that grace as God's free action is an action of the Lord who became incarnate for us and for our benefit, without in the least ceasing to be the Lord who has his freedom in himself and is not exhausted by what he does for us. McCormack's problematic thinking here is dictated by his belief that when Barth spoke of Jesus Christ *rather than* of the eternal Son as the subject of election, this had to refer to the fact that God's "eternal act of choosing to be God-for-us in Jesus Christ is the very act in which God *constitutes* himself as triune."[82] And this is meant to remind us that

> the Second Person of the Trinity is not the "eternal Son" in abstraction from the humanity he would assume. The eternal Son has a name and his name is Jesus. *Any talk of the eternal Son in abstraction from the humanity to be assumed is an exercise in mythologizing; there is no such eternal Son—and there never was.*[83]

Here once more we see very clearly the results of McCormack's inability to distinguish without separating the immanent and economic Trinity as Barth had done. If there never was an eternal Son without Jesus, then the only

---

[81]Importantly, Robert B. Price (*Letters of the Divine Word: The Perfections of God in Karl Barth's Church Dogmatics*, ed. John Webster, Ian A. McFarland and Ivor Davidson, T & T Clark Studies in Systematic Theology [New York: T & T Clark, 2011]) notices that McCormack's proposal that election should have logically preceded the Trinity in Barth's thought represents "an overemphasis on the divine loving (God's love for us) and a compromising of the divine freedom" (p. 11). More than that, Price astutely points out that "For McCormack, God's eternal election logically includes the incarnation" (p. 141) and that this position is in conflict with what Barth actually says, namely, that "The incarnation is as such the confirmation of the triunity of God" (II/1, p. 515) and "there is revealed in it [the incarnation] the distinction of the Father and the Son, and also their fellowship in the Holy Spirit" (II/1, p. 515). Price thinks that the many other statements about God's freedom that are in conflict with McCormack's thinking as it follows his logical reversal of election and triunity "would appear too numerous to represent a mere inconsistency in Barth's thought" (p. 142). The point is that for Barth "What God does in time is . . . a function of what he is in eternity—not the other way round" (p. 142). This, says Price, "is one of the most basic themes of Barth's exposition" (p. 142). According to Price, "To claim that it is God's interaction with the created order which determines his immanent life is to run counter not merely to isolated inconsistencies or residual elements of classical theism in II/1, but to its entire flow of thought" (p. 142). Price rightly concludes that "McCormack's is a striking constructive proposal in its own right. But it encounters only resistance from Barth's doctrine of the divine perfections" (p. 142). But resistance is also evident in Barth's statement that "The true and living God is gracious. He transcends Himself. He discloses and imparts Himself. He does this first in Himself, and then and on this basis to man in His eternal election and its temporal and historical fulfilment" (IV/3.1, p. 81). Here is another important instance of Barth basing God's eternal election in his triune being and act and not collapsing the former into the latter.
[82]McCormack, *Engaging the Doctrine of God*, p. 218, emphasis mine.
[83]Ibid., p. 219, emphasis mine.

option left is to assert that Jesus Christ, the God-man, is the subject of the incarnation itself, thus obviating both Jesus' true humanity and his true divinity. This, because it eliminates Jesus' humanity by implying that it always existed instead of stating clearly that it only comes into existence at a particular point in time, and it undermines Jesus' true divinity as an authentic, definitive and essential existence that has its fullness in itself without respect to the humanity to be assumed. All this will be discussed in more detail in chapter five below. But it is important here to see what happens when one refuses to acknowledge, as Barth himself always did, that God could have been God without us but freely chose not to.

Before ending this particular discussion, however, it is worth noting that because Barth's most basic insights about the divine freedom made in II/1 cannot be reconciled with McCormack's basic thesis that election and the Trinity need to be logically reversed, since it is in election that God gives himself his triune being, McCormack simply argues that these statements must be rejected. Hence, while Barth decisively disallowed any idea that God causes himself, by rejecting the thinking of Hermann Schell in II/1,[84] McCormack claims that Barth's remark that God's triune being "does not need any origination and constitution" (II/1, p. 306) "cannot be redeemed and should be rejected."[85] As is typical with McCormack, he admits that Barth does indeed reject the idea that God is the cause of himself but claims that "the question must remain open as to whether his later Christology would allow him to continue to do so."[86] Of course, in McCormack's thinking this is not an open question; it is answered repeatedly by his own assertions in many contexts that God gives himself his being in the act of election—something Barth never approved and never would approve. In fact, as Hunsinger writes, "The notion that the eternal Son was constituted by pretemporal election was something so bizarre, and obviously false, that Barth could see little point in pausing very long to refute it."[87] Nonetheless, Hunsinger does cite a very relevant remark that Barth did make: "Of course, the fact that Jesus Christ *is* the Son of God does not rest on election" (II/2, p. 107,

---

[84]See Molnar, "Can the Electing God Be God Without Us?" for a discussion of this issue.
[85]McCormack, "Election and the Trinity," p. 132.
[86]Ibid., p. 133.
[87]Hunsinger, "Election and the Trinity," p. 195.

emphasis added) and one that was noted above. Even here, McCormack alleges that at this early date Barth was ambivalent in rejecting Hermann Schell's thinking. Yet, even McCormack's own presentation shows that Barth was not at all ambivalent—he clearly rejected Schell's statement. But he did want to honor Schell's "special concern," which was to overcome "the scholastic equation of God with the unmoved Mover of Aristotle" (II/1, p. 305). Barth wanted to overcome the static and unmoved God of Aristotle because he consistently argued that the triune God was in reality the only self-moved being, since God was the living God (II/1, pp. 268-72). Torrance, too, wanted nothing to do with the unmoved Mover of Aristotle.[88]

Schell may have intended that. But the way he went about overcoming Aristotle's view was unacceptable to Barth because the only way forward was on the ground of what God actually revealed in his Word and Spirit. It is only too clear from the context that McCormack wants to argue that God does take his origin from himself and that if Barth could have abandoned his rejection of that point, his thinking would have moved closer to the thinking of John Zizioulas. Indeed, for McCormack, "God must give himself being eternally in the act in which he sets himself in relationship to Jesus Christ and, in turn, to the world."[89] Oblivious to the fact that Barth insisted that a God who had to give himself his being was limited by the fact that he needed to do this, McCormack simply asserts this point, which is the logical consequence of his having reduced the immanent to the economic Trinity, precisely by logically reversing the doctrines of election and the Trinity. Finally, according to McCormack, there are two other statements of Barth that must be rejected: (1) that "Jesus Christ has a beginning, but God has no beginning" (II/2, p. 102), and (2) that "We know God's will *apart* from predestination only as the act in which, from all eternity and in all eternity, God affirms and confirms Himself" (II/2, p. 155). We are told: "Once Barth makes his later Christology to be the epistemological basis for all that may be said of God, such an 'apart from' becomes a complete impossibility."[90] These additional assertions will be dealt with in our discussion of whether Barth changed his views in his later Christology. At this point what can and must be said is that it is wholly inappropriate simply to

---

[88]See, e.g., Molnar, *Thomas F. Torrance*, pp. 50-51, 81, 133.
[89]McCormack, "Election and the Trinity," p. 135.
[90]Ibid., p. 134.

dismiss those crucial statements made by Barth that demonstrate that he had no intention of arguing that election determines or constitutes God's triunity simply because they don't fit the logic of one's own position.

An Attempt to Mediate the Disagreements

For now I wish to explore exactly why I think Kevin Hector fails to convince in his latest attempt to resolve the controversy. Following Jüngel, Hector says that in the act of creation God repeats *ad extra* "the Father's eternal act of begetting the Son," while in reconciling us it is "the Son's eternal act of reflecting the Father's love" that is repeated *ad extra*, and in mediating this reconciliation God repeats *ad extra* "the Spirit's eternal act."[91] While it is true that God draws us into his eternal relations through grace and faith, it is more than a little ambiguous to suggest that God is repeating his eternal acts of begetting and so on when he relates with us, since in reality God is doing something new, new even for himself, when he acts outside himself for us. Hector at least is able to acknowledge that God would still be Father, Son and Holy Spirit if he did not determine to be God with us, so that he would not then "repeat" his being *ad extra*. But he also makes the strange assertion that since Barth claims that God has determined to be with us, therefore, "God has never been triune without appropriating creation to the Father, reconciliation to the Son and redemption to the Spirit."[92] It is this very statement that demonstrates that, while Hector attempts to separate himself from McCormack's mistaken view that we cannot say that the triune God could have existed without us without being any less God, he cannot separate himself from the thinking that is singularly unable to distinguish without separating the immanent and economic Trinity. For if God has *never* been triune without appropriating creation, reconciliation and redemption to himself, then, what is being suggested is that God in fact never existed without the world! And that, once again, is the old Origenist error coming back to haunt modern theology. Hector, like McCormack, is unable to distinguish clearly between God's internal and external actions. Things go downhill from here.

Hector proceeds to argue that both election and triunity are necessary to God in different ways. "Triunity is necessary to God in an absolute sense,

[91]Hector, "Immutability, Necessity and Triunity," p. 70.
[92]Ibid.

whereas election is not, since God could have been God without us."[93] But his thinking is still caught in the web of the reasoning that equates triunity with election, since he has already told us that God never exists as triune except in relation to us. And so Hector maintains that while election is not absolutely necessary to God, it is "*volitionally* necessary."[94] From where does Hector acquire this notion? He gets it from Harry Frankfurt and from his analysis "of the phenomenon of love." And it is very clear that his analysis is based on an exploration of human love. That in itself is a major problem from Barth's perspective, since he insisted that we could not come to a true understanding of God's love for us in Christ by examining human love. While humans need others to love, God does not; and in that sense God is truly free in a way that humans can never be. In any case, Hector argues that one's care for one's child means that one "could not bring oneself to act cruelly towards him or her" and thus it must be the case that one's care of another "imposes certain volitional necessities upon one, in the sense that one could not will otherwise."[95] From this he concludes that necessities that are self-imposed rather than imposed from without do not compromise one's freedom: "If I identify with this configuration of my will . . . then it follows that I am free with respect to it not because I could will otherwise, but precisely because this will is self-imposed."[96] Applying this thinking to the doctrine of election, Hector reaches the following conclusions: (1) "In electing to be with us, God identifies our interests as God's own and thus identifies with us"; (2) "That God identifies wholeheartedly with this identification"; (3) "In so identifying, God has imposed certain volitional necessities upon Godself, the most important of which is that God has made this identity itself *necessary* to Godself."[97]

A moment ago I pointed out that one could not understand God's free love by analyzing human love. That is and always remained Barth's view. And as I pointed out in a 1989 article on Barth's doctrine of the Trinity, Barth's thinking on this matter stood in conflict with Jüngel's idea that we could only understand God's love by first inquiring into the nature of human love.[98]

---

[93]Ibid., p. 71.
[94]Ibid.
[95]Ibid., p. 72.
[96]Ibid., p. 73.
[97]Ibid., emphasis mine.
[98]Paul D. Molnar, "The Function of the Immanent Trinity in the Theology of Karl Barth: Implica-

First, in electing to be with us, God does not elect our interests as his own. Rather God elects our rejection of him, which is not in our best interest, precisely in order to love us by judging us in his Son and freely rectifying the human situation. So, in loving us, God does not just identify with us—he calls us into question in his Son and empowers us to love on the basis of his free and undeserved loving of us while we were still sinners. He is not bound to this by any necessity but acts this way with a freedom that is unhindered by our self-will and opposition. Second, no necessity is placed on God when he acts graciously and lovingly and thus unconditionally toward us in sending his Son to be the Judge judged in our place. Barth never ceased insisting that our relations with God in his Word and Spirit never could be construed in terms of mutual necessity; any such thinking would at once deny and obscure the very meaning of grace as a free overflow of the divine love toward us. Third, and finally, the fact that God loves us in electing us simply cannot be construed as necessary to God without in fact making God dependent on this relation. That, of course, was bound to happen in Hector's analysis because there are such necessities imposed in all human relations. But there are never any such necessities imposed on God, because God's relations with us never were and never are necessary to God. There is an irreversible relation between God and us, and any idea at all that our relations with God mean that election is necessary to him has not in fact escaped the logic that follows the idea that election is indeed the ground of God's triunity. So it turns out that even though Hector formally rejects McCormack's idea that election and triunity should be logically reversed, his thinking still advances all that follows from that mistaken reversal, since by embracing the fact that human love needs others to activate itself and imposes necessities on those who love, his thinking compromises the fact that God himself acts with both inward and outward freedom in loving us. That, Barth rightly insists, is the very mark of divine love that enables us to distinguish it from human love. And that indeed is what makes God's love divinely effective in its movement toward us who are sinners in need of divine forgiveness.

Hector tries to ground this thinking in Barth's view that once God has determined to love us as he has, it is a necessity in light of the fact that it is a decision of God and therefore cannot be undone. Barth does indeed say that. But for Barth the all-important distinction here is between factual necessities and logical necessities. The former refer to facts that have been accomplished by God and so are what they are because God has freely executed them, and the latter refer to necessities imposed on God on the basis of which it is thought that God must conform to certain volitional or other necessities. Hector thus concludes, "God has freely limited God's possibilities . . . by ruling out the possibility of being otherwise than God-with-us."[99] So, while still paying lip service to the idea that God could still be God without us, Hector concludes that "properly speaking, God has no being-in-Godself apart from the covenant."[100] It is clear from the context and from the texts Hector cites from the *CD* that Barth wants to uphold the view that what God is toward us he is eternally in himself, and so God is not other than who he is in the covenant; this of course is the view that I wish to embrace, following both Barth and Torrance. But Hector's thought has moved beyond this with the claim that God has no being apart from the covenant. That very claim reduces God to what he does for us. This conclusion stands in stark contrast to Barth's continued insistence that God "reveals Himself as the One who, even though He did not love us and were not revealed to us, even though we did not exist at all, still loves in and for Himself as surely as He is and is God" (IV/2, p. 755). Hector's thought will not allow for this, because he has erroneously introduced necessity into the divine loving and thus compromised the freedom of God's grace.

While Hector argues that his notion of volitional necessity is compatible with Barth's thinking, this last statement by Barth demonstrates that it is not. And while Hector rightly insists that "election is a *determination* of God's being rather than *constitutive* of it," he also says, "there is no height or depth in which God is indifferent to this identification, such that God has no being-in-Godself apart from the covenant."[101] Here what is given with the right hand is taken away with the left. Election is indeed a determination of God's being, but that cannot mean that "God has no being-in-Godself apart from the covenant." When Barth spoke of the covenant of grace he meant that it was a freely established and freely maintained relation that God, who

---

[99]Hector, "Immutability, Necessity and Triunity," p. 74.
[100]Ibid., pp. 74-75.
[101]Ibid., p. 75.

has his life in himself and could have maintained that life without us, freely chose to be God in communion with us. Still, God retains his life in himself even in his closest relations with us. That is the crucial point that is lost by Hector and those whose thinking is in the grip of an untheological understanding of the immanent Trinity in its relation with the economic. While I agree with Hector that "God is unreservedly God-with-us," I think the idea of a volitional necessity collapses God's eternal being into his being for us and thus does not solve the problem he set out to solve.

Hector makes every effort to escape the errors that McCormack introduced by logically reversing the doctrines of election and the Trinity. But he seems unable to do so. So while he understands "the eternal *logos* as *incarnandus*," he also asserts that the *logos* cannot be understood as "'nothing but' *incarnandus*, since the Son could have been otherwise than *incarnandus* and since . . . the Son maintains the being he would have had apart from the covenant."[102] The problem embedded in this thinking is this: it is problematic to say that the Son maintains the being "he would have had apart from the covenant," because that suggests that he never really had a preexistent being in himself and thus apart from the covenant and apart from the incarnation. Why does Hector not say that the Son maintains the eternal relation with the Father that he had before the creation of the world and thus also before the covenant? Why can he not say, with Athanasius and with Torrance, that while God was always Father and always Son, he was not always creator and was not always incarnate? It seems the answer is that his own thinking will not allow him to assert a genuine eternal existence of the Son who actually did in fact exist otherwise than *incarnandus* as the eternally begotten Son within the immanent Trinity who freely chose to love us in his electing grace, without needing to. And the reason for this can be traced to his idea of a volitional necessity, which causes him to think both that "God has no being-in-Godself apart from the covenant" and that this implies that "his being-incarnate is nothing other than that which he has been from all eternity."[103] The obvious difficulty with this latter assertion is that if the Son has been incarnate from all eternity, then one cannot affirm, with Torrance and Barth, that while the Son was always the Son he was not in fact always incarnate. Such an idea

---

[102]Ibid., p. 76.
[103]Ibid., p. 75.

compromises both Jesus' full humanity and his full divinity. And the only way to avoid doing that, as I shall argue later in greater detail in the next chapter, is to acknowledge that the incarnation is something new even for God.

Having said this, however, it must be admitted that Hector seems to affirm the *Logos asarkos* in the proper sense when he says that this refers to "the Son's own-most relation to the Father, a relation which he would have enjoyed even if God had not determined to be with us, and which he continues to enjoy even in determining to be with us."[104] But there also seems to be a serious instability in his thought. On the one hand he quite properly and graciously acknowledges that his prior interpretation of what I had said in my previous book on the Trinity about this issue was mistaken. He thought I was espousing the idea that God not only could have been God without us but that "God *remains* God without us" so that "God remains isolated from election."[105] Here we both agree that election is a *determination* of the *triune* God for us but not an act that *constitutes* God's triunity. But, on the other hand, his idea of a volitional necessity problematically leads him to go on to say that "we should not accept Molnar's suggestion that 'when a theologian claims that creation or humanity are in *any sense* necessary to God, that claim is a sure sign that the true idea of contingence has been lost and a logical necessity has been introduced.'"[106] Rejecting this idea, Hector nevertheless thinks he has done justice to the spirit of my affirmation that "since God exists eternally as Father, Son and Holy Spirit and would so have existed even if he had never decided to create, save and redeem the world, his decision to be God for us could neither be deduced from his nature nor could it be seen as necessitated by any external constraints" so that he has avoided my "Hegelian scruples."[107]

Unfortunately, as I have already indicated, I am not so sure that he has avoided a Hegelian outcome, because his very idea of a volitional necessity causes just the problem I was seeking to avoid; it leads to statements that reduce God to what God does for us. This difficulty becomes especially clear when we see exactly how Hector attempts to defend McCormack's proposal against charges of subordinationism and from modalism, even though he

---

[104]Ibid., p. 77.
[105]Ibid.
[106]Ibid.
[107]Ibid., pp. 77-78.

properly acknowledges that McCormack's proposal is not compatible with Barth's position and thus "should not be understood as an elaboration of Barth" but should be understood as his own "novel contribution to contemporary trinitarianism."[108] Here I must admit that both Hector and McCormack have been misled by Barth himself to some extent with the element of subordinationism that was left over in his doctrine of the Trinity and with his own problematic introduction of a type of subordinationism into the immanent Trinity in his discussion of the Son's subordination and eternal obedience in *CD* IV/1. I will not treat that issue in detail in this chapter because I intend to address that in chapter seven by comparing what Torrance says about the Son's obedience with what Barth says about that in *CD* volume IV.

Here I would simply like to illustrate the problems embedded in Hector's defense of McCormack. Let us first address the issue of subordinationism. Hector notes that McCormack's proposal has been thought liable to this charge since he believes that the God who could have been God without us "would not necessarily be triune."[109] This idea could suggest that God might have been the Father without the Son and Spirit and thus that the Father alone would be God in the proper sense, and that would imply subordinationism and thus an undoing of trinitarian doctrine at its heart. Hector offers two reasons why he thinks McCormack's trinitarian contribution is not subordinationistic. It will be worthwhile to examine these reasons very carefully.

First, Hector notes that we must "distinguish subordination from subordinationism."[110] This assertion already is ambiguous since, without a clear distinction, without separation, of the immanent and economic Trinity, such an assertion will necessarily end in subordinationism. And sure enough Hector fails to make that distinction when he says that understanding the Son's eternal being from the economy of grace means that "one may conclude that the Son's dependence upon the Father—even for his very being—does not compromise the fullness of his divinity."[111] The results are catastrophic because he is led directly into several serious errors, the most important of which is that he concludes that the Son's being "is contingent upon the will

---

[108]Ibid., p. 78.
[109]Ibid.
[110]Ibid.
[111]Ibid., p. 79.

of the Father."[112] Yet, it is that very belief that was firmly rejected at Nicaea and by later theologians who accepted the teaching of Nicaea in the interest of affirming the *homoousion* of the Son with the Father from all eternity. If the Son's being is contingent on the Father's will, then and to that extent the Son would have to be conceptualized as needing to come into being, and then God's triunity would have been conceptualized as a result of God's decision to elect us. At this point we are right back into the heart of McCormack's trinitarian proposal, which, as noted at the beginning of this chapter, is extremely problematic! And the results here are disastrous. Instead of arguing that the Son is eternally begotten of the Father in the sense that the Father never existed and never could exist without the Son, Hector, following McCormack, maintains that "the Son's being is not necessary in the same way that the Father's is, but this would not entail that the Son is less divine."[113] Here it must be said very pointedly that if the Son's being is not necessary in the same way that the Father's is, then and to that extent his true oneness of being with the Father has been denied. What is the evidence for this assertion by Hector? This appears in Hector's second point.

He argues, "While McCormack's proposal may imply that the Son's being is not necessary in the way the Father's is, this does not necessarily entail that the Father could be the Father without the Son, since McCormack could claim that the (actual) Father's love for the Son *makes* the latter necessary."[114] Exactly as written here, this is the perfect assertion of Arian subordinationism![115] If the Son's being needs to be *made* necessary by the Father's actual love for the Son and is not eternally what it is as a *unity of being* between the Father and the Son in the unity of the Holy Spirit such that it does not need to be made necessary, we already have a Son who "once was not" necessary but had to and did become so! As seen above, this is exactly the thinking Athanasius rejected in rejecting the twin ideas that the Son exists by an act of the Father's will or by any necessity within or outside God. Things get even worse. We are told by Hector that "The Father could not be the Father without the Son . . . not because of some impersonal necessity imposed by the Son's being, but

---

[112]Ibid. See my discussion above about why Athanasius forcefully rejected this idea in his arguments against the Arians.

[113]Ibid.

[114]Ibid.

[115]See my discussion of Athanasius's position above.

because the Father loves the Son wholeheartedly and therefore *wills* not to be God in any other way than with him by his side."[116] The wording of this assertion is quite similar to McCormack's claim that election is the ground of God's triunity. And it is simply wrong from a trinitarian standpoint, because while the Son's being one with the Father is in no sense "impersonal," it is nevertheless necessary in the sense that God the Father never was without his Son and never could have existed without his Son, while both Father and Son did exist prior to the existence of human history and could have continued to do so but chose not to.

Here there is a confusion of the immanent and economic Trinity, and the result is indeed a form of subordinationism. Insofar as the Son is thought to exist as a consequence of the Father's will or the Father's love, his *homoousion* with the Father has been negated. There is no way around this. Hector thinks that by saying that "since the Father has never not loved the Son—just as he has never not loved us—so he has never been the Father without the Son and, in consequence of his love for the Son, *could* never have been the Father without the Son,"[117] he is upholding the Son's uniqueness within the immanent Trinity. But he has not done so, because he here equates the Son's eternal existence with the Father's love of us. This is the ultimate confusion of the immanent and economic Trinity that I consistently and forcefully opposed in my earlier book on the Trinity, because it is just here that Hector is unable to maintain what he himself insisted was crucial to affirm, namely, that God the Father, Son and Spirit could have been fully God without us but *freely* chose not to. Here, because God needs to give himself his being, that is, because the Father needs to give himself his being by willing (loving) the Son, he could never be without the Son only insofar as he wills to love us eternally along with the Son! So when Hector argues that McCormack could say that the Son's necessity "is a consequence not of his being, but of the Father's love,"[118] therein we have a fully embodied Arian position;[119] it undercuts the

---

[116]Hector, "Immutability, Necessity and Triunity," p. 79, emphasis mine.
[117]Ibid.
[118]Ibid.
[119]Athanasius saw this point with great clarity when he argued, "God is not as man; for men beget passibly, having a transitive nature, which waits for periods by reason of its weakness. But with God this cannot be; for He is not composed of parts, but being impassible and simple, He is impassibly and indivisibly Father of the Son" (*C. Ar.* I, 28). Athanasius continues by noting, "The Word is not begotten according to affection." And that is because his eternal generation

full divinity of each of the divine persons so that while each is fully divine, there are not on that account three Gods but only one God in three persons, and all subordination within the immanent Trinity is ruled out.[120] From the time of Nicaea it was crucial to assert the oneness in being of the Father and the Son in the eternal act of the Father's begetting the eternal Son. This act could not be confused with or made contingent on God's willed relations with us. But since McCormack's thinking does not operate apart from the idea that God's electing us is the ground of his triunity and God's triunity is the result of an act of will, this confusion becomes necessary and unequivocal. Hector's thinking clearly has not escaped from this difficulty. And, as already argued, I suspect that the reason for this is that he believes that God's relations with us can be understood properly by introducing a volitional necessity into the divine being in eternity. They cannot.[121]

---

from the Father was eternal and not the result of an act of will (C. Ar. I, 29).

[120]See, e.g., Torrance's statement, following Epiphanius, "There is no suggestion of any subordinationism in God, for whatever the Father is, this the Son is and this the Spirit is in the Godhead. . . . There never was when the Spirit was not" (Trinitarian Faith, p. 222). Further, Torrance insists, following Athanasius, that "there is a coinherent relation between the Holy Spirit and God the Son, just as there is a coinherent relation between the Son and the Father" (p. 233). Here of course Torrance objected to the idea that it was the first person of the Trinity who was the "sole Principle or Cause or Source of Deity," because this weakened Athanasius's view that "whatever we say of the Father we say of the Son and the Spirit except 'Father'" (p. 241). That is why one must say that each of the divine persons is fully God and Lord such that the divine monarchy resides in the being of God as one and three.

[121]Unfortunately, the idea that creation is in some sense necessary for God has become more and more attractive to a number of contemporary theologians. For example, Kevin Diller mistakenly considers that divine self-causation and divine self-determination are the same, in "Is God Necessarily Who God Is? Alternatives for the Trinity and Election Debate," SJT 66, no. 2 (2013): 209-20, p. 214. Following Barth, I have rejected the idea that God gives himself his own being in willing himself, and I have argued that God's self-determination in election is a determination freely willed by the triune God. Diller unfortunately equates election and triunity and so fails to maintain the fact that election is an eternally contingent act of the Trinity and is therefore not necessary to God. He writes, "Molnar argues that keeping the priority of election is necessary to maintain 'God's freedom to have existed from eternity without us'" (p. 215). Given the context, I suspect he meant to say that I argue that keeping the priority of triunity is important so that one could see that election is not necessary for God to be God. Still, aside from many problematic assertions, I simply note two that are important here: (1) Diller thinks election and triunity are mutually necessary so that "in a sense" one could say they are "grounded in each other" (p. 215) so that one could also say that they are "mutually dependent" (p. 218). Such a view does not escape the problem of making God's triunity dependent on his election of us. Saying that "Election is simply part of who God is" solves nothing and only makes matters worse. (2) Following distinctions he finds in Aristotle, Diller notes that McCormack's position seems to imply that creation is in some sense necessary. And he proceeds to argue that in some sense creation is indeed necessary to God, that is, it is a "necessary consequent of God's being" (p. 216). This leads him to think that God's love is "more significant or more at the heart

Hector offers a final point of defense: those who favor Barth's proposal, as he understands it, are no better off than McCormack. Once again, the confusion of the immanent and economic Trinity is in evidence. First, he says that Barthians claim that God does not change in electing to be God for us; second, he claims that God's election of us means that the Father freely decides to do so and the Son accepts "this determination as determining his very being"; and third, "God's antecedent triunity must be characterised by a free decision of the Father which determines the very being of the Son."[122] Here we have a major problem, because God's determination to be God for us is indeed a self-determination. But for Barth, it is not a determination in the sense that in this act God gives himself his eternal triunity, while for McCormack that is exactly what it is. Crucially, when Barth speaks of Jesus Christ in this connection he is referring to the Son of God "in His whole giving of Himself to the Son of Man, and the Son of Man in his utter oneness with the Son of God" as the realization of the decree which is the "very first thing" done in the resolve of God "which precedes the existence, the possibility and the reality of all His creatures" (II/2, p. 157). Here the Son is not the result of an eternal decision of the Father; rather God eternally exists in the act of being Father, Son and Holy Spirit, which does of course involve his decision. Yet, God is not the result of his decision, as noted above, because that is the error of those who believe God takes his origin from himself. Furthermore, God's eternal triune act also includes God's decisions, but the decision of God to act *ad extra* is eternally contingent, while the decision to affirm his own eternal existence is eternally necessary in the sense that God could not will not to be the Father of the Son since God cannot come into conflict with himself. The upshot of all this is that the distinction between

---

of who God is than the fact that God is uncreated and almighty" (pp. 218-19). Yet, since God is One who loves in freedom, any view that prioritizes love over freedom or freedom over love has missed the truth of who God is. See my discussion of Robert B. Price's view above, note 84. Beyond this, I think Barth's statement that "what can need existence, is not God Himself, or His reality, but the reality which is distinct from Himself" (II/1, p. 306) is decisive here. There is no sense in which God needs us. Any such idea is at variance with the fact that all God's relations with us are acts of free grace. Walter Kasper states this quite clearly: "If God needs the world in order to be able to be the one God, then he is not really God at all. The transcendence and freedom of God are perceived only if the world is not necessary for God to be himself" (*The God of Jesus Christ*, trans. Matthew J. O'Connell [New York: Crossroad, 1986], p. 294, citing Gregory of Nazianzus).

[122]Hector, "Immutability, Necessity and Triunity," pp. 79-80.

subordination and subordinationism is spurious—the subordination advanced here is nothing but subordinationism in modern guise.

Hector's defense of McCormack against the charge of modalism is no more successful than his attempted defense of McCormack against the charge of subordinationism. Hector begins his defense with respect to modalism by "assuming that subordinationism is no longer an issue."[123] While I have indicated why I think it still is an issue, it is worth listening to his views on modalism just the same. He says, "McCormack could claim that the God who elects to be with us, and so triunes Godself, is in fact the Father, and thereby acquit himself of the suspicion that the electing God is a 'fourth' behind the three hypostases."[124] That is the question. Can McCormack actually make this problematic assertion while avoiding both subordinationism and modalism? I have already indicated why I think his thinking cannot and does not avoid subordinationism. Here I will let Hector's own conclusion demonstrate why I think he does not escape from modalism, either. Hector writes, "While McCormack would still be unable in principle to say anything about what God would have been like if God had not elected to be God with us, he can say, unequivocally, that the actual God is wholeheartedly committed to us and has thus ruled out any other way of being God."[125] This assertion is seriously problematic simply because any statement that, in principle, one could not say anything about what God would have been like without election necessarily introduces the specter of an unknown God behind the being of the eternal Trinity. Such an assertion in reality denies the very idea that Hector's article was meant to uphold, namely, that God would have been the one and only triune God even if he never decided to relate with us. That is the issue that is at stake in claiming that God "triunes" himself in electing to be God for us. So while Hector thinks that McCormack's position can be acquitted of both subordinationism and modalism, his own conclusions demonstrate exactly the opposite. Moreover, as we shall see in chapter five, McCormack's Christology seems to open the door to a kind of modalism as well, since he believes that "The second 'person' of the Trinity is the God-man. So even in the act of hypostatic

[123]Ibid., p. 80.
[124]Ibid.
[125]Ibid.

uniting, the 'subject' who performs that action is the God-man, Jesus Christ in his divine-human unity."[126] Yet, Karl Barth astutely noted, "We must distinguish between God as such and God in His purpose (decree). From eternity the Son (as God *and man*) exists in God. But until the incarnation this has not happened. Nevertheless, this must be made clear; otherwise you have a fourth member of the Trinity."[127]

Hector's attempt to defend the "orthodoxy" of McCormack's position must be deemed a failure in light of his own stated position. Hector laments the fact that McCormack's proposal "has been subjected to endless critique."[128] Here I can only suggest that there may be some good theological reasons for that endless critique. Indeed, while Hector himself now realizes quite properly that McCormack's attempt to ground his proposal in the theology of Karl Barth is mistaken, he nonetheless demonstrates that his own thinking about God for us is in the grip of an untheological understanding of God in himself to the extent that he implicitly supposes that there is a right way to say a wrong thing. That is, he believes one could say, with McCormack, that God "triunes" himself in electing us and that one could also say there is no other being of God than God for us. I have explained in detail why I think both of those statements are problematic—the former statement undermines the eternal triune being of the three persons, while the latter reduces God's eternal triunity to his actions for us. Still, I do believe there is no gap between God in himself and God for us, because the God who eternally exists as Father, Son and Holy Spirit and thus as the one who loves in freedom is the very same God who meets us in revelation and in his reconciling activity for us in created history. To put it another way, I would say that what God is toward us he is eternally in himself. But that statement cannot be taken to mean that God in himself has now ceased to exist since God only exists for us. That is the problem that arises when it is thought that God can or does give himself his eternal triunity in an act that aims toward us. Before drawing this chapter to a close and before addressing the very thorny issue of whether there can be a before and after in God in the next chapter as it relates to election, let us discuss two other proposals in order to make clear exactly what I am affirming theologically and what I am rejecting.

---

[126]See below, p. 254.
[127]Godsey, *Table Talk,* p. 52.
[128]Ibid.

UNDERSTANDING GOD'S FREEDOM AND LOVE

Like Kevin Hector, Paul Dafydd Jones clearly and quite rightly opposes the idea that election constitutes God's triunity, as when he writes, "It would certainly be wrong to claim that 'God's pretemporal decision of election actually gave rise to the Trinity' or that 'The Holy Trinity is a function of God's pretemporal decision of election'"[129] since, as he again rightly argues, God's elective action is not required for God to be triune inasmuch as "God does not stand under obligations of this kind."[130] Nevertheless, his thinking is inspired by the basic moves made by McCormack in his actualistic reduction of the immanent to the economic Trinity, and to that extent he is conceptually unable to maintain the sense of his initial insight, namely, that "the Son's self-determination has its ground in the divine being who is complete in himself—'before' the incarnation." Hence, he concludes incorrectly that "God's triunity is distinguished, reaffirmed—perhaps even *intensified*—given the Son's self-determination to become and be the 'electing God' and 'elected human.'"[131] Jones recognizes that this is a "risky" statement that "stands at the farthest edges of interpretative propriety,"[132] and yet his thought is driven in that direction when he again rejects McCormack's claim "that election has logical priority over divine triunity" but grants "that the eternal identity of the Son encompasses and, in a sense, is *constituted* by the concrete life of Jesus Christ."[133]

Here the error embedded in McCormack's thinking continues to shape the thinking of Paul Jones in spite of his attempts to extricate himself from the idea that God needs the incarnation to be the God he eternally is. Jones wants to modify Barth's statement that the "Word is what he is even before and apart from his being flesh," made in I/2,[134] in light of Barth's later Christology. He thus suggests, against Hunsinger's belief that the "Son *qua* Son is *properly* defined without reference to his being *incarnandus*" and against his

---

[129]Paul Dafydd Jones, "Obedience, Trinity, and Election: Thinking with and Beyond the *Church Dogmatics*," in *Trinity and Election in Contemporary Theology*, p. 153.

[130]Ibid.

[131]Ibid., pp. 153-54. See Christopher R. J. Holmes, "The Person and Work of Christ Revisited: In Conversation with Karl Barth," *Anglican Theological Review* 95, no. 1 (2013): 37-55, p. 47, where Holmes writes, "We must not say with Jones that 'God's action *ad extra* has ramifications for God's immanent being.'" Holmes sees the positive intentions of Jones but rightly questions the thinking that suggests that God is in some way transformed by virtue of the incarnation.

[132]Ibid., p. 154.

[133]Ibld., p. 155, emphasis mine.

[134]Ibid., p. 152, citing I/2, p. 136.

wish to distinguish the "*Logos,* the *Logos incarnandus,* and the *Logos incar-natus*" that "the Son's becoming human has ontological ramifications for God. . . . God's elective self-determination bears back on God's eternal being."[135] So it turns out that, although Jones makes every effort to recognize and to maintain God's internal and external freedom as the one who loves, he is conceptually unable to do so consistently precisely because he mistakenly argues that "the incarnation, as an elective event of divine self-transformation, *intensifies* God's triune self-differentiation."[136] And this leads him into the misguided idea that we should think of the Son's life "in terms of a beginning, a middle, and an end that, in a mysterious way, bears back on God's being."[137] At this point I think it is important to regard Barth's statement that "Jesus Christ has a beginning, but God has no beginning" (II/2, p. 102) as decisive because it is precisely in that statement that the distinction advocated by Hunsinger implies a distinction without separation of the immanent and economic Trinity.

As we shall see at the end of this chapter, it is precisely because Mc-Cormack rejects that statement by Barth that he is then led to conclude that God "must give himself his being eternally in the act in which he sets himself in relationship to Jesus Christ and, in him, to the world" so that in that way there is "no metaphysical gap between God's being and his acting."[138] This

---

[135]Ibid. It should be noted here that it is exactly this wish that led Jürgen Moltmann to move beyond Rahner's axiom of identity to insist that "'the economic Trinity *is* the immanent Trinity, and vice versa.' . . . The thesis about the fundamental *identity* of the immanent and the economic Trinity of course remains open to misunderstanding as long as we cling to the distinction at all. . . . The economic Trinity not only reveals the immanent Trinity; it also has a retroactive effect on it" (Jürgen Moltmann, *The Trinity and the Kingdom, the Doctrine of God,* trans. Margaret Kohl [New York: Harper & Row, 1981], p. 151). It is this mutual conditioning that follows from the failure to distinguish the *Logos* as Hunsinger has suggested we must.
[136]Paul Daffyd Jones, *The Humanity of Christ: Christology in Karl Barth's Church Dogmatics* (New York: T & T Clark, 2008), p. 212.
[137]Jones, "Obedience, Trinity, and Election," p. 146.
[138]McCormack, "Trinity and Election," p. 135. This whole idea that Barth opened a metaphysical gap between the immanent and economic Trinity earlier in the *Church Dogmatics* that needed to be closed is a ruse invented by those who confuse and reverse the actions of the immanent and economic Trinity. Thus, e.g., Alan Lewis argues that Barth "illogically" drove a wedge between the economic and immanent Trinity when he maintained that God could have remained satisfied with his own eternal glory but chose not to (Alan E. Lewis, *Between Cross and Resurrection: A Theology of Holy Saturday* [Grand Rapids: Eerdmans, 2001], pp. 209-14). Lewis proceeds to argue that God needs the world, that God's nature needs perfecting, and that God could not have done anything other than what he did in Jesus, pp. 253, 210, 212-14. See Molnar, *Divine Freedom,* pp. 270-71, for more on this. See also David Lauber, *Barth on the Descent into*

is the idea that Jones wishes to advance without accepting McCormack's notion that God's triunity is constituted by his electing us; but as clearly seen, in Jones's ideas that the Son has a beginning, that the Son is transformed in the incarnation, and that God's triunity is intensified in his relations with us, he is clearly unable to distinguish consistently, without separating, God's internal and external actions. That is the problem that always follows from rejecting Barth's important recognition that God could have been God without us but freely chose not to. In this book, therefore, while the emphasis is on the working of God in the economy in his Word and Spirit, I am contending that it is always important to realize that God's being for us is in no way defined by, intensified by or limited by what he does for us in the economy. And it is for that very reason that we can speak forcefully about divine and human freedom in light of reconciliation and redemption.

It is crucial to realize at this juncture that a distinction between God's internal and external relations must be made. God's eternal Sonship is not "transformed" in his determination to be God for us in the incarnation, and then in his actually becoming incarnate and reconciling the world to himself in the life history of Jesus of Nazareth. Barth rejected this very notion, and it certainly was rejected by Athanasius and others in the patristic era. The Word was not transformed in the incarnation but became man in Jesus Christ without ceasing to be God in order to exist as the one Mediator between the Father and us. Barth's insistence on the distinction without separation of the immanent and economic Trinity was meant precisely to avoid the idea that God's own eternal being was intensified or transformed in the incarnation.[139] And it is just his

---

Hell: God, Atonement and the Christian Life (Aldershot, UK: Ashgate, 2004), for an interesting critique of Alan Lewis's thinking. The truth of the matter is that Barth distinguishes God's being and act within the immanent Trinity and in the economic Trinity so that God's eternal act of being Father, Son and Spirit simply cannot be reduced to God's actions and works *ad extra*. It should be noted that this distinction is missing even from what McCormack says here. That affects one's view of time and eternity and of election and triunity.

[139]While Jones admits that Barth's earlier understanding of kenosis, as the Son joining human nature to his divine being, is present in IV/1, he also claims that in IV/1 Barth argues that "God wills that the incarnation should prove ontologically transformative for the divine Son" (Jones, *Humanity of Christ*, p. 214). And even his citation from Barth's *Church Dogmatics* at that point in his argument does not seem to support his contention as Barth says of kenosis that this "does not mean that God ceases to be himself as human, but rather that God takes it upon himself to be something quite other . . . than that which corresponds and befits his divine form, his coequality with God" (IV/1, p. 180). Since Barth is here speaking of the incarnate Word and of the fact that his life lived for us is in reality God's action for us from the divine and human side,

continued belief that God did not need the incarnation for the Son's being to be actual that underscores this point (IV/2, p. 113).[140] This belief also underwrites our human freedom. Take away the Son's eternal freedom with the idea that God's being is "transformed" in the incarnation, and the *mystery* of revelation and reconciliation is undermined, and these divine actions, which establish and maintain our human freedom as reconciled sinners, can no longer be seen as free acts of grace. Whenever Jesus' human history is erroneously thought to constitute his being as the eternal Son, there can be no doubt that God's actions *ad extra* on our behalf as the one who loves in freedom have been reduced to his actions *ad extra*. This was the key problem I sought to address in my first book on the Trinity. And, although this issue has now taken the form of a discussion of the relationship between election and God's triunity, the fundamental problem remains the same.

Before closing this chapter and moving on to a discussion of how a proper understanding of the relationship between time and eternity might help resolve the issues we have been discussing, I think it might be helpful to explore very briefly one other proposal that has been offered in order to demonstrate one final time that whenever the logic embedded in the proposal to logically reverse election and triunity is at work, God's eternal being is made to be dependent on and thus to that extent reduced to what God does *ad extra*. Paul T. Nimmo believes that consideration of the Holy Spirit and of pneumatology have not received their proper due in this discussion. Seemingly uncommitted to what he calls a "strong" rather than a "weak" reading of Barth's view of this matter, the former referring to the opinion that Barth's thinking changed with II/2 and the latter referring to the belief that Barth continued to believe that the Trinity must precede election,[141] Nimmo immediately proceeds to endorse a "strong reading" of Barth, claiming, "In a primal, eternal act, God determines and disposes over not only the being of the covenant partner, but also the very essence of God itself."[142] We are told that, while

---

Barth is not suggesting that the Son is transformed in the incarnation but rather that the incarnate Word now exists as God and human for all eternity and thus is the one Mediator. See also IV/1, pp. 135-37.

[140]See the discussion above, pp. 133, 156, 295.

[141]See Paul T. Nimmo, "Barth and the Election-Trinity Debate: A Pneumatological View," in Dempsey, *Trinity and Election in Contemporary Theology*, p. 163.

[142]Ibid., p. 165.

Barth was not always consistent in affirming God's "self-constitution" in the act of election, nonetheless, based on two quotations, Nimmo must embrace the "strong reading." When, however, both quotations are read in context, they clearly refer, as Barth himself insists, to God's "primal decision" not to "remain satisfied with His own being in Himself" but to reach out "to something beyond, willing something more than His own being. He willed and posited the beginning of all things with Himself" (II/2, p. 168). Barth goes on to say that "Our starting-point must always be that in all His willing and choosing what God ultimately wills is Himself. All God's willing is primarily a determination of the love of the Father and the Son in the fellowship of the Holy Ghost" (II/2, p. 169). Hence, in willing something other than himself as the beginning of his ways and works *ad extra*, the content of that love cannot be anything other than something that is good and glorious, "a glory which is *new* and *distinctive* and *divine*" (II/2, p. 169, emphasis mine). Then he says that in God's "primal decision," which in Barth's thinking definitely refers to the beginning of his ways and works *ad extra*,

> God does not choose only Himself. In this choice of self He also chooses another, that other which is man. Man is the outward cause and object of this overflowing of the divine glory. God's goodness and favour are directed towards him. In this movement God has not chosen and willed a second god side by side with Himself, but a being distinct from Himself. (II/2, p. 169)

Note clearly that Barth never says God's triunity is constituted in his eternal election of us in this context. What he does say is that God *also* chooses us, and he clearly suggests that this is something new even as an eternal act of the triune God. So when Barth also says, "The deity of God, the divinity of His love and freedom, being confirmed and demonstrated by this offering of the Father and this self-offering of the Son [in the covenant]" he can also say,

> This choice was in the beginning. As the subject and object of this choice, Jesus Christ was at the beginning. But He was not at the beginning of God, for God has indeed no beginning. But he was at the beginning of all things, at the beginning of God's dealings with the reality which is distinct from Himself. (II/2, pp. 101-2)

It is not surprising, then, that Nimmo writes, "The election of God to be for humanity in Jesus Christ is eternal, an event that, Barth writes, 'precedes absolutely all other being and happening' (II/2, p. 99)."[143] Stating the matter this way not only leaves out Barth's crucial qualification that nothing precedes his eternal triune being, but it fails to note that Barth here once again is speaking about the beginning of God's ways and works *ad extra*, which is grounded in his eternal being and action as triune. He is saying that all God's works both internal and external depend on God's election. Election therefore "precedes absolutely all other being and happening" (II/2, p. 99). But this "all other being and happening" very clearly refers to the being and happening of all that is other than God. It does not refer to God's "self-constitution," as Nimmo mistakenly thinks.

Whatever the merits of focusing on the Spirit as Nimmo suggests—and there are some very good and important points that he makes—the fact remains that his thinking is still encumbered by a mindset that refuses to acknowledge that God's eternal act of election is a free, new action of God to do something that he had never done before, that is, to create, reconcile and redeem the human race and to do so in and through Jesus Christ. That is why Barth famously rejected the *decretum absolutum*. He did not want to detach God's love for us from Jesus Christ himself, who is God acting from the divine and human side as the Judge judged in our place, and therefore as the one who graciously elevates us into fellowship with himself.

A number of strange conclusions follow. First, Nimmo asks: "Can there be, for Barth, in any sense an existence of the Spirit that does not have the existence of the community of God in view?"[144] Second, while he then cites a number of texts that support the "weak reading," he insists that at crucial moments Barth's theology "seems to point in an altogether different direction" and that is to the idea that

> once obedience in a second mode of being of God is seen as being *both* the fulfillment of a decree and essential to the being of God, then the being of God itself in its Trinitarian modes of being is posited as being determined by the decree of election in which it is determined what God will be in time. In other words, election logically precedes the Trinity: the eternal act of election as an act of self-determination is primal and there is no triunity behind or without it.[145]

---

[143]Ibid.
[144]Ibid., p. 172.
[145]Ibid., p. 173.

A careful reading of what is said here reveals exactly the confusion of the immanent and economic Trinity that Barth sought to avoid even in *CD* volume IV. Barth never holds that the existence of God in his second mode of being as the Son was the *result* of his eternal decree to be God for us without exception; if he had, he never could have asserted, even in volume IV, that the *Logos asarkos* was necessary in order to assert God's freedom in his actions *ad extra* in connection with the doctrines of the Trinity and of Christology (IV/1, p. 52). It is a mistake to think that the Son's eternal relation to the Father could or should be seen as the fulfillment of the divine decree. What is fulfilled in the divine decree is the obedient condescension of the Son, in obedience to the Father, as God humiliating himself on our behalf in the incarnation, death and resurrection of Jesus Christ. What God is eternally in himself is the eternal Father, Son and Holy Spirit who could have been God without us but freely chose not to. Moreover, it is imperative to hold, with Athanasius, that while God was always Father he was not always creator, and that while God was always the Son he was not always incarnate. Hence, creation and incarnation were new acts, new even for God. Consequently, what God is in time does not define who God is in eternity, even by way of anticipation. Rather, what God does in time, even by way of anticipation, falls within the life of the eternal Trinity, but not in such a way that elements of the economy are indiscriminately read back into the immanent Trinity. In other words, one cannot confuse the order of the persons of the Trinity with their eternal being. Furthermore, Nimmo's question about whether there could be "an existence of the Spirit that does not have the existence of the community of God in view" seems to imply that there would be no Holy Spirit without the community since the Spirit might seemingly not exist without having the community in view. This is surely not Barth's view of the Spirit.

I will not discuss Barth's belief that "it belongs to the inner life of God that there should take place within it obedience" (IV/1, pp. 200-201) in detail here, because I will devote chapter seven to this issue by comparing the thought of Torrance and Barth on this very theme. It will suffice here to point out that Barth's intention was to avoid any notion that what God did in humbling himself for us in the incarnation was an arbitrary act. It was instead an act of loving condescension that took place in accordance with his primal decision to be God for us in Jesus Christ. Hence, I do not believe

Barth intended to reverse logically the doctrines of election and the Trinity. Barth never says or even suggests that "election logically precedes the Trinity," even in IV/1 when he speaks of a *prius* and a *posterius*, a super and subordination, and obedience in God. What I believe he intended to say was that the events that occurred in the economy fell within the eternal being of God himself and could not be held apart from God's being. But as we shall see later, I do believe that Barth incorrectly read back elements of the economy into the immanent Trinity, causing much of the confusion here, such as the idea that God's second mode of being resulted from his electing us and that God's self-determination for us is the fulfillment of the divine subordination.

A third strange conclusion is offered by Nimmo. He believes that "as the eternal determination to incarnation is part of the determination of the eternal being of the Son, so the mediating activity of the Spirit in time between Jesus Christ and the community of God is part of the eternal determination of the Spirit."[146] Therefore, "the temporal events of the covenant of grace in which the Spirit mediates between the Son and the community that is elect in him are *as fundamental to the being in action of the Spirit* as the mediating activity between the Father and the Son in the eternal life of the Trinity."[147] The only way that this could be a true statement is if the immanent Trinity is confused with the economic Trinity! The Holy Spirit is the Spirit of the Father and of the Son in eternity, that is, antecedently in God himself, and simply cannot be reduced to what the Spirit does in the covenant of grace, as implied in this remark. Indeed, when Nimmo claims that "for Barth, the Trinitarian self-determination of God is a consequence of the primal divine decision of election,"[148] this suggests once again that God would not and could not exist as triune without electing us.

Things get even more problematic when Nimmo develops his constructive proposals regarding the Spirit. Without acknowledging that Barth also insisted that the *Logos asarkos* had an important role in the construction of the doctrine of the Trinity and of Christology (IV/1, p. 52), Nimmo simply claims Barth rejects the concept and then concludes that "one could say that the Spirit without reference to the temporal activity of mediation between

---

[146]Ibid., pp. 174-75.
[147]Ibid., p. 175, emphasis mine.
[148]Ibid., p. 177.

Jesus Christ and the community can only ever be a conceptual placeholder."[149]
Such a statement is tantamount to implying that the Spirit has no antecedent
eternal existence of his own in relation to the Father and Son! This stands
opposed to Barth's statement that

> the reality of God which encounters us in His revelation is His reality in all
> the depths of eternity. . . . In connexion with the specific doctrine of the Holy
> Spirit this means that He is the Spirit of both the Father and the Son not just
> in His work *ad extra* and upon us, but that to all eternity—no limit or reser-
> vation is possible here—He is none other than the Spirit of both the Father
> and the Son. "And the Son" means that not merely for us, but in God Himself,
> there is no possibility of an opening and readiness and capacity for God in
> man—for this is the work of the Holy Ghost in revelation—unless it come
> from Him, the Father, who has revealed Himself in His Word, in Jesus Christ,
> and also, and no less necessarily, from Him who is His Word, Jesus Christ,
> who reveals the Father. (I/1, pp. 479-80)

For Barth it was crucial to hold that

> The Holy Spirit does not first become the Holy Spirit, the Spirit of God, in the
> event of revelation. The event of revelation has clarity and reality on its sub-
> jective side because the Holy Spirit, the subjective element in this event, is of
> the essence of God Himself. What He is in revelation He is antecedently in
> Himself. And what He is antecedently in Himself He is in revelation. (I/1, p. 466)

Indeed, "Within the deepest depths of deity, as the final thing to be said
about Him, God is God the Spirit as he is God the Father and God the Son"
(I/I, p. 466). Finally, Barth insists that God the Spirit

> is "antecedently in Himself" the act of communion, the act of impartation,
> love, gift. For this reason and in this way and on this basis He is so in His
> revelation. Not *vice versa*! We know Him thus in his revelation. But he is not
> this because He is it in His revelation; because He is it antecedently in Himself,
> He is it also in His revelation. (I/1, pp. 470-71)

Take away or weaken the "antecedently in Himself," and the Lordship of the
Holy Spirit is lost. What is also lost is the distinction between the Holy Spirit
and the human spirit such that once that happens it is no longer possible to

---

[149]Ibid., p. 178.

distinguish God's actions enabling us to participate in God's own knowledge and love from our own. That is the end of theology!

Barth certainly never retracted any of these statements and does not even imply that the antecedent existence of the Spirit is only a "placeholder" for what he says in the doctrine of reconciliation. Had he done so, he would have reduced God's eternal existence as Father, Son and Spirit to a conceptual placeholder for his descriptions of what God was supposedly doing in history. He never did that and never could without coming into conflict with his own understanding of God's love and freedom. In any case Nimmo proceeds to draw the unfortunate conclusions that follow when one reverses who God is in himself with who God is for us. He claims that "there is simply no third person of the Trinity *in abstracto*, no Spirit to be considered either in time or in eternity without the mediating activity between Jesus Christ and the community of God in view."[150] He repeats once again that the idea of a Spirit "without the community of God, a third person of the Trinity 'as such' can only be a conceptual placeholder and cannot be the subject of independent inquiry."[151] In the end Nimmo claims he is following Barth, when in his Christology, Barth insists that "the concept of Jesus' true humanity is therefore primarily and finally basic—an absolutely necessary concept—in exactly the same and not a lesser sense than that of His true deity."[152] Thus Nimmo thinks that this should mean that the "actualistic enchurchment of the Spirit might also be considered primarily and finally basic to the ontology of that Spirit."[153]

What he fails to note, however, is that for Barth, Jesus' humanity was absolutely necessary in virtue of the incarnation. It was not necessary in the sense that God needed that humanity in order to be God. Therein lies the difference of emphasis one will have whenever one fails to distinguish without separating the immanent and economic Trinity. Any claim that "enchurchment" is basic to the "ontology of the Spirit" has to suggest that the Spirit cannot really be the Lord and giver of life, because he is the Spirit of the Father and Son in eternity, one in being with God, as the church is not.

---

[150]Ibid.
[151]Ibid.
[152]Ibid., citing IV/2, p. 35.
[153]Ibid.

In light of God's grace we can and must say that God does not will to be without us; but that hardly means that the church defines the ontology of the Spirit any more than Jesus' humanity makes Jesus to be the eternal Son of the Father in eternity! We have now come full circle from the point where Ben Myers did indeed argue that Jesus makes God to be God to the much more sophisticated and nuanced presentations of Kevin Hector, Paul Dafydd Jones and Paul Nimmo. What I have tried to show is that whenever theologians think they can or must embrace the train of thought that follows from assuming that we can or should logically reverse the doctrines of election and of the Trinity, God's being *in se* inevitably is reduced to God's actions *ad extra*, and in some measure what we then have is a dependent deity; a deity whose very being is constituted, shaped or transformed by created history. But a dependent deity is truly incapable of acting decisively for us in history as the living God actually does. That is why I continue to reject this sort of thinking as I develop this new work with a view toward seeing what God is up to in the economy of salvation and thus as the Lord of the covenant of grace.

4

Origenism, Election,
and Time and Eternity

At this point it would be helpful to point out that much of the difficulty surrounding the issues discussed in the last chapter centers on how to relate God's external and internal activities and on the proper understanding of the relationship between time and eternity. Following Thomas F. Torrance and Karl Barth, I have argued that there is and must be a priority of the Father/Son relation over the creator/creature relation because what God is toward us he is eternally in himself; and in his sovereign actions of love for us in his Word and Spirit, the eternal generation of the Son and the procession of the Spirit cannot be confused with God's actions as creator, reconciler and redeemer. The ultimate indications of such a confusion would be any idea that the eternal generation of the Son and the eternal procession of the Spirit might be seen as the result of an act of will on God's part. God freely willed to relate with us by creating us, reconciling us and redeeming us. But these actions are an overflow of his eternal love and glory, not in any emanationist sense, but as acts of will expressing God's superabundance rather than any lack; thus they are not in any sense necessary to God. They are, as Torrance often said, acts of amazing grace.[1]

Importantly, then, any idea that what God is toward us is in any sense *constitutive* of God's eternal being as Father, Son and Holy Spirit would be a clear indication of the Origenist confusion of God's internal and external

---

[1]See, e.g., *Incarnation*, pp. 227-28.

relations. This is why, following Torrance especially, I have stressed that while God was eternally the Father he was not always creator, and that while God was always the Son he was not always incarnate.[2] Hence, creation and incarnation must be seen as *new* actions, *new* even for God. There is a delicate balance that is required here because once the incarnation has taken place, it is impossible to disjoin Christ's divinity and humanity; from then on he lives as the incarnate Word, and now he lives as the risen and ascended Lord of history and interacts with us as the eternal high priest and as the Mediator in both his human and divine natures in virtue of the hypostatic union. It is just at this point in Christology where it is imperative, however, that one distinguish between God's internal and external relations. Without this distinction the eternal being of the Son will be thought to be changed or *constituted* in some sense by his human history. Yet, his human history is the history of God acting for us in the world as the reconciler without ceasing to be the Word through whom God created the world and through whom God continues to uphold it in the power of his eternal Spirit. We have already seen that Athanasius insisted on the importance of this point by rejecting any idea that the Word came to exist by an act of will on the part of the Father.

Everything here depends on a proper dynamic understanding of the hypostatic union. As Torrance insists, Jesus' humanity is no mere instrument through which God works among us; his humanity has its existence in and through the Word who acts *as* man. Therefore his humanity is his free human existence, which develops from his birth and throughout his life of obedience in its true freedom and in its sinlessness precisely because it is the humanity of the Word. There can be no separation of his divinity from his humanity. But that cannot mean that his humanity can be thought to

---

[2]Torrance himself makes this connection explicitly by identifying process theology as a type of thinking that mistakenly supposes that "the external relations of God are held in some measure to be constitutive of what he is as God" (*Christian Doctrine of God*, p. 208). He links the basic error here to Origen and his inability to distinguish the eternal generation of the Son from creation and incarnation. Torrance then asserts Athanasius's insight that "God is always Father, but he is not always Creator, for in his creative activity God has to do with what is 'external' to his Being, freely giving existence to what did not exist before, and sustaining it by his will and grace" (p. 208). From this it follows that creation is something new even for God, and that incarnation and the outpouring of the Spirit are similarly new even for God, and that "His almighty power and freedom are not exhausted in what he has done, does do, and will do" (p. 209). All of this, Torrance says, means that there is "a 'before' and 'after' in God's activity, which calls for a consideration of the unique nature of 'time' in the eternal Life of God" (p. 209).

transform his divinity. That thinking, once again, would reintroduce the Origenist error and miss the fact that, without ceasing to be the eternal Son who remains impassible, he becomes incarnate and is affected by our pain and suffering out of love for us.[3] But he is this in such a way that through it all he brings to bear his divine power on our sinful flesh in order to overcome sin, suffering, evil and death as is manifest in his resurrection from the dead. Of course God does not change essentially in the incarnation, because in every new action God eternally remains who he ever was as Father, Son and Holy Spirit. The question of whether God changes in the incarnation becomes a fundamental issue for those who think that God's self-determination to be God for us has to mean that in that action for us God gave himself his eternal being as Father, Son and Spirit. With that assertion one could only hold that the divine being does not change in history only because what God does in history he already was and is from all eternity by virtue of having given himself his being in order to relate with us. This thinking is perhaps the most sophisticated version of Origenism available today. But, as I have already argued at length and will argue further in the next chapter, it is just this thinking that supposes that in determining to be God for us, God does indeed change in the sense that God might not have been triune without us but only became so in electing to be God for us. All the differences between my understanding of the Trinity and that of those who embrace this other thinking are traceable to this.

In this connection Bruce McCormack of course is attempting to do justice to what he sees as Barth's having made suffering and death essential to God.[4] But even this is a problematic assertion because Barth does not

---

[3]Torrance flatly rejects the Greek ideas of immutability and impassibility. These conceptions envision a God "as too exalted to act so as to himself descend in utter humiliation in order to save us in such a way that what he did really affected him, or meant anything at all for himself. God was, so to speak, a prisoner of his own immutability, and his own impassibility" (*Incarnation*, p. 227). But Torrance insists that God is both immutable and impassible in the sense that in suffering our judgment for us he maintained his "sovereign freedom and initiative, even when he gave himself up to the death of the cross" (p. 227). That was an act of self-giving, an act of grace on his part. Hence, for Torrance, God could be both immutable and impassible by exercising his sovereign faithfulness to us in his gracious love by being the Judge judged in our place. But he certainly can be affected by our afflictions in such a way that he could exercise his mercy by loving us more than he loves himself (*Christian Doctrine of God*, p. 244).

[4]Bruce L. McCormack, "The Doctrine of the Trinity After Barth: An Attempt to Reconstruct Barth's Doctrine in the Light of His Later Christology," in *Trinitarian Theology After Barth*, ed. Myk Habets and Phillip Tolliday (Eugene, OR: Pickwick, 2011), p. 105.

simply make suffering and death "essential" to God. Rather he sees them as features that are not his own, features that God takes to himself in the suffering and death of Jesus, in order to overcome them for us.

> It is not at all the case that God has no part in the suffering of Jesus Christ even in His mode of being as the Father. No, there is a *particula veri* in the teaching of the early Patripassians. This is that primarily it is God the Father who suffers in the offering and sending of His Son, in His abasement. The suffering is not His own, but the alien suffering of the creature, of man, which He takes to Himself in Him. But He does suffer it in the humiliation of His Son with a depth with which it never was or will be suffered by any man— apart from the One who is His Son. And He does so in order that, having been borne by Him in the offering and sending of His Son, it should not have to be suffered in this way by man. This fatherly fellow-suffering of God is the mystery, the basis, of the humiliation of His Son; the truth of that which takes place historically in His crucifixion. (IV/2, p. 357)

The real difficulty here is one that arises from failure to respect the mystery of the inner trinitarian relations *as* mystery. We simply cannot explain *how* God can be three persons, one being, or *how* God can be eternally the one who loves and could love without us but freely chose not to. Here, as Torrance says more than once, following Athanasius, "Thus far human knowledge goes. Here the cherubim spread the covering of their wings."[5] It is just at this point that McCormack's move to logically reverse the doctrines of election and the Trinity is very problematic. It leads him to assert that

> The act in which God determines himself essentially is *election*. If then this act is primordial, then election is primordial. There is no triunity in God apart from election, for the two occur in one and the same event. We might best put it this way: the command of the Father in the covenant of grace generates the Son as a second mode of being in which the one divine Subject could obey.[6]

What is missing in this assertion is any distinction between God's eternal existence as Father, Son and Spirit and God's free act of self-determination to be ours as the electing God of the covenant, a distinction that is crucial for Torrance, who speaks more carefully of *prothesis* and election in relation

---

[5]*Christian Doctrine of God*, p. 193.
[6]McCormack, "Doctrine of the Trinity After Barth," pp. 114-15.

to God's eternity.[7] Here the relation between eternity and time assumes massive importance in this discussion.

In one sense *prothesis* refers to the "infinite recession of the mystery of Christ into eternity" and thus "to the eternal abiding of the Son in the Father."[8] In another sense "*prothesis* understood as the setting forth of that eternal mystery in Christ, in God's oneness with man in Christ, and through Christ, is *election*."[9] In another context Torrance notes, "Properly regarded, divine election is the free sovereign decision and utterly contingent act of God's Love in pure liberality or unconditional Grace whether in creation or redemption."[10] It is neither arbitrary nor necessary because it flows from the purpose of God's eternal love and "is entirely unconditioned by any necessity."[11] Indeed the doctrine of election expresses

> the unqualified objectivity of God's Love and Grace toward us, and the ultimate invariant ground in God himself on which all our faith and trust in him for our salvation in life and death repose. It represents a strictly theonomous way of thinking, from a centre in God and not from a centre in ourselves.[12]

---

[7]Importantly, this is a distinction that remains crucial for Barth as well, even in IV/2, where Barth is at pains to stress the fact that God is not unaffected by the suffering of his creatures due to their sin and alienation from God. God himself is willing and able to be and to become the one humiliated and judged in our place so that we may be exalted in him for all eternity through the incarnation, death, resurrection and ascension of Jesus Christ. "He became and was and is man. But because He did so as the Son of God He is from the very first, *from all eternity in the election and decree of God, elect man, exalted in all the lowliness of His humanity, and revealed in His resurrection and ascension as man set in eternal fellowship with God, at the right hand of the Father. How can it be otherwise when He is the man who in all His humanity exists only as the Son of God, who as man is identical with the Son of God?* It was not only in appearance, or partially, that He, the Son of God, became man like us, but genuinely and totally. In His exaltation He does not cease to be man like us. Otherwise He would not be our Brother, nor could He represent us, nor bear and bear away our rejection in accordance with His election. But as He became and was and is a man as the Son of God, He became and was and is the one real and true and living and royal man; and it is as such that He represents us. The majesty of the Son of God is the mystery, the basis, of the exaltation of the Son of Man; of the fact that the man Jesus of Nazareth is called and is the Lord. Therefore 'Jesus is Victor' is simply a confession of the majesty of the incarnate Son of God" (IV/2, p. 358, emphasis mine).

[8]*Incarnation*, pp. 177-78.

[9]Ibid., p. 178. For a discussion of Torrance's doctrine of election, see Myk Habets, "The Doctrine of Election in Evangelical Calvinism: T. F. Torrance as a Case Study," in *Irish Theological Quarterly* 73 (2008): 334-54.

[10]Thomas F. Torrance, *Christian Theology and Scientific Culture: Comprising the Theological Lectures at the Queen's University, Belfast for 1980* (Eugene, OR: Wipf and Stock, 1998), p. 131.

[11]Ibid.

[12]Ibid., p. 132.

It secures our knowledge of God and our relations with God as well as our creaturely freedom in God's own unlimited freedom. Torrance believes that the New Testament witness to this, especially in Paul (in Timothy, Romans and Ephesians), may go back to Second Isaiah and to the mind of Christ himself. Hence, "Election rests on the relation of love between the Father and the Son, and election is the *prothesis*, the setting forth, the projection of that love in Christ the beloved Son of God, through whom we are adopted into Christ's eternal relation of sonship in love to the Father."[13] Indeed, "Jesus Christ is identical with God's decision and man's election in the divine love."[14] But here we are up against the mystery of the divine love as grounded in the eternal knowledge and love of the Father and Son so that we can say no more here than that God loves because he loves and that we see the eternal purpose of God's love in the incarnation, death, resurrection and ascension of Jesus Christ.[15]

Prothesis then is "the great eternal presupposition of all God's relations with man, and of man's relations with God," and so it "sums up the whole gospel of Christ."[16] As such it is "the eternal beginning of all the ways and works of God in Jesus Christ."[17] Because these important distinctions made by Torrance are missing in McCormack's thinking, his logical reversal of election and the Trinity causes ontological damage to the reality of God since he is forced to claim that "There is no triunity in God apart from election." The only way this statement could be true is if the beginning of God's ways and works *ad extra* was equated unequivocally with God's triune life. Yet that equation would have to mean reducing the eternal Trinity to what God wills to do and does for us as Lord of the covenant, as in the following statement: "*There is no longer any room left here for an abstract doc-*

---

[13]*Incarnation*, p. 178.

[14]Ibid. See Torrance, "Predestination in Christ," *Evangelical Quarterly* 13 (1941): 108-41, where he insists, "Christ is in His own Person the eternal decree of God—it is a false distinction to make Him only the *causa et medium* and not also the full ground of predestination" (p. 110).

[15]See Paul D. Molnar, *Thomas F. Torrance: Theologian of the Trinity* (Aldershot, UK: Ashgate, 2009), pp. 112-13, and esp. p. 148, and *Christian Doctrine of God*, p. 244. Also see "Predestination in Christ," where Torrance writes: "The reason why God loves us is love. To give any other reason for love than love itself, whether it be a reason in God Himself, such as an election according to some divine *prius* that precedes Grace, or whether it be in man, is to deny love, to disrupt the Christian apprehension of God and to condemn the world to chaos!" (p. 117). See also Thomas F. Torrance, *The Doctrine of Jesus Christ* (Eugene, OR: Wipf and Stock, 2002), pp. 87-91.

[16]*Incarnation*, p. 178.

[17]Ibid.

trine of the Trinity. There is a triune being of God—only in the covenant of grace."[18] Given what was said above, it is clear that the claim that God is and always remains the eternal Father, Son and Holy Spirit both internally and externally means that it is not an abstraction at all to assert that God was always Father and Son but *not always* creator and not always incarnate.[19] It is a mistake to think that the command of the Father in the covenant of grace "generates the Son as a second mode of being," because the generation of the Son, which takes place from all eternity, is the presupposition for the beginning of God's ways and works *ad extra* and does not therefore take place *in order that* the Son *could* obey the Father in the history of the covenant.[20] Such a suggestion in reality makes who and what God is as love dependent on the works of God *ad extra*. Any reversal of this kind means that God's free love has been confused with human love, which is indeed mutually conditioned in this way. God's will to condescend to help us in our distress is an act of humiliation in the incarnation for the purpose of our exaltation, and it rests on the fact that God loves us simply because he loves us; that is the mystery that was and is revealed in Jesus Christ. The Holy Spirit enables us to experience this and to know it.

Hence, while it is quite proper for Bruce McCormack to reject Hegel's idea that in understanding God's self-revelation one could suggest that "God cannot be God in any other way than through this becoming,"[21] it is more than

---

[18]Bruce L. McCormack, "Election and the Trinity: Theses in Response to George Hunsinger," in *Trinity and Election in Contemporary Theology*, ed. Michael T. Dempsey (Grand Rapids: Eerdmans, 2011), p. 128, emphasis mine.

[19]On this point see especially Bruce D. Marshall, "The Absolute and the Trinity," *Pro Ecclesia* 23, no. 2 (2014): 160-64, who insists that only if our understanding of God's relations with us is grounded in the reality of the immanent Trinity do our relations with God have meaning. Seeing the eternal Trinity therefore merely as a "counterfactual" means that "theologians now often suppose" that there is "nothing worth knowing about who the Triune God actually is, or what he has actually done" (p. 161). Losing this basis in the reality of God, theologians then argue that one can no longer hold the view that God might not have created a world, or having created it might not have reconciled the world to himself.

[20]Following Athanasius, Torrance rightly insists that the fact that creation is a new act of God does not mean that "God did not always have the power to create, nor is it to say that creation was not in the Mind of God before he actually brought it into being" (*Christian Doctrine of God*, p. 208). Also, even though "God was always able to become incarnate, he chose to become incarnate in what the Bible calls 'the fullness of time'" (p. 209).

[21]Bruce L. McCormack, "Introduction," in *Mapping Modern Theology: A Thematic and Historical Introduction*, ed. Kelly M. Kapic and Bruce L. McCormack (Grand Rapids: Baker Academic, 2012), p. 14.

a little problematic to suppose that Hegel's mistake is avoided with the idea that God's self-revelation is "the consequence of an eternal (in the sense of pretemporal) act of *Self*-determination that *constitutes* God's being as a being for revelation in time."[22] McCormack of course attributes this view to Barth and claims that the difference between Barth and Hegel is that for Barth the immanent Trinity is fully realized in pretemporal eternity, while for Hegel it was "understood as a strictly eschatological reality."[23] That is indeed the difference between Barth and Hegel. But McCormack goes on to claim that "God's being is grounded in an *Urentscheidung* (i.e., a 'primordial decision') in which *he gives to himself his own being as God*."[24] It is not clear to me how this last assertion escapes the problems associated with Hegel's view, especially since McCormack also claims that it is acceptable to say that God is triune only for the sake of his revelation,[25] that election is the ground of God's triunity[26] and that "*There is a triune being of God—only in the covenant of grace*."[27] The fact that God can reveal himself in time is a fact grounded in who God eternally is as the one who loves in freedom; it is not the result of a self-determination *for us* that supposedly constitutes his triunity.[28]

This insight is shaped by the fact that God could have been the triune God without us but freely chose not to. Hence, God's self-determination to be God for us is already the beginning of the triune God's actions *ad extra* and cannot be understood to be constitutive of God's triunity. The difference in accent here between saying that "There is a triune being of God—only in the covenant of grace," and saying that God could have been the triune God

---

[22]Ibid., emphasis mine.

[23]Ibid.

[24]Ibid., emphasis mine.

[25]See below, note 35.

[26]As McCormack puts it: "The *decision* for the covenant of grace is the ground of God's triunity and, therefore of the eternal generation of the Son and of the eternal procession of the Holy Spirit from the Father and Son. . . . The works of God *ad intra* (the trinitarian processions) find their ground in the *first* of the works of God *ad extra* (viz. election)" ("Grace and Being," in *The Cambridge Companion to Karl Barth*, ed. John Webster [Cambridge: Cambridge University Press, 2000], p. 103). See also McCormack, *Orthodox and Modern: Studies in the Theology of Karl Barth* (Grand Rapids: Baker Academic, 2008), p. 194.

[27]McCormack, "Election and the Trinity," p. 128, emphasis mine.

[28]In other words, it is crucial, with Barth, to distinguish between who God eternally is within the immanent Trinity in his fully realized being and action as Father, Son and Holy Spirit, and who God determines himself to be for us in creation, reconciliation and redemption. His determination to be for us, as I have been arguing, is a determination of his triune being and action in electing us in his Son, who would become incarnate in Jesus Christ.

without us but freely chose not to, is captured nicely in Torrance's remark that "Creation like redemption was a sheer act of God's inexplicable grace exhibited in his incarnate Son who was 'created a beginning of God's ways for his works'—it was in him through his saving activity that the hidden reason for creation was to be traced."[29] Torrance insists that, for the Nicene theologians, "No attempt was made to answer the question *how* the universe was created out of nothing," but since all things come from God they are not to be understood as emanating from God's being but as "the product of his will and the activity of his love."[30] What, then, is the relation of God to creation? It is, says Torrance, "neither a necessary relation, nor an arbitrary relation. God was *free* to create the universe, but he was also free not to create it."[31] Citing a number of early church fathers, Torrance insists that creation was no accident and did not arise on its own, but "was an intelligible product of the divine Mind." He could even say that creation was in the mind of God before he created,[32] but without implying that creation either was arbitrary or necessary for God. Instead, Torrance says that, in contrast to a static "unmoved mover," the living God who is revealed to us

> through his Son and in his Spirit is absolutely free to do what he had never done before, and free to be other than he was eternally: to be Almighty Creator, and even to become incarnate as a creature within his creation. . . . The fact that while God was always Father he freely chose to become Creator [and] . . . to become a creature within his creation, reveals something about the astonishing nature and freedom of God's dynamic Being, and the inconceivable way in which his ever-living acting Being is always *new* while always remaining what it ever was and is and ever will be. . . . His almighty power and freedom are not exhausted in what he has done, does do, and will do.[33]

---

[29] *Trinitarian Faith*, p. 92.

[30] Ibid.

[31] Ibid. Torrance repeats this important point, citing Athanasius and following Georges Florovsky, that we must think about creation's relation to God from God's side and from the human side as both contingent and independent. Hence, we must think in terms of a "double contingency," namely, that creation took place "in the free creative act of God who need not have done what he did, and in what he actually brought into being which need not have happened as it did or even have happened at all" (*Trinitarian Faith*, p. 105). But this does not mean that it was an irrational or arbitrary act, because there was a "divine reason" (p. 105).

[32] See *Christian Doctrine of God*, p. 208. See also *Trinitarian Faith*, p. 87.

[33] *Christian Doctrine of God*, pp. 208-9. Torrance unequivocally rejects any idea that creation or incarnation were necessary to God. See Thomas F. Torrance, *Divine and Contingent Order* (Edinburgh: T & T Clark, 1998), pp. vii, 6, 22, 71.

The fact that these acts are "new for God" means that "there is, if we may express it thus, a 'before' and 'after' in God's activity,"[34] which Torrance indicates demands a discussion of the unique nature of time in God's own eternal life. We will conclude this chapter with a discussion of God's eternal time.

For now it is important to note that any view that suggests that God "becomes" triune only for the sake of revelation[35] undercuts a genuine recognition that God *is* triune and thus can act as revealer without ceasing to be the Father, Son and Spirit he eternally is. Indeed, this type of thinking leads McCormack to the conclusion that "The concept of an eternal generation of the Son secures for the Son a participation in the being of the Father; all that the Father has (in the way of being and attributes), he gives to the Son so that the Son is 'fully God.'"[36] The way this sentence is constructed, when coupled with McCormack's belief that it is the Father "who gives himself his own being in the act of election,"[37] opens the door to a type of subordina-

---

[34]*Christian Doctrine of God*, p. 209.
[35]Bruce McCormack embraces this view when he writes: "the command of the Father in the covenant of grace generates the Son as a second mode of being in which the one divine Subject could obey" ("The Doctrine of the Trinity After Barth," pp. 114-15), and it is more than a little problematic because it implies that God could not be God without the covenant. It also implies that election determines God's triunity. Further, McCormack claims that Barth should have put to himself the question of the *logical* relation of election to God's triunity but did not (McCormack, "Grace and Being," p. 101). Barth himself directly denies that revelation is the basis of the Trinity "as though God were the triune God only in His revelation and only for the sake of His revelation" (I/1, p. 312), because he says revelation is the basis of the *doctrine* of the Trinity and not the Trinity itself. And McCormack rightly notes that for Barth, God is "triune in himself . . . and not just in his historical revelation. Were he triune *only* in his revelation, the immanent Trinity would collapse into the economic Trinity" ("Grace and Being," p. 101). Yet, he then asks how Barth could have denied that God is triune "*only for the sake of* his revelation" (p. 101) and concludes that Barth could not deny this without positing "a mode of existence in God above and prior to God's gracious election" (p. 102). This, he says, is Barth's error, and it was the error of Calvin before him. McCormack asks: "How can he [Barth] (or anyone else) *know* that God is triune in and for himself, independent of his eternal will to be revealed?" (p. 102). He thinks Barth needed to retract this earlier assertion but that he never did. And it is my contention that Barth never did because he never intended to reduce God's triunity to God's will to be revealed, as this argument implies. What is being confused here, in my view, is that *we* cannot know God's inner being apart from revelation and that God really is God apart from revelation. Barth thus can know this without claiming that God is triune *only for the sake of* his revelation, because what he learned from revelation is that God is and remains self-sufficient even as he eternally wills to be and then becomes God for us. This will be discussed further in chapter five.
[36]McCormack, "Introduction," p. 15.
[37]McCormack, "Seek God Where He May Be Found: A Response to Edwin Chr. van Driel," *SJT* 60, no. 1 (2007): 67.

tionism because it implies that the Son receives his being from the Father and that he receives it only because and to the extent that the Father elects to relate with his creation through the Son's obedience.[38]

This is problematic because the Father, Son and Spirit is eternally the one he is in the act of being, which consists in his eternal love, which is free within the immanent Trinity. It is that eternal God who elects us in his Son and unites us to himself in his Spirit. And while Athanasius did speak of the Son's participation in the being of the Father in certain contexts, he also rejected it in others because the Son did not just participate in the Father's being in some derivative sense, but the Son is fully God as the Father is fully God, the only distinction being that the Son is not the Father. That is why Torrance firmly and rightly rejects any idea that the divine being is caused by the Father's eternal act of begetting the Son. It is a mistake, therefore, to think that the Father gives being to the Son, because both are fully God as the Father begets the Son from all eternity in the unity of the Holy Spirit. The eternal generation of the Son takes place because that is how God exists as one who loves in freedom, and that is how God would exist even if he never decided to create, reconcile and redeem us.

The real issue here concerns how to think about the fact that election is an eternal act of God in a way that respects both God's eternity and God's freedom as the one who loves. How can one speak of incarnation as a *new act* even for God without suggesting either that it is eternal or that God changes in the incarnation? I think Torrance's theology provides the answer here in a way that solves this issue without intruding on the mystery of God's eternal act and being, and in a way that allows him to assert that God can suffer *as* God for us without introducing suffering and death into the essence of God in the manner suggested by McCormack. Torrance is also able to hold on to the notion of God's impassibility in a way that overcomes the ambiguity associated with philosophical determinism such that this must be taken to imply that God himself is "incapable of divine passion."[39] Because McCormack is entrapped by his own

---

[38]This is the subordination that we noted above that Hector was unable to escape in his analysis as it was shaped by the intentions that led McCormack to logically reverse the doctrines of election and the Trinity.

[39]Torrance, *Divine and Contingent Order*, p. 6.

actualistic metaphysics, he completely rejects any idea of impassibility as a relevant theological concept describing God's internal and external activities in order to advance his Christology.[40]

GOD'S TIME

Torrance says that there is such a thing as time in God. But that time is his unique time without the opposition of past, present and future and without the limitations associated with our created time. Hence, he can speak of a before and after in God as it relates to election and the Trinity without implying that God existed one way before and another way after he decided to be God for us. This allows Torrance to see election as the free act of love that God is but also as a *new* act for us. Both God's act of love as the eternal Father, Son and Spirit and God's election of us, then, could be seen as one eternal act of the triune God. But election and incarnation would be acknowledged as *new* acts, *new* even for God. One could also say, as noted above, that God's act of love as the eternal Father, Son and Holy Spirit is eternally necessary, while his eternal act of electing us is eternally contingent, since God would have been no less or other than the eternal Trinity even without us. Speaking of a before and after in God, then, for Torrance means that God is eternally acting in new ways while remaining the God he is because God is not subject to inertia, as might be supposed if the limitations of created time are read back in God's eternal being and action.

Barth and Torrance are very close here. Thus, Barth says

> Already in the eternal will and decree of God He was not to be, nor did He
> will to be, God only, but Emmanuel, God with man, and in fulfilment of this
> "with," according to the free choice of His grace, this man, Jesus of Nazareth.
> And in the act of God in time which corresponds to this eternal decree, when

---

[40]McCormack holds, for instance, that Barth had no doctrine of impassibility but only a concept of impassibility. But that concept, we are told, describes "a perfection that *might* have been God's . . . had he not chosen rejection, suffering, and death for himself" (Bruce L. McCormack, "Divine Impassibility or Simply Divine Constancy? Implications of Karl Barth's Later Christology for Debates over Impassibility," in *Divine Impassibility and the Mystery of Human Suffering*, ed. James F. Keating and Thomas Joseph White, O.P. [Grand Rapids: Eerdmans, 2009], p. 183). Barth thus speaks of possibilities never actualized, "only to underscore the freedom of God's self-determination to be a God 'for us' in Jesus Christ. *They are not considered as possessing reality in God's life*" (p. 183, emphasis mine). This issue will be considered in greater detail by comparing the views of Torrance, Robert Jenson and McCormack in chap. 5.

the Son of God became this man, He ceased to all eternity to be God only, receiving and having and maintaining to all eternity human essence as well. Thus the human essence of Jesus Christ, without becoming divine, in its very creatureliness, is placed at the side of the Creator. (IV/2, pp. 100-101)

With this Torrance fully agrees: "The man Jesus, Son of Mary, who lived a fully human life among us as one of us, is none other than God himself come to us as man, and for ever belongs to the innermost being and life of the Godhead."[41] For Torrance, "Jesus Christ is not just man participating in God but is himself essential Deity."[42]

There are crucial distinctions in evidence here that cannot be maintained when election and the Trinity are logically reversed. God's eternal love of us, which was a mystery hidden for all ages and was revealed in Christ, demonstrates the eternal purpose of God's love; it is grounded in his eternal will and decree to be "Emmanuel." That decree is carried out in the history of Jesus. But it is imperative to realize at this point that none of this means that "the humanity of Jesus is eternal" in the sense that "it was eternally pre-existent."[43] "It does mean that his person is eternal, that his person is not human, but divine," and it also means that "the humanity of Jesus was assumed into oneness with the eternal Son and shares eternally in the glory of the only begotten Son which he had before the world was created."[44] Torrance insists that the doctrine of the hypostatic union refers to "a union of natures in one person" but "does not assert the pre-existence and in that sense the eternity of the human nature."[45] This precise thinking is extremely

---

[41] *Trinitarian Faith*, p. 144.

[42] Ibid., p. 149. See also Molnar, *Thomas F. Torrance*, pp. 139, 185.

[43] *Incarnation*, p. 177. This is an enormously important point for our present discussion, and it is a point made decisively by Athanasius when he says, "He [Christ] was not man previously, but became man for the sake of saving man. And the Word was not in the beginning flesh, but has been made flesh subsequently (cf. Jn. 1.1)" (*On Luke 22 [Matt. XI 27]* §3). For Athanasius, then, the Son "was not man, and then became God, but He was God, and then became man" (*C. Ar.* I, 39). There is no doubt that Barth embraced these ideas but at times introduced ambiguity, as when he wrote: "In this free act of the election of grace the Son of the Father is no longer just the eternal Logos, but as such, as very God from all eternity He is also the very God and very man He will become in time" (IV/1, p. 66). While Barth clarified this in his insistence that we must distinguish between the fact that this is true of Jesus in the decree of God and that it did not become a reality until the Word actually became incarnate (see above p. 158n78 and pp. 174-75, where Barth distinguished between God "as such" and his decree and the incarnation). McCormack carries this ambiguity beyond what Barth claimed when he says that the subject of the incarnation is the God-man.

[44] Ibid.

[45] Ibid.

helpful for us because it enables us to see that while Jesus' human nature had no independent *hypostasis* "prior to the incarnation," it was given genuine personal being "in the eternal Word, in the eternal Son, in the eternal *hypostasis* of God the Son."[46] And in light of the resurrection and ascension we can and must say that the one Mediator, Jesus Christ, forever exists as the divine-human high priest, prophet and king, who has once and for all reconciled humanity to God and united us in his human nature to God so that we may participate in his new humanity and thus in the inner life of the Son's own relations of knowledge and love to the Father.

> Election rests on the relation of love between the Father and the Son, and election is the *prothesis*, the setting forth, the projection of that love in Christ the beloved Son, through whom we are adopted into Christ's eternal relation of sonship in love to the Father. Jesus Christ is identical with God's decision and man's election in the divine love. That *prothesis* is the great eternal presupposition of all God's relations with man, and man's relations with God, and so St Paul speaks of election as the act of God which sums up the whole gospel in Christ.[47]

In this sense "election means . . . the eternal beginning of all the ways and works of God in Jesus Christ."[48]

> Christ assumes our flesh, assumes our fallen estate, assumes our judgment . . . our reprobation, in order that we may participate in his glory, and share in the union of the Son with the Father. That is the eternal mystery, the great secret hid from the ages but now revealed in the gospel.[49]

Exactly at this point, however, care is required because if the fact of the incarnation discloses the free grace and free love of God to us, and it was a mystery hidden in the eternal being and act of the Father and Son, it would be an enormous mistake to read these historical events back into the inner life of God in an attempt to explain the mystery of the Trinity or the mystery of God's relations with us. That is the error that Barth clearly made when he reached the "astounding conclusion" that there is a divine obedience within the immanent Trinity as a presupposition of the obedience of the Son in humbling himself for

---

[46]Ibid.
[47]Ibid., p. 178.
[48]Ibid.
[49]Ibid.

our sakes.[50] This led Barth to assert that there is not only a divine obedience within the immanent Trinity but that there is an eternal subordination within the Trinity as well. Torrance, as we shall see, emphatically rejects both ideas because he consistently refused to read back elements of the economy into God in order to make sense of God's condescension for us.[51]

Two crucial implications follow from this: first, in the incarnation "something altogether *new* happened, even for God, for God the Son was not always man but he now became man . . . though without ceasing to be God."[52] Second, "the relation of the incarnate Son to the Father did not arise within time. The life of Christ on earth was the obverse of a heavenly deed, and the result of an eternal decision, an eternal *prothesis* which God had purposed in himself from all eternity."[53] How is this to be understood in a way that respects the fact that God's time is his eternally active and living being as Father, Son and Holy Spirit and thus as the one who loves, while at the same time it acknowledges that there can therefore be a "before" and "after" even within the eternal life and action of God with respect to election, creation, incarnation and redemption? It is worth following how Torrance explains these matters with respect to time and eternity.

TIME, ETERNITY AND ELECTION

The *first* important factor to notice is that for Torrance the love of God that meets us in Christ, that is, in the person of the incarnate Word "does not rest upon any eternal hinterground in the will of God that is not identical with the foreground in the actual person of the incarnate Son, Jesus Christ."[54] While *prothesis* indeed refers "back to the eternal hinterground of the will of God," it also tells us that "that is absolutely identical with the existence and action, with the will of Christ for us which he carried out on the cross";[55] hence,

> If the pre-existence of Christ means that what God is in Christ he is antecedently and eternally in himself, election means that what God is in himself as love he is fully and entirely in Christ Jesus who died for us, for in Christ Jesus

---

[50]IV/1, p. 202. See chap. 7 below for a discussion of this issue.
[51]See chap. 7 below.
[52]*Incarnation*, p. 177.
[53]Ibid.
[54]Ibid., p. 179.
[55]Ibid.

the grace of God has moved into time and *completes in time the movement of his love toward man*, gathering and involving humanity in that eternal movement between the Son and the Father, and the Father and the Son through the Holy Spirit.[56]

Notice that Torrance carefully stresses that what is completed in God's movement toward us is not the fulfillment of the divine being, but the fulfillment of the divine love in its purposes for us. What is completed in created time is the movement of his love for us that culminated on the cross and in the resurrection of Jesus Christ for our benefit. So for Torrance it is not only true that it is solely in Christ that we are "eternally loved and elected" but also that "Christ is the *way* in which we are loved and elected."[57] For that reason there is no other way of salvation and no other way to the Father except Jesus Christ himself. What this means to Torrance is that when God's love goes into action, so to speak, in time there takes place an analogous kind of communion or fellowship between Jesus and his disciples that is itself grounded in and reflective of the eternal love and fellowship or communion within the Father/Son relation of the eternal Trinity. Torrance has in mind Christ's prayer at the last supper as recounted in John 17; in sharing "the bread of the presence" with his disciples, he gave them to share "in his mystery and to be one with him as he was one with the Father."[58] And citing Revelation 3:20 Torrance writes: "Behold, I stand at the door and knock; if any one hears my voice and opens the door, I will come in to him and eat with him, and he with me." Thus, the election of grace "goes into action through fellowship," as can be seen in Jesus' own life when he ate and drank with publicans and sinners. That is the divine *prothesis*. But how does Torrance relate his thinking to eternity and time in connection with election?

The *second* important thing to notice is that Torrance insists that in Jesus Christ we are confronted with "the eternal decision of God's eternal love. In Jesus Christ, therefore, eternal election has become *temporal event*."[59] But that means that election is not "some static act in a still point of eternity." Rather it is "eternal *pre*-destination, moving out of its eternal *prius* into time

---

[56]Ibid., emphasis mine.
[57]Ibid.
[58]Ibid.
[59]Ibid., p. 180.

as living act that from moment to moment confronts people in Jesus Christ."[60] Hence, "the 'pre' in predestination refers neither to a temporal nor to a logical *prius*, but simply to God Himself, the Eternal."[61] This is a vital insight. For Torrance, while we tend to think of eternity "as strung out in an infinite line with past, present, and future though without beginning and without end, in the form of an elongated circular time," this must not lead us to suppose that there is a "worldly *prius*" in God, because that would introduce immediately a "logical one" as well.[62] If and when predestination is brought within the compass of created time, then it would be thought of within the "compass of the temporal-causal series" and "interpreted in terms of cause and effect," and this would necessarily lead to determinism, which is the very opposite of what is actually affirmed in the "pre" of predestination. Torrance says the "pre" in predestination, when rightly understood, is "the most vigorous protest against determinism" known to Christian theology.[63] Since the "pre" in predestination does not refer to a "*prius* to anything here in space and time," it cannot be construed as "the result of an inference from effect to first cause, or from relative to absolute, or to any world-principle."[64] Rather, because election is "in Jesus Christ," the "pre" does not take election "out of time" but "grounds it in an act of the Eternal which we can only describe as 'per se' or 'a se.'"[65] That means it is grounded "in the personal relations of the Trinity" so that "because we know God to be Father, Son and Holy Spirit, we know the Will of God to be supremely Personal—and it is to that Will that predestination tells us our salvation is to be referred."[66]

But we can make that reference only "if that Will has first come among us and been made personally known. That has happened (ἐγένετο) in Christ, and in Him the act of predestination is seen to be the act of creative Grace in the communion of the Holy Spirit."[67] Election thus refers to God's "choice or decision" and "guarantees to us the freedom of God. His sovereignty, His omnipotence is not one that acts arbitrarily, nor by necessity, but by personal

---

[60]Ibid.
[61]Torrance, "Predestination in Christ," p. 116.
[62]Ibid.
[63]Ibid.
[64]Ibid.
[65]Ibid.
[66]Ibid.
[67]Ibid.

decision. God is therefore no blind fate, no immanent force acting under the compulsion of some *prius* or unknown law within His being."[68] The importance of emphasizing choice here concerns the fact that election cannot involve any necessity without becoming immediately a form of determinism. Instead, election refers to God's freedom "to break the bondage of a sinful world, and to bring Himself into personal relations with man";[69] election refers to a personal action from God's side and from the human side. Hence it is an act that creates personal relations. While God freely creates our human personal relations, human freedom is "essentially dependent freedom," while "the divine freedom is independent, 'a se' freedom; the freedom of the Creator as distinguished from the freedom of the creature."[70] In this connection Torrance describes election as "an act of love." It means that "God has chosen us because He loves us, and that He loves us because He loves us."[71]

That may sound a bit strange. But it is a loaded comment, because what Torrance means is that if we try to get behind this act of God's love toward us to find a reason beyond the simple fact that God loves us because he does, we will end up turning God's free love of us into a necessity in one way or another and thus once again compromise both divine and human freedom in the process. So Torrance insists,

> The reason why God loves us is love. To give any other reason for love than love itself, whether it be a reason in God Himself, such as an election according to some divine *prius* that precedes Grace, or whether it be in man, is to deny love, to disrupt the Christian apprehension of God and to condemn the world to chaos![72]

> Election is Christ the beloved Son of the Father, and the act of election in him is once and for all, a *perfectum praesens*, an eternal decision that is ever present. God's eternal decision does not halt or come to rest at any particular point or result, but is dynamic, and ever takes the field in its identity with the living person of Christ.[73]

---

[68]Ibid., p. 117.
[69]Ibid.
[70]Ibid.
[71]Ibid.
[72]Ibid.
[73]*Incarnation*, p. 180.

Hence it is "contemporary with us" and summons us to decision as to who we say he is. Here we must confront more directly the relationship between time and eternity. How exactly can one maintain that election is an eternal decision without reducing the eternal love between the Father and Son to the love of God enacted in the history of Jesus Christ for us? How can one maintain the strength of Torrance's insight that creation and incarnation are new acts even for God without obviating the power contained in the assertion that Jesus Christ is the ever-present act of God's electing love?

SAVED BY ETERNITY

Torrance maintains that "when everything is boiled down the doctrine of predestination or election comes to this: I am saved by God, by the eternal God. But if I am saved by Eternity, I am saved from all eternity unto all eternity."[74] But what do we mean by eternity? Here controversies arise. One such controversy concerned the debate over whether election is supra- or infralapsarian, that is, whether God's foreknowledge of the fall preceded his decree of election or election preceded the fall. But, Torrance says, it is sometimes objected that "if salvation is eternally determined, what sense is there in saying that it took place before or after the Fall?"[75] To that Torrance replies that the objection presumes a view of eternity that is problematic because it supposes an eternity "for which the distinctions of time are unreal or docetic," and he asserts that such thinking "is even a worse fault than the view of the controversialists who, however distorted their views of eternity and time may have been, did see that time had significance for eternity!"[76] There was an additional problem for the traditional view: that those who embraced that view were unable to make a distinction between a "*totum simul* view of eternity, and a *per se* one."[77] For Torrance the latter one is the biblical view while the former is acceptable but only with certain restrictions. Torrance does not think the controversies can simply be dismissed as hairsplitting. But he does believe that there would have been much less controversy had theologians stuck to the main point of election, namely, that

---

[74]Torrance, "Predestination in Christ," p. 118.
[75]Ibid., p. 135.
[76]Ibid.
[77]Ibid.

"election is Christ" since it is only from Jesus Christ that Torrance thinks we can begin to discuss the meaning of eternity properly. That is because it is only as a result of his coming and his revelation and redemption that predestination has a place in theology in any case.

Here we get a glimpse of what Torrance means by eternity and time, and how his understanding of these categories can point the way forward in the continuing debate about the logical relation of election and God's triunity. He begins by stating that the incarnation of the Son of God "must mean the moving of eternity into time."[78] This Torrance spells out in relation to the incarnation, noting, "If God became man, then there was a movement of Eternity into time."[79] Torrance maintains that this is "*the* central fact, of the Incarnation."[80] Indeed, this is the message of the whole Bible, namely, that the living and acting God actively moves toward humanity. And that, says Torrance, is the "doctrine of *Grace*";[81] this means that "God in his sovereign freedom has taken the initiative of Love toward men."[82] That is also the meaning of revelation—God moves in the direction of humanity—not that humanity moves in the direction of God.[83] And this revelation is completely fulfilled in the incarnation. Prior to that God had drawn near. But in the incarnation "Eternity has moved into time and taken up an abode in time."[84] This does not mean that "a piece of eternity has entered time or has been inserted into time" so that it has an existence "in a section of time, therefore a certain circumscribed existence."[85] Were Torrance to accept such a view, he would be embracing the container or receptacle concept of space and time and would thereby undermine Christ's divinity and his eternal being above time *and* within time. That is what Torrance means when he repeatedly insists that, in becoming incarnate in the man Jesus, God

---

[78]Ibid., p. 118.
[79]Torrance, *Doctrine of Jesus Christ*, p. 74.
[80]Ibid.
[81]Ibid.
[82]Ibid.
[83]The weakness of all Christologies from below is that they do not conceptually respect the fact that God's movement is toward us in Christ, and that that movement took place while we were still sinners and thus incapable of moving toward God. That is why Torrance believes Christology from below always ends in some sort of what he calls Ebionite Christology, which eventually passes over into some form of Docetic Christology, with the result that both Jesus' person and his work will be misunderstood.
[84]Torrance, *The Doctrine of Jesus Christ*, p. 74.
[85]Ibid.

himself never ceases being God. Among other things that means that the Son through whom God created the universe continues to rule the universe even while incarnate within history. A moment ago we noted that Torrance used the word *egeneto* to speak of Eternity entering time. Here again he explains that when the Word became (*egeneto*) flesh and when Eternity entered time, this meant that "Eternity is what God is; Eternity is God-in-action."[86] Therefore the most important point to be made here is that "in the heart of Eternity there is motion. Eternity is not static."[87] Consequently, Torrance rejects outright Aristotle's view of God as the "unmoved Mover." And he rejects also any philosophical idea of God's impassibility.[88] But, because Torrance holds strictly to what he calls the "fact of Christ," by which he means that Jesus is both truly divine and truly human without separation, confusion or mixture of his natures,[89] he is free to assert that God is both impassible (in that God does not cease being God in the incarnation, death and resurrection of Jesus Christ) and passible (in that God himself can and does suffer and experience death in the incarnate Word *as* God and *as* man in Jesus Christ) because while suffering does not become part of God's nature, still God takes on our suffering and death and experiences them both divinely and humanly in order to remove them from us.[90] That is why Torrance insists that if one understands impassibility and passibility logically, one would have to say that God cannot suffer and die because either God is subject to suffering and death or not. But Torrance insists that these categories must be understood soteriologically on the ground of what God actually did for us in the incarnation: he brought his eternal serenity to bear on our sinful human nature and bore our suffering in order to save us from suffering and death. But he did this without ceasing to be God.[91]

---

[86]Ibid.

[87]Ibid.

[88]Ibid., p. 75.

[89]See *Incarnation*, where Torrance insists that theology "must be faithful to the whole fact of the mystery of Christ. It can never start from one aspect of that mystery such as the historical or the eschatological, or the transcendental—but from the dual fact, the whole mystery of true God and true man. That fact calls into radical question the basic assumption (of both idealism and liberalism) that no fact in the time series can have absolute and decisive significance, for the Christian faith pivots upon the fact that here in time we are confronted by the eternal in union with time" (pp. 7-8). He goes on to say, "Apart from that historical act of God in history, there is no knowledge of God, no real experience of God's help and redemption" (p. 8).

[90]See Molnar, *Thomas F. Torrance*, pp. 152-55.

[91]See *Trinitarian Faith*, p. 185.

Eternity, then, for Torrance is an "eternity of action"; it is a relation. Yet it is an action or a relation "of the One who is always himself, the *I am who I am*, the ever unchanging and abiding One, whose freedom is not conditioned, but who is ever free to be himself, and who is Love."[92] Torrance contends that for philosophy, which thinks in terms of an Absolute in which motions and actions disappear, the idea that "Eternity" could actually move into time without ceasing to be "Eternity" is an impossible thought. For philosophy, time tends to disappear either by being absorbed into timelessness or into some sort of timeless eternity. For that reason time is conceptualized only as an appearance and not as a reality. Accordingly, the universal or absolute, in philosophical understanding, can neither be thought of as having anything to do with time relations nor any relations in time itself. That is why Torrance is so adamant in consistently rejecting the God of Aristotle, "the unmoved Mover." Such a view of God is without motion and therefore without love. And Torrance believes there is no purpose in the God of Baruch Spinoza and neither personality nor reciprocal relations in Hegel's "Absolute." Since, for Hegel, the Absolute "is the All in All,"[93] time and eternity are conceptualized as correlatives and in the end the stronger (eternity) negates the weaker (time).

In opposition to this philosophical understanding Torrance thinks of time in light of the incarnation, which, once again, means "*the actual coming of the Eternal God into time*" so that "Eternity establishes relations, real relations with time."[94] Naturally, Torrance does not mean by this what Piet Schoonenberg means when he argues for real relations between God and us, since for him "God's real relations with us entail that change, emergence, and becoming must also be recognized in God, albeit in a completely divine way."[95] Of course Torrance also spoke of God's becoming only to indicate that God is a living God who acts and not an inertial deity incapable of action within himself or outside himself in relation to us. But for Torrance, God's becoming was not in any sense on the way toward being, since God is and remains fully God the Father, Son and Spirit in all his changes. The supreme example in his mind is the fact

---

[92]Torrance, *Doctrine of Jesus Christ*, p. 75.
[93]Ibid.
[94]Ibid.
[95]Piet Schoonenberg, S.J., *The Christ: A Study of the God-Man Relationship In the Whole of Creation and in Jesus Christ* (New York: Herder & Herder, 1971), p. 84.

that God could do something new, new even for himself without changing in his essence as Father, Son and Spirit. So he could even say that

> Athanasius rejected the idea that God is eternally Creator and its attendant idea that the creation eternally exists in the mind of God, for the creation of the world out of nothing meant that it had an absolute beginning. That implies, staggeringly, that even in the life of God there is change: God was not eternally Creator; he became Creator in the free act of creation. Nor was God eternally incarnate, for in Jesus Christ he became what he never was eternally, a creature, without of course ceasing to be the eternal God. In the incarnation, therefore, something new happened, even for God, when, out of his free, outgoing love, he moved outside of himself, and in the incarnation of his Son, he forever bound himself up indissolubly with our creaturely being—such was the staggering extent of his love for the world.[96]

PIET SCHOONENBERG AND CHANGE IN GOD

It is worth comparing this statement to Schoonenberg's thinking, since Schoonenberg rejects the idea of change in God to the extent that it implies a movement from potency to act; this could imply that there is a change in the Son "which is synonymous with creaturehood." And he cites Vatican I to the effect that "God as being [is] a completely unique and inalterable spiritual substance" that "excludes from him a pantheistic self-development."[97] Yet he continues by explaining that God can and must be able to change in relation to his creatures in order to have real relations with them. In this he follows Karl Rahner, who argued that God changes in the other (namely in the incarnation). Again, Schoonenberg rejects the idea that God changes "for his own fulfillment."[98] Like Torrance, Schoonenberg wants to stress that God

> moves in his movements, he changes in the causing of being and becoming of the reality outside himself, and he does so in a totally divine way, without compulsion or influence, from freedom, from love. The reason which forces us to assume such a change in God lies in the very reality of his relations. He becomes different for us.[99]

---

[96]Thomas F. Torrance, *The Ground and Grammar of Theology* (Charlottesville: University Press of Virginia, 1980), p. 66.
[97]Schoonenberg, *The Christ*, p. 84.
[98]Ibid., p. 85.
[99]Ibid.

Schoonenberg even wisely asks whether someone's own idea of perfection might keep them from seeing this active movement of God, which he considers to be important in this context. So far so good. But Schoonenberg then asserts that

> From this point of view it is not impossible that God becomes Trinity through communicating himself in a total way to, and being present in, the man Jesus as Word, and through being in the Church as Spirit. This means a becoming Trinity of God himself, thus a possession of divine hypostases in God's own being.[100]

Further, Schoonenberg says he sees in process thought "a 'resource' for Christian theology. . . . I wish to emphasize, however, that God's 'becoming' is in no sense univocal to a becoming by which a created being grows, evolves, and increases. It is only by giving, bestowing, creating that God is related and that he becomes or changes."[101] Finally, Schoonenberg states that

> I myself am convinced that the idea of God becoming triune through his salvific self-communications is possible. Therefore, I can go further than Karl Barth, who refers God's Trinity to a decision of God which, however, is a "primordial decision." . . . I can see God becoming triune by a historical decision of himself. This is what *we* know about God's Trinity. This vision however, cannot be absolutized by saying that God "originally" was not triune. On a Trinity in God from eternity and by necessity we as creatures cannot make any statements, either in the affirmative or in the negative.[102]

It is worth noting here that Bruce McCormack thinks Schoonenberg is to be counted among "the best 'post-Barthian' theologians," who understood that "theological ontology can be constructed on the basis of the narrated history of Jesus of Nazareth without the help of metaphysics" and who therefore "proceeded in a way reminiscent of Barth."[103] In any case, Schoonenberg carries through this logic in connection with the eternal Word when he writes: "it is pointless to ask whether the Word in God existed before the incarnation: in God there is no time. But we can speak of 'before' and 'after' insofar as God is concerned in our history, or rather: insofar as he refers

---

[100]Ibid.
[101]Ibid., pp. 85-86.
[102]Ibid., p. 86.
[103]See Kapic and McCormack, eds., *Mapping Modern Theology*, pp. 171-72.

himself to our history."[104] He will of course admit that God's Word for us has a prehistory. But that prehistory is "his pre-history in the Old Testament and in all human history."[105] So Schoonenberg concludes, "Whatever there is of its transcendent or pre-existent or eternal existence with God, the Word begins its existence as concerned with us in the pre-history of Jesus, when God speaks many times and in many ways to the fathers."[106]

My point here is this: Schoonenberg's thinking allows him to admit of change in God; but that change is not the change that Torrance has in mind, because Schoonenberg is unwilling or unable to maintain the priority of the Father/Son relation over the creator/creature relation. And his appeal to process thinking, which, as we have already seen, Torrance rightly considers a reversion to the Origenist error of confusing God's internal and external relations, leads Schoonenberg to imply that God's eternal triunity is constituted by his relations with us in history. No doubt Schoonenberg explicitly claims he does not intend to do that. But his assertion that God becomes triune through his self-communication suggests exactly that. The result is that he sees God attaining his triunity in his becoming within history and completely misses the all-important point that Torrance quite properly wishes to make—God can do something new, new even for himself because he is a living God and because, without any dependence on history and created time, he himself has his own eternal time (something Schoonenberg apparently rejects when he says time does not apply to God).

BEFORE AND AFTER IN GOD

Thus Torrance speaks about God's eternal time and also of a before and after in God with respect to God's acts of creation and incarnation. And he is able to do so without implying that God's eternal triune being changes, since for him God's eternal triunity is the act and being of the living God, whose being is not inert or unmoved. God is ever new and thus can and does do new things even for him, precisely because his unique time is not an eternal timeless *now* that would devalue our time; it is rather God's real eternal life as the triune God. While our time relations must never be read back into God, in Torrance's

---

[104]Schoonenberg, *The Christ*, p. 86.
[105]Ibid., pp. 84-85.
[106]Ibid., p. 86.

view, it is crucially important to recognize that God's active and eternal triune being is "characterised by *time*." This is not a time like our finite and created time, which is marked by a beginning and past, present and future as well as by an end.[107] This is why Torrance can hold, following Augustine, that God created our time, but without "any temporal movement in himself" and that God's time transcends ours as "the time of God's Life," which is "defined by his everlasting uncreated Nature in which he transcends our temporality while nevertheless holding it within the embrace of this divine time."[108] Torrance even speaks of God's continually "self-moving" life, which is not "immobile" as a life of love that is "from everlasting to everlasting without beginning or end" but "continually new and carries within it the eternal purpose of God's love, moving uninterruptedly toward its perfect fulfilment" in that "The eternal life of God has *direction*."[109] More importantly, Torrance can speak about "moments" in God's eternity in such a way as to make sense of the fact that there can be a before and after in God's own eternal being, such as his existence before and after creation and incarnation. It is this assertion as such that allows Torrance, with Barth, to speak of God's history[110] in the unique sense that God remains the living subject of this particular history. For that reason, "There is and can be no conflict between the unchanging constancy of God's eternal time and the movement and activity of God toward the fulfilment of his eternal purpose of love."[111] So when Torrance asserts that the eternal became time without ceasing to be eternal, he wants to stress that God's very nature as triune "is characterised by both repose and movement and that his eternal Being is also a divine *Becoming*."[112] Yet, even this divine becoming is unique because it is never to be seen as a becoming on the way toward being or on the way toward the "fullness of being." Instead it must be seen as "the eternal fullness and the overflowing of his eternal unlimited Being. Becoming expresses the dynamic nature of his Being."[113] All of this thinking

---

[107] *Christian Doctrine of God*, p. 241.

[108] Ibid.

[109] Ibid., p. 240. Torrance does not mean that God's eternal life needs fulfillment but that the purpose of his love for us includes the perfect fulfillment of his acts of reconciliation and re- demption.

[110] Ibid., p. 242.

[111] Ibid.

[112] Ibid.

[113] Ibid.

links up quite consistently with Torrance's view of election. God's eternal love does indeed have a *purpose* and a *direction*. But that purpose and direction can never be construed as constituting his eternal triune being and action simply because God loves only because he loves. And one can never explain God's love beyond the fact that God is gracious to us in that love. Moreover, just as Torrance consistently avoids projecting "the finite distinctions between word, act, and person that characterise human beings" into his understanding of God, so he insists that "our finite distinctions between past, present and future may not be projected into our thought of God's being and activity which transcend them altogether."[114]

Therefore, Torrance thinks that the eternal establishes real relations with us in time and that time is thus real for eternity. Because of the incarnation, then, time can never be considered as unreal and resolved away in our thinking about God and God's relations with us in history. Unable to explain why eternity does not annihilate time, we can only refer what happens in that event to "the Wonderful reality of the Love and Grace of God. That is what the Incarnation betokens, a gracious attitude of Eternity toward time, evident in the acts of God in forgiveness and reconciliation."[115] But that cannot be taken to mean that all is right with time and that "time is simply ratified and substantiated, or that the Incarnation of God guarantees to people that their existence in time is essentially in union with Eternity."[116] On the contrary, because the incarnation is the movement of eternity into time, it is the movement of God's salvific love into time "in a final and ab- solute way."[117] "Eternity has come in Christ means that we have here an act which is utterly unique and quite decisive for the world."[118] An event that is neither mythical nor necessary, the incarnation is a once-for-all historical and particular event because in Jesus Christ himself "Eternity enters directly into time," and this means the crisis of all history. This movement of eternity into time then means that "Eternity had to be set in motion in order to save and redeem mankind."[119] In fact just because the incarnation "originates in

---

[114]Ibid.

[115]Torrance, *Doctrine of Jesus Christ*, p. 75.

[116]Ibid.

[117]Ibid., p. 90.

[118]Ibid.

[119]Ibid., p. 76. Here Torrance forcefully rejects the view that even if there had been no sin or fall

Eternity alone, because it has no antecedents in time," it cannot be related to other events in history.[120] It is, as Torrance stresses, a *novum* that is "without analogy anywhere in human experience or knowledge."[121] And we must admit that "How we know Christ, we cannot say in terms of our capacities or abilities or any a priori understanding."[122] This is why we cannot build up to a knowledge of Christ, because that knowledge comes from him only through the Holy Spirit as a miracle. Hence, "In knowing Christ we acknowledge the fact that confronts us as a lordly act from above and beyond us, which we can only acknowledge."[123] In the incarnation, "The Word *became* flesh in such a way as not to cease being the eternal Word of God. This 'become' is clearly unique and miraculous event [*sic*], a pure act of God's wisdom and mercy which is ultimately unfathomable by us."[124] The very same Word that was in the beginning with and was God and was the one by whom and through whom all things were made has now become incarnate. Yet, "The creator did not always exist as a creature made out of nothing, but now having made the creature out of nothing, the creator himself becomes one of the creatures that he made."[125] This *egeneto*, this becoming incarnate of the Word who is the source and Lord of all existence, both foolishness to the Greek and offensive to the Jews, means that "this very act of becoming man is itself an act of reconciliation."[126]

---

there would have been an incarnation of God because this would imply that the incarnation was due to a "necessity within God's Being," to some "law in God" or to some "immanent principle" in God (p. 76). Interestingly, Torrance is somewhat ambivalent on this issue later on, saying, "we cannot and may not try to press our thought speculatively behind that Love [the incarnation] to what might have happened, had not the fall taken place. . . . We can no more do that than we can think beyond the ultimate Being of God in his inner divine Life." That is in line with the position just mentioned. But, he also says, "while clapping our hands upon our mouth, without knowing what we say, we may nevertheless feel urged to say that in his eternal purpose the immeasurable Love of God overflowing freely beyond himself which brought the creation into existence would have become incarnate within the creation even if we and our world were not in need of his redeeming grace" (*Christian Doctrine of God*, p. 210). For more on this see Molnar, *Thomas F. Torrance*, p. 118. It should be stressed that despite this ambiguity, Torrance's thought invariably operates on the assumption that the incarnation took place for the purpose of reconciliation and redemption. See, e.g., *Incarnation*, p. 246.

[120]Ibid., p. 90.
[121]*Incarnation*, p. 1.
[122]Ibid., p. 2.
[123]Ibid.
[124]Ibid., p. 65.
[125]Ibid.
[126]Ibid.

KENOSIS AND INCARNATION

How then does Torrance relate the kenosis to the incarnation? Referring to Philippians 2 as the "*locus classicus* on the servant Son in the New Testament," Torrance explains that Paul's words: "you know the grace of the Lord Jesus Christ, that though he was rich, yet for your sake he became poor, so that by his poverty you might become rich" (2 Cor 8:9) represent a summation of the entire doctrine of the incarnation.[127] Torrance understands the passage to mean that Jesus Christ "emptied *himself* out of a heavenly and glorious *morphē* into an earthly and inglorious *morphē*, that is, he made himself of no reputation, and humbled . . . himself."[128] This does not refer to any "metaphysical change in God the Son such as an emptying out of God the Son of any divine attributes or powers." Rather, he "emptied *himself* out of his divine form into a human form." Yet, the "form of the servant" does indeed correspond "to the real act of the Son, to his being in humanity. That human form was no outer garment, but a real existence in humanity assumed into oneness with the existence of the Son who here condescended to human estate."[129] This self-humbling on the part of the Son was God's act of incarnation for the purpose of saving and redeeming the human race from sin. The cross itself was grounded in this self-humbling of the Son for us as an act of grace and mercy. "The atonement begins in the will of the Son to become man—that is, in the 'lamb slain before the foundation of the world.'"[130] This act of pure grace fulfills itself

> in our human existence and its death. . . . Although the transcendent act of self-giving and self-humbling fulfils itself in our human estate, in the death of the cross, it does not cease to be transcendent act. Therefore it carries on through the cross and completes its movement in exaltation to the right hand of God the Father.[131]

Everything here depends on the fact that "What Jesus does in forgiveness is not just the work of man, but the work of God, and is therefore of final and ultimate validity. . . . It is God himself who acts in Jesus Christ, in his teaching

---

[127]Ibid., p. 74.
[128]Ibid., pp. 74-75.
[129]Ibid., p. 75.
[130]Ibid.
[131]Ibid.

and reconciliation."[132] Importantly, Torrance insists that we cannot simply say, "Jesus is divine," and neither can we say, "God is human"; instead we can and must say that "God has become man, such that he is now also man in Christ, and so we can say that Jesus is man and also God, but to talk about divine humanity is confusion, and a form of monophysite heresy: it is to deny his humanity."[133] This is a crucial point in Christology that is lost by those who suppose that the only act that the Son performs is in becoming man, while all the rest of the acts of the so-called God-man are acts of the man Jesus.[134] Here, because of Torrance's precise understanding of the hypostatic union mentioned above that upholds the fact that there is only one person, namely, the person of the Word who is divine, while his humanity is truly human in the person of the Word or Son, he offers a Christology that allows him to speak of God acting both from the divine and from the human side as our reconciler.[135] But he can say a number of other very important things as well.

First, in his self-humiliation for our benefit, the eternal Son who became incarnate in the man Jesus raised us up "not to become divine, but to share in the divine fellowship and life" so that by the amazing grace of God we are raised up beyond anything we could imagine—yet without ceasing to be the creatures that God made us to be.[136] Human nature is not divinized because, as Torrance notes,

> God became man in Christ, but man did not, or did not also, become God. In the assumption of man into unity with the divine being, human nature was not divinised, but only raised into union and communion with God. If the divine Son assumed human nature into unity with himself only then to divinise it, then that would mean that he had no sooner condescended to be our brother, than he broke off that brotherhood—the idea of a divinisation of the human nature thus makes nonsense of the incarnation and reconciliation.[137]

Second, Christ's human nature, which has no personal being at all apart from its being in the person of the Son (*anhypostatos*), becomes *enhypostatos* "in the *Logos*, who being pre-existent, in fact existent from all eternity, has

---

[132]Ibid., p. 187.
[133]Ibid.
[134]See chap. 5 for a full discussion of this point.
[135]*Incarnation*, pp. 126-29, 228.
[136]Ibid., p. 228.
[137]Ibid., pp. 222-23.

received in time the form of a servant (Phil 2.7), and assumed the seed of Abraham (Heb 2.16) as its shrine and instrument."[138] Together *anhypostasia* and *enhypostasia* indicate that the incarnation is an act of pure grace and repudiates "any form of adoptionism, that is the adoption of a pre-existing man to become the Son of God."[139] In other words there is only one person in Jesus Christ who is the incarnate Son of God. "This one person means that his human nature had *no independent subsistence* or *hypostasis*, no independent centre of personal being."[140] Jesus' human existence never existed even for a moment except in personal subsistence in the "personal subsistence of God the Son."[141] For this reason it is important to note that the personal existence of the man Jesus, that is his human person, "is not other than the person of the divine Son."[142] Our human nature is not and never could be united to the eternal Son of God. And that is the difference between Jesus and us. His human nature "was united to God in a unique way (hypostatically in one person) as our human nature is not."[143] While he is fully human as we are (except he did not sin), he is unlike us in that he is uniquely united with the one person of the Son of God. That, Torrance says, is the "baffling element in the virgin birth."[144]

Contrast this very clear Christology with the strange assertions offered by some. We have been told that

> The "person" is made to be composite not through adding something to a divine being that is complete in itself without reference to the human. No, the second "person" of the Trinity is himself "composite"; in himself he already is, by way of anticipation (as founded in election), what he will become in time through ontological receptivity. Thus, "Jesus Christ" (i.e., the God-human in his divine-human unity) is the identity of the second "person" of the Trinity— not only in time but also "in himself" (when, as yet, there was no creation standing in need of redemption).[145]

---

[138]Ibid., p. 229.
[139]Ibid.
[140]Ibid.
[141]Ibid.
[142]Ibid., p. 230.
[143]Ibid.
[144]Ibid.
[145]Kapic and McCormack, eds., *Mapping Modern Theology*, p. 171.

We are then told that Barth has dispensed with "the metaphysical conception of the 'person' of Christ altogether. There is no 'person' somehow 'beneath' the two natures as that in which they 'subsist.' The two 'natures'—really, divine and human *being*—are made one in a single human history."[146] We are told that Barth has here "affirmed that Jesus Christ is fully divine and fully human in one person."[147] Whether or not this is an accurate presentation of Barth's Christology is a question all its own that will be discussed in greater detail in the next chapter. It is doubtful, as we shall see. But as a presentation of the Christology so carefully advanced by Torrance, this interpretation of Barth's thinking is confusing at best. For Torrance, who follows the early church fathers, the mystery of Jesus Christ consists precisely in the fact that his humanity is hypostatically united to the person of the eternal Son whose being is eternally constituted without reference to his will to become incarnate for us. Hence none of the persons of the Trinity "is before or after another: none is greater or less than the other. But the whole three persons are co-eternal and co-equal. So that in all things . . . the unity in trinity, and the trinity in unity is to be worshipped";[148] the idea that the two natures "are made one in a single history" leads to the idea that

> the history of God (in which the divine "essence" is constituted) and the history of the royal human (in which human "essence" is constituted) are one and the same history. . . . And if it be true that this one history is constitutive of both divine and human "essence," then this participation is also, at the same time, a participation in the divine "essence."[149]

The problem with this conclusion is that it undermines the hypostatic union simply because it does not acknowledge that the humanity of Jesus is what it is as it is posited in the eternal *Logos* so that the miracle in question could then be seen to reside in the fact that God, without ceasing to be God the eternal Word, acts through the Holy Spirit to become man by assuming human nature into the divine being in an act of condescension on our behalf. Instead, it is suggested that the person of Jesus Christ is the mutually constituted history of both divine and human essence in Jesus Christ himself.

---

[146]Ibid.
[147]Ibid.
[148]*Incarnation*, p. 234.
[149]McCormack, "Divine Impassibility," pp. 179-80.

As this relates to the relationship between time and eternity, one can easily see how McCormack's thesis that election logically precedes triunity causes trouble both in that it undermines the full eternal deity of the Word and that it disallows what to Torrance was a most important idea, namely, that because God has his own unique eternal time, there is a before and an after in what he does when he does things that are new even for himself. Thus he can argue that God's eternal election of us is an eternal action that is revealed in the history of Jesus as a mystery hidden through the ages but disclosed in his life, death and resurrection. And it is disclosed in that he heals our time, overcoming the opposition between past, present and future precisely because he is the same yesterday, today and tomorrow. So while McCormack, claiming to follow the later Barth, argues that the incarnation is not a new act for God since God is eternally God and man,[150] Torrance rightly insists that God is eternally God who elects to love us and that the movement and purpose of that love is for the Son to move toward us in the incarnation as an act of free grace and mercy that is neither arbitrary nor necessary but new even for himself. Without that distinction one would have to say that God was always incarnate or that the history of the man Jesus constitutes the eternal being of the Son in some sense. Either of those assertions, of course, would amount to a denial both of Jesus' true humanity and of his true divinity. None of this is to deny the importance of understanding creation through the events of the incarnation and redemption. But that cannot mean that God is understood to have become triune in order to relate with us as the incarnate Word and redeeming Spirit.

TIME AND SPACE/TIME AND ETERNITY

Whereas Torrance speaks of God's eternal time in its uniqueness and in its distinction in relation to created time, which needs reconciliation or fulfillment in light of what Christ did in his lifetime of obedience in reconciling the world and its time so that there may, in the consummation be a new heaven and a new earth, Bruce McCormack offers a very different view of time and eternity. He claims that the relation of eternity to time should be

---

[150]See above, chap. 3, pp. 155-56, where McCormack thus claims that in IV/1 Barth does not believe the incarnation "is a new event in God when it happens in time" ("Doctrine of the Trinity After Barth," p. 108).

understood as "the relation of a founding 'moment' to all subsequent temporal moments."[151] Any such idea undercuts the fact that Eternity is the living, moving and acting life of the triune God who does not simply found time but who actually enters into time without ceasing to be the eternal God, and exercises his eternal power of love in the freedom that is his alone in order to heal time and to fulfill it. The idea that eternity is simply the founding moment of time would have to mean that God would be only the beginning of a series of moments and not the very condition of the possibility of the moments we are given as creatures. But more importantly, any such suggestion would also have to mean that all of the incarnate Word's actions in time would be actions of the man Jesus and not actions of God *as* man. Torrance rightly and repeatedly insists that there is

> a communication of the divine and human acts in the one person of Christ. In him there takes place such a union and communion between his divine and human natures, that the divine acts are acts in his human nature, and the human acts are acts in his divine person. Each nature in communion with the other performs acts appropriate to it, but performs them as acts of the one person who embraces both natures, and is the one subject of all the divine and human acts.[152]

Here Torrance's idea of time and eternity can really help resolve the issues introduced by a failure to escape the Origenism discussed above. Consider, for example, Torrance's comments about time and space in relation to the ascended Lord. He notes that Jesus ascended from our human place to God's place while yet in himself he is "the one place in our human and created reality" and thus within our space and time "where God and man fully meet."[153] Because we tend to think abstractly about space and time, Torrance notes that we are inclined to imagine space "as something abstract and as something in itself, as though space could exist or be an entity in itself quite apart from the things it 'contains.'"[154] This is a dualistic form of thinking in that we imagine space and the things that are thought to be in it. From this

---

[151]McCormack, "Seek God Where He May Be Found: A Response to Edwin Chr. van Driel," *SJT* 60, no. 1 (2007): 75-76.
[152]*Incarnation*, p. 226.
[153]*Atonement*, p. 288.
[154]Ibid., pp. 288-89.

it follows that there could be "empty space." But, Torrance says, just as time must be understood as

> *time for* something, the time in which we live our life, time for decision, time for repentance, time for action, and the "time" of God is understood as the time in which God lives his own life, the time which God has in himself for his own eternal will of love, so we must think of space as *room for* something, as place defined in terms of that which occupies it.[155]

Torrance therefore insists that time and space must be thought out relationally—they are not to be thought of as abstract realities,

> but only *in relation* to active agents and therefore relationally—they are not "receptacles" apart from bodies or forces, but are functions of events in the universe and forms of their orderly sequence and structure. Space and time are *relational* and *variational* or *differential* concepts defined in accordance with the nature of the force that gives them their field of determination. They are *relational* to the operating forces and therefore *vary* or *differ* in accordance with them as those forces themselves vary or differ.[156]

These are critically important distinctions. And they lead Torrance to the following conclusions: (1) we cannot separate time from space, and (2) we cannot separate location from time since "temporal relation belongs to location." In other words, "we must think of place as well as time in terms of that *for which* they exist or function."[157] Consequently, we must speak of our human place and God's place; but we must do so differently because of the different realities in question. And this is where things get interesting.

"Man's place," Torrance says, "is defined by the nature and activity of man as the room which mankind makes for itself in human life and movement," while "God's 'place' is defined by the nature and activity of God as the room for life and activity of God as God."[158] Human space and time are defined by the change and sequence "of coherent structures in which human beings live life" within this physical world, and that also includes the personal, social and mental life in a properly differential way.[159] Hence, words such as *was, before,*

---

[155]Ibid.
[156]Ibid.
[157]Ibid.
[158]Ibid., pp. 289-90.
[159]Ibid., p. 290.

when and *beginning*, especially when used to refer to the fact that while God was always Father but not always creator, even though creation was in the mind of God before he actually brought it into being by a "definite act of his will" and thus gave it a beginning, are "time-related."[160] They thus present us with problems when speaking of God, "for the time-relations they imply *may not be read back into God*."[161] Here Torrance makes an important distinction, arguing that these terms have one meaning when referring to God since they "are governed by the unique nature of God, and another sense when used of creatures in accordance with their transitory natures."[162] So when the Scriptures tell us that "in the beginning God created," the word *beginning* must be understood in two distinct ways: (1) with reference to God's creating act, and (2) with reference to his works or to what he has created.

This implies that behind the beginning of creation there is "an absolute or transcendent beginning by God who is himself eternally without beginning."[163] That, Torrance says, is what makes creation so baffling—

> It is not only that something absolutely new has begun to be, *new even for God* who created it by his Word and gave it a contingent reality and integrity outwith himself, but that in some incomprehensible way, to cite Athanasius again, "the Word himself *became* the Maker of the things that have a beginning." God was always Father, not always Creator, but now he is Creator as well as Father. It is in similar terms that we may speak of the eternal Son who *became* Man. The Son was always Son of God, but now he is Man as well as God. "He was not man previously, but he became man for our sake."[164]

These were new acts "external to God," while yet they were new in God's eternal life. For this reason creation and incarnation, especially if we interpret creation by incarnation, tell us that God "is free to do what he had never done before, and free to be other than he was eternally: to be the Almighty Creator, and even to become incarnate as a creature within his creation."[165] These ideas, Torrance says, are offensive to the Greek mind, for it was impossible for them to conceive of something entirely new taking place, even for God.

[160] *Trinitarian Faith*, p. 87.
[161] Ibid., pp. 87-88, citing Athanasius *C. Ar.* I, 11, 13. Emphasis mine.
[162] Ibid., p. 88.
[163] Ibid.
[164] Ibid., some emphases mine.
[165] Ibid., p. 89.

Incarnation and creation sharply conflicted with "Greek philosophical categories of the necessity, immobility and impassivity of God."[166]

> We do not speak of space-time in relation to God, but we may speak of the "place" and "time" of God in terms of his own eternal life and his eternal purpose in the divine love, where he wills his life and love to overflow to us whom he has made to share with him his life and love. "Time" for God himself can only be defined by the uncreated and creative life of God, and "place" for God can only be defined by the communion of the persons in the divine life—that is why we speak of the "*perichōresis*" (from *chōra* meaning space or room) or mutual indwelling of the Father, Son and Holy Spirit in the triunity of God.[167]

What then does all this mean for the doctrines of the Trinity and of election? By maintaining the priority of the Father/Son relation over the creator/creature relation, Torrance is able to speak forcefully of God's eternal purpose of love as continually self-moving but without beginning or end. That is a pivotal remark. Torrance never suggests that God's purpose of love for us in his eternal decision of election in Jesus Christ is an act whereby he gives himself his triune being. That, for Torrance, would introduce the error of Greek thinking, which posits logical necessities and then presumes that without election God would not be the eternally living triune God. For Torrance, by contrast, God is continually new because God is unencumbered by the limitations of created time, and yet God's uncreated time is the basis for his relations of love with us in history. Our creaturely time and our created time are "contingently grounded upon the eternal time of God."[168] But there is a purpose of the divine love that is continually new, and so God can and does do new things, new even for himself. So there are moments in God's eternal life, and we can thus speak meaningfully of a before and an after in God's eternal life, such as the before and after of creation and incarnation.

Yet, this understanding of God's time and our time yields a very positive result. Torrance is able to maintain that God could have remained God without us but in the eternal purpose of his love he willed to be God with us, and that act of will is the act of the eternal Father, Son and Holy Spirit. By making these distinctions between God's eternal time and created time

---

[166]Ibid.

[167]*Atonement*, p. 290.

[168]*Christian Doctrine of God*, p. 241.

and history, Torrance can thus speak of creation as proleptically interpreted in light of the incarnation. But he can do so without projecting the limitations of history and created time back into the immanent Trinity. And the hallmark indication of what he has thereby accomplished is that he can say that God's eternal election is a free act of love on the part of God as the beginning of his ways and works with us and for us; he can say that what God is toward us he is eternally in himself, and thus maintain that the immanent and economic Trinity is identical in content; he can further say that the incarnation was not a transient episode in history that will one day cease to include history and time in the inner life of God. But he can say all of these important things without making the claim that God's election of us logically preceded his being as the triune God. That logical reversal is exactly the idea that is eliminated when one sees and maintains consistently that while election is grounded in God's eternal purpose of love, it nonetheless is itself an act of the triune God. Consequently, the priority of the Father/Son relation not only pertains to the doctrine of election, but it ensures that all the acts of God *ad extra* are acts of grace that are not necessary for God to be or to become the God he is. Rather these are acts external to God, whose meaning can only be discerned in light of the existence of creation and the incarnation of his Word within creation. Torrance can thus say:

> God is not one thing in himself and another thing in Jesus Christ—what God is toward us in Jesus he is inherently and eternally in himself. . . . There is a oneness in Being and agency between Jesus Christ the incarnate Son and God the Father. What God is in eternity, Jesus Christ is in space and time, and what Jesus Christ is in space and time, God is in his eternity. . . . There is thus no God behind the back of Jesus Christ.[169]

The issues discussed in this chapter can be seen even more clearly when the perils of "historicizing" Christology are specified. To this we now turn.

---

[169]Ibid., p. 243.

5

The Perils of Embracing a
"Historicized Christology"

In this chapter I will suggest that theologians who advance a "historicized Christology" by arguing for the idea that Jesus' human history in some sense "constitutes" his being as the second person of the Trinity actually undermine Jesus' true divinity and fail to uphold key aspects of the church's Christology. I will develop this thesis by presenting the more traditional view of the incarnation offered by Thomas F. Torrance and then comparing his dynamic view of Christ's divinity, operative within space and time, with the views offered by Robert Jenson, who believes that "Instead of interpreting Christ's deity as a separate entity that always *was* . . . we should interpret it as a final *outcome*, and just *so* as eternal";[1] and Bruce McCormack, who believes that

> If, in Jesus Christ, God has elected to become human, then the human history of Jesus Christ is constitutive of the being and existence of God in the second of God's modes to the extent that the being and existence of the Second Person of the Trinity cannot be rightly thought of in the absence of this human history.[2]

I will argue that historicizing Jesus' being as the second person of the Trinity in the manner suggested by both Jenson and McCormack inevitably confuses both epistemology and ontology and the "processions" and "missions"

---

[1]Robert W. Jenson, *The Triune Identity: God According to the Gospel* (Philadelphia: Fortress, 1982), p. 140.
[2]Bruce L. McCormack, "Karl Barth's Historicized Christology: Just How 'Chalcedonian' Is It?" in McCormack, *Orthodox and Modern: Studies in the Theology of Karl Barth* (Grand Rapids: Baker Academic, 2008), p. 223.

of the trinitarian persons, thereby conceptually eliminating Christ's genuine preexistence. Such thinking unwittingly undermines the idea that the world was actually created by the Father *through* the Word, by inadvertently embracing some version of the idea that there was *once* when Jesus was not the Son. When it is asserted that Jesus' divinity is in any sense constituted by his human history or must be seen as the outcome of that human history and not as a reality that "always was," then and there it is impossible to uphold the true eternity of the Son.

THOMAS F. TORRANCE ON THE INCARNATION

We have already seen that Thomas F. Torrance rejects any idea that God's eternal triune being is in any sense constituted by his history with us. At this point I will not present a thorough view of the incarnation in Torrance's thinking. For the purposes of this chapter I would, however, like to explain precisely why I think Torrance's view of the incarnation excludes the idea that Jesus' human history constitutes his being as the second person of the Trinity. As seen above, in Torrance's thinking, Jesus is to be understood as uniquely divine and human from the outset because in him, as the incarnate Word, we are dealing with "a new and unique fact without analogy anywhere in human experience or knowledge."[3] Knowledge of this unique fact can come only from and through Christ himself and not through our experience or capacities for knowledge or intuition. Because Jesus really is "Lord and God" we can only know him as one who is truly divine and truly human by acknowledging him for who he is. Thus the starting point for Christology, in Torrance's view, is the mystery of Jesus himself, namely, "the mysterious duality in unity of Jesus Christ, God without reserve, man without reserve, the eternal truth in time, the Word of God made flesh."[4] Because Jesus himself is this mystery we cannot explain how we know him "in terms of our capacities or abilities or any a priori understanding."[5]

This means that we must begin thinking about Jesus by acknowledging the truth of his incarnation: This man Jesus is the Word of God present in space and time and present to us and for us as the reconciler. His humanity

---

[3]*Incarnation*, p. 1. See above, pp. 207n89 and 214.
[4]Ibid., p. 3.
[5]Ibid., p. 2.

is posited by an act of the Word, and thus it is "not consumed by his deity"[6] but rather has its historical actuality precisely because it is what it is humanly in and by the Word itself. We meet God in Jesus Christ because it is in him that God has forever joined himself together with us. But Torrance is adamant that *we* cannot join God and humanity together, and that this is what we see in Jesus Christ.

> Incarnation tells us plainly that all our efforts to go from humanity to God are useless and false. . . . God has done the impossible, the incredible thing in Jesus Christ, but it is only now that he has done it that we see how utterly impossible it actually is, impossible for us to accomplish from the side of humanity.[7]

From these reflections we can easily see why Torrance insists that

> If Jesus Christ is the Son of God become man, then the historical humanity of this particular man, Jesus, cannot be fully appreciated or understood apart from the fact that he is Son of God as well as Son of Man. We must therefore interpret Jesus in the light of the origin from which he came and without which he would not be.[8]

Jesus simply cannot be understood by historical analysis, then, because historians never take into account "the vertical movement in and through which Jesus came into being in history."[9] This can only happen through the Holy Spirit, Torrance believes, because "No one says that Jesus is Lord except by the Holy Spirit."[10]

A further important feature of Torrance's Christology concerns the fact that the Word incarnate in Jesus Christ does not cease being divine in the incarnation but assumes our sinful humanity in order to "heal, sanctify and redeem it."[11] In his view, if the Word or Son did not actually assume our

---

[6]Ibid., p. 9.

[7]Ibid., pp. 9-10.

[8]Ibid., p. 27. Note the similarities between what Torrance says here and Barth's explication of the grace of origin of his human existence: "The grace of His particular origin consists in the fact that He exists as man as in the mode of existence of the Son God Himself exists. It is only because God exists that this One exists as man" (IV/2, p. 90).

[9]Ibid.

[10]Ibid.

[11]Ibid., p. 62. Importantly, Torrance writes: "The incarnation was not necessary for God to be God and live as God: it flowed freely, unreservedly and unconditionally from the eternal movement of Love in God, the very Love which God is and in which God lives his Life as God; it took place in the sovereign ontological freedom of God to be other in his external relations than he eternally

sinful humanity, then God himself did not really come all the way to us where we are in our estrangement from God. He did this, however, "without ceasing to be the holy Son of God. He entered into complete solidarity with us in our sinful existence in order to save us, without becoming himself a sinner."[12] Consequently, for Torrance, "If God the Word became flesh, God the Word is the subject of the incarnation, and how could God sin? How could God deny God, be against himself, divest himself of his holiness and purity?"[13] This is why Torrance will not begin Christology from below or from above "but from below and from above at the same time."[14] Unless we understand Jesus' history from who and what he was and is above, and unless we understand who and what Jesus is as the eternal Son from his human history as the incarnate Word, we will fall into what Torrance labels either an Ebionite or a Docetic view of Jesus, and thus we will miss the

---

was, and is, and to do what he had never done before. Thus in his freedom God chose not to live alone entirely in and by himself, but to create others for fellowship with himself, and in his wisdom chose to become incarnate, condescending in sheer love and grace to be one with us and one of us in our world, in order to realise his saving love for us in our lost existence, yet in such a way that he remains undiminished in the transcendent Freedom, Nature and Mystery of his eternal Being" (*Christian Doctrine of God*, p. 108). As we just saw in the last chapter in connection with the Origenist error and as we shall see below, it is exactly when theologians confuse God's external and internal relations that they then resolve God's free, transcendent and eternal being into his being for us. They fail to deploy the careful distinctions that Torrance employs, which allow him to say quite forcefully that God really is toward us what he is in himself, but that God is in no way constituted by his love for us evident in the incarnation, suffering and death of his Son.

[12]Ibid. Thomas G. Weinandy, O.F.M. Cap., *Jesus the Christ* (Huntington, IN: Our Sunday Visitor Publishing Division, 2003), pp. 98-99, also notes the importance of affirming that "the Son of God did not assume some generic humanity but our own sinful humanity" precisely in order to "heal and save it" (p. 99). See also Weinandy, *In the Likeness of Sinful Flesh: An Essay on the Humanity of Christ* (New York: T & T Clark, 2006). The problem in Torrance's view here is that of Apollinarianism, according to which Jesus' human mind was replaced by "the divine mind." This meant that "It was therefore some sort of neutral humanity that the Son of God assumed, and not the actual humanity in which we sinners all share" (*Atonement*, p. 439). Importantly, Torrance contends, with the fathers, that what was not assumed was not saved and that because, according to the Greek fathers we are estranged from God in the depths of our being, that is, in our minds, which govern our thinking and our culture, "we have become estranged from the truth and hostile to God." It is there, in that hostility, "that we desperately need to be redeemed and healed" (*Atonement*, p. 439). That is what is lost whenever it is thought or implied that the Word did not assume our sinful humanity in order to heal it.

[13]*Incarnation*, p. 63. In answer to the question of whether Jesus could have sinned, Torrance unequivocally answers no, because if that were possible, then it would be possible for God to come into conflict with himself. Even though in the incarnation the Word assumed our fallen nature, Jesus himself did not share our original sin, and he himself never sinned. See Thomas F. Torrance, *The Doctrine of Jesus Christ* (Eugene, OR: Wipf and Stock, 2002), pp. 121-30, especially pp. 128-29.

[14]*Christian Doctrine of God*, p. 114.

unique revelation that takes place only in and through him. For Torrance, "The ebionite approach to Christ was from below, and the docetic approach to Christ was from above."[15] Both must be rejected because, for Torrance, we meet God himself in Jesus Christ, and

> The New Testament does not present Christ in contrast to God or alongside of God, or argue from one to the other, as in ebionite and docetic Christologies, but presents him in the unbroken relationship of his incarnate life and work to God to the Father, and thus in the undivided wholeness of his divine-human reality as the Son of God become man.[16]

But the most important point to be noted here is the fact that what God is for us in Jesus Christ, he is eternally in himself.[17] Yet for Torrance this could never mean that God's eternal Sonship was in any sense constituted by his being for us in the history of Jesus. When Torrance speaks of Jesus' human actions (his work of atonement in particular), he means to assert that his human actions have significance only because they are actions of the person of Christ whose person and work are indivisible because of the incarnation.[18] It is "the person of Christ revealing so that revelation cannot be separated off from his person. Similarly, it is the person of Christ atoning, so that atonement cannot be divided from Christ's person."[19] This is why Torrance maintains that in the atonement "God's action was translated into terms of human action, for only in so doing does it reach men and women and become relevant to them as saving act; but it remains God's action, for only so does it touch and lay hold of them, and raise them up to salvation in reconciliation with God."[20]

As noted above in chapter four, Torrance employs the Greek patristic terms *enhypostasis* and *anhypostasis* to assert that Jesus' human nature has

---

[15]Ibid. See also *Incarnation*, p. 98. Torrance notes that the virgin birth was inserted into the creed partially to "combat Docetism." But it "equally excludes Ebionism, that is, excludes the idea that the Son of God united himself with one who was already man, or that a human being, either in embryo or as already born, was at some point adopted to be the Son of God" (pp. 98-99).

[16]Ibid., p. 115.

[17]Thus, "God is not one thing in himself and another thing in Jesus Christ—what God is toward us in Jesus he is inherently and eternally in himself. . . . There is no *deus absconditus*, no dark inscrutable God, no arbitrary Deity of whom we can know nothing but before whom we can only tremble" (*Christian Doctrine of God*, p. 243). See also *Christian Doctrine of God*, p. 130, and *Trinitarian Faith*, p. 130.

[18]See *Incarnation*, p. 108.

[19]Ibid.

[20]Ibid., p. 195.

its reality in the *hypostasis* of the Son (*anhypostasis* thus emphasizes "the *general* humanity of Jesus, the human nature assumed by the Son with its *hypostasis* in the Son"), but that the *particular* humanity of the man Jesus is in fact none other than the humanity of one "whose person is not other than the person of the divine Son."[21] Thus, *enhypostasis* emphasizes Jesus' particular humanity as the humanity of the Word. Jesus' human nature then was united to the Son in a unique way and thus in a way that ours can never be—that indeed is the significance of the virgin birth for Torrance.

> While the Son of God assumed our human nature, and became fully and really like us, nevertheless his full and complete human nature was united to God in a unique way (hypostatically in one person) as our human nature is not, and never will be. Therefore he is unlike us, not unlike us as to the humanity of his human nature, but in the unique union of his human nature to the divine nature in the one person of God the Son. (This is the baffling element in the virgin birth, which tells us that while it is our very human nature he assumed, he did not assume it in the way we share in it, because he took it in a unique relation with his deity.)[22]

Importantly, while Torrance places great stress on the human history of Jesus, he never thinks of Jesus acting in history except as the Son of God, because his humanity is inseparably united with the person of the Son.[23] And he insists that this is a dynamic activity so that "Jesus Christ is not just an instrument in the hands of God arbitrarily to be taken up, used, and laid aside at will; he *is* God become man, and remains God even though he has come among us as man."[24] Torrance will even say, "The cross is the out-

---

[21]Ibid., p. 230.

[22]Ibid.

[23]See ibid., p. 67, where Torrance notes, "*Jesus exists as man only so far as he exists as God,* and yet as God he also has an existence as flesh or *sarx*. There would have been no Jesus apart from the incarnation, so that the existence of Jesus even as man is an existence only in the Word become flesh, but in that the Word became flesh, there now exists a man Jesus who is true man and exists as historical human beings exist." In Torrance's view this is a completed event that has taken place "once and for all in the union of God and man in Jesus Christ; but it is also a historical event, a dynamic event, a real happening in the time of this world which is coincident with the whole historical life of Jesus." This historical life of Jesus remains real and is eternally a happening in history just because it falls within the life of the eternal Word; while it is a past event, it breaks through the relativity of history, which is marked by sin and decay and makes itself accessible to us in that history.

[24]*Christian Doctrine of God*, p. 216. All of this depends on the fact that Jesus' human history is the history of oneness between us and God "in the one Person of Jesus Christ" (ibid.). Hence, Jesus

working of a divine decision that constitutes the person of the Mediator himself in the incarnation."[25]

Consequently, in the atonement "God has brought about an act at once from the side of God as God, *and* from the side of man as man: an act of real and final union between God and man."[26] But notice what he does not say. He does not say that the second person of the Trinity is constituted by his decision to be for us in this way or by what happens in Jesus' human history. He does not say what some today say, namely, that the only act of the Son in relation to his humanity is the act of giving it existence in his own existence so that all other acts of the incarnate Word are acts only of the man Jesus. And he does not say this because it is not history but the history of the Son of God that he is thinking about. And this means, for Torrance, that because "God was not always incarnate any more than he was always Creator, the incarnation and the creation are to be regarded as new even for God, although they result from the eternal outgoing movement of his Love."[27] But, as discussed in chapter four in connection with God's internal and external relations, Torrance insists that

we cannot think of the ontological Trinity as if it were constituted by or dependent on the economic Trinity, but must rather think of the economic Trinity as the freely predetermined manifestation in the history of salvation of the eternal Trinity which God himself was before the foundation of the world, and eternally is. Hence when we rightly speak of the oneness between the ontological Trinity and the economic Trinity, we may not speak of that oneness without distinguishing and delimiting it from the ontological Trinity—there are in any case . . . elements in the incarnate economy such as the time pattern of human life in this world which we may not read back into the eternal Life of God.[28]

---

is the presence of God's kingdom among us in action, and the way he acted according to the gospel is exactly the way "the Father Almighty acts." Consequently, "that is how God will always act throughout all space and time into the consummation of his purpose of love" (ibid.).

[25]*Incarnation*, p. 108.

[26]Ibid., p. 195. See also *Atonement*, pp. 68-69, 76-77, 103-4, 121-23, 228-29, 274.

[27]*Christian Doctrine of God*, p. 108. Thus, "Since the Father-Son relation subsists eternally within the Communion of the Holy Trinity we must think of the incarnation of the Son as falling within the eternal Life and Being of God, although, of course, the incarnation was not a timeless event like the generation of the Son from the Being of the Father, but must be regarded as new even for God, for the Son of God was not eternally Man any more than the Father was eternally Creator" (*Christian Doctrine of God*, p. 144).

[28]*Christian Doctrine of God*, pp. 108-9.

For Torrance, as we have seen, election is

> the *prothesis*, the setting forth, the projection of that love [the love between
> the Father and the Son] in Christ the beloved Son of God, through whom we
> are adopted into Christ's eternal relation of sonship in love to the Father. Jesus
> Christ is identical with God's decision and man's election in the divine love.
> That *prothesis* is the great eternal presupposition of all God's relations with
> man, and man's relations with God.[29]

As argued in chapter four, this thinking allows Torrance to maintain that
election and incarnation are new acts even for God without introducing the
limitations associated with created time into the Godhead. Thus, he makes
a crucial distinction that historicist perspectives do not make by insisting
that Jesus' humanity is *not* eternal in the sense that "it was eternally pre-
existent" because it is his person that is eternal, and "his person is not human,
but divine."[30] Hence, the hypostatic union refers to "a union of two natures
in one person" but "does not assert the pre-existence and in that sense the
eternity of the human nature."[31] After the incarnation, and in light of the
resurrection and ascension, we can and must say that Jesus Christ, the one
Mediator, exists forever as the divine-human high priest, prophet and king
who has once for all reconciled humanity to God and united us to God so
that we may participate in his new humanity. This is a crucial distinction
that is lost in historicized versions of Christology. And this is why when
Torrance is confronted by the question of whether God suffers in the suffering of Jesus on the cross, he insists that God must be seen as both passible
and impassible, because in the incarnation God did not cease being God but
freely subjected himself to human suffering out of love for us.[32] God is thus
not constituted by his suffering for us but becomes passible in virtue of his
impassibility and perfection in order that we might be reconciled with him.

For Torrance "logically impassibility and passibility exclude one another,"[33]
and we cannot get the right understanding here thinking about impassibility
in the Stoic sense. Rather we must understand that God in his impassibility

---

[29]*Incarnation*, p. 178.
[30]Ibid., p. 177.
[31]Ibid.
[32]See above, chap. 4, pp. 189 and 207 for more on this.
[33]*Trinitarian Faith*, p. 185.

has "stooped" down to us and has overcome our suffering, pain and guilt in the Mediator out of sheer divine love. By sharing our passion then—by experiencing in mind, heart, soul and divinity our God-forsakenness as exemplified in his cry of dereliction in Mark 15:34, a passage repeatedly cited by Torrance when discussing the incarnation and atonement, Christ enables us to share in his "imperturbability (ἀπάθεια)."[34] In fact it is just at this point that Torrance shows how a proper trinitarian understanding of this issue shows the way forward. Torrance stresses Mark 15:34 but at the same time links Jesus' cry of God-forsakenness on the cross with Luke 23:46 and says that his cry of dereliction is followed by his cry "Father, into thy hands I commend my spirit."[35] This is the epitome of Christ's vicarious humanity at work in human history for our benefit. Jesus Christ not only experienced our passibility or God-forsakenness, even though he himself was not a sinner, but he answered to God for us by experiencing God's own opposition to our self-will and sin in a complete life of obedience that consisted in a renewed relationship between creator and creatures, exemplified in his obedience to the will of God: "Not my will, but thine be done" (Lk 22:42).[36]

One further point needs to be made: for Torrance, "the humanity of Christ has no revealing or saving significance for us apart from his deity, and his deity has no revealing or saving significance for us apart from his humanity."[37] This, because his divine and human actions "*are truly and completely united in one person or hypostasis.*" Thus, "the presence of full and perfect deity does not impair or diminish or restrict the presence of full and perfect humanity."[38] Unless all Jesus' human actions are seen as the actions of "the one divine person," we will inevitably miss the fact that in this man God has come all the way to us in our human history. "It is only because Christ is himself personally God that his human speech and human actions, and his human forms of thought, are also divine revelation."[39] This is why Torrance maintains that God comes to us in Christ *as* man and not just in a

---

[34]Ibid., p. 186.
[35]*Christian Doctrine of God*, p. 251.
[36]Torrance, "Questioning in Christ," in Torrance, *Theology in Reconstruction* (London: SCM Press, 1965), p. 126.
[37]*Incarnation*, p. 191.
[38]Ibid.
[39]Ibid., pp. 192-93.

man.[40] This allows Torrance to say, "There are not two actions in the life and death of Jesus Christ, but one action of the God-man, one action which is at once manward and Godward."[41] Consequently, he adds that

> Only the Word through whom man was made, by himself becoming man, can act in man's place and for man in such a way as to restore that which man lost, and recover what man lost in the creator Word of God. The atonement is the work of the God-man, of God and man in hypostatic union, not simply an act of God in man, but an act of God *as* man.[42]

ROBERT W. JENSON

Now let us see where Robert Jenson is led in his thinking about Jesus and the Trinity by his belief that "Instead of interpreting Christ's deity as a separate entity that always *was* . . . we should interpret it as a final *outcome*, and just *so* as eternal." How did Jenson come to think in this way?

Without presenting a developed version of Jenson's Hegelianized Christianity,[43] which causes him to transfer the eternal existence of the Son to history with his belief that Jesus' Sonship comes from his resurrection, I would like to explore what happens to his view of Christ when he interprets his Sonship "as a final *outcome*." It certainly leads to his complete rejection of the *Logos asarkos* in favor of the idea that Jesus' eternal being is the being that will come into existence through his historical relations with the Father in the eschatological future. The adoptionist and indeed the Arian overtones here seem clear in that Jenson's Hegelian and historicist view of Jesus' person and work make it impossible for him to affirm an actually existent eternal Trinity, that is, an eternal Trinity that exists independently of history and prior to it. My point here is that Jenson's Hegelian metaphysics, which he believes resolves many of the tensions resident in traditional Christology and

---

[40]Ibid., p. 195.

[41]Ibid.

[42]Ibid. See also *Christian Doctrine of God*, pp. 40-41. This of course is why Torrance insists that hypostatic union and atonement belong together.

[43]For a full discussion and critique of what George Hunsinger rightly calls Jenson's "neo-Arian" and "Socinian" view of Christ's eternal Sonship and his separation of the cross from Christ's resurrection, as well as his "panentheistic" view of the Trinity, see George Hunsinger, "Robert Jenson's *Systematic Theology*: A Review Essay," *SJT* 55, no. 2 (2002): 161-200. For a sympathetic, yet critical, presentation of Jenson's theology, see Scott R. Swain, *The God of the Gospel* (Downers Grove, IL: InterVarsity Press, 2013).

trinitarian theology, actually ends with a historicized version of Christology that finally cannot uphold the truth of the church's Christology or of the doctrine of the Trinity in any consistent manner. His intention certainly is to uphold what he takes to be the central sense of those doctrines. But his emphasis on futurity and his consistent rejection of the *Logos asarkos* prevent him from doing so in a plausible and consistent fashion. I therefore agree with George Hunsinger, who claims that Jenson's "'Hegelian' metaphysics . . . is a version of panentheism" that "tends toward monism" or toward "a kind of 'dialectical historicism with a teleological contour.'"[44] Hunsinger demonstrates how this Hegelianism gives Jenson's Christology "its 'adoptionist' and 'Arian features'" that eventuate in a doctrine of the Trinity that displays elements of subordinationism and "perhaps tritheism."[45] This Hegelian metaphysics is what shapes Jenson's attempt to reinterpret the classical doctrines of Christology and of the Trinity. And that is how I believe he came to his problematic reinterpretation of Christ's eternal Sonship. The most problematic element in this Hegelian metaphysics is the panentheist idea that somehow events within history *constitute* God's eternal being. It is my contention in this book that any suggestion that events in history *constitute* God's eternal being in any sense at all finally makes God in some sense dependent on the world for his own existence and inevitably confuses time and eternity. This is the case even if those theologians who think history in some sense determines Jesus' eternal Sonship simultaneously assert the freedom of God.

On the one hand, following his ideas as expressed in his book *The Triune Identity*, he arrives at this thinking in an effort to explain that "the 'economic' Trinity *is* the 'immanent' Trinity, and vice versa." On the other hand, he argues that there is a "legitimate theological reason for the 'immanent'/'economic' distinction," and that reason is to preserve the "freedom of God." And so he writes: "it must be that God 'in himself' could have been the same God he is, and so triune, had there been no creation, or no saving of fallen creation."[46]

---

[44] George Hunsinger, "Robert Jenson's *Systematic Theology*," p. 175.

[45] Ibid., p. 187.

[46] Jenson, *Triune Identity*, p. 139. It should be noted that while Jenson still espoused something of this idea in *STI*, pp. 65, 221, and *Systematic Theology*, vol. 2 (New York: Oxford University Press, 1999), p. 23, with certain modifications, he now retracts this thinking because he believes it is nonsensical even to ask how the Trinity would have been the Trinity "if God had not created a world." See Robert W. Jenson, "Once More the *Logos Asarkos*," *IJST* 13, no. 2 (April 2011): 130-33, at p. 131. It is still worthwhile exploring his earlier thought to see how it was shaped in rela-

Jenson believes he can reconcile both of these statements if the identity of the immanent and the economic Trinity is understood eschatologically. In other words God's freedom will be preserved only if "the 'immanent' Trinity is simply the eschatological reality of the 'economic.'" But, in his view, this requires a radical reconstruction of the traditional view that Jesus' eternal existence could only be understood by positing "a reality that always *was* in God." Within this traditional idiom, theologians posited the idea of a "Logos *asarkos*," that is, "the 'not [yet] incarnate Word,' who always was in God and then *became* the one sent in flesh to us. The Logos' relation to the Father was described as a Father-Son relation, and rightly, since it is Jesus' relation to his Father that is to be interpreted."[47] Jenson objects to this traditional viewpoint, saying, "the begetting and being-begotten of *this* Father and *this* Son had to be timeless; thus this 'procession' could not in fact be the same as the temporal relation of Jesus to his Father, that is, as the 'mission.'"[48] He contends that the Greek Fathers mostly ignored this difficulty and thought of the processions and missions as occurring together. But when more rigid thinkers reflected on this, the difficulty "proved fatal." He therefore believes that this entire pattern must be reversed.

> Instead of interpreting Christ's deity as a separate entity that always *was*—and preceding analogously with the Spirit—we should interpret it as a final *outcome*, and just *so* as eternal, just so as the bracket around all beginnings and endings. Jesus' historical life was a sending by the Father; a filial relation between Jesus and the Transcendence to which he turned temporally in fact occurred. And this man is risen from the dead, so that his mission must triumph, so that his filial relation to his Father is unimpeachable. Thus Jesus'

---

tion to his conception of Christ's preexistence, especially since even in this later article he is still trying to uphold Christ's genuine preexistence while holding a view that clearly collapses the immanent into the economic Trinity, as when he says: "The Father's sending and Jesus' obedience *are* the second hypostasis in God" (p. 133). Strained to the limit, Jenson contends that it is this very relation that subsists before Mary's conception, claiming that the life of the immanent Trinity is "constituted in nothing but the web of such relations" (p. 133). That of course is the problem. If Jesus' obedience to his Father's sending constitutes the immanent Trinity, then in reality, there is no immanent Trinity, since God's eternal relations (processions) have been made to be dependent on the missions (the sending of the Son and the obedience of Jesus). All of this confusion follows Jenson's continued rejection of the *Logos asarkos* or of the Word who preexisted his incarnate life on earth.

[47]Ibid., p. 140.
[48]Ibid.

obedience to the Father, and their love for us which therein occurs, *will* prove unsurpassable events, which is the same as that they now *are* God-events, "processions" in God.[49]

Notice what has happened in Jenson's thought. Because he will only think of the immanent Trinity and thus of Christ's eternal being as the outcome of his human relations with his Father, he has lost what for Torrance was the most crucial element in Christology. He can only think of Christ's deity as the final outcome of his historical life on earth, whereas Torrance insisted that his entire human life was nothing other than the life of the eternal Son of God who was *always* Son but was not always incarnate.[50] While Torrance insists that everything Jesus does humanly he does as the Son of God because of the hypostatic union, Jenson thinks that the resurrection is what makes him the Son of God.[51] And that is not the end of it. Jenson proceeds to confuse the missions with the processions or the immanent and the economic Trinity, in spite of the fact that he himself stated that it is important to maintain God's freedom, namely, the fact that God could have been

---

[49]Ibid.

[50]It is just this important assertion by Torrance that Jenson rejects in his most recent attempt to rethink this issue. Jenson thinks he can say at one and the same time that there never was a time when the Son was not and that there was no *Logos asarkos* or Son who existed prior to his existence as Jesus, the incarnate Son. The idea that there is no Word prior to his incarnate life on earth must, however, imply either that Jesus always existed in his humanity (which would deny the incarnation as new act of God) or that the Son was never actually the Son without his human history. Either way, such thinking cannot avoid the appearance of adoptionism and Arianism.

[51]For Jenson, Christ's Sonship is neither determined by his birth nor by his preexistence but by his resurrection: "He is Son in that he is resurrected" (*STI*, p. 142). Further, "In that Christ's Sonship comes 'from' his Resurrection, it comes from God's future into which he is raised" (p. 143). Jenson also says "Jesus would not be the Word without the Resurrection" (p. 171). Indeed, Jenson claims that "*fully* reliable love can *only* be the resurrected life of one who has died for the beloved ones" (p. 199). Finally, we are told not only that "the way in which the triune God is eternal, is by the events of Jesus' death and resurrection" but that his "individuality is constitutive of the true God's infinity" (p. 219). The error in each of these assertions can be seen in the fact that Jenson is unable to say with Torrance, Barth and the tradition that the resurrection manifests Jesus as the Word, but it does not in any way constitute his being as the Word, since this is fully constituted within the immanent Trinity as the condition that enables God to love us in the events of Jesus' life history. Instead, in true historicist fashion, Jenson claims that God is only eternal in and by the events of Jesus' life history and that his "individuality" constitutes God's infinity. Here history is allowed to determine God's being, and this amounts to a collapse of the immanent into the economic Trinity. This remains unchanged in his latest reflections, as when he explains that the Son as a creature "is 'determined' to be 'the powerful Son of God' by action of the Spirit; and so not by divine origin as the christological tradition might make us expect, but rather by the resurrection, the supreme act of the Spirit who is 'Giver of Life'" (Jenson, "Once More the *Logos Asarkos*," p. 132).

triune without us, at least in his earlier reflections.

Jenson therefore concludes that

> the saving events, whose plot is stated by the doctrine of trinitarian relations,
> *are*, in their eschatological finality, God's transcendence of time, his eternity,
> so that we need posit no timelessly antecedent extra entities—Logos *asarkos*
> or not-yet given Spirit—to assert the unmitigated eternity of Son and Spirit.[52]

For Jenson, traditional trinitarian theology is captive of "an alien definition
of deity" and therefore will not allow us to say simply "that Jesus *is* 'the
eternal Son.'"[53] In other words, within this captive notion of deity we cannot
say that "what happens between the human Jesus and his Father and the
believing community *is* eternity" because we must think of Jesus as "the
dwelling and manifestation of his own preexistent Double—and with that
all the impossibilities [of the traditional view] present themselves." It is the
need for that "pre" that causes the problems, according to Jenson. It is because traditionally eternity is conceived "as Persistence of the first past" instead of as "Faithfulness to the last future" that the problems of thinking
correctly about Jesus and about the Trinity arise.[54] What, then, does Jenson's solution look like?

> Truly, the Trinity is simply the Father and the man Jesus and their Spirit as
> the Spirit of the believing community. This "economic" Trinity is *eschatologi-
> cally* God "himself," an "immanent" Trinity. And that assertion is no problem,
> for God *is* himself only eschatologically, since he is Spirit. . . . As for God's
> freedom, only this proposal fully asserts it. . . . Genuine freedom is the reality
> of possibility, is openness to the future; genuine freedom is Spirit.[55]

---

[52]Jenson, *Triune Identity*, pp. 140-41.
[53]Ibid., p. 141.
[54]Ibid.
[55]Ibid. What this means for the Trinity is this: "the Son's subsistence must therefore be as much from the Spirit as *telos* as from the Father as *arche*" (Jenson, "Once More the *Logos Asarkos*," p. 132). In my view this change in the order of the trinitarian relations is the result of Jenson's need to histo-ricize the eternal Son by claiming that his deity comes from his future by means of the Spirit in accordance with his Hegelianized metaphysics. In traditional trinitarian understanding the Spirit proceeds from the Father and the Son or from the Father through the Son in eternity. The idea that the Son is constituted either by the Father as *arche* or by the Spirit as *telos* undermines the fact that all three persons of the Trinity are equally and fully divine by virtue of their perichoretic rela-tions within the immanent Trinity. Put succinctly, the Father is the *arche* in that the Father is first in order within the Trinity of persons. But that should not imply that the Son and Spirit receive their being from the Father, since the generation of the Son and procession of the Spirit are eternal

THE TRINITY: THE FATHER AND THE MAN JESUS AND THEIR SPIRIT AS THE SPIRIT OF THE BELIEVING COMMUNITY

In light of what was said above with regard to Torrance's thought about the incarnation, I trust that the problems inherent in this solution will be quite evident. For Torrance, who I believe speaks in harmony with the tradition, one could never say that the Trinity is simply the Father and the man Jesus because, in virtue of the incarnation, we know that the Trinity is the eternal Father, Son and Holy Spirit who does not need to create or to become incarnate in order to be God. In Torrance's words, "God does not need the world to be God, so the Fatherhood of God is in no way dependent on or constituted by relation to what he has created outwith himself."[56] Rather, "The world needs God to be what it is, but God does not need the world to be what he is. . . . The Creator was free not to create."[57] Consequently, God does not merely have his existence from the future but from his eternal existence as Father who was always Father but not always Creator, and Son who was always Son and not always incarnate. To say that the Trinity is simply the Father and the man Jesus is to eradicate the eternal existence of the triune God and not to assert it. It undermines the very heart of the incarnation by implying that Jesus is not the Son before the incarnation or during his earthly life. Such thinking leads Simon Gathercole to conclude that Jenson's position is incoherent.[58] While Jenson intends to uphold an

---

acts that do not in the least mean that the Son and Spirit derive their deity from the Father, because all three persons are always already one in being. Therefore each is fully divine, and none of the persons thus becomes divine in their eternal actions *in se* or *ad extra*. Thus, any attempt to speak of the Son as from the Spirit as *telos* could, and in Jenson's thought, seems to open the door to the idea that the Son in some sense has his being from the Spirit's activities in history. Thus Jenson says, "Truly, the Trinity is simply the Father and the man Jesus and *their Spirit as the Spirit of the believing community*" (*Triune Identity*, p. 141, emphasis mine). And, as we have seen, he thinks of Jesus' being the Son or Word as deriving from the resurrection (above, note 51).

[56]*Christian Doctrine of God*, p. 207.

[57]Torrance, *Divine and Contingent Order*, p. 34.

[58]See Simon Gathercole, "Pre-existence, and the Freedom of the Son in Creation and Redemption: An Exposition in Dialogue with Robert Jenson," *IJST* 7, no. 1 (January 2005): 38-51, at p. 47. "Jenson's Christology fails in that it cannot accommodate a real, personal 'before and after' which the Son's free act entails" (p. 47). Captive to his historicism, Jenson claims "that an event happens to something does not entail that this something must be metaphysically or temporally prior to it" (*STI*, p. 221). The problem with this statement is that, in the case of the incarnation, unless the Son preexists his incarnate life on earth, metaphysically and temporally, then one can only either embrace adoptionism or deny that the incarnation is a new free act of God, who does not need to become incarnate in order to exist as triune.

existence for Jesus prior to his life on earth, that existence turns out to be a
"God-man" who has always existed and can no longer refer to the second
Person of the Trinity in himself. Hence, "'the Son' in trinitarian use" does
not "first denote a simply divine entity. Primally, it denotes the claim Jesus
makes for himself in addressing God as Father; as we will see, this Son is an
eternally divine Son only in and by this relation."[59] Clearly, Jenson is quite
literally unable to think of the Son existing within the immanent Trinity
pretemporally but can only say that the Son exists in and by the human relation of Jesus to the Father. He thus concludes, "There must be in God's
eternity—with Barth, in his eternal decision—a way in which the one Jesus
Christ as God precedes himself as man, in the very triune life which he lives
eternally as the God-man." Yet, "What in eternity precedes the Son's birth to
Mary is not an unincarnate *state* of the Son, but a pattern of movement
within the event of the Incarnation, the movement to incarnation, as itself
a pattern of God's triune life."[60] And this leads him to assert once again, "The
'hypostases' are Jesus and the transcendent Will he called 'Father' and the
Spirit of their future for us. . . . What happens between Jesus and his Father
and our future *happens in God*—that is the point."[61] Indeed, "God is what
happens between Jesus and his Father in their Spirit."[62]

Yes, what happens between Jesus and his Father happens in God only because of the incarnation. But, if that is true, then one could never say that the
"hypostases" are Jesus and the transcendent Will he called "Father" and "the
Spirit of their future for us," because the hypostases are the eternal Father, Son
and Spirit who preexisted creation and incarnation. And one could never

---

[59]*STI*, p. 77.

[60]Ibid., p. 141. Jenson now thinks this proposal is problematic not because it is "merely false" but
because it is "hopelessly vague" ("Once More the *Logos Asarkos*," p. 132). What is his suggestion
now? It is, as noted above, that "The Father's sending and Jesus' obedience *are* the second hypostasis in God" (p. 133). Nothing, of course, is solved with this remark because this statement
represents a complete collapse of the immanent into the economic Trinity; it represents a collapse of the processions into the missions. Once again Jenson ends his reflections by explicitly
rejecting the *Logos asarkos*, as he must, since for him the missions constitute the immanent
Trinity and as such this web of relations, he claims, subsists "'before' Mary's conception, in
whatever sense of 'before' obtains in the Trinity's immanent life. For that life is constituted in
nothing but the web of such relations, which as terms we are told to call Father, Son and Spirit.
In the divine life there is therefore no line on which the relation describable as God's sending
and Jesus' obedience could occupy a position 'after' anything" (p. 133).

[61]Jenson, *Triune Identity*, p. 106.

[62]*STI*, p. 221.

simply equate God's eternal triunity with what happens in history between Jesus and his Father in their Spirit. Furthermore, to say that the Spirit is simply the Spirit of the believing community is overtly to collapse the immanent into the economic Trinity.[63] If, however, we allow Torrance's more traditional thinking to shed light on the matter, we would have to say that the Spirit is the Spirit of the Father and Son within the immanent Trinity pretemporally and is in no way constituted by his relations with the community. God's relations with the community are relations of grace and love such that one could never say or imply that the Spirit is simply the Spirit of the believing community. The Spirit is *homoousion* with the Father and Son in eternity and therefore cannot be reduced to the Spirit of the believing community. So when Jenson says that the economic Trinity is eschatologically God himself, he misses the most important point of Christology and of the Trinity, namely, that what God is eternally in himself—Father, Son and Spirit—the one who loves freely—he is for us. To claim therefore that the economic Trinity will only be the immanent Trinity in the future (eschatologically) strips Jesus of his eternal Sonship by undercutting his real pretemporal existence and thus undermines the meaning of the hypostatic union. And the main reason for this is that Jesus' divinity has been historicized in Jenson's thought.

He refuses to think of Jesus' divinity as something that "always was" when in fact if Jesus is authentically, definitively and essentially divine (*homoousion* with the Father as Son), then his divinity precedes (both metaphysically and temporally) and is the basis for what he does for us and continues to do because he has been raised from the dead and mediates between us and the Father as the risen, ascended and advent Lord. Instead of allowing Jesus, truly divine and truly human, to determine his thought about the processions and missions, Jenson confuses the two and argues that the two must be the same. Instead of distinguishing the immanent and economic Trinity, a distinction that, he stated in his earlier work, was needed, Jenson collapses the one into the other and then argues that the immanent Trinity is the result of Jesus' human activity within history. This reasoning illustrates why I think George Hunsinger's depiction of Jenson's thinking as plagued by monophysite, adoptionist, subordinationist, tritheist and Arian ten-

---

[63] As noted in chap. 3, this seems to be where Paul Nimmo's thinking leads him as well.

dencies is quite plausible.[64] While the God we know in Jesus Christ is for-
evermore the incarnate Word, it is nevertheless necessary to affirm the *Logos
asarkos*, for without it the dangers of historicism loom large; whenever the
Logos asarkos is rejected, theologians always end up reducing the processions to the missions and then offer a view of Jesus' divinity that is dependent on and conditioned by his human history. Jenson's thinking displays some of the perils that follow any attempt to "historicize" the person
and work of Jesus Christ and then to speak relevantly about the Trinity. Let
us explore briefly one further attempt to historicize Christology in order to
make clearer the perils of such an endeavor.

BRUCE MCCORMACK

In his effort to understand Barth as a theologian attempting to be orthodox
as a modern thinker, Bruce McCormack argues that the later Barth historicized his Christology. What does that mean? First, it means that he could
not maintain that the Person of the Logos or Son was already fully constituted without reference to the historical existence of the man Jesus. In Mc-
Cormack's words:

> The root of Barth's Christology is to be found in his doctrine of election. . . .
> God determines himself to be, in a very real sense a "human" God. Thus
> divine election means the taking up of humanity into the *event* of God's
> being—the event, that is to say, in which God's own being receives its own
> most essential determination.[65]

Second, this leads McCormack to claim that Barth needed to retract his
earlier view that "His Word would still be His Word apart from this becoming
[incarnation], just as Father, Son and Holy Spirit would be none the less
eternal God, if no world had been created."[66] And McCormack believes this
because, in his understanding, this assertion seems to imply "that the being
of the Word is something complete in itself without respect to the 'becoming'
which he would undergo in entering time."[67] This is unacceptable because
from a modern perspective the one thing that cannot be said is what a "sub-

---

[64]See Hunsinger, "Robert Jenson's *Systematic Theology*," esp. pp. 167-75, 187-89, 193-95.
[65]McCormack, *Orthodox and Modern*, p. 223.
[66]Barth, I/2, p. 135. See McCormack, *Orthodox and Modern*, pp. 209-13.
[67]McCormack, *Orthodox and Modern*, p. 209.

stantialist form of ancient metaphysics" has to say, namely, that "a person 'is' something that is complete in and for itself, apart from and prior to all the decisions, acts, and relations that make up the sum total of the lived existence of the person in question."[68] He believes that this thinking drives a wedge between "essence" and "existence," and that it does so "in such a way that whatever happens on the level of existence has no effect on that which a person is essentially."[69]

Before proceeding, perhaps it would be helpful here simply to indicate why McCormack's depiction of a substantialist understanding of persons could never apply to the traditional doctrine of the Trinity. For McCormack, an "essentialist ontology" holds that "the 'essence' of the Logos (or, as we might prefer, the 'self-identical element' which makes the Logos to be the Subject that it is) is understood to be complete in itself apart from and prior to all actions and relations of that Subject."[70] There are, unfortunately, several mistakes embedded in this thinking. *First*, in Barth's trinitarian doctrine and in the ancient and mediaeval church doctrine of the Trinity, none of the great theologians (e.g., Athanasius, Gregory of Nyssa, Augustine, John of Damascus and Thomas Aquinas)[71] would have dreamt of saying that the Logos is essentially the Logos without his eternal relation to the Father in the Spirit. So, his claim that anyone adopting the theology of the early church would have to hold that the Logos is who he is without his eternal perichoretic activity and relation to the Father and Spirit is simply off the mark. *Second*, he does not distinguish between the activity of the Logos within the immanent Trinity and his actions *ad extra* in the economy.[72] Hence he concludes that his human activity must mean that his person as

---

[68]Ibid., p. 211.
[69]Ibid.
[70]Ibid., pp. 189-90, 211.
[71]See Barth, I/2, pp. 168-70.
[72]It is important to realize, as we noted in chap. 3, that "We do not understand the economy unless we take time to consider God who is, though creatures might not have been" (John Webster, "Trinity and Creation," *IJST* 12, no. 1 [January 2010]: 4-19, p. 7). With such a distinction in place one then could argue coherently that "God's *ad intra* activities are unceasing, not temporal or transient. They are not an act of self-constitution or self-causation (talk of God as *causa sui* makes no sense)" (p. 11). Just as "the triune God could be without the world" (p. 12), it is imperative to realize that God could have been God without becoming incarnate. All of God's activities *ad extra* are free actions in this sense. Without acknowledging that God was always Father but not always creator and always Son but not always incarnate, it is impossible to distinguish God from creation.

Logos was *constituted* by God's determination to become incarnate and then by his incarnate activities. This view, as we have seen already, Barth consistently rejects. And so did the traditional theologies of the early church. That is why the distinction between the immanent and economic Trinity was so important to Barth and to the early church theologians. With this distinction we can say, with Barth, that the Word needs no completion but condescends to become one of us out of free love, and so this becoming is itself a sovereign act of free grace—it expresses God's free love but does *not constitute* it. Thomas F. Torrance offers a fine interpretation of God's being and becoming that is fully in line with Barth's understanding: "His [God's] Becoming is not a becoming on the way toward being or toward a fullness of being, but is the eternal fullness and the overflowing of his eternal unlimited Being. Becoming expresses the dynamic nature of his Being."[73]

Third, and decisively, McCormack concludes that Jesus' human history is *constitutive* of his being as the second person of the Trinity. Hence,

> If, in Jesus Christ, God has elected to become human, then *the human history of Jesus Christ is constitutive of the being and existence of God in the second of God's modes* to the extent that the being and existence of the Second Person of the Trinity cannot be rightly thought of in the absence of this human history.[74]

This last statement clearly confuses epistemology and ontology. It is certainly true that we cannot know the second person of the Trinity correctly in the absence of his humanity. But that hardly means that it is his humanity that makes him to be the eternal Son. Had McCormack been able to distinguish

---

[73]*Christian Doctrine of God*, p. 242. Strangely, McCormack claims that the "center of gravity" of Barth's doctrine of the Trinity in I/1 "did not lie in the God-human, Jesus Christ—which is why this doctrine of the Trinity is *not* Christologically grounded" (Bruce L. McCormack, "God *Is* His Decision: The Jüngel-Gollwitzer 'Debate' Revisited," in *Theology as Conversation: The Significance of Dialogue in Historical and Contemporary Theology, A Festschrift for Daniel L. Migliore*, ed. Bruce L. McCormack and Kimlyn J. Bender [Grand Rapids: Eerdmans, 2009], pp. 48-66, at p. 63). This is indeed a peculiar remark in light of Barth's statement that "we have to accept the simple presupposition on which the New Testament statement [concerning his divinity] rests, namely, that Jesus Christ is the Son because He is. . . . With this presupposition all thinking about Jesus, which means at once all thinking about God, must begin and end. No reflection can try to prove this presupposition, no reflection can call this presupposition in question. All reflection can only start with it and return to it" (I/1, p. 415). This statement and Barth's development of thought based on this certainly give every appearance of being a christologically grounded understanding of the Trinity. It is definitely not a "historicized" understanding in McCormack's sense. But neither is Barth's later Christology historicized in McCormack's sense. We will discuss this in greater detail in the next chapter.
[74]McCormack, *Orthodox and Modern*, p. 223, emphasis mine.

the immanent and economic Trinity as Barth and Torrance both did, he could have said what they say, namely, that what God is toward us, he is eternally in himself; hence, as seen above, Torrance insists that there is "no God behind the back of Jesus Christ."[75] With such a distinction this could have been said without the misguided historicist conclusion that Jesus' human history actually constitutes the Son's divine being. All three of these important ideas are shaped, to some extent, by McCormack's most basic assumption, which he inaccurately ascribes to Barth, namely, that "divine election [is] the ground of the mode of being we typically refer to as the second 'person' of the Trinity."[76] It is important to realize that this very problematic assertion, about God giving himself his eternal triune being in the act of electing us, originally was inspired by a conversation McCormack had with Robert Jenson about the "*Extra Calvinisticum*."[77]

With respect to whether Barth thinks of God as impassible, McCormack

---

[75]See, e.g., *Christian Doctrine of God*, pp. 243, 199, 24.

[76]Bruce L. McCormack, "Divine Impassibility or Simply Divine Constancy? Implications of Karl Barth's Later Christology for Debates over Impassibility," in *Divine Impassibility and the Mystery of Human Suffering*, ed. James F. Keating and Thomas Joseph White, O.P. (Grand Rapids: Eerdmans, 2009), p. 174. As seen above in chap. 3, this notion that election is the ground of God's triunity first arose in McCormack's essay "Grace and Being," in *The Cambridge Companion to Karl Barth*, ed. John Webster (Cambridge: Cambridge University Press, 2000), pp. 92-110. That essay, as noted above, was reprinted in *Orthodox and Modern* in a slightly revised form, pp. 183-200. As is well known by now, I have questioned this thinking in Paul D. Molnar, *Divine Freedom and the Doctrine of the Immanent Trinity: In Dialogue with Karl Barth and Contemporary Theology* (New York: T & T Clark, 2005), pp. 62-64, and in "Can the Electing God Be God Without Us? Some Implications of Bruce McCormack's Understanding of Barth's Doctrine of Election for the Doctrine of the Trinity," *NZSTh* 49, no. 2 (November 2007): 199-222. As seen above, this thinking also has been questioned by George Hunsinger in "Election and the Trinity: Twenty-Five Theses on the Theology of Karl Barth," *Modern Theology* 24, no. 2 (April 2008): 179-98. See *Trinity and Election in Contemporary Theology*, ed. Michael T. Dempsey (Grand Rapids: Eerdmans, 2011), for a full discussion of this subject. See also Price, *Letters of the Divine Word*, pp. 10-11 and 140-43, where he notes that McCormack overstresses God's love at the expense of his freedom and that his views run counter to Barth's view of the divine perfections discussed in *CD* II/1, which were developed *after* Barth's doctrine of election expressed in *CD* II/2.

[77]Ibid., p. 170. McCormack writes: "My essay ["Grace and Being"] on Barth's ontology was my way of answering a critical question posed to me in private conversation by Jenson," who was "the hidden conversation-partner throughout." The idea is developed extensively in *Orthodox and Modern*, pp. 191-95, where McCormack attempts to distinguish his and Barth's thinking from Hegel's, noting that for Barth the immanent Trinity is complete in itself without regard to the historical process. Yet, as noted above, McCormack's thesis that God's "*decision* for the covenant of grace is the ground of God's triunity" (*Orthodox and Modern*, p. 194) leads him to a view of historicization that goes beyond Barth by asserting that Jesus' human history constitutes his eternal being since it constitutes the person of the Son. This assertion cannot and does not maintain, with Barth, that the immanent Trinity is complete in itself without regard to the historical process.

therefore concludes that in all probability his concept of divine impassibility functions descriptively "of a road not traveled."[78] Barth thus has a *concept* of divine impassibility but not a *doctrine* of divine impassibility. And what that concept describes is "a perfection that *might* have been God's . . . had he not chosen rejection, suffering, and death for himself."[79] Therefore, in choosing to suffer and die for us on the cross God surrenders nothing essential, since both "majesty and humility, a being omnipotent and impotent" are essential to him. Why? Because "that which is *essential* to God is that which God has chosen for himself." Both "are equally original."[80] Thus, one may not even suggest that God surrendered his impassibility because God cannot surrender something "that was never God's." Consequently, Barth speaks of possibilities never actualized "only to underscore the freedom of God's self-determination to be a God 'for us' in Jesus Christ. *They are not considered as possessing reality in God's life.*"[81]

This last remark is extremely revealing, because if it is placed within the context of Barth's trinitarian theology, it suggests that when Barth maintained, as he did, that God was in fact the triune God prior to the existence of the world and would be that same God even without his creating, reconciling and redeeming the world, he must have been referring to something that possessed no reality! It is hard to believe Barth would agree with that. There is a fine line here that McCormack has crossed. And the fact that he has crossed it is illustrated by his belief that God's decision to humble himself for our sake makes God to be the God he will be throughout eternity. While McCormack claims that he has escaped Hegel's thinking in espousing this view, it is only too clear that he has not. And the fact that he has not can be seen when he claims that God never actually was impassible. It is important, however, to realize that Barth does not say what McCormack claims he is saying. Barth never says that God's self-humiliation on our behalf *constitutes* his eternal triune being. In fact he says the opposite. Even where Barth speaks of obedience and subordination in the inner life of God, he is far more careful than McCormack because he insists that

---

[78]Ibid., p. 158.
[79]Ibid., p. 183.
[80]Ibid.
[81]Ibid., emphasis mine.

> God did not need this otherness of the world and man. In order not to be
> alone, single, enclosed within Himself, God did not need co-existence with
> the creature.... Without the creature he has all this originally in Himself, and
> it is His free grace, and not an urgent necessity to stand in a relationship of
> reciprocity to something other outside Himself, if He allows the creature to
> participate in it.... In superfluity—we have to say this because we are in fact
> dealing with an overflowing, not with a filling up of the perfection of God
> which needs no filling. (IV/1, p. 201)

Notice the difference here between Barth and McCormack. McCormack
argues that God's determination to be for us is the *ground* of his eternal
being, so that any statement that God is or could be God without us is really
an empty statement. Hence, God actually assigns himself his being in determining to be God for us,[82] or more pointedly, "it is God's act of determining
himself to be God for us in Jesus Christ which constitutes God as triune,"[83]
and "the 'Father' [is] the subject who gives himself his own being in the act
of election."[84] Moreover, God realizes his being in suffering for us.[85] By
contrast, Barth maintains that God is fully who he is in himself as one who
commands and obeys, and does not need us in order to be the perfect God
he is. Hence, God does not realize his being in suffering for us; rather he
realizes his purposes of love for us as the reconciler in this way. As we shall
see in chapter seven, there is some ambiguity in Barth's thought about these
matters because he does introduce obedience and an element of subordination into the immanent Trinity in order to speak of what God does for us
in the economy. And this ambiguity certainly opens the door to those who
wish to read Barth as having confused the "missions" with the "processions,"
as seen above and as we shall see in more detail below.

Despite the fact that Barth himself says, "The true humanity of Jesus
Christ, as the humanity of the Son, was and is and will be the primary
content of God's eternal election of grace, i.e., of the divine decision and

---

[82]See McCormack, *Orthodox and Modern*, pp. 191, 216.

[83]McCormack, "Seek God Where He May Be Found: A Response to Edwin Chr. van Driel," *SJT* 60, no. 1: 62-79, at p. 67.

[84]Ibid.

[85]See McCormack, *Orthodox and Modern*, p. 225. "God does so in fulfillment of that for which God has eternally determined himself. He gives himself over to that [suffering and death] in and through which his true being is realized."

action which are not preceded by any higher *apart from the trinitarian happening of the life of God*" (IV/2, p. 31, emphasis mine),[86] McCormack argues that "If God 'essences' himself as Father, Son and Spirit in the act of divine election and the history to which it gives rise, then a presupposed 'essence' must constitute limit-language; something we must say in particular contexts but which always has something improper about it."[87] Therefore McCormack is smoothing out Barth's thinking by shifting attention from a "*presupposed* divine 'essence'" to focus on "the act of 'essence-ing,'" in order to show that "divine suffering in time [is] the outworking of an eternal humility that is truly *essential* to God."[88] Here there is no room for divine impassibility, just as "there is no 'eternal Son' if by that is meant a mode of being in God which is not identical with Jesus Christ."[89] Despite the fact that McCormack insists that for Barth and for him there is indeed a *Logos asarkos* in the sense that the preexistent Logos is *Logos incarnandus*, the fact is that, since his thinking compels him to conclude that God really has no other existence than his existence as God for us (as when he says "*There is a triune being of God—only in the covenant of grace*"[90]) he reaches this conclusion. This conclusion is conspicuously similar to Robert Jenson's belief that he too can maintain God's freedom without recourse to a *Logos asarkos* whose existence is complete without reference to the history he decides to have and then does have with us.[91] Thinking along these lines, however,

---

[86]It is very evident to me that Barth continues to wish to acknowledge God's own immanent freedom in this passage in a way that McCormack cannot. This is because McCormack's metaphysics is dictated by his ontological actualism that refuses to acknowledge God's freedom as just described. See also and especially Barth's statement that "Godhead, divine nature, divine essence does not exist and is not actual in and for itself" because "Even Godhead exists only in and with the existence of the Father, Son and Holy Ghost, only as the common predicate of this triune Subject in its modes of existence. Only the One who is God has Godhead" (IV/2, p. 65). This is important because if God is only Godhead and not the eternal Trinity then God really could not have become incarnate. But because the divine essence became flesh in the Son, then because of the action of this Subject, God really can exist as this man and therefore for us as the reconciler. Hence, contrary to McCormack's thesis that Barth had completely changed the language of Chalcedon in *CD* IV, Barth asserts: "The whole doctrine of the two natures in the strict sense depends on this primary and proper union and unity as it is described in Jn. 1:14" (IV/2, pp. 65-66).

[87]McCormack, "Divine Impassibility," p. 173.

[88]Ibid.

[89]McCormack, *Orthodox and Modern*, p. 219.

[90]McCormack, "Election and the Trinity," in Dempsey, p. 128, emphasis mine. See also above, chap. 3.

[91]It is no accident, then, that some readers of Bruce McCormack have concluded that for him "there

leads McCormack to distort Barth's own thought. He analyzes an important text from Barth that reads as follows:

> As God was in Christ, far from being against Himself, or at disunity with Himself, He has put into effect the freedom of His divine love, the love in which he is divinely free. He has therefore done and revealed that which corresponds to His divine nature. His immutability does not stand in the way of this. It must not be denied, but this possibility is included in His unalterable being. He is absolute, infinite, exalted, active, impassible, transcendent, but in all this He is the One who loves in freedom, the One who is free in His love, and therefore not His own prisoner. He is all this as the Lord, and in such a way that He embraces the opposites of these concepts even while He is superior to them.... He can be God and act as God in an absolute way and also a relative, in an infinite and also a finite, in an exalted and also a lowly, in an active and also a passive, in a transcendent and also an immanent, and finally, in a divine and also a human . . . and all without giving up His own form, the *forma Dei*, and His own

is no eternal Logos *in abstraction* (no *logos asarkos*), but only the Logos manifest eternally in the incarnation of Jesus Christ (i.e., *logos ensarkos*)" (Peter Goodwin Heltzel and Christian T. Collins Winn, "Karl Barth, Reconciliation, and the Triune God," in *Cambridge Companion to the Trinity*, ed. Peter C. Phan [Cambridge: Cambridge University Press, 2011], p. 190). Here one may see once more the similarity between McCormack's thinking and Jenson's. Both theologians consider the question of whether God would have been the triune God had he not created the world to be nonsensical because they think it arises from "metaphysics" and thus from natural theology. Yet it is precisely McCormack's insistence that election is the act that "constitutes" the triune being of God, based on his idea that he must logically reverse election and the Trinity, that has ontological implications here, as elsewhere. McCormack admits that Thomas Aquinas gave logical priority to the processions over the missions (as did Barth and most of the Catholic and Protestant tradition following Nicaea, I would add). But he wishes to give logical priority to the missions over the processions. And my point is that this, too, has ontological implications because it leads McCormack and his followers to think that one cannot define God's freedom "over against necessity" because he does not see freedom and necessity "as oppositional terms" (Bruce L. McCormack, "Processions and Missions: A Point of Convergence between Thomas Aquinas and Karl Barth," pp. 99-126, in *Thomas Aquinas and Karl Barth: An Unofficial Catholic-Protestant Dialogue*, ed. Bruce L. McCormack and Thomas Joseph White, O.P. [Grand Rapids: Eerdmans, 2013], pp. 122-23). He thus concludes that "God is free in the one act of self-constituting electing grace. And that means that his freedom is a freedom for that to which he gives himself, a freedom to realize his electing purposes" (p. 124). It is just this thinking that misses God's freedom because it reduces his freedom to his act of election as the beginning of his ways and works *ad extra*. God's electing grace is God's free love of us, which was not necessary to his eternal being as the triune God who loves in freedom. But, as we have seen repeatedly, this is just the assertion that must be rejected by those who reduce the *Logos asarkos* to the *Logos incarnandus* because they do indeed allow a certain priority to the missions over the processions. Since the missions are an expression of God's free grace, and thus of his movement to his purposes of love for us, that cannot possibly be an acceptable view of the divine freedom. As Robert Price has noted, this thinking overemphasizes the divine loving (God's love for us) and compromises the divine freedom.

glory, but adopting the form and cause of man into the most perfect communion with His own . . . God can do this. (IV/1, p. 186-87)

It seems quite clear that what Barth is saying here and from the context of his
reflections on the previous pages is that God can be both transcendent *and*
immanent, passible *and* impassible because he is not a prisoner of his own
freedom, but is one who is loving in his freedom so that it corresponds to his
love and mercy that he can befriend sinners and overcome their suffering from
within without coming into conflict with himself. But McCormack draws quite
a different conclusion. He claims that God's impassibility (*unberührbar*), which
he prefers to translate as "unaffected," is being used by Barth

> to describe what God might have been had he not chosen to be God for us in
> Jesus Christ. It is descriptive, in other words, of a possibility that was never
> actualized—which can only be talked about, if at all, in terms of that which
> was rejected by God and put aside.[92]

But that is not what Barth says here at all. Barth explicitly maintains that God
can be and is *both* possible *and* impassible, transcendent *and* immanent, infinite *and* finite, exalted *and* lowly, and all without surrendering his glory, but
in a way that corresponds to who he is as one who is both loving and free. This
is just one more instance where McCormack has crossed that thin line between
seeing God acting for us in history *as* God and reducing God to God's actions
for us in history. And he consistently makes this mistake because he unfailingly
reduces the immanent to the economic Trinity, while Barth refused to do so.

McCormack argues that impassibility and passibility are metaphysical
concepts founded in the former instance in cosmology and in the latter in
anthropology, and as such describe nothing but a "*this-worldly* dialectic."
Consequently, their foundation is "other than Christology," and following
Barth we must have none of it by suggesting some sort of apophatic gesture,
"a merely *conceptual* relocation of divine being above and beyond the dialectic of impassibility and passibility." Rather the dialectic itself must be
dissolved "by means of sustained concentration on the God who suffers on
the cross."[93] McCormack concludes that there is no room for any doctrine
of divine impassibility in the later Barth. My point here is that this is simply

---

[92]McCormack, "Divine Impassibility," p. 167.
[93]Ibid., pp. 182-83.

another version of McCormack's thesis that Barth can no longer say that God would have been triune without us and without the incarnation. We must be clear that there is a great deal at stake here. When McCormack claims that impassiblity and passibility are founded in cosmology and anthropology and not Christology, he is making a dubious assertion, because one could also claim that *homoousion* also was not founded in Christology. Yet *homoousion*, an unbiblical term, was used in the fourth century in order to express the very heart of the Nicene faith, as it still does today.

TORRANCE, JENSON AND MCCORMACK

The most renowned contemporary theologian to focus on the *homoousion* of course is Thomas F. Torrance. And Torrance is far more judicious in the way he thinks about God's impassibility. Moreover, his thinking is strictly Christological, since his understanding of God's impassibility is dictated by his faith in Jesus Christ and not by any independent metaphysics.[94] Furthermore, Torrance's thinking is closer to Barth's own intentions than the thinking espoused by McCormack. Torrance insists that God is both passible and impassible precisely because what he suffers for us in the freedom of his love must be understood dynamically on soteriological grounds and not at all in a logical way.[95] God does not surrender his transcendence in becoming incarnate, and he does not surrender his impassibility when he experiences suffering, even as God for our sakes. Thus,

> There is certainly a sense in which we must think of God as impassible . . . for he is not subject to the passions that characterise human and creaturely existence, but that is not to say that he is not afflicted in all the afflictions of his people or that he is untouched by their sufferings. . . . We cannot think of the sufferings of Christ as external to the Person of the Logos. It is the very same Person who suffered and who saved us, not just man but the Lord as man; both his divine and his human acts are acts of one and the same Person. . . . Thus we may say of God in Christ that he both suffered and did not suffer, for through the eternal tranquility of his divine impassibility he took upon himself our passibility and redeemed it.[96]

---

[94]See above, chap. 4, pp. 197-98 and 207.
[95]See *Trinitarian Faith*, p. 185, and above, chap. 4.
[96]*Trinitarian Faith*, pp. 184-85.

Here it will be helpful to move on from discussing Barth's thinking to reflect briefly on some serious issues that arise between the thinking of Mc-
Cormack and Torrance. First, in his Christology, McCormack argues, "The
only act of the Son of God in relation to his humanity is the act in which he
gives it existence in his own being and existence. All subsequent acts of the
God-man made possible by *this singular act* are acts performed by the man
Jesus."[97] This is a problematic statement because, while Torrance would agree
with McCormack that we should move away from a static Chalcedonian view
of Jesus,[98] he would also insist, as we saw above in chapter four, that all Jesus'
human actions are also mysteriously actions of the Son or Word.[99] This is why
Torrance insists that the more meek and mild Jesus was, the more violent the
crowd became in resentment against him. On his human way of obedience
to the Father, which led to the cross, "The more like a lamb he is, the more
like ravening wolves they become."[100] And, "Jesus is the embodiment of the
still small voice of God: he is the Word made flesh, the Word that is able to
divide soul and spirit asunder. That voice, that Word of God in Jesus pene-
trated as never before into the secrets of humanity and exposed them."[101] To
restrict the Son's action to the first moment of incarnation is to suggest that
even though the man Jesus is, in McCormack's words, the "performative
agent of all that is done by the God-human,"[102] nonetheless, the Son no longer
has any active role. The contrast between the two theologians can be seen

---

[97]McCormack, "Divine Impassibility," p. 177.

[98]*Incarnation*, pp. 335-36.

[99]See, e.g., ibid., pp. 60-61. This is why Torrance speaks of Jesus' meekness, the gospel of grace
and vicarious suffering as "*the most powerful deed the world has ever known*" (p. 150). Indeed,
for Torrance, God does not just wipe away the evil in our hearts by smiting it away violently
"by a stroke of his hand." Rather, he enters it "from within" and proceeds "into the very heart
of the blackest evil, and [makes] its own sorrow and guilt and suffering his own" (p. 150). This
intervention in meekness, Torrance says, "has violent and explosive force. It is the very power
of God. And so the cross with all its incredible meekness and patience and compassion is no
deed of passive and beautiful heroism simply, but the most potent and aggressive deed that
heaven and earth have ever known: the attack of God's holy love upon the inhumanity of man
and the tyranny of evil, upon all the piled up contradiction of sin" (p. 150). See also *Atonement*,
pp. 76-77, where Torrance says that the doctrine of *anhypostasia* and *enhypostasia* is crucially
important because it means that "even as man in atoning action, Christ is act of God, and that
atonement is in no sense Pelagian propitiation of God," and "even as God in atoning action,
Christ is act of man, and that atonement is man's act of obedient self-offering to God. . . . Atonement is the act of God himself, at once from the side of God and from the side of humanity."

[100]*Incarnation*, p. 151.

[101]Ibid.

[102]McCormack, "Divine Impassibility," p. 177.

most clearly when Torrance upholds the idea that Christ indeed raised himself from the dead in perfect Amen to the Father and that this is not in conflict with the fact that the Father and the Spirit also were said to have raised him from the dead.[103] McCormack rejects such thinking as an instrumentalization of Jesus' humanity,[104] while Torrance himself unequivocally rejects any understanding of Jesus' humanity as instrumentalized,[105] and his thinking consistently bears that out. Perhaps even more importantly, Torrance insists that in the atonement we have God acting both from the side of God and from the side of humanity in the man Jesus.[106] If we follow Torrance's thinking, as I believe we should, we may achieve McCormack's laudable goal of presenting a more dynamic Christology, but without restricting the act of the Son or Word to the first moment of incarnation. Torrance himself accomplishes this without adopting any sort of Apollinarianism, or any sort of Nestorian thinking, either.

McCormack, however, avoids the clutches of Apollinarianism only to fall into the open arms of Nestorian thinking (that could at any moment become monophysite) by claiming that the subject of all subsequent acts of the God-

---

[103]Thus "he raised himself up from the dead in perfect Amen to the Father's Will, acquiescing in his verdict upon our sin but responding in complete trust and love to the Father" (Thomas F. Torrance, *Space, Time and Resurrection* [Edinburgh: T & T Clark, 1998], pp. 67-68). Torrance does not here appeal to a biblical text but rather to Cyril of Alexandria. See ibid., p. 32n7. Torrance also refers to the fact that Calvin did not hesitate to state that, in addition to his being raised by the Father, "He rose again Himself as Conqueror." And he mentions that *The Larger Catechism* unambiguously says, "He rose again from the dead the third day by His own power" (*The School of Faith: The Catechisms of the Reformed Church*, trans. and ed. with an introduction by Thomas F. Torrance [Eugene, OR: Wipf and Stock, 1996], pp. lxxvi-lxxvii). For Torrance it is important to say that Christ also rose by his own power to avoid any suggestion of Nestorian separation of his divinity and humanity in the act of atonement. In virtue of the fact that the whole Trinity is involved in the economic actions *ad extra* (*opera trinitatis ad extra sunt indivisa*), it might well be appropriate to hold the view espoused by Torrance and Cyril. And there can be little doubt that Cyril had in mind Jn 2:19-22, where Jesus' reference to destroying the temple and raising it up in three days is interpreted to refer to his resurrection. Hence, Jesus says: "Destroy this Temple, and in three days I will raise it up. . . . He was speaking of the Temple that was his body, and when Jesus rose from the dead, his disciples remembered that he had said this, and they believed the scripture and what he had said." In fact, Cyril says, referring to the incarnate Word that "as God he is life and life-giver, and so he raised up his own temple" (St. Cyril of Alexandria, *On the Unity of Christ*, trans. John Anthony McGuckin [Crestwood, NY: St. Vladimir's Seminary Press, 1995], p. 118), and in a direct reference to Jn 2:19 on the very next page, Cyril describes Christ's actions as the "life-giving power of the Father" (p. 119). There seems no reason to ignore this as a biblical warrant for including Christ's own activity in the resurrection.
[104]McCormack, "Divine Impassibility," p. 168.
[105]*Christian Doctrine of God*, p. 216, and above.
[106]See *Incarnation*, p. 195; *Trinitarian Faith*, p. 159; and above p. 231n27.

man is the man Jesus, in what he calls a kind of Cyrillean Christology in reverse, since for Cyril the Word was the subject of the activities of the incarnate Word. This leads to the second issue. In a manner reminiscent of Robert Jenson once again, McCormack argues that

> Because Barth "collapses," if you will, the relation of "command" and "obedience" that structures the divine election into the eternal processions, the modality of receptivity vis-à-vis the man Jesus is not merely an economic relationship; it is rather that which constitutes God's second "mode of being" already in eternity-past. The second "person" of the Trinity is not a Logos *asarkos* considered in abstraction from the human "nature" to be assumed. The second "person" of the Trinity is the God-man. So even in the act of hypostatic *uniting*, the "subject" who performs that action is the God-man, Jesus Christ in his divine-human unity.[107]

Here McCormack is not only at odds with Torrance, but he has misconstrued Barth. When Barth speaks of command and obedience within the immanent Trinity, he does not mean to suggest that there is obedience within God because it is constituted by what happened or was to happen in Jesus' human history. Rather he meant to say that what happened in Jesus' human history corresponded to what God was like within himself. This is not to say that Barth himself did not get carried away, as when he wrote that Jesus' obedient humility was not done "without any correspondence to, but as the strangely logical final continuation of, the history in which He is God" (IV/1, p. 203).[108] My objection here is not to Barth's attempt to find a basis for the obedience of the incarnate Word in the inner divine life by saying that the Son was obedient and therefore that his human humiliation fell within the life of the Trinity. My objection rather is to the idea that this was a "logical continuation" of God's eternal history.[109] Such thinking is at variance with Barth's own continued affirmation that none of these acts of

---

[107]McCormack, "Divine Impassibility," p. 178.

[108]Even if one translates the original *wunderbar konsequenter letzter Fortsetzung* (*KD* IV/1, p. 223) saying "wonderfully consistent final continuation," or perhaps even "miraculously final continuation," instead of "logical final continuation," and even if one stresses, as Barth does, that this is in "correspondence" with God's eternal history, there still remains the difficulty attached to the word *Fortsetzung* (continuation), which seems to suggest a blurring of the distinction between God's internal and external actions.

[109]For a full discussion of how Barth and Torrance differ with regard to this issue, see below chap. 7.

free love could be seen as logically necessary for God to be God. In any case, McCormack reaches the strange conclusion that the second person of the Trinity is "the God-man," when in fact for Barth the second person of the Trinity is the eternal Son of the Father.

> The content of the doctrine of the Trinity . . . is not that God in His relation to man is Creator, Mediator and Redeemer, but that God in Himself is eternally God the Father, Son and Holy Spirit. . . . [God acting as Emmanuel] cannot be dissolved into His work and activity. (I/2, pp. 878-79)[110]

McCormack's conclusion is quite similar to Jenson's ill-advised statement that the Trinity is the Father, the man Jesus and their Spirit as the Spirit of the believing community. This cannot be acceptable, since such thinking represents the final collapse of the immanent into the economic Trinity, something which Barth always rightly rejected, even later in the *CD*.[111]

But even more ominously, McCormack's thinking conflicts with Barth's view of the hypostatic union. McCormack well understands that for Barth, it was the eternal Son who was God, who assumed human nature into union with his divine being. Presumably, that is why he says, as noted above, that the only act that the Son of God performs in relation to his humanity is that act of giving it being and existence in his own being and existence. Here his own reflections are in conflict, since one cannot simultaneously claim that the *Logos asarkos* is already and only *incarnandus*, that the subject of the act of hypostatic uniting is the God-man *and* that the Son's only action was to unite humanity to his being and existence as the Son. For this latter statement to make any sense, Jesus would have had to exist prior to the incarnation as the only begotten Son. In other words, Jesus had to have existed as the *Logos asarkos*, who then also came to exist as *incarnandus* and *incarnatus*. Therefore one cannot meaningfully claim that the subject of the hypostatic union was the God-man. But McCormack's historicized version of this event prevents a genuine hypostatic union from occurring within history at this

---

[110]Had McCormack been able to accept Hunsinger's careful and nuanced understanding of Jesus Christ as the subject of election in "Election and the Trinity," pp. 182-84, he could have avoided this misunderstanding.

[111]This leads to the following injudicious statement, as I have already noted a number of times: "There is a triune being of God—only in the covenant of grace" (McCormack, "Election and the Trinity," p. 128).

point in his reflections because, in his thinking, the subject of the hypostatic union cannot be the eternal Son who is not yet the man Jesus, but must be the God-man. The only possible conclusion one can reach from this suggestion is that since the Son was always incarnate, therefore the incarnation cannot be something new either for God or for Jesus. If the subject of the incarnation was the God-man, as McCormack claims, then what exactly happened in the incarnation? Again, such a supposition is even in conflict with the restricted sense in which McCormack will speak of the Son acting only in the sense that he assumed human nature into union with his divine being. There is a further similarity here with Robert Jenson. Both theologians appear to intend to say that the missions are the same as the processions. Yet that is precisely what neither Barth nor Torrance ever said or would ever want to say, because they both always rejected any idea that Jesus' human history was constitutive of his divine being.[112]

This matter becomes especially clear when we compare the idea that the missions are the same as the processions to Torrance's position. Torrance insists that the Father would still be the Father without being creator, and the Son would still be the Son without becoming incarnate. And, as argued in chapter four, Torrance insists that creation and incarnation are new events, new even for God himself. To him this means that God can do something entirely new without changing in his essence because he always remains the one he is, namely, the eternal Father, Son and Spirit. Torrance thus repeatedly can assert that what God is toward us in Christ and his Spirit he is eternally in himself. But at the same time he maintains that what God is for us does not *constitute* who God is in eternity. And the advantage of Torrance's position over the position advocated by McCormack is that Torrance actually can distinguish the eternal Trinity from the economic Trinity and thus avoid reducing the immanent Trinity (processions) to the economic Trinity (missions). Torrance will never say or imply that Jesus' human history constitutes his being as the second person of the Trinity, because his human history is *enhypostatic* by virtue of the miracle of Christmas. Any

---

[112]This does not mean that Barth was always consistent in that regard, because in reality he did occasionally read back elements of the economy into the immanent Trinity in ways that Torrance would reject, as when he argued for a *prius* and *posterius* as well as subordination and obedience within the immanent Trinity. See below, chap. 7.

idea that Jesus' human history constitutes his being as the second person of the Trinity is a sure sign that one's Christology and trinitarian theology have fallen prey to a view of history and modernity that simply cannot accept the fact that God alone has the fullness of his being in himself and is not constituted personally in the slightest by his relations with us. In fact, without a clear recognition of this freedom of God, all of God's supposed actions for us in history become indistinguishable from our relations with ourselves. And that is no longer good news because when, in these circumstances, we claim that God has saved us from sin and death, such a claim represents no more than our own conversation with ourselves.

While both Barth and Torrance would agree with McCormack that there is no distinction in content between the immanent and economic Trinity, they would nonetheless insist, against McCormack, that there is need for a heuristic distinction, since what God does for us in history is always a free act of grace. McCormack too insists on the freedom of grace. But his historicist perspective obliterates this freedom by making God dependent on history for the realization of his being. Without such a heuristic distinction one will always be in danger of collapsing the immanent into the economic Trinity and then historicizing Christology by claiming that Jesus' human history constitutes his being as the eternal Son. That McCormack does exactly this can be seen when he says that, in his single-subject Christology in which the "God-human in his divine-human unity" is the subject, we must say that

> the history of God (in which the divine "essence" is constituted) and the history of the royal human (in which human "essence" is constituted) are one and the same history. . . . And if it be true that this one history is constitutive of both divine and human "essence," then this participation is also, at the same time, a participation in the divine "essence."[113]

There is only one problem here, and it is this. If God's essence is constituted in any sense as part of a single history in which humanity and divinity are constituted together, then the incarnation can no longer be seen as a free, new act of God coming into history from outside, and the immanent Trinity must in fact be understood, with Robert Jenson, as the eschatological reality that results from Jesus' human historical interaction with his Father. This thinking,

---

[113]McCormack, "Divine Impassibility," pp. 179-80.

however, gives the appearance of tending toward an adoptionism that ultimately makes it more difficult to recognize and to maintain the true divinity
of the Son. That could explain why Jenson thinks Jesus' Sonship results *from*
his resurrection. And that could explain why McCormack has great difficulty
allowing the Word to be the continuing subject of the event of incarnation,
with his virtual elimination of any continuing function for the *Logos asarkos*
and his belief that Jesus' human history in some sense *constitutes* his being as
the second person of the Trinity. It also explains why Jenson, in his latest
thinking, will not acknowledge that the Son would be who he is apart from
creation and salvation. Those are just some of the perils of historicizing Christology today. It is not easy to avoid these sorts of problems once it is claimed
that "the divine decision which sets in motion the economy of salvation is the
act which *constitutes* God as God."[114] Of course both Jenson and McCormack
could argue that their similarities on some issues are outweighed by their dis-
similarities on others. On the one hand Jenson could claim that his Hegel is
"Christianized" via eschatology, and McCormack could claim that his Hegel is
Christianized via election.[115] And indeed that is what they do argue in their
different ways. Yet, on the other hand, given the evidence adduced here, I
think it might be more accurate to say that Jenson's Christianity is Hegelianized via eschatology while McCormack's is Hegelianized via election.

Whatever the situation with their historicized Christologies, however, it is
important to maintain, with Athanasius and against these approaches, that
the Son is the one through whom God created all things and that the Son is
not begotten by choice, that is, by an act of will, but rather we are the ones
created by an act of will on the part of God.[116] These insights remain crucial

---

[114]Ibid., p. 171.

[115]For a sympathetic but critical discussion of the differences and similarities of Jenson and Mc-
Cormack, see Swain, *God of the Gospel*, chaps. 9 and 10. One of the key differences he notes is
that McCormack's attempts at "trinitarian orthodoxy" are "protologically oriented," while Jenson's are "eschatologically oriented" (p. 232). Ultimately, while stating that he believes McCormack's thinking is more secure with respect to Nicaea and Chalcedon than is the thinking of
Jenson, Swain concludes that neither "proposal adequately preserves the proper evangelical
relation between God's triune being and the events of the gospel" (ibid.). In particular Swain
quite rightly opposes the idea of "self-realization" with respect to the being and act of the triune
God, and, citing Thomas Aquinas, he rightly says that "God does not act in order to constitute
his natural paternity, filiation and spiration" (p. 233).

[116]See Athanasius, *C. Ar.* III, 60-67, in *A Select Library of Nicene and Post-Nicene Fathers of the
Christian Church Second Series*, trans. and ed. Philip Schaff and Henry Wace, volume IV, *St.
Athanasius: Select Works and Letters* (Edinburgh: T & T Clark, 1987).

today for those who see the importance of distinguishing, without separating, the immanent and the economic Trinity and for that very reason refuse to historicize the persons of the Trinity in ways that make it more difficult to recognize and to affirm the true deity of the Son and Spirit. It is just here that I think it would be helpful to consider Karl Barth's early and later Christology with a view toward showing why I believe that Barth never did embrace the kind of historicist Christology discussed and questioned in this chapter.

6

Can Jesus' Divinity Be Recognized as "Definitive, Authentic and Essential" if it is Grounded in Election? Just How Far did the Later Barth Historicize Christology?

The issue that I would like to explore in this chapter is whether and to what extent Barth's view of the incarnation changed or remained the same between his presentations in *CD* I/2 and *CD* IV/1 and IV/2. We have already seen that there is a view today that enthusiastically claims that Barth so changed his thinking with the publication of his doctrine of election in *CD* II/2 that, by the time he wrote *CD* IV/1 and IV/2, he had so historicized God's being that he could no longer say important things that were crucial to his thinking earlier in the *Church Dogmatics*. As already mentioned above, it has been said that Barth should have seen that election is the *ground* of God's triunity[1] and that therefore it was and is impermissible to maintain that God ever could have been the triune God without us.[2] God could have been *God* without us, we are

---

[1] See Bruce L. McCormack, "Grace and Being," in McCormack, *Orthodox and Modern: Studies in the Theology of Karl Barth* (Grand Rapids: Baker Academic, 2008), p. 194. See also McCormack, "Divine Impassibility or Simply Divine Constancy? Implications of Karl Barth's Later Christology for Debates over Impassibility," in *Divine Impassibility and the Mystery of Human Suffering*, ed. James F. Keating and Thomas Joseph White, O.P. (Grand Rapids: Eerdmans, 2009), p. 174, where he carries that thinking through with respect to Christology, saying "divine election [is] the ground of the mode of being we typically refer to as the second 'person' of the Trinity."

[2] See McCormack, "Seek God Where He May Be Found: A Response to Edwin Chr. van Driel," in

told, but the moment anyone says that the *triune God* could have been God without us, then something has gone wrong in one's thinking because such a person has failed to realize that, although God might be triune without us, we have no way of knowing that; all we actually have according to this view is the God who gives himself to us in revelation, no other. Those who take this position reject Barth's claim that the *Logos asarkos* or the "second 'person' of the Godhead in Himself and as such . . . is not revealed to us" together with his view that "He [the *Logos asarkos*] is the content of a necessary and important concept in trinitarian doctrine when we have to understand the revelation and dealings of God in the light of their free basis in the inner being and essence of God" (IV/1, p. 52). To put the matter bluntly, those who reject the idea that this *Logos asarkos* is a necessary concept that acknowledges God's freedom sometimes insist that Barth never should have espoused such a view at all.[3] Never mind that this last statement by Barth was made in *CD* IV/1. Never mind that it is completely consistent with his earlier statement that "His Word would still be His Word apart from this becoming [incarnation], just as Father, Son and Holy Spirit would be none the less eternal God, if no world had been created" (I/2, p. 135). Never mind the fact that even when Barth describes the atonement in *CD* IV he continues to insist that God could and did cross the abyss between himself and us but that his incarnation and our reconciliation result from

> the coming of God to man which is grounded only in itself and can be known only by itself, the taking place of the atonement willed and accomplished by Him, the sovereign act which God did not owe to Himself or the world or any man, on which no one could bank, yet which has in fact taken place and been made manifest. (IV/1, p. 83)

Any acknowledgment that God could be triune without us is still, some think, incompatible with the historicization of the divine being that took place when Barth claimed that Jesus Christ and not the Logos was the subject of election.

Orthodox and Modern, pp. 261-77. McCormack claims, "A statement which took the form 'God would be God without us' would be a true statement and one whose truth must be upheld. . . . If we were to go further and seek to specify precisely what God would be without us—as occurs, for example, when Molnar says that God would still be triune without us—then we would make ourselves guilty of the kind of metaphysical speculation which was the bane of early-church theology" (p. 274). See also *Orthodox and Modern*, p. 297.

[3] As McCormack puts it: "What context could there possibly be which would justify speaking in this way?" *Orthodox and Modern*, p. 193.

Needless to say, I consistently oppose this reading of Barth for a number of
crucial reasons, not least of which is the fact that I do not believe that Barth
changed his mind about God's freedom between *CD* I/2 and IV/1 and IV/2.
While I certainly agree that there is a change of emphasis in volume IV of the
Church Dogmatics, I would argue that that change of emphasis results from
the fact that in that volume Barth is presenting the doctrine of reconciliation
proper and so he is not there focusing on the doctrines of the Trinity and
Christology as the theological presuppositions of the doctrine in the same
way.[4] And he does attempt to rethink the Christology of Chalcedon, which he
accepts as normative[5] in more historical and actualistic categories, so that he
is able to think of God's movement toward us and our movement toward God
in Christ as a history in partnership rather than a series of static states that
occur and might be left behind. In the doctrine of reconciliation, then, he
focuses on the actual events in history through which reconciliation and revelation occur and will occur. That is part of what I hope to show in this chapter.

But I also hope to show why it is imperative to see where this erroneous
reading of Barth comes from and where it leads. In my view it comes from
a serious misreading of Barth's doctrine of the Trinity. It leads to a disso-
lution of the Nicene faith because, although its proponents claim to be upholding Christ's true humanity and true divinity, their basic contention that
history *constitutes* the Person of the Son, as we saw to some extent in the last
chapter, undermines Barth's fundamental assertion that Jesus' divinity must
be acknowledged as "definitive, authentic and essential" (I/1, p. 400).[6] It had
to be acknowledged further that the statements of Christology are basic and
not derivative statements in that one can only begin reflecting on Jesus'

---

[4]Even when Barth says that he does not want to offer a "Special Christology" in IV/1, pp. 123-24,
that is not because he rejected the Christology he presented in *CD* I/2. It is because he did not
want to separate Christ's person and work, as he believed could easily happen if one focused only
on Christ's Person. And so while Barth notes that he cannot avoid the old formula when speaking historically about Jesus as "very God, very man, very God-man," he notes that he wants to
stress that he is the subject of the act of reconciliation between God and us and that atonement
actually takes place in him as God become man: "Jesus Christ is not what He is—very God, very
man, very God-man—in order as such to mean and do and accomplish something else which is
atonement. But His being as God and man and God-man consists in the completed act of the
reconciliation of man with God" (IV/1, pp. 126-27).
[5]See, e.g., IV/1, p. 133.
[6]In the last chapter we saw how this difficulty developed in the thinking of Robert Jenson and
Bruce McCormack by comparing their views to the thinking of Thomas F. Torrance. Here we
will focus specifically on Barth's early and later Christology.

person and work in faith by acknowledging his true divinity. That, as I have argued, is one of the basic themes of this book: unless our thinking about what God is doing for us in the economy is thinking that takes place in faith by acknowledging who God is in his Word and Spirit, it is, strictly speaking, not a theology that is shaped by the action of the Holy Spirit. It is instead a type of thinking that is not only abstract but that logically interprets revelation from the standpoint of its assumptions. Therefore, it is important to realize, with Barth, that one could not under any circumstances attempt to derive statements of Christology from anyone or anything other than the incarnate Word himself.[7]

That, together with our discussion of the perils of embracing a "historicized" Christology, should be enough to make clear that there is a great deal at stake in this particular issue. After briefly rehearsing key elements of Barth's understanding of the incarnation in *CD* I/2 and IV/1 and IV/2, I will compare Barth's understanding of the divine freedom in both and draw critical conclusions related to the thesis that Barth should have abandoned his earlier conception of the divine freedom. I will argue that he not only should not have abandoned his earlier conceptions, but that his very conception of the incarnation in *CD* IV was possible only because of his consistent perception of the divine freedom. Furthermore, I will show that a number of crucial insights that structured Barth's Christology are noticeably missing from those Christologies that attempt to historicize the Person of the Son with the claim that his eternal Sonship was constituted by his electing to be and then becoming God for us. I do not think this is accidental, as we have already had occasion to note. Throughout the *Church Dogmatics* Barth rejected any notion of mutual conditioning of divine and human being and action; he rejected the idea that Jesus was the revealer in his humanity as such; he stressed the fact that the incarnation and reconciliation (which for him are really synonymous since incarnation by its very nature means that God was in Christ reconciling the world to himself) were miraculous acts of God within history that therefore could not be explained from the human side; and he rejected all forms of what he labeled Ebionite and Docetic Christology.

---

[7]See I/1, pp. 414-15, and II/1, pp. 625-29 as this relates to the relationship between eternity and time.

DIVINE FREEDOM AND THE DOCTRINE OF THE INCARNATION

Before exploring what Barth has to say specifically about the incarnation in *CD* I/2, let me describe briefly Barth's understanding of the "Problem of Christology" and why he embraced the traditional Christologies as opposed to those modern approaches that question these. Barth begins by referring back to *CD* I/1 where he had spoken of God the Son as Reconciler and as the eternal Son, §11, and *CD* I/2 where he spoke of Jesus Christ as the objective reality of revelation, §13. It will be remembered that Barth begins in the former section by saying that

> The one God reveals Himself according to Scripture as the Reconciler, i.e., as the Lord in the midst of our enmity towards Him. As such He is the Son of God who has come to us or the Word of God that has been spoken to us, because He is so antecedently in Himself as the Son or Word of the Father. (I/1, p. 399)

Here Barth insists that the unity of the Son with the Father attested in Scripture "and therefore the deity of Jesus Christ, is to be understood as definitive, authentic and essential" (I/1, p. 400). Barth also maintains, against Bultmann, who one-sidedly spoke only in terms of Jesus' sayings, that Jesus' sayings can be properly understood only together with the miraculous actions that accompany them: "The acts which invariably speak and are to be heard as well are miraculous acts" (I/1, p. 400). In IV/1 Barth points out that he presents that part-volume "in an intensive, although for the most part quiet debate with Rudolf Bultmann" (IV/1, p. ix).[8] And as it relates to the theme of this chapter it is important to note that in *CD* IV/2, Barth tells us that in the twenty-three years since he began work on the *Church Dogmatics*, as far as he could see, there had been

---

[8]This debate is epitomized in his rejection of Bultmann's interpretation of the resurrection as the rise of the disciples' Easter faith and his direct rejection of Bultmann's identification of the work of Christ with our human act of faith. Barth insists that Christ makes himself "the object and origin" of Christian faith "in the work of His Holy Spirit" and we must take note of this, cling to it and respond to it in faith "without itself [faith] being the thing which accomplishes it, without any identity between the redemptive act of God and faith as the free act of man. Jesus Christ and his death and resurrection do not cease to be its object and origin. . . . What is Bultmann's conception but an existentialist translation of the sacramentalist teaching of the Roman Church, according to which, at the climax of the mass, with the transubstantiation of the elements—in metaphysical identity with what took place then and there—there is a 'bloodless repetition' of the sacrifice on Golgotha?" (IV/1, p. 767). Barth here opposes all thinking that absorbs justification into sanctification, noting that that is perhaps why Hans Urs von Balthasar had accused him of a "christological constriction" in his own understanding (IV/1, p. 768). See also chap. 1 above, p. 43-44.

no important breaks or contradictions in the presentation; no retractions have been necessary (except in detail). . . . I have always found myself content with the broad lines of Christian tradition. . . . My contemporaries (and even perhaps successors) ought to speak at least more circumspectly when at this point or that they think they have discovered a "new Barth." . . . there is perhaps more inward and outward continuity in the matter than some hasty observers and rash interjectors can at first sight credit. (IV/2, p. xi)

Here also in *CD* I/1 Barth decisively rejects any sort of Ebionite or Docetic understanding of Jesus' deity as thought lines that arose by the second century and were ultimately rejected by the church, claiming that

> The New Testament statement about the unity of the Son with the Father, i.e., the deity of Christ cannot possibly be understood in terms of the presupposition that the original view and declaration of the New Testament witnesses was that a human being was either exalted as such to deity or appeared among us as the personification and symbol of a divine being. (I/1, p. 402)

An Ebionite understanding of this matter would suggest that for the New Testament authors "knowledge of a historical figure came first and a transforming of this into faith in the heavenly Son of God came second" (I/1, p. 402). The problem with this is that Jesus' deity becomes simply a way of presenting "the apotheosis of a man" so that there "inevitably arose the impression and idea that He was a God"; such thinking supposes that at some point in his life and ministry "God appointed the man Jesus to this dignity and adopted Him as His Son." To the eye of faith this man "was idealised upwards as God, as could happen and actually had happened to other heroes. This is Ebionite Christology, or Christology historically reconstructed along the lines of Ebionitism" (I/1, p. 403). A Docetic understanding sees Jesus merely as the "personification of a familiar idea or general truth," so that one's thinking is not bound by the particular man Jesus. Rather Jesus is believed in "as theophany or myth, as the embodiment of a general truth." The "eye of faith" had fallen on him, but "what was in view was the idea, not the Rabbi of Nazareth . . . whom there was at any rate a desire to know only for the sake of the idea" (I/1, p. 403). "This," Barth writes, "is Docetic Christology, or Christology historically reconstructed along the lines of Docetism" (I/1, p. 403). All of this is meant to underscore the fact that Christology must begin with Jesus Christ himself and him alone, because he alone really was and is the Lord. When we say Jesus *is* the Lord, Barth believes that we affirm with those who first uttered this something that "cannot be deduced, or proved, or discussed, but can only be affirmed in an analytic proposition as the beginning of all thinking about him" (I/1, p. 406). Because this man is fully and truly God, he is so "without reduction or limitation, without more or less. Any such restriction would not merely weaken His deity; it would deny it" (I/1, p. 406).

But what is revealed in the fact that Jesus is Lord? Because he is the true Son of God, "He also reveals Himself as the Son of the Father," and what takes place "is an act of God" that "signifies something very different from the activity of God the Creator" (I/1, p. 406), since in this act God turns to us not simply as creator to creature but as one who "seeks us as those who can let themselves be found. He converses with us as those who are capable of hearing, understanding and obeying" (I/1, p. 407). He deals with us as creator but "as a person with persons, not as a power over things." This, Barth says, is "miraculous," because God actually establishes intercourse between himself and us precisely by overcoming our enmity against him. But the fact that we are God's enemies, Barth insists, is not an insight that can arise from general anthropology; it arises only

> from the fact that God has actually established that intercourse with us. But precisely on the assumption of the factuality of this event we can regard this event itself only as miraculous. The Word of God whose revelation is attested in Scripture tells man that he is a rebel who has wantonly abandoned the fellowship between himself as creature and God as Creator and set himself in a place where this fellowship is impossible. (I/1, pp. 407-8)

This is a point Barth would continue to stress in his doctrine of reconciliation.[9] We know, then, from revelation that we are in fact disobedient; we are closed to what God's Word has to say to us, and that our being closed to God's Word "is simply an expression of the wrath of God resting upon [us]" (I/1, p. 408). In

---

[9]Barth writes: "Christology cannot and must not take as its starting-point a knowledge of man in general. On the contrary (cf. *CD* III/2, §43, 2, and *passim*), a genuine knowledge of man in general, a theological anthropology, and therefore a theological doctrine of the sin and misery of man, can be based only on the particular knowledge of the man Jesus Christ, and therefore on Christology" (IV/2, p. 27). Barth makes the same point with fuller implications in IV/2, pp. 140-54.

these circumstances Barth says that if we hear the Word of God then "the Nevertheless of our hearing as a possibility which ('in some way') we still have left or which can still be fashioned by us" must be rejected. The fact that we do actually hear the Word of God is "a sheer miracle both subjectively and objectively, as the Nevertheless of grace which has on our side no complement or precondition" (I/1, p. 408). Because revelation involves God speaking to us in his Word, and this further involves the wrath of God on us as sinners, Barth insists that when this happens "it takes place miraculously in and in spite of human darkness" so that for him revelation is synonymous with reconciliation.[10]

In this context Barth contends that revelation as reconciliation cannot be understood "as the completion of creation but as a miracle in and on the fallen world" (I/1, p. 412). Hence, "There is no abstract person of the Revealer, but the person of the Revealer is the person of Jesus Christ, who is subordinate to the Creator revealed by it, yet who is also indissolubly co-ordinate with Him, who is with Him; in this person the revelation is a reality" (I/1, p. 412). Here Barth makes a number of crucial points from which he never retreated. *First*, he insisted that Jesus is able to reveal and reconcile us to the Father "because He reveals Himself as the One He is. He does not first become God's Son or Word in the event of revelation. . . . Jesus Christ reveals Himself as the One He already was before, apart from this event in Himself too" (I/1, p. 414). Crucially, one might say, this same insight plays a role in Barth's thought later on when he speaks of the incarnation as magnifying God's glory in the world, but that he neither owed this to the world nor did he owe the world his "accepting unity and solidarity with sinful man." Moreover, he did not owe this to himself, Barth says:

> Because nothing would be lacking in His inward being as God in glory, as the Father, Son and Holy Spirit, as the One who loves in freedom, if He did not show Himself to the world, if He allowed it to complete its course to nothingness: just as nothing would be lacking to His glory if He had refrained from giving it being when He created it out of nothingness. That He does, in fact, will to reconcile it with Himself, and to save it, and therefore to magnify His glory in it and to it, is from every standpoint the sovereign will of His

---

[10]Referring to revelation, Barth says, "The term reconciliation is another word for the same thing" (I/1, p. 409).

mercy. We cannot deduce it or count on it from any side. (IV/1, p. 213)[11]

Second, Barth insists that "God is God the Son as He is God the Father," and he is so "Down to the very depths of deity . . . as the ultimate thing that is to be said about God." In other words, "Jesus Christ is the Son because He is (not because He makes this impression on us, not because He does what we think is to be expected of a God, but because He is)" (I/1, pp. 414-15). *Third,* because the Son is God just as is God the Father, Barth insists we must accept the presupposition on which the New Testament statement about Christ's deity rests, namely, that "all thinking about Jesus, which means at once all thinking about God, must begin and end." And importantly, he adds, "No reflection can try to prove this presupposition," and "no reflection can call this presupposition in question" (I/1, p. 415). Reflection can only begin here and return to this fact.

Barth notes that the dogma of the Trinity adds to the New Testament the fact that Jesus Christ can reveal God to us and reconcile because he reveals himself as "the One He is." Barth also says that while dogma only has "human pedagogic dignity" and not "divine dignity," so he might not have had to affirm it on the basis of Scripture, he nonetheless was led toward the dogma of the early church by the New Testament witness. Barth notes that the dogma is not in the biblical texts, but that as an interpretation of the Bible the dogma is correct in affirming Christ's true and eternal deity. And he insists that we see this true and eternal deity "in His work in revelation and reconciliation." "But," and here is the crucial point that becomes obscure

---

[11]This kind of remark is made frequently by Barth: "We have to do with the being of the one and entire Jesus Christ whose humiliation detracts nothing and whose exaltation adds nothing. And in this being we have to do with His action, the work and event of atonement" (IV/1, p. 133). As "the eternal Son of the Father, as the eternal Word," Jesus did not "stand in need of exaltation, nor was He capable of it" (IV/1, p. 135). See also IV/2, pp. 150-51 where, in connection with Christ's humiliation and exaltation in his divine-human unity, Barth maintains that "as the Son of God He did not need to be exalted. In fact, He could not be exalted." This thinking is in continuity with his earlier thinking. With reference to the incarnation Barth said, "While this event as a happening in and on the created world makes, magnifies and enhances the glory of God outwardly, inwardly it neither increases nor diminishes His glory, His divine being. For this is neither capable nor in need of increase or decrease. God did not and does not owe this happening to the world or to us any more than He did creation or the history of salvation. . . . It was not the case, nor is it, that His being necessitated Him to do it" (II/1, pp. 513-14). And in his Christology, Barth claimed, "He is the Lord who . . . never ceases in the very slightest to be God, who does not give His glory to another. In this, as Creator, Reconciler and Redeemer, He is a truly loving, serving God. He is the King of all kings just when He enters into the profoundest hiddenness in 'meekness of heart'" (I/2, p. 133). Thus Barth held that "In His majesty as the Son of God, which he did not forfeit but exercised, he became man. . . He was never greater as Lord than in this depth of His servanthood" (IV/2, p. 150).

in the thinking that I am contesting, Barth insists that "revelation and reconciliation do not create His deity. His deity creates revelation and reconciliation" (I/1, p. 415). This is why Barth adamantly maintains that the content of the doctrine of the Trinity

> is not that God in His relation to man is Creator, Mediator and Redeemer, but that God in Himself is eternally God the Father, Son and Holy Spirit. The doctrine of the Trinity, opposing dangerous and destructive errors, affirms securely that even in this differentiation of God in His revelation—not merely in a hiddenness of God over and above His revelation, but because in His hiddenness, genuinely in His revelation too—we have to do with God Himself. . . . This Subject God Himself cannot be dissolved into His work and activity, but wills to be known and recognised as this Subject in this work and activity. (I/2, pp. 878-79)

Barth therefore rejects what he calls "Modernist Protestantism" because it discredits Christ's antecedent existence as a kind of "untheological metaphysical speculation" (I/1, p. 416). With this series of insights Barth carries through his initial insistence that when we think about "God for us" we must think about his actions for us by distinguishing without separating the immanent and economic Trinity:

> We have to be very clear that we are not engaged in correlation-theology, i.e., in a theology in which God swings up or down in His relation to us, either from below upwards so that God becomes a predicate of man, or from above downwards so that man becomes a requisite in God's nature. In the thinking necessary in correlating God and man we *must not think away the free basis that this correlation has in God* . . . as Bultmann in my view can hardly avoid doing. If we are not to do this, then it is not just good sense but absolutely essential that along with all older theology we make a deliberate and sharp distinction between the Trinity of God as we may know it in the Word of God revealed, written and proclaimed, and God's immanent Trinity, i.e., between "God in Himself" and "God for us," between the "eternal history of God" and His temporal acts. . . . "God for us" does not arise as a matter of course out of the "God in Himself," . . . it is not true as a state of God which we can fix and assert on the basis of the concept of man participating in His revelation, but . . . is true as an act of God, as a step which God takes towards man and by which man becomes the man that participates in His revelation. This becoming on man's part is conditioned from without, by God, whereas

God in making the step by which the whole correlation is first fashioned is not conditioned from without, by man. For this reason . . . theology cannot speak of man in himself in isolation from God. But *as in the strict doctrine of the Trinity as the presupposition of Christology, it must speak of God in Himself, in isolation from man.* (I/1, p. 172, emphasis mine)[12]

Here Barth insists that our knowledge of God is indirect and takes place in faith because there is no direct identity between what God is in himself and what he is for us in the humanity of Christ; while God is indeed identical with us in the man Jesus in the sense that one cannot separate Jesus' divinity and humanity, one cannot simply equate his divinity and humanity, as might occur in a Christology that supposes that Jesus is revealer in his humanity as such. Therefore Barth insists that we must distinguish between the humanity and divinity of Christ "between the *terminus ad quem* and the *terminus a quo*" (I/1, p. 173). Because God's Word is hidden in the humanity of Christ, we must constantly seek and find it there; we do not have it directly, Barth insists, and therefore Barth also maintains that whenever we know the immanent Trinity, without confusing God in his eternal essence with his works *ad extra*, we know it as a miraculous act in which we do not confuse the secular form with the Word, but we also recognize that we do not have the Word of God without the secular form. In other words, the "coincidence of the two is clear to God but is not discernible by us" (I/1, p. 175). "Faith means recognising that synthesis cannot be attained [because then we would be attempting to do God's miraculous act ourselves] and committing it to God and seeking and finding it in Him" (I/1, p. 175).

IS JESUS THE REVEALER IN HIS HUMANITY AS SUCH?

This thinking by Barth is carried through with his insight concerning what he considered to be one of the hardest problems in Christology, namely, whether Jesus is the revealer in his humanity as such. He agrees that we must seek and find God in the humanity of Christ and only there. But he again argues that because God did not identify himself directly with the human Jesus in such a way that his eternal being could be resolved into his actions

---

[12]Of course, Barth never meant by this that God remains isolated from us. What he meant was that unless God is recognized as God who has his life in himself and from himself alone, we will always confuse God with ourselves in one way or another.

as God for us, we must respect the miraculous nature of God's action in the incarnation. Barth asks:

> Can the incarnation of the Word according to the biblical witnesses mean that the existence of the man Jesus of Nazareth was as it were in itself, in its own power and continuity, the revealing Word of God? Is the *humanitas Christi* as such the revelation? Does the divine sonship of Jesus Christ mean that God's revealing has now been transmitted as it were to the existence of the man Jesus of Nazareth, that this has thus become identical with it? (I/1, p. 323)[13]

In answer to these questions Barth asserts that wherever such a view has been held, then the holiness of God's revelation so important in the Old Testament witness is obscured, because when people think this way they are really attempting to grasp at God and become his master by setting themselves "on the same platform as God" (I/1, p. 323). They are, Barth says, attempting to come to terms with God's presence in Christ "and to take control of it with the help of certain conceptions deriving from the humanity" (I/1, p. 323). Here Barth answers this, the hardest question of Christology, by asserting that because of God's holiness, God himself is not so immanent in the humanity of Jesus Christ that the power and continuity of the revealed Word could be identified with the power and continuity of Jesus' human existence. In fact Barth insists that Jesus

> did not become revelation to all who met Him but only to a few. Even these few could also deny and leave Him and one of them could be His betrayer. Revealing could obviously not be ascribed to His existence as such. His existence as such is indeed given up to death, and it is in this way, from death, from this frontier, since the Crucified was raised again, that He is manifested as the Son of God. Nor is his resurrection described as an operation proper to the *humanitas Christi* but rather as something done to it, as a being raised from the dead by God. (I/1, p. 323)

Barth concludes by saying that "the Godhead is not so immanent in Christ's humanity that it does not also remain transcendent to it, that its immanence ceases to be an event in the Old Testament sense, always a new thing, something that God actually brings into being in specific circumstances" (I/1, p. 323).

---

[13]On this issue see also II/1, p. 56, and IV/2, pp. 76-84. and 87, where Barth opposes the idea that Jesus' humanity is divinized for this very reason.

The importance of this statement is this: Paul's statement that God was in Christ reconciling the world to himself (2 Cor 5:19) must be interpreted in such a way that one should not so emphasize the "was" that the connection with the verb "reconciling" is overlooked. "This reconciling action of God is the *being* of God in Christ, but it is this reconciling *action* that is the being. The Son 'glorifies' the Father, yet not without the Father glorifying Him, the Son (Jn. 17:1)" (I/1, p. 323). The point here then is that the power of the Word incarnate in and as Jesus of Nazareth cannot be understood statically to have been transmitted to his humanity in such a way that God's presence in Christ can be seen, understood or explained simply by referring to his humanity, which, in and of itself, is thought to be identical with the power of the *action* of the Word speaking and reconciling humanity to God in Christ there and then and here and now. There is in reality a distinction between the humanity and divinity of Christ, without separation or confusion that must be maintained conceptually at this point and all along the line when thinking about Jesus Christ, the incarnate Word.

"THE SON OF GOD IN HIMSELF AND FOR ME"

Now perhaps Barth's statement regarding Christ's Sonship will be clearer. When Barth speaks of the fact that the dogma of Christ's deity has to do with the mystery in which God acts toward us as the reconciler, we fail to respect this mystery as God's miraculous action for us in this history if we fail to distinguish between "the Son of God in Himself and for me. On the distinction between the 'in Himself' and 'for me' depends the acknowledgment of the freedom and unindebtedness of God's grace, i.e., the very thing that really makes it grace" (I/1, p. 420). Here Barth makes a decisive point. He maintains that the church dogma of Christ's true and eternal divinity with its "antecedently in Himself" denies and prohibits "an untheologically speculative understanding of the 'for us'" (I/1, p. 420). In what would such an untheological speculative understanding consist? In other words, what would happen in the thinking of those who do not distinguish without separating our knowledge of the immanent and the economic Trinity?

First, those who fail to properly acknowledge Christ's true deity in this way end up turning God's being for us "into a necessary attribute of God. God's being is then essentially limited and conditioned as a being revealed, i.e., as a relation of God to man. Man is thus thought of as indispensable to God" (I/1, p. 421). But according to Barth "this destroys God's freedom in the act of revelation and reconciliation, i.e., it destroys the gracious character of this act. It is thus God's nature (*c'est son métier,* Voltaire) to have to forgive us. And it is man's nature to have a God from whom he receives forgiveness" (I/1, p. 421).[14]

Second, Barth asserts that if we "accept only the Son of God for us without remembering that He is antecedently the Son of God in Himself," this would not only be another form of untheological speculation, but it would not even be knowledge of faith. Why? Because faith acknowledges the mystery that God's speech is a divine act, a coming forth of God and an unveiling of God by his own act. It must therefore arise out of the silence of God "as an actual event between a *terminus a quo* and a *terminus ad quem* and not otherwise" (I/1, p. 421). We cannot therefore understand the benefits of Christ apart from this act of God, which must, as noted above, continually become an act of God for us.

Third, if we restrict our knowledge of God only to what God is for us, then "the criterion will have to be something man himself has brought" (I/1, p. 421). In this case Barth says we might "on the basis of our value judgment, call [Jesus] the Son of God." But when this happens Barth claims, "We are thus confronted again by the two christological types which we have learned to know as the Ebionite and the Docetic" (I/1, p. 421). And in Barth's thinking that would have to mean that we would have failed to note and to allow for the fact in our own understanding that Jesus is God in a "definitive, authentic and essential" way. Here Barth claims that "the knowledge of Christ's deity can only be the beginning and not the result of our thought" (I/1, p. 422). Hence it is this truth that disallows any attempt on the theologian's part to reduce the Son's existence

---

[14]Because it has been said that Barth's view of God's freedom changed after *CD* II/2, it is imperative to note here that Barth wanted to break the spell of an idea of God that was either mutable or immutable in the sense that God could not humble himself in Jesus Christ but that in the "supreme exercise" of his essence he could, as the immutable (constant) God, accomplish reconciliation for us. Nonetheless, Barth insists even here, "It is not that it is part of His divine essence, and therefore necessary, to become and be the God of man, Himself man. That He wills to be and becomes and is this God, and as such man, takes place in His freedom. It is His own decree and act. Nor is there anything in the essence of man to make necessary this divine decree or act" (IV/2, p. 85). What, then, is the divine essence that remains unchanged in all of this, Barth asks? He says, "It is the free love, the omnipotent mercy, the holy patience of the Father, Son and Holy Spirit. And it is the God of *this* divine essence who has and maintains the initiative in this event. He is not, therefore, subject to any higher force when He gives Himself up to the lowliness of the human being of the Son of God" (IV/2, p. 86).

to his existence for us. And preeminently, in Barth's mind, this means that when, with the Nicene Creed, we acknowledge Christ's lordship, we know that we are not just analyzing "the meaning of Jesus Christ for us as this is manifested to us in faith" (I/1, p. 424). Rather, it means that "grounded in Himself, and apart from what He means for us, Jesus Christ is what He means for us, and that He can mean this for us because quite apart therefrom He is it antecedently in Himself" (I/1, p. 424). Barth takes this to mean that "Jesus Christ does not first become God's Son when He is it for us. He becomes it from eternity; He becomes it as the eternal Son of the eternal Father" (I/1, p. 427).

When the Nicene Creed therefore speaks of the fact that before all time he was begotten of the Father, Barth says this should not be regarded as a temporal statement and cites the Fourth Lateran Council of 1215 to underscore this insight: "From the beginning, always and without end: the Father begetting, the Son begotten, and the Holy Spirit proceeding."[15] Barth further clarifies his thinking by asserting that the begetting of the Son is a perpetual becoming but a becoming that *"rules out every need of this being for completion*. Indeed this becoming simply confirms the perfection of this being" (I/1, p. 427, emphasis mine). Barth reiterates this important point a little later, noting that there is indeed a real, eternal becoming of Jesus Christ. But it is "His eternal becoming appropriate to Him as God" (I/1, p. 430). In other words Christ's being from the Father as God does not take place as ours does, namely, by creation. While this certainly can be said of Jesus' human nature (that it exists by creation),

> it cannot be said of Him who here assumes human nature, of Him who here exists as man ("for us men," as *Nic. Const.* says later) but does not allow His being and essence to be exhausted or imprisoned in His humanity, who is also in the full sense *not* man in this humanity, who is the Revealer and Reconciler in His humanity by virtue of that wherein He is not man. (I/1, p. 430)

Indeed it is "Because the One who here became man is God, God in this mode of being, therefore, and not otherwise, His humanity is effective as revelation and reconciliation" (I/1, p. 430). Barth even describes the "indestructible fellowship" between the Father and Son by noting that this fellowship "is not grounded in choice but in their two-sided existence" (I/1, p. 432).

While Barth thinks that the begetting of the Son "is certainly to be under-

---

[15]This is a translation of the Latin in the original.

stood as an act of will," it is a free act in which "God wills Himself and in virtue of this will of His is Himself" (I/1, p. 434). However, the begetting of the Son, Barth says, "is not an act of the divine will to the degree that freedom to will this or that is expressed in the concept of will" (I/1, p. 434). It is precisely here at the heart of Barth's trinitarian theology that the difference between him and those who claim that God's triunity is the result of his will to be for us may be seen. Barth insists that God "cannot not be Father and cannot be without the Son" so that "His freedom or aseity in respect of Himself consists in His freedom, not determined by anything but Himself, to be God, and that means to be the Father of the Son. A freedom to be able not to be this would be an abrogation of His freedom" (I/1, p. 434). The begetting of the Son, Barth notes, is a work of nature and "could not not happen just as God could not not be God." But creation is a work of God's will such that "it could also not happen and yet God would not be on that account any the less God" (I/1, p. 434). The same applies *mutatis mutandis* to the doctrine of election: it is not God's determination to be God for us that *constitutes* his triunity; this might not have happened and God would still be Father, Son and Spirit. That it did happen means that we may know God only on the ground of God's free self-determination to be ours in Christ and his Spirit. In other words, the Father begets the Son through his will but not because of it. Now let us see how some of these issues play out in Barth's view of the incarnation in *CD* I/2 and in *CD* IV. Here we shall focus on key aspects of his thinking as they relate to our theme.

INCARNATION IN *CD* I/2 AND *CD* IV

Commenting on what it means to say that "the Word became flesh," Barth insists that this took place in the "divine freedom of the Word" (I/2, p. 135). What did he mean by this? "As it is not to be explained in terms of the world-process, so it does not rest upon any necessity in the divine nature or upon the relation between the Father, Son and Holy Spirit that God becomes man" (I/2, p. 135). Think about the implications of what Barth has said. The incarnation can neither be explained from the world-process, nor does it rest on any necessity in the divine nature. Moreover, it does not even rest on the relation of the Father, Son and Holy Spirit that this event in history occurs. We might even say that in Barth's thinking here this event is so utterly new and free that it can in no way be explained in terms of anything perceptible within the range of our experience at all. Here we gain a glimpse into how Barth's doctrine of the Trinity structured his thinking about all other doctrines, including revelation, incarnation and reconciliation. Barth maintains that it is certainly right to say that God's love is "originally grounded upon the eternal relation of God, Father and Son." But, he continues: "this love is already free and unconstrained in God Himself" (I/2, p. 135). Consequently, he claims it is only when we see things in this order that we recognize that it is "free in its realisation towards man" (I/2, p. 135). Barth therefore insists that

> God acts with inward freedom and not in fulfillment of a law to which He is supposedly subject. His Word will still be His Word apart from this becoming, just as Father, Son and Holy Spirit would be none the less eternal God, if no world had been created. The miracle of this becoming does not follow of necessity from this or that attribute of God. Further, it does not follow either from creation, in the sense that God was in duty bound to it or to Himself to command a halt to its destruction through sin by a fresh creation. *If He has actually done this, we have to recognise His free good will in doing so*, and nothing else. (I/2, p. 135, emphasis mine)[16]

This is a fairly typical statement by Barth that acknowledges God's freedom as the freedom that is his alone as the one who loves in freedom without being a prisoner of his freedom so that, as one who loves self-sufficiently, God must be understood to be the only self-moved being (II/1, pp. 268-69). It is crucial to realize that this is no isolated or occasional remark made by Barth; in fact, as seen above and as will be seen below, he makes statements like this quite frequently throughout the *Church Dogmatics* in order to underscore the truth that all of God's actions *ad extra* are free actions and are thus not

---

[16]Interestingly, at this point Barth is critical of Athanasius and Anselm for not thinking this matter through consistently. The former says that God became human since it would have been unseemly and incompatible with God's goodness for him to allow the destruction of the human race, and the latter argues that the fall demanded a corresponding satisfaction, that it was impossible that God would allow his finest work (humanity) to be destroyed, and that God needed to restore the heavenly order disrupted by Lucifer and the wicked angels "for which a corresponding number of redeemed men was required." "There is a wrong note in all of this," Barth writes, "as everyone must admit." But then Barth notes that Anselm's intention was not as wrong as it sounds because for him "*necessitas*" was not the last word "either noetically (in the recognition of an object of faith) or ontically (in this object's existence prior to faith's recognition). But the last word is had by and is *veritas* itself, God, for whom and over whose will there is no necessity." Thus, "God does nothing by necessity since He can by no means be compelled or prohibited from doing anything" (I/2, p. 135). This last sentence is a translation of the Latin original.

necessary to his eternal becoming as Father, Son and Holy Spirit within the immanent Trinity. We have already seen a number of these remarks above.[17]

Importantly, Barth here insists that God's inward freedom consists in the freedom of his acts as Father, Son and Spirit; this means that in election and then in the incarnation God acts as the subject of those events and is not subject to some actualistic law that he must fulfill.[18] Barth goes on to say that God's Word would still be his Word "apart from this becoming" because this particular becoming is a miracle and cannot be deduced either from God's nature or from creation in any way, but could only be acknowledged as a fact created and disclosed by God's own act of revelation in his Word and Spirit.[19] According to Eberhard Busch, when Barth makes such statements he is not arguing that God is and remains independent of us and therefore that God wills actually to exist without us.[20] Rather, he makes this statement in order to underscore the fact that

---

[17]Here I was critical of Eberhard Jüngel in my *Divine Freedom and the Doctrine of the Immanent Trinity: In Dialogue with Karl Barth and Contemporary Theology* (New York: T & T Clark, 2005), pp. 263-69. Jüngel's idea that we can understand God's love only on the basis of our preunderstanding of love may be a manifestation more of a Bultmannian than a Barthian approach to theology. John Webster astutely notes that Jüngel was more radically "historical" than many who follow Barth and that, "as a pupil of Bultmann," he was also "deeply interested in the *existential reality of God.*" Webster notes that this aspect of Jüngel's work "has not received the thorough critical discussion it deserves." He also notes that Barth would not make concessions to existentialism, nor did Barth use the doctrines of incarnation and reconciliation to "ground any kind of existential interests." Webster believes that one of the most important questions to ask of Jüngel's early work on the Trinity, *God's Being Is in Becoming*, is whether his handling of the relation between Barth and Bultmann can be supported. See Eberhard Jüngel, "Translator's Introduction," in *God's Being Is in Becoming: The Trinitarian Being of God in the Theology of Karl Barth. A Paraphrase*, trans. John Webster (Grand Rapids: Eerdmans, 2001), pp. xx-xxi.

[18]Even in *CD* IV/2 Barth continued to speak of the Son of God as the acting Subject: "On the one hand there is the acting Subject, God Himself in His mode of existence as the Son, who is of one divine essence with the Father and the Holy Spirit. And on the other hand there is human essence, to which the Son of God gives (His own) existence and actuality, no longer being only the Son of God in this act, but becoming and being also the Son of Man" (IV/2, p. 84). This is where Barth speaks of God's determination of himself to be our God in election; it is first, he says, a determination of himself and then of us. But, as argued above in chapter three and later, Barth never says that in determining himself for us in this way God gave himself his triune being.

[19]For Barth, "revelation denotes the Word of God itself in the act of its being spoken in time. . . . It is the condition which conditions all things without itself being conditioned. . . . [It] means the unveiling of what is veiled. . . . Revelation as such is not relative. Revelation in fact does not differ from the person of Jesus Christ nor from the reconciliation accomplished in him. To say revelation is to say 'The Word became flesh'" (I/I, pp. 118-19). This of course is what is revealed in the resurrection and ascension of Jesus Christ, the incarnate Word (IV/2, p. 149).

[20]See Eberhard Busch, *The Great Passion: An Introduction to Karl Barth's Theology*, trans. Geoffrey W. Bromiley, ed. and annotated Darrell L. Guder and Judith J. Guder (Grand Rapids: Eerdmans, 2004), pp. 121-27.

God's becoming *ad extra* is freely willed and is not the result of any necessity within or without the divine being and action of the Trinity.

REVISITING BARTH'S "HISTORICIZED CHRISTOLOGY"

Now the question that has been raised about this text by Bruce McCormack[21] can be formulated as follows. He believes that when Barth made this statement he had lapsed into what he calls "metaphysical thinking," which he was able to excise more thoroughly and consistently from his later theology. Nonetheless this particular thinking, according to McCormack, is in conflict with his later theology (*Orthodox and Modern*, pp. 207, 209).[22] The statement of God's freedom made here, McCormack maintains, was rendered questionable by Barth's doctrine of election, when Barth made Jesus Christ rather than the Logos the one who elects as well as the one elected. It

---

[21]See McCormack, "Karl Barth's Historicized Christology: Just How 'Chalcedonian' Is It?" in *Orthodox and Modern*, pp. 201-33. References to this chapter in *Orthodox and Modern* will be in the text.

[22]In "The Actuality of God: Karl Barth in Conversation with Open Theism" in *Engaging the Doctrine of God: Contemporary Protestant Perspectives*, ed. Bruce L. McCormack (Grand Rapids: Baker Academic, 2008), pp. 185-242, McCormack claims there was an instability in Barth's doctrine of God that led to these sorts of assertions. So when Barth insisted that God's omnipotence could not be collapsed into his omnicausality, since God is who he is in his works but cannot be resolved into his works *ad extra*, McCormack claims that Barth's talk of omnicausality in II/1, pp. 526-27 is "dangerous" ("Actuality of God," p. 235), and that the "residue of classical metaphysics" expressed in that distinction "had to be eliminated." McCormack identifies the "instability" in Barth's doctrine of God with his continued desire to "preserve in God a triunity that is complete in itself above and prior to the eternal act of self-determination in which God chose himself for the human race" ("Actuality of God," pp. 237-38). This is a problem for McCormack because he believes that when God determined to be for us he actually gave "to himself his own being" (p. 239). Because Barth refused to say this, McCormack claims that this refusal reflects "the confusions which lie at the heart of Barth's doctrine of God in *Church Dogmatics*, II/1" ("Actuality of God," p. 239). The real difference between McCormack and Barth can be seen when Barth says, "will and being are equally real in God, but they are not opposed to one another in the sense that the will can or must precede or follow the being of God or the being the will" (II/1, p. 548). And McCormack criticizes this, saying, "I would say, on the contrary, 'It is as He wills that He is God,' and leave it at that" ("Actuality of God," p. 239). But the reason Barth did not leave it at that is because he did not believe that God gave himself his being, since he simply exists eternally in the unity of nature and will as the one he is, namely, the eternal Father, Son and Holy Spirit. A God who needed to give himself his being would be limited by the fact that he was not yet who he needed to become by choosing to be God for us. I discuss this issue in detail in "Can the Electing God Be God Without Us? Some Implications of Bruce McCormack's Understanding of Barth's Doctrine of Election for the Doctrine of the Trinity," *NZSTh* 49 (2007): 199-222, pp. 213-17; and "The Trinity, Election and God's Ontological Freedom: A Response to Kevin W. Hector," *IJST* 8, no. 2 (July 2006): 294-306, esp. pp. 296-97, 302, 306, and above chap. 3, esp. pp. 158-63. For my positive suggestion about how to think more accurately about election and the Trinity see above, chap. 4, esp. pp. 197-224.

was further marginalized by his doctrine of reconciliation, in which Barth abandoned the idea of a special Christology and held the view that God never existed except in relationship to us (*Orthodox and Modern*, p. 207).[23] For McCormack, as we have already seen more than once, Barth's affirmation of God's freedom in *CD* I/2 seems to imply "that the being of the Word is something complete in itself without respect to the 'becoming' which he would undergo in entering time" (*Orthodox and Modern*, p. 209).[24] Indeed Barth's statement that the Son's becoming "rules out every need of this being for completion" (I/1, p. 427 and above) supports just this insight.

Clearly, this is an extremely important point that needs to be analyzed. First of all, it is correct to speak about God's being that is in becoming for Barth, as Eberhard Jüngel has shown. But, secondly, it is imprecise and therefore incorrect to blur the distinction between God's becoming within the immanent Trinity and his becoming *ad extra* as noted above. It is specifically because McCormack regularly blurs this distinction in his presentation of Barth's thought that he claims that Barth was inconsistent in his thinking and that he therefore abandoned his previous positions when he presented his later views. It is of course my position that Barth's conception of God's freedom is the very factor that allows him to present his

---

[23] As noted above, it is my view that when Barth said in *CD* IV/1 that he did not want to fasten on a special Christology (IV/1, pp. 123-24), his intention was not to reject what he had written about the incarnation in *CD* I/2 but to insist, in a way that the tradition did not, that one could not separate treatments of the Person of Christ from his work.

[24] For a discussion of McCormack's view of this "essentialist ontology" and its implications, along with a critique, see above, chap. 5, pp. 242-50. It is important to note that McCormack has his own peculiar view of metaphysics in that he will not equate ontology with metaphysics. This, because for him metaphysics is only an attempt to speak of "supramundane" realities and as such it "begins with general concepts rather than concrete particulars," and for that reason only refers to ideas and not to realities (*Mapping Modern Theology: A Thematic and Historical Introduction*, ed. Kelly M. Kapic & Bruce L. McCormack [Grand Rapids: Baker Academic, 2012], p. 168n54). He wants to argue that one can only give an account of reality based on an individual, namely, Jesus Christ, since this was "made necessary by the belief that Jesus Christ is God incarnate. In him that which 'deity' is and that which 'humanity' is are 'universals' made concretely real *in an individual.*" This starting point, then, is not considered metaphysical because it does not develop its thinking from general concepts; as such this is what McCormack labels ontology. Indeed it is what he calls a "postmetaphysical" ontology, because it was "an option that was only recognized after the failings of both classical and modern metaphysics had become clear" (ibid.). The problem in McCormack's thinking of course concerns the fact that his "ontology" is in reality a type of historicized metaphysics in the sense that it constructs a view of God that is in some sense constituted by Jesus' human history and to that extent is not the particular God who did indeed become incarnate in Jesus of Nazareth.

doctrine of the incarnation both in *CD* I/2 and in *CD* IV/1 and *CD* IV/2 consistently and with power. Let me give an example.

With respect to Barth's treatment of the incarnation in *CD* I/2, Mc-Cormack notes that Barth first treats the fact that the Word is the subject of the event of incarnation. He then considers that to which the Word is united (our humanity) and concludes by considering the union of natures. He agrees that when Barth stresses that the Word became incarnate, it is a free and sovereign act of the Word and that Barth would still affirm this in his doctrine of reconciliation. Furthermore, he agrees that Barth's intention in stating that the Word would still be the Word even without the incarnation was to stress that the Word was not transformed into a creature in that becoming, and that there is an irreversible relation between Christ's divinity and his humanity, such that the Word always has priority. In other words, the completed event of the incarnation has historical reality only because of the activity of the Word. McCormack rightly contends that both of these concerns are honored later on in the doctrine of reconciliation. In treating the fact that Jesus is also truly human, he maintains that the *enhypostasis* and the *anhypostasis* played an important role for Barth: "*Anhypostasis* makes the negative, antiadoptionistic point that this human 'nature' had no independent existence alongside the Word. *Enhypostasis* is the positive corollary. It says that this human nature acquired its existence in the existence of God, in the mode of being of the eternal Son" (*Orthodox and Modern,* p. 211). This thinking also corresponds with Torrance's understanding of these concepts as noted above in chapter five. McCormack approves of Barth's statement that "God Himself in person is the Subject of a real human being and acting,"[25] but he believes that Barth begins to slip into a type of substantialist metaphysics with regard to his Christology when he then proceeds to distinguish unambiguously between the becoming of the Word and human becoming. What he fails to take into account in this context, however, is the fact that for Barth we are dealing with a miracle, as described above. Therefore what happens in the incarnation simply cannot be explained from the human side. If we could accomplish that, then we would have obviated the need for God to actively disclose this to us here and now. Moreover,

---

[25]This quotation appears in I/2, p. 151.

Barth here insists that the becoming of the Word in the incarnation "is not an event which in any sense befalls Him, in which in any sense He is determined from without by something else" (I/2, p. 160). And Barth goes on to say, "If it includes in itself His suffering, His veiling and humiliation unto death—and it does include this in itself—even so, as suffering, it is His will and work. It is not composed of action and reaction. . . . He did not become humbled, but He humbled Himself" (I/1, p. 160).[26]

Because this is a miracle, Barth contends it is something that is inconceivable but not absurd. "The inconceivable fact in it is that without ceasing to be God the Word of God is among us in such a way that He takes over human being, which is His creature, into His own being and to that extent makes it His own being" (I/2, pp. 160-61). Barth prefers to speak of the Word's assuming human nature to avoid the idea that in the incarnation a third thing arises between humanity and divinity. Were that third thing to arise, then God would cease being God, and God certainly would not be a human being like us. But Barth states that Jesus is both God and man.

> It is not the act of the human being and nature. How can it be capable of such an act? Nor is the act either of the divine being and nature as such. It is not the divine nature that acts where God acts. But it is the triune God in His divine nature, One in the three modes of existence of Father, Son and Holy Spirit. (I/2, p. 161)

Here it is the Word by means of his own will and power along with the will and power of the Father and Spirit who becomes flesh. Barth thus insists that the Word who is with the Father and Spirit is "the unchangeable God Himself and so incapable of any change or admixture. Unity with Him, the 'becoming' of the Word, cannot therefore mean the origination of a third between Word and flesh, but only the assumption of the flesh by the Word" (I/2, p. 161).[27] Hence, "This 'and' is the inconceivable act of the 'becoming' in the incarnation." Saying this, Barth is simply affirming what he had established in his trinitarian doctrine, namely, that God does not need us but nevertheless he freely wills to exist with us and for us in Christ and through his Spirit. And as we saw above, Barth makes this identical statement in the heart of *CD* IV/2.

---

[26]Barth maintains this same emphasis later in *CD* IV/2.

[27]Barth maintains exactly these same points in IV/1, p. 135, and again *CD* IV/2, as we shall see.

Here is where things get interesting. Barth maintains that the incarnation does not mean that "in Jesus Christ, God and a man were really side by side, but it means that Jesus Christ, the Son of God and thus Himself true God, is also a true Man. But this Man exists inasmuch as the Son of God is this Man—not otherwise" (I/2, p. 150). In *CD* I/2 he does not spell out how Jesus' human existence is what it is in reconciliation with the same detail or historical emphasis that he gives in *CD* IV/2. But Jesus' humanity is nonetheless pivotal in *CD* I/2, as can be seen from this statement. It is in relation to this discussion that McCormack observes that when substantialist or "ancient forms of metaphysics" are applied to "the problem of an ontology of the person" it is supposed that

> what a person "is" is something that is complete in and for itself, apart from and prior to all the decisions, acts, and relations that make up the sum total of the lived existence of the person in question. In other words, a wedge is driven between "essence" and "existence" in such a way that whatever happens on the level of existence has no effect on that which a person is essentially.[28]

Given what was said above concerning Barth's trinitarian doctrine and Christology, it seems clear that in his desire to eradicate the type of metaphysical thinking he believes led Barth to assert that the Word would still be the Word without the incarnation, McCormack ends up substituting an abstract metaphysics for the revelation of God in Jesus Christ. He embraces the thinking that Barth identified for us as "untheological metaphysical speculation." And he does so precisely because he is here blurring the distinction that Barth made between God's being and acts within the immanent Trinity and God's being and acts *ad extra*. This is the heart of the matter.

In his trinitarian doctrine, Barth contends that the person of the Son or, as he prefers to say, the mode of being of the Son, is constituted by his eternal relation to the Father in the Spirit. There is therefore an eternal becoming of the triune God. But God does not need to become God for us in order to exist as triune. This is repeated by Barth even in his doctrine of reconciliation:

> In the triune God there is no stillness in which He desires and must seek movement, or movement in which He desires and must seek stillness. This God has no need of us. This God is self-sufficient. This God knows perfect beatitude in Himself. He is not under any need or constraint. It takes place in

---

[28]*Orthodox and Modern*, p. 211. See above chap. 5, pp. 242-44.

an inconceivably free overflowing of His goodness if He determines to co-exist
with a reality distinct from Himself, with the world of creatures, ourselves; and
if He determines that we should co-exist with Him. . . . God does not have to
will and do all this. But He does will and do it. And because He is the God of
triune life, He does not will and do anything strange by so doing. In it He lives
in the repetition and confirmation of what He is in Himself. (IV/2, p. 346)

Barth therefore maintains that God would be this God without us but that
he freely chose to be God for us nonetheless. And he insists that it is imperative that this be acknowledged; otherwise God would be reduced to his
being for us. So for Barth the person of the Son is the perfect expression of
who God is. Therefore the Word is not *constituted* by his decision to be for
us or by his actions for us in the incarnation and reconciliation. In Barth's
words: "revelation and reconciliation do not create his deity." It is the other
way around. This is what makes grace grace, according to Barth, as seen
above. Barth has not here driven a wedge between essence and existence.[29]
Instead, he has distinguished between the essence and existence of the
Father, Son and Spirit in eternity and this God's essence and existence as our
God by virtue of his electing grace and by virtue of his subsequent actions
of creation, incarnation, reconciliation and redemption. That is exactly why
Barth can say that God is who he is in his works *ad extra* but that he is not
only who he is in these works; he remains superior to them as their subject.[30]

IMMANENT/ ECONOMIC TRINITY

McCormack has backed himself into a corner on this issue precisely because
he is unable to distinguish the immanent and economic Trinity in his doctrine of God. In this context he assumes that Christ's lived existence as a man

---

[29]Incidentally, as noted above, p. 177n138, McCormack is the not the first to allege that Barth had
driven a wedge between the immanent and the economic Trinity by not allowing for history to
determine God's eternal being. This allegation was first made by Alan Lewis. See Alan E. Lewis,
Between Cross and Resurrection: A Theology of Holy Saturday (Grand Rapids: Eerdmans, 2001),
pp. 209-14. I have criticized this thinking in my *Divine Freedom*, pp. 270-71, and above in chap.
3, p. 177n138. While David Lauber, *Barth on the Descent into Hell: God, Atonement and the
Christian Life* (Aldershot, UK: Ashgate, 2004), also alertly criticizes Lewis on this issue, he did
not make the connection between McCormack's thinking and the weaknesses of Lewis's thinking. This may be because McCormack had not yet drawn out the implications as fully in his
Cambridge Companion piece on election as he now has.

[30]For Barth, God "is not, therefore, who He is only in His works. Yet in Himself He is not another
than He is in His works" (II/1, p. 260).

for us must determine the person that he is in eternity, just as he assumes that God's election of us constitutes his being as triune. We saw the implications of this thinking in chapter five. And this is the thinking that Barth consistently rejected, because the divine and human natures in the one Mediator were indeed irreversibly related since the Word was not in fact transformed into a man in the incarnation. God remained fully God and fully human at the same time, so that Barth could bluntly assert, "This Man Jesus Christ is identical with God because the Word became flesh. . . . Therefore He does not only live through God and with God. He is Himself God" (I/2, p. 162). Barth explains that Christ's humanity is the predicate of his Godhead, or more basically "the predicate, assumed in inconceivable condescension, of the Word acting upon us, the Word who is the Lord" (I/2, p. 162). It is perfectly appropriate for Barth to argue that God is fully God for us but that he is this precisely in virtue of his being the eternal Son of the Father who draws his life from himself and not from created history. In Barth's words:

> "Begotten of the Father before all time" means that He did not come into being in time as such. . . . That the Son of God becomes man and that He is known by other men in His humanity as the Son of God are events, even if absolutely distinctive events, in time. . . . *But their distinction does not itself derive or come from time* . . . because the power of God's immanence is here the power of His transcendence, their subject must be understood as being before all time, as the eternal Subject.[31]

Here one must make a choice. One may either adopt an actualistic and modern ontology that is just another form of metaphysics based on a particular view of history and of personhood that allows events in history to determine who God is in eternity and thus who Christ is as the second person of the Trinity. Or one may recognize God's grace in faith and thus refrain from constructing an ontology that demands that something must happen *to* the Logos by virtue of the incarnation. This should not, of course, be taken to mean that for Barth, God is not affected by our plight of suffering. He is, of course, as Barth even insisted in *CD* I/2 and *CD* II/1 and elsewhere.[32] But the fact that he is results from God's self-moved com-

---

[31]I/1, pp. 426-27, emphasis mine.
[32]See, e.g., II/1, pp. 303, 309-15, 370-73, 496, 510-11, and IV/2, p. 85, where Barth rejects the Greek conception of God that saw him as too exalted to have the incarnation mean anything for

passion and mercy expressed in the incarnation, cross and completed in the resurrection and ascension. He is not affected because he exists in a mutually constitutive relationship with us, as seems necessary in actualistic and modern ontologies that fail to note this particular shape of the divine freedom. He is affected because he actively humbles himself on our behalf since he is gracious within his inner being even as he is holy. McCormack has missed the essential point that Barth wanted to stress in his commentary on the meaning of the becoming spoken of in John 1:14.

He contends that this position advanced by Barth in *CD* I/2 "calls into question Barth's entire christological edifice. . . . In spite of his explicit rejection of Nestorianism, Barth drifts unintentionally in that direction by making the human nature be a subject in its own right, a subject of its own becoming, thus setting up a 'double Christ'" (*Orthodox and Modern*, p. 212). But if one follows Barth's thinking carefully, it is clear that Barth has not set up a twofold Christ with the claim that the becoming of the divine Word is inconceivable. In fact Barth insists that the man Jesus is the reality of God among us. Yet he also wants to say that this is and remains God's own act and is not determined by anything outside of God, and that God's becoming incarnate means no surrender of deity but rather its exercise. When Barth says, "In the sense of the concept familiar to us, we can therefore assert 'becoming' only of the human being, in order by that very means to give expression to the inconceivable becoming of the divine Word" (I/2, p. 160), he is not headed toward Nestorianism. Instead, he is stressing that the becoming incarnate of the Word cannot be explained by any analysis of becoming we might be familiar with. And in actuality he argues that this miraculous becoming contradicts what we might ordinarily suppose, namely, that God actually does make human being his own being, but without surrendering his divinity (I/2, pp. 160-61).

Barth therefore insists that this becoming is not an event that *befalls* him because it is an event that he actively embraces and establishes as human reality for our benefit. This becoming, then, is not an event "in which in any

---

himself in a way that "would affect His Godhead" (IV/2, p. 85). For them "He was the prisoner of His own Godhead" (p. 85). See also III/3, p. 285, and II/2, pp. 101-2. See also George Hunsinger, *How to Read Karl Barth: The Shape of His Theology* (New York: Oxford University Press, 1991), p. 158.

sense He is determined from without by something else" (I/2, p. 160). Barth
can even say that

> Every question concerning the Word which is directed away from Jesus of
> Nazareth, the human being of Christ, is necessarily and wholly directed away
> from Himself, the Word, and therefore from God Himself, because the Word,
> and therefore God Himself, does not exist for us apart from the human being
> of Christ. (I/2, p. 166)

But because Barth does not believe that the Word ceased being the Word in
this event, he rejects any idea of mutual conditioning between the divinity
and humanity of Christ, and so he asks: "On the assumption of . . . a mutual
conditioning does it not mean that either the *vere Deus* or the *vere homo* is
taken less than seriously, is in fact weakened down and altered in meaning?"
(I/2, p. 167).[33] Barth's understanding here seems very different from the
picture conveyed by McCormack.

Barth wanted to stress the very same point he makes here in *CD* IV,
namely, that the Word does not surrender his divinity in becoming incarnate; rather the Word exercises his divinity in a miraculous act of mercy
on the part of God that simply cannot be explained from the human side
but can only be acknowledged as a mystery. Indeed it is certainly worth
noting in this context that Barth's commentary on John 1:14 in *CD* IV/1
closely resembles the points that he makes here: he follows his own thinking
in *CD* I/2 §15, 2 by noting that the virgin birth does not explain how Jesus

---

[33]It is worth repeating that this thinking is determinative for Barth's view of God's freedom in *CD*
II/1. For Barth, God's being "does not need any origination and constitution. He cannot 'need'
His own being because He affirms it in being who He is. . . . What needs origination and constitution in order to be . . . is not God Himself . . . but the reality which is distinct from Himself"
(p. 306). And "by His existence He simply reaffirms Himself. It is not that He needs to reaffirm
Himself, but that, being who He is, He does in fact reaffirm Himself and His existence. . . . He
Himself, in being, is His own basis, and that as such He differentiates His being from what He
is not. . . . It is not that His being needs this confirmation, but that the very fact of His being,
free from all need, is in fact this confirmation. This is the first primary meaning of God's being
in freedom, in aseity" (p. 306, emphasis mine). And there is a second meaning for Barth, i.e.,
"When we have established this first proposition that God is He who is free in Himself, we can
express His aseity in a second proposition, that He is the One who is free from all origination,
conditioning or determination from without, by that which is not Himself. The fact that in every
way He is independent of all other reality does not in itself constitute God's freedom but its
exercise. It does not constitute His divinity, but He is divine in it. . . . God is, whether everything
else is or is not, whether it is in this way or some other. If there is something other, it cannot
precede God, it cannot place God in dependence upon itself, and it cannot limit God or change
God" (pp. 307-8).

became the Son of God but represents a statement about the "basis and condition of His divine Sonship. It is a description of the way in which the Son of God became man" (IV/1, p. 207). As a sign of this mystery, which differs from all other human beginnings, this indicator points toward "a creative act of divine omnipotence, in which the will and work of man in the form of a human father is completely excluded from the basis and beginning of the human existence of the Son of God" (IV/1, p. 207). For Barth, the virgin birth and the empty tomb point to the mystery of Jesus' divine Sonship and his incarnation; they are attestations that "are based on His divine Sonship, not His divine Sonship on these attestations. They have a great deal to do with it noetically, but nothing at all ontically" (IV/1, p. 207). Jesus shows himself to be the Son of God by living a life of perfect obedience in the flesh. But

> The fact that He shows Himself to be the Son of God in this way does not mean that He becomes the Son of God thereby, let alone by the miracle which attests Him as such. He shows Himself the One He is by the obedience which He renders as man. . . . The One who in this obedience is the perfect image of the ruling God is Himself—as distinct from every human and creaturely kind—God by nature, God in His relationship to Himself, i.e., God in His mode of being as the Son in relation to God in his mode of being as the Father, One with the Father and of one essence. (IV/1, pp. 208-9)

Barth explains that, according to John's Gospel, the history that Jesus inaugurates "is inaugurated from above, from heaven and by God" so that

> As the Son of the Father, He speaks what He has heard of Him (8:26, 40), what He has been commissioned by Him to speak (12:49). . . . It is the indwelling Father who does [the works] (14:10). . . . As the One who glorifies the Father, He Himself is glorified by Him (12:23, 13:31, 17:1f.). This twofold glorification, however takes place as He is in the Father and the Father in Him . . . as He and the Father are one. . . . It is in this fellowship of action and being with God that the man Jesus is the Revealer, the light, the Witness of the truth. To believe in Him is thus to know that what He says and does is said and done in this fellowship. (IV/3.1, p. 234)

Barth then notes that the mystery of the divine freedom on which Jesus' human activities as Revealer rest can be founded only

on the divine disposition which precedes all history and indeed the creation
of the world, and which is the theme of the Prologue and of later passages
which either refer to this or are in harmony with it. But since the inner divine
disposition as such is grounded in the freedom of God and not in a compulsion to which He is subject, so is its historical actualisation, the temporal
event of the incarnation of the Word. This is the absolutely sovereign act of
God which in John's Gospel is continually described as the Father's sending
of the Son or the Son's being sent by the Father. (IV/3.1, pp. 234-35)

In this context Barth asks the question of what the Jesus of the fourth Gospel
reveals, and answers that

> He reveals Himself as the One who as the Son of God exists in this fellowship
> of action and being with the Father, by whom the Father's work is done, and
> who for His part wills to do and does this work. His glory consists in the fact
> that He glorifies the Father and . . . is Himself glorified by Him. It consists in
> the fact that the Father is in Him and He in the Father, that He and the Father
> are one. (IV/3.1, p. 235)

Barth notes that it is the perfection of the Father's love for the Son and the
Son's love for the Father that is revealed by Jesus to the world. And he continues by asking this important question: "Is this, then, the revelation of the
inner divine mystery?" He answers by saying:

> It is this, too, and it is because it is the revelation of perfect love in God
> Himself that even in its conflict with darkness it has and maintains its positive
> character, its superiority and invincibility. . . . The revelation of this mystery
> can and does take place only because it does not remain this inner divine
> mystery, but discloses itself within the reality distinct from God, the Word
> being made flesh, the Son who loves and is loved by the Father becoming
> identical with the man Jesus. (IV/3.1, p. 235)

According to McCormack, then, Barth is inconsistent because he claims
that God, the acting Subject, is the Subject of a real human being and action,
but this claim is rendered null and void by distinguishing between a becoming of the human nature and a becoming of the Word (*Orthodox and
Modern*, p. 212). Barth's error was to fail to ascribe "'becoming' to the Word
in a realistic sense" (*Orthodox and Modern*, p. 212). But as we have just seen,
what this means to McCormack is that Jesus' being as the eternal Word must

be seen as *constituted* by events that occur in history, namely, the incarnation and the historical events of Jesus' life. Yet, as we have also seen, this is exactly the point that Barth rejected in *CD* I/2 and throughout the *CD* in order to affirm the fact that what occurs here is a mystery and miracle as a divine action in the humanity of Jesus himself; in Barth's view, such thinking as espoused by McCormack would have to mean the humanizing of God or the divinizing of man. This is indeed a strange predicament because McCormack rightly spends a great deal of time and energy explaining why Barth rejected any notion of divinization. In any case we need to ask—what is the "root of this inconsistency"?

Not surprisingly, that root is traced to Barth's doctrine of the Trinity where "the problem of substantialistic thinking first reared its head" (*Orthodox and Modern*, p. 212). The problem he reiterates is captured in Barth's statement that "God's Word would still be his Word even if the incarnation had never happened" (*Orthodox and Modern*, p. 212). Thus Barth had to drive "a wedge between what the Divine Word truly is (in and for himself) and what he might seem to be (but is not!) through the verbal ascription to him of acts and experiences which are not really his own" (*Orthodox and Modern*, p. 212). This, of course, discounts Barth's insistence that the human acts of the incarnate Word really are his own, but as miraculous acts of grace they do not constitute his antecedent being as the Word. It is the other way around. The Word becomes flesh in order to reconcile and redeem us. To be fair to Barth at this point, however, this metaphysical moment in Barth's thought is said to be just a moment "in what was otherwise an antimetaphysical mode of reflection" (*Orthodox and Modern*, p. 212). Here I appeal to what was said above about Barth's trinitarian doctrine to assert as forcefully as possible that Barth's affirmation of the divine freedom, indicated by his assertion that the Word would still be God's Word even without the incarnation, is no mere moment in his thought. It is the very foundation for all he says from the beginning to the end of the *CD*. As seen above, the antimetaphysical thinking ascribed to Barth undoes the very substance of Barth's argument that any undermining whatsoever of Christ's antecedent existence as the eternal Son of the Father, with the idea that his divinity is conditioned (constituted) by his humanity or by history generally, has to mean that the actions of God *for us* are now being viewed through the vision of one whose thinking is in the grip of an untheologically speculative grasp of the *for us*. That is where the heart of this discussion rests.

McCORMACK'S MAJOR THESIS REVISITED

I will not rehearse the claims that Barth's thinking changed radically with the doctrine of election, such that by thinking of Jesus Christ as the subject of election and not exclusively of the Son or Word, Barth had now overtly embraced the idea that there could no longer be a God who could have been the Word without becoming incarnate. These issues have been discussed above and in detail by me and by George Hunsinger.[34] Let us move at once to McCormack's main conclusions that I regard as problematic, namely, the claim that because the covenant of grace is an act of divine self-determination, it is an act in which

> God has elected to be God in the covenant of grace and to be God in no other way. This is not a decision for mere role-play; it is a decision with ontological significance. It is a free act in which God assigned to himself the being God would have for all eternity. (*Orthodox and Modern*, p. 216)

The mistakes in this reasoning are easily cleared away once one realizes that McCormack's ontology is one that embraces mutual conditioning, while Barth's does not.

First, it is true to say that God's covenant relations with us are based in an act of divine self-determination. Second, Barth admits, even in *CD* I/2, that with the incarnation as grounded in election, God remains truly divine and human from and to all eternity. And he stresses this point in *CD* IV as well. But he did not mean by this to excise God's pretemporal eternity from the discussion. Instead he attempted to uphold God's pretemporal, supratemporal and posttemporal existence in a way that corresponded to his eternal

---

[34]See Molnar, *Divine Freedom*, pp. 61-64, 81, and "Can the Electing God Be God Without Us?"; McCormack, *Orthodox and Modern*, pp. 183-277; and George Hunsinger "Election and the Trinity: Twenty-Five Theses on the Theology of Karl Barth," *Modern Theology* 24, no. 2 (April 2008): 179-98. In notes 1 and 2 of "Election and the Trinity" Hunsinger provides a full bibliography related to this discussion. Hunsinger correctly maintains that for Barth, God's being and act "are equally and primordially basic" (p. 180) so that it is incorrect for McCormack to claim that for Barth God's act "constitutes" God's being. But Barth makes a distinction between act and work so that he will not reduce God to his works *ad extra*. Nor will he claim that God's works constitute God's being. Act refers to God's eternal triune being (p. 180), while work refers to his acts *ad extra* in this context. Additional discussion of these issues can be seen in chaps. 3 and 5 above.

trinitarian being and action as actions of one who loves in freedom. Third, when McCormack says that God's self-determination to be God for us has ontological implications, he is compelled by the logic of his philosophy to insist that this must have ontological implications for God's eternal being. What does he conclude? He concludes that this act of God is a free act "in which God assigned himself the being God would have for all eternity." It is an act of "Self-*limitation*" (*Orthodox and Modern*, p. 216). Here then is the heart of the matter. For Barth, a God who assigns himself his being is in fact not God at all because he is limited by the fact that he might have been different and thus needed to assign a being to himself. For Barth, as seen above, God eternally wills himself but is not free to choose to do this or not to do it; were this the case, he would not truly be one who is loving *and* free.

From this error on McCormack's part follows a second error. He claims that with his doctrine of election, God is so much Lord "that he is even the Lord over his own 'essence'" (*Orthodox and Modern*, p. 216). With this of course I agree. But I do not agree with the sense that McCormack gives to this assertion. He uses this assertion to embrace the idea that this allows Barth to say later on in *CD* IV/1 that "God is not by accident a suffering God but is so 'essentially'" (*Orthodox and Modern*, p. 216; the reference here is to IV/1, p. 164). And from this he concludes that the truly revolutionary nature of Barth's doctrine of election is not that Jesus Christ is the object of election; that would only imply that he had a role to play in determining to be God for us. McCormack says, "It is easy to understand how Jesus Christ, the God-human in his divine-human unity, could be the object of an eternal decision made by a Triune God composed of Father, Son, and Holy Spirit" (*Orthodox and Modern*, p. 216).[35] But such thinking simply follows the logic of classical theology, which suggested that the eternal Son participated in the decision that would give him a role to play in the economy and that this would lead to his incarnation. McCormack says Barth rejected this thinking in *CD* IV/1 because it created "an ontological gap" between "that which the eternal Son is in and for himself and that which he becomes by virtue of this decision— which also leads to a differentiation between the immanent and economic Trinities" (*Orthodox and Modern*, p. 217). And this would have to lead to the

---

[35]Of course in traditional trinitarian doctrine God is not composed of anything since God is simple even in his triunity. Partialism is thus excluded as a possibility.

idea that "What the Word is as incarnate would therefore have no ontological significance for the *true* being of the Word in his eternal mode of being" (*Orthodox and Modern*, p. 217). Moreover, we have already seen that, in light of McCormack's own ontology, this has to mean that history must determine the ontological reality of the eternal Word. To carry out Barth's assertion that Jesus Christ is the subject of election would have to mean that the logic of classical theology is swept aside. And this means that we must

> bid farewell to the distinction between the eternal Word and the incarnate Word. An eternal Word or eternal Son which had no regard for the humanity to be assumed on the most basic level of personal identity would, in this view, have to be regarded as a metaphysical abstraction with no reality attached to it. (*Orthodox and Modern*, pp. 217-18)

Here McCormack claims Barth's actualism has been pushed back into the "very being of God" (*Orthodox and Modern*, p. 218). Here, he asserts, Barth was able to identify the immanent and economic Trinity in content and thus make sense of his assertion that God is "essentially" a suffering God. "Jesus Christ as the One who suffers in time is what God is 'essentially'" (*Orthodox and Modern*, p. 218).

From here McCormack attempts to explain himself further. In answer to possible critics who might ask how Jesus Christ could be the subject of a decision that gives him his own being, he responds that such a question itself has snapped back into "metaphysical thinking." But his reasoned answer nonetheless is that since the triune God is a single subject, when we say that Jesus Christ is the electing God, we must mean that "'God determined to be God in a second mode of being.' It lies close to hand to recognize that it is precisely the primal decision of God in election which constitutes the event in which God differentiates himself into three modes of being. Election thus has a certain logical priority even over the triunity of God" (*Orthodox and Modern*, p. 218).[36] Thus, following Jüngel, McCormack says the event in

---

[36]The error in this thinking once again is to fail to note that Barth very subtly distinguishes without separating the immanent and economic Trinity, even here when he writes: "To the extent that this step obviously means something new in God, a self-distinction of God from Himself, a being of God in a mode of being that is different from though not subordinate to His first and hidden mode of being as God, in a mode of being, of course, in which He can also exist for us" (I/1, p. 316). McCormack did not seem to notice that when Barth spoke of the second mode of existence (the Son) even here, he said "he can exist for us," clearly implying that he did not have

which God "constitutes himself as triune is identical with the event in which he chooses to be God for the human race. Thus the 'gap' between the 'eternal Son' and 'Jesus Christ' is overcome, the distinction between them eliminated" (*Orthodox and Modern*, p. 218). This electing decision on God's part has thus "never *not* already taken place. So there is no 'eternal Son' if by that is meant a mode of being in God which is not identical with Jesus Christ. Therefore Jesus Christ is the electing God" (*Orthodox and Modern*, p. 219).

Without going further into the details of this argument, we may simply ask where this thinking leads. Predictably, it leads to the following assertions:

> The root of Barth's Christology is to be found in his doctrine of election. . . . God determines himself to be, in a very real sense a "human" God. Thus divine election means the taking up of humanity into the *event* of God's being—the event, that is to say, in which God's own being receives its own most essential determination. . . . If, in Jesus Christ, God has elected to become human, then *the human history of Jesus Christ is constitutive of the being and existence of God in the second of God's modes* to the extent that the being and existence of the Second Person of the Trinity cannot be rightly thought of in the absence of this human history. (*Orthodox and Modern*, p. 223, emphasis mine)

We have already seen how and why this statement represents an illegitimate historicizing of the Word.[37] Yet, on this basis McCormack claims that Barth's Christology in *CD* IV is Chalcedonian only in the formal sense that he still maintains that there is in Jesus Christ a true humanity and a true divinity, but that it is incorrect to speak simply of Barth's Chalcedonian Christology. And the hallmark of this new Christology is that "we cannot think about the Second Person of the Trinity in isolation from his history, for it is in his history that he is *constituted* the 'person' that he is" (*Orthodox and Modern*, p. 224, emphasis mine).[38] Moreover, while McCormack, Barth and I certainly agree that in the incarnation God gives himself over to suffering and death and yet does not cease being God but bears his own wrath on our behalf, I do not think Barth would agree with the conclusion Mc-

---

to be incarnate in order to be God in that second mode of being.

[37]See above, chap. 5.

[38]It is just with respect to this statement that I noted above in chap. 5 that Torrance's more precise understanding offers a better way forward when he argued that the Person of the Son is eternal but the humanity of Jesus Christ is not eternal in the sense that it existed prior to the incarnation.

Cormack thus reaches: that "God does so in fulfillment of that for which God has eternally determined himself. He gives himself over to that in and through which his true being is realized" (*Orthodox and Modern*, p. 225). Here we reach the point that we knew we had to reach when we were told that for substantialist metaphysics the persons of the Trinity had to be seen as complete in themselves, while in an actualist metaphysics they had to be seen as constituted by their existences and actions within history. The point that I wish to argue here, as I did in chapters three and five, is that McCormack has presented Barth on the procrustean bed of his own actualistic ontology without regard for what Barth actually says in his doctrine of the Trinity and in his doctrine of the incarnation.

DISTINGUISHING WITHOUT SEPARATING OR CONFUSING THE IMMANENT AND ECONOMIC TRINITY

For Barth it was imperative that a careful distinction be made between the immanent and economic Trinity because God's actions for us did not arise as a matter of course out of his trinitarian being and action. This is crucial to see. McCormack has in fact collapsed the immanent into the economic Trinity, and the sure signs that this has happened are his views that (1) the human history of Jesus *constitutes* his divinity; (2) there is no longer a second Person of the Trinity existing in and for himself in relation to the Father and the Spirit (this is the virtual elimination of the *Logos asarkos*); (3) God's suffering for us is not only part of God's essential nature; but (4) God's being is actually realized through his suffering for us.

He cites a number of texts from *CD* IV/1 and *CD* IV/2 to support his claims. In each citation he fails to note important qualifications offered by Barth. Let us take the first statement, i.e., that Jesus' human history constitutes his divine being. We saw above that for Barth it is exactly the other way around; his divine history is the basis of what happens in human history as a series of free divine actions on our behalf, beginning with his election of the human race. Therefore even in *CD* IV Barth is very careful never to embrace a mutually conditioning and mutually conditioned notion of God's relations with us as the incarnate Word. Barth continues to maintain that "in itself and as such the humanity of Jesus Christ is a predicate without a subject" (IV/2, p. 102). And for him the incarnation does not constitute Jesus'

Sonship, but God is disclosed in and through his human actions as actions of the Word. Thus Barth writes:

> In the inner life of God, as the eternal essence of Father, Son and Holy Ghost, the divine essence does not of course, need any actualisation. On the contrary, it is the creative ground of all other, i.e., all creaturely actualisations. Even as the divine essence of the Son it did not need His incarnation, His existence as man . . . to become actual. (IV/2, p. 113)[39]

This statement by Barth is fully in accord with the Christology developed in *CD* I/1 and *CD* I/2 and is the direct antithesis of the position advanced by McCormack. It is not Jesus' human history as the incarnate Word that determines who he is within the immanent Trinity. That is determined from all eternity by his unique relation with the Father and Spirit, and that being and action would still be his even if he had not become incarnate. Therefore Barth was quite justified in making that assertion, and indeed he would have contradicted his own view of the Trinity had he not done so.

Perhaps even more directly, one could observe that Barth rejected all forms of Ebionite and Docetic Christology exactly because such approaches to the person of Christ were grounded within history in the form of the community's response to Jesus based on its experiences or ideas. But the most important point to note in this context is that a Jesus whose divinity is *constituted* by events in his life history as the incarnate Word can no longer be recognized as "definitive, authentic and essential." In other words, his divinity, in such a view, needs the incarnation or the resurrection in order to be fully realized. This is a surprisingly frequent assertion among a number of contemporary theologians and, as I have shown in my book *Divine Freedom* and again in this work, it leads to the idea of a dependent deity,[40] that is, a God whose being is becoming what it will be only by virtue of its relations with us. Such a deity in the long run, however, ultimately becomes

---

[39] And, importantly, in *CD* IV/1 Barth insists in relation to the incarnation that "God is always free in His love, transcendent God. He does not cease to be God transcendent when He makes it His glory to be in the depths, in order to make peace on earth to the men of His good will. In His Godhead, as the eternal Son of the Father, as the eternal Word, Jesus Christ never ceased to be transcendent free and sovereign. He did not stand in need of exaltation, nor was He capable of it. But He did as man—it is here again that we come up against that which is not self-evident in Jesus Christ" (IV/1, pp. 134-35).

[40] See esp. Molnar, *Divine Freedom*, pp. 70-81.

indistinguishable from history and so is no longer recognizable as the basis of our human freedom, which was a constant theme for Barth, especially in *CD* IV, as we shall see in chapter eight.

Against all such thinking Barth insisted, "The triune life of God which is free life in the fact that it is Spirit, is the basis of His whole will and action even *ad extra*, as the living act which He directs to us" (IV/2, p. 345). And Barth can say that "the reason and compelling power of [Christ's] history" is "the fact that the Subject of atonement and therefore of incarnation, Jesus Christ, is the Son of God. . . . There can be no question of the human essence assumed and adopted by Him being the subject here" (IV/2, p. 65). Indeed, "He gives the human essence a part in His divine, and the human essence receives this part in the divine from Him. This means that the word mutual cannot be understood in the sense of interchangeable. The relationship between them is not reversible" (IV/2, pp. 70-71). Crucially, as noted above, Barth consistently claims, "The fact that He shows Himself to be the Son of God in this way does not mean that He becomes the Son of God thereby, let alone by the miracle which attests Him as such. He shows Himself the One He is by the obedience which He renders as man" (IV/1, p. 208). And this indeed becomes a significant emphasis in Barth's Christology in *CD* IV/2, so that Barth does indeed seek to stress the fact that Jesus' true humanity is absolutely necessary in exactly the same way that his deity is necessary (IV/2, p. 35).

In addition, he departs from traditional Reformed thinking in attempting to think through the implications of Chalcedon more actualistically than was done in the past, because he wanted to move away from a static conception of the person of Christ (IV/2, pp. 105-16). In a play on words that obviates Athanasius's traditional rendering, Barth writes, "God becomes man in order that man may—not become God, but come to God" (IV/2, p. 106).[41] Barth here wants to stress that in Jesus Christ, God humiliates himself for us in order to exalt us in the human history of Jesus into fellowship with God. That indeed is our reconciliation with God himself, namely, the fact that the man Jesus does what none of us do or can do; he obeys God to the end and therefore lives solely

---

[41]Torrance regarded Athanasius's statement that God became incarnate "in order to make us divine" as unfortunate if it is interpreted ontologically, because then it would obliterate the distinction between creator and creature, which was important for classical and contemporary theology. See Paul D. Molnar, *Thomas F. Torrance: Theologian of the Trinity* (Aldershot, UK: Ashgate, 2009), pp. 78 and 157.

by the grace of God as our representative and Lord and by the power of the
Holy Spirit. Barth does not want to the think of Jesus' true divinity and true
humanity as two states because that, he says, would tear apart the unity of
Christ as humiliated and as exalted. Even in this context Barth accepts Chalcedon as normative and attempts to think historically about Christ's divinity
and humanity as a union without mixture, change, division or separation, a
union or movement that is in itself inconceivable (IV/2, p. 109).

RECONSIDERING THE *LOGOS ASARKOS*

Espousing a notion of a "dependent deity" is closely connected with the idea
that Christ's Sonship is constituted by his resurrection.[42] In this context it is
important to see that Barth did not dismiss the idea that Jesus was the Son
even as *Logos asarkos*, although he is very clear that he was not only this. He
even says that the New Testament writers wished to say that the power and
wisdom of God belonged also to the eternal Son or Word of God as such, but
not only to him, since they also had in view Jesus Christ as the one through
whom creation took place. Barth even notes that the whole concept of the
Logos asarkos or second Person of the Trinity as such is an "abstraction" that
has "shown itself necessary to the Christological and trinitarian reflections
of the Church. Even to-day it is indispensable for dogmatic inquiry and presentation, and it is often touched upon in the New Testament, though nowhere expounded directly" (III/1, p. 54). Speaking of the *Logos asarkos* as an
abstraction, Barth did not mean to suggest that it had no reality.[43] Rather, he

---

[42]As documented in my *Divine Freedom*, Moltmann, Jenson and Pannenberg all espouse some
version of this view. Apparently Jüngel does as well in his *God as the Mystery of the World: On
the Foundation of the Theology of the Crucified One in the Dispute Between Theism and Atheism*,
trans. Darrell L. Guder (Grand Rapids: Eerdmans, 1983), p. 369. See Molnar, *Divine Freedom*,
p. 269. See also McCormack's remark that "The unity of God with Jesus takes place in the event
of identification, which Jüngel locates at the end of Jesus' life *rather than* at its beginning" (*Orthodox and Modern*, p. 255, emphasis mine). Does not such an idea undermine the very fact that
Jesus' entire life is a life of atoning reconciliation, beginning with his conception by the Holy
Spirit of the Virgin Mary and thus beginning at Christmas and culminating on Easter? If God
is not identified with the man Jesus from the beginning of his earthly life, how can one possibly
avoid the adoptionist perspective that seems intrinsic to Nestorian Christologies? This is a question that I address in my *Incarnation and Resurrection: Toward a Contemporary Understanding*
(Grand Rapids: Eerdmans, 2007). See, e.g., my discussion of Pannenberg's idea that "Jesus would
not have been who he was [the Word] without the Easter event" (ibid., pp. 283-84) and his explicit affirmation of a "dependent deity."
[43]See John Webster's criticism of Barth for this, above chap. 3, p. 139n28 and my response. See
also chap. 8, p. 381n7.

meant that one could not focus on that Word without the incarnation and still properly understand reconciliation and redemption as well as theological anthropology. Hence, there is no doubt that Barth does not want to substitute some formless idea of Christ for Jesus Christ who is the Mediator even before the creation of the world and is as such the basis of God's dealings with us in history. But there is also no doubt that when theologians simply dismiss the *Logos asarkos* altogether either directly by dismissing it outright or by claiming to uphold it while merely paying lip service to it by reducing the *Logos asarkos* to the *Logos incarnandus*, then the idea of a dependent deity is not far behind. This is a difficult issue. But there is no question that Barth did not wish to dispense with the idea that the Son or Word of God or "second mode of existence ('person')" also refers to "the inner divine reality in itself and as such" (III/1, p. 50). In Barth's thinking the inner divine reality always referred to the eternal relations of the Father, Son and Holy Spirit. Hence, the immanent Trinity for Barth was not an abstraction in the sense that it was not very real as a reference to the triune God who loves in freedom and is free in his love (II/1, 317). Yet, one also could never separate the immanent from the economic Trinity in his thinking, either.

In fact, Barth wants to say that in his inner divine love as the triune God, the creator turns to us and creates us in his Son Jesus Christ and through his Spirit. This means, however, that God's creating us through his Word and Spirit implies that it is with a view toward his incarnate Son, his suffering, death and indeed his resurrection and all that is implied in those events for us, that God creates the world and holds it together in his love and freedom through his Spirit. So Barth also insists that the understanding of creation as an act of the Trinity in the sense that the Father acts through his Word or Son as such is inadequate and must be coordinated with his decree that his Son would humble himself as the incarnate Word. That is what Barth means when he says that while the New Testament undoubtedly had in view a *Logos asarkos*, the one who shaped their understanding of God's love for us was the incarnate Word. Again, that does not mean that Barth simply jettisoned the concept of the Word as such; rather he apprehended it together with, and held it in close relation to, the fact that this God determined himself to be God for us. And the necessity of this concept could be seen in his polemic against those who claimed that knowledge of Christ's antecedent existence was untheological metaphysical speculation by countering and saying that those who rejected this were engaging in untheological speculative understanding, as seen above. Perhaps it would be most accurate to describe Barth's view of this matter by noting his statement that "The Son is both *logos ensarkos* and *logos asarkos*. Do we not have to say this afresh and for the first time truly the moment we speak about the union of God and man in revelation lest we forget that we stand here before the miracle of God? Can we ever have said it enough?"[44]

Is God Essentially a Suffering God?

What about McCormack's claim that for Barth, God is not by accident a suffering God but that he is so "essentially" (*Orthodox and Modern*, p. 216)? He cites a text in IV/1 where Barth speaks of Christ as the suffering servant and therefore as one who does not merely suffer humanly but does so as the Son of God. Therefore this suffering is not merely accidental or incidental. It was not done merely to show his mind or disposition. Nor was it merely a foil for stressing his glory. "But necessarily and, as it were, essentially, and so far as can be seen without meaning or purpose. He is a suffering servant who wills this profoundly unsatisfactory being, who cannot will anything other in the obedience in which He shows Himself the Son of God" (IV/1, p. 164). Has Barth here introduced a necessity into the free being and action of God? Has Barth here introduced suffering and death directly into God's being in such a way that God has lost his freedom and can no longer save us from suffering and death? In other words, has Barth opened the door to a kind of modalistic patripassianism in view of the fact that all actions of the Trinity are one? Barth explains that what he means here is that when the Word became incarnate he became sinful flesh and that since he obeys his Father as the Son who actively humbled himself for us, therefore it could not be otherwise. He humbled himself in the sense of Philippians 2. He gave his life up in order to give life. No one took his life from him (Jn 10:18), but he gave it freely and he had the power to take it up again.

This thinking is wholly in line with what Barth maintained in *CD* I/2 when he wrote that the becoming incarnate and the suffering of the Word who became incarnate were not events that "befell" Jesus such that he was

---

[44]Karl Barth, *The Göttingen Dogmatics: Instruction in the Christian Religion*, vol. 1, ed. Hannelotte Reiffen, trans. Geoffrey W. Bromiley (Grand Rapids: Eerdmans, 1991), p. 160.

determined from without (I/2, p. 160). Rather, "it is His will and work. . . .
He did not become humbled, but He humbled Himself" (I/2, p. 160). Barth
also says, "Jesus would not be Jesus if His way could be different or bear a
different character" (IV/1, p. 166). This is similar to Barth's statement in
another context that the power of death could not hold Jesus and that he
had to rise from the dead because of who he was. But most importantly, to
say, as McCormack does, that "Jesus Christ as the One who suffers in time
is what God is 'essentially,'" opens the door once again to a confusion of the
immanent and economic Trinity by making suffering and death part of
God's eternal nature. If God is essentially one who suffers, then how does he
have the power to overcome our suffering and death? As seen above, Barth
answered these questions with extraordinary care and skill when he wrote:

> It is not at all the case that God has no part in the suffering of Jesus Christ
> even in His mode of being as the Father. No, there is a *particula veri* in the
> teaching of the early Patripassians. This is that primarily it is God the Father
> who suffers in the offering and sending of His Son, in His abasement. The
> suffering is not His own, but the alien suffering of the creature, of man, which
> He takes to Himself in Him. But He does suffer it in the humiliation of His
> Son with a depth with which it never was or will be suffered by any man—
> apart from the One who is His Son. And He does so in order that, having been
> borne by Him in the offering and sending of His Son, it should not have to be
> suffered in this way by man. This fatherly fellow-suffering of God is the
> mystery, the basis, of the humiliation of His Son; the truth of that which takes
> place historically in His crucifixion. (IV/2, p. 357)

Here it becomes clear that for Barth suffering is not part of God's essence,
but that God makes our suffering his own in a real and therefore in an essential way in the incarnation by assuming our sinful humanity and experiencing God-forsakenness in our place, in order to overcome our suffering
and death in and through these human actions of Jesus Christ. Earlier
Barth indicated that

> The Son of God suffers—the final extreme is also and primarily true of Him—He
> was crucified, dead and buried. . . . This is all to be said, not of a man called Jesus
> who was different from God, but of the Son of God who is of one essence with
> the Father and the Holy Ghost. For all this is an event and true and actual in Jesus
> Christ as the real participation of the Son of God in human essence. (IV/2, p. 74)

Our suffering is something God takes to himself in his Son out of love for us in order to overcome suffering and death for us. This is a free act of God's grace. Indeed, "God finds no suffering in himself. And no cause outside God can cause him suffering if he does not will it so" (II/1, p. 370). And the fact that he does will this to be so is a manifestation of his free grace and love. While there is no ontological gap in Barth's thinking between the immanent and the economic Trinity either early or later in the *CD*, his distinction without separation of the immanent and economic Trinity is imperative, since without such a distinction the freedom of God's actions for us become necessities. No wonder McCormack argues that if there is a "differentiation between the immanent and economic Trinities" this would lead to the idea that what the incarnate Word is would have "no ontological significance for the *true* being of the Word in his eternal mode of being" (*Orthodox and Modern*, p. 217).

DISTINGUISHING THE ETERNAL WORD AND THE INCARNATE WORD

Here choices must be made. Must we assume that history determines the eternal Word in order to take the incarnation seriously? Or must we acknowledge that the Word actively makes our history his own without surrendering his deity? The choice McCormack offers is clear. He wishes to bid farewell to the distinction between the eternal Word and the incarnate Word. But it is my claim that bidding farewell to this distinction means bidding farewell to the fact that God freely steps out of his inaccessibility by becoming incarnate in accordance with his having elected us from eternity in Jesus Christ. It means bidding farewell to the distinctions between God's pretemporal, supratemporal and posttemporal existence. It means bidding farewell to the fact that God has his own independent existence even as he exists as God for us in his Word and Spirit. In short it means that God's freedom to be eternally Father, Son and Spirit has been collapsed into his actions *ad extra*; in other words, the doctrine of the Trinity has become exactly what Barth thought it was not.

For Barth, as we saw above, "The content of the doctrine of the Trinity . . . is not that God in His relation to man is Creator, Mediator and Redeemer, but that God in Himself is eternally God the Father, Son and Holy Spirit. . . . [God acting as Emmanuel] cannot be dissolved into His work and activity" (I/2, pp. 878-79). When God's actions *ad extra* are seen against the background of his freedom to have been God himself without us, then his actions in history through which we know that he has in fact chosen to be God for us are respected as mysterious and miraculous acts of free love. Whenever this distinction is not respected, then incarnation and creation will be portrayed, wittingly or unwittingly, as essential and necessary for God's existence as God. There is a lot at stake in this decision. While we have seen that Barth refused to discredit the fact that the Son has an eternal existence that cannot simply be reduced to his existence as God for us, McCormack argues that "there is no 'eternal Son' if by that is meant a mode of being in God which is not identical with Jesus Christ" (*Orthodox and Modern*, p. 219).

Because McCormack makes this decision he concludes that God's being is realized through the events of incarnation and suffering for us. But if he had been able to make this distinction, with Barth, he might have been able to say that what is realized in these events is the eternal decision on God's part to be God for us.[45] God did not need this decision, nor did God need us. That is why Barth constantly reiterates this throughout the *Dogmatics*. He prefaces all his important dogmatic sketches by the phrase that God did not need us and does not need us, but nonetheless he did not in fact will to be without us. Wherever that distinction is not made, then the imprecision that is introduced always leads to some version of the idea that somehow God's being itself is realized by means of his relations with us. Barth never endorsed such an idea and could not have, given his view of God's freedom and love.

A further point needs to be mentioned. According to McCormack, when Barth considered the incarnation in *CD* IV/2 he came to the position that "the human history of Jesus Christ is *constitutive* of the being and existence of God in the second of God's modes to the extent that the being and existence of the Second Person of the Trinity cannot be rightly thought of in the absence of this human history" (*Orthodox and Modern*, p. 223, emphasis mine, referring to IV/2, p. 43). Ultimately, the problem here, as indicated in chapter five, concerns the fact that McCormack has confused

---

[45]"This is the work of the eternal Son, determined in God's eternal decree and taking place in time, as the meaning and basis and power of the reconciliation of the world with God" (IV/2, p. 44). This is why, as noted above, Barth insisted that the Son's eternal begetting is a perpetual becoming that "rules out every need of this being for completion. Indeed this becoming simply confirms the perfection of this being" (I/1, p. 427). With this, as seen above in chap. 5, p. 244, Thomas F. Torrance fully agrees (*Christian Doctrine of God*, p. 242).

epistemology and ontology by saying that because *we* cannot know the eternal Trinity without the human Jesus as the Word of God incarnate, therefore we must hold that Jesus' human history *constitutes* his being as the second person of the Trinity. I believe that we are indeed limited to the human Jesus as the incarnate Word to know who God is, but that the God we know in him is constituted eternally within the immanent Trinity and not by his relation to us in history, just as I believe his being is not realized through his humiliation on our behalf. What is realized are his purposes of love for us. Therefore it is correct to say that in light of God's act of incarnation and reconciliation and thus in light of God's self-humiliation on our behalf, we can no longer think of the second person of the Trinity unless we do so by thinking of this history of the incarnate Word. But it is incorrect to read this back into the immanent Trinity as McCormack has done, because in *CD* IV/2 Barth was as emphatic as he was in *CD* I/2 in insisting on the irreversibility of the divine and human natures in Christ:

> His unity with it [the unity of the Word and flesh] became and is irreversible. And so the statement in Jn. 1:14 is irreversible. . . . Abstract declaration about flesh as the Word is quite impossible. Flesh became and is the Word only to the extent that the Word became flesh. The exaltation which came to man in this unity took place and is always grounded in God's humiliation. In it it *did* take place, and it *is* grounded—it is work and actuality—but only in it. . . . Hence the movement from below to above which takes place originally in this man does not compete with the movement of God from above to below. It takes place because and as the latter takes place. (IV/2, p. 47)

Barth was still concerned, as he was in *CD* I/2, to avoid having a third reality arise between God and human being in the incarnation, and so he also insisted that

> if what God willed and resolved from all eternity took place as an event between Himself and man in time, this is not partly conditioned by an act of man, nor is it the outworking of a necessity which binds Himself to man and man to Himself, but it is the work of His own free initiative and act, of His grace. . . . The unity achieved in this history has to be described, not as two-sided, but as founded and consisting absolutely and exclusively in Him. He is the One who did not and does not will to be the One He is—the eternal Son—without also being the Son of Man. (IV/2, p. 46)

Note that Barth is still thinking of the person of the Son as the subject of the incarnation even here. His thinking remains Chacledonian in the sense that he maintains the unity in distinction without separation, division or confusion of natures in Christ and never compromises the full deity or full humanity of Jesus. And his thinking is even Chalcedonian in the sense that his view of the unity of justification and sanctification is explicitly patterned after the union and distinction just mentioned.[46]

This makes McCormack's criticism of George Hunsinger for speaking of a Chalcedonian pattern in connection with the doctrine of reconciliation somewhat puzzling. He criticizes Hunsinger because he claims Hunsinger failed to treat the "problem of the ontology of the *subject* of the twofold history of humiliation and exaltation. . . . If Barth were really 'Chalcedonian,' it would surely be incumbent upon Hunsinger to have done this" (*Orthodox and Modern*, p. 223). But what really is at stake in this criticism? It is clear that what McCormack is looking for from Hunsinger in this context is some illustration of the fact that Jesus' human history *constitutes* his being as the eternal Son. The only problem is that, as we have been seeing, Barth does not espouse this view. Barth continues to hold the view that the "eternal Son," or the person of the Son in Chalcedonian terms, is the subject of the event of incarnation and that he is "The Father's Son, by nature God, A guest this world of ours He trod" (IV/2, p. 47, quoting Luther). Barth continues: "It is not that divine and human-creaturely essence are found and united in Him simply and directly, but that He who is 'by nature God' with the Father and the Holy Ghost took human essence to Himself and united it with His divine nature" (IV/2, p. 47). That sounds awfully Chalcedonian to me.[47] And Barth says, as he did in *CD* I/2, "He *assumed* and adopted that which is so completely different from His divine nature, so alien to it. He is the One who founds and sustains this union, who

---

[46]See, e.g., IV/2, p. 505.

[47]Consider also Barth's rejection of the idea that Jesus is directly in his humanity as such to be seen as the unique Son of God, as when he considered the "question whether the humanity of Jesus Christ as conceived in this way is not one long abstraction: abstracted, that is, from the history to which we cannot even for a moment cease to cling if we are to see and think and confess 'Jesus Christ'; abstracted from the one true Son of God and Son of Man in whom the divine and human are genuinely united, without admixture or separation" (IV/2, p. 80). This is why Barth rejects the idea that Jesus' humanity is divinized. McCormack discusses this also (*Orthodox and Modern*, pp. 227-28) and claims Barth had to reject this because of his "newly revised doctrine of election" (*Orthodox and Modern*, p. 227). But Barth rejected this idea already in *CD* I/1 when he rejected the idea that Jesus is revealer in his humanity as such, as noted above.

makes this different and alien thing, His being as man, both possible and actual as His own" (IV/2, p. 47, emphasis mine).[48] It will be remembered that Barth chooses the word "assumed" in order to stress that the Word was not transformed into man in the incarnation.

It is noteworthy that Barth carefully distinguishes without separating the immanent and economic Trinity even here. Not only does Barth maintain that "The true humanity of Jesus Christ, as the humanity of the Son, was and is and will be the primary content of God's eternal election of grace, i.e., of the divine decision and action which are not preceded by any higher *apart from the trinitarian happening of the life of God*" (IV/2, p. 31, emphasis mine),[49] but Barth speaks here of the "inter-trinitarian background" of the humility that God experiences for us in humbling himself in the incarnation and says that God

> exists even in Himself as God, not only in the majesty of the Father, but also and in the same reality and Godhead as the Son begotten of the Father and following Him and ordered in accordance with Him. In itself and as such, then, humility is not alien to the nature of the true God, but supremely proper to Him in His mode of being as the Son. What God does in this assumption of human being into unity with His own is of course, as an *opus ad extra*, as an act of grace of God to His creature, as His divine action in temporal history, an application and exercise and revelation of the divine humility, the newness and strangeness of

---

[48]Barth deliberately still embraces here "the concept of *assumptio carnis* as it was applied in all older dogmatics to describe the incarnation" (IV/2, p. 42). God became man in Jesus Christ, and this act of humility, to be treated in the second part of Barth's doctrine of reconciliation, presupposes the first part of the doctrine in which God became man and "went into the far country" but that God did this "without ceasing to be God" (IV/2, p. 42). "He is not a prisoner of His own exalted status, but can also be lowly—not in the surrender but the affirmation of His divine majesty" (IV/2, p. 42). Note that lowliness and therefore suffering is not part of God's nature; it becomes his in his act of incarnation on our behalf.

[49]It is very evident to me that Barth continues to wish to acknowledge God's own immanent freedom in this passage in a way that Jüngel and McCormack cannot. As we shall see in a moment, Barth here holds the view espoused by Alan Torrance and rejected by McCormack exactly because McCormack's metaphysics is dictated by his ontological actualism that refuses to acknowledge God's freedom as just described. See also and especially Barth's statement that there is no Godhead because "Even Godhead exists only in and with the existence of the Father, Son and Holy Ghost, only as the common predicate of this triune Subject in its modes of existence" (IV/2, p. 65). This is important because if God is only Godhead and not the eternal Trinity, then God really could not have become incarnate. But because the divine essence became flesh in the Son, then because of the action of this Subject, God really can exist as this man and therefore for us as the reconciler. Hence, contrary to McCormack's thesis that Barth had completely changed the language of Chalcedon in *CD* IV, Barth asserts: "The whole doctrine of the two natures in the strict sense depends on this primary and proper union and unity as it is described in Jn. 1:14" (IV/2, pp. 65-66).

which as the content of this free divine decree ought not to be put into the shade or weakened by this reference to its inter-trinitarian background. (IV/2, p. 42)

What happens in history then corresponds to the unique ability of the Son not to grasp at equality with God but to *humble himself*, and this, Barth says, is the reason for the incarnation. "For the reconciliation of the estranged world with Himself He, the Creator, willed to exist also as a creature Himself" (IV/2, p. 43). Barth continues:

> We can only say that in its great inconceivability—always new and surprising when we try to conceive it—this reason is holy and righteous and worthy of God because it corresponds to the humility of the eternal Son as it takes place in supreme reality in the intra-trinitarian life of God Himself; and although it cannot be deduced from this, in the light of it it can be recognised as a reason which is in itself both clear and well-founded. (IV/2, p. 43)[50]

In *CD* IV/2 Barth is also still concerned, as he was in *CD* I/2, with the fact that God does not change in the incarnation: "It is not that in Him a changed God who loses His deity becomes and is a changed man who loses his humanity, but the one unchangeably true God becomes and is unchangeably true man" (IV/2, pp. 40-41). And here Barth acknowledges the divine freedom in a way that is missing from all accounts that require that Jesus' human history *constituted* his divine person: "God did not owe it to man. He did not owe it even to the man Jesus. He did not owe it either in His eternal counsel or in its execution. He did not owe it to Himself to an inner dialectic of His Godhead" (IV/2, p. 41). Barth continues to insist that "it is founded only in His freedom, in His free love to the world. Only in virtue of His free decision did it take place that as true God He willed to be and became and is true man as well" (IV/2, p. 41). This action of God, Barth asserts, has neither a basis nor a possibility and "certainly no necessity, apart from His gracious good-pleasure" (IV/2, p. 41). And perhaps most importantly in this context, Barth finally contends that the occurrence of this becoming incarnate of the Son cannot be "perceived or understood or deduced from *any ontology which embraces Himself and the world, Himself and man, or from any higher standpoint whatsoever*" (IV/2, p. 41, emphasis mine).

---

[50]Barth clearly has in view Phil 2:7 when he presents his thoughts here. And therefore he means to refer to humility on the part of the Son not to have to grasp at his equality with God but to be able to exercise his freedom to become a creature in order to reconcile us to God.

The question then to be asked of those who believe they can explain how God "became" triune by attributing both God's triunity and the eternal being of the Son to God's eternal act of electing to be God for us is whether and to what extent they have attempted to explain the mystery of God's eternal being as Father, Son and Spirit by means of an ontology that encompasses God *and* created history. To what extent have they therefore attempted to understand God and creation from a higher standpoint than God's eternal being in act as the triune God who was God before he created the world, before he became incarnate and who would have been this very God even if he never decided to create, reconcile and redeem the world. Put another way, that is the question to be asked of those who claim that Barth abandoned and so must we abandon a Chalcedonian ontology that sees the incarnation as a unique, free and sovereign action of the Word or Son in becoming flesh in favor of an actualistic ontology that demands that the person of the Son cannot be fixed from all eternity but must itself be *constituted* by his human history as God for us. This is the crux of my disagreement with McCormack in wishing to apply his thesis that election is the ground of God's triunity even to his Christology. Once the logic of that assertion is accepted, God's freedom must vanish into his life as God for us. And once that happens, one can modify Barth's understanding of the divine freedom to mean that God cannot and could not exist in any other way than as God for us. Barth does not hold this position, and the way he avoids such a conclusion, as we have seen, is precisely by insisting that the Word would still be the Word even if he never became incarnate. He did of course become incarnate. But this was an act of divine freedom that is inconceivable to us apart from the faith that recognizes that God remains God in himself even as he acts divinely for us as our reconciler and redeemer in the history of the man Jesus from Nazareth. Here once again we see how important it is to speak of the knowledge of faith and to acknowledge that this means a knowledge that is inconceivably enabled by the Holy Spirit, a knowledge that is grounded in the incomprehensible turning of God to us sinners who need his reconciling grace in order to understand his free love for us.

Two final points need to be mentioned. First, McCormack is very critical of Alan Torrance's account of the Trinity[51] because Torrance holds that

---

[51]See Alan Torrance, "The Trinity," in *The Cambridge Companion to Karl Barth*, ed. John Webster (Cambridge: Cambridge University Press, 2000), pp. 72-91.

"God's eternal being is constituted as a 'non-temporal' becoming, an essential act of Self-relatedness that is complete in itself without regard for God's Self-communication in history" (*Orthodox and Modern*, p. 220). Torrance's error, we are told, rests in his attempt to overcome a metaphysics of divine unity with "an equally metaphysical account of the relationality of the Triune God" (*Orthodox and Modern*, p. 220). And Torrance is said to have seriously misunderstood Jüngel, who held that God's essence is actually decided "precisely in his will" (*Orthodox and Modern*, p. 220). Torrance's error is that he makes God's triunity a reality anterior to "the differentiated reality of God encountered in his work of the world" (*Orthodox and Modern*, p. 220). And so Alan Torrance's citation of the following crucial statement by Barth is deemed to be impermissible in light of Barth's doctrine of reconciliation:

> God is who He is in His works. He is the same even in Himself, even before and after and over His works, and without them. They are bound to Him, but He is not bound to them. They are nothing without Him. But He is who He is without them. He is not, therefore, who He is only in His works. (II/1, p. 260)[52]

Any appeal to statements such as this are in direct conflict with McCormack's question: "For when has God ever been anything other than God the Reconciler?" (*Orthodox and Modern*, p. 220). That question demonstrates his failure to understand that Barth's doctrine of the Trinity is first a teaching about who God is, which *we* learn about only from the economy but that, when we learn it, teaches us that God is in himself eternally the Father, Son and Holy Spirit and that while he was God without us, since the Father is always Father but not always Creator, and while he could have chosen to remain God without us, nevertheless, he *freely* chose to be God for us. Any

---

[52]I have commented at length on the importance of this passage for Barth's thought. See Molnar, "Can the Electing God Be God Without Us?" pp. 203-4. In discussing Barth's "actualism" George Hunsinger, *How to Read Karl Barth*, gets it just right: "The being of God in act is a being in love and freedom. God, who does not need us to be the living God, is perfectly complete without us. For God is alive in the active relations of love and freedom which constitute God's being in and for itself. These are the active relations of God's trinitarian self-differentiation. . . . Actualism emphasizes the sovereign activity of God in patterns of love and freedom—not only in God's self-relationship, but also in relationship to others" (p. 30). By abandoning God's being in and for itself, McCormack has not only abandoned Barth's positive understanding of God's love and freedom, but he has made it impossible to distinguish God's internal actions from his actions *ad extra*. This is certainly not the actualism Barth had in mind in the *Church Dogmatics*. This statement by Barth is cited by Alan Torrance, "The Trinity," p. 90n28.

other statement in this context necessarily reduces God to his actions *ad extra*. And that clearly is the point that Alan Torrance correctly wished to stress. I agree with Alan Torrance not because either of us wants to separate the immanent and economic Trinity but because the doctrine of the Trinity is not a teaching about God as creator, reconciler and redeemer, but about who God is as Father, Son and Spirit. This, I suggest, is an important point that is inevitably lost, as we have seen in chapter three above, by those who wholeheartedly embrace McCormack's thinking. As we have seen, it is also lost by those who are rightly critical of McCormack's thesis about the logical reversal of election and the Trinity, but who nonetheless embrace in some fashion the thinking that follows that reversal.

Second, and closely related to this mistake by McCormack, is his erroneous understanding of several key passages in *CD* IV/1. Barth's claim that there is a *Logos asarkos* who is not revealed to us is evidence, from McCormack's perspective, that Barth was inconsistent in maintaining that there never was a time when God was not the reconciler. So he can make no allowance for the following statements.

> In this context we must not refer to the second "person" of the Trinity as such, to the eternal Son or the eternal Word of God *in abstracto*, and therefore to the so-called λόγος ἄσαρκος. . . . The second "person" of the Godhead in Himself and as such is not God the Reconciler. In Himself and as such He is not revealed to us. In Himself and as such He is not *Deus pro nobis*, either ontologically or epistemologically. He is the content of a necessary and important concept in trinitarian doctrine when we have to understand the revelation and dealings of God in the light of their free basis in the inner being and essence of God. But since we are now concerned with the revelation and dealings of God, and particularly with the atonement, with the person and work of the Mediator, it is pointless, as it is impermissible, to return to the inner being and essence of God and especially to the second person of the Trinity as such, in such a way that we ascribe to this person another form than that which God Himself has given in willing to reveal Himself and to act outwards. (IV/1, p. 52)

Barth does not here deny that the Word exists also in this form. Rather he insists that in the context of the doctrine of reconciliation we must not retreat to this form so as to exclude the fact that God really has become our

Mediator by becoming incarnate in Jesus Christ. We must not give another form to Christ that would allow us to evade his humanity or his divinity as it is revealed in his self-humiliation on our behalf and our exaltation in him. Barth insists that we are not permitted to return to a *Logos asarkos* in this context in order to "ascribe to this person another form than that which God Himself has given in willing to reveal Himself and to act outwards" (IV/1, p. 52). What Barth opposes here once more is any inventing of a Word who is not this Word in this particular form. He is opposing a natural theology that might attempt to speak about the Word apart from knowledge of that Word through the historical Jesus who was himself that Word incarnate as the revealer and reconciler. But that does not mean that Barth wanted to say that God ceased to exist in his form as the eternal Father, Son and Spirit, and that is why he also insisted on the same page that the second person of the Godhead in himself and as such is not God the Reconciler. That is why he notes, "He, the Son of God, is the One who was and is and will be, existing in the pre-temporality, the co-temporality and the post-temporality of God Himself" (IV/2, pp. 74-75). But he does impart himself to human essence in Jesus Christ, and in Jesus Christ human essence becomes his: "As He is, it takes place that the divine essence in all its distinctiveness is gifted to the human, and the human in all its distinctiveness receives the divine" (IV/2, p. 75). We have to do with God in this form, and we must not use a concept of the *Logos asarkos* to evade this fact. That does not mean that Barth has here reduced God's eternal being to his being for us.[53]

---

[53]Importantly, in his summary of his own doctrine of election offered in *CD* IV/2, Barth once again does not simply dismiss the *Logos asarkos* but argues that in light of the various biblical texts attesting our election in Christ before the foundation of the world, the reference is to Jesus Christ who is truly Son of God and Son of Man and as such is the beginning of God's ways and works *ad extra*. The world was created with a view toward Jesus Christ, who would be the one in whom the world would find its true basis, meaning and goal. Thus Barth writes: "The declarations of predestination from v. 15 onwards (Col. 1:15ff.) cannot, therefore, relate only to the Son of God, to a λόγος ἄσαρκος" (IV/2, p. 33). Also, with regard to the prologue of John, Barth writes: "The event attested in Jn. 1:14 is one to which the whole Prologue looks back. So, then, the whole Prologue (with the possible exception of the first phrase of v. 1)—although it certainly speaks of the eternal Logos—speaks also of the man Jesus" (IV/2, p. 33). He explains this further on the next page. His point clearly illustrates what he means in *CD* IV/1 when he says we must not retreat to a *Logos asarkos* in the context of the doctrine of reconciliation. The reason is that since God became incarnate in Jesus Christ, he is and remains truly divine and truly human to all eternity. It is not, as Scotus Erigena suggested, a passing episode that might one day end (IV/2, p. 35).

Here is where Barth and McCormack are in clear conflict. For Mc-Cormack the unity of the two natures in Christ is grounded in God's election, and so for him "it is the concrete unity of a decision in which God gives both to himself and to humanity his and their essential being" (*Orthodox and Modern*, p. 228). But for Barth, God does not have to give himself his essential being because he already has it and is it as the eternal Father, Son and Spirit. Nonetheless, he does take form for us in the incarnation in accordance with his eternal election, and so he gives our human existence its essential being in his Son Jesus Christ as an act of gracious election, incarnation, reconciliation and redemption. The difference here once again can be seen when McCormack says, "It is in and through the *one* history of the man Jesus that what is essential to both God and humanity is concretely realized" (*Orthodox and Modern*, p. 228). For Barth, God does not need to realize his being, not even as the Son who does not need to be incarnate in order to be who he is (IV/2, pp. 51, 53, 54, 63). But our humanity does need to be realized, and it is indeed true that this is what happens in Christ the Mediator for us.

Importantly, the disagreement over how to read Barth in this matter is, to an extent, the result of Barth's own argument that in order to avoid modalism and subordinationism it is important to realize that there is an eternal obedience of the Son. Now in one sense Barth is absolutely right, since the Son now lives eternally as the one who was sent by his Father and as the one who in his life of obedience as God become man did indeed reconcile us to the Father and now intercedes for us before the Father as prophet, priest and king. But in another sense it seems that Barth unfortunately and unnecessarily read back elements of the economy into the immanent Trinity in order to stress that Jesus' human life history fell within the life of the immanent Trinity. A careful analysis of this difficulty, with the help of Thomas F. Torrance, I hope will lead to an understanding of what Barth's positive intentions were and exactly how his thinking became problematic at that point and needs to be corrected.

In the next chapter therefore we will carefully compare the thinking of T. F. Torrance and Karl Barth on the obedience of the Son with a view toward seeing that they both consider it to be extremely important to ground the Son's condescension to be God for us in the mutual love of the Father and

Son in the unity of the Holy Spirit. Yet, I will argue that we must at the same time guard against confusing the order of the trinitarian persons with their being. In other words, we must avoid reading back elements of the economy into the immanent Trinity, thus blurring any distinction between the processions and missions. With the help of Torrance's thinking I hope to show that when Barth read back subordination and obedience into the inner trinitarian relations, he tended to blur just this distinction, even though he really did not need to do that in order to make his most important points regarding the doctrine of reconciliation.

The Obedience of the Son in the Theology of Karl Barth and of Thomas F. Torrance

M y goal in this chapter is to think as clearly and as rigorously as possible about what Karl Barth and Thomas F. Torrance mean when they speak of the obedience of the Son. I intend to illustrate that when a clear union and distinction between the actions of the immanent and economic Trinity is maintained consistently, then we can appreciate the power of God's actions in the economy in a way that is impossible when elements of the economy are inappropriately read back into the eternal life of the Trinity. In order to accomplish this I will offer a close reading of some of what each theologian says, with a view toward making an assessment of what appears to be a disagreement in the midst of wide agreement regarding the doctrines of the atonement and of the Trinity. The disagreement concerns the question of whether, with Barth, we should affirm "as essential to the being of God the offensive fact that there is in God Himself an above and a below, a *prius* and a *posterius*, a superiority and a subordination."[1]

The question that must be asked is whether this thinking represents an improper reading back of elements of the economy into God's eternal being, thus disrupting rather than strengthening the trinitarian basis for understanding atonement as an act of God within history in the incarnate Word. There is no doubt that both Barth and Torrance wanted to stress that obedience, humiliation and subordination were not simply experiences of the

---

[1]IV/1, pp. 200-201.

human Jesus but were experienced by God the Son in his divine nature as well. That I regard as one of their strengths. The question that I will be raising is whether it is acceptable to find obedience and subordination within the immanent Trinity as the basis for the Son's actions *ad extra*. Barth does this of course in volume IV of the *CD* and sees God's actions *ad extra* in the incarnation and atonement as corresponding to who and what God is within the immanent Trinity. This is a thorny issue because both Barth and Torrance thoroughly agree that what God is toward us he is eternally in himself, and what he is eternally in himself he is toward us. Still, they do not agree completely about how to interpret this, as we shall see. The question will concern whether we are in a position to explain how God's actions for us are grounded in the inner being of God beyond acknowledging that they are grounded in the mystery of the eternal, free, mutual love of the Father, Son and Holy Spirit and thus in God's free decision to be God for us, a decision that is indeed eternal but is not constitutive of the divine being.

This is a daunting topic. If I were to develop in detail what each theologian says about the obedience of the Son, this chapter would become much too long. Therefore I will discuss several important issues related to the obedience of the Son that I believe will lead us to see exactly how and why what is at stake in this discussion is not only a proper view of Christology and atonement but also a proper view of the relationship between the immanent and economic Trinity, since, as Torrance says and Barth would agree, Christology and the Trinity are intimately related doctrines. *First*, I will illustrate that both theologians agree that when we speak of the obedience of the Son we are speaking of the Son's condescension to become incarnate for our sake. That is important because it suggests that the obedience of the Son as a divine and human act concerns the Son's mission to be God for us. *Second*, we will have to explain why each theologian insists that the incarnation is a free action of God such that God does not cease in any way being the transcendent God but rather acts in a hidden way as God for us, and this is disclosed to us in the resurrection of Jesus from the dead. In order to understand how each theologian thinks about God's freedom and love as well as the relationship of the immanent and economic Trinity, we will consider how each of them understands the *Extra Calvinisticum*. *Finally*, we must consider how and why each theologian opposes subordi-

nationism and modalism and explain why it is imperative that the order of
the inner trinitarian relations not be confused with the being of the trinitarian persons. To do so always leads to some form of subordinationism or
modalism and could open the door to monism and dualism as well.

THE OBEDIENCE OF THE SON AS CONDESCENSION FOR BARTH

Barth speaks about the obedience of the Son in connection with God's
election of and reconciliation of the human race. Atonement, Barth says, is
a very special history, so special, in fact, that it takes precedence over all
other history. It is of course "the very special history of God with man" and
"the very special history of man with God" (IV/1, p. 157). For Barth, we actually take part here and now in the history of Jesus Christ himself, and what
takes place in that history is "the new obedience of man" (IV/1, p. 158) as the
work of God himself who condescended to become one with us in the incarnation. In the Holy Spirit this is actually a present event for us.

Obedience here means that, while remaining God, that is, without ceasing
to be God who alone has his life in himself, God comes to sinful creatures
and interests himself in them "in Jesus Christ"; God comes "without any
merit or deserving" and freely, "from outside, from above—which is to say,
from God's standpoint, the aspect of His grace in which He does something
unnecessary and extravagant, binding and limiting and compromising and
offering Himself in relation to man by having dealings with him and making
Himself his God" (IV/1, p. 158). By condescending to become one of us, God
in Jesus Christ thus goes "into the far country" (IV/1, p. 158), into the world
of evil that was created by our rebellion against God. God makes this situation his own for our sake, without in the least surrendering his deity but in
this way demonstrating it. God is able to humiliate himself for us to overcome
sin as the "human act of pride" (IV/1, p. 145). Hence, "God is not proud. In
His high majesty He is humble" (IV/1, p. 159) because in Jesus Christ the Lord
acts for us as a servant.[2] Barth insists that the incarnation does not just mean
the act of the Son assuming flesh; though it certainly means that, it also

---

[2]This statement could be seen as comparable to Torrance's statement that God who gives *himself*
to us, who "dies our death, descends into the chasm or abyss of our alienation from him in order
to effect atonement and propitiation . . . reveals that he loves us more than he loves himself"
(*Christian Doctrine of God*, pp. 215, 166).

means that "At every point we shall be dealing with the action and work of the Lord God" (IV/1, p. 159). Thus, in the form of an obedient servant, we meet the Lord God himself, who is our reconciler. Surrendering to God's will, Jesus put into effect "His freedom to finish His work, to execute the divine judgment by undergoing it Himself, to punish the sin of the world by bearing it Himself, by taking it away from the world in His own person, in his death" (IV/1, p. 271). This had to happen because this was the way that God would liberate the human race from sin and evil once and for all.

What happens in the incarnation of God, then, is the "divine conde-scension"—God goes "into the far country" (IV/1, p. 168). This is the God of the covenant, "The Father who is one with the man Jesus His Son (Jn. 10:30)" (IV/1, p. 168). In this one Israelite, God is not only the giver of grace as electing creator but its recipient as elected creature; God does not just command, but he is the one "who is called and pledged to obedience" (IV/1, p. 170). The character of God's grace and revelation is that of "election," and so Barth claims it involves "a self-limitation and a self-humiliation on the part of God" (IV/1, p. 170). Jesus accepted his election as the Word made flesh. Israel testifies to God's election, and this alone shows us "who and what is man—his unfaith-fulness, his disobedience, his fall, his sin, his enmity against God" (IV/1, p. 171). All of this Jesus, the Son of God, took on himself in order to repent perfectly in our place. This is the action of God's grace that shows us to be God's en-emies; in light of this we must acknowledge ourselves as transgressors (IV/1, p. 172). Jesus had to be the friend of publicans and sinners because "God was already the God who loved His enemies, who 'endured such contradiction of sinners against Himself'" (IV/1, p. 172; Heb 12:3). As sinners, then, God's elect who negate God in their sin are negated; they are rejected by God's grace. Because they are rejected by God's grace, this takes place in an act of faith-fulness toward those who are unfaithful. God's grace is concealed within this judgment. But that ultimately means that Jesus himself is the Judge judged in our place, and that is the form of God's saving grace.

Barth always stresses that Jesus acts both divinely and humanly so that we never have simply a human or a divine being in Jesus. Jesus' sacrifice for us "is, of course, a human action—but in and with the human action it is also a divine action, in which . . . the true and effective sacrifice is made" (IV/1, p. 280). In Jesus we see the true meaning of suffering and death. While there was suffering and death in Israel, in Jesus these become "the work of God Himself" (IV/1, p. 175). Against the idea, discussed above, that the only act that the Son of God performed was in assuming flesh so that all the rest of the acts of the God-man were performed by the man Jesus,[3] Barth repeatedly insists, as does Torrance, that "The Son of God in his unity with this man exists in solidarity with the humanity of Israel suffering under the mighty hand of God" (IV/1, p. 175). As such he suffers Israel's suffering as "children chastised by their Father"; in him God entered the vicious circle of human suffering by allowing the divine sentence to fall on himself. "He, the electing eternal God, willed Himself to be rejected and therefore perishing man" (IV/1, p. 175). This, then, is the mystery of Christ's deity. God was truly willing, able and ready "to condescend, to humble Himself in this way" (IV/1, p. 177). This understanding of God "cannot be gathered from any notion of supreme, absolute, non-worldly being." Jesus' divine nature and therefore the true God himself can only be known through "His becoming flesh and His existence in the flesh" (IV/1, p. 177).

Notably, for Barth, "There is no lowliness which is divine in itself and as such" (IV/1, p. 191) since the cross is no mere symbol of some pessimistic outlook on life. Humanity's limitations are one thing. But "God's visitation of us" within those limitations is quite another. Consequently, "Salvation is not in those limits, but in the concrete event of this visitation, in what took place in the man Jesus" (IV/1, p. 192). Indeed, "The Godhead revealed and active in this event is His Godhead" (IV/1, p. 192). But the Godhead that is attested in him is *his alone,* according to the New Testament—our suffering and dying with Christ is a posteriori and not a priori—it follows him and indirectly indicates him. Therefore what happens in the life of the believer "stands or falls" with what happened and happens in the life of Jesus. And what exactly was that? "Jesus Christ is the Son of God and as such, in conformity with the divine nature, the Most High who humbles Himself and in that way is exalted and very high" (IV/1, p. 192). Thus Christians are in Christ and delivered by God from darkness and into the kingdom of his Son (Col 1:13). The Christian life, then, allows, "follows and confirms" the fact that "It

---

[3]See above, chap. 4, p. 216, chap. 5, pp. 231 and 252, and Bruce L. McCormack, "Divine Impassibility or Simply Divine Constancy? Implications of Karl Barth's Later Christology for Debates over Impassibility," in *Divine Impassibility and the Mystery of Human Suffering,* ed. James F. Keating and Thomas Joseph White, O.P. (Grand Rapids: Eerdmans, 2009), p. 177.

is only because He is the Son of God in this sense that they are called and empowered in fellowship with Him to choose the [lowliness] of mind which is natural to the children of God" (IV/1, p. 192).

In this sense, for Barth, the way of the Son into the far country is the "way of obedience" (IV/1, p. 192). This is "the first and inner moment of the mystery of the deity of Christ" (IV/1, p. 192). This is a mystery, and one that *offends* because we learn here that "for God it is just as natural to be lowly as it is to be high, to be near as it is to be far, to be little as it is to be great" (IV/1, p. 192). Barth emphasizes that God is true to himself acting this way in the freedom of his love (IV/1, p. 193). God is never to be seen as in contradiction with himself; that is a false alternative that refuses to acknowledge that God really was in Christ reconciling the world. God "does not have to choose and do this. He is free in relation to it" (IV/1, p. 193). Thus we are dealing with the real thing "when He does choose and do this" (IV/1, p. 193). Here we have to do with "God Himself in His true deity" (IV/1, p. 193). In his distinctive way Barth argues that what God is toward us he is eternally in himself. And so he says that this humility in which God reveals himself to us is a new mystery for us because it conflicts with our false ideas of God. But Barth claims it is not a new mystery for God. What does this mean?

It could not mean that God was always incarnate; such a concept would undermine his own understanding of God's transcendence. It seems reasonable that Barth means that God acts *ad extra* in accordance with his decision to be for us in his pretemporal eternal existence; he elected in free grace to have covenant relations with us, and therefore what Jesus does as the Word incarnate is not arbitrary but necessary in the sense that he can do nothing other than obey God's will; that is his freedom. That is why, attempting to overcome any nominalistic view of the divine perfections, Barth could argue at one and the same time that grace is God's free and unmerited movement toward us in order to have communion with us, and it is part of God's very nature to be gracious.[4] The fact, then, that God seeks and creates fellowship with us is grounded in God's love and freedom as Father, Son and Holy Spirit; God *is* the One who loves in

---

[4]See II/1, p. 357. Barth writes: "It is in this way, graciously, that God not only acts outwardly towards His creature, but is in Himself from eternity to eternity." For an important discussion of the implications of Barth's attempts to overcome nominalism, see D. Stephen Long, "From the Hidden God to the God of Glory: Barth, Balthasar and Nominalism," *Pro Ecclesia* 20, no. 2 (Spring 2011): 167-85.

freedom, and that means that in a way known only to God in his inner being, God is free positively and negatively. God's freedom as creator, reconciler and redeemer is "not exhausted in the fact that in His revelation it consists throughout in this freedom from external compulsion . . . it is only manifested in all this. For He has it in Himself quite apart from His relation to another from whom He is free" (II/1, p. 301). That is why Barth sees the atoning act of God for us as a "sovereign act which God did not owe to Himself or the world or any man, on which no one could bank, yet which has in fact taken place and been made manifest" (IV/1, p. 83). Hence, the "grace of God" is "exclusively His grace, His sovereign act, His free turning to man as new and strange every morning" (IV/1, p. 84). This frequently repeated insight safeguards God's freedom in his love. And it is based within the Trinity itself: "In the inner life of God, as the eternal essence of Father, Son and Holy Ghost, the divine essence does not, of course, need any actualisation. . . . Even as the divine essence of the Son it did not need His incarnation . . . to become actual" (IV/2, p. 113). This is important, as seen above,[5] because from revelation we learn that God is gracious to sinners and that his good will for us is "unimpeded" by our sin and resistance.

THE OBEDIENCE OF THE SON AS CONDESCENSION IN THE THEOLOGY OF THOMAS F. TORRANCE

In Torrance's theology, the Son's obedience is often described as his descent into our sinful history in order to "live out from within it a life of pure obedience, fulfilling the covenant will of God, and bringing humanity back from estrangement to communion with the Father."[6] Torrance also emphasizes the Son's active and passive obedience in order to avoid a purely forensic or judicial idea of justification. He does this by insisting that in the incarnation God experiences our alienation from within the person of the Mediator, and by living a life of perfect obedience, the Son bends our wills and converts our minds back toward God in his once-for-all actions of justification and sanctification (*Atonement*, p. 70).[7] He also stresses that what Christ does actively for our benefit is to establish positive communion, filial love and worship that reflect the Father's own love. For Torrance,

---

[5]See above, e.g., chap. 3, pp. 133, 156, and chap. 6, p. 295.
[6]*Incarnation*, p. 114.
[7]See also *Incarnation*, p. 115.

the involvement of the Son in our lowly condition is to be understood as an act of pure condescension on his part and not as an indication of an imperfection in him. He was not creaturely or space-conditioned in his own eternal Being, but he humbled himself to be one with us and to take our finite nature upon himself, *all for our sakes*.[8]

This, Torrance says, is what patristic theology "called his 'economic condescension,' that is, the way in which God chose out of transcendent freedom and grace to effect the salvation of mankind."[9]

As with Barth, Torrance insisted on holding together Christ's person and work in revelation and in atonement.[10] Torrance thus insists that the eternal Son of God "intervenes" into our sinful existence as it is alienated from God "as our mediator, as true God and true man in one person who acts as judging God and judged man, as loving God and as obedient man" (*Atonement*, p. 75). He insists that we "must think of the work of Christ in terms of a mediation which fully represents both the divine and human side" (*Atonement*, p. 75). Hence, Christ

> does not act as man reconciling God or as man appeasing God. He acts as God who enters into the place of humanity, and brings himself into reconciliation with humanity and brings them into reconciliation with himself. . . . [This] is not an act just done over their head, but an act that is fully and entirely human act, issuing out of the depth of their humanity and directed from humanity toward God the Father. . . . Even as man in atoning action, Christ is act of God . . . [and] even as God in atoning action, Christ is act of man. . . . Atonement is man's act of obedient self-offering to God. (*Atonement*, pp. 76-77)

In his obedience to the will of God he lives humanly in the way in which we were intended by God to be: a reflection of God's own glory by being truly righteous and holy (*Incarnation*, p. 122). The Son of God came, Torrance says, "to live out . . . in the midst of our disobedience a life of obedience, and so to live the perfect life in communion with the perfect God" (*Incarnation*, p. 123).

---

[8]Thomas F. Torrance, *Divine Meaning: Studies in Patristic Hermeneutics* (Edinburgh: T & T Clark, 1995), p. 344.

[9]Ibid.

[10]Thus, "The significance of the cross . . . lies in the fact that the person of Christ is the one who sheds his blood for our sin—it lies in the identity of his person and work. . . . The cross is the outworking of a divine decision that constitutes the person of the Mediator himself in the incarnation" (*Incarnation*, p. 108).

But he was to live this "not simply as Son of God but as Son of God become *man*, as Son of Man, that is to live it out from beginning to end within the limitations of our creaturely humanity . . . in the house of bondage" (*Incarnation*, p. 123). In obedience he "laid aside his glory in order that within our frailty and weakness, where we are assaulted by all the attacks and temptations of the evil one, he might perfectly fulfill the Father's will of love and holiness" (*Incarnation*, p. 123). Jesus chose to live out his mission, which led to the cross; as the mediator, he increasingly exposed the evil in the human heart so that he came to be more and more despised simply for being there as savior, helper and friend (*Incarnation*, pp. 235-56). In his perfect obedience and life of faith in relation to the Father as his beloved Son among sinners, "he opened the kingdom of heaven to all believers" (*Incarnation*, p. 125).

Jesus' human life of obedience, Torrance insists, was not simply instrumental "*but an integral and essential part of that divine revelation and reconciliation*" in the sense that he was at one and the same time "the complete revelation of God to man and the perfect correspondence on man's part to that revelation" (*Incarnation*, p. 126). In his doctrine of atonement, Torrance stresses not only that God in Christ acts *as* man (*Atonement*, p. 123) but that "even as man in atoning action, Christ is *act of God*" (*Atonement*, p. 77). Hence, for Torrance, God justifies us in his act of reestablishing relations with us, and God reconciles in "pure condescension" by living a life under judgment for us (*Atonement*, p. 145).

Jesus was not only the perfect image and reflection of God because his whole human life "was in entire agreement with the mind and will of the Father" (*Incarnation*, p. 127), but "he *was* the very God he imaged and reflected in his human life" (*Incarnation*, p. 127). Because of this "his activity on earth *was itself* the saving activity of God himself" (*Incarnation*, p. 127). Jesus' act

> in laying down his life is grounded upon the entire solidarity and mutuality between the Father and the Son, so that all that he does in his human life is identical with the act of God himself, but also so that nothing is done in his human life except what issues out of the love of the Father for the Son and the Son for the Father. (*Incarnation*, p. 127)

Because of that relation, Jesus' perfect human life is identical "with the saving truth and love of God the Father" (*Incarnation*, p. 127). Because reconciliation is "the great positive enactment of the divine love" (*Atonement*, p. 147), we may see that God's purpose in turning toward us in our sin was to reconcile himself to humanity "in order to turn humanity to himself, in order to reconcile humanity to himself" (*Atonement*, p. 148).

In virtue of this condescension on the part of God, "Jesus Christ is in himself the hypostatic union of the judge and the man judged" (*Atonement*, pp. 148, 124-25, 145), both God the judge and the "sin-bearer who bore our judgment and the penalty for our sin in his own life and death" (*Atonement*, p. 148). Christ was so at one with God that "what he did, God did, for he was none other than God himself acting thus in our humanity. And therefore there is no other God for us than this God, and no other action of God toward us than this action in which he stood in our place and acted on our behalf" (*Atonement*, p. 152, also pp. 76-77). But since he was also one with us,

> when he died we died, for he did not die for himself but for us, and he did not die alone, but we died in him as those whom he had bound to himself inseparably by his incarnation. Therefore when he rose again we rose in him and with him . . . we are already accepted of God in him once and for all. (*Atonement*, p. 152)

For Torrance, as for Barth, God in no way was transformed in the incarnation but rather exercised his majesty in the form of an "incredible act of condescension" that not only meant that the Son of God assumed the form of a servant but that the incarnation was "an act of utter self-abasement and humiliation in which he assumed our abject servile condition" (*Trinitarian Faith*, p. 153). Hence, kenosis was not to be understood "in any metaphysical way as involving a contraction, diminution or self-limitation of God's infinite being" (*Trinitarian Faith*, p. 153). Rather it was to be understood as God's "self-abnegating love in the inexpressible mystery of the *tapeinosis* . . . impoverishment or abasement, which he freely took upon himself in what he became and did in Christ entirely for our sake" (*Trinitarian Faith*, p. 153).

The main point to be made then in connection with Torrance's understanding of incarnation as condescension is this: for God to relate with us who are at enmity with him because of our sin, which is our self-centeredness, he humbled himself to take the form of a servant in order to exercise his judgment by being the Judge judged in our place (see *Atonement*, pp. 184-85). That is his grace and love expressed in and toward a sinful world. In the Son's life of perfect obedience, which he renders in Jesus' human life, the gulf that separates God and humanity is overcome, and we are enabled not only to know the meaning of sin and salvation but God himself in his own inner relations.[11] The Son of the Father not only entered and obeyed the Father in that life "but by a life in which he personally through compassion and revelation brought his relations with sinners to their completion and then acted for them as their mediator before God" (*Atonement*, p. 162). The resurrection was the apex of Christ's active obedience in the form of his Amen to the Father by raising himself from the dead;[12] one cannot so emphasize God's act of grace here as to eliminate from the incarnate Word this perfect Amen to the Father that also takes place within our human existence in Jesus' resurrection.

A genuine personal union was achieved between God and humanity in the person of his Son, Jesus Christ, that was both noetic and ontic because it was "carried through his conscious personal relations as well as his union in being with God" (*Atonement*, p. 162). It is within the ontic relation and thus "within the hypostatic union, that the *noetic* or 'knowing' relation has its place" (*Atonement*, p. 162). It is noetic in the sense that the divine Logos revealed himself "within our humanity" and also enabled "our humanity to receive his revelation personally, in love and faith and understanding" (*Atonement*, p. 162). But we must also think of this, Torrance says, "as the condescension of the Word, to enter into our humanity and within our humanity to accommodate himself to us in reconciling revelation. Thus the eternal Word or Son of God veiled his effulgence of glory" that we might see this in the lowliness of Jesus' human activity. In other words, in the incarnation he "stooped down to enter our flesh" and thus "brought divine omnipotence within the compass of our littleness, frailty and weakness. . . . The eternal Word and truth of God entered into the darkness of our ignorance in order to redeem us from the power of darkness and ignorance, in order

---

[11]In *Space, Time and Resurrection* (Edinburgh: T & T Clark, 1998), Torrance insists that apart from the resurrection we could not say that we creatures of space and time truly know God the Father in his own ultimate being and reality (p. 71). "The resurrection is therefore our pledge that statements about God in Jesus Christ have an objective reference in God, and are not just projections . . . objectifying forms of thought in which we fashion a God in terms of the creaturely content of our own ideas" (pp. 72-73).

[12]See, e.g., *Space, Time and Resurrection*, pp. 53, 32; Paul D. Molnar, *Thomas F. Torrance: Theologian of the Trinity* (Aldershot, UK: Ashgate, 2009), pp. 230-31, and above, chap. 5, p. 253.

to deliver us from untruth and to make us free for and in the truth of God"
(*Atonement*, pp. 162-63; also *Trinitarian Faith*, pp. 186-87).[13]

EXTRA CALVINISTICUM AND THE RELATION OF THE IMMANENT AND ECONOMIC TRINITY

Barth, like Torrance, appeals to Matthew 11:25-30 and Luke 10:21-24 and
asserts that the form of revelation (Jesus' human existence and actions) does
not correspond to who and what he is "as the human bearer of that unlimited omnipotence [he receives from the Father], and who and what is the
One who has given it to Him" (IV/1, p. 178). This revelation cannot be deduced from its form and cannot be "judged and evaluated from without"
(IV/1, p. 178). It is indeed more likely that this will not be recognized in this
form because "this door to the majesty of Jesus can open only from within"
(IV/1, p. 178). And what is disclosed here is "the strange form of the divine
majesty, the humility in which God is God and the Son the Son, and to that
extent the Father the Father, the alien life in which He is manifest *only to
Himself* alone" (IV/1, p. 178, emphasis mine).

As Barth's interpretation of the Son's obedience reaches its climax, he does
not just present the incarnate Son as obedient to the Father by humbling
himself for us as the Judge judged in our place. He goes further and claims
that the basis for what the incarnate Son does for us is found in the obedience
of the Son within the immanent Trinity. The incarnation informs Barth's
understanding of the inner trinitarian relations here. Barth insists that the
incarnation is a free divine action. Thus, "God is always God even in this
humiliation" (IV/1, p. 179). As does Torrance, Barth maintains that there is
no change, diminution or transformation of the divine being into something
else (IV/1, p. 180).[14] Understanding Philippians 2:7 as its own commentary,
Barth insists that it was not a necessity that the Son must exist "only in that
form of God, only to be God . . . only to be the eternal Word and not flesh.

---

[13]Hence, "Redemption was not accomplished just by a downright *fiat* of God, nor by a mere divine
'nod,' but by an intimate, personal movement of the Son of God himself into the heart of our
creaturely being and into the inner recesses of the human mind, in order to save us from within
and from below" (*Trinitarian Faith*, pp. 187-88). See also *Atonement*, pp. 440-47. It is crucial that
in the atonement we know that our minds were healed so that we could know God and obey
God in freedom.

[14]Consequently, "He humbled Himself, but He did not do it by ceasing to be who He is," Barth
says (IV/1, p. 180).

. . . In addition to His form in the likeness of God He could also . . . take the form of a servant" (IV/1, p. 180). This incarnation is his movement into the far country. Following Gregory of Nyssa and Calvin, Barth notes, however, that "An absolute *inclusio* of the Logos in the creature, the man Jesus, would mean a subordination of the Word to the flesh, a limitation and therefore an alteration of His divine nature, and therefore of God Himself" (IV/1, p. 180).[15]

This assertion came to be called the *Extra Calvinisticum*, since later in history Calvinists and not Lutherans affirmed this insight and were suspected by the Lutherans of Nestorian tendencies because of it. It is exceedingly important to see exactly what Barth means when he both affirms this *Extra Calvinisticum* and claims there is something unsatisfactory about it. This could help explain why Barth both affirms the *Logos asarkos* in the limited sense that it points to the fact that God has his own proper life (IV/1, p. 52) but also rejects it as something we cannot return to in an attempt to understand the atoning work of the incarnate Word. The problem with the *Extra Calvinisticum* is that it could lead and has in fact led "to fatal speculation about the being and work of the λόγος ἄσαρκος, or a God whom we think we can know elsewhere, and whose divine being we can define from elsewhere than in and from the contemplation of His presence and activity as the Word made flesh" (IV/1, p. 181). So when Barth rejected Brunner's *Logos asarkos* during a conversation,[16] he was not overturning his other statements that affirm its necessity for recognizing the freedom of God in the doctrines of the Trinity and Christology; rather he was rejecting any sort of natural theology—any attempt to subject Jesus Christ, the incarnate Word and the reconciler, to a criterion other than himself. Therefore it is crucial to see that Barth does not deny this form of the *Logos*'s existence but emphatically rejects any idea that the *Logos* can be detached from the form of revelation and still be known as the true Son who humbled himself for us (IV/1, p. 52).

Modern kenoticism, which espoused the idea that the divine Son had to renounce his attributes of majesty for those of humility, also suggested that

---

[15]This is fully in accord with Barth's earlier statement that "the Godhead is not so immanent in Christ's humanity that it does not also remain transcendent to it, that its immanence ceases to be an event in the Old Testament sense, always a new thing, something that God actually brings into being in specific circumstances" (I/1, p. 323).

[16]See *Karl Barth's Table Talk*, recorded and ed. John Godsey (Richmond, VA: John Knox, 1962), p. 49.

Jesus' Godhead no longer remained "intact and unaltered." And that, Barth says, is a clear departure from all earlier tradition, because it eliminated the fact that "God was in Christ" in favor of a historical understanding of the incarnation (IV/1, p. 183). Barth insists that the identity of the man Jesus with God "tells us that God for His part is God in His unity with this creature, this man, in His human and creaturely nature—and this without ceasing to be God, without any alteration or diminution of His divine nature" (IV/1, p. 183).

In answer to the question of how God became man, Barth unequivocally rejects any idea that in humbling himself for our salvation God comes into conflict with himself. If God were thought of as setting himself in self-contradiction, then noetically and logically what happened in the incarnation would be an absolute paradox and a completely new mystery—new in the sense there would be a rift in God between his being and essence or his being and activity such that what God is in himself would differ from what he is in the economy. As I have been arguing throughout this book, both Barth and Torrance firmly reject any sort of dualistic understanding of the relation of the immanent and economic Trinity by affirming that what God is toward us in the economy, he is eternally in himself. Any such dualistic split would leave us only with a God who could not in fact be tempted or be truly present among us in our sinful condition; such a God could not in reality be omnipresent, eternal and glorious but only lowly and open to attack (IV/1, p. 184). In assuming the form of a servant, God did not give up being God as he would have done had he come into conflict with himself. In the incarnation, God comes into conflict with sin and death for our benefit by living as the Judge judged in our place; but God himself never sins, since that would place him in opposition to himself and miss the point of the incarnation. Hence, in subjecting himself to God-forsakenness, God does not make common cause with us as sinners but exercises his Lordship over this contradiction (IV/1, p. 185). While God in Christ mingles with sinners "he does not sin," and when he dies in his unity with the man Jesus, "death does not gain any power over him. He exists as God in the righteousness and the life, the obedience and the resurrection of this man" (IV/1, p. 185). In other words, God is true to himself in this condescension. And it is the risen Lord who discloses this.

While Barth insists that God is not "at disunity with himself" (IV/1, p. 186), he is also very careful not to deny God's immutability and argues that what God did in the incarnation "corresponds to His divine nature" (IV/1, p. 187). Barth maintains, as seen above in chapter five, that God "is absolute, infinite, exalted, active, impassible, transcendent, but in all this He is the One who loves in freedom" (IV/1, p. 187). Consequently, God is free to be *both* infinite and finite, divine and human, exalted and lowly "without giving up His own form, the *forma Dei*, and His own glory" (IV/1, p. 187). Therefore it corresponds to the divine nature and is grounded in it when in free grace God sacrifices himself in his Son for us. God is "not His own prisoner" (IV/1, p. 187), and thus God can be temporal and can suffer and die without ceasing to be eternal and without having suffering and death gain control over him (IV/1, p. 188).

As Barth digs deeper to understand the connection between God's inner being and what God does for us in the economy, he reaches the conclusion that Christ's human acts of obedience and humility must imply that "there is a humility grounded in the being of God" so that "something else is grounded in the being of God Himself" (IV/1, p. 193). Barth wants to say that Christ's obedience cannot be a "capricious choice of lowliness, suffering and dying" because it is "a free choice made in recognition of an appointed order . . . which was intended to be obeyed" (IV/1, p. 193). Accordingly, if "God is in Christ" that must mean that "what the man Jesus does is God's own work" so that his act of "self-emptying and self-humbling . . . cannot be alien to God" (IV/1, p. 193). Again, Barth turns to Philippians 2:8 and other texts to refer to Christ's learning obedience and notes that through obedience we are made righteous, according to Paul (Rom 5:19). Unless what we say here about the man Jesus is also said about God, Barth believes that his atoning life, suffering and death would only be seen as "accidental events of nature or destiny" (IV/1, p. 194). But Barth's whole argument rests on the fact that Jesus cannot do anything other than what he does because here he acts with the freedom of God himself, "making use of a possibility grounded in the being of God" (IV/1, p. 194). God's freedom to be God in hidden and lowly form and also to be God in himself "and known only to Himself" (IV/1, p. 194) is not arbitrary; it is not something God might or might not do. Rather "if 'the Father's Son, by nature God, A guest this world of ours He trod' (Luther), if God made use of His freedom in this sense" (IV/1, p. 194), then God is not a victim of circumstances so to speak but the one who freely acted in obedience for us.

Here, God chose to make use of his freedom to fulfill his own decision to
be our God in Christ. Therefore it does not take place, as we discussed above
in chapter three in another context, "in the play of a sovereign *liberum arbitrium*" because "there is no possibility of something quite different happening"; it is not the result of "one of the throws in a game of chance which
takes place in the divine being" (IV/1, p. 195). Rather, we have to do here with
the foundation of a divine decision that is fulfilled in this event as we have
it and not otherwise. This itself is a decision of obedience, and for that
reason it can demand our obedience. Otherwise, as an arbitrary act, we
could not have confidence in it. Once again at this point we are confronted
with the mystery of Christ's deity. His human obedience is grounded in "His
divine nature and therefore in God Himself" (IV/1, p. 195). Now Barth asks:
does this lead to an impenetrable mystery or to "knowledge of it as an open
secret?" (IV/1, p. 195). Here Barth makes the move from the economic to the
immanent Trinity again. Only now he maintains that there must be an "obedience which takes place in God Himself" (IV/1, p. 195). Noting that this is
both a "difficult" and an "elusive" thing to speak about, Barth argues that
"obedience implies an above and a below, a *prius* [before] and a *posterius*
[after], a superior and a junior and subordinate" (IV/1, p. 195). Do not these
ideas compromise the unity and equality of the divine being, Barth asks?
How can God be one and also "above and below, the superior and the subordinate"? Barth asks again (IV/1, p. 195). Does this not mean that we have
here two divine beings, one only improperly divine because he exists on the
created side of reality and is thus not really God in the true sense?

Things now start to get interesting. Here I believe Barth makes a subtle
mistake that places his thinking in conflict with itself. He is absolutely
correct to argue that God can be one and also "above and below, superior
and subordinate" in the incarnation and the mission of the Son of God
obeying God for us. But why does Barth think he must ascribe superiority
and subordination to God's inner life in order to make this assertion? Why
does he embrace a concept that he himself once stoutly rejected, when he
wrote: "If revelation is to be taken seriously as God's presence, if there is to
be a valid belief in revelation, then *in no sense can Christ and the Spirit be
subordinate hypostases*" (I/1, p. 353, emphasis mine)? Torrance also believes
that what God is toward us he is in himself, but never once does he attempt

to ground this assertion in a superiority and subordination within the immanent Trinity; nor does he claim there is a *prius* or a *posterius* in God's inner being. In fact, following Calvin, he writes:

> The *principium* of the Father does not import an ontological priority, or some *prius aut posterius* in God, but has to do only with a "form of order" (*ratio ordinis*) or "arrangement" (*dispositio*) of inner trinitarian relations governed by the Father/Son relationship, which in the nature of the case is irreversible, together with the relationship of the Father and the Son to the Spirit who is the Spirit of the Father and the Spirit of the Son. (*Trinitarian Perspectives*, p. 66)[17]

Consequently, Torrance firmly argues that "the subordination of Christ to the Father in his incarnate and saving economy cannot be read back into the eternal personal relations and distinctions subsisting in the Holy Trinity" (*Trinitarian Perspectives*, p. 67). What is going on here?

SUBORDINATIONISM AND MODALISM

As noted above, both Barth and Torrance unequivocally reject subordinationism and modalism as false alternatives that cannot do justice to the fact that God can be God on high and in a lowly form for us in the incarnation without ceasing to be God. When Barth rejects subordinationism at this point in *CD* IV/1, he insists that we cannot have in the incarnate Christ a being of lesser dignity than the Father, for that would destroy the doctrine of atonement. And he opposes modalism because such thinking admits there is a commanding and an obeying here of the divine being, but "only as worldly forms or appearances of the true Godhead, and therefore only in the sphere of the improper being of Godhead" (IV/1, p. 196). If, however, God is somewhere behind this economy of action, then this history does not really bring us into contact with God himself. The true Godhead, in this view, does not appear in this world because suffering, humiliation, death, and above and below are only appearances and cannot be seen as actions of the incarnate God at all. This modalistic view makes a "distinction between a proper and an improper being of God, an immanent and a *purely* economic" (IV/1, p. 197, emphasis mine). Importantly, Barth is not here aban-

---

[17]See also Thomas F. Torrance, "The Doctrine of the Holy Trinity in Gregory Nazianzen and John Calvin," in *Trinitarian Perspectives*, pp. 21-40, esp. pp. 28-36; also "Calvin's Doctrine of the Trinity," p. 71. See also pp. 118-20 and 133 of the same volume.

doning the distinction between the immanent and economic Trinity for which he argued in *CD* I/1, II/1 and elsewhere.[18] Previously, he never espoused a purely economic doctrine of the Trinity, but always grounded God's actions *ad extra* in the antecedent reality of God's being as Father, Son and Holy Spirit. And he always maintained that God is constantly the one he is in all his works, and so God himself never changes even in the incarnation. He thus wanted to stress that God's actions *ad extra* as creator, reconciler and redeemer are free actions that are not necessitated by his nature or any necessity outside or apart from his own free love (I/1, p. 172).

Significantly, his argument depended on his assertion that God's being and act are one. In other words, Barth would want to say that God is who he is in his works but not only in his works.[19] He also wanted to make a clear distinction in the incarnation between Jesus' divinity and his humanity without separating or confusing them. That is why he could speak of a correspondence between Jesus' human actions and his being within the immanent Trinity. We should note that the problem here was present even in Barth's earlier thought with respect to his understanding of grace. On the one hand, Barth says grace is God's seeking and creating fellowship with us in condescension. On the other hand, he says grace is part of God's eternal being (II/1, pp. 354, 357). But if grace is the former, then one cannot make the latter statement without implying that God could not be gracious without us. Barth himself recognized this problem and asked how there can be grace as this seeking and creating fellowship with us in God's eternal being without this implication.

---

[18]See above, e.g., chap. 6, pp. 267-70. Also, Barth wrote, "We must distinguish between God as such and God in His purpose (decree). From eternity the Son (as God *and man*) exists in God. But until the incarnation this has not happened. Nevertheless, this must be made clear; otherwise you have a fourth member of the Trinity" (Godsey, *Table Talk*, p. 52).

[19]For Barth, as seen in chap. 6 above, "God is who He is in His works. He is the same even in Himself, even before and after and over His works, and without them. They are bound to Him, but He is not bound to them. They are nothing without Him. But He is who He is without them. He is not, therefore, who He is only in His works. Yet in Himself He is not another than He is in His works. In the light of what He is in His works it is no longer an open question what He is in Himself" (II/1, p. 260). All of this is true because God's being and act are one, and revelation is God's act for us (II/1, p. 261). As noted in chap. 6, Alan Torrance rightly sees this as a key point in Barth's doctrine of the Trinity in "The Trinity," in *The Cambridge Companion to Karl Barth*, ed. John Webster (Cambridge: Cambridge University Press, 2000), pp. 72-91, esp. p. 90. See also Molnar, "Can the Electing God Be God Without Us?" *NZSTh* 49, no. 1 (2007): 199-222, and above, chap. 6.

He answered that we could not know the form that grace has in the inner life of God because only God knows that.[20] That assertion is in keeping with his often-repeated insight that we cannot know *how* God can be three persons or modes while yet remaining one in being and we cannot know *how* God can be truly divine and truly human at the same time. These are ineffable mysteries that we can only acknowledge and then understand. Barth is no agnostic here; he simply means to say that, when we know God's inner being through revelation, what is known is and remains a mystery to us because we cannot control God and cannot know God as God knows himself. Any attempt to pry into the inner being of God could lead us to read back elements of the economy into the divine being and thus inadvertently lead us to introduce subtle elements of subordinationism and/or modalism into the discussion. This is all well and good. But when Barth ascribed grace, which is God's turning toward us in condescension, to God's inner being, he already confused who God is in eternity with God's free actions of love for us. Barth is right to argue that God is who he is when he acts in grace toward us as the one who loves us, because that is the form God's grace (love) takes in relation to us. And God does this because he is loving *and* free in himself; in other words, the Son's eternal love for the Father, and its receptivity, is the eternal ground for the love shown in his act of kenosis in obedience to the Father.[21] Since this is the case, there is no need to go beyond this to ascribe subordination and obedience to the eternal Son as a condition of the possibility of his being obedient to the Father for our sakes as the reconciler.

Barth is no subordinationist or modalist. But he creates a major problem here by conceptually introducing hierarchy into the divine being.[22] I say conceptually because even here Barth's description of the trinitarian relations notably stresses the oneness in being of the persons (modes of being) of the Trinity. Barth's reason for doing this is so that he can affirm that God

---

[20]See II/1, p. 357. Hence, "There is not in fact any scope for the form which grace takes in its manifestations to us. *The form in which grace exists in God Himself and is actual as God is in point of fact hidden from us and incomprehensible to us.* For this very reason even in its manifestation and effectiveness for our sakes and towards us it is for us always the mystery which can thus be appropriated only as such and in faith. For this very reason grace can be revealed and imparted to us only by grace" (emphasis mine).

[21]I am grateful to George Hunsinger for helping me to see this point with clarity.

[22]Barth of course explicitly rejects such thinking as Origenist in I/1, p. 352.

FAITH, FREEDOM AND THE SPIRIT

really is incarnate as the one who suffers and dies for us. In Jesus Christ we do have to do with "an 'economy,'" Barth says, but not one in which God's true and proper being "remains behind an improper being, a being 'as if'" (IV/1, p. 198). Here too Barth and Torrance are at one, as when Torrance insists, "We cannot go behind the incarnation, for there is in fact no God behind the back of Jesus Christ, and no God apart from his own self-revelation";[23] "there is no God but this God . . . who is completely one with Jesus Christ in Word and act."[24] For this reason both Barth and Torrance insist that God himself experiences our forsakenness from within the person of the mediator and so converts us back to himself from within the depths of our human nature as it is turned in on itself in sin. Here the one true being of God himself is

> the subject of the act of atonement. . . . His presence and action as the Reconciler of the world coincide and are indeed identical with the existence of the humiliated and lowly and obedient man Jesus of Nazareth. . . . The true God [is] identical with this man—He humbles Himself and becomes lowly and obedient . . . [without] being in contradiction to his divine nature. (IV/1, p. 199)

Because of this, God is "not therefore exposed to the postulate that he can become and be this only as a creature" (IV/1, p. 199). This is not just an appearance as in modalism, but the reality of God condescending to act for us within our sinful humanity. Barth says, "God chooses condescension." God also chooses "humiliation, lowliness and obedience . . . in order to convert man and the world to Himself" (IV/1, p. 199). Therefore we must see the humiliation, lowliness and especially the obedience of Christ "as the dominating moment in our conception of God" (IV/1, p. 199). Christ's obedience unto death must inform our view of God's nature.

Certainly, subordinationism and modalism deal with the christological mystery by "juggling it away" (IV/1, p. 200), as Barth maintains. But why does Barth, who explicitly asserts that he wants to remain faithful to the thinking of Athanasius and Nicaea here, think he must speak of a subordi-

---

[23]See Thomas F. Torrance, "The Christian Apprehension of God the Father," in *Speaking the Christian God: The Holy Trinity and the Challenge of Feminism*, ed. Alvin F. Kimel Jr. (Grand Rapids: Eerdmans, 1992), p. 136.

[24]Thomas F. Torrance, *Karl Barth, Biblical and Evangelical Theologian* (Edinburgh: T & T Clark, 1990), p. 201.

nation as part of God's eternal being, even though he theoretically rejects subordinationism here and firmly rejected subordination especially in *CD* I/1?[25] The answer seems to be that he intends to say that the obedience of the incarnate Son acting for us is an act of God himself; therefore he claims that "a below, a *posterius*, a subordination . . . belongs to the inner life of God" (IV/1, p. 201). Hence, there is also obedience within God's inner life. Consequently, for Barth, God's unity "consists in the fact that in Himself He is both One who is obeyed and Another who obeys" (IV/1, p. 201). With this thinking we must ask the hard question: Has Barth successfully avoided both subordinationism and modalism at this point? Has Barth blurred the distinction between the immanent and economic Trinity for which he continues to argue on this very page when he says,

> God did not need this otherness of the world and man. In order to not be alone, single, enclosed within Himself, God did not need co-existence with the creature. . . . Without the creature He has all this originally in Himself, and it is His free grace, and not an urgent necessity to stand in a relationship of reciprocity to something other outside Himself. (IV/1, p. 201)

---

[25]For Barth, "All Subordinationism rests on the intention of making the One who reveals Himself there the kind of subject we ourselves are, a creature whose Thouness has limits we can survey, grasp and master, which can be objectified, in face of which the I can assert itself" (I/1, p. 381). See also I/1, pp. 353 and 439. Barth also says, "there is a command in the incarnation, and there is a relation of God as Lord and God as Servant. There is no subordination, however" (Godsey, *Table Talk*, p. 52). Interestingly, Barth speaks of super- and subordination even in I/1. But there he clearly is referring to the sequence of actions of the creator and reconciler so that in reconciliation the Son is acting as man in subordination to the Father for us (p. 413). Nonetheless, his statement in this context is not completely without ambiguity because on the one hand he says clearly that "this *subordination* and sequence cannot imply any distinction of being; it can only signify a distinction in the mode of being" (I/1, p. 413, emphasis mine). But on the other hand he says, "Here, then, sonship as well as fatherhood, in and with the *super-* and *subordination* expressed thereby, is to be understood as unrestrictedly true deity" (I/1, p. 414, emphasis mine). This would explain why he has been read to suggest that there is a kind of subordination even within the immanent Trinity in *CD* I/1. Thus Adam Johnson maintains that Barth "distinguishes between two forms of subordination within the Trinity." First, "Subordination [*Unterordnungsverhältnis*] regarding their deity" (I/1, p. 393), which Barth unequivocally rejects, and second, "the relation of subordination [*Unterordnungsverhältnis*]" (I/1, p. 413), which Barth favors as "a matter of the distinction and relationality between the various modes of being of the one essence" (Adam J. Johnson, *God's Being in Reconciliation: The Theological Basis of the Unity and Diversity of the Atonement in the Theology of Karl Barth* [New York: T & T Clark, 2012], pp. 73-74n37). Johnson concludes by saying, "Barth reaffirms and more fully explores the nature of this Trinitarian subordination in *CD* IV/1, 200-10" (p. 74). I am claiming that a problem arises because Barth thinks he needs to find some sort of subordination within the immanent Trinity at all. Additionally, when he continues to speak of subordination within the immanent Trinity as the basis of the economic actions of God in IV/2, pp. 351-52, Barth seems to confuse the missions with the processions once more.

COMPARISON OF BARTH AND TORRANCE

I propose to answer this question by comparing what Barth says here to what Thomas F. Torrance says about this same issue. But before doing this in detail, let us hear Barth's own reasoning. Demonstrating a strong sense of the immanent Trinity existing in freedom, Barth asserts, "Primarily and originally and properly it is not the cosmos or man which is the other, the counterpart of God, that which co-exists with God. Primarily and originally and properly God is all this in Himself" (IV/1, p. 201). Thus it is myth to divide God conceptually into "two gods of unequal divinity" (IV/1, p. 201). That confuses "the world and man with God" and projects this created differentiation into the Godhead by supposing there is a superior god in heaven and a "subordinate goddess of earth" (IV/1, p. 201). Opposing this, Barth insists that God exists in equal, not unequal, unity and cannot be divided; and so God is "One and also Another, His own counterpart, co-existent with Himself" (IV/1, p. 201). All of this is well stated. But from this Barth reckons that we therefore can say God "exists as a first and as a second, above and below, *a priori* and *a posteriori*" (IV/1, pp. 201-2). Importantly, and strangely, Barth here ceases to make a distinction that was in evidence earlier. That is, he no longer says that God humbles himself to become lowly in order to go into the far country for us so that we may be exalted. He now introduces obedience and subordination into God's inner being as the presupposition for God's humbling himself on our behalf. Before pursuing this thought, let us listen to two important clarifications that Barth offers here.

First, we must think rightly about God's unity, which cannot be equated "with being in and for oneself" (IV/1, p. 202). God is not imprisoned in his own being as one who is single and solitary. While God's unity is exclusively his, it is not this kind of unity—the kind that sees him imprisoned in solitariness. God's unity "is open and free and active in itself—a unity in more than one mode of being, a unity of the One with Another, of a first with a second, an above with a below, an origin and its consequences" (IV/1, p. 202). It is dynamic and not static. Second, Barth says we must abandon the idea that because there is in God a first and a second, an above and a below, this would have to imply "a gradation, a degradation and an inferiority in God" which would obviate the *homoousia* of the different modes of being (IV/1, p. 202). Barth thinks this is all too human a way of thinking and asks: "Does subordination in God necessarily involve an inferiority, and therefore a deprivation, a lack?" (IV/1, p. 202). Significantly, Barth indicates that we may think of an "inner order" here with a "direction downwards" that maintains God's equality and unity (IV/1, p. 202). At this juncture Barth asks why should not our way of "finding a lesser dignity and significance in what takes the second and subordinate place (the wife to her husband) need to be corrected in the light of the *homoousia* of the modes of divine being?" (IV/1, p. 202).

Here we reach the heart of the problem. The fact that there is an order within the immanent Trinity is a particularly important insight that Torrance emphasizes, relying on Athanasius, Augustine and Calvin. But according to Torrance this fact cannot imply any sort of subordination within the Trinity. Yes, the incarnate Son subordinates himself to the Father *for us* in obedience. But one cannot read this back indiscriminately into the immanent Trinity without causing problems. What is noticeably missing in Barth's presentation at this point in the *Dogmatics* is any account of *perichoresis*, which was an important trinitarian principle he developed in *CD* I/1, a principle complemented by the principles *opera trinitatis ad extra sunt indivisa* and appropriation. Torrance does deal with the order of the trinitarian relations precisely by using the concept of *perichoresis*. And, as we shall see, that makes an enormous difference to his interpretation of the trinitarian relations. In any case, Barth continues by claiming that a look at Jesus Christ forces him to the "astounding conclusion of a divine obedience" (IV/1, p. 202). God thus is "One who rules and commands in majesty and One who obeys in humility" (IV/1, p. 202). God is a first and a second in equal Godhead and in perfect unity and equality because "He is also a third, the One who affirms the one and equal Godhead through and by and in the two modes of being, the One who makes possible and maintains His fellowship with Himself as the one and the other" (IV/1, pp. 202-3). By virtue of the Holy Spirit there is no division or conflict or contradiction among the modes, and God is whole in each. All of this is well stated from the standpoint of classical trinitarian theology, except that when Barth says God is one who rules and commands and one who obeys, he appears to divide the Father from the Son by assigning majesty to the Father and not to the Son. He does not do this consistently. But he does do it here.

GOD'S HISTORY WITH US AS A LOGICAL CONTINUATION OF HIS INNER HISTORY

God acting *ad extra* gives us a part in the history in which God is God. In reconciliation "the inward divine relationship between the One who rules and commands in majesty and the One who obeys in humility is identical with the very different relationship between God and one of His creatures, a man" (IV/1, p. 203). Barth believes, "God goes into the far country for this to happen. He becomes what He had not previously been. . . . To do this He empties Himself, He humbles Himself" (IV/1, p. 203). But this action *ad extra*, like God's action of creation, has a "basis in His own being, in His own inner life." God "does not do it without any correspondence to, but as the *strangely logical final continuation* of, the history in which He is God" (IV/1, p. 203, emphasis mine). The point obviously is that God does not abandon his deity to condescend to us in order to be God for us, and God does not change from being who he is when he becomes incarnate.[26] Yet, Barth's solution here is not without difficulties. Is he able to fully excise all subordination from his view of the Trinity as he believes he has? To answer this question one need only consider his view of the divine majesty. Sometimes Barth applies this concept to the Son in his divinity.[27] That is why he speaks of the concealment of his majesty in his life of humble obedience. But other times Barth refers to One who commands in majesty and one who obeys in humility in a way that clearly intends to refer to the first and second persons of the Trinity. Is this not an example of what Torrance called the element of subordination in Barth's doctrine of the Trinity? Just consider these words from Torrance:

> The subjection of Christ to the Father in his incarnate economy as the suffering and obedient Servant cannot be read back into the eternal hypostatic relations and distinctions subsisting in the Holy Trinity. The mediatorial office of Christ, as Calvin once expressed it, does not detract from his divine Majesty.[28]

What difference does it make that Barth reads this mediatorial activity of the Son back into the immanent Trinity? I think it makes a great deal of difference.

---

[26]See above, chap. 5, p. 254n108, for a discussion of this phrase used by Barth and its implications.

[27]See, e.g., I/2, pp. 31-32, 37, 160, 165-66, 168; also IV/1, pp. 47, 53, 138, 161-63, 176, 178, 180-82, 209.

[28]*Christian Doctrine of God*, p. 180. Importantly, Torrance here appeals to 1 Cor 15:24ff. and Phil 2:7-10 as well as to John Calvin in his *Institutes* 1:13, pp. 24, 26.

While Barth wants to uphold the all-important point that what God is toward us he is in himself, here his thinking is problematic in at least two ways.

On the one hand, Barth's reference to the subordination of wives to husbands leaves one with the impression that we may speak of subordination in God as a "downward direction" without obviating the full equality of the modes of being. Has Barth not conceived the Trinity here in an all-too-human way? Earlier Barth insisted that the *how* of the trinitarian relations remained a mystery to us even in our understanding of God's inner nature as the one who loves in freedom in his being as Father, Son and Spirit. Now, it seems, Barth has illegitimately read back into the Godhead the order he thinks he found in male-female relations. Of course he has not done this without insisting that this needs to be clarified by the perfect equality within the triune being of God. But that does not alleviate the problem, because Barth has in fact conceived the inner Trinity in terms of a hierarchy, and that is, according to Torrance, damaging not only to the doctrine of the Trinity but to our relations with God in the economy. Whether or not it is Barth's "sexism" or his social and cultural mores that have gotten him into trouble here is beside the point.[29] It is nonetheless a problem, and it distorts his own understanding of obedience, because for him obedience must involve super- and subordination as well as a "downward direction." It would have been better if he simply said that God can experience super- and subordination, suffering and obedience *as God for us* because he loves in freedom in himself in a way that transcends all superiority and subordination as well as all suffering and need for obedience. For that reason, and since God is not a prisoner of his own freedom, God can be and is gracious to us in such a way that his act for us cannot be detached from his being, so that grace is seen as God himself turning toward us "not in equality, but in condescension" (II/1, p. 354). But then Barth could not claim that grace as condescension and free movement toward us pertains to God's inner being as God; it pertains rather to God's free movement toward us.[30]

---

[29]This is what Paul Dafydd Jones thinks (*The Humanity of Christ: Christology in Karl Barth's Church Dogmatics* [New York: T & T Clark, 2008], pp. 212-13). In spite of my disagreement with Jones's understanding of the *Logos asarkos* in Barth and his mistaken idea that God "transforms" himself and "organizes" himself and constitutes himself by way of election and incarnation, I do think he is right to point out this weakness in Barth's understanding of the divine obedience, even though he did not seem to notice that Barth intended to equalize human relations in light of the divine relations.

[30]This is especially confusing because Barth defines grace as "the distinctive mode of God's being in so far as it seeks and creates fellowship by its own free inclination and favour, unconditioned by any merit

This would alleviate the strain evident in Barth's own thinking about this, as noted above when he himself sees this problem and responds that the form of grace in God's eternal being is hidden from us.[31] In other words, a clearer distinction between the trinitarian processions and missions at this point would have helped Barth to ground the obedience and humiliation of the Son for us in his inner grace and mercy without conceptually confusing the fact that God is lowly for us with a lowliness in the divine being itself as a condition for that free action *ad extra*.

On the other hand, when Barth speaks of a correspondence between what happens *ad extra* and what God is and does *ad intra*, does he not commit the very error of dualism he claims to have overcome with this "dif-

---

or claim in the beloved, but also unhindered by any unworthiness or opposition" (II/1, p. 353). If only Barth could have been as clear as Torrance here when Torrance consistently and repeatedly argued that the Gift and Giver of grace cannot be separated from each other and that grace is God's own personal action for us in Jesus Christ. See, e.g., Molnar, *Thomas F. Torrance*, pp. 10, 46, 58, 170, 200, 293. That does not mean that elsewhere Barth is not crystal clear that the Gift cannot be separated from the Giver, as when he asserts concerning the incarnate Word as the "true Witness" that as a "concrete man" he lives and is at work "expressing the truth" in our time and place "in the promise of the Spirit." This, Barth says, is "the second form of his coming again as the Revealer" (IV/3.1, p. 378). His first form was his resurrection, and his third form is the goal and the "end of days." He does this all "as this man" who "cannot be replaced by any distinct and distilled significance, power, influence or effects of His person and work. Nor can he be replaced by any truth which appeared in Him but may now be asserted independently, by any idea bound up with Him only as its first proponent, by any correct human doctrine concerning Him. . . . The Lord Himself in His Word is the promised and promising Spirit. Neither the truth nor its expression can be separated or even distinguished from Him. To be the true Witness, therefore, He does not need to be confirmed nor authorised by any other. . . . He does not need to be interpreted by any generally known truth nor any specific, i.e., ecclesiastical truth deduced from His appearance. As He Himself lives and acts in the form of the promise of the Spirit, He is the true Witness. He is Himself the truth and its expression. And in His existence and life as such He unmasks every other man" (IV/3.1, p. 378). One could scarcely get a clearer expression of the fact that grace as truth cannot be separated from the giver! Just the same, Barth very clearly expresses the unity of grace with the Giver (Jesus Christ), saying, "everything depends on the simplicity of heart which is read to let the grace of God be exclusively His grace, His sovereign act, His free turning to man as new and strange every morning, so that it does not know anything higher or better or more intimate or real than the fact that quite apart from anything that he can contribute to God or become and be in contrast to Him, unreservedly therefore and undeservedly, man can hold fast to God and live by and in this holding fast to Him" (IV/1, p. 84). For this reason Barth rejected the Roman Catholic view of grace, which he believed negated this unity of grace with the Giver: "It is the negation of the unity of grace as His grace in Jesus Christ" (IV/1, p. 84). What he objected to was the attempt to speak about uncreated and created grace as though God's grace given always in the act of Christ through his Spirit could pass out of God's active control and into us as something that becomes ours in some sense. For Barth this would open the door to some sort of self-justification and self-sanctification in the name of grace. Torrance held quite a similar view. See Molnar, *Thomas F. Torrance*, pp. 10, 46, 57-58, 78 and 207.

[31]See above, p. 331.

ficult" and "elusive" (IV/1, p. 195) and even "astounding" (IV/1, p. 202) idea of an obedience taking place in God himself? There is no question that both Barth and Torrance intend to say and do say that God is obedient as the incarnate Word and that therefore the atonement is an act of God *as* man. It is not a purely human act so that God is somewhere behind the back of Jesus Christ. But Torrance will not read back certain aspects of the economy into the immanent Trinity because he conceptually respects God's mystery even in revelation at this point. Both theologians also say that the incarnation falls within the inner life of God.[32] But I think Barth confuses the order of the trinitarian persons or modes with his ideas of an above and a below, which he clearly takes from God's relations with us. Yes, in the incarnation God demonstrates that he has the ability to exist above in himself and below with us in humility. God does humble himself and obey and subordinate himself in his existence for us. But to read these categories back into the immanent Trinity smacks of exactly the error Barth repeatedly attempted to avoid; it reverses what God is for us with what God eternally is in himself by advancing the idea that God is eternally subordinate and that there is thus by implication an eternal hierarchy within the Trinity.[33]

---

[32]See especially Torrance on God's suffering, *Christian Doctrine of God*, pp. 246-54.

[33]In his article "Barth and Subordinationism," *SJT* 64, no. 3 (2011): 327-46, Kevin Giles rightly notes that Barth repeatedly rejected subordinationism and that he also inexorably attempted to avoid reading back elements of the economy into the immanent Trinity. Yet, even he found Barth's discussion of subordination and obedience as applying to the eternal Son "who fulfils the divine subordination" and the Father who "fulfils the divine superiority" to be "breathtaking" to the point that his thinking reached the "breaking point" (p. 344). He does not push Barth any further than to say that, faced with the dilemma of espousing eternal subordination within the Trinity or subordination only of Christ's human nature in the incarnation, Barth produced "one of his most colourful pieces of abstruse rhetoric in his *Church Dogmatics*, suggesting that what is logically impossible is possible in God" (p. 345). Of course, with the help of Torrance, I am claiming that Barth did indeed mistakenly read back elements of the economy at this point in this thinking. For more on this issue as it concerns the divine Monarchy, see Paul D. Molnar, "Theological Issues Involved in the *Filioque*," in *Ecumenical Perspectives on the Filioque for the 21st Century*, ed. Myk Habets (New York: T & T Clark, 2014), pp. 20-39, esp. pp. 34-39. There I discuss the problems embedded in the thinking of those who attempt to ascribe "ontological priority and absolute authority" to the Father. See, e.g., Benjamin Dean, "Person and Being: Conversation with T. F. Torrance About the Monarchy of God," *IJST* 15 (January 2013): 58-77, p. 69. For a view that attempts to appreciate the importance of what Barth says in order to affirm "that obedience constitutes the proper form of the Son's divine work in the economy of salvation" so that one does not have to jettison "classical Catholic and Reformed trinitarian tradition," see Scott Swain and Michael Allen, "The Obedience of the Eternal Son," *IJST* 15, no. 2 (April 2013): 114-34, p. 116. The authors certainly do not wish to confuse the missions and the processions (pp. 131-32). With this I agree. But in repeatedly conceptualizing the missions as an "ex-

It is just this sort of thinking that has led some contemporary theologians to confuse the missions and the processions and thus to argue in various ways that Jesus' divine Sonship will not be fully what it is until salvation history is complete. Theoretically, Barth would reject this conclusion. But this apparently abstruse error in conceptualizing the trinitarian relations leads directly to this conclusion! Not only that, but when Barth develops his idea of correspondence by saying that this takes place "as the *strangely logical final continuation* of the history in which He is God" (IV/1, p. 203, emphasis mine), has he not said too much? If what God does out of love for us is a logical continuation of his immanent divine love in any sense, is Barth not inadvertently suggesting that, in the end, God could not be God without us?[34] To be sure, Barth continues to insist that it remains true that God could have been God without us and does not need us, even in *CD* IV. And his thinking frequently bears that out. But by describing this as a *logical* (or any other sort of) *continuation* of God's love within the immanent Trinity at this point, Barth has made his own positive understanding of God's love and freedom more than a little problematic.[35] He opens the door to interpretations of the Trinity that go far beyond what he would countenance in arguing that what God does for us determines who he is in his inner life and that Jesus' human history in some sense constitutes his being as the second person of the Trinity.

---

tension" of the processions, one wonders whether the all-important distinction for which they argue can be consistently maintained. In any case this article does not specifically address the question of whether Barth had inadvertently read elements of the economy into the immanent Trinity with his concepts of obedience and subordination. I am arguing, with Torrance, that we do not have to and should not ascribe eternal obedience and subordination to the Son in his receptivity within the immanent Trinity in order to understand his actions for us and for our salvation as acts of obedient condescension. Such thinking, as I have been arguing, tends to advance some version of the idea that the Son has his being from the person of the Father as a "derived deity." And this confuses the order of the persons with their being. For more on this issue, see my "The Importance of the Doctrine of Justification in the Theology of Thomas F. Torrance and of Karl Barth," forthcoming in *SJT*; *Divine Freedom and the Doctrine of the Immanent Trinity: In Dialogue with Karl Barth and Contemporary Theology* (New York: T & T Clark, 2005), pp. 326-30; and "Theological Issues Involved in the *Filioque*."

[34]See above, chap. 5, p. 254n108, for an alternative translation of this phrase that might alleviate some of the difficulty here, but not all of it.

[35]Twenty-five years ago when I discussed the function of the immanent Trinity in the theology of Karl Barth, I stated that he was generally quite consistent in distinguishing without separating the immanent and economic Trinity. But I noted that there were instances when he apparently failed to do so. This is one of those instances. Torrance helps us see what the real problems here are. See Paul D. Molnar, "The Function of the Immanent Trinity in the Theology of Karl Barth: Implications for Today," *SJT* 42 (1989): 367-99.

TORRANCE'S CAREFUL DISTINCTION BETWEEN CHRIST'S VICARIOUS ACTIVITY FOR US AND HIS INNER BEING AS WORD

Barth's mistake can be explained even better with the help of Thomas F. Torrance's refusal to read back Christ's mediatorial activity directly into the immanent Trinity. Torrance insists, "The statement of Jesus, 'My Father is greater than I,' is to be interpreted not ontologically but soteriologically, or 'economically. . . . ' as Gregory Nazianzen, Cyril of Alexandria and Augustine all understood it" (*Christian Doctrine of God*, p. 180). Similarly, while Torrance argues that the incarnation and Christ's mediatorial activity fall "within the life of God" (*Christian Doctrine of God*, pp. 246, 144), and even that Christ's suffering and dereliction were "suffered by God in his innermost Being for our sake" (*Christian Doctrine of God*, p. 249) because "it cannot be said that Christ suffered only in his humanity and not in his divinity" (*Christian Doctrine of God*, p. 252), nonetheless he also made important distinctions. Torrance insisted that "the incarnation was not a timeless event like the generation of the Son from the Being of the Father" (*Christian Doctrine of God*, p. 144). And he asked, "how far and in what way may we read his suffering back into the ultimate Being of God which he the Son of God fully shared"? (*Christian Doctrine of God*, p. 252). As it happens, Torrance thinks we cannot simply attribute Christ's physical and emotional suffering to God. But there was a deeper suffering, Torrance says, and a more terrible suffering "behind the suffering of the incarnate Son" (*Christian Doctrine of God*, p. 252). That was the suffering of the Father in giving up his Son for us. God takes on himself our afflictions out of love for us. Consequently, "What pains God above all is the sin and wickedness of his human creatures, their rebellion against his holy will" and their "rejection of his grace" (*Christian Doctrine of God*, p. 248).

Torrance then insists that God by nature is impassible, but not in the sense that he is remote from our suffering. Understood soteriologically and not logically, Torrance can say that in Christ, God is both impassible and passible because he takes our suffering and pain to himself to remove them, and he does so effectively because he remains the impassible God who brings his divine serenity to bear on our human nature in such a way as to heal us of our sin and self-will.[36] Hence, Torrance claims, "The passion of

---

[36]For a full discussion of Torrance's understanding of impassibility and passibility, see above, chap. 4, p. 207.

Christ considered apart altogether from the passion of the Father would be no more than the noblest martyrdom for it would be empty of ultimate divine validity. It is in his perfect oneness in being with God that the passion of Christ is saving" (*Christian Doctrine of God*, p. 252). Torrance and Barth are very close here. Both reject patripassianism. But both think there is an element of truth in it. So, as seen already in chapter six, Barth can say,

> It is not at all the case that God has no part in the suffering of Jesus Christ even in His mode of being as the Father. No, there is a *particula veri* in the teaching of the early Patripassians. This is that primarily it is God the Father who suffers in the offering and sending of His Son, in His abasement. The suffering is not His own, but the alien suffering of the creature, of man, which He takes to Himself in Him. But He does suffer it in the humiliation of His Son with a depth with which it never was or will be suffered by any man— apart from the One who is His Son. . . . This fatherly fellow-suffering of God is the mystery, the basis, of the humiliation of His Son; the truth of that which takes place historically in His crucifixion. (IV/2, p. 357)[37]

Notice here that Barth distinguishes more carefully than he does when he ascribes subordination and obedience to the inner life of the Trinity.[38] Here

---

[37]As mentioned above in chap. 6, Barth carefully notes, "God finds no suffering in Himself. And no cause outside God can cause Him suffering if He does not will it so. But it is, in fact, a question of sympathy with the suffering of another in the full scope of God's own personal freedom" (II/1, p. 370). As noted above in chap. 6, Barth wishes to avoid any sort of mutually conditioned notion of God's activity in relation to us. But Barth also insists that God's impassibility cannot mean that he cannot feel compassion for us in our sin. No. In his inmost being, Barth insists, God feels our distress and seeks to remove it. That is his grace (II/1, p. 371).

[38]The tensions in evidence in IV/1 remain in IV/2, however, since Barth also argues a very traditional view, namely, that in virtue of Mt 11:27, we must say that there is a genuine "history in partnership" between the Father and the Son in eternity and that the Holy Spirit is the one who draws us into this history of love in which the persons of the Trinity are at a distance, without separation, conflict or confusion as a presupposition for what takes place *ad extra* (pp. 344-46). But the problem that arises in IV/1 is also in evidence because Barth thinks that the antithesis that is on display in Christ, the antithesis between Jesus as God's Son and Jesus who "was executed and destroyed, disappearing into the night of death" (IV/2, p. 349), already existed within the eternal Trinity, which included a "here and there, before and after, above and below . . . in their original and proper form, quite apart from us and before the world was" (IV/2, p. 343). While Barth rightly insists that God as Father and Son is both "in equal Godhead" and inseparably so in a mutual relationship of love and knowledge and that he in no sense needs us (IV/2, p. 346), he is clearly importing antitheses that become visible between God and us in the history of Jesus Christ into the immanent Trinity, as when he says, "This is His divine here and there, before and after, above and below" (IV/2, p. 343). He says God knew this problem and solved it even before the world existed in and by the action of the Spirit (IV/2, p. 344). And while it is true that God knew of these antitheses before creation, it is not true that the relations of distance and interaction among the trinitarian persons included a problem (of

he distinguishes between the inner being of God, whose nature does not include suffering, but who can suffer as God by taking our suffering to himself in the incarnation. This fatherly fellow-suffering is the mystery and the basis of the humiliation of his Son, which takes place economically, of course, on the cross for us. Torrance cites this text himself approvingly to make essentially the same point (*Christian Doctrine of God*, p. 249).

But importantly, Torrance does not feel compelled to introduce subordination and obedience into the immanent Trinity to reach this conclusion. Indeed, because Torrance at this point, unlike Barth, adamantly claims that the *how* of the incarnation cannot be explained, he consistently interprets Philippians 2:7 to mean that in the incarnation the Son humbled himself for us. And he insists that any attempt to explain the *how* of the incarnation would necessarily lead to the errors of kenotic thinking that would either divinize the humanity of Christ or humanize God's eternal divine being, which cannot change in the incarnation.[39] Torrance himself avoids patripassianism and subordinationism by thinking perichoretically of the inner and outer relations of the Trinity. Hence, he says that because the whole undivided Trinity is involved in the work of salvation, God the Father and God the Spirit were also involved in Christ's atoning passion "in their different but coordinated ways" (*Christian Doctrine of God*, p. 252). Torrance grounds the very suffering and love of the Son in union with the Father and Spirit in "the eternal Love that God is," saying, "The Gospel does not rest

---

a before and after and superiority and subordination) that needed solution by the Spirit. There is no problem in God, as Barth suggests here, even according to his own understanding of the Trinity; but God does love us with his eternal love and so experiences these antitheses in his relations with us in order to reconcile us to himself. Barth's strength is in saying that "The triune life of God, which is free life in the fact that it is Spirit, is the basis of His whole will and action even *ad extra*" (IV/2, p. 345). But his weakness is in reading back elements of the economy illegitimately into the inner life of God, as when he then says Jesus' human obedience as the incarnate Son corresponds with and witnesses to the fact that "there is height and depth, superiority and subordination, command and willingness, authority and obedience, in God Himself—not in identity, but in a real differentiation, because He attests the height and superiority and command and authority of the Father rather than Himself, and the depth and subordination and willingness and obedience which He attests are His own and not the Father's" (IV/2, p. 351). Yet the subordination and willingness here are the subordination and willingness of the Son to be obedient to the Father in becoming incarnate for us and for our salvation, even according to Barth's own understanding (IV/2, p. 351). Hence, the problem remains: Why does Barth think he needs to read these back into the immanent Trinity to avoid separating the immanent and economic Trinity at this point?

[39]See Thomas F. Torrance, *The Doctrine of Jesus Christ* (Eugene, OR: Wipf and Stock, 2002), pp. 108-15.

simply on the fact that God loves us, but on the fact that he loves us with the very same Love which he is in the eternal Communion of Love which God is in his Triune Being" (*Christian Doctrine of God*, p. 253).[40] Thus it is imperative to "note the oneness (incomprehensible though it is) between the passion of God the incarnate Son in his union with us in history and the transcendent passion of God the Father" (*Christian Doctrine of God*, p. 253).

CONSIDERING THE *EXTRA CALVINISTICUM* AND THE RELATION OF THE IMMANENT AND ECONOMIC TRINITY AGAIN

Let us briefly explore Torrance's view of the *Extra Calvinisticum* and of the relationship between the immanent and economic Trinity in order to make my critique of Barth's position clearer. Torrance is absolutely consistent on this issue. Whenever he speaks of the Son's obedience to the Father, he always refers to the mission of the Son acting as God for us. As we have just seen, Torrance insists that in his humility Christ suffers both divinely and humanly. But by not reading back elements of the economy into the immanent Trinity, Torrance is able to overcome subordinationism and modalism in a way that leaves no doubt about whether or not one could ascribe any sort of subordination to the inner being of God. Here is where both theologians definitely argue for a distinction without separation of the immanent and economic Trinity. But on this issue I would have to judge Torrance more consistent than Barth.

It is common knowledge that Torrance directly criticized Barth for an "element of 'subordinationism' in his doctrine of the Holy Trinity" in the "earlier volumes of *Church Dogmatics*."[41] Unfortunately, Torrance did not offer any specific references when he made that statement. But he did say that he regarded the issue as "a hang-over from Latin theology" and also from "St Basil's doctrine of the Trinity" that affected one's stance toward the *filioque*, and he consistently rejected "subordinationism in Trinitarian

---

[40]Importantly, Torrance describes the inner trinitarian love as mutual love without importing problematic notions of hierarchy into the inner life of God as a precondition for his actions *ad extra*, so he can say, "It is out of that selfless self-giving Love which God is eternally in himself that he gave himself freely in surrendering his dear Son in atoning sacrifice for our sins. Thereby God has revealed that he does not keep himself to himself but loves us without any reserve, more, astonishingly, than he loves himself" (*Christian Doctrine of God*, p. 166).

[41]Torrance, *Karl Barth*, p. 131. See also Thomas F. Torrance, "My Interaction with Karl Barth," in *How Karl Barth Changed My Mind*, ed. Donald McKim (Grand Rapids: Eerdmans, 1986), pp. 61-62.

relations."[42] The question that I am raising in this chapter is whether any type of subordination within the inner life of God represents an illegitimate reading back into the immanent Trinity elements of the economy. As already noted, both Barth and Torrance unequivocally rejected an idea that was commonly expressed during the patristic era and sometimes even today, namely, that only the human Jesus suffered and thus experienced God-forsakenness.[43] Yet, we have also seen that Torrance does not simply read back Jesus' human suffering into the Godhead.

Torrance also explicitly says that "we cannot but think of the incarnation of the Son as *falling within the being and life of God*—although . . . the incarnation must be regarded as something 'new' even for God, for the Son was not eternally man any more than the Father was eternally Creator."[44] Barth too thinks of God's covenant with us as

> a new thing that in His unity with Himself from all eternity God wills to be the God of man and to make and have man as His man. This is the content of a particular act of will which has its basis neither in the essence of God nor in that of man, and which God does not owe either to Himself or to any other being, and least of all to man. (IV/1, p. 66)

But, in a manner similar to what he does when he projects obedience and subordination into the inner Trinity, Barth's thinking here also becomes a bit fuzzy.

On the one hand he says that in God's free election of grace as the beginning of his ways and works *ad extra*, in his pretemporal eternity "there is already present, and presumed, and assumed into unity with His own existence as God, the existence of the man [Jesus Christ] whom He intends and loves from the very first and in whom He intends and loves all other men." On the other hand he says, "In this free act of the election of grace the Son of the Father is no longer

[42]Torrance, *Karl Barth*, pp. 131-32, and "My Interaction," p. 61.

[43]Torrance rejects this thinking frequently. In *Atonement*, he rejects it as a "hyper-Calvinist" position, p. 184.

[44]*Trinitarian Faith*, p. 155. See also *Christian Doctrine of God*, p. 208. Because Jesus Christ "is himself God and man in one Person," two points follow from this: (1) "all his divine and human acts issue from his one Person," and (2) the "atoning mediation and redemption which he wrought for us, fall *within* his own being and life as the one Mediator between God and man" (*Trinitarian Faith*, p. 155). This thinking is completely in accord with Barth's view that God does not act toward us *ex machina* but personally from within the incarnate life history of Jesus himself, since God was in Christ reconciling the world to himself. See also *Incarnation*, pp. 177-80.

just the eternal Logos, but as such, as very God from all eternity He is also the very God and very man He will become in time" (IV/1, p. 66). How can God already be God and man before he becomes man in time? Barth's positive intention, of course, is to avoid having a God behind the back of Jesus Christ. But his thinking here unfortunately opens the door to a confusing idea, namely, the idea that Jesus Christ humanly existed before he actually came into existence by the power of the Spirit from the Virgin Mary. It is clear from the context that Barth meant to distinguish what in reality is God's predestination of himself to be born of the Virgin for us and for our salvation and what occurs in the fullness of time. But unfortunately he has been read here as collapsing the inner trinitarian relations once more into the processions.[45] He has not, of course. He simply wanted to say, against those whose thinking pushed Jesus Christ as the incarnate Word to the side when they thought of predestination as a pact between the Father and the Son, that God is one as Father, Son and Spirit, and as the one God decided to be for us in Jesus Christ, who himself was "the beginning of all the ways of God" (IV/1, p. 66). And there are other statements of his that suggest greater precision and nuance, as when he writes: "Jesus Christ was at the beginning. He was not at the beginning of God, for God has indeed no beginning. But He was at the beginning of all things, at the beginning of God's dealings with the reality which is distinct from Himself. . . . He was the election of God's grace as directed towards man" (II/2, p. 102).[46]

---

[45]See Wolfhart Pannenberg, *Systematic Theology*, vol. 2, trans. Geoffrey W. Bromiley (Grand Rapids: Eerdmans, 1994), p. 368, where he says that Barth "did not manage to define conceptually the connection between the preexistence of the eternal Son as such and the historical filial relation of Jesus to the Father. For the act of the election is part and parcel of the freedom of God's relation to the world, so that its content cannot be constitutive for the eternal identity of his divine essence. If it were, the world itself would be the correlate of this essence."

[46]George Hunsinger, "Election and the Trinity: Twenty-Five Theses on the Theology of Karl Barth," *Modern Theology* 24, no. 2 (April 2008): 179-98, pp. 181-83, explains perfectly that when Barth says that Jesus Christ is the subject of election he is not speaking without qualification. By analogy Hunsinger says that if one says, "The queen was born in 1819," one does not mean literally that Queen Victoria was queen of England at the moment of her birth; one is referring to an infant who would become queen. While she was not yet queen, she did become queen and thus became what she was ordained to be. Retrospectively, then one would say, "The queen was born in 1819." This is not meant to be taken literally, without qualification. Applied to what Barth says about Jesus then in the text cited here, he could be read as saying that the one who would be the incarnate Word in time is the very same one who was with God in the beginning, but this one is not yet incarnate. Retrospectively, however, in light of the incarnation, we can say that Jesus Christ was with God in the beginning. None of this, however, can be presented without further nuances, so that we have to say that "The eternal Son and the incarnate Son are numerically the same, but different in their modes of existence" (Hunsinger, p. 182). Yet only the Son *incarnatus* "is identical with Jesus Christ. . . . The eternal Son

Torrance also argues that "we cannot think of the ontological Trinity as if it were constituted by or dependent on the economic Trinity" (*Christian Doctrine of God*, pp. 108-9). Barth would agree with this, even though this judgment stands opposed to those who mistakenly claim that God the Son is somehow constituted as the second person of the Trinity by or through Jesus' human history or perhaps anticipatorily because of God's choice to relate with us through Jesus Christ. They would also agree that the incarnation was a free action of God, and that while it was only the Son and not the Godhead who became incarnate, the whole Trinity was involved in the incarnation and in atonement because the Trinity is undivided and was also at work in the incarnate life of Christ. Both Torrance and Barth, as we have seen, insist that the incarnation did not mean any surrender of deity or of God's transcendence; it did not involve "any compromising of his eternal freedom, or any renouncing of what he ever was before the foundation of the world, or any imprisoning of his eternal trinitarian relations within the space-time processes of our creaturely world" (*Christian Doctrine of God*, p. 108).[47]

---

qua eternal is not *incarnatus* but *incarnandus*. . . . The eternal Son qua Son, however, is not even *incarnandus*, because the Son qua Son is properly defined without reference to his being *incarnandus*" (p. 182). This is because the eternal Son as such is the second person of the Trinity, and for Barth his generation from the Father cannot be confused with who he freely chooses to be for us in the incarnation. In Hunsinger's words: "He is necessarily the eternal Son; he is only contingently *incarnandus*" (p. 183). Hence the second person of the Trinity "is, by a free divine decision, *also* the one determined from all eternity to be *incarnandus*" (p. 183). One thus can say that, in a certain respect, Jesus Christ is the subject of election. One cannot say this without qualification. As noted above, Barth's own statement about this matter confirms Hunsinger's interpretation: "We must distinguish between God as such and God in His purpose (decree). From eternity the Son (as God *and man*) exists in God. But until the incarnation this has not happened. Nevertheless, this must be made clear; otherwise you have a fourth member of the Trinity" (Godsey, *Table Talk*, p. 52).

[47]Torrance makes this point forcefully when he explains, in opposition to "kenoticism," that God exercised his omnipotence and thus "all the powers of full Divinity" when in the incarnation he lived a "lowly" life of humiliation as our savior (*Doctrine of Jesus Christ*, p. 112). And he did this precisely because he was Lord. His human actions were meaningful only because they were actions grounded in the person of the Son. That is why, in answer to the question of whether or not Jesus could sin, Torrance forthrightly and adamantly maintains that the question arises from a view of ethical goodness grounded in our fallen human nature. He thinks the question is illegitimate. But he answers it just the same. And his answer is compelling. Torrance maintains that Jesus could not sin because in his human actions, grounded in his Person in a union without confusion or separation of natures, he is God himself at work in human history overcoming our sin by experiencing temptation really and truly and overcoming this as the God-man. God cannot sin and God cannot come into conflict with himself. And since Jesus really is God incarnate reconciling the world to himself, we must conclude that his freedom was his freedom to do the good by obeying God and that it is not a neutral freedom that could choose between two alternatives. That latter view is the view that arises only from within our fallen natures. But even though in the incarnation the Word

Torrance maintains that what took place in the incarnation was a sover-
eignly free act of God "to be other in his external relations than he eternally
was, and is, and to do what he had never done before" (*Christian Doctrine
of God*, p. 108). To read this back into the immanent Trinity, however, could
suggest that humiliation and subordination were part of God's eternal being
before the incarnation. Such thinking would be problematic, because it
would in fact make time and eternity indistinguishable at the very point that
they are united without confusion, separation or mixture. This is why Torrance warns against inappropriate reading back into the immanent Trinity
elements of the economy. We must

> think of the economic Trinity as the freely predetermined manifestation in
> the history of salvation of the eternal Trinity which God himself was before
> the foundation of the world, and eternally is. Hence, when we rightly speak
> of the oneness between the ontological Trinity and the economic Trinity, we
> may not speak of that oneness without distinguishing and delimiting it from
> the ontological Trinity—there are in any case . . . elements in the incarnate
> economy such as the time pattern of human life in this world which we may
> not read back into the eternal Life of God. (*Christian Doctrine of God*, p. 109)[48]

Barth too argues for a distinction between the immanent and the economic Trinity, and his argument for this distinction is an argument for the
fact that what God does for us in the incarnation and atonement is always
a free, loving action that is neither necessitated by God's being nor by anything outside God. In Barth's words:

> it is not just good sense but absolutely essential that along with all older the-
> ology we make a deliberate and sharp distinction between the Trinity of God
> as we may know it in the Word of God revealed, written and proclaimed, and
> God's immanent Trinity, i.e., between "God in Himself" and "God for us,"
> between the "eternal history of God" and His temporal acts. . . . "God for us"
> does not arise as a matter of course out of the "God in Himself." . . . It is true
> as an act of God, as a step which God takes towards man. (I/1, p. 172)[49]

---

assumed our fallen nature, Jesus himself did not share our original sin, and he himself never
sinned. He could not sin (*Doctrine of Jesus Christ*, pp. 121-30, esp. pp. 128-29).

[48]In his understanding of election as *prothesis*, we have already seen above in chaps. 4 and 5 that
Torrance is very clear that Jesus' humanity is not eternal in the sense that it was preexistent, his
person is eternal, and "his person is not human but divine" (*Incarnation*, p. 177).

[49]This thinking continues even in IV/1, pp. 125-32.

However, when Barth introduces subordination into the immanent Trinity, even though he claims he has avoided any idea that there is inequality among the persons (modes) of the Trinity, he has in reality not only caused conceptual confusion, he has in fact introduced some sort of hierarchy into the immanent Trinity: "In His mode of being as the Son He fulfils the divine subordination, just as the Father in His mode of being as the Father fulfils the divine superiority" (IV/1, p. 209).[50] At this point Barth is unclear about the fact that what the Son fulfils in the incarnation and the events that follow is the eternal divine decree to be God for us in humility and in obedience and thus to reconcile the world through his cross and resurrection. To say simply that the Son fulfils his subordination and the Father his superiority without clearly and consistently stating that what is fulfilled is God's salvific purpose and activity *for us*, implies a need on the part of God for fulfillment. And that is something Barth theoretically rejected both earlier and later in the *CD*.[51] He even seems to get right back on track in this very context.

Even as the Son complies in humility, Barth says, he is the same in obedience as the Father is in origin. Indeed Barth says, "In His humility and compliance as the Son He has a supreme part in the majesty and disposing of the Father. The Father as the origin is never apart from Him as the consequence, the obedient One." The one who begets is never without the one who is begotten. And neither exist without "a mutual affirmation and love in the Holy Spirit" (IV/1, p. 209).[52]

---

[50]While I think much of Rowan Williams's critique of Barth is off the mark, his observation about this remark is interesting: "What, if anything, this can possibly mean, neither Barth nor his interpreters have succeded (*sic*) in telling us" ("Barth on the Triune God," in *Karl Barth: Studies of His Theological Method*, ed. S. W. Sykes [Oxford: Clarendon, 1979], p. 175). Here Barth and those who read him in a one-sidedly actualistic and historicist way stand opposed to Torrance who, incidentally with Barth, held that God's "Becoming is not a becoming on the way toward being or toward a fullness of being, but is the eternal fullness and the overflowing of his eternal unlimited Being. Becoming expresses the dynamic nature of his Being" (*Christian Doctrine of God*, p. 242). Here Torrance is able to combine a dynamic view of God's act and being without confusing his internal and external relations but instead holding them together on the basis of God's free outgoing love. Barth also did this pretty consistently, as when he insisted that the Son's eternal begetting is a perpetual becoming that "rules out every need of this being for completion. Indeed this becoming simply confirms the perfection of this being" (I/1, p. 427). But here he opens the door to the confusion Torrance identifies. And he does so, I suggest, just because he mistakenly imported a hierarchical set of concepts into the immanent Trinity.

[51]See especially his statements in II/1, pp. 306-21, his statements above chap. 3, p. 132-33 and chap. 6, pp. 272-75.

[52]Consequently, "The Son is therefore the One who in His obedience, as a divine and not a human work, shows and affirms and activates and reveals Himself—shows Himself to be the One He is—not another, a second God, but the Son of God, the one God in His mode of being as the Son" (IV/1, p. 209).

Once again, we all agree that the Son's obedience and revelation are the Son's divine work. But they embody the divine work of kenosis. They illustrate the necessary outworking of God's eternal decree to be for us in humility the God he has proven himself to be on the cross and in the incarnate Son's resurrection from the dead. Therefore, God is forever our God by virtue of his free choice to love us by creating, reconciling and redeeming us in and through his Son and Spirit. And while God will never go back on what he has become for us in the incarnation,[53] still, by pushing obedience back into the immanent Trinity, with the attendant notions of above, below, *prius* (before), *posterius* (after) and subordination, in order to achieve a proper understanding of Jesus' deity here, Barth has made it more difficult to say at this point in his presentation what both he and Torrance believe to be true. He has made it more difficult to say that the incarnation is something new even for God. That inability is a further consequence of reading back events in the economy indiscriminately into God's pretemporal being and existence.

I believe Torrance's thinking on this issue, while indebted to Barth in many ways, is more consistent than Barth's and points us to at least three extremely important insights. First, Torrance is absolutely clear that one cannot confuse the order of the persons of the Trinity with their being without also falling into the trap of reading elements of the economy back into the immanent Trinity thus undermining the true power of grace to overcome suffering, sin, evil and death. To confuse the order of the trinitarian Persons with the being of the Persons of the Trinity could open the door both to subordinationism and to modalism in some form or another; it might even open the door to monism or dualism. Second, Torrance insists that the incarnation (like creation) is something new, new even for God. Unless this statement is forcefully made and conceptually maintained by not reversing the actions of God for us with who God is in eternity, there will always be serious confusion regarding the Trinity and election because it will be thought that in some sense God constitutes his eternal triunity by and through deciding to and then relating with us. It could then be surmised that there is no longer any Son of God in himself and that God can no longer be said to be impassible as well as passible.[54]

---

[53]See, e.g., *Christian Doctrine of God*, p. 216.

[54]For such arguments, see above, chaps. 5 and 6. As also seen above, it could lead to thinking that negates the fact that the hypostatic union is the uniting of the divine Word with the human

Torrance, of course, maintains both insights on soteriological grounds and therefore does not embrace any sort of static idea that God cannot suffer without ceasing to be God. And I believe he is correct. Barth does as well, but he is not quite as consistent in this as is Torrance because he does inadvertently introduce a logical necessity into the discussion that then leads him to think that the Father needs to fulfill his superiority and the Son needs to fulfill his subordination. Third, Torrance seems to be more consistent than Barth in applying the *enhypostasis* and *anhypostasis*[55] in his thinking about the Person of the Son in his vicarious acts of obedience for us. He can thus clearly state that all of Jesus' human actions are actions of the Son. As we have seen, Barth also maintains this in his Christology. But when Barth ascribes subordination to the obedience of the eternal Son, he seems to have blurred a distinction that he elsewhere stressed and maintained, a distinction that Torrance consistently maintains. That distinction enables Torrance to emphasize Jesus' eternal high-priestly mediation between us and the Father in connection with every aspect of our lives so that he can say Jesus' human activities fall within the life of the immanent Trinity. But that is a far cry from ascribing super- and subordination to the inner life of God as the basis for his condescension to be humble for us and our salvation.

What difference does this make? In Torrance's view, Barth's failure to give due emphasis to Christ's high priestly mediation led him to revert to a form of dualistic thinking that he previously rejected when he presented his view of the sacrament of baptism.[56] It led to a number of other difficulties that cannot be discussed here, such as Barth's references in *CD* IV/3 to "the humanity of God" instead of to the specific humanity of the risen, ascended and advent Jesus Christ. Speaking only generally of the humanity of God undermines the need for a properly conceived eschatology that respects the fact that Jesus' humanity as the ascended and advent Lord is his own, and that he unites us to that humanity through his Spirit. This would explain why some followers of Barth actually have argued that the only body the

---

nature of Jesus Christ in the incarnation. Thus, "The second 'person' of the Trinity is the God-man. So even in the act of hypostatic *uniting*, the 'subject' who performs that action is the God-man, Jesus Christ in his divine-human unity" (McCormack, "Divine Impassibility," p. 178).

[55]As defined above, chaps. 4 and 5.

[56]See Torrance, "My Interaction," pp. 62-64, and *Karl Barth*, pp. 134-35.

risen Lord needs is the existence of the church.[57] By contrast Torrance
argues for an "eschatological reserve" that sees the unity in distinction between the ascended Lord in his true humanity and divinity and the church
as his body between the time of his first and second coming. In the interim
Jesus continues his high priestly mediation through the church's preaching
and the sacraments precisely by uniting us to his new humanity through the
Holy Spirit and in faith as we await his return.[58]

In summary, then, the question is this: In the incarnation, did the eternal
Son of God enter time and space "in such a way that he left the bosom of the
Father or left the throne of the universe?" (*Atonement*, p. 282). Put another
way, even in subjecting himself to the conditions of our existence in space
and time, did the Son of God continue "to rule the universe as the creator
Logos by whom all things were made?" (*Atonement*, p. 282). Torrance believes both patristic and Reformed theology held that the eternal *Logos* did
enter time and space "not merely as creator but as himself made creature"
and lived his life within those limits. And yet he "did not cease to be what
he was eternally in himself, the creator Word in whom and through whom
all things consist and by whom all things derive" (*Atonement*, p. 282). But
Torrance could hold together Christ's divinity and humanity without falling
into monophysitism or Apollinarianism precisely because he rejected the
container or receptacle notion of space, which always leads both to false
forms of kenoticism and to demythologizing.[59] Torrance thus maintained

---

[57]See Robert Jenson, whose thinking about Jesus' Sonship, resurrection and his body after the resurrection is confused, as when he writes: "In that Christ's Sonship comes 'from' his Resurrection, it
comes from God's future into which he is raised" (*STI*, p. 142). Jenson thinks that "the way in which
the triune God is eternal, is by the events of Jesus' death and resurrection," and that his "individuality is constitutive of the true God's infinity" (p. 219). Regarding Christ's risen body, he claims,
"Sacrament and church are *truly* Christ's body for us" because he makes himself available to us
through them. Hence, Jesus "needs no other body to be a risen man, body and soul" (p. 206).

[58]See, e.g., Thomas F. Torrance, *Royal Priesthood: A Theology of Ordained Ministry*, 2nd ed. (Edinburgh: T & T Clark, 1993), chap. 2, "The Function of the Body of Christ," and chap. 3, "The
Time of the Church."

[59]Interestingly, Torrance thinks that while Thomas Aquinas himself modified the receptacle notion of space when thinking of the incarnation in patristic terms, Luther failed to do so and so
allowed monophysitism in by the back door by extending the ubiquity of Christ (the human
receptacle) to contain his omnipresence with a strong form of the *communicatio idiomatum*
(*Space, Time and Incarnation*, [Edinburgh: T & T Clark, 1997], p. 62). For a clear statement of
the problems inherent in the container or receptacle view of space and time, see Molnar, *Thomas
F. Torrance*, pp. 124-35, and *Incarnation and Resurrection: Toward a Contemporary Understanding*
(Grand Rapids: Eerdmans, 2007), pp. 90-96.

both that "the Word of God is nowhere to be found except in inseparable union with Jesus, the babe of Bethlehem, the real and proper man" (*Atonement*, p. 284), *and* that "if we press that to mean that in the incarnation the Word was resolved into this Jesus without remainder, so to speak, then insuperable difficulties arise" (*Atonement*, p. 284). That is to say, this thinking would open the door to kenotic theories or to some sort of demythologizing. For Torrance, "we cannot say that the eternal *Logos* became flesh in such a way that part of the *Logos* was excluded . . . for the *Logos* was totally incarnate" (*Atonement*, p. 284). Nonetheless, "he remained wholly himself, the creator and ruler and preserver of the universe of all creaturely reality. He became man without ceasing to be God, and so entered space and time without leaving the throne of God" (*Atonement*, p. 284; also *Incarnation*, p. 218). So Torrance and Barth can readily say that once the incarnation has occurred, we cannot think of the Word apart from Jesus. But we must do so without eliminating the preexistent Word and the Word in its continued transcendence, either.[60] We must, then, affirm two realities in a complementary way: (1) "The Word cannot be subordinated to the flesh it assumes" (*Incarnation*, p. 220) as would happen if the Word were thought of as "limited by the creaturely reality with which it is united," because then it would have to have been "altered in its transcendence and divine nature" (*Incarnation*, p. 220); and (2) all monophysitism would have to be rejected; that is, any idea that Christ's human nature was "absorbed into the divine nature" via the incarnation (*Incarnation*, p. 220).

Because the Word is not resolved without remainder into the man Jesus either in pretemporal, supratemporal or posttemporal eternity, the Word could be said to exist in different forms without losing his divinity and without being confused with the humanity of Jesus in the incarnation. But because his humanity is both *enhypostatic* and *anhypostatic*, one could say that he is fully human and not divinized just because of the action of the Word; all that he does humanly has no independent meaning since it is the action of the man Jesus in union with the Word. These are both crucial in-

---

[60]Barth's continued reference to the *Logos asarkos* as necessary even in IV/1, p. 52, then could be seen as an attempt to maintain the "Calvinist extra" and would make sense as long as it was not understood using a receptacle or container view of space, which might lead to the false conclusion that there is indeed a God behind the back of Jesus Christ.

sights that Torrance and Barth exploit with great effect in their theologies. And they are able to do this just because they acknowledge that the Word continues to exist in his own unique way within the immanent Trinity even as he is *ensarkos* for us and for our salvation. As we have seen, each thread of their thinking immediately leads to another complete fabric of ideas that illustrates the inner workings and interrelatedness of the doctrines treated here and throughout this book. But the key point I hope to have established is that when the divine freedom is properly conceived on the basis of God's freedom for us in his Word and Spirit, then we can have a consistently developed notion of what God is up to in the economy. And we can do this without the need to historicize or perhaps modernize the second person of the Trinity by claiming that his eternal being is constituted in some sense by his human history as the incarnate Word. With this in place, I would now like to demonstrate what a view of human freedom properly grounded in the trinitarian actions of God in history might look like.

A Theology of Grace

Living In and From the Holy Spirit

We have already seen how important it is to understand that faith means faith in Christ alone in the sense that it is not our faith that enables us to live as those who are justified and sanctified by God alone in Christ and through his Spirit, but God himself actively enabling us to do so. And we have seen that it is crucial all along the line never to attempt to know God or the meaning of salvation apart from the act of the Holy Spirit uniting us to Christ and thus to the Father. We have also seen that it is vital to recognize and to respect the fact that the God who is for us in his Word and Spirit could have been God without us but freely chose not to, and so we may know and live as those who are objectively justified and sanctified already in Christ's vicarious human life of obedience, which includes us. And in the power of his resurrection the risen Lord enables us now, in the power of his Spirit, not only to recognize that, but to live in and from Christ's own faith and obedience. This can be recognized and lived, however, only with a proper eschatological reserve that appreciates that living by faith and hope means that we know that, objectively, our reconciliation is a reality in the life, death, resurrection and ascension of Jesus himself, but that this will not be conclusively disclosed to everyone until Christ returns to complete the redemption of the world. In this chapter I would like to show exactly what it might mean to live by grace and faith within a trinitarian context that pays due attention to the action of the Holy Spirit in the economy precisely by acknowledging grace as the act of God in his Word and Spirit. This means that grace can never be detached from the Giver. This chapter will explore the positive and negative implications of this assertion. In order to accomplish this I will first discuss how Barth holds together God's grace with God's act in his Word and Spirit and what some implications of this might be. Then I will discuss how Thomas F. Torrance understands what he calls "cheap and costly grace" in order to apply this to our understanding of just how human action is free precisely because of God's free mercy and love.

KNOWLEDGE OF GOD

We may begin with the simple but profound recognition that for Barth and Torrance the doctrine of justification by faith, which can also be categorized as the doctrine of justification by grace, means that hearing God's Word and therefore knowing God in truth and acting accordingly cannot be ascribed in any sense to our own viewing and conceiving or to any of our experiences, even our experiences of grace and faith. One might suppose, therefore, that there is no basis in our experience for knowing and loving God and our neighbors. And that would be a correct supposition, because while we can have no knowledge of God without an experience of faith, grace and revelation, the basis of that experience is and always remains a miraculous act of God's free mercy and love.[1]

---

[1]Among contemporary theologians, George Hunsinger understands and calls attention to this important aspect of Barth's theology best. Thus he writes, "Those who are awakened to lifelong conversion by the Spirit never cease to be sinners in themselves. Yet despite their continuing sinfulness, the miracle of grace never ceases in their hearts" ("The Mediator of Communion: Karl Barth's Doctrine of the Holy Spirit," in *The Cambridge Companion to Karl Barth*, ed. John Webster [Cambridge: Cambridge University Press, 2000], pp. 177-94, on p. 183. This is why Barth opposes any idea that "Christian love would be a prolongation of divine love" (p. 183). Such a view would deny the fact that Christian love is a free human action enabled by the Spirit—the Spirit does not "take from man his own proper activity, or . . . make it simply a function of His own overpowering control. Where he is present, there is no servitude but freedom" (IV/2, p. 785). It is never a question of "determinism" or "free will" for Barth, because God himself is the enabling condition of our freedom. Barth also consistently rejects any sort of "synergism" (Hunsinger, pp. 183-84). This would include any view that suggests that "human freedom 'cooperates' with divine grace in effecting salvation" (Hunsinger, p. 183). Barth rejects both Augustinian and Thomistic versions of synergism, the former suggesting that divine and human activity are "indirectly identical," and the latter suggesting that the divine act is the material cause and the human act the instrumental cause in such a way that they "cooperate in effecting salvation" (Hunsinger, pp. 183-84). This is why Barth rejected Brunner's idea of a point of contact in human experience for revelation and grace. All these views underestimate the importance of understanding that grace is a miraculous act of God that engenders human freedom without supplanting human actions and without being confused with them or becoming dependent on them, either.

Early on in the *Church Dogmatics*, Barth objects to any confusion of God's act with the human actions of those who believe: "On the one side we have to say that the being of the Church is *actus purus*, i.e., a divine action which is self-originating and which is to be understood only in terms of itself and not therefore in terms of any prior anthropology," while "on the other side we have also to say that the being of the church is *actus purus*, but with the accent now on *actus*, i.e., a free action and not a constantly available connexion, grace being the event of personal address and not a transmitted condition" (I/1, p. 41). For Barth the being of the church "is identical with Jesus Christ" (I/1, p. 41), and for that reason neither grace nor revelation could be detached from Jesus Christ as the acting subject and located within human experience; grace in particular simply could not be conceptualized as "a transmitted condition" without in reality detaching grace from the Giver, that is, from Jesus Christ himself as the living Lord of the church. Any attempt to describe dogmatic knowledge, then, on the basis of some prior anthropological possibility would lead to an *analogia entis* that could be seen and explained apart from faith. Indeed, any attempt to understand dogmatic knowledge as "a subsequent ecclesiastical reality" would miss the fact that grace refers to "the present moment of the speaking and hearing of Jesus Christ Himself, the divine creation of light in our hearts" (I/1, p. 41). This insight was carried through by Barth in his discussion of God's Word and experience.

Here it is important to recognize that knowledge means "the confirmation of human acquaintance with an object whereby its truth becomes a determination of the existence of the man who has the knowledge" (I/1, p. 198). This pivotal insight means that there is no such thing as "abstract" knowledge, that is, knowledge detached from our human involvement. This is what Barth means by experience (*Erfahrung*). It means that people exist only "in determinations of [their] existence by objects, by things outside of [them] and distinct from [them]" (I/1, p. 198). With this in mind it is imperative to recognize and to maintain several important insights. First, human beings can be determined by God's Word. But that cannot be taken to mean mere passivity on their part, as if they give up their ability to determine themselves. It means, instead, that their self-determination is freely accomplished in free obedience to the determination of the Word that alone actually empowers their freedom, since all acts of self-determination that occur apart from the Word heard and believed are acts of self-reliance or self-justification or acts of human beings who in and of themselves are sinful since the fall of Adam. Second, under no circumstances can the determination of human existence by the Word of God be confused with or identified with "a determination man can give to his own existence" (I/1, p. 199). Even though our experience of God's Word always takes place "in an act of human self-determination . . . it is not experience of the Word of God *as this act*" (I/1, p. 199, emphasis mine). Not only this, but there can be no "cooperation between divine determining and human self-determining" so that it might be assumed that human beings do what they can and then leave the rest to God to determine (I/1, p. 199). And Barth was most forceful in rejecting what he took to be the view of Augustine, namely, that the proper understanding of God's determination and our self-determination is one of "simultaneity, interrelation and unity in tension between the divine and human determining" so that "What is seen from the one side as grace is freedom when seen from the other side and *vice versa*" (I/1, p. 199).

Each of these theories is unacceptable because any genuine experience of the Word means that people experience themselves as having a Lord, as being creatures of the Lord, as being lost sinners who are blessed by the Lord and as people who await redemption, and thus who are strangers in this world as it is. Indeed, any real experience of the Word in the biblical sense would have to mean that no one could ascribe even the possibility of this experience to himself or herself. The main issue here in Barth's thinking is that anyone without faith is bound to attempt to understand the relation between divine and human determination neutrally (outside of standing within "the event of real knowledge of the Word of God as this man is presented to us by Holy Scripture") and thus in a disinterested manner as "an external onlooker" (I/1, pp. 199-200) who sees this event in a way that might construe divine and human determination as "rivals of one another" (I/1, p. 199). Seen in this way, the only reasonable thing to do is to conceive these two determinations as coexisting by attempting "a synthesis between them" so as to "maintain the self-determination of man in face of the determination of man by God" (I/1, p. 200). In other words, any attempt to understand what it truly means to experience God's Word outside faith would have to mean an attempt to set in opposition or to confuse divine and human freedom. Any such perspective, however, will always fail to see that the coexistence that occurs between God and us, in any genuine experience of God's Word, simply cannot be seen from a higher level, because the coexistence between them is not in any sense "on the same level" (I/1, p. 200). So where does that leave us?

There is only one alternative. And that is to cease any attempt to try to maintain our human self-determination, as Barth says, "even dialectically, over against the determination of man by God. Our very self-determination needs this determination by God in order to be experience of God" (I/1, p. 200). This genuine human need, which cannot be seen or understood apart from revelation, faith and grace, is really a relation of "total subjection and need *vis-à-vis* determination by God," and "it cannot possibly replace this," Barth says, "as Pelagius wished, or co-operate with it, as the Semi-Pelagians wished, or be secretly identical with it, as Augustine wished" (I/1, p. 200). All these mistaken views are possible with respect to "competing determinations of man or of an object" (I/1, p. 200). But when speaking of a human determination by God and by us, they are all useless. Yet again, none of this can mean that our human self-determination is eliminated by the divine determination. And it cannot mean that human self-determination is reduced to "a state of partial or total receptivity or passivity" (I/1, p. 200). This is a decisive point because in Barth's thinking any such viewpoint immediately suggests a retreat to a form of self-reliance or self-justification that signifies once more the attempt to escape from the only possible source of true human freedom, that is, the freedom that comes to us from God and enables our freedom; then we no longer behave as spectators but as those who are truly free for God and for our neighbors. One either hears the Word and obeys in and through one's free decision of faith, or one hears the Word wrongly and disobeys. But whether one's hearing is obedient or disobedient cannot be decided by us at all. Rather, "As he decides, as he resolves and determines, he is rather in the secret judgment of the grace or disfavor of God, to whom alone his obedience or disobedience is manifest. And this is the overlapping determination by God which befalls his self-determination" (I/1, p. 201).

Knowledge of God: Acknowledgment and Miracle

The key word that Barth uses to describe this human activity is *acknowledgment*. We have already seen how important this is in connection with our discussion of faith in chapter one and how that relates to our connection with the rest of the Christian community and ultimately to our relationship with Jesus Christ himself, the living Lord who wins people for himself through the witness of Christians. Here we simply note that for Barth faith as acknowledgment means knowledge, because it is a communication of person (God) to person (us) and therefore must involve rational communication in speech. It also means that because the acknowledgment is an experience of one person (God) and another (us) it does refer to a fact, but not to "a fact of nature" but one that is "created and presented by a person or persons"; human determination thus means determination "by God's person" (I/1, p. 205). Acknowledgment also means "not only subjection to necessity, but adaptation to the meaningfulness of this necessity, approval of it, not just involvement in it by acceptance of it" (I/1, p. 205). In other words, people must accept the Word of God as truth that is valid for them; this must mean accepting God's purpose for them as God acts in specific ways as God for us. It also implies that revelation comes to us "in its contingent contemporaneity" as "Holy Scripture and Church proclamation." What happened there and then becomes present here and now. "Jesus Christ Himself lives in the message of His witnesses, lives in the proclamation of His Church on the basis of this message, strides forward as the Lord of grace and judgment to meet the existence of the hearer of the Word" (I/1, p. 206). Experience of the Word therefore means experience of his presence—but since "this presence does not rest on man's act of recollection but on God's making Himself present in the life of a man, it is acknowledgment of His presence" (I/1, p. 206). This experience once again is one of obedience and submission on the part of human beings, because it is not a relationship of equals and it comes to us "as Law or Gospel, as command or promise . . . in such a way as to bend man, and indeed his conscience and will no less than his intellect and feeling. It does not break him; it really bends him, brings him into conformity with itself" (I/1, p. 206). In addition, acknowledgment means decision: God's free choice, God's act of good pleasure to come to us is an act of "divine freedom and choice" (I/1, p. 206). But it comes to us as grace or judgment so that in obedience our experience is indeed an experience of God's Word of grace; in disobedience or unbelief, however, while there is indeed an acknowledgment of God's Word, it takes place "against man's will and to his perdition" so that "Even in his disobedience man characterizes himself as the man he is before God's Word"

(I/1, p. 206). Experience of God's Word, then, is decision, and that is why Barth says we can and must "be summoned in the Church to ever new experience and therefore to decision" (I/1, p. 206).

Acknowledgment also means "halting before an enigma, acquiescence in a situation which is not open but which is unexplained from the standpoint of him who does the acknowledging" (I/1, p. 207). This means that because revelation encounters us in the secular form of human activity and human conceptuality, its true meaning will always remain concealed to us and can only be seen and understood when God acts to unveil himself to us in and through that secular form. When that actually occurs it is a miracle, that is, a

> special new direct act of God in time and in history. In the form in which it acquires temporal historical actuality, biblically attested revelation is always a miracle, and therefore the witness to it, whether direct or indirect in its course, is a narrative of miracles that happened. Miracle is thus an attribute of revelation. (I/2, pp. 63-64)

Because we are always dependent on God to speak to us and thus to make himself known to us as his own act, we must always respect the fact that mystery and miracle here are intrinsically related. Revelation can only be understood as a miracle because according to the New Testament it is "revelation in the resurrection of Jesus Christ from the dead" (I/2, p. 64). This is an important insight because it means that since revelation is an act of lordship on each of us, "who must face it as God's enemy, who is the darkness that did not and also cannot comprehend the light—it follows that if revelation nevertheless takes place it can only take place in the form of a miracle" (I/2, p. 64).

Barth goes further and insists that if revelation nevertheless is an event for us that we can confess by saying, "God reveals Himself," then "it can only be the confession of a miracle that has happened, but not the expression of an insight into a content, which he can also explain otherwise than by the special new direct act of God" (I/2, p. 64). Any attempts therefore to weaken or conjure away "the miraculous character of revelation are to be rejected in principle" (I/2, p. 64). This applies most especially in Barth's thinking to the life-of-Jesus research, whether this takes place in the form of the

> mildest conservatism to the most imaginative or else most unimaginative, "hypercriticism," to uncover out of the New Testament, by means of a series of

combinations, restorations and also and particularly deletions, the figure of
the mere man Jesus, the so-called "historical Jesus," as he might have lived in
the years 1-30. (I/2, p. 64)

Furthermore, acknowledgment of the mystery of God's Word is such that it
can only be made as required, and thus it cannot be "resolved into an attitude"
(I/1, p. 207). It means always being led to recognize that God's Word encounters us in the veil of secondary objectivity and unveils itself to us through
that sphere—this involves hearing both the veiling and the unveiling without
any attempt at a synthesis. Finally, acknowledgment means that the person
who acknowledges God's Word yields him- or herself "before the thing or
person he acknowledges. He submits to the authority of the other" (I/1, p. 207).
This, one might say, is the high point Barth's understanding of acknowledgment in this context: "In the act of acknowledgment, the life of man,
without ceasing to be the self-determining life of this man, has now its centre,
its whence, the meaning of its attitude, and the criterion whether this attitude
really has the corresponding meaning—it has all this outside itself, in the thing
or person acknowledged" (I/1, pp. 207-8). The point to be made here then is
that while the human act of self-determination is established and maintained
by God himself, this has to imply that what truly determines this human
action can never be ascribed directly to the human action itself. Hearing the
Word of God, therefore, is itself a "gift of the Holy Spirit"; therefore, it is "the
Word's own act on man" (I/1, p. 208). Here we get a very clear picture of what
Barth means by grace and faith. Grace, as God's free act of love and mercy
toward us, never becomes a possibility that is proper to human being as such,
even of the human being pardoned by God in Christ. It can never be seen as
"a kind of divine emanation towards man, or, from man's standpoint, a divine
influxus whose outcome is the possibility in question" (I/1, p. 210).

   Miracle, grace and faith therefore are all connected in Barth's thought in
such a way that we must recognize that grace can never be detached from
the act of God and therefore from the living Jesus Christ himself, the risen
Lord who in his Spirit is active here and now in the form of the historical
witness that takes place in acknowledgment. This is a miracle—and a miracle
that could be explained from the human side would not be a miracle at
all—an act of God that can only be acknowledged and then understood in
faith, which itself, even as a human act, is determined in truth by the act of

God overcoming our enmity with God and empowering our true under-standing and thus our proper living as Christians.

This thinking can be seen most clearly in Barth's conviction that our knowledge of God does not rest on any capacity of ours but only on our being justified by grace itself. That is precisely why Barth insists that knowledge of God is an event enclosed within the mystery of the divine Trinity. Barth not only applies the doctrine of justification by faith to his understanding of our experience of the Word; he applies it to our knowledge of God, and so he insists that we only know God truly in acknowledgment, and that is why we have to recognize "the lofty but simple lesson that it is by God that God is known . . . [and that this] was neither an axiom of reason nor a datum of experience. In the measure that a doctrine of God draws on these sources, it betrays the fact that its subject is not really God but a hypostatized reflection of man" (II/2, p. 3). Not only is God hidden in himself, but even when we know God in Christ he remains hidden in the sense that it is not our expe-rience that becomes the focus of our attention, but God alone as the enabling condition of our knowledge of him and our experience of him.

George Hunsinger captures Barth's attitude toward experience well by noting that we cannot understand our salvation "by looking directly at our-selves" because our being is hidden with Christ in God.[2] And he helpfully notes that, for Barth,

> We believe in Christ . . . not in our experience of Christ; in the gospel, not in our experience of the gospel; in salvation, not in our experience of salvation. Jesus Christ is not an experience but an event, the gospel is not an experience but the news of an event, and the presence of salvation is "not an experience, precisely because and as it is the divine decision concerning us."[3]

Here the action of the Holy Spirit must be acknowledged, respected and noted:

> This being of ours is thus enclosed in the act of God. . . . We cannot as it were look back and try to contemplate . . . this being of ours as God's redeemed. . . . To have the Holy Spirit is to let God rather than our having God be our confi-dence. . . . It lies in the nature of the *regnum gratiae*, that having *God* and our

---

[2]George Hunsinger, *How to Read Karl Barth: The Shape of His Theology* (New York: Oxford Uni-versity Press, 1991), p. 121.
[3]Ibid. Hunsinger is quoting from I/2, p. 532.

having God are two very different things. . . . We believe our future being. We believe in an eternal life even in the midst of the valley of death. In this way, in this futurity, we have it. . . . The assurance of faith means concretely the assurance of hope. . . . The man we know does not live an eternal life. This is and remains the predicate of God, of the Holy Spirit. . . . Both [becoming rich in God and poor in ourselves] become our experience. . . . But we do not have the divine and spiritual riches and the divine and spiritual poverty in our experience [because] God remains the Lord even and precisely when He Himself comes into our hearts. . . . The deity of the Holy Spirit is thus demanded. (I/1, pp. 462-65)[4]

Here we recall that

Revelation would not be revelation if any man were in a position to advance and to establish against others the claim that he specifically speaks of and from revelation. If we know what revelation is, even in deliberately speaking about it we shall be content to let revelation speak for itself. (I/1, pp. 346-47)

For Barth, then, "what God says to us specifically remains His secret which will be disclosed in the event of His actual speaking" (I/1, p. 143). All of this thinking shows that for Barth our knowledge of God is "an event enclosed in the mystery of the divine Trinity" (II/1, p. 181).

Knowledge of God . . . as the knowledge of God which is objectively and subjectively established and led to its goal by God Himself, the knowledge of God whose subject and object is God the Father and the Son through the Holy Spirit, is the basis—and indeed the only basis—of the love of God which comes to us and the praise of God which is expected of us. (II/1, p. 180)

Because this God remains hidden even in his revelation and even as we participate in that event and therefore even as we participate in the very history of Jesus himself made present here and now in the Spirit, we must stress once again how important it is to acknowledge that "Knowledge of God is then an event enclosed in the bosom of the divine Trinity" (II/1, p. 205). Hence, Barth's objection to natural theology cannot be explained merely in terms of his political outlook or in terms of some aversion to philosophy; it rests rather on the fact that true theology is and remains grounded in the triune God, and in him alone as he has acted for us as the

---

[4]See also I/2, p. 249.

reconciler and redeemer in his Word and Spirit and acts even now in the power of his Spirit, the power of the risen Lord who is coming again.

THE HOLY SPIRIT, THE GIVER OF LIFE

Having said all of this, it is just here that I would like to make the connection between the Holy Spirit and our relationship with God as those who are justified and sanctified by God himself in his Word and Spirit. The point of this chapter is to show exactly how we relate humanly with God by grace, through faith and by revelation in a way that respects the freedom of grace as God's own continued action for us as the risen and ascended Lord, a continued action that really frees us to live as those who decide for God, who acknowledge that God is in the right in establishing our relations with him through union with Christ. Here it is important to mention Barth's rejection of what he calls "indirect Christian Cartesianism" in *CD* I/1. Because he opposes the idea that grace and revelation can be reproduced out of our experience, he insists that the possibility for experiencing the Word of God cannot be conceptualized as something that is "given by God to the religious man, the Christian believer, that is handed over to him by God, that we are thus to seek it in him, in his own personal experience of faith as such, in his 'word-bound ego,' among the contents of his consciousness" (I/1, p. 215). This view resists the view mentioned above, that is, the Augustinian view that would describe acknowledgment of the Word as an "emanation from the Word of God spoken to man or an *influxus* into the man addressed by the Word" so that it becomes "man's own, a predicate of his existence, a content of his consciousness, his possession" (I/1, p. 214).

Any such thinking, however, makes it impossible to be certain that it is the Word of God that is experienced and known. Just as we saw in chapter two that there could be no apodictically certain knowledge of God if that knowledge is ascribed to us in any sense instead of to the action of the Holy Spirit uniting us to Christ and thus to the Father, so here Barth insists, "When we try to find the content of the divine Spirit in the (pardoned) consciousness of man, are we not like the man who wanted to scoop out in a sieve the reflection of the beautiful silvery moon from a pond?" (I/1, p. 216). The only thing that can be discovered in this way is a philosophical reflection on the phenomenon of human activities that in and of themselves cannot irrefutably demonstrate that we have indeed experienced and known the Word of God. It is important to realize here that we are sinners who are reconciled to God in Christ and that it is therefore only in him that we can have that certainty. That is why our involvement in revelation, which includes our whole existence, can never become the object of reflection if we are to speak properly about the promise and claim of God's grace on us. "Not for a moment or in any respect will he rely upon the fact that he is involved, orientate himself by it, or take from it the standard for understanding the reality in which he stands: he will not want to reflect on it but will simply be in it" (I/1, p. 220). No one who actually has acknowledged the Word of God will ever attempt to cling to this experience because "The judgment of the divine Word is passed on his involvement even as it takes place" (I/1, p. 220). And this does not mean that our activity in this regard is merely shown to be imperfect or inadequate; it is rather shown to be futile and corrupt and completely incapable of being anything but an invention of our hearts and minds without the forgiving grace of God himself. The only basis for true acknowledgment of the Word here, then, is that which comes to us "by grace" on our work, which in and of itself is "corrupt and dead through sin." And it comes to us "for Christ's sake and not for the sake of [our] inner disposition" (I/1, p. 220). The crucial point here then is this:

> Precisely when we describe both the conformity of man to God that takes place in faith and also the point of contact for the Word of God posited in this conformity, not as an inborn or acquired property of man but only as the work of the actual grace of God, our only final word at this point can be that God acts on man in His Word. Because man's work in faith is that on which God's work is done, man can know the Word of God. He knows as he is known by God. (I/1, p. 244)

Everything here depends all along the line on allowing God's knowing of us to be the determining factor in our knowing God. That is indeed what faith means. Barth's discussion of faith in *CD* I/1 is thus linked to his discussion offered in *CD* IV/1, already presented in chapter one above and then discussed in connection with the action of the Holy Spirit in chapter two. This is why it is so important to recognize and to acknowledge the priority of the Father/Son relation over the creator/creature relation, as I argued in subsequent chapters. That obviates any attempt to make God's being and action contingent on history. Faith, therefore, is the human action that corresponds to the divine action that alone awakens, enables and completes our hearing of the Word as well as our knowledge of God. But the ultimate factor in all of this is the action of the Holy Spirit, the Spirit of Christ uniting us to him in his lived obedience to the Father and empowering our faith as obedience and thus as acknowledgment. This is not just a theoretical statement but a statement of exactly how we live by grace and by faith. The fact that all of this happens and can happen again and again is a miracle to us precisely because the *how* of this occurrence cannot be explained from the human side but only in faith as an act of God judging our sinful attempts to ground knowledge of him in ourselves and actually enabling us to participate in the knowledge of the Son, who alone knows the Father and reveals him to us. At this point I'd like to make the connection between our experience of God and God's own action more precise by developing a few concepts Barth presents in *CD* IV/3.

KNOWLEDGE OF JESUS, THE LIGHT

The first point to be made is the powerful and decisive one, namely, that Jesus Christ himself is the "light of life" (IV/3.1, §69/2, pp. 38-165). This refers to his prophetic office in connection with the doctrine of reconciliation. And so Barth says he both begins with and must continue with Christ himself by noting that "continuation with Him can proceed only from a specific beginning with Him, i.e., from a christological foundation in the narrower sense" (IV/3.1, p. 38). This statement cannot be overstressed because, as seen above in chapter six, it has been argued that in *CD* IV/1 Barth is no longer interested in Christology in the narrower sense but only in the history of Jesus for us. Any such argument is not only opposed to Barth's thinking, as shown above, but is completely undermined by Barth's presentation in this section. Revelation, reconciliation and thus grace itself take place in him and cannot be detached even momentarily from the one who alone in his life action "is identical with that of God Himself, His history with the divine history" (IV/3.1, p. 40). Barth's thinking in this context stresses both that Jesus Christ himself is the true Son of God, that is, God from God, and the true man that he is as the one who humbles himself so that we might be exalted to fellowship with God in him. Hence Barth insists,

As Jesus Christ lives, there takes place in Him both creative actualisation of being, yet also in and with it creaturely actualisation; creative and creaturely life together, without the transformation of the one into the other, the admixture of the one with the other, or separation or division between them. This is how Jesus Christ is seen and attested in Scripture. (IV/3.1, p. 40)[5]

There can be little doubt that Barth's thinking about Jesus as the Word of God incarnate, the reconciler, is shaped by both the scriptural witness and by the characterizations espoused at the Council of Chalcedon. For Barth, God does not just come into a man, but "God does what this man does. Or rather, this man does what God does" (IV/3.1, p. 41). Jesus Christ lives his life for us "in the sovereign power proper to Him as the free Subject of this occurrence. And he is the Servant as the One who wholly and utterly subjects Himself to, and serves, this divine power of life even to the point of obedience unto death. This is how Jesus Christ lives" (IV/3.1, p. 41). Indeed Barth maintains that in "His own life-act, which is directly that of God Himself fulfilled as man, there take place all the life-acts of those who as free subjects (within their determined limits) are the creatures of God" (IV/3.1, p. 41). When anyone who attempts to live life uses the freedom "given by the fact that he is an I and not an It, he declares that in some sense he belongs to the territory in which Another, this One, is Lord and Servant, to the sphere in which God Himself says I in this Other, and as man makes effective and not merely tentative use of His divine freedom" (IV/3.1, p. 41).

This does not mean that God as Father, Son and Spirit ceases to live on high in his eternally free life and love, which are not subject to any restrictions, needs or conditions. It means, rather, that this very God determines to act and does indeed act graciously toward us. Hence, it is because we meet this very God who is "eloquent and radiant" and "does not merely become this when we perceive and accept Him as such" (IV/3.1, p. 79) that we can be certain that Jesus Christ himself is the light of life, that he is the truth, which we can never question as Pilate did by asking, "What is truth?" (Jn 18:27)—"Every one that is of the truth heareth my voice" (IV/3.1, p. 77-78). This means that whoever genuinely hears the voice of Christ as the light and truth of God for us will never be asking, "whether and how this voice will

---

[5]Notice here the Chalcedonian pattern, which George Hunsinger frequently refers to in Barth's thought.

show itself to be the voice of truth, but whether and how he himself will
show himself to be its hearer" (IV/3.1, p. 78). Anyone, therefore, who demands a confirmation of who Jesus was and is and will be with Pilate's
question "What is truth?" in practice has already demonstrated the inability
yet to hear the Word of truth. What Barth wishes to avoid at all costs here is
any idea that understanding Jesus as *the* light of the world, *the* truth and *the*
prophet in distinction from all other prophets can be equated with the idea
that "we merely 'ascribed' these things to Him, as many historians think that
other functions and titles were later ascribed" (IV/3.1, p. 72). Barth explicitly
maintains that any such position really amounts only to a "modification of
the old question of Ludwig Feuerbach" (IV/3.1, p. 72). In such a perspective
one might wonder whether his truth is seen as

> no more than that of a category under which we try to grasp the importance
> of His work ... His Logos no more than what we regard as the *ratio* of our own
> life-action . . . [his revelation] only another word for the creative insight in
> which, with reference to and therefore with the help of His figure, we achieve
> awareness of the problem of our own existence, and the solution of this
> problem [indeed] his prophecy [becomes] no more than the power and au-
> thority of our own self-declaration for which we find an evident confirmation
> and to which we lend dignity and weight by understanding and describing it
> as the declaration of this person documented in the Bible. (IV/3.1, p. 72)

The key question here concerns whether there really is any place from
which we can ask "whether Jesus Christ is the light, the revelation, the Word,
the Prophet?" (IV/3.1, p. 73). Any attempt to attribute to ourselves the ability
to pose such questions means that in that very way we have already denied
that his life "is light, His work truth, His history revelation, His act the Word
of God" (IV/3.1, p. 73). The only way to avoid the kinds of answers given by
Feuerbach is to recognize that these can never be the questions asked by
someone who has really acknowledged Jesus Christ as the light, the truth,
the revelation of God and indeed the Logos of God himself; we are in fact
"unfitted to play the role of questioners" (IV/3.1, p. 73). Any supposition that
it is the task of Christians to attempt to demonstrate perhaps some "anthropological problem to which we can find the answer in Him alone" or to seek
"the confessional demonstration of the direct experience which compels us
to recognise and proclaim His Word as the Word of God" will always mean

that we are thinking "in the spirit of Feuerbach" and on the way to "denying the very thing which we are trying to demonstrate" (IV/3.1, p. 74).

Whoever truly acknowledges Jesus Christ does so "in a freedom which neither belongs to him nor is to be won by him, but is given him" (IV/3.1, p. 74). Thus even to raise such questions already means that we have forfeited the freedom actually given to us by the living Christ himself because we think that we must in some way guarantee its truth and validity. In reality, however, what we learn from revelation is that we have no competence to do this—the very thing we attempt to demonstrate in this way is undermined by the fact that in this pursuit we show that we really do not regard him as the truth, the light and the prophet inasmuch as we think we must help him in this fashion. In fact he has shown himself to be the one he is and spoken for himself and does not need our reasons "to bring true conviction as to His status" (IV/3.1, p. 75). All of this represents Barth's way of asserting that there is literally no authority for believing in Jesus Christ other than Jesus himself who is the way, the truth and the life. Hence, when we confess him, it is he himself who is

> the One who asks. . . . We do not have to answer ourselves or other men; we have to answer Him. We do not have to give an account to ourselves or other men; we have to give an account to Him. And as, reached by His light, participant in His revelation, conscious of His truth and encircled by the glory of His prophecy, we give an account of Him, not as those who ask but as those who are asked, we know what we are doing in confessing Him, and our confession achieves the substance, the solidity, the specific weight of knowledge, which it must have if it is not to be a futile beating of the air. (IV/3.1, p. 77)

Because the starting point here is and must be the fact that in the life of Christ we really are dealing with the "presence and action of God," that we say that he is "light, truth, revelation, Word and glory"—not that he might be, but that he *is*—not that we suppose that he is—but that he *is* "indisputably." And this can and must be said because "it is so primarily and intrinsically and not just secondarily and derivatively. . . . In this life God Himself is present as acting Subject" (IV/3.1, p. 79). Because here in this life it is a matter of God himself, Barth rightly insists that "we can only see ourselves as those who are asked concerning our acknowledgment and respect, concerning our praise of God" (IV/3.1, p. 79).

Where God is present as the active Subject as in the life of Christ, "life is not just possibly or secondarily but definitely and primarily declaration, and therefore light, truth, Word and glory" (IV/3.1, p. 79). A God who is mute or obscure is nothing but an idol, Barth says. A God who is mute and obscure to us "is another matter" (IV/3.1, p. 79). Whether we know it or accept it, God

> is eloquent and radiant. He does not merely become this when we perceive and accept Him as such. . . . If He is eloquent and radiant in creation and history, this is on the basis of, and in correspondence with, the fact that from all eternity He is not merely the Father, but also the eternal Word as the Son of the Father, and that in the Son He has the reflection of His own glory. (IV/3.1, pp. 79-80)

Because of this it is "essential and proper" to God "to declare Himself." This is not something that is "accidental or external to Him" (IV/3.1, p. 80), because God is by nature glorious, that is, it is God's right to make himself known as the one he is and as the one he wills to be for us. Jesus Christ himself lives in the glory of God. Importantly, Barth goes on to add,

> there is no beginning before God, no height above Him, no depth beneath Him, no ground outside Him. But as His life has no whence or wherefore, so His light and speech have no basis or authority, apart from the fact that the life is His life, that as such it cannot be concealed but impels and summons to revelation, that it wills to be recognised and known as such, that it can be recognised and known only through itself, and that it is therefore self-disclosing life. (IV/3.1, p. 80)

Barth says that his reference to God's trinitarian being

> cannot be deduced from any principle, but can only describe and explain the fact that God Himself and He alone is the principle and source from which all that He is, and therefore the fact that He is self-disclosing life, does not "derive" as in the case of a logical deduction, but is eternally repeated and confirmed in the act of His existence as the living God. (IV/3.1, p. 80)

This is the very life that discloses itself "in the act of His existence that is lived by Jesus Christ as the Son of God" (IV/3.1, p. 80). For this reason when we have to do with Jesus Christ we have to do with the eternal Word of God, the truth itself, with eternal light that shines of its own accord. If we take this seriously, then "our conduct will be right, for it will be required by the matter itself," and we will thus show ourselves to be "those to whom the truth has confirmed itself as truth, who are 'of the truth' and children of the light" (IV/3.1, p. 80).

Jesus' Human Life—the Covenant of Grace

In the context of the present discussion, it is necessary to note that Jesus' human life is the life of the "covenant of grace willed and determined by God and addressed and given by Him to the man for whom and to whom it is active" (IV/3.1, p. 81). He is God's grace as God's "action to man," and this is "as such God's self-disclosure and self-impartation as it takes place toward man but is grounded in his own divine being." It is, says Barth, "the choice and act of His own incomprehensible freedom to be the Almighty and the Holy One, not only in and for Himself, not only in His own transcendence and self-originating life, but also beyond this in the depths" (IV/3.1, p. 81). Barth says: "In this freedom He is God" (IV/3.1, p. 81). This critical remark demonstrates with clarity that for Barth it is impossible to reduce God's freedom to what God does for us. This is exactly what was argued in chapters three through six above. As an act of grace this is a free action of the God who continues to exist in and for himself, but *not only* in and for himself; God exists in his transcendence but *not only* in transcendence but within the depths of our life marked by sin and death. That is God's grace. God's eternal choice to disclose himself and to impart himself to us and in the historical event in which he actually does this

> on the basis of the fact that to be gracious, to disclose and impart Himself, is already His own freedom, the freedom of the Father to be in and for Himself, yet *not to be only in and for Himself*, but eternally to disclose and impart Himself in the Son, and with the Son in the Holy Ghost. (IV/3.1, p. 81, emphasis mine)

Barth insists that no idea of God invented by us could possibly be gracious in himself and to us. But "The true and living God is gracious. He transcends Himself. He discloses and imparts Himself. He does this first in Himself, and then and on this basis to man in His eternal election and its temporal and historical fulfilment" (IV/3.1, p. 81).

God's act of grace is his freedom to "disclose and impart Himself" (IV/3.1, p. 81). This is God's eloquent and radiant life. "Grace would not be grace if it were to remain mute and obscure, or could try to be in and for itself alone" (IV/3.1, p. 81). This is consistent with Barth's statement in II/1 that God can be and is gracious to us in such a way that his act for us cannot be detached from his being, so that grace is seen as God himself turning toward us "not in equality, but in condescension" (II/1, p. 354).[6] Here, Barth says, this is prophecy, "the prophecy of the life of Jesus Christ" (IV/3.1, p. 81). "Grace is the election and act of God which is not to be expected or demanded by man, which cannot be provoked, let alone projected or produced by him, but which simply comes to him, affects him and determines him, which is quite undeserved but addressed to him without and in spite of his deserving" (IV/3.1, pp. 81-82). Barth's assertion then that Jesus is "light and prophecy" means to him that his life is the life of "God among us; God with us; and God for us" (IV/3.1, p. 82). This cannot be and must not be established or justified "from some other point" because "this life is grace, and grace is radiant as such" (IV/3.1, p. 82). Here, then, is Barth's crucial assertion that the gift (freedom, knowledge of the truth, participation in God's own self-disclosure, eternal life) cannot be separated from the Giver, and that for that very reason anyone who is in the truth and living by God's grace will never attempt to justify God's life for us from any point outside that actual gracious activity that takes place in his Word and Spirit.

LIVING IN THE TRUTH

What, then, does it mean to be in the truth? It means above all to live in the promise of the Spirit. But this means to live in the truth. How can this happen if we are sinners, fallen in Adam, if we, as Barth says in *CD* I/1, are not merely no longer living in the image of God, because that image is completely annihilated in light of the fall and is restored and therefore a reality only in Jesus Christ himself? Here we must come to grips with Barth's often-repeated assertion that grace meets us in judgment and in promise. Our sin, our falsehood is "sin against the grace of God," and thus it is "falsehood as it is also pride and sloth" (IV/3.1, p. 372). It is of course the truth itself that "unmasks" us as sinners. In other words, apart from the revelation and reconciliation that have already taken place for all in Jesus Christ himself—in him as God acting for us both

---

[6]This was discussed in relation to Barth's conception of the Son's eternal obedience in chap. 7.

from the divine and human side—we would not see the fact that we are sinners who are now at one with God in him. In Barth's words,

> the truth unmasks, discovers, accuses and judges the man of sin as such. But the truth which does this in all circumstances (whether men realise it or not) and irresistibly (whatever they attempt against it) is Jesus Christ Himself as the true Witness of His true deity and humanity, as the authentic Witness of the saving grace of God which has appeared in Him justifying and sanctifying man. (IV/3.1, p. 371)

Just as we may know God himself in history only as we are known by him in the miraculous action of the Holy Spirit of Jesus Christ himself, and therefore only in union with Christ by grace and through faith, so we may live freely, that is, in and from the truth itself, as we live our reconciled lives and our new humanity in and from Christ alone, and therefore in faith and hope and thus also in love by loving God and our neighbors. Jesus Christ himself "in and with the promise of the Holy Spirit" goes with us on our way through history "from His resurrection as in the promise of the same Spirit He also comes towards us on this way in intimation and anticipation of His final coming" (IV/3.1, p. 371). He himself is the law of God, the norm by which we are shown to be transgressors, deceivers and even liars. By virtue of the fact that Jesus himself has risen from the dead and confronts each and every person through his Spirit and therefore in and through the scriptural witness or the witness of others to what is there attested, all human beings find themselves in this encounter with the risen Lord. It is in this encounter that we know of our sin and recognize it for what it is—the impossible possibility! In fact, in this encounter, sin itself comes alive so to speak: "It awakens, lives and acts in opposition to Him" (IV/3.1, p. 371). Sin itself is dreadful and incomprehensible, and what makes it so is the fact that it "is the denial, perversion and falsification of what is said to man as God's Word in Him, the Son of God and Man" (IV/3.1, p. 371). The limitation of sin, however, is also revealed in Jesus Christ so that it can never overcome what is a reality in him, that is, the union of God and humanity that has taken place in his history for our benefit. Sin, therefore, can be no more than a "shadow and not true light" (IV/3.1, p. 371) in its relation to Jesus Christ, the true light of the world. Sin is, as Barth says, no match in relation to Jesus

Christ. While sinners can deny Jesus Christ as the Word of God, they cannot silence him. Sin is still terrible even in its limitation. It is transitory in its relation to Christ, but it is still awful and fearful for what it is, and it must be recognized in the "deeds and misdeeds of man" (IV/3.1, p. 372).

As Barth discusses at length elsewhere in the doctrine of reconciliation, sin takes the form of pride and sloth. But in this context it exists "as it were in a third dimension." It exists as falsehood, as lying and therefore as an act which is an

> arbitrary, unfounded, unjustifiable and wicked breaking out from the reality
> of the covenant which on the basis of His eternal election of grace God has
> founded already in and with the creation of all things, which He has fulfilled
> to His own glory and man's salvation in the humiliation and exaltation, in the
> true deity and humanity, of Jesus Christ, and which He has thus established
> and unshakeably confirmed as the promise made to all men but also as the
> norm and criterion of all human conduct. (IV/3.1, p. 372)

We are, of course, guilty of falsehood in our pride in that in opposition to the "humility of the Son of God, [we seek] to occupy the place of God and play a divine role," and in sloth in our opposition to the majesty "of the royal man Jesus, [we seek] to divest [ourselves] of the dignity of his divinely given nature" (IV/3.1, p. 372). Our falsehood that is disclosed to us only in Jesus Christ himself in his resurrection from the dead is something that in our pride and sloth we will never admit to ourselves, and so we conceal this from ourselves by pretending that our sin is in some sense "necessary, righteous and holy" (IV/3.1, p. 372). But in relation to the truth itself our sin as falsehood, pride and sloth is exposed for what it is—falsehood is thus seen to be "the common exponent in which they both [pride and sloth] necessarily betray and express themselves as sin" (IV/3.1, p. 372).

Barth makes a very interesting distinction here, noting that while pride and sloth are our human works as sinners, falsehood "forms itself into a word," and in this form too it expresses itself as opposition to the grace of God that is addressed to us as human beings. It expresses itself as opposition to the threefold character of Christ's office and work. Indeed it is precisely in this way that it confirms the fact that it has no independent existence or originality in relation to the will and work of God. It cannot free itself from this "downward flight to nothingness. The devil has nothing of his own to oppose to God, but only falsifying imitations" (IV/3.1, p. 373). How then does falsehood arise? Here Barth brilliantly explains that as the Lord of the covenant of grace that is fulfilled in Christ himself, God continues his action as reconciler by speaking to us and by telling us "what He is for [us] in His grace and what [we] may be for God in gratitude for His grace" (IV/3.1, p. 373). He notes that God has already done this prior to the fulfillment of the covenant in the prophecy of the history of Israel, which itself only "intimates the history of Jesus Christ" as this is illustrated in the language and history of the Old Testament in relation to the elect people of God. In the prophecy of Jesus Christ himself "as the Word of His fulfilled will and action there is still heard the voice of the rule of God as it moves to its fulfilment, the Word of the old covenant as the promise of the new" (IV/3.1, p. 373).

This history of salvation, which was enacted once and for all and is thus a completed history, Barth says, "has as it were a spearhead in which it continually takes place as it is also a living Word speaking of and for itself beyond its own particular age" (IV/3.1, p. 373). This is the form *"post Christum"* in which it reaches us here and now: "The revelation of Jesus Christ, His work as the true Witness of God in this intervening time, is the promise of the Holy Spirit" (IV/3.1, p. 373). What he means, of course, is that there are three forms of Christ's presence to us in history as the man who reveals and reconciles us to God in his incarnate life as the Word, and therefore as the "true Witness" and as the one who cannot be replaced by anyone or anything else: (1) his resurrection, (2) his coming again as the revealer and (3) the goal and the end of days. All of this he does as the man he was and is in his person and work, who cannot be replaced by anyone or anything else. He does this as "The Lord Himself in His Word is the promised and promising Spirit. Neither the truth nor its expression can be separated or even distinguished from Him. . . . As He Himself lives and acts in the form of the promise of the Spirit, He is the true Witness. He is Himself the truth and its expression" (IV/3.1, p. 378).

The work of Jesus Christ as the true witness, the revealer, the Word of God himself, addresses people of this "intervening time" together with those "of the time of the Old Testament witness," and these people are "forced to make" an answer; and this answer "is sin in the form of falsehood" (IV/3.1, p. 373). This did not have to happen this way. God's Word discloses to all people their justification and sanctification "as they have taken place in Jesus Christ" (IV/3.1, p. 373). And this means that each of us has been told that "as the man of sin he is displaced, vanquished, dead and buried in the life and death of Jesus Christ, so that he is freed not only for the reality but also for the truth of his reconciliation, for knowledge of it" (IV/3.1, p. 373). We are told then that we do not have to remain those who are proud and slothful or those who "persist in falsehood" (IV/3.1, pp. 373-74). All that the sinful person needed to do and needs to do is "to give place to the Word of God encountering him as the promise of the Spirit, to give to it the place which rightfully belongs to it in his heart and conscience and whole existence, and he would immediately have found himself in agreement with it" (IV/3.1, p. 374).

What then? Then our answer would have been our own "free, sponta-neous and quite unequivocal Yes, corresponding to what is said to [us] by God" (IV/3.1, p. 374). Had this happened, then, this time between the resur-rection of Jesus Christ and his second coming, the time left to us as "the time of grace," the "Christian era," would have acquired its proper meaning for humanity. A person responding in this way to the completed action of rec-onciliation could have and would have moved "towards the goal and end of this time in His final and conclusive revelation. . . . That he may give this answer to God, freedom is also given him in this sphere" (IV/3.1, p. 374). But the problem is that we do not give this answer. In light of the time of grace given and the freedom given with it, it is incomprehensible that we would continue to give as our answer our own falsehood, that is, our own "attempt not to allow to be true that which is true between God and [us], to set aside the truth which is told to [us] by God, to produce instead [our] own truth, which as such, opposing and replacing the Yes which [we owe] to God and which God has made [us] free to utter, can only be [our] untruth" (IV/3.1, p. 374). Just as incomprehensibly, we also continue in our pride and sloth as well. But this third form of sin is sin in "its most highly developed form" (IV/3.1, p. 374). What discloses this sin in its most highly developed form is the "prophecy of Jesus Christ" during the Christian era.

Even as sinners, of course, we cannot free ourselves from God. Even in our falsehood we still can only live by the truth of God himself. The untruth in which we as sinners answer the truth "can only have the form and content of a travesty of the truth. Only the truth immediately and incontrovertibly

unmasks him as a liar" (IV/3.1, pp. 374-75). The truth itself in the form of
Christ's prophetic work unmasks us as sinners, as liars. But Barth offers
spectacular analysis and description to illustrate just how falsehood takes
the shape of confusing the truth with doctrine, ideas, principles or systems,
even though it is and remains identical with the risen, ascended and coming
Lord himself. Even doctrine, which is necessary and important, as the work
of sinners "is always a dubious and equivocal phenomenon" (IV/3.1, p. 376).
Even as a statement that is entirely correct "it can be or become falsehood,"
because "no doctrine has of itself the power to unmask the sinner, i.e., the
power of the event in which he is irresistibly detected and exposed as a liar"
(IV/3.1, p. 376). Only the truth itself can do this, and that truth is Jesus Christ
himself in the promise of the Spirit. Doctrine therefore is true and participates in the truth or not to the extent that it "teaches Him or fails to do so"
(IV/3.1, p. 376). Moreover, the truth that is identical with Jesus Christ himself
as he comes to us as the true witness is not something that we encounter "as
a phenomenon which is immediately and directly illuminating." Strange as
it may seem, if we were to conceptualize the truth of the prophecy of Jesus
Christ this way, namely, as something that comes to us "easily and smoothly,"
Barth says that "He would not be who he is if the promise of the Spirit" came
to us in that way (IV/3.1, p. 376). The truth tells us of the message of our
reconciliation with God and of our justification, sanctification and freedom
as well as our true being as new human beings in him.

But this message is new, strange and unsettling compared to what we are
in ourselves (sinners) and therefore apart from our being in Jesus Christ and
therefore apart from what we would regard as true, acceptable and pleasing.
Barth insists that we really need to become completely other than what we
are in ourselves. In this regard the truth that comes to us in Jesus Christ does
not in the first instance address us, but "it contradicts us and demands our
contradiction" (IV/3.1, p. 377). For that very reason it does not come to us
easily, and it does not disclose "itself to us cheaply and otherwise than in a
desperate conflict of decision" (IV/3.1, p. 377). Things that come to us easily
and cheaply and self-evidently "might well be kindly and good and even true
within the sphere of a creaturely life, but they would certainly not be the
truth of God" (IV/3.1, p. 377). And that is the case because God's truth as
grace comes to us precisely by unmasking us as the sinners we are in our-

selves, summoning us to knowledge of God's grace as well as to faith and obedience. Indeed Barth insists that the glory of the Mediator is "concealed in its opposite, in invisibility, in repellent shame" (IV/3.1, p. 377). It does not meet us in a "splendour which wins [us] easily and impresses [us] naturally." This Mediator meets us rather as the risen but crucified Lord and thus "in the despicable and forbidding form of the Slain and Crucified of Golgotha"; in this particular one our life is "hidden and secured in God" (IV/3.1, p. 377).

It is vital to see that Jesus Christ himself continues to be with us in the promise of his Spirit precisely as the one who was judged in our place. As the one who was denied by Peter, betrayed by Judas and deserted by his own disciples, and who was "accused by the congregation of saints as a blasphemer and condemned by the civil authorities as a rebel . . . who offered up His life, who shed His blood," he attests the truth and "unmasks us as liars" (IV/3.1, p. 390). It is precisely as this one that he is "alive in the promise of the Spirit" (IV/3.1, p. 390). It is in this form that he addresses his community and did so from the first as the risen Lord. And it is in this form that he continues to do so even as this is a stumbling block to the Jews and foolishness to the Greeks (1 Cor 1:23). Barth insists, "He encounters us in this form or not at all" (IV/3.1, p. 391). One can speak of God's grace and love and love of neighbor, or the coming of the kingdom; but any assertion of a Christian truth "alongside or outside this Word" will always mean that what is presented "cannot possibly be His Word nor have the meaning and power which such words can have only if they are His Word" (IV/3.1, p. 391). Even today Jesus Christ meets us in this form and as such exposes all of us as enmeshed in human falsehood because and to the extent that we are implicated as those who are of the same stock as those who brought him to the cross. We live in the sphere of the gospel and in the sphere of the light that shines in darkness, but darkness still opposes the light since the world is not yet redeemed. Sin and darkness have been overcome in the life of Jesus Christ, but they are still a threat and temptation even now. While the light might grow brighter as history progresses, the problem of sin and its threat is still present, and in the time between Christ's first and second coming it is a threat that is even more unyielding. The time and place in which we live *post Christum* therefore is not a time and place of "a decrease of darkness, as we might suppose, but rather of its intensification and increase" (IV/3.1, p. 392). We are those who are seriously challenged by the Word of the crucified and risen Lord himself, and we are alarmed by the fact that we have been displaced in him. This time and history in which this genuine conflict takes place is the time and history willed by God. In this time and history each of us is given the opportunity

> under the promise of the Spirit to participate in reconciliation as an active subject, namely, as a recipient and bearer of the Word of reconciliation. And this good will of God inevitably includes the fact that the human sin which Jesus Christ has already deprived of all right and power still has in this sphere of ours a theatre in which to act with all its destructive consequences. (IV/3.1, pp. 392-93)

CHRIST'S VICTORY OVER EVIL

All of this occurs within the limits set by God. But does God will this evil that is directed against himself? Or does God merely permit it? In analogy with Exodus 9:15-16, which refers to God raising up the Pharaoh to show his power in him, Barth says that evil is allowed to run its course even now so that God's glory demonstrated in Jesus Christ may be increased and magnified. In the history that moves from the cross forward to the second coming, "humanity, or many of its members, should have the opportunity under the leadership of this Victor, and as hearers and doers of the Word, of playing an active part in this conflict, in His prophetic work, and therefore secondarily in the divine act of reconciliation" (IV/3.1, p. 393). Even though Jesus who was crucified has already won the war against sin and evil, he is still despised, harassed and smitten in our time and history as the true witness who unmasks the falsehood of us all. In this sense, Barth says, "He must still take up and carry His cross" (IV/3.1, p. 393). Jesus must do this because he

> has to wrestle with the good will of God, recognising and honouring as His will, and therefore as His good will, the fact that the man of sin is not yet abolished, that this frightful liberty of action is still allowed to him. . . . Jesus Christ is thus not merely the One who suffers, but, as in Gethsemane and on Golgotha, He is the One who is smitten and afflicted by God, and it is in this way alone that he is the true Witness. (IV/3.1, p. 394)

One often hears what, from the human point of view, is the strange assertion that God's power is revealed in Jesus' works in weakness, that is, in the weakness of the cross, of the one who refused to come down from the cross when asked to prove his divine Sonship. Well, this is what that strange assertion means in the ongoing history of Christ's presence to us as the true witness who, as the crucified, risen and coming Lord, enables our free participation in reconciliation even now prior to the redemption of the world. This Jesus Christ is the witness to the limit of all sin and evil that still plague this world; "He is a radiant and liberating Witness to our solid and definitive fellowship with God and therefore with one another" (IV/3.1, p. 394). Interestingly, Barth maintains that even in the most questionable feature of the Roman Catholic Mass, which is said to have the character of "a representation of the sacrifice of Golgotha, we must acknowledge that it does at least make this clear" (IV/3.1, p. 395) and that evangelical preaching must never "lag behind in this respect." At this point Barth makes some interesting distinctions.

He insists that Jesus also exists in "the pure, divine form," which is "the meaning and power of His form of suffering" (IV/3.1, p. 395). But in this form he is seen and known "only by God" and remains a mystery to us. He is thus "concealed in this pure form and exists among and for us in the form of suffering in which the pure form is at work" (IV/3.1, p. 395). Here Barth is taking the fact that the incarnation meant that the Word assumed our sinful flesh seriously, and he is taking it seriously because he insists that "Solely and abstractly as the eternal Word and Son of God, in the form in which the Father alone sees and knows Him, He would necessarily be remote and strange, and could give neither comfort nor direction for all His glory" (IV/3.1, p. 395).[7]

---

[7]This statement is fully in line with Barth's remark in IV/1, p. 52, that the *Logos asarkos* in and of itself is neither revealed to us as such nor is the reconciler. While Barth refers to the *Logos asarkos* as an abstraction here and in III/1, p. 54, and again in IV/3.1, p. 395, it seems clear that he does not mean to suggest that the eternally begotten Son through whom God created the world was simply an "abstraction" in the sense that the Son as such was just a conceptual placeholder with no real existence within the immanent Trinity or simply a "counterfactual." As he indicates here in IV/3.1, p. 395, what he means is that to speak of the *Logos asarkos* in the context of creation and reconciliation is to "abstract" from his being as the incarnate Son in the sense that one is then speaking of the Son "in the form in which the Father alone sees and knows Him." That is hardly a disavowal of his eternal existence in that form. It is simply a recognition of the fact that God meets us in the form of the incarnate Son and not directly in his eternal being as it exists within the immanent Trinity. If this is taken into account, then John Webster's criticism of Barth on this point ("Trinity and Creation," *IJST* 12, no. 1 [January 2010]: 4-19, p. 18), could be set aside, since he is really arguing for something quite similar to what Barth is arguing for here, namely, for the following creedal sequence, i.e., "Jesus, Lord and Messiah, is traced to his origin in the eternal relation of Father and Son, his participation in the divine essence is affirmed, and on that basis he is acclaimed as pantokrator" (p. 17). See also above, chap. 3, pp. 297-98.

We ourselves would be unable to receive what the Word has to say to us about our reconciliation with God (our justification and sanctification) if he did not tell us that he still bears our burdens as he did in his suffering on the cross for us and "thus is with us when we have to carry our burdens and experience our sorrows. But He does say this. It is not merely that He was once 'touched with the feeling of our infirmities'; He is still so" (IV/3.1, p. 395). He was not only once tempted as we are, but "He is with us and before us, tempted as we are" (Heb 4:15). He is present with us even today

> in all our confusion, aberration and abandonment, before all our locked prison doors, at all our sick-beds and gravesides, and, of course, with questioning, warning, restraint and delimitation, in all our genuine or less genuine triumphs. He is still the Friend of publicans and sinners whose very family think that He is mad, who is accused of blasphemy and sedition, who is reckoned with male-factors and crucified with them, who is forsaken by His disciples and our God. (IV/3.1, pp. 395-96)

Jesus certainly suffered and died as the Judge judged in our place once and for all. But "He did not do it once only," since as the risen Lord "He lives and takes it to heart with undiminished severity. This is His passion to-day" (IV/3.1, p. 396). Does this mean that we can only relate with the true witness, Jesus Christ, in his form as the one who was crucified? Is there a truth behind the suffering Christ that is the real truth? Such a question as this, Barth says, might even be suggested by the distinction he makes between "the pure form of Jesus Christ in which God sees and knows Him from the form of suffering in which He encounters us as the true Witness" (IV/3.1, p. 396). But, as he did in his developed doctrine of the Trinity, Barth insists that while there is a distinction between the immanent and economic Trinity in the sense just described, there can be no separation between God in his "pure form" and God "for us," because what the eternal God did, in electing us and in becoming incarnate and revealing himself to us as the reconciler and as the coming redeemer in the power of his Spirit, was not a temporary action of God in history. As the incarnate Son who suffered and died, he never ceases to live as God the Son who was and is truly divine and human to all eternity.

At this point, as he did in *CD* IV/1, Barth wonders whether we should "ask concerning the proper truth of the former [the pure form of Jesus Christ as

Logos asarkos], of the Word or Son of God in Himself and as such." He says
the answer must be a definite "no," precisely because "distinction does not
mean separation. It is as the Word or Son of God that He exists as the man
of Gethsemane and Golgotha" (IV/3.1, p. 396). Notice that Barth does not
take the view espoused, either explicitly or implicitly, by a number of those
theologians discussed in chapter three that, in light of the incarnation and
reconciliation of the world in Christ, there is no longer any *Logos asarkos*.
Barth does not deny the continued reality of the *Logos asarkos*, as I argued
in chapter five. What he denies is that the *Logos asarkos* can be detached
from the suffering Jesus Christ, who is God acting for us in history and
enabling our human freedom to live as those who really are reconciled with
God in the power of the Spirit. And so Barth argues, "It is in His pure form
that He is the secret, power and meaning of His form of suffering" (IV/3.1,
p. 396). It is in this unity, Barth says, that Christ exists for us. But because it
is a real unity of humanity in its fallen condition with the divinity of the Son
or Word, we cannot suppose that there is another truth behind what the
crucified Son is and does for us. Any such question would immediately
presuppose a separation of the Word from his human being and history, and
would destroy both the doctrines of revelation and reconciliation. It would
undermine the fact that for us to be truly human must mean that we live the
freedom that is already ours in the achieved unity between God and humanity disclosed in the resurrection of Jesus Christ from the dead. We live
in freedom as we accept in faith the truth that our suffering and pain became
his, so that when he actually experienced God's active opposition to humanity in its sin and enmity against God, he did that so that we would not
have to experience that ultimate judgment and God-forsakenness. In this
setting one can see that Barth still maintains what George Hunsinger has
called the "Chalcedonian Pattern," as when he argues that

> In the unity between His pure form in which He is hidden from us and the form
> of suffering in which He is revealed, He exists primarily before the eyes and in
> the knowledge of God, and therefore properly, and from and to all eternity. That
> God alone sees and knows Him in His pure form does not mean that God
> knows Him only in this form, so that before and for God, and therefore in
> proper truth, He is an anonymous λòγός ἄσαρκος, quite different from the One
> who encounters us in the alien and puzzling form of His passion. (IV/3.1, p. 397)

What this means is that if anyone were to claim or imply that God himself does not participate in our human suffering caused by sin, then any such suggestion or implication would amount to a statement that God remains remote from us and at a distance from us as we really are; God would only be seen as a spectator "in the events between Jesus Christ and us and therefore in His prophetic work" (IV/3.1, p. 397). This is what Barth quite rightly opposes here and elsewhere because God, the eternal Word and Son who is known only to the Father in his pure form, "exists *as* the man of Gethsemane and Golgotha known to us, and is present to us in this very form" (IV/3.1, p. 397, emphasis mine). Here the important point once again is that one cannot separate the form of revelation and reconciliation from the content, which is that God acts as the man Jesus and what Jesus does as man is therefore what God himself does in and for us in our fallen and sinful humanity. Because this man was raised from the dead and ascended into heaven, we have, Barth says, "an unchangeable priesthood," because he continues forever to act as the suffering and afflicted one that he was and is, to live and to "make intercession" for us (Heb 7:24-25) (IV/3.1, p. 397). Barth insists, "The Lamb slain not only stood, but still stands, between the throne of God and the heavenly and earthly cosmos (Rev. 5:6)," and this lamb who was slain is the "priest for ever after the order of Melchisedec (Heb. 7:17)," who is not just a witness to another transcendent and remote truth; rather, "He is the medium, vehicle and witness of His own truth and therefore of the truth beside and above which there is none other either on earth or in heaven, for us or for and before God" (IV/3.1, p. 397).

Because of this it is extremely important for Barth to maintain that "In His mercy God's own mercy is present and active. God Himself suffers with us as He suffers" (IV/3.1, p. 397). But does this thinking not make suffering and death part of God's own nature so that God himself now is seen to be powerless to overcome suffering and death? Does this not obscure the good news that our sin and death have been overcome once and for all in the death and resurrection of Christ himself? The answer to both these questions is an emphatic "no" because there is a unity in distinction here. On the one hand, God himself experiences God-forsakenness as man in such a way that the man of sin is now destroyed. On the other hand, we have the new man, the man who, having risen from the dead, lives eternally as the ascended and advent Lord and is present and active here and now in his prophetic witness to this truth. He is present, Barth maintains,

> in the promise of the Spirit. . . . He is present in His form of suffering, wherein the pure form in which God alone sees and knows Him active but also concealed. It is in this form that He is the true and authentic declaration of the truth, because in it He is Himself the truth beside which there is no other or higher truth whether on earth or in heaven, in time or from and to all eternity, for us or for God. (IV/3.1, p. 408)

But this truth itself is God's grace. Indeed it is a miraculous action, which "is the truth speaking for itself" (IV/3.1, p. 410). Because it is the "miraculous power of God Himself" that is active here, it is not based in any way on our religious convictions, some authoritative tradition or even some church authority. It is certainly not based on anyone's faith. The only basis for actually believing and knowing and living in harmony with the Word of God, which makes itself known miraculously (that is, without any proof from the human side), is the movement of God toward us "which God does not owe [us] but in fact gives [us]" (IV/3.1, p. 410). But God never gives this in such a way that he is captive to our own thought and expression. We cannot reach this truth by arguing with others, as Pannenberg thinks,[8] because "Only the truth itself and therefore God Himself can vouch for it" (IV/3.1, p. 410). Because this truth can only be acquired through the miraculous action of God himself, one can only pray "in intercession that God will vouch for it. . . . In prayer there may be given without hesitation, vacillation or doubt, without the slightest uncertainty, the answer that the crucified Jesus Christ does speak; for as he speaks God speaks" (IV/3.1, p. 410). Here Barth maintains a point that he consistently asserted, namely, that because it is God himself speaking for himself here as Jesus himself speaks, "This man and therefore God would speak even though there were no human hearing and no affirmation by human confession" (IV/3.1, p. 411). This robust statement is certainly opposed to the view of Paul Tillich, who thinks "the believing reception of Jesus *as* the Christ, calls for equal emphasis. Without this reception the Christ would not have been the Christ, namely, the manifestation of the New Being in time and space."[9]

---

[8]See Paul D. Molnar, "Some Problems with Pannenberg's Solution to Barth's 'Faith Subjectivism,'" *SJT* 48, no. 3 (1995): 315-39.

[9]Paul Tillich, *Systematic Theology* (Chicago: University of Chicago Press, 1957), 2:99.

MUTUAL CONDITIONING

Barth's assertion here has a power that is voided in any conceptuality that asserts some sort of mutual conditioning between us and the Word of God or
between faith and revelation. This is no small issue, because it is precisely here
that major differences can be seen between the Roman Catholic view of grace
as espoused by Karl Rahner and the Reformed view as espoused by both Barth
and Torrance. For instance, the notion of created grace is central to Rahner's
concept of the "supernatural existential," and it shapes his view that natural
theology and revealed theology mutually condition each other.[10] Hence, he
thinks uncreated grace and created grace mutually condition each other with
the result that he believes God's relation to us via uncreated grace, i.e., "(God's
communication of himself to man, the indwelling of the Spirit)" which "implies a new *relation* of God to man . . . can only be conceived of as founded
upon an absolute *entitative* modification of man himself, which modification
is the real basis of the new relation of man to God upon which rests the relation of God to man" (*TI* 1:324, last emphasis mine). For Rahner, "This absolute entitative modification and determination of man is created grace" (*TI*
1:324). This, Rahner describes as the Scholastic view in this matter, which he
believes to be acceptable (*TI* 1:325). "Grace, being supernaturally divinizing,
must rather be thought of as a change in the structure of human consciousness"
(*TI* 5:103). All of this both Barth and Torrance would reject because such
thinking detaches grace from the Giver of grace, namely, from Jesus Christ
himself acting miraculously here and now as the only factor that enables us
to know and love him and our neighbors without changing "entitatively," so it
might then be supposed that we could reflect on ourselves as those who are
justified and sanctified, to arrive at a proper view of revelation and faith.[11]

While for Rahner revelation "presupposes as a condition of its own possibility the one to whom this revelation remains unowed" (*TI* 6:75), Barth is
here stating unequivocally that revelation is and remains identical with the
fact that God speaks *as* Jesus Christ the risen and ascended Lord speaks, and
does so even without any human hearing or affirmation. Hence, he un-

---

[10]For Rahner, "the revealed Word and natural knowledge of God mutually condition each other"
(*TI* 1:98).

[11]As seen earlier in this chapter, Barth rejects any such notion of an "entitative" change in us so
that we might reflect on ourselves to know of God and our relations with God, because our
justification and sanctification are real in Christ and cannot be found directly within us.

equivocally rejects any notion of mutual conditioning when he says, "His speaking is the basis of human hearing and confession, not *vice versa*" (IV/3.1, pp. 411, 418-19).[12] Indeed he goes on to assert,

> Whether or not men hear and affirm by confession, the fact that it is uttered and breaks the silence of death distinguishes His speech from all other human speech as the human Word which is pronounced with the superior power possessed only by God, and therefore as the declaration of the truth, as the speech of the true Witness. (IV/3.1, p. 411)

Torrance explicitly rejects the idea of grace as "a transferable quality infused into and adhering in finite being, raising it to a different gradation where it can grasp God by a connatural proportion of being."[13] Ultimately, Torrance's positive point is to assert that "Grace is not something that can be detached from God and made to inhere in creaturely being as 'created grace.'"[14] Instead, grace is identical with Christ himself, the Giver of grace. That is why the Gift and the Giver must not be separated, as in the thinking that detaches grace from Christ and makes it inhere in creaturely being.[15]

GRACE AS MIRACLE

What, then, are some practical implications of Barth's view of grace as a miraculous act of God acting and speaking to us as man in the crucified and risen Lord in such a way that grace can never be separated from its Giver? *First*, Barth insists that Jesus' suffering and death for us are not to be seen as some unfortunate accident or the result of fate: "What men decree and execute against Him [Jesus] in supreme corruption and iniquity takes place according to the holy and gracious counsel of God" (IV/3.1, p. 413). God willed that this man should pay the price of experiencing God-forsakenness because God himself must turn away from sinful human beings and thus

---

[12]The God who speaks as the crucified and risen Lord, Barth insists, is not "the prisoner of a necessary reciprocity between His divine speaking and our human hearing" (IV/3.1, p. 418). "Whether He is heard or not, He speaks in His own freedom and power. When God speaks; when the crucified man Jesus Christ speaks, He does so—for what else does speaking mean, and how else should we know that He speaks?—not merely with the intention of being heard by us, but also with the power to make Himself heard" (IV/3.1, pp. 418-19).

[13]Torrance, "The Word of God and the Nature of Man," in Torrance, *Theology in Reconstruction* (London: SCM Press, 1965), p. 114.

[14]Torrance, "The Roman Doctrine of Grace," in *Theology in Reconstruction*, p. 182.

[15]See, for example, *Trinitarian Faith*, pp. 24 and 140-41, and *Christian Doctrine of God*, p. 147.

against the "One who knows no sin but shows to Him only obedience and gratitude. The bitter implication is that He puts Him in the place of us all, that He makes Him His Lamb (Jn. 1:29)" (IV/3.1, p. 413). It is important here to note that Barth does not make suffering and death part of God's eternal nature, as happens in the thinking of Moltmann. Rather, Jesus' experience of God-forsakenness means that he experiences the "death-cry of the man who dies in Him and the birth-cry of the man who comes to life in Him" (IV/3.1, p. 413). Barth says that, in relation to the Jews and Romans who brought about his death, Jesus says, "Father, forgive them; for they know not what they do" (Lk 23:34) while in relation to God he says, "My God, my God, why hast thou forsaken me?" This question, Barth says, corresponds to the dreadful situation in which God forsook this man as no other. But what does this mean? It means that "He turned against Him as never before or since against any—against the One who was for Him as none other, just as God for His part was for Him as He never was nor is nor will be for any other" (IV/3.1, pp. 413-14). What Barth wants to say here is that as the eternal Son of the Father, Jesus Christ experiences God's wrath and judgment on human sin for us and thus for our benefit; God is thus not remote and detached from us as the sinners we are so that "With the eternal Son the eternal Father has also to bear what falls on the Son as He gives Himself to identity with the man Jesus of Nazareth, thus lifting it away from us to Himself in order that it should not fall on us" (IV/3.1, p. 414). Here Barth makes an all-important but subtle distinction missing from other more provocative expressions of Christ's suffering and death. He asserts,

> In Jesus Christ God Himself, the God who is the one true God, the Father with the Son in the unity of the Spirit, has suffered what it befell this man to suffer to the bitter end. It was first and supremely in Himself that the conflict between Himself and this man, and the affliction which threatened this man, were experienced and borne. (IV/3.1, p. 414)

Notice that, as indicated above, the suffering is not God's own but the suffering of human beings marked by sin and death that he takes to himself in the incarnate Son.[16] God took this suffering and death on himself so that it should no longer be ours, because in doing this he restored peace between us and God.

---

[16]See above, chap. 3, p. 157, chap. 4, pp. 189-90, chap. 6, pp. 299-301, and chap. 7, pp. 341-43.

Second, because the only power that actually enables reciprocity between us and God, that is, that enables us to hear God's Word in truth, is a miraculous act of God, it can never be equated with doctrine, however important that is, precisely because doctrine can only point to the Word, which does its own speaking miraculously here and now. But what exactly is this miraculous power in this context? It is, according to Barth, power and work of the Holy Spirit: "The power of our hearing was simply the power of His speaking, as the power of His speaking became that of our hearing. It was the work of the Holy Spirit that we heard and therefore could hear" (IV/3.1, p. 420). This assertion and the power embedded in it are the result of a view of grace, faith and revelation that never detaches its understanding of these actions from the action of God himself acting as man within the contours of history and time that is reconciled to God in Christ and awaiting its redemption in him at his second coming. We know and experience the truth of revelation only in and by the power of the Holy Spirit. It is only in the promise of the Spirit, and the promise of the Spirit yet to come, who acted in the first form of Jesus' coming in his resurrection and will act in his coming again at the "goal and end of all history" (IV/3.1, p. 420), that we encounter the grace and love of God. This is an important presupposition for all theology. But it is not one that Christians can provide or achieve of themselves, because this is a matter of "God's free act of grace and revelation present in a way which we cannot control, though known and experienced by us in its accomplishment. This presupposition is the activity of the Holy Spirit" (IV/3.1, p. 421). Here we are confronted by the freedom of God's grace, which is none other than the prophetic witness of the risen and ascended Lord himself empowering faith, knowledge and obedience as free spontaneous acts of those who are renewed by his Spirit.

Third, Jesus Christ comes to us now in the Holy Spirit "as the man who came once and then came again first in His resurrection from the dead, as the man of Gethsemane and Golgotha, as the Crucified" (IV/3.1, p. 421). In this form he is the truth and "so declares it that it is received as such" (IV/3.1, p. 421). Only in this form does he speak the truth in the work of the Spirit. This is a crucial point because it implies that any reference to the Holy Spirit that is not at once a reference to the crucified and risen Lord who is alive now and speaking his Word of truth would simply be another example of human falsehood expressing itself; it would represent just another attempt to minimize the significance of Jesus Christ himself as the only one who can speak for himself! What is it that distinguishes the work of the Holy Spirit from the works of "other very active spirits"? The answer is that, because in the work of the Holy Spirit, Jesus Christ as the one who was crucified and is the Word of God and thus the truth itself "speaks out and is declared and active" (IV/3.1, p. 421). "The Holy Spirit is simply but most distinctly the renewing power of the breath of His mouth which as such is the breath of the sovereign God and victorious truth" (IV/3.1, p. 421). Notice how even here it is important for Barth to distinguish the work of the Spirit from the work of the Word without in any way separating them. Indeed, because it is the power of the Holy Spirit who is this renewing power in Christ's speaking his own Word to us here and now, Barth can also say that it is in this power that the Word of truth "is not only in Him, but where and when He wills [it] goes out also to us men, not returning to Him empty but with the booty or increase of our faith and knowledge and obedience" (IV/3.1, p. 421). And this occurs again and again so that there is established between him and us real communication and a genuine history of "mutual giving and receiving" (IV/3.1, p. 421). But again, Barth insists that what occurs here is "the miraculous work of God which cannot be attained by any human contemplation or comprehension, thought or utterance, nor enclosed in any theory, namely, the majestic autonomy and freedom of His grace, which is the mystery of the existence and work of the true Witness" (IV/3.1, p. 421). Confronted by this true witness "existing and active in this mystery, the falsehood of sinful man is necessarily unmasked and disqualified" (IV/3.1, p. 421).

This sinful activity is the "impotent counterpart of the divine act of revelation in process of fulfilment in Jesus Christ" (IV/3.1, p. 434). The first form of falsehood, according to Barth, is "evasion." Just as the knowledge of faith, hope and love can only occur in relation to Jesus Christ, so it is in that same relation that falsehood arises. This is the form sin takes "in the Christian age which begins with the resurrection of Jesus Christ and which is determined by the action of the Holy Spirit and teleologically by the outcome of this action in the final appearance of Jesus Christ" (IV/3.1, p. 435). People prefer to escape the encounter with Jesus Christ, in whom they are justified and sanctified only by God's grace; they fear this and would rather live from themselves. "Evasion means trying to find another place where truth can no longer reach or affect [us], where [we are] secure from the invading hand of its knowledge, and from its implications" (IV/3.1, p. 435). But it is just this that is impossible because there is no escape from the truth itself—the true witness, Barth says, will follow us who are tenacious evaders of the truth into whatever new places we find in an attempt to evade the truth and set us this same dilemma once again, namely, exposing our falsehood and confronting us with the truth that we are covenant partners who are at one with God in him. The real power of this evasion lies in its attempt to use the truth itself to evade the truth by making it something that is "tolerable and useful" (IV/3.1, p. 436). Importantly, no matter how we, as sinners, may seek to evade the truth and transform it even as we claim to acknowledge it in its identity with Jesus Christ, nothing can change the fact that the truth is and remains always identical with Jesus Christ himself as the Word who as reconciler and redeemer is active here and now in the promise of his Spirit. He differentiates himself from all attempts to depict him. The truth that Christ attests once again is the reconciliation of the world with God, the fulfilled covenant in him, as well as his justifying and sanctifying grace

> as dwelling and effective in Him, as alive in His fellowship with man and the fellowship of man with Him. He attests this *truth* as He attests Himself. But He attests it as He attests *Himself*. We do not encounter Him without at once encountering this *truth*. But we do not encounter this truth without at once encountering *Him*. (IV/3.1, p. 440)

GIFT AND GIVER

Once again, the pivotal point that must be stressed here is that grace is inseparable from the Giver of grace so that in this context, as Barth rightly affirms, there would be no offense at all in the idea of God's gracious interaction with us and ours with God. But there is indeed offense and, as Barth puts it, "Boundless offence" (IV/3.1, p. 441), when the person of the witness to the truth is identical with the truth itself. In Barth's words: "The painful and scandalising thing which man wishes to avoid is the identity between this man and this truth, between this truth and this man" (IV/3.1, p. 441). In face of this fact, any attempt to conceptualize Jesus Christ as the supreme mani-

festation or most impressive symbol of the truth means that in those characterizations we have already attempted to evade the truth itself, which is inseparable from Jesus Christ himself. This is the key to human sin; sinful
creatures will always try to evade this identity of the truth and of grace with
the truth itself and with the Giver of grace. And the moment that occurs, true
human freedom, as grounded in the divine freedom of God's grace and love
actualized in the life, death, resurrection and in the form of Christ's coming
again as the true witness and the true prophet, becomes obscure and shaky
once more. It cannot be stated too strongly at this point that all attempts to
separate grace from the Giver and truth from the truth itself as it is in Jesus
Christ will always be manifest by the fact that Jesus himself causes no offense
or discomfort whenever his work is reinterpreted so that it can be understood
apart from his actual disclosure of its truth as a miraculous divine action that
can only be acknowledged in faith. It is precisely the "work of falsehood,"
Barth says, that attempts to "silence, suppress and eliminate their identity,"
that is, the identity of the truth with Jesus Christ himself (IV/3.1, p. 441).

This is why Thomas F. Torrance could and did argue that a secularized
Christianity that can be communicated directly to people without their
having to give up all their self-reliance and turn exclusively toward Christ is
a Christianity that "has become a harmless superficial thing, capable neither
of inflicting deep wounds nor of healing them," because in Torrance's words,
"it has nothing to say to men which they do not already know. . . . The more
the Church tries to get 'with it' the more it makes itself an otiose relic of the
past."[17] The point here is that what needs to be said to people is that they are
already free; they are already justified and sanctified in Christ himself and
therefore their salvation is in no sense conditional on what they do or how
they think about Jesus, as they might by conceiving him as the highest instance or symbol of the truth of God's grace and revelation. He is neither of
these, because he himself is the grace and truth of God, which cannot be
located in the church, in the experience of salvation or in our faith, love or
hope. That is and remains the offensive element in revelation.

This point was crucial to Torrance and to Barth for good reason. To hear
the crucified Christ who now lives as the risen and ascended Lord is to hear

---

[17]Torrance, *God and Rationality* (London: Oxford University Press, 1971; reissued Edinburgh:
T & T Clark, 1997), p. 71.

the voice of one who became obedient by humbling himself for our benefit; it is to "hear the sigh of this One judged in our place . . . to see this One condemned, expelled and rejected in our place . . . to realise that His place ought to have been ours . . . to take up and bear our much smaller crosses, and not to be able to escape this requirement" (IV/3.1, p. 442). In other words, confronted by God's judgment and grace revealed in the human rejection of Jesus Christ, our only possible response can be to accept and obey the grace and command that meet us in this one. Yet, of ourselves, that is exactly what we cannot and do not do. We can only receive this news as a gift and act and miracle of the Holy Spirit, and receive this gift with the resolute act of conversion of the lost son. Barth says, "We do not want dealings with the Holy Spirit and His gift and the reception of this gift. Both seem to us absurd, the one as a miracle we cannot really expect and the other as a demand we cannot really concede" (IV/3.1, p. 444). Instead of surrendering ourselves to Christ himself, we attempt to explain this mystery and miracle away; instead of recognizing that here in Jesus Christ we have "two partners who are from the very first and unchangeably unequal, namely, God and man," we attempt to obscure this as much as possible without denying it outright precisely by replacing it "by the less unsettling notion of a *continuous co-existence* of the two" (IV/3.1, p. 444, emphasis mine).

Instead of accepting the genuine relationship of fellowship between us and God established in the cross and resurrection of this particular man, we try to think of a correlation between God and us by making the distinction between us and God "as loose as possible," so that in the end the distinction between Jesus Christ as the true witness and us, in which the distinction between God and us is quite clear and obvious, "must be relativised in such sort that man generally is regarded as a *potential Christ*" (IV/3.1, p. 445, emphasis mine). Has Barth gone too far here? Just think of the statement by Elizabeth Johnson on the basis of which she thinks we ought to reflect on God in female categories because in her thinking, "women . . . can freely represent Christ, being themselves, in the Spirit, other Christs."[18] Or think of the statement by Catherine

---

[18]Elizabeth A. Johnson, *She Who Is: The Mystery of God in Feminist Theological Discourse* (New York: Crossroad, 1992), p. 167. While Johnson speaks of the "scandal of particularity," she does not have in mind the fact that Jesus is offensive to us because of who he is as the very Word of God speaking and acting here and now. For her this scandal refers not to "Jesus' historical sex" but "the scandal of his option for the poor and marginalized in the Spirit of his compassionate, liberating

LaCugna that "Ministry properly exercised activates the vocation and mission of *every* member of the church to become Christ."[19] These contemporary assertions suggest quite firmly that Barth has not gone too far at all. Any implication that we are or could be other Christs immediately obscures the identity of grace with the Giver of grace; it obscures the identity of the truth with the only true witness himself. Any implication that our vocation is to become Christ immediately obscures the all-important fact that vocation is the life each of us lives in relation to the specific call of the true witness and the enabling but miraculous power of the Holy Spirit permitting us to hear that witness and to live it here and now.

TRUE FREEDOM

Here finally we see the true picture of divine and human freedom active within the economy in a way that does not displace the action of the Holy Spirit as the Spirit of Christ himself freely active here and now, but in such a way that there can be no possibility of confusing the Holy Spirit with the human spirit, which, marked by sin, will always attempt to level up the relation of inequality that exists between God and those whose sin has been overcome by grace itself in judgment and forgiveness. In the sovereign freedom of his love God makes himself known to us as our "loving Father and Lord, Friend and Helper, who opens up to [us] the fulness of his treasures. But He does this in absolute independence of all presuppositions distinct from Himself, of all psychic or moral principles, laws, criteria or stan-

---

Sophia-God. That is the scandal that really matters" (ibid.). Having shifted the scandal from an encounter with Jesus himself as the very Word of grace and judgment, she argues that "feminist theological speech about Jesus as the Wisdom of God" shifts focus from "maleness" onto the significance of the "Christ event" and concludes that Jesus "in his human, historical specificity is confessed as Sophia incarnate, revelatory of the liberating graciousness of God imaged as female" (ibid.). But God "imaged as female" is clearly not the triune God, who is not, as Johnson believes, *like* a trinity, but is the one true God in his unique eternal being, beyond all gender, existing and acting as the eternal Father, Son and Holy Spirit. This God is not a symbol we can use to create the society we want, but the God who is incarnate in and active in his Word and Spirit, uniting us to himself through union with Jesus, the risen, ascended and coming Lord. See above, chap. 2, p. 90.
[19]Catherine Mowry LaCugna, *God for Us: The Trinity and Christian Life* (San Francisco: HarperSanFrancisco, 1991), p. 402. Compare this to the following statement by Feuerbach, "We are all supposed to be one in Christ. Christ is the consciousness of our unity. Therefore, whoever loves man for the sake of man, whoever rises to the love of the species, to the universal love adequate to the nature of the species, is a Christian; he is Christ himself" (*The Essence of Christianity* [New York: Harper Torchbooks, 1957], p. xviii). This is what Barth rejects consistently (see above pp. 368-69).

dards" (IV/3.1, p. 446). He does this as the "source and norm of all good . . .
in His self-determination and therefore in His freedom" (IV/3.1, p. 446).
And this means that: (1) because the truth is and remains identical with Jesus
Christ himself as the true witness, we human beings are "prevented *a limine*
from occupying a place where [we] can make meaningful objections or even
reservations in relation to this Witness and His testimony"; (2) the Word of
the cross as the form of Jesus' witness and testimony alone refers and drives
us "directly to the only means of deliverance in the grace of God as the Lord
of life and death"; therefore there exists (3) "the indissolubly differentiated
relation between the speaking of God and the hearing and answering of man,
between the gift and the reception of the Holy Spirit as the fellowship into
which God enters with man and man is taken up by God" (IV/3.1, p. 446).
All of this occurs as "an absolutely sovereign grasping of man by God," which
is sovereign because we have "no possibility of encountering God from a
position which is not that posited and secured for [us] by God Himself
through His Word and Spirit." We thus have no recourse whatsoever to any
other norm for what is good or true or of what salvation, peace or our well-
being might consist in, so that we might use any or all of these to consider
God, to wrestle with God or to grasp or even evade God or argue with God
(IV/3.1, pp. 446-47). Because we are dealing here with God's love, we are
dealing with God's free love, and that means with his free self-determination
to meet us and establish fellowship with us in the form of his incarnate Son,
who alone reveals God to us and "gives [us] information and direction concerning Himself, and therefore concerning [us]" (IV/3.1, p. 447).

Our freedom, then, consists simply in this: "to cleave freely to this free God.
Freely, for God's sovereign grasping of man is not an act of force to induce a
sacrficium intellectus et voluntatis" (IV/3.1, p. 447). On the contrary, God's act
of grasping us in the love of his Word and Spirit "evokes and establishes the
intellectus and the *voluntas fidei*" (IV/3.1, p. 447). For all those who mistakenly
suppose that Barth's theology is fideistic, this very assertion completely undermines any such misguided thinking. Had Barth really been a fideist, he
never would have argued for the fact that we have genuine free relations with
God in union and distinction from him in and through the relations that God
himself has established and establishes in his Word and Spirit, and thus
through the miraculous action of his grace, love and forgiveness. He never

would have been able to assert and express what it means to experience God on the basis of God's own sovereign actions in the economy in his Son Jesus Christ and now through the actions of the risen and ascended Lord, who includes us in genuinely free relations of knowledge and love with him in the promise of the Spirit. He never would have been able to make sense of the fact that our decisions to accept his grace and love as these are evoked and established by the Holy Spirit are free actions of obedience shaped by our acknowledgment of the truth that God is for us and therefore no one and nothing can be against us. The God who frees us for this free activity is the God who was and is active in Jesus Christ himself; who is concerned for us and who wills to free us not as puppets but as those who are "born again to freedom and therefore to self-determination, i.e., to that which accrues to [us]" as responsible covenant-partners "of the free and self-determining God, as His creature, as the one who is loved by Him" (IV/3.1, p. 447).

Our freedom, then, which is both given and required of us, "is the freedom of one who belongs to the free God and is freed by Him" (IV/3.1, p. 447). This means that we are truly freed by God from all limiting and arbitrary notions about God and about ourselves; in this sense we are freed from ourselves. It means "attraction and activity in relation to the information and direction received from the One who gives and requires this freedom" (IV/3.1, p. 447). It also means that we are given, and therefore we have, the "courage and joy to make the only possible and meaningful use of it corresponding to its nature, i.e., the only use which can be considered in view of the fact that it is given and required by the free God" (IV/3.1, p. 447). We are God's covenant partners, and we are therefore free to live as his children and as those who have been elected by him. "It is a matter of the freedom to elect Him as elected by Him. It is a matter of the freedom of responsibility to Him" (IV/3.1, p. 447).

Sin is still visible to the extent that we draw back from this freedom in various ways but most especially by changing the confrontation between us as sinners with the one who freed us from sin in Jesus Christ through conceptualizing our relations with God in terms of the infinite and finite. In that way we coordinate this confrontation into a system of two essences, one infinite and absolute, and the other finite and relative, and in thinking just this way we blunt the reality of what actually has taken place in our confrontation with the free God who freely fulfilled the covenant by justifying and sanctifying us in Jesus Christ himself. Thinking of God and creatures in these categories means there can no longer be any question "of a true giving and receiving or commanding and obeying" (IV/3.1, p. 448). No longer would we then refer to a true liberation of sinful creatures for freedom grounded in God's own freedom for us. There could no longer take place a confrontation in which there is

> the passing of the old or emergence of the new. This elimination of the freedom of God and man, this depriving of the confrontation of God and man of all force and tension by the notion of an order overruling and comprehending them both, is the general alleviation which the falsehood of the man of sin has in view. (IV/3.1, p. 448)

In this perspective, God certainly would be highly honored as a supreme being. This being would be one who *via eminentiae* may be understood as the "sum of all notions of the good, the true and the beautiful, of love, righteousness and wisdom" (IV/3.1, p. 448). Or this supreme being might be thought of *via negationis* "as the sum of the limit and transcendence of all finite being and occurrence, as the sum of a being independent of that of all other entities, as the sum of what is knowable only in its unkowableness to our knowledge which is orientated on the finite and therefore itself finite" (IV/3.1, p. 448). But in Barth's estimation, in light of the revelation of God in Jesus Christ, this thinking would represent no more and no less than "the ideal picture in which man tries to see and understand his own being and its order and mystery" (IV/3.1, p. 449). This is the picture that sinful man gives himself, since "This supreme being has too close an affinity to the supreme content of man's understanding of the world and himself" (IV/3.1, p. 449). The very idea of God as the "supreme being" is the attempt on our part as sinners to secure ourselves from the true freedom of God and thus from our actual freedom which was and is enabled by God himself in his Word and Spirit. Here we see quite plainly the difference it makes if one pursues knowledge of God via natural theology or as a free act of acknowledging who God really is in his free actions within the economy as the God who established, maintains and fulfills the covenant of grace precisely by uniting us to himself through the Spirit and thus through union with Christ himself. When Christ is left out of the picture as the truth and only source of true freedom, as he always is when conceptualized by sinners apart from faith, grace and revelation, we miss both divine and human freedom, which can be seen and experienced only in the confrontation between God's grace, which judged human sin on the cross and revealed the union of forgiven sinners with God himself in him.

HOMINUM CONFUSIONE ET DEI PROVIDENTIA

By way of closing our discussion of experience and knowledge of God in the freedom of grace within the economy with emphasis on the Holy Spirit, it is worth considering briefly our human relations with God within the context of world occurrence. Following Barth's lead, we will discuss a few implications of God's providence as it relates to us and the confusion caused by our human thinking and action marked by sin and death between the time of Christ's resurrection, ascension and second coming. Barth notes that if these were the only alternatives, then Christians would be caught in a situation where they would look to God as the Lord of history on the one hand with courage and confidence, and then to world occurrence in history on the other hand with anxiety and fear in light of the fact that they might find moments of meaning within history but also moments of confusion. Is this the way things must be? It has often been depicted thus from a Christian perspective, that is, that Christians exist in a world in which there is a tension or even a dialectic between two principles or two kingdoms, namely, God's Lordship and human confusion, which could be categorized as the distinction between a theologically ideal perspective and a realistic or prac- tical one. The result would be a view that portrayed matters "As if all the birds in their different ways were not voicing the same song from every roof!" (IV/3.2, p. 702). But Barth will have none of this, precisely because it really says nothing new that could not be said by anyone who had not really heard the voice of the true witness at all. Instead Barth maintains that there is in fact a third way. While it is important to recognize both of these factors, namely, the providence of God and the confusion of human beings, it is imperative to note that this third way is superior to both and that it is only in light of this that Christians can say what should be said to the world.

Care is necessary, however, in presenting this third way, because it could easily lead to the Hegelian idea that the third way is the way of a synthesis of a thesis (*providentia*) and antithesis (*confusione hominum*) "which takes the contradiction into itself, integrates the two sides and thus overcomes it" (IV/3.2, p. 703). But the problem with this perspective is that it then would see the two factors as "elements of one and the same reality," and this would imply that both God's providence and the confusion of human beings would be divested of the mystery that characterizes them in quite different ways. In that case, then, "we could not seriously speak either of a mystery of God over world history or a mystery of iniquity within it," because ultimately they would be seen as "moments of history which are intrinsically perceptible, understandable and explicable" (IV/3.2, p. 704). Such thinking would make it impossible to assert what needs to be asserted, namely, that it is God's providence alone that must be absolutely honored, affirmed and indeed adored, while human confusion must be unequivocally negated and detested. Such thinking would open the door to seeing the two factors as positively related such that one might even suppose that there was a relation of dependence between them. And this would lead to the idea that God positively willed not only creation but also sin and "the human confusion of creation with nothingness" (IV/3.2, p. 704). Then it would follow that the proper Christian view would be to bring God's providence and human confusion "under a common denominator . . . validating both in their higher unity" (IV/3.2, p. 704). Further, Christians then might feel compelled "with sighs perhaps but also perhaps with cheerfulness, to affirm the human confusion justified and sanctified by its connexion with the providence of God"! (IV/3.2, p. 704). Unfortunately, however, it is just this manner of thinking that illustrates human confusion and not true knowledge of God in his relations with us in history. In fact it is in just such a synthesis of nothingness with God's good creation that human confusion arises in the first place. In Barth's words,

> Christ Himself would then have been brought into agreement and harmony with Belial (2 Cor. 6:15). And the proclamation of this agreement and harmony would be the glad tidings which the Christian has to transmit to the world. As though the world had any need to listen to such tidings! For is it not the familiar confusion of men which in this message comes to it in the form of the confusion of Christians? (IV/3.2, p. 705)

This thinking would make Christianity superfluous. And that is why Barth says it must be avoided at all costs. But it must be avoided not because this is where it leads but because of where such thinking began. It began with the assumption that we can overcome the antithesis between the good, creative will of God and nothingness by relying on ourselves, by creating a worldview that sets us above both God and ourselves in a way that sees the two together and combines them together. This move itself, Barth says, is an act of arrogance that substantiates the fact that we are fallen creatures—creatures "fallen away from God and fallen out with [our] neighbor and [ourselves]" (IV/3.2, p. 706). With this starting point, only confusion follows, not clarity.

This thinking brilliantly demonstrates exactly the nature of grace and its connection with the miraculous action of God, because grace means that we are both judged by the fact that our self-reliance has been overcome in Jesus Christ as the one who reconciled us to God by being judged in our place, and we are freed by grace to live as those who may now love God and our neighbors with a freedom that comes to us from the risen and ascended Lord in the power of his Spirit. But this grace is revealed in and through his cross and resurrection as the new act of God visible only to faith, which itself comes from the Holy Spirit. All along the line we are totally dependent on God's active love as the revealer and reconciler to know of this third way through this problem. This is the offensive element in the Word of grace, because it strikes us "from without and from a superior height," and in virtue of this we can only understand ourselves as we are understood (IV/3.1, p. 257). God does not say "No" to us but "Yes," and it is only on the basis of this "Yes" that is said to us by the living Christ himself that our yes to ourselves can be secure. Creating a worldview is one of the ways in which the "opposing element" in us attempts to neutralize God's judgment and therefore God's grace in his completed act of reconciliation, of having fulfilled the covenant on our behalf; this is in addition to indifference and using an apparent but only an apparent acceptance of grace as a guise for continued self-reliance in the form of basically rendering the Word of grace innocuous.[20] This, Barth rightly says, cheapens grace "so that it is declared cheaply and may be heard and had cheaply." This occurs by assimilating it to Chris-

---

[20]See IV/3.1, pp. 257-60, and Paul D. Molnar, *Incarnation and Resurrection: Toward a Contemporary Understanding* (Grand Rapids: Eerdmans, 2007), p. 334.

tians in their experiences of faith and thus by "softening its rough edges" and suppressing or softening

> the strangeness of its declaration, so that it is now trivial and familiar, and the divine Yes has become curiously like the Yes which man is always about to say to himself, and it has become a kind of world-view, facilitating, supporting and even furthering man's evasion and escape from its message in perhaps the most respectable and unchallengeable form. (IV/3.1, p. 259)

Creating worldviews is a kind of pride that sets itself against the prophetic truth of Jesus Christ himself, and the hallmark of this activity of sinful human beings is that "no world-views can find any place for Jesus Christ" (IV/3.1, p. 257). Certainly they can indeed find a place for "an abstract God and an abstract man, but not for Him, the God-man." They can certainly find a place for a "historical Jesus distilled out of the witness of the New Testament, or for a Christ-idea attained by a similar process of abstraction, but not for the living Lord, for the High-priest, the King and especially the Prophet Jesus Christ" (IV/3.1, p. 257). The living Christ is of no use to those who rely on their worldviews. "He would not be who He is if He were" (IV/3.1, p. 257). He calls into question all, really all human attempts at self-understanding and self-reliance precisely by telling us that we are free to live from grace and thus from our new life in and from him alone and thus by faith. While our will and intention may be the best in thinking this way, it will always lead to confusion because, as Barth puts it, "The wisdom of serpents will always produce the work of serpents" (IV/3.2, p. 706).

The solution to this problem is "childishly simple." And it is this: "The reality and truth of the grace of God addressed to the world in Jesus Christ is the third word which the Christian community is both required and authorised to consider and attest beyond and in integration of the first two as it turns its gaze on world-occurrence" (IV/3.2, p. 706). Here Barth's thinking offers us the heart of what it means to say that the truth is what it is in its identity with the living Jesus Christ, who alone speaks for himself. For this very reason "the grace of God shown to the world in Him is not a principle which man can perceive, affirm and appropriate as such, and then logically develop and apply to transcend and overcome all possible antitheses" (IV/3.2, p. 706). This is the sense in which grace is costly—costly to God, who experiences his own opposition to sin in the cross of Christ, but also costly to us in that we must surrender ourselves to his having set us free from sin and thus from self-reliance in the reconciliation accomplished on the cross and revealed in his resurrection from the dead. It is worth noting that Torrance captures this point perfectly in a chapter titled "Cheap and Costly Grace"[21] when he rejects John A. T. Robinson's attempt to think about God by projecting mythological images from ourselves instead of thinking from a center in God himself as Jesus Christ actively reveals this to us. For this reason Robinson thinks of God "as the ground of our being." But "this is to think out of a centre in the depth of man rather than out of a centre in God himself,"[22] and this procedure makes it impossible to distinguish ourselves from God. Torrance identifies Robinson's ultimate mistake as allowing himself to be

> thrown back upon himself to give content to his notion of God, as what is of
> ultimate concern *for* him in the depth and significance of his own being. But
> when he does that by looking about for a new way of speaking about God that
> will satisfy that concern of his and so get the "God" that he wants, how can
> he avoid making God a predicate of himself or "using God" for his own ends
> and satisfactions, which is precisely the kind of "God" that Bonhoeffer ex-
> posed as idolatrous projection and that must be given up?[23]

This, Torrance says, is the kind of thinking that is out for "cheap grace," that is for the God people want, "one to suit themselves and modern 'secular' man, rather than the God of *costly grace* who calls for the renewing of our minds in which we are not schematized to the patterns of this world but are transformed in conformity with His own self-revelation in Jesus Christ."[24] Such thinking balks at Jesus Christ "where He asks them to renounce themselves, take up the cross and follow Him unreservedly all along the road to crucifixion and resurrection."[25]

The similarity between Torrance's thinking and Barth's is striking. And they are both right. Both theologians are employing the insight that grace cannot be detached from the living Word of God, that is, from the living Christ himself

---

[21]Torrance, *God and Rationality*, chap. 3.
[22]Ibid., p. 80.
[23]Ibid., pp. 81-82.
[24]Ibid., p. 82.
[25]Ibid.

and then understood. Whenever that happens, grace itself is cheapened. But the important point to be made here is that whenever grace is cheapened, then and there our human freedom, which is truly grounded in God's freedom for us as the one who created us and who distinguishes himself from us and frees us to live in dependence on him alone, is also cheapened and obscured.

God's Self-Disclosure—a "New" Reality

To return to the train of thought offered by Barth, we may draw this discussion to a close noting that the providence of God and the confusion of human beings can be understood properly only when God's grace is respected as his free and sovereign act of disclosing to us the truth itself as his own self-disclosing truth. It is free, Barth says, because "it finds its actualisation in the sovereign, divine-human acts of the life and death of Jesus Christ"; because "it is revealed in the resurrection of the same divine-human person of Jesus Christ"; because "as a Word spoken in the power of His Holy Spirit, who blows where He lists" he obviates the need and even the possibility of becoming "the object of speculation and disposition" (IV/3.2, p. 706). The grace of God that is addressed to the world in Jesus Christ in a unique way, as that which exists supremely, is addressed to us only "on the basis of God's eternal love and election and faithfulness as it was and is and will be event, inaccessible to all human or even Christian *hybris*, recognisable only in gratitude for the fact that it is real and true, and in prayer for ever new recognition of its reality and truth" (IV/3.2, pp. 706-7). Here Barth's emphasis on mystery and miracle is crucial once more because he insists that, whenever the grace of God is treated as something we can understand as if it were a problem set before us that we can solve by overcoming the antithesis between divine providence and human confusion, it will never be seen for what it is. "Where grace is actually present and active, it is enveloped by the mystery of its royal freedom" (IV/3.2, p. 707). Only if this is respected will human freedom be properly understood in this context. What difference does this thinking make for perceiving the truth of human freedom grounded in the divine freedom for us demonstrated in the history of Jesus Christ?

The community will recognize that there is no possibility of harmonizing the good, creative will of God with the confusion created by human sinners; there is in fact "no possibility of understanding the one as the basis of the

other, or the other as grounded in it" (IV/3.2, p. 708). The community lives
from a "new thing" in relation to the opposing situation of God the creator
and Lord of humanity and of world history and the confusion of fallen humanity creating havoc between them and God and their neighbors. It derives from this "new thing" that it did not and could not create. Indeed the
community has not discovered this new thing on its own and thus cannot
control it in any way. Rather this "new thing" has made itself known to the
community "as the work of God for the world and His Word to it" (IV/3.2,
p. 709). The community therefore lives in freedom as the community freed
from this antithesis precisely by attesting this "new thing" to the world. In
what might be called a specifically anti-Pelagian stance, Barth consistently
affirms that this "new thing" came to the community, enabling it to see and
hear the truth, and that the community did not come to it. It is thus truly
something new that occurs within world history, something that is "beyond
the antithesis" and yet within history as the first and final word concerning
it (IV/3.2, p. 709). What exactly is this new thing?

It is "the grace of God addressed to it [the community]" (IV/3.2, p. 709).
What the community knows, therefore, is that while the antithesis between
God the creator and Lord and humanity and a world marked by the fall and
by sin is not removed, and the seriousness of the conflict is not lessened; it
is "relativised, loosened and in a definite sense broken through by the fact
that God not only confronts the world as its Creator, Lord and Governor,
but in this great superiority of His has turned to it as gracious Father, that
apart from and even in spite of its deserts He is kind towards it in the free
omnipotence of His mercy" (IV/3.2, p. 709). Because of this, the world does
not just exist in a condition of confusion created by fallen creatures, but it
also exists under God's gracious address to it. This is the new thing that is
both an event and a revelation within history that may be known by all and
is in reality known by the community that lives by faith. Here the key point
to be noted is that grace alone effectively makes itself known as the grace of
God himself that strikes us in the midst of our human confusion and opens
up before us "a new heaven" from which God rules and acts towards us with
loving kindness, and indeed a "new earth" under heaven that exists because
of God's loving kindness. This is the new and positive "sign" that is given to
the community so that it may see "God and the world and therefore history"

(IV/3.2, p. 710). But as long as this "new thing" is described in the neutral category of a "thing" even as the grace of God described just now, it could easily become just another kind of human speculation about God, the world, humanity and history unless and until it is recognized in its identity with the "unique person of Jesus Christ" (IV/3.2, p. 710).

Here once again, the freedom of human beings to live by the assurance of grace and therefore to be able to attain true assurance, not a merely dialectical vacillation between acknowledging God's goodness on the one side and the confusion of humanity on the other, can be seen. But the assurance here is guaranteed only by the fact that grace itself is identical with the name of this person, that is, Jesus Christ himself. The "new thing" is the "grace of God addressed to the world in Him. And this 'in Him,' the name of Jesus Christ, indicates more than the means, instrument or vehicle used by God in addressing His grace to the world" (IV/3.2, p. 710). What difference does it make to hold the gift (grace) together with the Giver (Jesus Christ himself)? It means that we cannot look past him or through him to find God's gracious address to the world because he himself is "God, the Son of the Father, of one essence with Him. He is Himself God in His gracious address to the world. He is Himself the grace in which God addresses Himself and which He addresses to the world" (IV/3.2, p. 711).

This is a crucial point because in looking only to Jesus Christ as the grace of God to and for the world, Christians are prevented from looking upward or downward in an attempt to resolve the antithesis mentioned above. And what they actually recognize and realize is that by looking at Jesus Christ himself, his life, death and resurrection, they can see and understand the "true and radical alteration of this situation" (IV/3.2, p. 711). Jesus Christ himself is the "new person," the one in whom the entire human situation and world history itself have been altered. That is the grace of God active within history. Because Jesus Christ is no ideal or theory but is God himself acting as man and indeed as man who has fallen away from God and is thus subject to confusion, but also as the one man who does not acquiesce in that sin, we can see in him the resolution of this conflict. In Barth's words,

> The event indicated by the name of Jesus Christ and identical with His person
> is that the true Son of God, of one essence with the Father, has in this One
> assumed humanity, and very concretely this humanity, to unity with Himself,

that He not only became one with it and adopted its creaturely nature but took
to Himself its whole sin as though He had committed it and were its Author,
that in His death He bore it away instead, thus achieving in its place the obedience to the Father which the humanity of the first Adam had refused and
still refuses. (IV/3.2, pp. 711-12)

Here, then, is the only possibility of true human freedom—it is the freedom
of those who have been freed from sin to obey the God who is for them and
not against them in his Son Jesus Christ. In him the world is truly reconciled
with God; we are truly justified and sanctified in him. All people have been
justified and sanctified in him. And therefore it is in this human being who
is the Son of God acting as man for our benefit that human confusion is cut
off at its root and order has been restored. And it is in and through his Holy
Spirit that the power of his resurrection, in and through which our humanity
is corrected and reformed and not just illuminated within world history, that
we not only perceive this truth in faith but live it as we live in the free obedience of faith, hope and love as tied to him alone. Only a Christianity that
is blind, Barth says, could recognize theoretically that sin, the devil and
death really were overcome for the entire human race in the life, death and
resurrection of Jesus Christ and then act "as though everything were otherwise" (IV/3.2, p. 712).

The open secret is that in Jesus Christ "the transcendent God who yet
loves, elects and liberates the world and lowly man who is yet loved, elected
and liberated by Him, are indeed distinct and yet are not separated or two,
but one" (IV/3.2, p. 712). Moreover, the covenant between God and humanity "has not merely been kept by God and broken by man, but kept by
both, so that it is the fulfilled covenant" (IV/3.2, p. 712). This is an enormous
point that Torrance stresses throughout his work, namely, that God has not
only acted to justify and sanctify us in Jesus Christ from the divine side but
also from the human side. And because of this there is and never can be any
other mediator between us and God the Father in heaven or on earth. It is
always the case, Torrance rightly believed, that when Jesus' human mediation as the eternal Word acting in our place and thus for us in his priestly,
kingly and/or prophetic actions is displaced, that other mediators enter and
self-justification takes hold and suppresses our justification by grace and by
faith. Such thinking always pushes Jesus Christ himself as the only source

of truth and freedom to the side, and always does so by displacing the Holy Spirit from the picture by separating the Spirit from Jesus Christ and confusing the Holy Spirit with the human spirit. This can take many forms, from the search for other mediators to utter self-reliance in which each person himself or herself becomes their own mediator by relying on their own experiences of faith and hope.

Here the point is simply this:

> In Him there is not the clash of two kingdoms but the one kingdom of God in reality. This is the new thing which the Christian community has not sought and found at random, let alone invented in a fit of inspiration, but which has disclosed itself to it and by which it has thus been found as the Word or call of Jesus Christ has come to it and has been received by it. (IV/3.2, p. 712)

Notice that in Barth's thinking there really is never any separation of the humanity and divinity of Jesus Christ as the acting subject in reconciliation and redemption. It is never only the man Jesus acting here and now as revealer and reconciler. It is always the man Jesus acting as the Word because it is the Word acting as the man he is, representing us and enabling our freedom, as those who are who they now are in and from him alone. This is the grace of God addressed to the world, which stands within world history and before the witness of the community. Because of this it is the final thing the community has to say to the world exactly because it is at the same time the very first thing it must say; "it is the source from which it derives its own existence and life" (IV/3.2, p. 712).

In Jesus Christ, therefore, the new reality of world history exists so that the real test concerning whether Christians see and live this new reality is whether they simply keep to this fact and this alone. So the fact that it is in him that "world history really and properly takes place" is not just a new opinion or theory; rather "it is the work of deliverance and liberation which God Himself has accomplished and completed in and on the world, its reconciliation to Him" and therefore our justification and sanctification with him in the fulfilled covenant (IV/3.2, p. 713). Crucially, it is important to stress that the community does not see in Jesus Christ something that "might be, or ought to be, or one day will be." It sees "what is, what has come into being in Him and by Him" (IV/3.2, p. 713). Here Christianity stands or falls, because if the community did not have this to say to the world, then it would have nothing more to say to the world than what the world already knows of itself. But this really is the new thing that the community does have to say to the world, namely, that in Jesus Christ there is a genuinely completed alteration of the human situation that is identical with the coming of the kingdom in him. If the community either did not know or did not say to the world that this absolutely new thing, the lordship of God, was already established in world history, then it would have no advantage at all over the world and nothing new to say to the world.

But here the critical point must be made and held fast once more: that it is only in Jesus Christ that this new thing and new reality have appeared and therefore that "what has happened in Him has the dignity, power and validity of the *first* and *last thing* in world-occurrence" (IV/3.2, p. 713, emphasis mine). Even though this new thing may be hidden from the community and the world, it will come to light "as the reality of all history" (IV/3.2, p. 713). In the time between the revelation of this new reality in the resurrection of Jesus Christ and his second coming when this will come to light, there still remains the history in which there is the confusion of human beings and the providence of God. Why is this the case? Because Jesus Christ himself has not merged into world-occurrence, and world-occurrence has not merged into him—they remain two separate things. This very fact obviates any sort of Christomonism. The real Christomonism that Barth considered an "unlovely term" is the Christomonism that confuses Jesus' continued action as the risen and ascended Lord on his way from his resurrection to his return and thus to redemption, with world history itself. What might be the perfect example of what Barth is rejecting here? It is, I think, the example of Karl Rahner, who reached the astounding conclusion that self-acceptance is the same as accepting Jesus Christ and espoused the theory of anonymous Christianity that flows from that assumption.[26] Nothing could be further from the truth because the only possibility for our acceptance is the reality of reconciliation that has occurred in the life, death and resurrection of Jesus himself. And there is no such thing as an anonymous Christian because to be a Christian is to recognize explicitly what has happened in history in this particular history.

---

[26]See, e.g., Molnar, *Divine Freedom and the Doctrine of the Immanent Trinity: In Dialogue with Karl Barth and Contemporary Theology* (New York: T & T Clark, 2005), pp. 49-58 and *passim*.

But in light of this third way that acknowledges the new thing that has occurred in the history of Jesus Christ, the confusion of human beings and the providence of God lose the appearance of an irreconcilable antithesis or conflict "simply because God and man are still different even in their unity in Jesus Christ" (IV/3.2, p. 713). Pointing to Jesus Christ in this way, the twin character of world-occurrence "no longer points to a menacing abyss" so that "we are no longer tempted either to invoke a *Deus ex machina* or to bridge it by speculative or dialectical juggling" (IV/3.2, p. 713). Why is this the case? Simply because "The one Jesus Christ has already represented God to man and man to God." Jesus Christ "has already restored order between God and man and concluded peace between them" (IV/3.2, p. 713). What the community knows when it hears the Word of this man Jesus Christ, the risen Lord who was crucified, whose cross and empty tomb signify the fact that his life is the reality of world history in its twofold form because of what is accomplished by him and in him, is something the world does not know. This is something only known by the community. And this is the case because "His call, which underlies and sustains it [the community], has already made it known to it, and continually does so" (IV/3.2, p. 714). Here a proper distinction must be made because world history and the history of the people of God are not at an end; they haven't yet reached the goal of God's work. This, because even after the appearance of Jesus Christ time and history continue. But during this time and in this history the community proclaims "the Word of Jesus Christ and what has taken place in Him," and the world has time to "receive this Word; space for the history of the prophecy of Jesus Christ." This means, however, that the new reality of world history—the reconciliation of the world with God, the new creation as the new order between God and creation, the fulfilled covenant—"is known even to the community only in Jesus Christ and cannot therefore be known to the world which does not participate in the knowledge of Jesus Christ. It cannot be known" (IV/3.2, p. 714).

THE KINGDOM—NOW AND TO COME

Here, then, one can see with great clarity the difference between the knowledge of faith and knowledge that does not recognize or does not realize that Jesus Christ himself is the kingdom of God present in history and therefore the one in whom the new reality of world history has been created and exists; it is

present in him and "is lacking in nothing" (IV/3.2, p. 714). Without faith one
simply cannot see this third way—this new reality. One will therefore only see
the twofold antithesis between the confusion of humanity and the providence
of God apart from faith. "Apart from Jesus Christ Himself [this] is still the
hidden reality of world history. . . . To blind eyes it is not yet the new reality,
and to no eyes at all is it yet the new form of this new reality" (IV/3.2, p. 714).
Even though Barth admits that there are signs or intimations of this new reality in history, namely, signs "of the grace of God addressed to the world in
Jesus Christ," such as "the history of Holy Scripture, of the Church and of the
Jews," and even though the new reality itself might occasionally intimate itself
"as the first and final meaning of the whole even at what seems to be the farthest
remove from the occurrence of the specific history of salvation" (IV/3.2,
pp. 714-15), the fact remains that these cannot become and are not the foundation for knowledge of this new reality. This is the case because "they are
relevant only for those to whom the new reality of history has already made
itself known directly in a very different way" (IV/3.2, p. 715). In light of world
history itself, however, "neither Christians nor non-Christians could suspect
the reconciliation of the world to God in which the distinction between them
is robbed of the sting of division, nor the divine covenant with man fulfilled
by God Himself, nor the reconstituted order between the two, nor the kingdom
of God inaugurated" (IV/3.2, p. 715). Inklings concerning these facts, Barth
says, "are not to be restrained." But the community cannot be built on such
inklings without running the risk of "the radical defection of attempted
Christian philosophies of history and the related practical experiments"
(IV/3.2, p. 715). This cannot happen because the movement from faith to sight
is not something that the community can achieve; it is something it must await
as the act of Jesus Christ himself. One simply cannot yet see the kingdom of
God itself, that is, the new reality, "in world-occurrence itself" because even
now in the best of situations we can only see this "in that twofold form and
not in its true and proper sense" (IV/3.2, p. 715).

Here Barth is stressing the importance of seeing and understanding the new
creation in history, as it now exists between the time of Christ's resurrection
and second coming, with what Torrance calls "eschatological reserve." This is
required because "the kingdom for which we now pray will be its manifestation,
the final, universal and definitive manifestation of Jesus Christ and of what has

already taken place in Him," which for the community will be its "transition from faith to sight" (IV/3.2, p. 715). But there is a restriction here, and it is that in history as it exists at present, what has really and fully taken place in Jesus Christ, that is, the kingdom that has come, "is known only to the community, and to the community only in His appearance and person and *not in world-occurrence as such*" (IV/3.2, p. 715, emphasis mine). For that reason even the community has to pray for the coming of the kingdom. It is vital to recognize that this new reality, of the world reconciled with God, is not hidden to the community but is revealed and therefore is knowable in Jesus Christ, but only in him because it is revealed only by him as the one in whom God has acted both from the divine and human side to fulfill his covenant of grace. The community that does actually believe in him "does actually see in Him, in His appearance and person, the first and the last, the atonement already made in Him, the covenant already fulfilled, the order restored" (IV/3.2, p. 715). What the community sees and knows in this way is the new creation, the new heaven and the new earth "already given in relation to Him" (IV/3.2, p. 715). This distinguishes the community from the rest of the world, which does not participate in the knowledge of Jesus Christ and what has already become reality in him. And it is this very distinction "which capacitates it for witness to the world, and commits it to this witness" (IV/3.2, p. 715). This faith and knowledge take the form of obedience that accepts the fact that the new creation has already become reality in Jesus Christ and will be disclosed to all at his return. This faith and knowledge as obedience "is a resolute being and attitude and action" that distinguishes it as Christian action (IV/3.2, p. 716).

This means that Christians have a very definite confidence—a confidence "in Jesus Christ and Him alone" (IV/3.2, p. 716). Christians see in world history no more than others the conflict between light and darkness, between God and creation caused by sin, and so they see very clearly, even more clearly than others, "the antithesis between the rule of God and the confusion of men. But it sees the same things differently" (IV/3.2, pp. 716-17). And that difference is that the community can always behave with complete confidence in the fact that for all appearances the world is already reconciled to God in Jesus Christ. Yet the community will have no illusions—it will not, for instance, share

the enthusiasm of those who regard the old form [of history which has been judged, removed and outmoded as the passing form of this world] as capable of true and radical improvement nor the skepticism of those who in view of the impossibility of perfecting the old form think they are compelled to doubt the possibility of a new form. (IV/3.2, p. 717)

The community is not called to judge others because it is "sure of the one fact that Jesus Christ has lived and died and risen again for them too" (IV/3.2, p. 717). And because this is true, Christians are not left to themselves in face of the virtues, accomplishments, faults, blasphemies and even crimes of human beings, but have confidence that "the demolition and rebuilding [of humanity] which have already taken place in Jesus Christ and only wait to be manifested in the world on behalf of which they have been accomplished" is the very confidence with which they are to confront the world and history, which do not share in this. It cannot fear the humanity that continues to act as though none of this has already taken place. It cannot hate this humanity, either, Barth says, because it can only love and therefore only be for humanity "since God in Jesus Christ is and has decided for them. It [the community] cannot be *anti*, i.e., against even individuals" (IV/3.2, pp. 717-18). This confidence is not something that is discussed or debated because it is simply not "marketable." Nor does the community "resolve to maintain it." This is the case because, as the community called by Jesus Christ himself, as it knows him, it also knows that "the decision has been made for it. It has no option but to maintain it. In all the necessity of its commitment to and orientation on Him, it can do no other" (IV/3.2, p. 718). That is how the community lives in confidence in face of the present antithesis between light and darkness. This implies that the community cannot simply act as a spectator might in face of world affairs, taking a position

> high above the antithesis between God and sinful man. All mere meditation or discussion for discussion's sake is now ruled out. Serving both the glory of God and the salvation of man, the decision taken in Him is unequivocally and definitively a decision for the world government of God and therefore against the confusion of men, for the good creation of God and therefore against nothingness. (IV/3.2, p. 718)

This, because fallen human beings who have fallen away from God, fallen out with their neighbors and caused great confusion in world occurrence, have been done away with in the obedient life, death and resurrection of Jesus

Christ himself. "A new man, free in obedience to God, has been born and introduced. The act of God in Jesus Christ is a clear decision for this new man living at peace with God and therefore honouring the goodness of His creation" (IV/3.2, p. 718). This decision the community sees, keeps and follows in the sphere of world history in active obedience and not as an inactive spectator.

THE ENABLING OF THE HOLY SPIRIT

But how exactly does this happen? It happens when the Holy Spirit enables us to live our justification and sanctification, which is real only in Christ and therefore only in union with Christ and only in faith. Here a proper theological anthropology is discerned and can be seen as pivotal in understanding that true humanity has been established once and for all in Jesus Christ himself and that all really are elect in him, but also rejected in the sense that they can only live by grace and therefore in gratitude for the freedom granted them in him as the one who experienced God's judgment in our place. In this way he obeyed God in his vicarious life of obedience, and through his Spirit we are enabled to live as those who have been freed to do so by him; indeed he himself is present now in his Spirit as the enabling power (the power of his own resurrection) to empower us to live as part of the new creation. The problem, however, is that all people, including Christians (and Christians see just this when they understand their sinful nature that has been changed in the reconciliation of God in Jesus Christ) continue to resist grace inexplicably and thus to live as those who slip back into doing the impossible possibility (sin) in the form of sloth, which expresses human unbelief most forcefully in "the rejection of the man Jesus" (IV/2, p. 406).

This is an important insight. For very few people do not absolutely oppose the idea of a "supreme being," or the idea of being committed to such a being, or the idea that there is something that transcends us or even the idea that we should enter into some sort of relation with this transcendent other. Most people, as Barth rightly observes, "will never seriously or basically reject altogether religion or piety in one form or another, nor will [they] finally or totally cease to exercise or practise them in open or disguised form" (IV/2, p. 406). In reality it is quite the opposite. The very tendency by people to "escape to religion, to adoring faith in a congenial higher being, is the purest and ripest and most appropriate possibility at which [someone] grasps in [that person's]

sloth" (IV/2, p. 406). This is a powerful articulation of Barth's own understanding of the *simul justus et peccator*; we are righteous, free and sanctified
in Jesus Christ now and to eternity—but unless we live in that freedom in and
through the Spirit of Christ, we continue to rely on ourselves (and thus on our
sinful nature that has been radically eliminated in Christ and only in Christ).
It has been changed or eliminated, and as long as we live, as Torrance might
say, from a center in ourselves instead of from a center in God (incarnate in
his Son and present in his Spirit) we continue to live as those who are in conflict with our true selves as revealed and as truly actualized in Jesus himself.

But how then can it become clear to us that we really do reject God
himself by rendering him innocuous in religion and piety as we submit to a
"supreme being"? This happens only when this rejection becomes fully serious and weighty. And this occurs finally and decisively "when man definitely will not accept in relation to himself the reality and presence and
action of God in the existence of the man Jesus, and the claim of God which
they involve" (IV/2, p. 406). They do not accept these as God's real presence
and action here and now "which refer absolutely and exclusively and totally
and directly to him, and make on him an absolute, exclusive, total and direct
demand" (IV/2, p. 406). These are extremely forceful words because what
they demonstrate is that all people, including Christians, tend to resist exactly this—the fact that they are claimed exclusively and absolutely by God
himself in the man Jesus and only in him. How many people today are
perfectly willing to see in Jesus an important illustration of what it means
to sacrifice humanly for others so that they may also claim that wherever
such human self-sacrifice is present there too we find God actively present
for us? A "supreme being" might tolerate us. And it certainly will allow us
to remain undisturbed and to an extent at peace. It will never question us or
disturb us because it will always be tolerated by us. But when we are confronted by God in Jesus Christ we find that we are truly offended and not
tolerated as we are! We are not confirmed in our search for a "supreme being"
and for a peace that takes the form of an equilibrium stemming from our
relation to this self-chosen idea of God. In him we are offended because we
are "basically illuminated and radically questioned and disturbed and
therefore offended by the deity of God in the concrete phenomenon of the
existence of this man" (IV/2, p. 406). To put the matter bluntly and directly:

human rejection of God in its most unequivocal form "finds expression" in one's "relation to this man. Tested in this way, he will unhesitatingly avoid God even as the religious or pious man." But this means that "he will unhesitatingly resist God" (IV/2, p. 406).

The problem with sin as sloth, then, is the fact that we hesitate to accept the free grace of God, the freedom that is already ours in Jesus Christ, because we are offended at the fact that God has acted in this decisive way by loving us as the true and living God exclusively in the human phenomenon of Jesus Christ. Our sloth, namely, our inaction, hesitation and withdrawal into ourselves in confrontation with the man Jesus, signifies that we wish to choose to will for ourselves who we should be, what our vocation should be. But this is a choice that God in Christ has not left and does not leave to us, since it always leads back to sin, unbelief, pride, sloth, untruth (even to ourselves). We sinful human beings do not want to be disturbed in making our free choice of the God we want and of the life we want to live. But it is we who are now, and always will be, disturbed by the God who has the name of Jesus Christ. When we come face to face with the will of God in this man, we come "to the frontier which [we] can cross only if [we] will give up [ourselves] and [our] congenial deities and find God and [ourselves] in this Other" (IV/2, p. 407).

Vocation

Barth's understanding of human vocation, as the clearest expression of his developed theological anthropology, is still compelling today. It pinpoints and expresses divine and human freedom in a way that sees the problem of sin only because it sees its true solution from the divine and human side as executed by God in Jesus Christ. It also pointedly sees that human vocation means preeminently to be called by this Jesus Christ and empowered to live as his witness in different historical circumstances according to God's will, which frees people to exercise their free self-determination in diverse ways.

> No matter where, when or how it occurs, vocation is thus the work of God or Jesus Christ towards man in time, itself a temporal work. That it is God or Jesus Christ who calls makes the vocation of man, no matter where or when or how it occurs, an act of powerful grace and gracious power different from every other act. (IV/3.2, p. 497)

This calling comes into history from outside in the history of Jesus as God's call in the history of Israel and of Jesus himself. In virtue of his resurrection, Jesus becomes the contemporary of each of us in our own histories, which never become identical with his. This insight is of paramount importance because here one must never confuse the Holy Spirit with the human spirit.

Briefly put, the point here is this. Whenever the objective elements of Christian knowledge and dogmatics are marginalized, as they necessarily are when our focus on the truth of God's grace and love is sought in piety and religion instead of in revelation and faith (in Jesus Christ, not in ourselves), then theology becomes abstract as an anthropology that in a certain sense reached its zenith in the thinking of Schleiermacher (cf. IV/3.2, p. 498). In this way a proper doctrine of the Trinity, election (predestination) and Christology become and have become marginalized. Here, as Barth wisely points out, we must learn once again that "the Holy Spirit is the Lord and Master of the Christian spirit and not simply identical with it, and that the Word of God is His Word and therefore cannot be understood merely as the self-declaration of the Christian spirit" (IV/3.2, p. 498). It is in this way that Barth rightly wanted to avoid what he called "Christianocentrism," namely, a theology that really is self-grounded rather than grounded in the action of the Holy Spirit and therefore in the Word of God active and present in the risen Lord himself. It is right to react against this "anthropocentric" theology. But it is wrong to overreact so that one might conclude that vocation as an event that occurs in human history has only to do with some transcendentalized existence beyond and above history. It is important to note here, as Barth himself did, that

> The object and theme of theology and the content of the Christian message is neither a subjective nor an objective element in isolation. That is to say, it is neither an isolated man nor an isolated God, but God and man in their divinely established and effected encounter, the dealings of God with the Christian and the Christian with God. (IV/3.2, p. 498)

God's work on us does not merely touch us from beyond and thus from without; it is necessary that our vocation take place here and now within history and not simply as a foreordination or predisposition. We must not think docetically here, Barth rightly insists: "To do this is tantamount to thinking that the star which guided the wise men to Bethlehem finally shone upon an empty manger"

(IV/3.2, p. 498). God's being does not just hover over us like a "soap-bubble," but it leads to something that really happens in us so that "there is a Christian ordination and disposition of man's being in time" (IV/3.2, p. 498).

CONCLUDING REMARKS

We close this chapter by noting that none of this can be known and explicated without faith in the Word of God incarnate in Jesus Christ and thus without the enabling power of the Holy Spirit uniting us to the risen, ascended and coming Lord. None of this can be controlled by us. This grace of God was actualized in the election of Jesus Christ and the realization of our reconciliation in his life, death and resurrection. This was a miracle, and it remains a miraculous action of the Holy Spirit even now when it occurs in our history in the manner just described. It is a miracle because it cannot be explained from the human side but can only be acknowledged and then understood in a way that demonstrates exactly what it means to live in freedom and thus as part of the new creation as it is a reality in the new humanity of Jesus himself. We might say at this point, then, that it is important to stress the Holy Spirit, who enlightens us about the fact that all time and history are "potentially the time of grace" and salvation because the Lord of all time and history, Jesus Christ himself, "the Mediator and Prophet of grace and salvation, is actually on the way to His goal, namely, to His victory in His conclusive self-declaration" (IV/3.2, p. 500). Our vocation or calling by this Jesus "is not merely internal but external; it is not merely spiritual but moral, social and political; it is not merely invisible but also visible" (IV/3.2, p. 500). But this is a spiritual process that can be described only in and through the Holy Spirit because "As the Spirit of the Father and the Son He is the power of the Gospel itself to call and enlighten and sanctify and preserve man in the true faith" (IV/3.2, p. 501). Importantly, then, "The only free God, who is the Father of Jesus Christ, is the Creator and basis of all freedom worthy of the name" (III/3, p. 130). Any supposed freedom that might suggest that the creature is wholly independent of *this* God would open the door to the idea that we must look to "a field of force or a system of norms instead of to Him!" (III/3, p. 131). But this is what must never happen, because it is not God as a first cause whose power then could be equated with the natural law or some other cosmic law who is our God; it is the Father of Jesus Christ who is the Lord over all things, and this particular God is omnipotent precisely in his faithfulness to us. Hence this God does not let go of us and does not allow us to fall

> not for a single moment or in any respect. This God does not allow Himself to be mocked or trifled with. This God has taken into His own hands the relationship between Himself and the creature, and he has no time for representatives or vice-regents. *This God is directly present to the creature always and in all places by the Holy Spirit.* (III/3, p. 131, emphasis mine)

Conclusion

As noted in the Preface, my aim was to explore divine and human relations within the economy with a proper emphasis on the Holy Spirit and therefore on faith, grace and revelation. I wanted to demonstrate exactly how and why experience of and knowledge of God take on an entirely different character and meaning when they never attempt to move outside the sphere of faith in God's Word and Spirit. As the title of the book suggests, I intended to stress that the freedom of Christians is enabled by God's freedom for us in his Word and Spirit. Hence, it is a freedom that is actualized in faith as enabled by the Holy Spirit. It is a freedom grounded in God's eternal election as the election of the triune God. To those who sincerely believe that some apologetic approach to theology built on general human experience, history, psychology, sociology or philosophy is required before engaging in a strictly dogmatic theology, this book will certainly offer a challenge—the challenge to see the difference between a theology that is deliberately unwilling to base its reflections on anyone or anything other than God himself as confessed in the Nicene Creed.

In order to accomplish that goal I deliberately stressed the need to focus on the Holy Spirit as the enabling condition of both faith and knowledge of God. With a clear view of the Holy Spirit I have argued that one not only may but must speak clearly and precisely about our human experience of God within the economy. My aim was not to forget what was learned about the importance of the doctrine of the immanent Trinity. This, because it is only when the God of whom we speak in the economy is recognized as the eternal Father, Son and Holy Spirit who has his life in himself as the one who loves in freedom that we are able to recognize and to speak forcefully of this God as the one who can and does act in the sovereign freedom of his grace as creator, reconciler and redeemer. But, having learned why it is vital to recognize that the God who is for us, Emmanuel, has his own unique self-sufficient existence, one can then understand that God's presence within history interacting with us is a very particular presence that is actualized and maintained in his Word and Spirit. Consequently, any theological reflections on our relationship with God as it takes place within history must clearly articulate who God is in himself in order to speak clearly about who God is for us and what God actually is doing here and now.

Anyone who is familiar with my approach to theology will know immediately and see again in this book that I find Karl Barth's thinking extremely helpful. Not only among contemporary theologians does his thinking stand out as among the most rigorous and helpful, but he ranks as one of the truly great theologians of history. His thinking has great ecumenical significance, since his theology was meant to be a dogmatics for the entire church, Catholic and Protestant. It has been said that in him for the first time the Protestant Reformation was able to speak with clarity not only to Protestant colleagues but to Catholic theologians. And according to Thomas F. Torrance, Pope Paul VI spoke of Karl Barth as the greatest theologian since Thomas Aquinas.[1] That is certainly high praise, and it is praise that is justified by the monumental contributions Barth made to theology in the twentieth century. And if Torrance is right in counting Barth's theology among the greatest in church history, that is, among the great theologians such as Augustine, Athanasius, Thomas Aquinas and John Calvin, then I think he is also right to say that Barth's theology has had a greater impact on the Roman Catholic church than "four hundred years of Protestantism."[2] Having said this, one can see why I chose to rely heavily on the thinking of Karl Barth in order to explicate the themes treated in this book. Since I am not simply presenting the theology of Karl Barth in this book, I also turned to the thinking of Torrance himself, who, as a student of Karl Barth, understood his work as well as anyone and

---

[1]Thomas F. Torrance, *Karl Barth, Biblical and Evangelical Theologian* (Edinburgh: T & T Clark, 1990), pp. 1 and 26.
[2]Ibid., p. 1.

who was not afraid to raise critical questions to Barth's thinking where appropriate. What we have seen in this book is that Torrance can and does help theologians today appreciate both Barth's strengths and some of his weaknesses. But he also helps us see with great clarity why it is fruitful to think about God only from a center in God and therefore never from a center in ourselves.[3] That is the basic theme that runs through this work. Whenever theologians allow history and experience to dictate the content of Christian theology, then and to that extent God's grace and revelation tend to become dependent on and indistinguishable from our experience within the economy. This, one might even say, is still one of the burning issues in contemporary theology, as can be seen by some of the very different interpretations of Barth's theology that are discussed in the text.

Following my stated method, then, I began the discussion with an extensive and detailed analysis of faith and the knowledge of God. I followed the premise that if theology simply focused on one center, namely, God and thus was resolved into a mere teaching about God's action in relation to us, it would become, as Barth put it, "metaphysics," that is, a teaching about a God who could be known by analyzing being with the intention of equating the results of that analysis with God himself (some version of an *analogia entis*). On the one hand, such thinking might leave us with a God who is far removed from us in our experiences within history, with the result that we would be left to ourselves to define and redefine our view of God in order to make sense of history. Or it might leave us with a God who is ultimately indistinguishable from us, in which case there would be no true knowledge of God at all—anyone or anything could be divine. On the other hand, a theology that sought to resolve itself only into a teaching about our action in relation to God and thus into a pure teaching of the Spirit would end in mysticism, or in the attempt to know God directly by reflecting on our experiences instead of knowing God as the one who chose to make himself known mediately through

---

[3]Thinking from a center in God of course does not mean we have to reach beyond the sphere of history and experience to know God. Indeed, this cannot possibly happen since God has come into history in the incarnation to enable us to know him from the center in God present in his Word and Spirit within history and experience. That is why Torrance could argue that without the resurrection there would be no true knowledge of God. This is the opposite of Karl Rahner's claim that the main approach to faith is "a man's direct confrontation with himself." Such thinking only leads to the idea that self-acceptance is the same as accepting Christ. And this too is the opposite of a theology that thinks from a center in God.

history as attested in the Old and New Testament witness and through his own incarnation in history in Jesus Christ himself. I have chosen to argue that a proper theology of the Holy Spirit would allow us to begin with a focus on human experience. But I began by stressing that such a theology is always a theology that makes it clear that we are brought face to face with God by God himself, who graciously acts as the one who loves us not only as creator but as reconciler and redeemer. Since the Holy Spirit is decisive in such reflections, I have argued that the only way for that to be recognized is by understanding that the Spirit is the Spirit of the Word, and so the true center of theology must always be Jesus Christ himself, the very Word of God speaking and acting even here and now as the risen, ascended and advent Lord. Through the miraculous action of the Holy Spirit, who is *homoousion* with the Son and with the Father, we have access to God and thus we experience God and come to know God in faith. Hence one can say with Barth that knowledge of God is indeed an event enclosed within the mystery of the Trinity.

It is within this context that, while I noted some formal similarities in statements made by both Barth and Rahner, I still needed to explain why I could not accept Rahner's apologetic approach to theology and then demonstrate exactly the differences in emphasis and insight that follow from a more consistently theological approach. The main differences between Barth and Rahner concern the fact that Rahner thinks one can and must find some verification for the truth of faith within human experience, while Barth insists that such verification comes from the Holy Spirit uniting us to Christ and thus to the Father. I explained why I thought Barth's position makes more sense because he takes sin and the need for reconciliation seriously. By that I meant that, in light of the cross and resurrection, he recognized that we have no capacity to relate with the triune God because, as a result of the fall and humanity's rejection of Christ that led to the cross, we are shown to be God's enemies who, in spite of their rejection of Christ, are reconciled to God only by God's free grace as disclosed in the resurrection itself. That means that to know God is to allow God's reconciling grace to determine the truth of what is said about God and ourselves all along the line. This cannot happen when some effort to justify faith is attempted from a point outside or apart from the object of faith itself, which alone justifies and sanctifies us in all our self-determinations.

Consequently, this cannot happen when it is thought, with Rahner, that one can have an anonymous knowledge of God in Christ or an anonymous experience of the resurrection or that one can or must construct an a priori anthropology in order to make belief in Jesus reasonable. Such thinking is akin to the thinking of Paul Tillich, which, as we saw, equated knowledge of God with knowledge of ourselves at the deepest level. This amounted to what Torrance categorized as non-conceptual symbolic knowledge of God, which in his view amounted to an unscientific view of God, that is, one that was not shaped by the nature of the true God confessed by Christians in the Nicene Creed. That is why both Torrance and Barth argued firmly against any sort of unthematic or non-conceptual knowledge of God. Any such approach denies the mediated knowledge of God that comes to us in the specific form of revelation in its identity with the historical Jesus and the testimonies to him offered in Scripture and made effective through the Holy Spirit. The main point of that first chapter was to illustrate exactly what theological knowledge that is completely dependent on grace and the action of the Holy Spirit looks like. One does not have to be a fideist to think about the truth of our experience of God in this way. Indeed one cannot possibly be a fideist to hold this position because faith is knowledge of the truth that comes from the truth itself and therefore is not blind obedience without insight, knowledge or understanding that is simply rendered as an emotional response or an act of will. It is instead an act that includes our acknowledgment, recognition and confession.

Within this framework, I then offered a detailed description of what an understanding of God that takes place on the basis of a properly functioning pneumatology looks like. Here I argued that while everyone has some natural knowledge of God, in light of the revelation of God in Jesus Christ and through his Spirit, we know that we cannot rely on such knowledge in order to know God accurately and in truth. Natural theology is always a theology that is built on the "sinking sand" of a knowledge untouched by the recognition of our justification and sanctification as these have already occurred for us in the life, death and resurrection of Jesus himself. Again, that is why faith is necessary. But this necessary faith is not a general characteristic of humanity. Rather it is a gift of the Holy Spirit that unites us to Christ and thus to the Father. I therefore argued that whenever it is supposed that natural theology and revealed theology mutually condition each other, there and then a proper theology, which can only consist in faith in the very Word of God in its identity with the man Jesus Christ, becomes distorted and confused. Then, nature and grace as well as reason and revelation become confused, and humanity once again is directed to itself instead of to God the revealer and reconciler for true knowledge of God and knowledge of our reconciliation with God and with our neighbor. Any such thinking, I have argued, will never be able to recognize or understand the real meaning of divine or human freedom since human freedom is the freedom that is enabled by God the reconciler and redeemer. From this it follows that even those theologians who do explicitly recognize that Christian theology must find its center in Christ through his Holy Spirit but still imply, suggest or claim that history in some sense constitutes who Jesus Christ was and is, miss some of the most important aspects of divine and human freedom.

With this last insight in mind, therefore, I considered divine freedom once again as I had in my first book, *Divine Freedom and the Doctrine of the Immanent Trinity*. But this time I explored in detail some of the criticisms of what I said in that previous work to explain why I believe those criticisms were not only unfounded but why they were criticisms that stemmed from a misunderstanding of some of Karl Barth's most central insights. In this context I addressed an issue that only received scant attention in my 2002 book on the Trinity, namely, the proper relation between election and God's triunity. My initial argument that one cannot logically reverse election and the Trinity without doing serious damage both to our knowledge of Christ's true deity and humanity and to our knowledge of God's eternal being as Father, Son and Holy Spirit was correct. But it clearly needed further discussion—discussion that has ensued over the last twelve years or so. In order to take this discussion seriously and to advance it beyond a mere shouting back and forth of proponents of opposite views, I spent a good deal of time exploring what I take to be the main issues involved in the discussion, and showing how and why I think those who still believe that Barth should have logically reversed the doctrines of election and the Trinity are simply out of step with his own thought. Today there is wide agreement that this is an accurate position. In spite of this, however, I have explained why I think that those theologians who want to move beyond Barth and argue for some version of the idea that there is a sense in which creation is necessary to God or that the eternal Word is transformed by virtue of the incarnation are mistaken. Any such thinking obscures the reality of God's grace and revelation, and undermines God's freedom for us as well as our human freedom, which is enabled only by God himself. In this vein I explained why I thought that those whose thinking allows for such ideas tend to continue to open the door to subordinationism and to modalism in their understanding of the triune God, in spite of their belief that they have avoided these difficulties.

Relying on the thought of Thomas F. Torrance, I then proceeded to explain exactly how and why I believe that his understanding of the doctrine of election is one that not only respects God's freedom *in se* and God's free actions for us in the economy, but one that can actually point us beyond the impasse evident in the current discussion of the relation of the doctrines of election and the Trinity. I identified the chief issue here as the reemergence of a kind of Origenism, because those who embrace the thinking implied in the logical reversal of these doctrines, even if they explicitly recognize the theoretical problem in this reversal, always tend to confuse God's internal being with his external actions. Expressed differently, they always confuse the missions with the processions, thus reducing the latter to the former. Torrance's thinking is immensely helpful in that he demonstrates what a proper understanding of time and eternity might look like if we are willing to acknowledge that God's eternal being does not exclude time but includes time as it is in God in an utterly unique sense, because God is not limited by created time or by the opposition of past, present and future. Yet within God there is a before and an after, such that while God was always Father and always Son, he was not always creator and not always incarnate. This idea of a before and after in God's time should not be confused with the notion that there might be a *prius* and *posterius* in the eternal relations of the trinitarian persons. As we have seen this is an idea that Torrance consistently rejects.

Based on these important insights and the critical distinctions that follow (such as the distinctions between the eternal Person of the Son/Word and his existence as the Word who became incarnate for us and for our salvation), I argued that both creation and incarnation must be seen as *new* actions, *new* even for God, to make sense of the doctrines of Christology and of atonement. All thinking marked by the notion that God in some sense needs creation, is

constituted by his relations with us in history, or that God needs us as his
creatures within the created world misses this important insight and always
presents God's being as somehow dependent on his relations with us. In this
book I consistently reject any such thinking, because it not only obscures
who God is in himself, but it makes impossible any genuine recognition of
God's actions as free actions of love occurring within history for our benefit.
My point in this fourth chapter was to illustrate that one can and must say
that what God is toward us in the economy, God is eternally in himself.
Hence, there is no God behind the back of Jesus Christ—since he *is* God
acting for us in history. But this important insight is lost when the miracle of
the incarnation is undermined with the idea that the eternal being of the
Word was somehow constituted by the humanity he assumed through the
power of the Holy Spirit when he was born of the Virgin Mary, and perhaps
even prior to that in his eternal act of election.

Closely connected with the issues that arose in connection with the problematic reemergence of a kind of twenty-first-century Origenism, I then
compared the thinking of Thomas F. Torrance, Robert Jenson and Bruce
McCormack, focusing on one very specific issue in order to illustrate my
point that when history is allowed to shape who Jesus is as the eternally
begotten Son of the Father, then problems arise for theologians attempting
to conceptualize God's free actions for us within the economy. That specific
issue, of course, was and is the question of whether and how we should think
of the *Logos asarkos*. With the help of Torrance's more traditional Christology, I pointed out some of the perils involved in embracing a "historicized" Christology, namely, a Christology that attempts to explain Jesus'
uniqueness either by explicitly rejecting the notion of a *Logos asarkos*
(Jenson) or by reducing the *Logos asarkos* to the *Logos incarnandus* (Mc-
Cormack). Both of these views, I argued, led to confused and confusing
statements about Jesus' true divinity and true humanity. I then proposed
that confusion could be avoided if we followed the thinking of Torrance,
who escaped the errors of suggesting either that Jesus' deity is the outcome
of his human life on earth or that the subject of the incarnation is the God-
man precisely because he distinguished Jesus' existence as the eternal Word,
through whom God created the world, from his eternal existence as the
divine-human mediator, who exists eternally in God's eternal decree but

only exists eternally in his divine and human being after the incarnation as the incarnate, risen, ascended and advent Lord. In other words, Torrance did not reduce the processions of the trinitarian persons to the missions of the Word and Spirit acting in the economy.

Following this important discussion, I focused on just how Barth's early and later Christology should be understood, because it has been suggested that Barth's rather firm assertion that God's Word would still be God's Word even without the incarnation and that the Father, Son and Holy Spirit would have been no less divine even if God never decided to create, needed to be retracted in light of his later Christology. This issue has become something of a flashpoint among contemporary theologians. With respect to Barth's own theology, there is an internal debate among Barth scholars about whether he changed this earlier view. I take the position, based on the evidence that I present, that Barth not only never changed his view regarding this matter, but that it is precisely because he was able to recognize and maintain the fact that God could have been the triune God he eternally is even without us that he was able to present a powerful understanding of human freedom based on God's freedom for us in his grace and thus in the actions of his Word and Spirit in the economy. Had Barth rejected his earlier view, he then would have undermined what I take to be one of his most significant insights, namely, that Jesus' divinity must be recognized as definitive, authentic and essential if incarnation, reconciliation and redemption, as well as the actions of the Holy Spirit, are to make sense in a way that accords with the Nicene faith.

Still focusing on our relations with God in the economy, I then proceeded to explore exactly how Karl Barth and Thomas F. Torrance conceptualized the obedience of the Son. This is and remains a pivotal issue for contemporary theologians, because while I believe that all theologians would want to say with Torrance and Barth that what God is toward us, he is eternally in himself, everything depends on how that is conceptualized. For instance, Torrance did accept Rahner's axiom concerning the identity of the immanent and economic Trinity. But he also believed, as I noted in my previous book on the doctrine of the Trinity, that Rahner had introduced logical necessities into his understanding of the Trinity. In this book, I do not focus on Rahner's thinking at this point but on the thinking of Karl Barth in order to explain how and why I believe he mistakenly read back elements of the economy into the immanent Trinity. This occurs with his claim that the obedience of the Son as an act of condescension for us had to imply that there was an eternal obedience and thus some sort of subordination or *prius* and *posterius* in the eternal relations of the trinitarian persons on the basis of which he could be for us the obedient Son in the economy. With the help of key distinctions provided by Torrance, I explain why it is so very important for theologians today not to confuse the order of the persons within the Trinity with their being, by introducing some idea of causality or hierarchy into the immanent Trinity. I argued that that is exactly what happened to Barth at that point in his thinking and that Torrance shows us the way forward with a more consistent and precise understanding that allows us to see that the very Son of God can and does become obedient to the Father in his mission of condescension to act for us as the reconciler. Thus one does not have to embrace any kind of modalism by holding the view that God himself could not be obedient in the incarnation and act as man for us in reconciling us to the Father. For both theologians it was imperative to hold both to the idea that God himself experienced our suffering and death because he acted in obedience to the Father as God and as man and that he did so to remove these threats from us. All of this I argued could and should be recognized. But this can only be recognized with clarity if and to the extent that we acknowledge that God's gracious act of condescension for us is grounded in the mystery of God's free love within the eternal Trinity. In other words, one does not have to read back super- and subordination into the immanent Trinity in order to make that quite proper assertion.

Finally, in order to illustrate how human beings may live in freedom within the economy on the basis of God's actions for us in his Word and Spirit, I concluded the book by presenting a detailed description of what human freedom under the Word might look like when the activity of the Holy Spirit in union with God the Father and Son is noted and emphasized. In that final chapter I discussed in detail how the doctrine of justification by faith relates to the living of the Christian life in the power of the Spirit. Here too I relied on the thinking of Thomas F. Torrance and of Karl Barth to stress that human freedom is the freedom to live by the grace of God. But living by the grace of God, I argue, cannot be done cheaply or easily, because it is not something within our power or under our control. To live by grace means literally to surrender ourselves to

God in Christ, who alone, through his Spirit, can enable us to live as he intended us to live—as his free and joyous covenant partners.

Because of the problem of sin and the need for reconciliation, we are utterly dependent on the Holy Spirit to actualize God's reconciling action that took place once for all in the history of Jesus, the incarnate Word, in us here and now. How does one know that he or she is acting in and through the Holy Spirit? The answer is that one can only know that to the extent that one exists explicitly in union with Christ himself. Any talk of human freedom, therefore, as in any way self-grounded, or any claim to have the Spirit that results in thinking or acting that separates the Spirit from Christ in any way, shape or form, will be clear evidence that one is not in reality speaking of the Holy Spirit confessed by Christians in the Nicene Creed. Any confusion of the Holy Spirit with the human spirit that might then refer us to our own self-experience as the basis for speaking about God, revelation, grace or reconciliation will be clear evidence that one is not in reality speaking of the Holy Spirit. One simply cannot know God and relate with God by equating knowledge of God or love of God with love of one's neighbor. Love of neighbor, I argue, necessarily follows from love of God. But such love is not a means for loving God, since that would only be another form of self-justification. This chapter provides a nice finish to the book because it indicates in detail how and why it is so important never to detach who God his from his being and action in the incarnate Word. Whenever that happens, either theoretically or practically, then and there true knowledge of both divine and human freedom becomes impossible because then, as the sinners we are apart from our new being in Christ, we hide behind the idea that God is a "supreme being" in order to secure freedom for ourselves, thus avoiding the true freedom that is freely given and thus already ours in Christ and through his Spirit. Positively stated, the point of this book was and remains that we really can have experience of God's saving grace, and indeed we must have this if we are to know the true meaning of divine and human freedom. But we can and do have this only in faith as the Holy Spirit enables us to live as those we already are in Jesus Christ himself and thus through union with the living Christ. That is why prayer for the coming of the Holy Spirit is so central and necessary for living the Christian life.

Select Bibliography

Aquinas, Thomas. *Summa Contra Gentiles*. Translated by Anton C. Pegis. New York: Doubleday, 1955.

Athanasius. *A Select Library of Nicene and Post-Nicene Fathers of the Christian Church*. Vol. IV, *St. Athanasius: Select Works and Letters*. Translated by Philip Schaff and Henry Wace. Edinburgh: T & T Clark, 1987.

Barth, Karl. *Church Dogmatics*. 4 vols. in 13 pts.

———. Vol. I, pt. 1. *The Doctrine of the Word of God*. Edited by G. W. Bromiley and T. F. Torrance. Translated by G. W. Bromiley. Edinburgh: T & T Clark, 1975.

———. Vol. I, pt. 2. *The Doctrine of the Word of God*. Edited by G. W. Bromiley and T. F. Torrance. Translated by G. T. Thomson and Harold Knight. Edinburgh: T & T Clark, 1970.

———. Vol. II, pt. 1. *The Doctrine of God*. Edited by G. W. Bromiley and T. F. Torrance. Translated by T. H. L. Parker, W. B. Johnston, H. Knight and J. L. M. Harie. Edinburgh: T & T Clark, 1964.

———. Vol. II, pt. 2. *The Doctrine of God*. Edited by G. W. Bromiley and T. F. Torrance. Translated by G. W. Bromiley, J. C. Campbell, Iain Wilson, J. Strathearn McNab, Harold Knight and R. A. Stewart. Edinburgh: T & T Clark, 1967.

———. Vol. III, pt. 1. *The Doctrine of Creation*. Edited by G. W. Bromiley and T. F. Torrance. Translated by J. W. Edwards, O. Bussey and Harold Knight. Edinburgh: T & T Clark, 1970.

———. Vol. III, pt. 2. *The Doctrine of Creation*. Edited by G. W. Bromiley and T. F. Torrance. Translated by Harold Knight, G. W. Bromiley, J. K. S. Reid and R. H. Fuller. Edinburgh: T & T Clark, 1968.

———. Vol. III, pt. 3. *The Doctrine of Creation*. Edited by G. W. Bromiley and T. F. Torrance. Translated by G. W. Bromiley and R. J. Ehrlich. Edinburgh: T & T Clark, 1976.

———. Vol. III, pt. 4. *The Doctrine of Creation*. Edited by G. W. Bromiley and T. F. Torrance. Translated by A. T. MacKay, T. H. L. Parker, Harold Knight, Henry A. Kennedy and John Marks. Edinburgh: T & T Clark, 1969.

———. Vol. IV, pt. 1. *The Doctrine of Reconciliation*. Edited by G. W. Bromiley and T. F. Torrance. Translated by G. W. Bromiley. Edinburgh: T & T Clark, 1974.

———. Vol. IV, pt. 2. *The Doctrine of Reconciliation*. Edited by G. W. Bromiley and T. F. Torrance. Translated by G. W. Bromiley. Edinburgh: T & T Clark, 1967.

———. Vol. IV, pt. 3. *The Doctrine of Reconciliation*. First half. Edited by G. W. Bromiley and T. F. Torrance. Translated by G. W. Bromiley. Edinburgh: T & T Clark, 1976.

———. Vol. IV, pt. 3. *The Doctrine of Reconciliation*. Second half. Edited by G. W. Bromiley and T. F. Torrance. Translated by G. W. Bromiley. Edinburgh: T & T Clark, 1969.

———. Vol. IV, pt. 4. *The Doctrine of Reconciliation*. Fragment. *Baptism as the Foundation of the Christian Life*. Edited by G. W. Bromiley and T. F. Torrance. Translated by G. W. Bromiley. Edinburgh: T & T Clark, 1969.

———. Vol. IV, pt. 4. *The Christian Life*. Lecture Fragments. Translated by Geoffrey W. Bromiley. Grand Rapids: Eerdmans, 1981.

———. *Credo*. Translated by Robert McAfee Brown. New York: Charles Scribner's Sons, 1962.

———. *Die Kirchliche Dogmatik*. Vierter Band. *Die Lehre Von Der Versöhnung*. Erster Teil. Evangelischer Verlag AG. Zollikon-Zürich, 1953.

———. *The Göttingen Dogmatics: Instruction in the Christian Religion Volume One*. Edited by Hannelotte Reiffen. Translated by Geoffrey W. Bromiley. Grand Rapids: Eerdmans, 1991.

———. *The Humanity of God*. Translated by Thomas Wieser and John Newton Thomas. Richmond, VA: John Knox Press, 1968.

———. *The Knowledge of God and the Service of God According to the Teaching of the Reformation*. Translated by J. L. M. Haire and Ian Henderson. London: Hodder and Stoughton, 1949.

———. *Letters 1961–1968*. Edited by Jürgen Fangemeier and Hinrich Stoevesandt. Translated and edited by Geoffrey W. Bromiley. Grand Rapids: Eerdmans, 1981.

———. *Protestant Theology in the Nineteenth Century: Its Background and History*. Translated by Brian Cozens and John Bowden. Valley Forge, PA: Judson Press, 1973.

Busch, Eberhard. *The Great Passion: An Introduction to Karl Barth's Theology*. Edited by Darrell L. Guder and Judith J. Guder. Translated by Geoffrey W. Bromiley. Grand Rapids: Eerdmans, 2004.

Congar, Yves. *I Believe in the Holy Spirit*. Vol. III. Translated by David Smith. New York: Crossroad, 1997.

Cyril of Alexandria. *On the Unity of Christ*. Translated by John Anthony Mc-Guckin. Crestwood, NY: St. Vladimir's Seminary Press, 1995.

Dean, Benjamin. "Person and Being: Conversation with T. F. Torrance About the Monarchy of God," *International Journal of Systematic Theology* 15 (January 2013): 58-77.

Dempsey, Michael T., ed. *Trinity and Election in Contemporary Theology*. Grand Rapids: Eerdmans, 2011.

Diller, Kevin. "Is God *Necessarily* Who God Is? Alternatives for the Trinity and Election Debate." *SJT* 66, no. 2 (2013): 209-20.

Doyle, Brian M. "Review of *Divine Freedom and the Doctrine of the Immanent Trinity*." *Horizons, The Journal of the College Theology Society* 36, no. 2 (2009): 356-57.

Duffy, Stephen J. "Experience of Grace." In *The Cambridge Companion to Karl Rahner*. Edited by Declan Marmion and Mary E. Hines, pp. 43-62. Cambridge: Cambridge University Press, 2005.

Dulles, Avery, S.J. *The Assurance of Things Hoped For: A Theology of Christian Faith*. New York: Oxford University Press, 1994.

———. *The Craft of Theology: From Symbol to System*. New York: Crossroad, 1992.

Dych, William V., S.J. *Karl Rahner*. Collegeville, MN: Liturgical Press, 1992.

Egan, Harvey D. "Theology and Spirituality." In *The Cambridge Companion to Karl Rahner*. Edited by Declan Marmion and Mary E. Hines, pp. 13-28. Cambridge: Cambridge University Press, 2005.

Feuerbach, Ludwig. *The Essence of Christianity*. Translated by George Eliot. New York: Harper Torchbooks, 1957.

Galvin, John P. *The Invitation of Grace*. In *A World of Grace: An Introduction to the Themes and Foundations of Karl Rahner's Theology*. Edited by Leo J. O'Donovan, S.J., pp. 64-75. New York: Crossroad, 1981.

Gathercole, Simon. "Pre-existence, and the Freedom of the Son in Creation and Redemption: An Exposition in Dialogue with Robert Jenson." *International Journal of Systematic Theology* 7, no. 1 (January 2005): 38-51.

Giles, Kevin. *The Eternal Generation of the Son: Maintaining Orthodoxy in Trinitarian Theology*. Downers Grove, IL: InterVarsity Press, 2012.

———. "Barth and Subordinationism." *SJT* 64, no. 3 (2011): 327-46.

Godsey, John, ed. *Karl Barth's Table Talk*. Richmond, VA: John Knox, 1962.

Grenz, Stanley J. *Rediscovering the Triune God: The Trinity in Contemporary Theology*. Minneapolis: Fortress, 2004.

Habets, Myk. "The Doctrine of Election in Evangelical Calvinism: T. F. Torrance as a Case Study." *Irish Theological Quarterly* 73 (2008): 334-54.

Habets, Myk and Phillip Tolliday, eds. *Trinitarian Theology After Barth*. Eugene, OR: Pickwick, 2011.

Haught, John. *What Is God? How to Think About the Divine*. New York: Paulist, 1986.

Healy, Nicholas. *Thomas Aquinas: Theologian of the Christian Life*. Aldershot, UK: Ashgate, 2007.

Hector, Kevin. "Immutability, Necessity and Triunity: Towards a Resolution of the Trinity and Election Controversy." *Scottish Journal of Theology* 65, no. 1 (2012): 64-81.

Heltzel, Peter Goodwin, and Christian T. Collins Winn. "Karl Barth, Reconciliation, and the Triune God." In *Cambridge Companion to the Trinity*, edited by Peter C. Phan, pp. 171-91. Cambridge: Cambridge University Press, 2011.

St. Hilary of Poitiers. *A Select Library of Nicene and Post-Nicene Fathers of The Christian Church*. Second Series. Edited by Philip Schaff and Henry Wace. Volume IX, *Hilary of Poitiers and John of Damascus*. Edited by W. Sanday. Translated by E. W. Watson, L. Pullan, et al. Grand Rapids: Eerdmans, 1997.

Holmes, Christopher R. J. "The Person and Work of Christ Revisited: In Conversation with Karl Barth." *Anglican Theological Review* 95, no. 1 (Winter 2013): 37-55.

Hunsinger, George. "Election and the Trinity: Twenty-Five Theses on the Theology of Karl Barth." *Modern Theology* 24, no. 2 (April 2008): 179-98.

———. "Election and the Trinity: Twenty-Five Theses on the Theology of Karl Barth." In *Trinity and Election in Contemporary Theology*. Edited by Michael T. Dempsey, pp. 91-114. Grand Rapids: Eerdmans, 2011.

———. *How to Read Karl Barth: The Shape of His Theology*. New York: Oxford University Press, 1991.

———. "Karl Barth's Doctrine of the Trinity, and Some Protestant Doctrines After Barth." In *The Oxford Handbook of The Trinity*. Edited by Gilles Emery, O.P., and Matthew Levering, pp. 294-313. New York: Oxford University Press, 2011.

———. "The Mediator of Communion: Karl Barth's Doctrine of the Holy Spirit." In *Cambridge Companion to Karl Barth*. Edited by John Webster, pp. 177-94. Cambridge: Cambridge University Press, 2000.

———. "Robert Jenson's *Systematic Theology*: A Review Essay." *Scottish Journal of Theology* 55, no. 2 (2002): 161-200.

Jenson, Robert W. "Once More the *Logos Asarkos*." *International Journal of Systematic Theology* 13, no. 2 (April 2011): 130-33.

———. *Systematic Theology*. Vol. I, *The Triune God*. New York: Oxford University Press, 1997.

———. *Systematic Theology*. Vol. II, *The Works of God*. New York: Oxford University Press, 1999.

———. *The Triune Identity: God According to the Gospel*. Philadelphia: Fortress, 1982.

Johnson, Adam J. *God's Being in Reconciliation: The Theological Basis of the Unity and Diversity of the Atonement in the Theology of Karl Barth*. New York: T & T Clark, 2012.

Johnson, Elizabeth A. *Quest for the Living God: Mapping Frontiers in the Theology of God*. New York: Continuum, 2008.

———. *She Who Is: The Mystery of God in Feminist Theological Discourse*. New York: Crossroad, 1992.

Jones, Paul Dafydd. *The Humanity of Christ: Christology in Karl Barth's Church Dogmatics*. New York: T & T Clark, 2008.

———. "Obedience, Trinity, and Election: Thinking with and Beyond the *Church Dogmatics*." In *Trinity and Election in Contemporary Theology*. Edited by Michael T. Dempsey, pp. 138-61. Grand Rapids: Eerdmans, 2011.

Jüngel, Eberhard. *God as the Mystery of the World: On the Foundation of the Theology of the Crucified One in the Dispute Between Theism and Atheism*. Translated by Darrell L. Guder. Grand Rapids: Eerdmans, 1983.

———. *God's Being Is in Becoming: The Trinitarian Being of God in the Theology of Karl Barth, A Paraphrase*. Translated by John Webster. Grand Rapids: Eerdmans, 2001.

Kantzer Komline, Han-Luen. "Friendship and Being: Election and Trinitarian Freedom in Moltmann and Barth." *Modern Theology* 29, no. 1 (January 2013): 1-17.

Kasper, Walter. *The God of Jesus Christ*. Translated by Matthew J. O'Connell. New York: Crossroad, 1986.

Kaufman, Gordon. *Theology for a Nuclear Age*. Philadelphia: Westminster Press, 1985.

LaCugna, Catherine Mowry. *God for Us: The Trinity and Christian Life*. San Francisco: HarperSanFrancisco, 1991.

Lauber, David. *Barth on the Descent into Hell: God, Atonement and the Christian Life*. Aldershot, UK: Ashgate, 2004.

Lewis, Alan E. *Between Cross and Resurrection: A Theology of Holy Saturday*. Grand Rapids: Eerdmans, 2001.

Long, D. Stephen. "From the Hidden God to the God of Glory: Barth, Balthasar and Nominalism." *Pro Ecclesia* 20, no. 2 (Spring 2011): 167-85.

Marshall, Bruce D. "The Absolute and the Trinity." *Pro Ecclesia* 23, no. 2 (Spring 2014): 147-64.

———. *Trinity and Truth*. Cambridge: Cambridge University Press, 2000.

McCormack, Bruce L. "The Actuality of God: Karl Barth in Conversation with Open Theism." In *Engaging the Doctrine of God: Contemporary Protestant Perspectives*. Edited by Bruce L. McCormack, pp. 185-244. Grand Rapids: Eerdmans, 2008.

———. "Divine Impassibility or Simply Divine Constancy? Implications of Karl Barth's Later Christology for Debates over Impassibility." In *Divine Impassibility and the Mystery of Human Suffering*. Edited by James F. Keating and Thomas Joseph White, O.P., pp. 150-86. Grand Rapids: Eerdmans, 2009.

———. "The Doctrine of the Trinity After Barth: An Attempt to Reconstruct Barth's Doctrine in the Light of His Later Christology." In *Trinitarian Theology After Barth*. Edited by Myk Habets and Phillip Tolliday, pp. 87-120. Eugene, OR: Pickwick, 2011.

———. "Election and the Trinity: Theses in Response to George Hunsinger." *Scottish Journal of Theology* 63, no. 2 (2010): 203-24.

———. "Election and the Trinity: Theses in Response to George Hunsinger." In *Trinity and Election in Contemporary Theology*. Edited by Michael T. Dempsey, pp. 115-37. Grand Rapids: Eerdmans, 2011.

———, ed. *Engaging the Doctrine of God: Contemporary Protestant Perspectives*. Grand Rapids: Baker Academic, 2008.

———. "God *Is* His Decision: The Jüngel-Gollwitzer 'Debate' Revisited." In *Theology as Conversation: The Significance of Dialogue in Historical and Contemporary Theology, A Festschrift for Daniel L. Migliore*. Edited by Bruce L. McCormack & Kimlyn J. Bender, pp. 48-66. Grand Rapids: Eerdmans, 2009.

———. "Grace and Being: The Role of God's Gracious Election in Karl Barth's Theological Ontology." In *The Cambridge Companion to Karl Barth*. Edited by John Webster, pp. 92-110. Cambridge: Cambridge University Press, 2000.

———. "Grace and Being: The Role of God's Gracious Election in Karl Barth's Theological Ontology." In *Orthodox and Modern: Studies in the Theology of Karl Barth*, pp. 183-200. Grand Rapids: Baker Academic, 2008.

———. "Karl Barth's Historicized Christology: Just How 'Chalcedonian' Is It?" In *Orthodox and Modern: Studies in the Theology of Karl Barth*. Grand Rapids: Baker Academic, 2008.

———. "The Lord and Giver of Life: A 'Barthian' Defense of the *Filioque*." In

Rethinking Trinitarian Theology: Disputed Questions and Contemporary Issues in Trinitarian Theology. Edited by Robert J. Woźniak and Giulio Maspero, pp. 230-53. New York: T & T Clark, 2012.

———. *Mapping Modern Theology: A Thematic and Historical Introduction*. Edited by Kelly M. Kapic and Bruce L. McCormack. Grand Rapids: Baker Academic, 2012.

———. *Orthodox and Modern: Studies in the Theology of Karl Barth*. Grand Rapids: Baker Academic, 2008.

———. "Processions and Missions: A Point of Convergence between Thomas Aquinas and Karl Barth." In *Thomas Aquinas and Karl Barth: An Unofficial Catholic-Protestant Dialogue*. Edited by Bruce L. McCormack and Thomas Joseph White, O.P, pp. 99-126. Grand Rapids: Eerdmans, 2013.

———. "Seek God Where He May Be Found: A Response to Edwin Chr. van Driel." *Scottish Journal of Theology* 60, no. 1 (2007): 62-79.

———. "Seek God Where He May Be Found: A Response to Edwin Chr. van Driel." In *Orthodox and Modern: Studies in the Theology of Karl Barth*, pp. 261-77. Grand Rapids: Baker Academic, 2008.

McGrath, Alister E. "Karl Barth's Doctrine of Justification from an Evangelical Perspective." In *Karl Barth and Evangelical Theology: Convergences and Divergences*. Edited by Sung Wook Chung, pp. 172-90. Grand Rapids: Baker Academic, 2006.

McKim, Donald K. *Westminster Dictionary of Theological Terms*. Louisville, KY: Westminster John Knox, 1996.

Molnar, Paul D. "Can the Electing God Be God Without Us? Some Implications of Bruce McCormack's Understanding of the Doctrine of Election for the Doctrine of the Trinity." *Neue Zeitschrift für Systematische Theologie und Religionsphilosophie* 49, no. 2 (2007): 199-222.

———. "Can the Electing God Be God Without Us? Some Implications of Bruce McCormack's Understanding of the Doctrine of Election for the Doctrine of the Trinity." In *Trinity and Election in Contemporary Theology*. Edited by Michael T. Dempsey, pp. 63-90. Grand Rapids: Eerdmans, 2011.

———. *Divine Freedom and the Doctrine of the Immanent Trinity: In Dialogue with Karl Barth and Contemporary Theology*. New York: T & T Clark, 2002.

———. "The Function of the Immanent Trinity in the Theology of Karl Barth: Implications For Today." *Scottish Journal of Theology* 42, no. 3 (1989): 367-99.

———. "The Importance of the Doctrine of Justification in the Theology of Thomas F. Torrance and of Karl Barth." *Scottish Journal of Theology* (forthcoming).

438 Faith, Freedom and the Spirit

———. *Incarnation and Resurrection: Toward a Contemporary Understanding*. Grand Rapids: Eerdmans, 2007.

———. "Is God Essentially Different from His Creatures? Rahner's Explanation from Revelation." *The Thomist* 51, no. 4 (October 1987): 575-631.

———. "Natural Theology Revisited: A Comparison of T. F. Torrance and Karl Barth." *Zeitshcrift Für Dialektische Theologie* 20, no. 1 (December 2005): 53-83.

———. "A Response: Beyond Hegel with Karl Barth and T. F. Torrance." *Pro Ecclesia* 23, no. 2 (Spring 2014): 165-73.

———. "Some Problems with Pannenberg's Solution to Barth's 'Faith Subjectivism.'" *Scottish Journal of Theology* 48, no. 3 (1995): 315-39.

———. "Theological Issues Involved in the *Filioque*." In *Ecumenical Perspectives on the Filioque for the 21st Century*. Edited by Myk Habets, pp. 20-39. New York: T & T Clark, 2014.

———. *Thomas F. Torrance: Theologian of the Trinity*. Aldershot, UK: Ashgate, 2009.

———. "'Thy Word Is Truth': The Role of Faith in Reading Scripture Theologically with Karl Barth." *Scottish Journal of Theology* 63, no. 1 (2010): 70-92.

———. "The Trinity, Election and God's Ontological Freedom: A Response to Kevin W. Hector." *International Journal of Systematic Theology* 8, no. 3 (2006): 294-306.

———. "The Trinity, Election and God's Ontological Freedom: A Response to Kevin W. Hector." In *Trinity and Election in Contemporary Theology*. Edited by Michael T. Dempsey, pp. 47-62. Grand Rapids: Eerdmans, 2011.

———. "What Does It Mean to Say That Jesus Christ Is Indispensable to a Properly Conceived Doctrine of the Immanent Trinity?" *Scottish Journal Theology* 61, no. 1 (2008): 96-106.

Moltmann, Jürgen. *The Trinity and the Kingdom: The Doctrine of God*. Translated by Margaret Kohl. New York: Harper & Row, 1981.

Murray, John Courtney, S.J. *The Problem of God Yesterday and Today*. New Haven, CT: Yale University Press, 1965.

Myers, Benjamin. "Election, Trinity, and the History of Jesus: Reading Barth with Rowan Williams." In *Trinitarian Theology After Barth*. Edited by Myk Habets and Phillip Tolliday, pp. 121-37. Eugene, OR: Pickwick, 2011.

Nimmo, Paul T. "Barth and the Election-Trinity Debate: A Pneumatological View." In *The Trinity and Election in Contemporary Theology*. Edited by Michael T. Dempsey, pp. 162-81. Grand Rapids: Eerdmans, 2011.

———. *Being in Action: The Theological Shape of Barth's Ethical Vision*. New York: T & T Clark, 2007.

Nordling, Cherith Fee. *Knowing God by Name: A Conversation between Elizabeth A. Johnson and Karl Barth.* New York: Peter Lang, 2010

Pannenberg, Wolfhart. *Systematic Theology.* Vol. 1. Translated by Geoffrey W. Bromiley. Grand Rapids: Eerdmans, 1991.

———. *Systematic Theology.* Vol. 2. Translated by Geoffrey W. Bromiley. Grand Rapids: Eerdmans, 1994.

Price, Robert B. *Letters of the Divine Word: The Perfections of God in Karl Barth's Church Dogmatics.* New York: T & T Clark, 2011.

Rahner, Karl, ed. *Encyclopedia of Theology. The Concise Sacramentum Mundi.* New York: Seabury, 1975.

———. *Foundations of Christian Faith: An Introduction to the Idea of Christianity.* Translated by William V. Dych. New York: Seabury, 1978.

———. *Theological Investigations.* 23 vols.

———. Vol. 1, *God, Christ, Mary and Grace.* Translated by Cornelius Ernst, O.P. Baltimore: Helicon, 1961.

———. Vol. 4, *More Recent Writings.* Translated by Kevin Smyth. Baltimore: Helicon, 1966.

———. Vol. 6, *Concerning Vatican Council II.* Translated by Karl-H. Kruger and Boniface Kruger. Baltimore: Helicon, 1969.

———. Vol. 7, *Further Theology of the Spiritual Life.* Translated by David Bourke. New York: Herder and Herder, 1971.

———. Vol. 9, *Writings of 1965–1967.* Translated by Graham Harrison. New York: Herder and Herder, 1972.

———. Vol. 16, *Experience of the Spirit: Source of Theology.* Translated by David Morland. New York: Seabury, 1976.

———. Vol. 17, *Jesus, Man, and the Church.* Translated by Margaret Kohl. New York: Crossroad, 1981.

———. Vol. 21, *Science and Christian Faith.* Translated by Hugh M. Riley. New York: Crossroad, 1988.

——— and Karl-Heinz Weger. *Our Christian Faith: Answers for the Future.* Translated by Francis McDonagh. New York: Crossroad, 1981.

Robinson, John A. T. *Honest to God.* Philadelphia: Westminster Press, 1963.

Rogers, Eugene F. *Thomas Aquinas and Karl Barth: Sacred Doctrine and the Natural Knowledge of God.* Notre Dame, IN: University of Notre Dame Press, 1995.

Schoonenberg, Piet, S.J. *The Christ: A Study of the God-Man Relationship in the Whole of Creation and in Jesus Christ.* New York: Herder & Herder, 1971.

Swain, Scott R. *The God of the Gospel: Robert Jenson's Trinitarian Theology.* Downers Grove, IL: InterVarsity Press, 2013.

Swain, Scott R., and Allen, Michael. "The Obedience of the Eternal Son." *International Journal of Systematic Theology* 15, no. 2 (April 2013): 114-34.

Taylor, Iain. *Pannenberg on the Triune God.* New York: T & T Clark, 2007.

Tillich, Paul. *The Shaking of the Foundations.* New York: Charles Scribner's Sons, 1948.

——. *Systematic Theology: Three Volumes in One.* Chicago: University of Chicago Press, 1967.

Torrance, Alan. *Persons in Communion: Trinitarian Description and Human Participation.* Edinburgh: T & T Clark, 1996.

——. "The Trinity." In *The Cambridge Companion to Karl Barth.* Edited by John Webster, pp. 72-91. Cambridge: Cambridge University Press, 2000.

Torrance, Thomas F. *Atonement: The Person and Work of Christ.* Edited by Robert T. Walker. Downers Grove, IL: IVP Academic, 2009.

——. "The Christian Apprehension of God the Father." In *Speaking the Christian God: The Holy Trinity and the Challenge of Feminism.* Edited by Alvin F. Kimel Jr., pp. 120-43. Grand Rapids: Eerdmans, 1992.

——. *The Christian Doctrine of God: One Being Three Persons.* Edinburgh: T & T Clark, 1996.

——. *Christian Theology and Scientific Culture: Comprising The Theological Lectures at The Queen's University, Belfast for 1980.* Eugene, OR: Wipf and Stock, 1998.

——. *Divine and Contingent Order.* Edinburgh: T & T Clark, 1998.

——. *Divine Meaning: Studies in Patristic Hermeneutics.* Edinburgh: T & T Clark, 1995.

——. *The Doctrine of Jesus Christ.* Eugene, OR: Wipf and Stock, 2002.

——. *God and Rationality.* London: Oxford University Press, 1971; reissued, Edinburgh: T & T Clark, 1997.

——. *The Ground and Grammar of Theology.* Charlottesville: University Press of Virginia, 1980.

——. *Incarnation: The Person and Life of Christ.* Edited by Robert T. Walker. Downers Grove, IL: IVP Academic, 2008.

——. *Karl Barth, Biblical and Evangelical Theologian.* Edinburgh: T & T Clark, 1990.

——. "My Interaction with Karl Barth." In *How Karl Barth Changed My Mind.* Edited by Donald McKim, pp. 52-64. Grand Rapids: Eerdmans, 1986.

——. "Predestination in Christ." *Evangelical Quarterly*, 1941.

———. *Royal Priesthood: A Theology of Ordained Ministry.* 2nd ed. Edinburgh: T & T Clark, 1993.

———, trans. and ed. *The School of Faith: The Catechisms of the Reformed Church.* Eugene, OR: Wipf and Stock, 1996.

———. *Space, Time and Incarnation.* London: Oxford University Press, 1969; reissued, Edinburgh: T & T Clark, 1997.

———. *Space, Time and Resurrection.* Edinburgh: T & T Clark, 1998.

———. *Theology in Reconstruction.* London: SCM Press, 1965.

———. *The Trinitarian Faith: The Evangelical Theology of the Ancient Catholic Church.* Edinburgh: T & T Clark, 1988.

———. *Trinitarian Perspectives: Toward Doctrinal Agreement.* Edinburgh: T & T Clark, 1994.

Webster, John. "Review of *Divine Freedom and the Doctrine of the Immanent Trinity: In Dialogue with Karl Barth and Contemporary Theology.*" *The Journal of Theological Studies* 56, part 1 (April 2005): 289-90.

———. "Trinity and Creation." *International Journal of Systematic Theology* 12, no. 1 (January 2010): 4-19.

Weinandy, Thomas G., O.F.M. Cap. *In the Likeness of Sinful Flesh: An Essay on the Humanity of Christ.* New York: T & T Clark, 2006.

———. *Jesus the Christ.* Huntington, IN: Our Sunday Visitor Publishing Division, 2003.

Williams, Rowan. "Barth on the Triune God." In *Karl Barth: Studies of His Theological Method.* Edited by S. W. Sykes, pp. 147-93. Oxford: Clarendon, 1979.

Name Index

Subject Index